MARKET
SHARE
REPORTER

ISSN 1052-9578

MARKET SHARE REPORTER

AN ANNUAL COMPILATION
OF REPORTED MARKET SHARE
DATA ON COMPANIES,
PRODUCTS, AND SERVICES

1999

ROBERT S. LAZICH

GALE

DETROIT · LONDON

Robert S. Lazich, *Editor*

Editorial Code & Data Inc. Staff

David Smith and Susan Turner, *Contributing Editors*
Joyce Piwowarski, *Programmer*

Gale Research Inc. Staff

Donna Wood, *Coordinating Editor*

Mary Beth Trimper, *Production Director*
Deborah Milliken, *Production Assistant*

Barbara J. Yarrow, *Graphic Services Supervisor*
Christine O'Bryan, *Desktop Publisher*

Address until September 15, 1998:
835 Penobscot Building
645 Griswold St.
Detroit, MI 48226-4094

Address after September 15, 1998:
27500 Drake Rd.
Farmington Hills, MI 48331-3535

ISBN 0-7876-2448-9
ISSN 1052-9578

Printed in the United States of America
Published in the United States
by Gale Research

TABLE OF CONTENTS

TABLE OF TOPICS

The *Table of Topics* lists all topics used in *Market Share Reporter* in alphabetical order. One or more page references follow each topic; the page references identify the starting point where the topic is shown. The same topic name may be used under different SICs; therefore, in some cases, more than one page reference is provided.

INTRODUCTION

Market Share Reporter (MSR) is a compilation of market share reports from periodical literature. The ninth edition covers the period 1995 through 1998; while dates overlap slightly with the eighth edition, the ninth edition of *MSR* has completely new and updated entries. As shown by reviews of previous editions plus correspondence and telephone contact with many users, this is a unique resource for competitive analysis, diversification planning, marketing research, and other forms of economic and policy analysis. Features of the 1999 edition include—

- 2,000 entries, all new or updated.

- SIC classification, with entries arranged under 440 SIC codes.

- Corporate, brand, product, service and commodity market shares.

- Coverage of private and public sector activities.

- North American coverage.

- Comprehensive indexes, including products, companies, brands, places, sources, and SICs.

- Table of Topics showing topical subdivisions of chapters with page references.

- Graphics.

- Annotated source listing—provides publishers' information for journals cited in this edition of *MSR*.

MSR is a one-of-a-kind resource for ready reference, marketing research, economic analysis, planning, and a host of other disciplines.

Categories of Market Shares

Entries in *Market Share Reporter* fall into four broad categories. Items were included if they showed the relative strengths of participants in a market or provided subdivisions of economic activity in some manner that could assist the analyst.

- *Corporate market shares* show the names of companies that participate in an industry, produce a product, or provide a service. Each company's market share is shown as a percent of total industry or product sales for a defined period, usually a year. In some cases, the company's share represents the share of the sales of the companies shown (group total)—because shares of the total market were not cited in the source or were not relevant. In some corporate share tables, brand information appears behind company names in parentheses. In these cases, the tables can be located using either the company or the brand index.

- *Institutional shares* are like corporate shares but show the shares of other kinds of organizations. The most common institutional entries in *MSR* display the shares of states, provinces, or regions in an activity. The shares of not-for-profit organizations in some economic or service functions fall under this heading.

- *Brand market shares* are similar to corporate shares with the difference that brand names are shown. Brand names include equivalent categories such as the names of television programs, magazines, publishers' imprints, etc. In some cases, the names of corporations appear in parentheses behind the brand name; in these cases, tables can be located using either the brand or the company index.

- *Product, commodity, service, and facility* shares feature a broad category (e.g. household appliances) and show how the category is subdivided into components (e.g. refrigerators, ranges, washing machines, dryers, and dishwashers). Entries under this category cover products (autos, lawnmowers, polyethylene, etc.), commodities (cattle, grains, crops), services (telephone, child care), and facilities (port berths, hotel suites, etc.). Subdivisions may be products, categories of services (long-distance telephone, residential phone service, 800-service), types of commodities (varieties of grain), size categories (e.g., horsepower ranges), modes (rail, air, barge), types of facilities (categories of hospitals, ports, and the like), or other subdivisions.

- *Other shares.* MSR includes a number of entries that show subdivisions, breakdowns, and shares that do not fit neatly into the above categorizations but properly belong in such a book because they shed light on public policy, foreign trade, and other subjects of general interest. These items include, for instance, subdivisions of governmental expenditures, environmental issues, and the like.

Coverage

The ninth edition of *Market Share Reporter* covers essentially the same range of industries as previous editions. However, all tables are *new* or represent *updated* information (more recent or revised data). Also, coverage in detail is different in certain industries, meaning that more or fewer SICs are covered or product details *within* SICs may be different. For

these reasons, it is recommended that previous editions of *MSR* be retained rather than replaced.

Changes in Coverage. Beginning with the fifth edition, *MSR*'s geographic area of coverage became North America—Canada, the United States, and Mexico. As in all past editions, the vast majority of entries are for the United States. In the first four editions of *MSR*, international data were included at greater or lesser intensity depending on availability of space. This necessitated, among other things, frequent exclusion of data organized by states or regions of the United States—which are popular with users.

In order to provide better service to users, a companion publication, called *World Market Share Reporter* (*WMSR*), is available. *WMSR* features global market share information as well as country-specific market share and/or market size information outside North America. At the same time, *MSR* features more geographical market shares in the North American area.

MSR reports on *published* market shares rather than attempting exhaustive coverage of the market shares, say, of all major corporations and of all products and services. Despite this limitation, *MSR* holds share information on nearly 4,500 companies, more than 1,100 brands, and more than 1,100 product, commodity, service, and facility categories. Several entries are usually available for each industry group in the SIC classification; omitted groups are those that do not play a conventional role in the market, e.g., Private Households (SIC 88).

Coverage by SIC is roughly the same as the eighth edition: 440 SIC categories versus 511 last year. Variation in coverage from previous editions is due in part to publication cycles of sources and a different mix of brokerage house reports for the period covered (due to shifting interests within the investment community).

As pointed out in previous editions, *MSR* tends to reflect the current concerns of the business press. In addition to being a source of market share data, it mirrors journalistic preoccupations, issues in the business community, and events abroad. Important and controversial industries and activities get most of the ink. Heavy coverage is provided in those areas that are—

- large, important, basic (autos, chemicals)
- on the leading edge of technological change (computers, electronics, software)
- very competitive (toiletries, beer, soft drinks)
- in the news because of product recalls, new product introductions, mergers and acquisitions, lawsuits, and for other reasons
- relate to popular issues (environment, crime), or have excellent coverage in their respective trade press.

In many cases, several entries are provided on a subject each citing the same companies. No attempt was made to eliminate such seeming duplication if the publishing and/or original sources were different and the market shares were not identical. Those who work with such data know that market share reports are often little more than the "best guesses" of knowledgeable observers rather than precise measurements. To the planner or analyst, variant reports about an industry's market shares are useful for interpreting the data.

Publications appearing in the May 1997 to July 1998 period were used in preparing *MSR*. As a rule, material on market share data for 1998 were used by preference; in response to reader requests, we have included historical data when available. In some instances, information for earlier years was included if the category was unique or if the earlier year was necessary for context. In a few other cases, projections for 1999 and later years were also included.

"Unusual" Market Shares

Some reviewers of the first edition questioned—sometimes tongue-in-cheek, sometimes seriously—the inclusion of tables on such topics as computer crime, endangered species of fish, children's allowances, governmental budgets, and weapons system stockpiles. Indeed, some of these categories do not fit the sober meaning of "market share." A few tables on such subjects are present every edition—because they provide market information, albeit indirectly, or because they are the "market share equivalents" in an industrial classification which is in the public sector or dominated by the public sector's purchasing power.

Organization of Chapters

Market Share Reporter is organized into chapters by 2-digit SIC categories (industry groups). The exception is the first chapter, entitled *General Interest and Broad Topics*; this chapter holds all entries that bridge two or more 2-digit SIC industry codes (e.g. retailing in general, beverage containers, advanced materials, etc.) and cannot, therefore, be classified using the SIC system without distortion. Please note, however, that a topic in this chapter will often have one or more additional entries later—where the table could be assigned to a detailed industry. Thus, in addition to several tables on transportation in the first chapter, numerous tables appear later on cargo shipments, trucking, courier services, etc.

Within each chapter, entries are shown by 4-digit SIC (industry level). Within blocks of 4-digit SIC entries, entries are sorted alphabetically by topic, then alphabetically by title.

SIC and Topic Assignments

MSR's SIC classifications are based on the coding as defined in the *Standard Industrial Classification Manual* for 1987, issued by the Bureau of the Census, Department of Commerce. This 1987 classification system introduced significant revisions to the 1972 classification (as slightly modified in 1977); the 1972 system is still in widespread use (even by the Federal government); care should be used in comparing data classified in the new and in the old way.

The closest appropriate 4-digit SIC was assigned to each table. In many cases, a 3-digit SIC had to be used because the substance of the table was broader than the nearest 4-digit SIC category. Such SICs always end with a zero. In yet other cases, the closest classification possible was at the 2-digit level; these SICs terminate with double-zero. If the content of the table did not fit the 2-digit level, it was assigned to the first chapter of *MSR* and classified by topic only.

Topic assignments are based on terminology for commodities, products, industries, and services in the SIC Manual; however, in many cases phrasing has been simplified, shortened, or updated; in general, journalistically succinct rather than bureaucratically exhaustive phraseology was used throughout.

Organization of Entries

Entries are organized in a uniform manner. A sample entry is provided below. Explanations for each part of an entry, shown in boxes, are provided on the facing page.

1   *Entry Number.* A numeral between star symbols. Used for locating an entry from the index.

2   *Topic.* Second line, small type. Gives the

★ 41 ★   1
Corn (SIC 0115)   2   3
Leading Corn Seed Producers   4

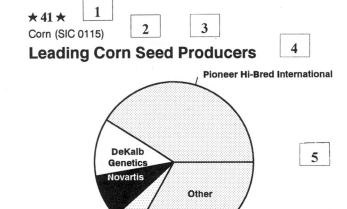

Shares are estimated. Novartis includes Ciba Seeds and Northrop King.   6

	1996	1997
Pioneer Hi-Bred International . . .	44.0%	42.0%
DeKalb Genetics	11.0	11.5
Novartis	8.0	8.5
Mycogen	5.0	4.5
Other	32.0	33.5

Source: *Wall Street Journal*, August 8, 1997, p. A3, from NatWest Securities.   9

broad or general product or service category of the entry. The topic for Leading Corn Seed Producers is Corn.

3   *SIC Code.* Second line, small type, follows the topic. General entries in the first chapter do not have an SIC code.

4   *Title.* Third line, large type. Describes the entry with a headline.

5   *Graphic.* When a graphic is present, it follows the title. Some entries will be illustrated with a pie or bar chart. The information used to create the graphic is always shown below the pie or bar chart.

6   *Note Block.* When present, follows the title and is in italic type. The note provides contextual information about the entry to make the data more understandable. Special notes about the data, information about time periods covered, market totals, and other comments are provided. Self-explanatory entries do not have a note block.

7   *Column headers.* Follow the note block. Some entries have more than one column or the single column requires a header. In these cases, column headers are used to describe information covered in the column. In most cases, column headers are years (1997) or indicators of type and magnitude ($ mil.). Column headers are shown only when necessary for clarity of presentation.

8   *Body.* Follows the note block or the column header and shows the actual data in two or more columns. In most cases, individual rows of data in the body are arranged in descending order, with the largest market share holder heading the list. Collective shares, usually labelled "Others" are placed last.

9   *Source.* Follows the body. All entries cite the source of the table, the date of publication, and the page number (if given). In many cases, the publisher obtained the information from another source (original source); in all such cases, the original source is also shown.

Continued entries. Entries that extend over two adjacent columns on the same page are not marked to indicate continuation but continue in the second column. Entries that extend over two pages are marked *Continued on the next page.* Entries carried over from the previous page repeat the entry number, topic (followed by the word *continued*), title, and column header (if any).

Use of Names

Company Names. The editors reproduced company names as they appeared in the source unless it was clearly evident from the name and the context that a name had been misspelled in the original. Large companies, of course, tend to appear in a large number of entries and in variant renditions. General Electric Corporation may appear as GE, General Electric, General Electric Corp., GE Corp., and other variants. No attempt was made to enforce a uniform rendition of names in the entries. In the Company Index, variant renditions were reduced to a single version or cross-referenced.

Use of Numbers

Throughout *MSR*, tables showing percentage breakdowns may add to less than 100 or fractionally more than 100 due to rounding. In those cases where only a few leading participants in a market are shown, the total of the shares may be substantially less than 100.

Numbers in the note block showing the total size of the market are provided with as many significant digits as possible in order to permit the user to calculate the sales of a particular company by multiplying the market total by the market share.

In a relatively small number of entries, actual unit or dollar information is provided rather than share information in percent. In such cases, the denomination of the unit (tons, gallons, $) and its magnitude (000 indicates multiply by 1,000; mil., multiply by 1,000,000) are mentioned in the note block or shown in the column header.

Data in some entries are based on different kinds of currencies and different weight and liquid measures. Where necessary, the unit is identified in the note block or in the column header. Examples are long tons, short tons, metric tons or Canadian dollars, etc.

Graphics

Pie and bar charts are used to illustrate some of the entries. The graphics show the names of companies, products, and services when they fit on the charts. When room is insufficient to accommodate the label, the first word of a full name is used followed by three periods (...) to indicate omission of the rest of the label.

In the case of bar charts, the largest share is always the width of the column, and smaller shares are drawn in proportion. Two bar charts, consequently, should not be compared to one another.

Sources

The majority of entries were extracted from newspapers and from general purpose, trade, and techni-

cal periodicals normally available in larger public, special, or university libraries. All told, 951 sources were used; of these, 291 were primary print sources, while 38 were taken from the Internet. Many more sources were reviewed but lacked coverage of the subject. These primary sources, in turn, used 622 original sources.

In many cases, the primary source in which the entry was published cites another source for the data, the original source. Original sources include other publications, brokerage houses, consultancies and research organizations, associations, government agencies, special surveys, and the like.

Since many primary sources appear as original sources elsewhere, and vice-versa, primary and original sources are shown in a single Source Index under two headings. Primary sources included in *MSR* almost always used the market share data as illustrative material for narratives covering many aspects of the subject. We hope that this book will also serve as a guide to those articles.

Indexes

Market Share Reporter features five indexes and two appendices.

- **Source Index.** This index holds 951 references in two groupings. *Primary sources* (329) are publications where the data were found. *Original sources* (622) are sources cited in the primary sources. Each item in the index is followed by one or more entry numbers arranged sequentially, beginning with the first mention of the source.

- **Place Names Index.** This index provides references to more than 230 cities, states, and regions in North America and elsewhere. References are to entry numbers.

- **Products, Services, and Issues Index.** This index holds more than 1,100 references to products and services in alphabetical order. The index also lists subject categories that do not fit the definition of a product or service but properly belong in the index. Examples include *budgets, conglomerates, crime, defense spending, economies, lotteries,* and the like. Some listings are abbreviations for chemical substances, computer software, etc. which may not be meaningful to those unfamiliar with the industries. Wherever possible, the full name is also provided for abbreviations commonly in use. Each listing is followed by one or more references to entry numbers.

- **Company Index.** This index shows references to nearly 4,500 company names by entry number. Companies are arranged in alphabetical order. In some cases, the market share table from which the company name was derived showed the share for a combination of two or more companies; these combinations are reproduced in the index.

- **Brand Index.** The Brand Index shows references to more than 1,100 brands by entry number. The arrangement is alphabetical. Brands include names of publications, computer software, operating systems, etc., as well as the more conventional brand names (Coca Cola, Maxwell House, Budweiser, etc.)

- **Appendix I - SIC Coverage.** The first appendix shows SICs covered by *Market Share Reporter.* The listing shows major SIC groupings at the 2-digit level as bold-face headings followed by 4-digit SIC numbers, the names of the SIC, and a *page* reference (rather than a reference to an entry number, as in the indexes). The page shows the

first occurrence of the SIC in the book. *MSR*'s SIC coverage is quite comprehensive, as shown in the appendix. However, many 4-digit SIC categories are further divided into major product groupings. Not all of these have corresponding entries in the book.

- **Appendix II - Annotated Source List.** The second appendix provides publisher names, addresses, telephone and fax numbers, and publication frequency of primary sources cited in *Market Share Reporter,* 9th Edition. As a new feature in this edition, the costs of the publications are also provided in some of the entries.

Available in Electronic Formats

Diskette/Magnetic Tape. *Market Share Reporter* is available for licensing on magnetic tape or diskette in a fielded format. The complete database may be ordered. The database is available for internal data processing and nonpublishing purposes only. For more information, call 800-877-GALE.

Online. *Market Share Reporter* is accessible online as File MKTSHR through LEXIS-NEXIS and as part of the MarkIntel service offered by Thomson Financial Services' I/PLUS Direct. For more information, contact LEXIS-NEXIS, P.O. Box 933, Dayton, OH 45401-0933, phone: (937)865-6800, toll-free: 800-227-4908, website: http://www.lexis-nexis.com; or Thomson Financial Services, 22 Pittsburgh St., Boston, MA 02210, phone: (617)345-2701, toll-free: 800-662-7878.

CD-ROM. *Market Share Reporter* is available on CD-ROM as part of Market Share Reporter and Business Rankings Worldwide. For more information, call 800-877-GALE.

Market Share Reporter information is also available through GaleNet and on CD-ROM as part of Gale Business Resources.

Acknowledgements

Market Share Reporter is something of a collective enterprise which involves not only the editorial team but also many users who share comments, criticisms, and suggestions over the telephone. Their help and encouragement is very much appreciated. *MSR* could not have been produced without the help of many people in and outside of Gale Research. The editors would like to express their special appreciation to Ms. Donna Wood (Senior Editor, Gale Research) and to the staff of Editorial Code and Data, Inc.

Comments and Suggestions

Comments on *MSR* or suggestions for improvement of its usefulness, format, and coverage are always welcome. Although every effort is made to maintain accuracy, errors may occasionally occur; the editors will be grateful if these are called to their attention. Please contact:

Editors
Market Share Reporter
Gale Research Inc.

Address until September 15, 1998:
835 Penobscot Building
645 Griswold St.
Detroit, Michigan 48226-4094
Phone: (313) 961-2242 or (800) 347-GALE
Fax: (313) 961-6815

Address after September 15, 1998:
27500 Drake Rd.
Farmington Hills, MI 48331-3535
Phone:(248)699-GALE or (800)347-GALE

MARKET
SHARE
REPORTER

General Interest and Broad Topics

★ 1 ★
Baby Care

Baby Care Market

The table shows sales in millions of dollars at drug stores, department stores and mass merchandisers. Figures do not include baby food, car seats, strollers, furniture, clothing and similar items.

Disposable diapers	$ 3,643
Infant formula	2,622
Baby wipes	492
Baby feeding equipment	400
Baby needs	351
Cotton swabs	210
Baby shampoo	43
Teething remedies	27

Source: *Drug Topics*, December 3, 1997, p. 66, from A.C. Nielsen and industry sources.

★ 2 ★
Bar Codes

Leading Consumers of Healthcare Bar Codes

Shares are shown based on sales.

Wholesales	30.0%
Transportation	22.0
Healthcare	13.0
Finance/banking	5.0
Insurance	5.0
Telecommunications	5.0
Utilities	5.0
Construction	2.0
Education	2.0
Other	5.0

Source: *Reseller Management*, November 1, 1997, p. 138.

★ 3 ★
Bill Payment

Check Writing in the United States - 1997

Distribution is shown in percent.

Individual to business	48.0%
Business to business	23.0
Business to individual	16.0
Individual to individual	6.0
Other	7.0

Source: *American Demographics*, March 1998, p. 9, from Nilson Report, Green Sheet, Bank Administration Institute, and Mentis Corporation.

★ 4 ★
Cargo Transport

U.S. Expedited Cargo Market - 1997

The estimated $69.56 billion market is shown in percent. Figures are based on revenues.

Domestic air	37.5%
Domestic LTL	26.1
Domestic ground parcel	22.9
Air export	13.4

Source: *Distribution*, July 1997, p. 54, from Colography Group Inc.

★ 5 ★
Consumer Spending

Consumer Spending on Media - 2001

The table shows spending on media in percent. Per person media spending is projected to reach $685.18 a year.

Subscription video	28.7%
Home video	16.6
Consumer books	15.0
Interactive digital media	11.1
Recorded music	10.4
Consumer magazines	6.0
Films in theaters	4.0
Other	8.2

Source: *Financial Times*, July 29, 1997, p. 6, from Veronis, Suhler & Associates.

★ 6 ★
Consumer Spending

Holiday Spending per U.S. Household

Regions are ranked by average household spending on holiday gifts. The national average for holiday spending is $465.

New England	$ 593
Middle Atlantic	514
East North Central	488
South Atlantic	457
East South Central	453
West South Central	444
Pacific	438
Mountain	411
West North Central	395

Source: *Christian Science Monitor*, November 21, 1997, p. 3, from The Conference Board.

★ 7 ★
Consumer Spending

Leading Methods of Consumer Payments

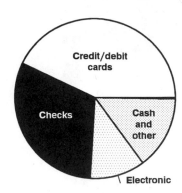

Methods of payment are shown ranked as a percent of total consumer transactions for 1995, 2000, and 2005.

	1995	2000	2005
Credit/debit cards	21.0%	33.0%	43.0%
Checks	55.0	44.0	31.0
Electronic	2.0	5.0	11.0
Cash and other	22.0	18.0	15.0

Source: *Banks Systems + Technology*, January 1998, p. 37, from The Nilson Report.

★ 8 ★
Contraceptives

Leading Contraceptive Brands - 1997

Shares are shown based on $262.3 million in sales for the 52 weeks ended December 7, 1997.

Trojan	25.6%
Trojan Enz	18.3
LifeStyles	11.3
Conceptrol	4.1
Sheik	3.6
Kling Tite Naturalamb	2.8
Ortho Gynol II	2.7
Class Act	2.2
Ramses Ultra	2.1
Other	27.3

Source: *Supermarket Business*, January 1998, p. 76, from Information Resources Inc.

★ 9 ★

Disasters

Most Costly U.S. Insured Disasters

Events are ranked by by estimated insured loss in billions of dollars.

Hurricane Andrew (1992)	$ 15.5
Northridge CA earthquake (1994)	12.5
Hurricane Hugo (1989)	4.2
Hurricane Opal (1995)	2.1
20-state winter storm (1993)	1.8

Source: *USA TODAY*, March 13, 1998, p. 4B, from American Insurance Services Group.

★ 10 ★

Flooring

U.S. Flooring Market

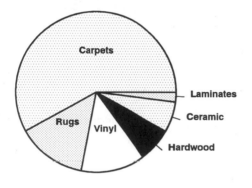

The market is shown by segment.

Carpets	58.2%
Rugs	13.6
Vinyl	13.0
Hardwood	7.1
Ceramic	6.1
Laminates	2.0

Source: *Wall Street Journal*, March 31, 1998, p. B1, from *Floor Focus*.

★ 11 ★

Foreign Markets

Foreign Presence in Canada's Cultural Markets

The table shows the foreign share of cultural markets in Canada.

Movies screened	95.0%
Music recordings sold	84.0
Magazines sold at newsstands	83.0
Book sold	70.0
Music played on radio stations	70.0
English-language television programming . .	60.0

Source: *Wall Street Journal*, February 4, 1998, p. A18, from Heritage Canada.

★ 12 ★

Hair Removal

Women's Hair Removal Market

The market is shown in percent.

Blade shavers	70.0%
Women's shavers	15.0
Depilatories	10.0
Appliances	5.0

Source: *HFN*, March 9, 1998, p. 36.

★ 13 ★

Home Automation

Advanced Home Controller Market by Segment - 2000

Shares of the $2.1 million market are shown in percent. HVAC stands for heating, ventillation and air conditioning.

Communications	40.5%
Central controller	23.0
HVAC	21.0
Security	10.7
Lighting	4.8

Source: *Professional Builder*, January 1998, p. 42, from Parks Association.

★ 14 ★

Home Renovation

Home Renovation Spending - Canada

Canadian provinces are ranked by spending in billions of U.S. dollars for 1996 and 1997. Data are forecasted.

	1996	1997
Ontario	$ 5.1	$ 5.4
Quebec	3.2	3.2
British Columbia	1.9	2.1
Alberta	1.1	1.3
Atlantic Provinces	1.0	1.1
Manitoba	0.4	0.5
Saskatchewan	0.4	0.4

Source: *National Trade Data Bank*, January 16, 1997, p. ISA961201, from Clayton Research Associates.

★ 15 ★

Leisure Activities

Popular Leisure Activities

The table shows number of hours the average adult devotes to each activity per week.

Watch television	15.0
Socialize (visits, meals, parties)	6.7
Communicate (phone, mail, talk)	4.4
Read	2.8
Hobby	2.7
Education	2.2
Recreation/sports	2.2
Groups	1.2
Cultural events	0.9
Religion	0.9
Radio/recordings	0.4

Source: *USA TODAY*, September 16, 1997, p. 1A, from *Time for Life*.

★ 16 ★

Licensed Merchandise

Largest Licensed Sports Merchandise Firms - 1997

Organizations are ranked by sales in millions of dollars.

VF Corp. Licensing	$ 326
Starter	270
Logo	262
Fruit of the Loom Sports & Licensing	230
Champion	185
Nike	140
Russell Licensed Products	122
Haddad (Mighty Mac)	100
New Era	88
Sports Specialties	69

Source: *Sportstyle*, May 1998, p. 33.

★ 17 ★

Licensed Merchandise

Licensed Merchandise Sales - 1997

Retail sales reached $73.23 billion in the United States and Canada.

Entertainment	22.0%
Trademarks and brands	22.0
Sports	19.0
Fashion	18.0
Art	7.0
Other	12.0

Source: *New York Times*, June 12, 1998, p. C1, from *The Licensing Letter*.

★ 18 ★
Licensed Merchandise

Licensed Products Sales by Category - 1996

Product categories are ranked by retail sales in billions of dollars. Data are for the U.S. and Canada.

Apparel	$ 11.58
Toys/games	7.85
Gifts/novelties	6.94
Accessories	6.83
Food/beverage	6.08
Domestics	4.78
Publishing	4.35
Health/beauty	4.26
Stationery/paper	3.58
Video games/software	2.98
Housewares	2.50
Infant products	2.49
Sporting goods	2.43
Footwear	2.19
Music/video	1.27
Electronics	1.17
Furniture/home furnishings	0.84
Other	0.16

Source: *Discount Merchandiser*, June 1997, p. 3, from *The Licensing Letter*.

★ 19 ★
Licensed Merchandise

Licensed Products Sales by Property - 1996

The table shows retail sales in billions of dollars. Data are for the U.S. and Canada.

Entertainment/character	$ 16.70
Trademarks/brands	15.11
Sports	13.79
Fashion	12.60
Art	5.20
Toys/games	2.71
Celebrities/estates	2.57
Publishing	1.64
Music	1.03
Nonprofit	0.70
Other	0.23

Source: *Discount Merchandiser*, June 1997, p. 3, from *The Licensing Letter*.

★ 20 ★
Licensed Merchandise

Licensed Sports Merchandise - 1997

Organizations are ranked by sales in millions of dollars.

NFL	$ 2,865
Collegiate Licensing Company	2,500
NBA	2,400
MLB	1,740
NHL	1,150
NASCAR	800

Source: *Sportstyle*, May 1998, p. 33.

★ 21 ★
Media

Largest Entertainment Firms

Firms are ranked by revenue in millions of dollars.

Walt Disney	$ 22,473
Viacom	13,505
Time Warner	13,294
CBS	9,632

Source: *Fortune*, April 27, 1998, pp. F-47.

★ 22 ★
Media

Top Media Firms - 1996

Firms are ranked by revenues in billions of dollars. Where parent companies are shown, top media divisions are in parentheses. Data for General Electric, General Motors, Sony, and Westinghouse represent media revenue only.

Time Warner Inc.	$ 20.9
The Walt Disney Co.	18.7
News Corp. Ltd. (Fox)	14.3
Viacom Inc. (Paramount)	12.1
Tele-Communications Inc.	8.0
Sony Corp. (Columbia)	7.9
General Electric Co. (NBC)	5.2
Westinghouse Electric Corp. (CBS)	5.2

Continued on next page.

★ 22 ★ *Continued*

Media

Top Media Firms - 1996

Firms are ranked by revenues in billions of dollars. Where parent companies are shown, top media divisions are in parentheses. Data for General Electric, General Motors, Sony, and Westinghouse represent media revenue only.

Gannett Co. . . . .$ 4.4
General Motors (Hughes Electronics) . . . 4.1

Source: *Broadcasting & Cable*, July 7, 1997, p. 4.

★ 23 ★

Media

Yellow Pages Media Firms - 1996

Firms are ranked by Yellow Pages revenue in millions of dollars.

SBC Communications . . . . $ 1,985.0
BellSouth Corp. 1,742.0
GTE Corp. 1,527.0
Bell Atlantic 1,222.5
U.S. West 1,120.0
Nynex Corp. 969.5
Ameritech Corp. 860.1
DonTech 408.9
Dun & Bradstreet Corp. 377.5
Sprint 309.0

Source: *Advertising Age*, August 18, 1997, p. S8.

★ 24 ★

Packaging

Caps and Closures Demand - 2001

Demand is shown by material. Data are based on an estimated total demand of 150 billion units.

Plastic .62.7%
Metal 34.0
Other 3.3

Source: *Plastics News*, November 10, 1997, p. 3, from The Freedonia Group Inc.

★ 25 ★

Packaging

Types of Containers Used for Soft Drinks - 2001

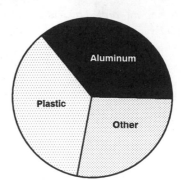

Sales are shown by type of container. Figures are estimated.

Aluminum 36.0%
Plastic 36.0
Other 28.0

Source: *Business Week*, October 6, 1997, p. 108, from Alcan Aluminium Ltd.

★ 26 ★

Personal Care Products

Health & Beauty Care Sales

Sales are shown in percent.

OTC remedies 28.5%
Hair care 12.8
Oral hygiene 10.9
Feminine hygiene 8.2
Vitamins/supplements 6.0
Cosmetics & nail care 5.3
Personal deodorants 5.1
Shaving needs 4.3
Skin/sun tan 3.9
Other 15.0

Source: *Supermarket Business*, May 1998, p. 112.

★ 27 ★
Pets

Small Pet Ownership - 1996

Data show the number of U.S. households that own each pet.

	Number	Share
Rabbits	1,878,000	41.04%
Hamsters	1,008,000	22.03
Guinea pigs	583,000	12.74
Ferrets	395,000	8.63
Gerbils	277,000	6.05
Other	435,000	9.51

Source: *Pet Product News*, March 1998, p. 35, from American Veterinary Medical Association.

★ 28 ★
Plumbing Fixtures

Plumbing Fixtures by Material - 1996

Data show shipments in percent.

Fiberglass plastic	47.0%
Vitreous china	30.0
Metal	21.0
Other	4.0

Source: *Ceramic Industry*, August 1997, p. 28, from U.S. Department of Commerce.

★ 29 ★
Private Label

Leading Non-Foods Categories for Private Label Products - 1996

Data show dollar shares and unit shares for non-food, private label categories as a percent of each category's total market. Figures refer to supermarket sales.

	Dollar share	Unit share
Cotton balls	41.34%	51.75%
Vitamins	33.47	43.83
First aid treatment	24.89%	60.79%
Moist towelettes	22.73	28.60
Cold/allergy/sinus liquids	21.23	30.41
Miscellaneous health treatments	19.57	40.27
Internal analgesics	19.05	25.24
Nasal spray	17.76	28.61
Baby needs	17.14	22.09
Mouthwash	16.95	25.69

Source: *Nonfoods Merchandising*, November 1997, p. 23, from Information Resources Inc.

★ 30 ★
Private Label

Top Private Label Categories in Supermarkets - 1996

Data show dollar volume in millions of dollars.

Milk	$ 6,200
Fresh bread & rolls	1,900
Cheese	1,800
Fresh eggs	1,600
Ice cream	976
Carbonated beverages	856
Frozen plain vegetables	740
Sugar	689
Juice, refrigerated	643

Source: *Prepared Foods*, November 1997, p. 18, from Information Resources Inc. and Private Label Manufacturers Association.

★ 31 ★
Smart Cards

Smart Card Use by Application

Data represent millions of dollars for 1996 and 2001. The United States has an estimated 6% of the global smart card product market.

	1996	2001	Share
Transaction processing	$ 15	$ 575	37.10%
Automatic ID & security	50	400	25.81
Communications	10	250	16.13
Government	50	150	9.68
Other	20	175	11.29

Source: *Security*, August 1997, p. 32, from The Freedonia Group.

★ 32 ★
Smart Cards

Smart Cards by Application - 1996

Data show millions of cards issued for each application.

	Cards (mil.)	Share
Phone	668	79.0%
Financial	65	8.0
Health	46	5.0
Mobile phone	28	3.0
Pay television	28	3.0
Transportation/travel	9	1.0
Other	2	1.0

Source: *USA TODAY*, October 21, 1997, p. 7B, from Faulkner's Gray *Card Technology*.

★ 33 ★
Transportation

Freight Transportation

Figures are shown for tonnage carried less than 100 miles.

Private	49.0%
For-hire	28.0
Rail	7.0
Water	3.0
Other	13.0

Source: *Purchasing*, April 9, 1998, p. 41, from Standard & Poor's DRI and American Trucking Association.

★ 34 ★
Transportation

How Freight is Transported

Shipments are shown in percent.

	1996	2001
Truck	82.3%	82.4%
Rail	7.0	6.6
Pipeline	4.4	4.0
Air	3.2	3.9
Water	1.8	1.6
Rail intermodal	1.3	1.4

Source: *Traffic World*, January 5, 1998, p. 9.

★ 35 ★
Transportation

Passenger Land Transportation

Data are based on passengers travelling 3,910.3 billion miles. Excluding the auto & light truck category, the school bus segment jumps to 55.7% of the market.

Auto & light truck	95.6%
School bus	2.4
Transit bus & rail	1.1
Intercity bus	0.7
Amtrak	0.1

Source: From the Internet, http:// www.publicpurpose.com, 1995, p. 1, from U.S. Department of Transportation.

★ 36 ★
Weddings

Bridal Market

The market is shown in billions of dollars.

	($ bil.)	Share
Wedding-related	$ 16.4	51.25%
Home furnishings	7.8	24.38
Honeymoon travel	4.5	14.06
Engagement/wedding rings . . .	3.3	10.31

Source: *HFN*, April 20, 1998, p. 13, from *Bride's* and Power of Two.

★ 37 ★
Windows & Doors

Windows & Door Market

Demand is shown in millions of dollars.

	1996 ($ mil.)	2001 ($ mil.)	Share
Millwork . . . . . . ding	$ 12,050	$ 14,520	54.69%
Metal	7,884	8,505	32.03
Vinyl & other	2,359	3,525	13.28

Source: *Wood & Wood Products*, December 1997, p. 17, from Freedonia Group.

SIC 01 - Agricultural Production - Crops

★ 38 ★

Produce (SIC 0100)

Produce Market by Sales - 1996

Data show sales in percent.

Apples	10.5%
Potatoes	7.0
Tomatoes	6.6
Bananas	6.2
Citrus fruits	5.9
Lettuce	5.5
Onions	2.9
Celery	1.9
Carrots	1.5
Mushrooms	1.5
Corn	1.1
Wild bird seed	0.6
Floral	0.4
Other fruits	12.6
Other vegetables	35.8

Source: *Supermarket Business*, October 1997, p. 88.

★ 39 ★

Grain (SIC 0110)

Largest Grain Handlers in Canada - 1997

Firms are ranked by revenues in millions of dollars.

Saskatchewan Wheat Pool	$ 4,229
Alberta Wheat Pool	2,052
Manitoba Pool Elevators	1,355
United Grain Growers	220

Source: *Globe and Mail*, April 22, 1998, p. B1, from companies.

★ 40 ★

Grain (SIC 0110)

Leading Grain Companies - Canada

Shares are shown in percent for 1996.

Saskatchewan Wheat Pool	31.0%
Alberta Wheat Pool	17.0
United Grain Growers	17.0
Cargill Inc.	10.0
Pioneer	10.0
Manitoba Pool Elevators	7.0
Others	8.0

Source: *Globe and Mail's Report on Business Magazine*, June 1997, p. 36.

★ 41 ★
Corn (SIC 0115)

Leading Corn Seed Producers

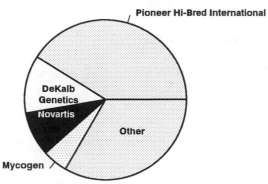

Shares are estimated. Novartis includes Ciba Seeds and Northrop King.

	1996	1997
Pioneer Hi-Bred International . . .	44.0%	42.0%
DeKalb Genetics	11.0	11.5
Novartis	8.0	8.5
Mycogen	5.0	4.5
Other	32.0	33.5

Source: *Wall Street Journal*, August 8, 1997, p. A3, from NatWest Securities.

★ 42 ★
Corn (SIC 0115)

Top Corn Harvesting States - 1996

States are shown ranked by millions of acres harvested.

Iowa	12.4
Illinois	10.8
Nebraska	8.3
Minnesota	6.9
Indiana	5.4
South Dakota	3.7
Wisconsin	3.0

Source: *San Juan Star*, September 17, 1997, p. B51, from United States Department of Agriculture.

★ 43 ★
Tobacco (SIC 0132)

Top Tobacco-Producing States - 1995

States are ranked by cash receipts in millions of dollars.

North Carolina	$ 871
Kentucky	615
South Carolina	187
Tennessee	178
Virginia	147
Georgia	133
Florida	31
Ohio	28
Indiana	25
Pennsylvania	22

Source: *USA TODAY*, June 23, 1997, p. 3B.

★ 44 ★
Vegetables (SIC 0161)

Largest Vegetable Farms - North

Companies in the northern U.S. are ranked by 1997 acreage.

R.D. Offutt Co.	53,000
Hartung Brmiscs. Inc.	24,877
Heartland Farms Inc.	8,300
A&W Farms	8,168
Paramount Farms Inc.	7,600
Black Gold Farms	7,200
Empire Farms Inc.	6,145
Charles H. West Farms Inc.	6,041
Wysocki Farms Inc.	5,874
Okray Family Farms	5,292
Torrey Farms Inc.	5,040
Anthony Farms Inc.	4,455

Source: *American Vegetable Grower*, October 1997, p. 13.

★ 45 ★
Vegetables (SIC 0161)

Largest Vegetable Farms - Southeast

Companies in the southeastern U.S. are ranked by 1997 acreage.

A. Duda & Sons Inc.	20,000
Dimare-Homestead	17,370
Pacific Tomato Growers Ltd./Triple E Produce Corp.	17,216

Continued on next page.

★ 45 ★ *Continued*
Vegetables (SIC 0161)

Largest Vegetable Farms - Southeast

Companies in the southeastern U.S. are ranked by 1997 acreage.

Six L's Packing Co. Inc.	13,550
Hundley Farms Inc.	11,575
Thomas Produce Co.	11,475
Zellwin Farms Co.	9,021
Pero Family Farms Inc.	6,188
Long Farms Inc.	6,010
NTGargiulo L.P.	6,000

Source: *American Vegetable Grower*, October 1997, p. 17.

★ 46 ★
Vegetables (SIC 0161)

Largest Vegetable Farms - Southwest

Companies in the southwestern U.S. are ranked by 1997 acreage.

Navajo Agricultural Products Industry	16,227
Martori Farms	8,650
Rousseau Farming Co.	6,072
Greer Farms	5,900
Sharyland Plantation	5,835
Pasquinelli Produce Co.	5,156
Starr Produce Co.	3,850
Barkley Co.	3,650
Sakata Farms Inc.	3,300
Holden Wallace Inc.	3,295

Source: *American Vegetable Grower*, October 1997, p. 21.

★ 47 ★
Vegetables (SIC 0161)

Largest Vegetable Farms - West

Companies in the western U.S. are ranked by 1997 acreage.

Grimmway Farms	41,000
Tanimura & Antle	35,115
Bruce Church Inc.	21,922
Blaine Larsen Farms	21,550
D'Arrigo Bros. Co. of California Inc.	20,209
Boskovich Farms Inc.	16,730
P.J. Taggares Co.	15,650
Dresick Farms Inc.	14,250

Ocean Mist Farms/Boutonnet Farms	14,248
Nunes Vegetables Inc.	13,680

Source: *American Vegetable Grower*, October 1997, p. 23.

★ 48 ★
Berries (SIC 0171)

Top Berry Growers

Companies are ranked by total acreage devoted to berry production.

Cherryfield Foods, Inc.	8,600
Jasper Wyman & Son	7,009
Northland Cranberries, Inc.	3,607
Merrill Blueberry Farms, Inc.	2,201
A.D. Makepeace Co.	1,574
Atlantic Blueberry Co.	1,320
Haines & Haines, Inc.	1,115
Coastal Berry Company	950
Reiter Bros. Inc.	820
Beaton Cranberries, Inc.	800
Adkin Blue Ribbon Pkg. Co. Inc.	790
A.R. DeMarco Enterprises, Inc.	740

Source: *Fruit Grower*, August 1997, p. 11.

★ 49 ★
Fruit (SIC 0171)

Blueberry Production by State - 1997

Production is shown in millions of pounds.

Michigan	76.0
New Jersey	32.0
Oregon	21.0
Georgia	14.0
Washington	8.7
North Carolina	8.6

Source: *Business North Carolina*, May 1998, p. 84, from United States Department of Agriculture.

★ 50 ★

Fruit (SIC 0171)

Strawberry Production by State - 1997

Production is shown in millions of pounds.

California	1,333.4
Florida	176.9
Oregon	50.0
North Carolina	18.0
Michigan	9.8
Washington	9.8

Source: *Business North Carolina*, May 1998, p. 84, from United States Department of Agriculture.

★ 51 ★

Fruit (SIC 0172)

Top Grape Growers

Companies are ranked by total acreage devoted to grape production.

E. & J. Gallo Winery	15,000
Giumarra Vineyards Corp.	10,000
Golden State Vintners	9,500
The McCarty Co.	7,500
Delicato Vineyards/San Bernabe Vineyard	7,103
Dole Food Company, Inc.	7,000
Sun World	6,871
Vino Farms, Inc.	6,423
Met West Agribusiness	5,735
Sutter Home Winery	5,217
John Kautz Farms	5,200
Scheid Vineyards and Management Co.	4,600

Source: *Fruit Grower*, August 1997, p. 10.

★ 52 ★

Nuts (SIC 0173)

Top Nut Growers

Companies are ranked by total acreage devoted to nut production.

Paramount Farming Co./Paramount Citrus	40,713
Diamond AgraIndustries	8,619
Dole Food Company, Inc.	8,300
Farmland Management Services	8,202
Farmers Investment Co.	6,958
Ka'U Agribusiness Co., Inc.	6,604
Braden Farms, Inc.	6,419

Lassen Land Co.	5,610
Premiere Partners III/Westchester Group, Inc.	4,915
Montpelier Orchard Management	4,728
Pecan Valley Nut Company	4,500
Capital Agricultural Property Services Inc.	4,490

Source: *Fruit Grower*, August 1997, p. 10.

★ 53 ★

Fruit (SIC 0175)

Apple Production by State - 1997

Production is shown in millions of pounds. Total sales in the U.S. reached 10.2 billion pounds.

Washington	4,900
New York	1,120
Michigan	1,050
California	975
Pennsylvania	475
Virginia	240
Oregon	155
North Carolina	150
Idaho	130
West Virginia	100

Source: *Business North Carolina*, May 1998, p. 84, from United States Department of Agriculture.

★ 54 ★

Fruit (SIC 0175)

Cherry Production by State - 1997

Production is shown in tons.

Washington State	92,000
Oregon	50,000
California	49,200
Michigan	27,000
Idaho	1,300
Montana	1,300

Source: *Fruit Grower*, April 1998, p. 36, from Untied States Department of Agriculture.

★ 55 ★

Fruit (SIC 0175)

Top Apple & Pear Growers

Companies are ranked by total acreage devoted to apple and pear production.

Naumes, Inc.	5,956
Stemilt Management Inc.	5,770
Brewster Heights Packing	5,150
Evans Fruit Farm	4,482
Broetje Orchards	4,000
Fruit Hill Orchard, Inc.	3,147
Bowman Agricultural Enterprises, LLC	3,100
Northwestern Fruit and Produce Co.	2,999
Borton & Sons, Inc.	2,767
Kropf Orchards & Storage Inc.	2,500
Capital Agricultural Property Services Inc.	2,358
Fowler Brothers, Inc.	2,310

Source: *Fruit Grower*, August 1997, p. 9.

★ 56 ★

Fruit (SIC 0175)

Top Apple Producing States

Data show production in thousands of 42-pound bushels for 1996 and 1997.

	1996	1997
Washington	130,952	128,571
New York	24,524	25,714
Michigan	17,262	25,000
California	21,429	21,429
Pennsylvania	9,310	11,310
Virginia	6,548	5,952
North Carolina	4,762	4,048
Oregon	3,310	3,690
Idaho	4,285	3,095
West Virginia	2,500	2,738

Source: *Fruit Grower*, September 1997, p. 8, from United States Department of Agriculture.

★ 57 ★

Fruit (SIC 0175)

Top Non-Citrus Fruit Growers

Companies are ranked by total acreage devoted to non-citrus fruit production.

Paramount Farming	41,605
Dole Food Co.	17,900
E. & J. Gallo Winery	16,200
Met West Agribusiness	11,340
Sun World	10,402
Giumarra Vineyards Corp.	10,350
Capital Agricultural Property Services Inc.	10,070
Golden State Vintners	9,500
Diamond AgraIndustries	9,338
Farmland Mgt. Services	9,132
Cherryfield Foods, Inc.	8,600
Beringer Wine Estates	8,579

Source: *Fruit Grower*, August 1997, p. 9.

★ 58 ★

Fruit (SIC 0175)

Top Pear Producers

Production is shown in thousands of tons.

	1996	1997
California	287	300
Washington	105	190
Oregon	70	45

Source: From the Internet, http://www.usda.gov, June 12, 1997, p. 1, from United States Department of Agriculture.

★ 59 ★

Fruit (SIC 0175)

Top Stone Fruit Growers

Companies are ranked by total acreage devoted to stone fruit production.

Gerawan Farming	4,800
Sun World	3,531
Lane Packing Co.	3,500
California Prune Packing	3,162
Taylor Orchards	3,054
Evans Farms	2,952
ITO Packing Co., Inc.	2,906
Fowler Packing Co. Inc.	2,660
J.W. Yonce & Sons Farms, Inc.	2,100
J.R. Wood, Inc.	1,997
R.W. Dubose & Sons, Inc.	1,900
Chappell Farms Inc.	1,800

Source: *Fruit Grower*, August 1997, p. 9.

★ 60 ★

Floriculture (SIC 0180)

Green Goods Sales - 1998

Total sales are expected to reach $21.6 billion.
Distribution is shown in percent.

Evergreens	39.7%
Shade/flowering trees	17.9
Bedding/garden plants	16.3
Flowering plants	11.7
Fruit/nut plants	7.4
Foliage plants	4.4
Bulbs	2.6

Source: *Nursery Retailer*, February/March 1998, p. 62.

★ 61 ★

Floriculture (SIC 0181)

Leading Flower Importers

Colombia	
Netherlands	
Ecuador	
Mexico	
Costa Rica	
Other	

Countries are shown ranked by share of flower
imports to the United States.

Colombia	63%
Netherlands	12
Ecuador	10
Mexico	4
Costa Rica	3
Other	8

Source: *Air Cargo World*, January 1998, p. 30, from
Society of American Florists.

★ 62 ★

Floriculture (SIC 0181)

Ohio's Green Goods Industry

The industry is shown by segment.

Landscape construction and installation	29.86%
Garden centers	28.99
Landscape maintenance	18.40
Wholesale	16.13
Other	6.62

Source: From the Internet, http:// www.hcs.ohio-
state.edu, 1997, p. 1.

★ 63 ★

Vegetables (SIC 0182)

Top States for Greenhouse Tomatoes

States are ranked by acres devoted to greenhouse
tomatoes.

Colorado	94
Texas	72
Pennsylvania	56
Arizona	44
New York	35
California	30
Ohio	20
Tennessee	20
Mississippi	16
New Jersey	15
Nevada	12
North Carolina	10
Florida	7

Source: *American Vegetable Grower*, August 1997, p. 10,
from Richard Snyder, Mississippi State University
Cooperative Extension.

SIC 02 - Agricultural Production - Livestock

★ 64 ★

Hogs (SIC 0213)

Largest Pork Producers - 1997

Companies are shown ranked by sows in production.

Murphy Family Farms	297,200
Carroll's Foods	144,800
Smithfield Foods	120,000
Cargill	115,000
Prestage Farms	115,000
Tyson Foods	111,500
Premium Standard Farms	110,000
Seaboard Corporation	108,750
DeKalb Swine Breeders	97,000
Iowa Select Farms	82,000
Goldsboro Hog Farm	60,000
Heartland Pork Enterprises	56,000
Continental Grain Company	52,000
Hanor Company	40,000
Land O'Lakes	34,000

Source: *Successful Farming*, October 1997, p. 23.

★ 65 ★

Eggs (SIC 0252)

Top Egg Producers - 1997

Data show production in millions of layers.

	(mil.)
Michael Foods, Inc.	20.3
Cal-Maine Foods, Inc.	17.2
Rose Acre Farms, Inc.	14.2
Buckeye Egg Farm	10.0
DeCoster Egg Farms	9.0
Fort Recovery Equity	7.5
ISE America	5.0
Mahard Egg Farms	4.8
Moark Productions, Inc.	4.5
Hillandale Poultry Services L.P.	4.1

Source: *Egg Industry*, January 1998, p. 6.

★ 66 ★

Poultry (SIC 0259)

North Carolina's Top Game-Bird Farms - 1996

Quail Valley	
Shady Knoll Gamebird Farm	
Mauney's Quail Farm	
Campbell's Quail Farm	
Chriscoe's Gamebird Farm	

Farms are shown ranked by birds raised. Animals include quail, chukar and pheasant.

Quail Valley	250,000
Shady Knoll Gamebird Farm	110,000
Mauney's Quail Farm	80,000
Campbell's Quail Farm	55,000
Chriscoe's Gamebird Farm	55,000

Source: *Business North Carolina*, April 1997, p. 68, from Gary Davis, N.C. State University, and farms.

★ 67 ★

Honey (SIC 0279)

Honey Production by State

Production is shown in thousands of pounds.

California	400
North Dakota	245
Florida	240
South Dakota	240
Minnesota	145
Idaho	120
Minnesota	107

Source: *Bee Culture*, May 1998, p. 13, from United States Department of Agriculture.

★ 68 ★

Honey (SIC 0279)

Leading Honey Importers to the United States - 1997

Figures are in metric tons.

Argentina	43,132
China	15,351
Mexico	7,920
Canada	4,734
India	1,593
Australia	1,082
Vietnam	1,066

Source: *Bee Culture*, April 1998, p. 19, from United States Bureau of Census.

SIC 07 - Agricultural Services

★ 69 ★

Farm Management (SIC 0762)

Largest Farm Management Firms

Firms are ranked by total acres managed.

NationsBank	2,480,689
Bank One Farm and Ranch Management	1,478,000
Farmers National Co.	1,203,186
Texas Pacific Land Trust	1,096,756
Norwest Bank Farm Management	1,030,215
U.S. Bancorp	725,000
Hall and Hall Incorporated	631,000
Am South Bank	570,400
Capital Agricultural Property Services Inc.	475,803
N.E. Agri Serv	423,000

Source: *Agri Finance*, November 1997, p. 3.

SIC 08 - Forestry

★ 70 ★

Timber (SIC 0811)

Largest Timberland Sales - 1997

Sales are shown in thousands of acres. Acquirers are shown in parentheses.

Kimberly-Clark (Alliance Forest)	400
Blandin Paper (Kymmene)	192
International Paper (Forest Investment)	175
Fort James (Champion International)	140
Georgia Pacific (Sierra Pacific)	127
James River (Hancock Timber)	95

Source: *Pulp & Paper*, January 1998, p. 67, from *International Woodfiber Report*.

★ 71 ★

Timber (SIC 0811)

Top Timber Producing Counties - North Carolina

Data show counties ranked by timber harvested in thousands of dollars.

Beaufort	$ 33,923
Columbus	33,915
Gladen	30,482
Moore	26,127
Pender	25,134
Sampson	$ 24,448
Brunswick	18,740
Onslaw	15,695
Wilkes	9,631
Randolph	7,872

Source: *Business North Carolina*, July 1997, p. 12, from N.C. State University.

SIC 09 - Fishing, Hunting, and Trapping

★ 72 ★

Fishing (SIC 0912)

Tuna Fishing - 1996

Data show U.S. commercial Pacific Ocean tuna catches in metric tons.

Skipjack	128,300
Yellowfin	41,900
Albacore	19,000
Bigeye	10,300
Bluefin	3,100

Source: *Tuna Newsletter* at http:// swfsc.ucsd.edu/ tunanews/feb97.html#production, February 1997, p. 1.

★ 73 ★

Shellfish (SIC 0913)

Shrimp Landings by State

Data show the number of landings for the first three months of the year.

Florida	3,879
Texas	2,656
Louisiana	2,085
Alabama	908
Mississippi	325

Source: From the Internet, http:// remora.ssp.nmfs.gov/ market_news/doc45.txt, March 1998, p. 1.

★ 74 ★

Fishing (SIC 0971)

Popular Fishing Catches - Canada

Types of fish caught are shown in percent. Canadian anglers catch approximately 300 million fish per year.

Trout	29.0%
Walleye	15.0
Pike	11.0
Bass	10.0
Smelt	8.0
Other	27.0

Source: *National Trade Data Bank*, July 2, 1997, p. IMI970630.

★ 75 ★

Hunting (SIC 0971)

Popular Types of Game

Data show millions of hunters, by type of game.

Big game (deer, elk)	11.3
Small game (rabbits, squirrels)	6.9
Fowl	3.0
Other (fox, raccoon)	1.5

Source: *Washington Post*, May 9, 1998, p. C2, from U.S. Department of the Interior and U.S. Department of Commerce.

★ 76 ★

Hunting (SIC 0971)

Top States for Hunting

Texas	
Michigan	
California	
New York	
Pennsylvania	
Wisconsin	
Mississippi	
Tennessee	
Louisiana	
Colorado	

Data show retail sales in thousands of dollars.

Texas	$ 1,072,943
Michigan	841,809
California	538,139
New York	541,325
Pennsylvania	514,374
Wisconsin	446,016
Mississippi	415,128
Tennessee	346,294
Louisiana	322,852
Colorado	311,934

Source: *Business North Carolina*, April 1997, p. 68, from Southwick Associates.

★ 77 ★

Hunting (SIC 0971)

What States Spend on Hunting - 1996

Spending is shown in billions of dollars. Figures reflect money spent by residents both in and outside their home states. Data are based on a national survey of state residents age 16 or older, conducted every four years.

California	$ 5.68
Texas	5.41
Michigan	3.73
Florida	3.46
Illinois	3.18
New York	2.80

Minnesota	$ 2.32
North Carolina	2.32
Wisconsin	2.20
Georgia	2.15

Source: *Wall Street Journal*, May 8, 1998, p. W8, from 1996 National Survey of Fishing, Hunting and Wildlife-Associated Recreation and U.S. Fish and Wildlife Service.

SIC 10 - Metal Mining

★ 78 ★
Mining (SIC 1000)

Leading Integrated Mining Companies - Canada

Companies are ranked by revenues in thousands of Canadian dollars. Figures for Alcan Aluminium and Inco Ltd. represent thousands of U.S. dollars.

Alcan Aluminium	$ 7,689,000
Inco Ltd.	3,139,000
Falconbridge Ltd.	2,290,122
Cominco Ltd.	1,911,855
Inmet Mining	954,504
Cameco Corp.	592,854
Hudson Bay Mining & Smelting	490,958
Sherritt International	300,093

Source: *Globe and Mail's Report on Business Magazine,* July 1997, p. 160.

★ 79 ★
Gold (SIC 1041)

Canada's Gold Producers

Companies are ranked by revenues in thousands of U.S. dollars. Figures for Teck Corp., Echo Bay Mines, and Homestake Canada represent thousands of Canadian dollars.

Barrick Gold	$ 1,318,000
Placer Dome	1,223,000
Teck Corp.	1,018,774
Placer Dome Canada	466,000
Echo Bay Mines	348,600
Cambior Inc.	314,942
Homestake Canada	405,039
Pegasus Gold	245,984
Kinross Gold	207,731
TVX Gold	195,108

Source: *Globe and Mail's Report on Business Magazine,* July 1997, p. 160.

★ 80 ★
Gold (SIC 1041)

Gold Production by State - 1996

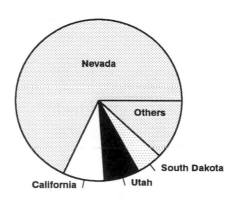

Total production was valued at $4 billion.

Nevada	68.0%
California	8.0
Utah	7.0
South Dakota	5.0
Others	12.0

Source: *Mining Engineering,* December 1997, p. 57.

★ 81 ★
Silver (SIC 1044)

Top Silver Producing States

Figures are in millions of ounces.

Nevada	21.0
Arizona	5.5
Idaho	5.2

Source: *USA TODAY,* February 6, 1998, p. 3B.

★ 82 ★
Uranium (SIC 1094)

Largest Uranium Production Centers - 1997

Production is shown in millions of pounds.

Highland (Wyoming)	1.56
Crow Butte (Nebraska)	0.78
Irigaray/Christensen (Wyoming)	0.70
Uncle Sam (Louisiana)	0.70
Kingsville Dome (Texas)	0.60
Donaldsville (Louisiana)	0.40
White Mesa (Utah)	0.35

Source: *Engineering & Mining Journal*, March 1998, p. 69.

★ 83 ★
Bauxite (SIC 1099)

Bauxite Consumption by Industry - 1996

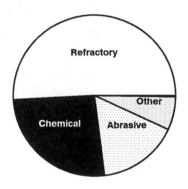

Consumption is shown in percent based on 760 thousand tons.

Refractory	50.8%
Chemical	26.4
Abrasive	15.5
Other	7.2

Source: *Ceramic Industry*, January 1998, p. 40, from U.S. Geological Survey.

★ 84 ★
Yttrium (SIC 1099)

Yttrium Demand - 1995

Demand is shown in percent. CRT stands for cathode ray tube.

Lamp/CRT phosphors	66.0%
Structural ceramics	29.0
Oxygen sensors, laser	5.0

Source: *Ceramic Industry*, January 1998, p. 45, from U.S. Geological Society.

SIC 12 - Coal Mining

★ 85 ★

Coal (SIC 1200)

Coal Production - Canada

| Alberta |
| British Columbia |
| Saskatchewan |
| Nova Scotia |
| New Brunswick |

Canadian provinces are shown ranked by coal production in millions of tons. Figures include metallurgical and thermal coal.

Alberta	. 36.2
British Columbia	. 25.4
Saskatchewan	. 10.9
Nova Scotia	. 3.1
New Brunswick	0.3

Source: *Globe and Mail*, August 19, 1997, p. B6.

★ 86 ★

Coal (SIC 1220)

Largest Coal Mines in West Virginia - 1997

Data are in millions of short tons.

Mountaineer	. 5.6
McElroy	. 5.4
Loveridge	. 4.8
Robinson Run No. 95	. 4.8
Shoemaker	. 4.8
Left Fork No. 2	. 4.7
UBBMC Montcoal Eagle	. 4.6
Federal No. 2	. 4.4
Samples	. 4.4
Camp Creek Mine No. 1	. 4.1

Source: *Mining Engineering*, May 1998, p. 113.

SIC 13 - Oil and Gas Extraction

★ 87 ★
Natural Gas (SIC 1311)

Largest Gas Producers in Texas - 1996

Data show production in millions of cubic feet.

Exxon Corp.	281,636,946
Union Pacific Resources Company	272,538,680
Shell Western E & P Inc.	180,779,869
Transtexas Gas Corporation	171,105,730
Texaco E & P Inc.	156,714,809
Mobil Producing Texas & New Mexico Inc.	149,267,297
Chevron U.S.A. Inc.	145,144,666
Phillips Petroleum Company	130,637,220
Enron Oil & Gas Company	127,081,116
Conoco Inc.	109,912,316

Source: From the Internet, http:// www.rrc.state.tx.us/ divisions/og/information-data/stats/ogist96.html, December 1, 1997, p. 1.

★ 88 ★
Natural Gas (SIC 1311)

Natural Gas Production by State - 1997

Production is shown in millions of cubic feet per day.

Texas	17,754
Louisiana	14,728
Oklahoma	4,623
New Mexico	4,242
Kansas	1,924
Wyoming	1,861
Colorado	1,590
Alaska	1,325
Alabama	1,027
Michigan	836

Source: *Oil & Gas Journal*, January 26, 1998, p. 71.

★ 89 ★
Oil (SIC 1311)

Largest Oil Producers in Texas - 1996

Companies are ranked by barrels of oil produced.

Amoco Production Company	40,137,089
Exxon Corp.	29,215,774
Shell Western E & P Inc.	22,300,219
Marathon Oil Company	20,269,378
Texaco E & P Inc.	18,918,878
Mobil Producing Texas & New Mexico Inc.	18,880,420
Chevron U.S.A. Inc.	16,908,787
Parker & Parsley Development L.P.	15,208,330
Amerada Hess Corporation	13,250,518
Union Pacific Resources Company	9,250,077

Source: From the Internet, http:// www.rrc.state.tx.us/ divisions/og/information-data/stats/ogist96.html, December 1, 1997, p. 2.

★ 90 ★
Oil (SIC 1311)

Oil Consumption by End Use

Distribution is shown in percent.

Personal vehicle travel	33.9%
Petrochemicals	11.5
Industrial fuel	8.3
Air transport	7.6
Heating and electrical generating	7.3
Water transport	2.7
Other land transport	20.7
Other nonfuel	4.3
Other	3.8

Source: *Investor's Business Daily*, January 23, 1998, p. 4, from American Petroleum Institute.

★ 91 ★
Oil and Gas (SIC 1311)

Leading Oil and Gas Firms - Canada

Firms are ranked by revenues in thousands of Canadian dollars. Figure for Amoco Canada Petroleum represents thousands of U.S. dollars.

Amoco Canada Petroleum	$ 4,512,000
PanCanadian Petroleum Ltd.	2,957,600
Imperial Oil Resources	2,501,000
Talisman Energy	1,468,600
Norcen Energy Resources	1,444,000
Cdn. Occidental Petroleum	1,398,000
Chevron Canada Resources	1,359,205
Alberta Energy Co.	1,124,800
Gulf Canada Resources	975,000

Source: *Globe and Mail's Report on Business Magazine*, July 1997, p. 158.

★ 92 ★
Oil and Gas (SIC 1321)

Oil Rig Activity by State - 1997

Data show number of wells.

Texas	357.0
Louisiana	193.1
Oklahoma	103.4
New Mexico	52.5
California	31.7

Source: *Oil & Gas Journal*, January 26, 1998, p. 71.

★ 93 ★
Oil Field Services (SIC 1389)

Leading Oil and Gas Field Service Companies - Canada

Nowsco Well Service
Canadian Fracmaster
CE Franklin
Ensign Resource Service Group
Dreco Energy Services
Precision Drilling Corp.

Companies are ranked by revenues in thousands of Canadian dollars. Figures for CE Franklin and Dreco Energy Services represent thousands of U.S. dollars.

Nowsco Well Service	$ 483,036
Canadian Fracmaster	348,540
CE Franklin	259,900
Ensign Resource Service Group	245,429
Dreco Energy Services	130,258
Precision Drilling Corp.	163,483

Source: *Globe and Mail's Report on Business Magazine*, July 1997, p. 158.

SIC 14 - Nonmetallic Minerals, Except Fuels

★ 94 ★

Dolomite (SIC 1411)

Top Dolomite Producing States

States are ranked by production in millions of metric tons.

Pennsylvania	16.0
Ohio	14.9
Illinois	13.4
Michigan	8.1
Indiana	6.8

Source: *The American Ceramic Society Bulletin*, June 1997, p. 95.

★ 95 ★

Sand and Gravel (SIC 1440)

Industrial Sand and Gravel Consumption by End Use - 1995

Data show consumption in thousands of metric tons.

	(000)	Share
Glass sands, all types	10,700	37.94%
Foundry sands	6,760	23.97
Abrasive (blast sand)	1,770	6.28
Hydraulic fracturing sand	1,580	5.60
Ceramics	253	0.90
Other	7,140	25.32

Source: *The American Ceramic Society Bulletin*, June 1997, p. 130.

★ 96 ★

Clays (SIC 1450)

Domestic Clay Production - 1997

Production is shown in kilotons.

Kaolin	9,180
Bentonite	3,780
Fuller's earth	2,570
Ball clay	1,030
Fire clay	403

Source: *Mining Engineering*, June 1998, p. 35, from U.S. Geological Survey Mineral Commodity Summaries.

★ 97 ★

Clays (SIC 1455)

Top Clay Producing States - 1996

States are ranked by production in thousands of metric tons.

	(000)	Share
Georgia	10,500	23.87%
Alabama	3,360	7.64
Wyoming	3,210	7.30
Texas	2,600	5.91
North Carolina	2,440	5.55
Ohio	2,170	4.93
California	1,780	4.05
South Carolina	1,690	3.84
Missouri	1,530	3.48
Arkansas	1,340	3.05
Tennessee	1,260	2.86
Other	12,100	27.51

Source: *The American Ceramic Society Bulletin*, June 1997, p. 91.

★ 98 ★

Kaolin (SIC 1455)

Airfloated Kaolin Consumption

Data show 1.4 million short tons of airfloated kaolin distributed by end use. Leading companies include Albion Kaolin, Evans Clay, Feldspar Corp., M&M Clay, W.R. Grace and Wilkinson Minerals.

Fiberglass	29.4%
Rubber/elastomeric	25.6
Sanitary	13.2
Filler/extender	12.8
Refractories	5.9
Dinnerware	2.9
Ceramic tile	1.8
Electrical porcelain	1.1
Other	7.3

Source: *The American Ceramic Society Bulletin*, June 1997, p. 105.

★ 99 ★

Potash (SIC 1474)

Top Potash Producers

Companies are ranked by capacity in thousands of short tons per year.

	(000)	Share
IMC Kalium	360	28.26%
Mississippi Potash West	335	26.30
Mississippi Potash East	255	20.02
Eddy Potash	200	15.70
Reilly Industries	70	5.49
Potash Corporation of Saskatchewan	54	4.24

Source: *Chemical Market Reporter*, June 23, 1997, p. 37.

★ 100 ★

Soda Ash (SIC 1474)

Largest Soda Ash Producers - 1997

Firms are ranked by production in short tons per year.

	(Tons)	Share
FMC Corp.	3.55	26.39%
General Chemical	2.50	18.59
OCI	2.30	17.10
Solvay	2.30	17.10
NA Chemical	1.50	11.15
Tg Soda	1.30	9.67

Source: *Engineering & Mining Journal*, March 1998, p. 64.

★ 101 ★

Fluorspar (SIC 1479)

Leading End Uses for Fluorspar - 1996

Shares are shown in percent.

Hydrofluoric manufacturers	91.0%
Steel manufacturers	6.0
Enamel, glass, foundry and others	3.6

Source: *Ceramic Industry*, January 1998, p. 43.

★ 102 ★

Mica (SIC 1499)

Ground Mica Consumption by End Use - 1996

Data show consumption in metric tons.

	Tons	Share
Joint compound	46,000	46.00%
Paint	20,000	20.00
Plastics	4,000	4.00
Well-drilling mud	4,000	4.00
Other	26,000	26.00

Source: *The American Ceramic Society Bulletin*, June 1997, p. 116.

SIC 15 - General Building Contractors

★ 103 ★
Building Construction (SIC 1500)
Construction Market - 1998

Spending is shown in billions of dollars.

Retail	$ 46.0
Institutional	45.6
Education (private & public)	39.1
Office	32.8
Multifamily	21.3
Health care (public & private)	19.3
Hotel	14.0

Source: *Building Design & Construction*, January 1998, p. 27, from Reed Elsevier Business Economics.

★ 104 ★
Building Construction (SIC 1500)
Largest Design Firms - 1997

Fluor Daniel Inc.
Bechtel Group Inc.
Brown & Root Inc.
Parsons Corp.
Raytheon Engineers & Constructors
Foster Wheeler Corp.
URS Greiner Woodward-Clyde
CH2M Hill Cos.
ABB Lummus Global Inc.
Black & Veatch

Firms are ranked by billings in millions of dollars.

Fluor Daniel Inc.	$ 1,652.0
Bechtel Group Inc.	1,203.0
Brown & Root Inc.	1,022.0
Parsons Corp.	977.3
Raytheon Engineers & Constructors	876.0
Foster Wheeler Corp.	796.9
URS Greiner Woodward-Clyde	766.5
CH2M Hill Cos.	753.3

ABB Lummus Global Inc.	$ 644.1
Black & Veatch	635.0

Source: *Engineering News Record*, April 20, 1998, p. 53.

★ 105 ★
Building Construction (SIC 1520)
Top General Contractors in North Carolina - 1997

Firms are ranked by revenues in millions of dollars.

Edifice Inc.	$ 70.0
Renentenbach Constructors Inc.	65.0
Weaver Construction LLC	65.0
C.C. Mangum Inc.	58.0
R.N. Rouse & Co.	53.0
J.M. Thompson Co.	50.0
Nello L. Teer Co.	50.0
Sebrell/Griffin & Co.	50.0

Source: *Business North Carolina*, May 1998, p. 14.

★ 106 ★
Residential Construction (SIC 1521)
Condominium Building in Canada - 1998

Data show units under construction for the first quarter of the year.

Vancouver	6,998
Toronto	3,545
Calgary	1,288
Montreal	983
Edmonton	613

Source: *Globe and Mail*, May 19, 1998, p. B10, from *Clayton Housing Report*.

★ 107 ★
Residential Construction (SIC 1521)

Housing Permits by State - 1997

Florida	132,813
Texas	123,985
California	109,908
Georgia	76,870
North Carolina	73,404
Arizona	57,843
Michigan	47,935
Illinois	46,833
Ohio	46,077
Virginia	45,178

Source: *Contractor*, April 1998, p. 3, from United States Department of Commerce.

★ 108 ★
Residential Construction (SIC 1521)

Top Attached For-Sale Leaders

Companies are ranked by number of units.

NVR	2,687
Universal Constructors	2,277
Hunt Building Corp.	1,585
U.S. Home Corp.	1,536
K. Hovnanian Enterprises	1,234
Centex Corp.	976
The Rottlund Co.	949
Lennar Corp.	826
Pasquinelli Construction Co.	621
Brookfield Homes	576

Source: *Builder*, May 1998, p. 96.

★ 109 ★
Residential Construction (SIC 1521)

Top Builders in Austin, TX - 1997

Companies are ranked by sales.

Milburn Homes	1,171
Buffington/Wilshire Homes	672
Ryland Homes	333
Newmark Homes	287
Main Street Homes	275

Source: *Builder*, May 1998, p. 218, from American Metro Study Group.

★ 110 ★
Residential Construction (SIC 1521)

Top Builders in Boston, MA - 1997

Companies are ranked by closings.

Toll Brothers	152
Pulte Home Corp. of Mass.	125
Vazza Properties	87
Commons Development Group	76
Modern Continental Enterprises	72

Source: *Builder*, May 1998, p. 222, from *Boston Business Journal* and Dun & Bradstreet Information Services.

★ 111 ★
Residential Construction (SIC 1521)

Top Builders in Cincinnati, OH - 1997

Companies are ranked by sales.

The Drees Co.	508
Fischer Homes	340
Zaring Homes	339
M/I Schottenstein Homes	274
Crossmann Communities	249

Source: *Builder*, May 1998, p. 218, from Robert Binns Associates.

★ 112 ★
Residential Construction (SIC 1521)

Top Builders in Denver, CO - 1997

Shares are shown based on 17,262 single-family permits.

Richmond American Homes	10.6%
Melody Homes	5.5
U.S. Home	4.7
Kaufman & Broad	4.7
Oakwood Homes	3.6
Village Homes	3.0
PrideMark Homes	3.0
Continental Homes	2.8
Pulte Home Corp.	2.7

Continued on next page.

★ 112 ★ *Continued*
Residential Construction (SIC 1521)

Top Builders in Denver, CO - 1997

Shares are shown based on 17,262 single-family permits.

Engle Homes	2.1%
Other	57.3

Source: *Professional Builder*, April 1998, p. 96, from Genesis Group.

★ 113 ★
Residential Construction (SIC 1521)

Top Builders in Greenville-Spartanburg, SC - 1997

Companies are ranked by number of closings.

Pulte Home Corp.	351
Seppala Homes	153
Centex Homes	134
Ryland Homes	130
Torrey Homes	125

Source: *Builder*, May 1998, p. 222, from Market Opportunity Research Enterprises.

★ 114 ★
Residential Construction (SIC 1521)

Top Builders in Houston, TX - 1997

Shares are shown based on 16,553 single-family permits.

MHI Homes	7.2%
Village Builders	5.9
Royce Homes	5.5
Pulte Home Corp.	4.4
Perry Homes	4.3
David Weekley Homes	4.3
Kimball Hill Homes	3.9
Ryland Homes	3.9
Lennar Homes	3.3
Dover/Ideal Homes	3.2
Other	54.1

Source: *Professional Builder*, April 1998, p. 100, from American Metro/Study Corp.

★ 115 ★
Residential Construction (SIC 1521)

Top Builders in Jacksonville, FL - 1997

D.W. Hutson

Atlantic Builders

SEDA Construction

Panitz Homes

Centex Homes

Companies are ranked by sales.

D.W. Hutson	721
Atlantic Builders	708
SEDA Construction	376
Panitz Homes	312
Centex Homes	224

Source: *Builder*, May 1998, p. 218, from Northeast Florida Builders Association.

★ 116 ★
Residential Construction (SIC 1521)

Top Builders in Las Vegas, NV - 1997

Shares are shown based on 18,737 single-family permits.

Lewis Homes	8.0%
Del Webb Corp.	7.7
Pulte Home Corp.	3.3
Rhodes Homes	3.3
American West Homes	3.3
Pardee Homes	3.0
Woodside Homes	2.6
Kaufman & Broad	2.5
Beazer Homes	2.3
Developers of Nevada	2.3
Other	65.0

Source: *Professional Builder*, April 1998, p. 96, from The Meyers Group.

★ 117 ★
Residential Construction (SIC 1521)

Top Builders in Los Angeles, CA - 1997

Companies are ranked by number of sales.

Kaufman and Broad 336
S & S Construction 271
William Lyon Co. 238
Centex Homes 202
Lewis Homes 171

Source: *Builder*, May 1998, p. 220, from The Meyers Group.

★ 118 ★
Residential Construction (SIC 1521)

Top Builders in Louisville, KY - 1997

Companies are ranked by number of closings.

Peter Built Homes 76
Monsour Builders 72
Mareli Development 68
Southeast Development 66
WKB Associates 56

Source: *Builder*, May 1998, p. 224, from HBA of Louisville.

★ 119 ★
Residential Construction (SIC 1521)

Top Builders in Memphis, TN - 1997

Companies are ranked by number of closings.

Bowden Building Co. 388
Lenox Homes 183
W.V. Richerson Co. 136
Hyneman Homes 96
Chamberlain & McCreery 93

Source: *Builder*, May 1998, p. 220, from Gamer Chandler/Chandler Reports.

★ 120 ★
Residential Construction (SIC 1521)

Top Builders in Miami, FL - 1997

Lennar Homes
Caribe Group
Shoma Homes
Weitzer Homes
Continental Homes

Companies are ranked by number of closings.

Lennar Homes 762
Caribe Group 364
Shoma Homes 268
Weitzer Homes 246
Continental Homes 225

Source: *Builder*, May 1998, p. 224, from Price Waterhouse.

★ 121 ★
Residential Construction (SIC 1521)

Top Builders in Oakland, CA - 1997

Companies are ranked by sales.

Kaufman and Broad 867
Centex Homes 421
Greystone Homes 384
Signature Properties 361
Ponderosa Homes 286

Source: *Builder*, May 1998, p. 216, from The Meyers Group.

★ 122 ★
Residential Construction (SIC 1521)

Top Builders in Pittsburgh, PA - 1997

Companies are ranked by number of closings.

Maronda Homes 275
Ryan Homes 254
Heartland Homes 66
Washington Homes 45
RWS Construction 41

Source: *Builder*, May 1998, p. 224, from Howard Hanna Real Estate Services.

★ 123 ★

Residential Construction (SIC 1521)

Top Builders in Richmond, VA - 1997

Companies are ranked by closings.

Ryan Homes	206
Emerald Homes	158
Eagle Construction	147
Teal Builders	129
Tomac Corp.	110

Source: *Builder*, May 1998, p. 222, from Rountry & Associates.

★ 124 ★

Residential Construction (SIC 1521)

Top Builders in Tucson, AZ - 1997

Companies are ranked by number of sales.

Estes Homebuilding	461
U.S. Home Corp.	453
Pulte Home Corp.	400
Richmond American	386
Robson Communities	313

Source: *Builder*, May 1998, p. 224, from The Meyers Group.

★ 125 ★

Residential Construction (SIC 1521)

Top Builders in Washington D.C. - 1997

Shares are shown based on 19,978 single-family permits.

Ryan Homes	10.8%
Pulte Home Corp.	5.2
Richmond American	4.7
NVHomes	3.2
Washington Homes	2.9
Regency Homes	2.8
Ryland Group	2.7
Winchester Homes	2.7
Trafalgar House	2.4
Toll Brothers	2.1
Other	60.5

Source: *Professional Builder*, April 1998, p. 100, from Meyers Housing Data Reports.

★ 126 ★

Residential Construction (SIC 1521)

Top Detached For-Sale Leaders

Companies are ranked by number of units.

Pulte Home Corp.	15,322
Centex Corp.	11,981
Kaufman and Broad Home Corp.	11,443
Lennar Corp.	8,943
The Ryland Group	8,377
U.S. Home Corp.	7,496
Del Webb Corp.	5,955
Beazer Homes USA	5,710
D.R. Horton	5,593
Continental Homes Holding Corp.	5,204

Source: *Builder*, May 1998, p. 96.

★ 127 ★

Residential Construction (SIC 1521)

Top Home Builders - 1997

Firms are ranked by revenues in billions of dollars.

Pulte Corp.	$ 2.47
Centex Corp.	2.27
Kaufman & Broad	1.82
Champion Enterprises Inc.	1.67
Lennar Corp.	1.65
The Ryland Group Inc.	1.52
Fleetwood Enterprises Inc.	1.43
U.S. Home Corp.	1.27
NVR Inc.	1.15
Del Webb Corp.	1.14

Source: *Professional Builder*, April 1998, p. 95.

★ 128 ★

Residential Construction (SIC 1521)

Top Home Builders in Atlanta, GA - 1997

Shares are shown based on 28,537 single-family closings.

D.R. Horton/Torrey Homes	3.8%
John Wiedland Homes	2.8
Pulte Home Corp.	2.7
Colony Homes	2.6
Ryland Homes	1.5
Bowen & Bowen Construction	1.1
Homeland Construction	1.1

Continued on next page.

★ 128 ★ *Continued*
Residential Construction (SIC 1521)

Top Home Builders in Atlanta, GA - 1997

Shares are shown based on 28,537 single-family closings.

McCar Development	1.0%
Centex Homes	0.9
Ashton Woods Homes	0.8
Other	81.7

Source: *Professional Builder*, April 1998, p. 95, from Magellan-Home Data Corp. and Farmer & Associates.

★ 129 ★
Residential Construction (SIC 1521)

Top Home Builders in Charlotte, NC - 1997

Companies are ranked by number of closings.

Pulte Home Corp.	576
Ryland Homes	455
Squires Homes	411
Centex Homes	390
Ryan Homes	381

Source: *Builder*, May 1998, p. 210, from Market Opportunity Research Enterprises.

★ 130 ★
Residential Construction (SIC 1521)

Top Home Builders in Chicago, IL - 1997

Shares are shown based on 2,225 single-family closings.

Cambridge Cos.	5.6%
Concord Development Co.	4.3
Lakewood Homes	3.9
Town & Country Homes	3.8
Kimball Hill Homes	3.5
Pulte Home Corp.	3.3
Sundance Homes	3.0
Neumann Homes	2.7
Ryland Homes	2.5
Pasquinelli Construction Co.	2.1
Other	65.3

Source: *Professional Builder*, April 1998, p. 95, from Tracy Cross & Associates Inc.

★ 131 ★
Residential Construction (SIC 1521)

Top Home Builders in Detroit, MI - 1997

Companies are ranked by sales.

Pulte Home Corp.	684
Crosswinds Communities	505
Tri Mount-Vincenti Cos.	354
Anthony Lombardo Cos.	293
Moceri Cos.	284

Source: *Builder*, May 1998, p. 208, from Housing Consultants.

★ 132 ★
Residential Construction (SIC 1521)

Top Home Builders in Orlando, FL - 1997

Market shares are shown based on 8,421 single-family closings.

Centex Homes	7.7%
Maronda Homes	6.6
American Heritage Homes	6.4
Eagle Homes	5.4
Lennar Homes	4.3
Landstar Development	4.1
Ryland Group	4.1
Cambridge Homes	3.7
Pulte Home Corp.	3.5
Morrison Homes	3.4
Others	50.8

Source: *Professional Builder*, April 1998, p. 100, from Charles Wayne Consulting Inc.

★ 133 ★
Residential Construction (SIC 1521)

Top Home Builders in Philadelphia, PA - 1997

Companies are ranked by sales.

Toll Brothers	744
Ryan Homes	458
Pulte Home Corp.	300
David Cutler Group	250
FPA/Orleans Builders	193

Source: *Builder*, May 1998, p. 208, from The Meyers Group.

★ 134 ★

Residential Construction (SIC 1521)

Top Home Builders in Phoenix/Mesa, AZ - 1997

Market shares are shown based on 31,359 single-family closings.

Continental Homes	6.6%
UDC Homes	5.0
Shea Homes	4.9
Del Webb Communities	4.0
Beazer Homes	4.0
Richmond American	2.8
Trend Homes/Key	2.7
Pulte Homes Corp.	2.7
Fulton Homes	2.6
Kaufman & Broad	2.4
Other	62.3

Source: *Professional Builder*, April 1998, p. 100, from R.L. Brown Housing Reports and Cahners Economics.

★ 135 ★

Residential Construction (SIC 1521)

Top Home Builders in Portland, OR - 1997

Companies are ranked by number of closings.

RMP Properties	485
West Hills Development	359
Aho Construction	278
New Tradition Homes	235
Centex Homes	220

Source: *Builder*, May 1998, p. 212.

★ 136 ★

Residential Construction (SIC 1521)

Top Rental Leaders

Companies are ranked by number of units.

A.G. Spanos Cos.	11,560
Trammell Crow Residential	7,987
JPI Construction	6,000
Lincoln Property Co.	5,462
Picerne Real Estate Group	4,050
Post Properties	2,943
Colson & Colson Construction Co.	2,776
The Related Cos.	2,447

Brisben Cos.	2,053
The Morgan Group	1,996

Source: *Builder*, May 1998, p. 96.

★ 137 ★

Siding (SIC 1521)

Siding Demand - 1996

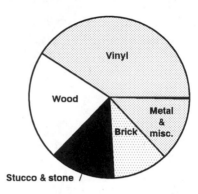

Demand is shown in percent, based on a total of 91.6 million squares.

Vinyl	41.0%
Wood	22.0
Stucco & stone	13.0
Brick	11.0
Metal & misc.	13.0

Source: *Do-It-Yourself Retailing*, March 1998, p. 90, from Freedonia Group.

★ 138 ★

Siding (SIC 1521)

Siding Market - 2005

The market is estimated in percent.

Fiber cement	30.0%
Solid wood/composite	20.0
Vinyl	17.0
Metal	1.0
Other	32.0

Source: *Wood Technology*, January/February 1998, p. 53.

★ 139 ★

Nonresidential Construction (SIC 1540)

Nonresidential Construction Spending

Types of nonresidential construction are shown ranked by 1996, 1997, and 1998 spending in billions of dollars.

	1996	1997	1998
Institutional	$ 92.7	$ 100.7	$ 102.0
Commercial	81.4	91.4	91.8
Office	25.2	30.3	29.5
Retail	45.0	47.6	47.5
Hotel/motel	11.2	13.5	14.8
Industrial	30.1	29.8	28.8

Source: *Supply House Times*, August 1997, p. 9, from U.S. Department of Commerce and Cahners Economics.

SIC 16 - Heavy Construction, Except Building

★ 140 ★

Heavy Construction (SIC 1600)

Heavy Construction Spending - 1998

Spending is shown in billions of dollars.

	($ bil.)	Share
Highways & streets	$ 41.5	34.87%
Water/sewer	16.2	13.61
Telecommunications	12.3	10.34
Other public construction	20.8	17.48
Utility & other private construction	28.2	23.70

Source: *Construction Equipment*, January 1998, p. 64.

★ 141 ★

Street and Highway Construction (SIC 1611)

New Road Construction by Region

Contract plans are shown in millions of dollars.

South	$ 4,037
Mississippi to Rockies	890
Mid-Atlantic	600
Far West	653
Midwest	587
New England	49

Source: *Engineering News Record*, January 26, 1998, p. 60.

★ 142 ★

Bridge Construction (SIC 1622)

New Bridge Construction by Region

Contract plans are shown in millions of dollars.

South	$ 1,227
Mississippi to Rockies	289
Mid-Atlantic	216
Midwest	171
New England	127
Far West	76

Source: *Engineering News Record*, January 26, 1998, p. 60.

SIC 17 - Special Trade Contractors

★ 143 ★

Contracting (SIC 1700)

Top Contractors - 1996

Contractors are ranked by dollar value of construction for which they were responsible. Data show millions of dollars.

The Turner Corp.	$ 2,684.58
BE&K Inc.	1,532.99
Bovis Inc.	1,475.35
Bechtel Group Inc.	1,313.66
Fluor Daniel Inc.	1,186.02
The Clark Construction Group Inc.	1,153.62
Centex Construction Group	1,031.33
McCarthy	1,027.00
Hoffman Construction Co.	1,023.15
Beers Construction Co.	963.00

Source: *Building Design & Construction*, July 1997, p. 40.

★ 144 ★

Contracting - Specialty (SIC 1700)

Top Specialty Contractors - 1996

Firms are ranked by dollar value of construction for which they were responsible. Data show millions of dollars.

EMCOR GROUP Inc.	$ 747.50
Poole and Kent Organization	703.00
Limbach Constructors Inc.	259.87
Harmon Ltd.	240.00
MMC Corp.	239.24
Shambaugh & Son Inc.	167.20
BUCON Inc.	167.00
Air Conditioning Co.	157.00
Natkin Contracting LLC	130.00
Murphy Co.	127.61

Source: *Building Design & Construction*, July 1997, p. 70.

★ 145 ★

Contracting - Mechanical (SIC 1711)

Leading Mechanical Contractors

Firms are ranked by 1996 revenues in millions of dollars.

EMCOR Group Inc.	$ 734.5
The Poole and Kent Co.	406.1
The Kinetics Group Inc.	278.0
Limbach Constructors Inc.	259.9
MMC Corp.	239.2
Air Conditioning Co. Inc.	157.1
Fullman Co.	145.2
Scott Co. of California	138.6
Murphy Co. Mechanical Contractors & Engineers	137.8
Southland Industries	137.5

Source: *Engineering News Record*, October 6, 1997, p. 59.

★ 146 ★

Contracting - Painting (SIC 1721)

Top Painting Contractors

Firms are ranked by 1996 revenues in millions of dollars.

Cannon Sline Inc.	$ 40.6
J.L. Manta Inc.	29.9
M.L. McDonald Co.	28.0
Techno Coatings Inc.	25.4
Robison-Prezioso Inc.	25.1
Swanson & Youngdale Inc.	21.3
Certified Coatings of California	16.7
Ascher Brothers Co. Inc.	16.5
The Vulcan Group	14.3
Fine Painting & Decorating Co. Inc.	13.1

Source: *Engineering News Record*, October 6, 1997, p. 68.

★ 147 ★
Contracting - Electrical (SIC 1731)

Leading Electrical Contractors

Firms are ranked by 1996 revenues in millions of dollars.

EMCOR Group Inc. . . . . $ 901.4
SASCO Group 348.0
MYR Group Inc. 291.9
Mass. Electric Construction Co. 247.1
L.K. Comstock & Co. Inc. 189.3
Sachs Electric Co. 147.5
Fischbach & Moore Inc. 139.6
Cupertino Electric Inc. 132.0
Fisk Electric Co. 118.4
Rosendin Electric Inc. 116.0

Source: *Engineering News Record*, October 6, 1997, p. 56.

★ 148 ★
Contracting - Masonry (SIC 1741)

Leading Masonry Contractors

The Western Group

Dee Brown Inc.

Seedorff Masonry Inc.

Pyramid Masonry Contractors Inc.

WASCO Inc.

Leonard Masonry Inc.

Sun Valley Masonry Co.

John J. Smith Masonry Co.

Thorleif Larsen & Son Inc.

Culbertson Enterprises Inc.

Firms are ranked by 1996 revenues in millions of dollars.

The Western Group . . . . $ 39.5
Dee Brown Inc. 33.4
Seedorff Masonry Inc. 30.9
Pyramid Masonry Contractors Inc. 28.1
WASCO Inc. 27.6
Leonard Masonry Inc. 22.5
Sun Valley Masonry Co. 21.0
John J. Smith Masonry Co. 20.6
Thorleif Larsen & Son Inc. 19.4
Culbertson Enterprises Inc. 19.0

Source: *Engineering News Record*, October 6, 1997, p. 60.

★ 149 ★
Contracting - Wall and Ceiling (SIC 1742)

Leading Wall and Ceiling Contractors

Firms are ranked by 1996 revenues in millions of dollars.

Performance Contracting Group Inc. . . . $ 153.2
Cleveland Construction Inc. 152.5
National Construction Enterprises Inc. . . . 87.6
Ellason & Knuth Cos. Inc. 69.9
Nastasi & Associates Inc. 65.1
Nastasi-White Inc. 60.1
F.L. Crane & Sons Inc. 60.0
Midwest Drywall Co. Inc. 59.4
Keenan, Hopkins, Schmidt & Stowell
  Contractors 52.6
Anson Industries Inc. 41.8

Source: *Engineering News Record*, October 6, 1997, p. 68.

★ 150 ★
Contracting - Roofing (SIC 1761)

Reroofing Materials for Commercial Buildings - 1996

Data represent 1996 spending in billions of dollars.

Single ply . . . . $ 3.25
Built-up roofing 2.99
Modified bitumen 2.41
Aphalt shingles 0.71
Sprayed polyurethane foam (SPF) 0.36
Metal 0.27
Liquid applied 0.21
Tile 0.11
Other 0.09

Source: *AS&U*, June 1997, p. 38, from National Roofing Contractors Association.

★ 151 ★
Contracting - Roofing (SIC 1761)

Steep-Slope Roofing Sales - 1997

The market is shown by type of material. Figures are for new construction.

Fiber/asphalt shingle 36.3%
Metal 17.0
Organic asphalt shingle 7.0
Concrete tile 5.1

Continued on next page.

Contracting - Roofing (SIC 1761)

Steep-Slope Roofing Sales - 1997

The market is shown by type of material. Figures are for new construction.

Clay tile	3.8%
Wood shingle	3.3
Slate	2.9
Composite/synthetic	0.4
Other	24.2

Source: *Custom Builder*, 1998, p. 70.

★ 152 ★

Contracting - Sheet Metal (SIC 1761)

Leading Sheet Metal Contractors

Firms are ranked by 1996 revenues in millions of dollars.

Kirk & Blum	$ 63.7
Scott Co. of California	59.4
Hill Mechanical Corp.	44.4
EMCOR Group Inc.	33.4
Crown Corr Inc.	32.9
TDIndustries	31.3
Heating & Plumbing Engineers Inc.	26.9
The Egan Cos.	24.0
Anson Industries Inc.	22.1
Holaday-Parks Inc.	21.7

Source: *Engineering News Record*, October 6, 1997, p. 65.

★ 153 ★

Contracting - Concrete (SIC 1771)

Leading Concrete Contractors

Firms are ranked by 1996 revenues in millions of dollars.

Baker Concrete Contruction Inc.	$ 187.0
Ceco Concrete Construction Corp.	94.2
Miller & Long Co. Inc.	85.0
The Western Group	74.9
T.A.S. Construction Inc.	54.6
Capform Inc.	51.6

Bomel Construction Co. Inc.	$ 43.5
Structural Preservation Systems Inc.	43.2
VSI Corp.	40.0
Strescon Industries Inc.	38.4

Source: *Engineering News Record*, October 6, 1997, p. 60.

★ 154 ★

Contracting - Steel Erection (SIC 1791)

Leading Steel Erection Contractors

Firms are ranked by 1996 revenues in millions of dollars.

Midwest Steel Inc.	$ 108.0
Schuff Steel Co.	103.9
Broad, Vogt & Conant Inc.	74.5
The Williams Group Inc.	66.3
J.L. Davidson Co. Inc.	39.5
Interstate Iron Works Corp.	36.0
Adams & Smith Inc.	34.6
L.H. Sowles Co.	33.6
Washington Iron Works Inc.	32.2
Derr Construction Co.	28.1

Source: *Engineering News Record*, October 6, 1997, p. 62.

★ 155 ★

Contracting - Glazing & Curtain Wall (SIC 1793)

Leading Glazing/Curtain Wall Contractors

Firms are ranked by 1996 revenues in millions of dollars.

Harmon Ltd.	$ 379.0
Flour City Architecture Metals Inc.	47.0
Waltcrs & Wolf	38.1
MTH Industries	25.4
Masonry Arts Inc.	15.9
Cartner Glass Systems Inc.	13.7
Karas & Karas Glass Co. Inc.	13.7
Elward Construction Co.	13.4
National Glass & Metal Co. Inc.	11.5
Atlantic Plate Glass Co. Inc.	10.2

Source: *Engineering News Record*, October 6, 1997, p. 67.

★ 156 ★
Contracting - Excavation & Foundation (SIC 1794)

Leading Excavation/Foundation Contractors

Firms are ranked by 1996 revenues in millions of dollars.

Hayward Baker Inc.	$ 73.7
Ryan Inc. Central	71.2
Malcolm Drilling Co.	64.5
McKinney Drilling Co.	55.3
Nicholson Construction Co.	46.8
Berkel & Co. Contractors Inc.	45.0
Case Foundation Co.	43.8
Allwaste Inc.	42.0
The Beaver Excavating Co.	37.8
Richard Goettle Inc.	35.7

Source: *Engineering News Record*, October 6, 1997, p. 62.

★ 157 ★
Contracting - Demolition (SIC 1795)

Leading Wrecking Firms

Firms are ranked by 1996 revenues in millions of dollars.

Penhall International Inc.	$ 76.4
Cleveland Wrecking Co.	52.4
Integrated Waste Special Services Inc.	39.0
Bierlein Cos.	38.1
Philip Services Corp.	34.0
Iroquois Corp.	26.3
SCS Group L.C.	24.0
Olshan Demolishing Inc.	23.7
Midwest Steel Co. Inc.	21.7
Aman Environmental Construction Inc.	21.0

Source: *Engineering News Record*, October 6, 1997, p. 72.

★ 158 ★
Contracting - Asbestos Abatement (SIC 1799)

Leading Asbestos Abatement Contractors

Firms are ranked by 1996 revenues in millions of dollars.

NSC Corp.	$ 105.3
LVI Environmental Services Group Inc.	74.1

Chempower Inc.	$ 42.8
AC and S Inc.	32.4
Specialty Systems Inc. & Affiliated Cos.	22.1
PDG Environmental Inc.	17.1
Performance Contracting Group	16.1
Philip Services Corp.	14.9
Spray Systems Environmental Inc.	10.8
Anco Industries Inc.	10.0

Source: *Engineering News Record*, October 6, 1997, p. 72.

★ 159 ★
Contracting - Utility (SIC 1799)

Leading Utility Contractors

Firms are ranked by 1996 revenues in millions of dollars.

Kimmins Contracting Corp.	$ 73.8
Utilx Corp.	64.9
RCI Construction Group	62.4
Garney Cos. Inc.	53.3
Kearney Development Co. Inc.	51.4
Davis H. Elliot Co. Inc.	41.2
Insituform Technologies Inc.	32.2
Hydro Group Inc.	25.6
New River Electrical Corp.	24.5
Hooper Corp.	21.5

Source: *Engineering News Record*, October 6, 1997, p. 67.

★ 160 ★
Swimming Pools (SIC 1799)

Leading Swimming Pool Builders in Maricopa County, AZ - 1996

Shares are shown in percent.

Shasta Industries Inc.	20.4%
Paddock Pool Construction Co.	13.9
Hawaiian Pools Inc.	12.7
California Pools	10.9
Rondo Pools Inc.	3.3
Executive Pools & Spas Inc.	2.3
Dolphin Pool Construction Co. Inc.	2.2
Majestic Pools & Spas Inc.	1.9
Mossman Brothers Pools Inc.	1.5
Presidential Pools & Spas Inc.	1.5
La Paz Pools Ltd.	1.4
Hop Cassidy Pools Inc.	1.2

Continued on next page.

Swimming Pools (SIC 1799)

Leading Swimming Pool Builders in Maricopa County, AZ - 1996

Shares are shown in percent.

Swan Pools Inc.	1.2%
Sun Valley Pools	1.1
Malibu Pools & Spas	1.0
Other	23.5

Source: *The Business Journal - Serving Phoenix and the Valley of the Sun*, July 11, 1997, p. 19, from Jim Daniel.

SIC 20 - Food and Kindred Products

★ 161 ★
Food (SIC 2000)

Best-Selling Grocery Items - Los Angeles, CA

Sales are shown in millions of dollars for the third quarter of 1997.

Alcoholic beverages	$ 969.5
Milk	656.8
Meat and deli	584.5
Carbonated beverages	551.3
Bread & baked goods	546.7
Cereal	380.4
Prepared foods, frozen	318.3
Baby food	254.6
Pet food	244.6
Ice cream	196.9

Source: *Grocery Headquarters*, December 1997, p. 11, from A.C. Nielsen.

★ 162 ★
Food (SIC 2000)

Best-Selling Grocery Items - New York City, NY

Bread & baked goods
Carbonated beverages
Meat
Milk
Cereal
Prepared foods, frozen
Pet food
Cookies

Sales are shown in millions of dollars for the third quarter of 1997.

Bread & baked goods	$ 691.5
Carbonated beverages	532.2
Meat	468.5

Milk	$ 453.3
Cereal	422.2
Prepared foods, frozen	308.3
Pet food	296.3
Cookies	289.3

Source: *Grocery Headquarters*, December 1997, p. 11, from A.C. Nielsen.

★ 163 ★
Food (SIC 2000)

Best-Selling Grocery Items - San Francisco, CA

Sales are shown in millions of dollars for the third quarter of 1997.

Alcoholic beverages	$ 558.5
Meat and deli	298.7
Bread & baked goods	297.3
Milk	291.6
Carbonated beverages	215.5
Prepared foods, frozen	179.2
Cereal	171.2
Ice cream	121.2
Pet food	110.8
Cookies	95.2

Source: *Grocery Headquarters*, December 1997, p. 11.

★ 164 ★

Food (SIC 2000)

Enhanced Health Food Market

The retail market is shown by segment.

	($ bil.)	Share
Conventional foods	$ 387.4	86.7%
Lesser-evil foods	37.7	8.4
Functional foods	14.3	3.2
Natural/organic foods	7.3	1.6

Source: *Prepared Foods*, February 1998, p. 40, from *Nutrition Business Journal*.

★ 165 ★

Food (SIC 2000)

Largest Food Companies - 1997

Firms are ranked by revenues in millions of dollars.

ConAgra	$ 24,002
Sara Lee	19,734
RJR Nabisco Holdings	17,057
Archer Daniels Midland	13,853
IBP	13,259
Bestfoods	9,818
H.J. Heinz	9,357
Farmland Industries	9,148
Campbell Soup	7,964
Kellogg	6,830

Source: *Fortune*, April 27, 1998, pp. F-50.

★ 166 ★

Food (SIC 2000)

Largest Private Food Companies - 1996

Firms are ranked by food and beverage sales in millions of dollars. Figures are for United States and Canada.

Cargill Inc.	$ 20,400
Mars Inc.	13,000
Mid-America Dairymen Inc.	4,085
Farmland Industries Inc.	3,221
Borden Inc. and Affiliates	3,150
McCain Foods Ltd.	3,032

Associated Milk Producers Inc.	.$ 2,154
Perdue Farms Inc.	2,120
Specialty Foods Corp.	2,022
Keystone Foods Corp.	2,000

Source: *Prepared Foods*, December 1997, p. 11, from Cahners Food and Lodging Group Research Dept.

★ 167 ★

Food (SIC 2000)

Largest Public Food Companies - 1996

Firms are ranked by food and beverage sales in millions of dollars. Figures are for United States and Canada.

Philip Morris Companies Inc.	$ 32,277
PepsiCo.	20,204
Coca-Cola Co.	18,546
ConAgra Inc.	18,249
IBP Inc.	12,539
Anheuser-Busch Companies Inc.	10,144
Sara Lee Corp.	9,426
H.J. Heinz Co.	9,112
Nabisco Inc.	8,889
CPC International Inc.	8,477

Source: *Prepared Foods*, December 1997, p. 11, from Cahners Food and Lodging Group Research Dept.

★ 168 ★

Food (SIC 2000)

Natural Products Industry - 1996

The market is shown in percent. The $15 billion category includes fresh and organic foods and beverages, nutraceuticals, vitamins, dietary supplements, and all-natural personal care products.

Traditional foods	.85.7%
Low fat/no-fat foods	8.5
Functional foods	4.0
All natural/organic foods	1.8

Source: *Progressive Grocer*, March 1998, p. 87, from Willard Bishop Consultintg.

★ 169 ★

Lunch Meat (SIC 2013)

Popular Lunch Meat Brands

Data show selected sales in millions of dollars.

Oscar Mayer	$ 702.4
Louis Rich	252.1

Source: *Brandweek*, June 15, 1998, p. S52, from Information Resources Inc.

★ 170 ★

Sausage (SIC 2013)

Refrigerated Dinner Sausage Market

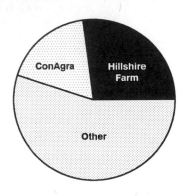

Shares are shown for the year ended April 27, 1997.

Hillshire Farm	27.4%
ConAgra	17.8
Other	54.8

Source: *Brandweek*, June 2, 1997, p. 4, from Information Resources Inc.

★ 171 ★

Poultry (SIC 2015)

Top Integrated Broiler Companies - 1997

Data show average weekly ready-to-cook production in millions of pounds. Shares are shown based on 581.7 million pounds produced by the top 46 companies.

	(mil.)	Share
Tyson Foods, Inc.	120.80	20.78%
Gold Kist, Inc.	53.30	9.17
Perdue Farms, Inc.	45.31	7.79
Pilgrim's Pride Corporation	34.60	5.95
ConAgra Poultry Company	31.85	5.48

	(mil.)	Share
Hudson Foods, Inc.	30.58	5.26%
Wayne Poultry/Continental Grain	24.96	4.29
Cagle's, Inc.	16.37	2.82
Foster Farms	14.53	2.50
Seaboard Farms, Inc.	14.09	2.42
Other	195.04	33.54

Source: *Broiler Industry*, January 1998, p. 18C.

★ 172 ★

Dairy Foods (SIC 2020)

Frozen Dairy Market - 1997

Sales are shown in percent.

Regular fat ice cream	73.2%
Reduced, light & low-fat ice cream	10.4
Frozen yogurt	7.5
Nonfat ice cream	4.2
Sherbet	3.5
Sorbet	0.6
Other	0.6

Source: *Dairy Foods*, March 1998, p. 82, from A.C. Nielsen and International Ice Cream Assn.

★ 173 ★

Dairy Products (SIC 2020)

Top North American Dairy Food Companies - 1996

Data show sales of finished dairy products in millions of dollars.

Kraft Foods	$ 4,100
Dean Foods Co.	1,611
Borden Inc.	1,200
Leprino Foods Co.	1,150
Schreiber Foods Inc.	1,100
Ault Foods Ltd.	989
ConAgra Inc.	970
Good Humor-Breyers Ice Cream	910
Bols Wessanen U.S.A. Inc.	870
Stella Foods Inc.	800
Dreyer's/Edy's Grand Ice Cream Inc.	792
Great Lakes Cheese Co.	607
Besnier USA Inc.	600
Baskin-Robbins U.S.A. Co.	550
Dannon Company Inc.	550

Source: *Dairy Foods*, July 1997, p. 11.

★ 174 ★
Dairy Products (SIC 2020)

Use of Milk Solids - 1996

The table shows the use of milk solids in percent.

Cheese	45.0%
Fluid milk	29.0
Butter	7.0
Ice cream	7.0
Powdered milk	4.0
Other	8.0

Source: *Hoard's Dairyman*, July 1997, p. 519, from National All-Jersey.

★ 175 ★
Cheese (SIC 2022)

Leading Cheese Makers - 1998

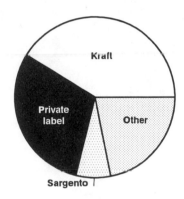

Market shares are shown based on supermarket sales of a year ended February 1, 1998. The entire market is valued at $6.5 billion.

Kraft	41.0%
Private label	30.0
Sargento	7.0
Other	22.0

Source: *Chicago Tribune*, March 30, 1998, p. 3, from Information Resources Inc.

★ 176 ★
Cheese (SIC 2022)

Supermarket Cheese Sales - 1997

Sales are shown for the year ended November 29, 1997.

	(mil.)	Share
Regular fat	1,267	79.19%
Lower fat	250	15.63
Nonfat	83	5.19

Source: *Dairy Foods*, April 1998, p. E, from A.C. Nielsen.

★ 177 ★
Macaroni & Cheese (SIC 2023)

Macaroni & Cheese Mix Market

The $597.6 million market is shown in percent.

Kraft Foods	78.9%
Private label	16.9
Other	4.2

Source: *Advertising Age*, March 30, 1998, p. 4, from Information Resources Inc.

★ 178 ★
Milk (SIC 2023)

Evaporated/Condensed Milk Market Leaders - 1997

Shares of the $292.9 million market are shown for the year ended May 25, 1997.

	Sales ($ mil.)	Share
Carnation	$80.6	27.52%
Eagle Brand	61.5	21.00
Private label	99.8	34.07
Other	51.0	17.41

Source: *Brandweek*, June 30, 1997, p. 4, from Information Resources Inc.

★ 179 ★
Frozen Desserts (SIC 2024)

Frozen Cheesecake Market

Shares are shown for the year ended March 29, 1998.
Data refer to supermarket sales.

Sara Lee	65.2%
Other	34.8

Source: *Brandweek*, April 27, 1998, p. 3, from
Information Resources Inc.

★ 180 ★
Frozen Yogurt (SIC 2024)

Top Frozen Yogurt Brands - 1996

Shares are shown based on a $475.6 million market
for the year ended December 1, 1996.

Ben & Jerry's	8.8%
Kemps	7.4
Dreyer's	6.6
Breyer's	5.8
Haagen-Dazs	5.8
Turkey Hill	4.7
Dreyer's/Edy's	4.3
Dreyer's/Edy's Grand	4.1
Dannon	2.3
Private label	17.8
Other	32.4

Source: *Dairy Foods*, March 1997, p. 82, from
Information Resources Inc.

★ 181 ★
Ice Cream (SIC 2024)

Ice Cream Leaders

Sales are shown in millions of dollars for the year
ended December 7, 1997.

Breyer's	$ 407.0
Dreyer's/Edy's	328.5
Blue Bell	174.2
Haagen-Dazs	152.7
Private label	856.9

Source: *Dairy Foods*, March 1998, p. 83, from
Information Resources Inc.

★ 182 ★
Ice Cream (SIC 2024)

Top High-Priced Ice Cream Brands - 1997

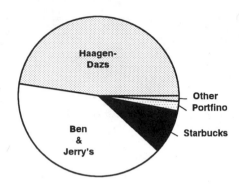

Market shares are shown in percent.

Haagen-Dazs	47.5%
Ben & Jerry's	40.7
Starbucks	9.2
Portfino	1.8
Other	0.8

Source: *New York Times*, May 22, 1998, p. C1, from A.C.
Nielsen via Haagen Dazs and Ben & Jerry's.

★ 183 ★
Ice Cream (SIC 2024)

Top Ice Cream Brands - 1998

Brands are ranked by sales in millions of dollars.
Figures are for the year ended April 26, 1998.

	Sales ($ mil.)	Market Share
Breyers	$ 406.5	11.9%
Dreyers Edy's Grand	365.8	10.7
Blue Bell	180.2	5.3
Haagen-Dazs	157.2	4.6
Ben & Jerry's	120.4	3.5
Healthy Choice	102.0	3.0
Dreyers Edy's Grand Light	87.7	2.6
Turkey Hill	78.6	2.3
Wells Bluebunny	68.5	2.0
Store brands	823.5	24.1

Source: *New York Times*, May 22, 1998, p. C3, from
Information Resources Inc.

★ 184 ★
Ice Cream (SIC 2024)

Top Ice Cream Makers - 1998

Shares of the $3.3 billion market are shown for the year ended March 29, 1998.

Edy's/Dreyer's	16.2%
Unilever	14.9
Private label	25.6
Others	43.3

Source: *Advertising Age*, April 27, 1998, p. 32, from Information Resources Inc.

★ 185 ★
Ice Cream (SIC 2024)

Top Sherbert/Sorbet Brands - 1996

Shares are shown based on a $195.9 million market for the year ended December 1, 1996.

Haagen-Dazs	22.7%
Ben & Jerry's	7.9
Dreyer's	4.2
Blue Bell	3.4
Breyers	3.2
Real Fruit	3.2
Dreyer's/Edy's	2.7
Deans	1.3
Kemps	1.3
Private label	26.2
Other	23.9

Source: *Dairy Foods*, March 1997, p. 84, from Information Resources Inc.

★ 186 ★
Coffee Creamers (SIC 2026)

Leading Refrigerated Coffee Creamer Brands - 1997

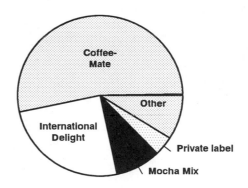

Brands are ranked by sales in millions of dollars for the 52 weeks ended October 12, 1997. Top producers include Nestle and Suiza/Morningstar.

	Sales ($ mil.)	Share
Coffee-Mate	$ 164.4	53.08%
International Delight	77.1	24.90
Mocha Mix	28.5	9.20
Private label	11.2	3.62
Other	28.5	9.20

Source: *Dairy Foods*, March 1998, p. 41.

★ 187 ★
Dairy Products (SIC 2026)

Cultured Product Sales

Sales are shown in thousands of dollars.

Yogurt	$ 1,693
Cottage cheese	737
Sour cream	481
Refrigerated dips	255

Source: *Dairy Foods*, April 1998, p. 29, from A.C. Nielsen and International Dairy Foods Association.

★ 188 ★
Milk (SIC 2026)

Canada's Milk Sales - 1997

Sales are shown for the year ended September 12, 1997.

	($ mil.)	Share
2%	$ 563.5	44.74%
1%	249.9	19.84
Homo	190.4	15.12
Skim	146.8	11.66
Filtered	67.2	5.34
Chocolate	41.7	3.31

Source: *Marketing Magazine*, June 1, 1998, p. 14, from A.C. Nielsen and New MarketTrack.

★ 189 ★
Milk (SIC 2026)

Milk Production in the Northeast - 1997

Production is shown for the last six months of the year. Data are in millions of pounds.

Vermont	1,300
Maine	329
Connecticut	253
Massachusetts	214
New Hampshire	161
Rhode Island	15

Source: *Dairy Herd Management*, May 1998, p. 44, from Bliming and Associates.

★ 190 ★
Milk (SIC 2026)

Milk Sales by Container - 1997

Total white milk sales reached $9.1 billion.

Gallon	69.20%
Half gallon	25.40
Quart	5.00
Pint	0.40
Half pint	0.03
Other	0.01

Source: *Dairy Foods*, May 1998, p. 10, from A.C. Nielsen.

★ 191 ★
Milk (SIC 2026)

Quebec's Milk Market

Market shares are shown in percent.

Natrel	55.0%
Other	45.0

Source: *Marketing Magazine*, May 25, 1998, p. 3.

★ 192 ★
Milk (SIC 2026)

Top Flavored Milk Brands - 1997

Brands are ranked by sales in millions of dollars for the 52 weeks ended November 9, 1997.

	Sales ($ mil.)	Share
Nestle Quik	$ 56.2	13.16%
Borden	12.4	2.90
Dean	10.4	2.44
Kemps	10.1	2.36
Private label	132.6	31.05
Other	205.4	48.09

Source: *Dairy Foods*, March 1998, p. 41.

★ 193 ★
Yogurt (SIC 2026)

Leading Yogurt Makers - 1997

Companies are shown ranked by sales in millions of dollars for the 52 weeks ended March 2, 1997.

	Sales ($ mil.)	Share
Dannon	$ 596.6	35.9%
Yoplait	342.5	20.6
Unilever	105.3	6.3
Kraft	67.4	4.1
Colombo	54.2	3.3
Nabisco	46.8	2.8
Stonyfield	28.0	1.7
Borden	21.2	1.3
Private label	251.8	15.2

Source: *Dairy Foods*, June 1997, p. 63, from Information Resources Inc.

★ 194 ★

Baby Food (SIC 2032)

Baby Food and Snack Producers - 1997

Companies are shown ranked by sales in millions of dollars for the 52 weeks ended September 14, 1997.

	Sales ($ mil.)	Share
Gerber Products Co.	$ 478.7	66.8%
Beech-Nut Corp.	116.5	16.3
Heinz USA	111.5	15.5
Nabisco Foods Group	9.4	1.3

Source: *Los Angeles Times*, October 30, 1997, p. D5, from Information Resources Inc.

★ 195 ★

Baby Food (SIC 2032)

Baby Food Market - Canada

Market shares are shown in percent.

Heinz	80.0%
Gerber Canada	20.0

Source: *Financial Times*, May 1, 1998, p. 8.

★ 196 ★

Canned Food (SIC 2032)

Canned Pasta Market

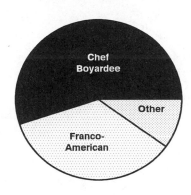

Shares of the $526.6 million market are shown for the year ended April 27, 1997.

	Sales ($ mil.)	Share
Chef Boyardee	$ 291.5	55.4%
Franco-American	183.7	34.9
Other	51.4	9.7

Source: *Brandweek*, June 2, 1997, p. 13, from Information Resources Inc.

★ 197 ★

Canned Food (SIC 2032)

Leading Canned Meat Brands

Shares of the $149.9 million market are shown in percent.

	($ mil.)	Share
Spam	$ 72.6	48.43%
Bridgeford	23.1	15.41
Other	54.2	36.16

Source: *Brandweek*, May 18, 1998, p. 6, from Information Resources Inc.

★ 198 ★

Soups (SIC 2032)

Canned Soup Market - 1997

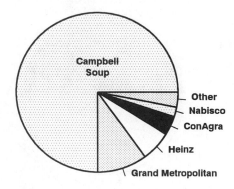

Market shares are shown in percent for the 52 weeks ended August 3, 1997.

Campbell Soup 75.0%
Grand Metropolitan 10.0
Heinz 6.0
ConAgra 4.0
Nabisco 2.0
Other 3.0

Source: *New York Times*, September 10, 1997, p. C8, from Campbell Soup Company.

★ 199 ★

Canned Food (SIC 2033)

Best-Selling Canned Fruits - 1996

Data show retail sales in thousands of dollars.

	($000)	Share
Peaches	$ 387,574	19.23%
Applesauce	336,331	16.69
Fruit cocktail	287,798	14.28
Pineapple	248,469	12.33
Pears	186,784	9.27
Cranberries	128,404	6.37
Citrus	65,529	3.25
Apricots	33,219	1.65
Other canned fruit	341,606	16.95

Source: *Supermarket Business*, September 1997, p. 42.

★ 200 ★

Canned Food (SIC 2033)

Best-Selling Canned Meats and Specialty Foods - 1996

Data show retail sales in thousands of dollars.

	($ 000)	Share
Poultry	$ 177,657	10.42%
Ham	166,244	9.75
Lunch meats	159,409	9.35
Sausages & frankfurters . . .	158,171	9.28
Beef hash	96,209	5.64
Meat spreads	83,284	4.88
Corned beef	56,236	3.30
Other canned meats	808,104	47.39

Source: *Supermarket Business*, September 1997, p. 42.

★ 201 ★

Canned Food (SIC 2033)

Best-Selling Canned Vegetables - 1996

Data show retail sales in thousands of dollars.

Corn	$ 631,503
Beans with pork or sauce	492,099
Tomatoes	489,460
Beans (waxed & green)	476,477
Tomato sauce	365,040
Peas	308,861
Mushrooms	237,447
Tomato paste	155,829
Potatoes	123,765
Asparagus	89,716
Beets	84,105
Sauerkraut	69,100
Tomato puree	49,776
Other canned vegetables	52,729

Source: *Supermarket Business*, September 1997, p. 42.

★ 202 ★

Juices (SIC 2033)

Best-Selling Canned/Bottled Juices & Drinks - 1996

Data show retail sales in thousands of dollars. Data include full strength and concentrated juices that are non-carbonated.

	($ 000)	Share
Fruit drinks	$ 2,737,817	39.85%
Apple cider & juice	1,168,902	17.01
Aseptic juices & drinks . . .	1,021,681	14.87
Iced tea, ready-to-drink . . .	443,141	6.45
Cranberry juice	435,871	6.34
Vegetable juice	374,315	5.45
Prune juice	136,634	1.99
Aseptic juices & drink concentrates	131,243	1.91
Grape juice	107,433	1.56
Orange juice	87,626	1.28
Nectars	87,420	1.27
Pineapple juice	87,245	1.27
Other fruit juices	51,499	0.75

Source: *Supermarket Business*, September 1997, p. 42.

★ 203 ★

Juices (SIC 2033)

Best-Selling Juices - 1997

Sales are shown based on sales of $3.44 billion for the year ended August 17, 1997.

	($ mil.)	Share
Orange juice	$ 2,332.5	67.80%
Fruit drinks	628.3	18.26
Fruit juices, blended	172.8	5.02
Grapefruit juice/cocktail drink . .	98.8	2.87
Lemonade	53.7	1.56
Cider	39.4	1.15
Apple juices	13.1	0.38
Cranberry juice/juice blend/ cocktail drink	8.9	0.26
Pineapple	7.7	0.22
Grape juice	7.2	0.21
Other	77.9	2.26

Source: *Beverage Industry*, November 1997, p. 4, from Information Resources Inc.

★ 204 ★

Juices (SIC 2033)

Best-Selling Orange Juice Brands - 1997

Shares are shown for the 52-week period ended June 22, 1997.

Tropicana Pure Premium	25.7%
Minute Maid	11.8
Tropicana Season's Best	7.5
Florida's Natural	6.5
Minute Maid Premium	5.2
Tropicana Pure Premium Plus	1.8
Other	41.5

Source: *Advertising Age*, August 18, 1997, p. 30, from Information Resources Inc.

★ 205 ★

Juices (SIC 2033)

Bottled Juice Sales - 1996

Manufacturers are ranked by sales in millions of cases. One case is 24 16-ounce bottles.

Snapple	23.6
Mistic	9.3
Fruitopia	7.4
Arizona	6.4
Ocean Spray	3.7
Odwalla	2.6
Nantucket Nectars	2.3

Source: *New York Times*, September 17, 1997, p. C1.

★ 206 ★

Juices (SIC 2033)

Canada's Orange Juice Market

Market shares are shown in percent.

Tropicana	60.0%
Lassonde	18.0
Other	22.0

Source: *Toronto Star*, March 29, 1998, p. D5.

★ 207 ★

Juices (SIC 2033)

Top Aseptic Juice Brands - 1996

Total sales reached $571.3 million for the year ended August 11, 1996.

	($ mil.)	Share
Capri Sun	$ 171.6	30.04%
Hi-C	127.0	22.23
Kool Aid Kool Bursts	43.9	7.68
Squeezit	33.9	5.93
Mondo	31.6	5.53
Ocean Spray	18.2	3.19
Other	145.1	25.40

Source: *Beverage Industry Annual Manual*, Special Issue 1997-1998, p. 35.

★ 208 ★

Juices (SIC 2033)

Top Canned Juice Brands - 1996

Total sales reached $114.2 million for the year ended August 11, 1996.

	($ mil.)	Share
Hawaiian Punch	$ 34.4	34.40%
Hi C	32.0	32.00
Jumex	7.4	7.40
Kerns	7.0	7.00
Ocean Spray	6.0	6.00
Arizona	4.1	4.10
Hansen's	3.5	3.50
Other	5.6	5.60

Source: *Beverage Industry Annual Manual*, Special Issue 1997-1998, p. 35, from Information Resources Inc.

★ 209 ★

Juices (SIC 2033)

Top Orange Juice Brands - 1997

Market shares are shown based on sales of $2.33 billion for the year ended August 17, 1997.

Tropicana Pure Premium	30.2%
Minute Maid	12.0
Minute Maid Premium	7.8
Florida's Natural	7.0
Tropicana's Seasons Best	6.8
Tropicana Pure Premium Plus	2.2
Florida Gold	1.6
Citrus World Donald Duck	0.7

Florida's Natural Grower's Pride	0.6%
Private label	24.4
Other	6.7

Source: *Beverage Industry*, November 1997, p. 4, from Information Resources Inc.

★ 210 ★

Juices (SIC 2033)

Top Shelf-Stable Juice Makers - 1997

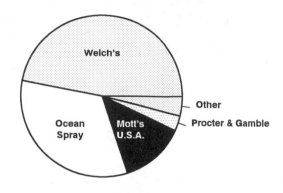

Sales are shown based on sales of $96.4 million for the year ended August 17, 1997.

	Sales ($ mil.)	Share
Welch's	$ 45.2	46.9%
Ocean Spray	31.8	33.0
Mott's U.S.A.	12.5	13.0
Procter & Gamble	3.1	3.2
Other	3.8	3.9

Source: *Beverage Industry*, November 1997, p. 16, from Information Resources Inc.

★ 211 ★

Juices (SIC 2033)

Top Shelf-Stable Juices - 1997

Sales are shown based on sales of $3.01 billion for the year ended August 17, 1997.

	($ mil.)	Share
Cranberry juice/juice cocktail/ juice drink	$ 859.8	28.51%
Fruit drinks	612.8	20.32
Apple juice	479.0	15.88
Grapefruit juice/cocktail	246.0	8.16
Grape juice	171.2	5.68
Fruit juice blend	117.2	3.89

Continued on next page.

★ 211 ★ *Continued*
Juices (SIC 2033)

Top Shelf-Stable Juices - 1997

Sales are shown based on sales of $3.01 billion for the year ended August 17, 1997.

	($ mil.)	Share
Tomato/vegetable juice/ cocktail	$ 108.4	3.59%
Prune/fig juice	88.0	2.92
Lemonade	79.0	2.62
Lemon/lime juice	78.4	2.60
Other	176.1	5.84

Source: *Beverage Industry*, November 1997, p. 16, from Information Resources Inc.

★ 212 ★
Ketchup (SIC 2033)

Canada's Ketchup Market

Market shares are shown in percent.

Heinz	73.0%
Other	27.0

Source: From the Internet, http:// www.prnewswire.com/cnoc/HNZbrand.html, 1997, p. 2.

★ 213 ★
Baking Needs (SIC 2035)

Baking Product Sales

Sales are shown in millions of dollars.

Sugar	$ 1,266.1
Baking mixes	446.9
Flour	419.0
Cake mixes, dry	390.0
Puddings/pie fillings, mixes, ready-to-eat	359.2
Canned milk	309.8
Whipped topping	297.9
Artificial sweeteners	292.2
Brownie/cookie mix	229.3

Source: *Supermarket Business*, March 1998, p. 26, from A.C. Nielsen.

★ 214 ★
Mayonnaise (SIC 2035)

Top Mayonnaise Brands - 1998

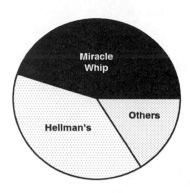

Shares of the $979.9 million market are shown in percent for the year ended March 29, 1998. Figures refer to supermarket sales.

Miracle Whip	45.3%
Hellman's	38.8
Others	15.9

Source: *Brandweek*, May 18, 1998, p. 13.

★ 215 ★
Mustard (SIC 2035)

Top Mustard Brands - 1998

Shares of the $261.9 million market are shown as of March 29, 1998.

	($ mil.)	Share
French's	$ 68.8	26.27%
Grey Poupon	42.8	16.34
Gulden's	19.5	7.45
Private label	44.6	17.03
Other	86.2	32.91

Source: *Brandweek*, May 4, 1998, p. 4, from Information Resources Inc.

★ 216 ★
Salad Dressings (SIC 2035)

Popular Salad Dressings

Data show selected sales in millions of dollars.

Kraft . . . . $ 380.5
Wish-Bone 211.9
Hidden Valley Ranch 164.6

Source: *Brandweek*, June 15, 1998, p. S52, from
Information Resources Inc.

★ 217 ★
Sauces (SIC 2035)

Pasta Sauce Market

*Shares are shown in percent. Brand names for
Borden and Hunt Wesson sauces were not specified.*

Ragu (Unilever) 36.8%
Prego (Campbell Soup Co.) 22.5
Hunt Wesson brands 10.9
Borden brands 10.8
Other 19.0

Source: *Advertising Age*, November 24, 1997, p. 8, from
Information Resources Inc.

★ 218 ★
Frozen Fruit (SIC 2037)

Frozen Fruit Sales - 1996

*Sales are shown in milllions of pounds. Total sales
reached 1.01 billion pounds. Other includes non-
citrus purees.*

	(mil.)	Share
Strawberries	387.0	38.05%
Apples	114.3	11.24
Peaches	109.5	10.76
Blueberries	109.0	10.72
Red raspberries	23.3	2.29
Blackberries	20.4	2.01
Apricots	17.7	1.74
Cherries	14.9	1.46
Boysenberries	5.2	0.51
Black raspberries	1.7	0.17
Plums & prunes	1.7	0.17
Other	212.5	20.89

Source: *Quick Frozen Foods International*, October 1997,
p. A18.

★ 219 ★
Frozen Vegetables (SIC 2037)

Frozen Potato Leaders - 1997

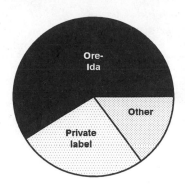

*Shares are shown of the $756.6 million market for
the year ended March 1, 1998.*

Ore-Ida 58.9%
Private label 25.7
Other 15.4

Source: *Advertising Age*, April 20, 1998, p. 2, from
Information Resources Inc.

★ 220 ★
Frozen Vegetables (SIC 2037)

Frozen Vegetable Market - 1997

*Shares of the $1.6 billion market are shown in
percent.*

	Sales ($ mil.)	Share
Green Giant	$ 337.9	21.12%
Birds Eye	258.2	16.14
Other	1,003.9	62.74

Source: *Brandweek*, June 23, 1997, p. 4, from
Information Resources Inc.

★ 221 ★
Frozen Vegetables (SIC 2037)

Frozen Vegetable Sales - 1996

*Sales are shown in milllions of pounds. Total
production reached 11.277 billion pounds.*

	(mil.)	Share
Potato products	8,443.5	74.87%
Corn products	959.7	8.51
Green beans	320.8	2.84

Continued on next page.

★ 221 ★ *Continued*
Frozen Vegetables (SIC 2037)

Frozen Vegetable Sales - 1996

Sales are shown in milllions of pounds. Total production reached 11.277 billion pounds.

	(mil.)	Share
Carrots	300.0	2.66%
Green peas	296.0	2.62
Spinach	182.9	1.62
Broccoli	144.5	1.28
Onions	98.5	0.87
Lima beans	93.3	0.83
Okra	63.4	0.56
Other	375.1	3.33

Source: *Quick Frozen Foods International*, October 1997, p. A17.

★ 222 ★
Frozen Desserts (SIC 2038)

Top Frozen Novelty Brands - 1996

Shares are shown based on a $1.55 billion market for the year ended December 1, 1996.

Klondike	6.6%
Popsicle	6.0
Drumstick	4.8
Haagen-Dazs	4.1
Good Humor	2.6
Dole	2.5
Dove	2.2
Wells' Blue Bunny	2.1
Nestle	2.0
Private label	15.9
Other	51.2

Source: *Dairy Foods*, March 1997, p. 81, from Information Resources Inc.

★ 223 ★
Frozen Foods (SIC 2038)

Leading Frozen Appetizers and Snack Rolls - 1997

Brands are ranked by sales in millions of dollars for the 52-week period ended October 12, 1997.

	Sales ($ mil.)	Share
Totino's	$ 115.6	31.4%
Bagel Bites	63.9	17.3
Farm Rich	22.1	6.0
Hot Pockets	17.4	4.7
Cheese Bites	13.2	3.6
La Choy	12.9	3.5
Dyna Bites	11.4	3.1
Jack's Pizza Bursts	7.3	2.0
Hot Bites	7.2	2.0
Poppers	7.1	1.9
Other	90.6	24.5

Source: *Snack Food & Wholesale Bakery*, December 1997, p. 18, from Information Resources Inc.

★ 224 ★
Frozen Foods (SIC 2038)

Popular Frozen Pizza Brands

Data show selected sales in millions of dollars.

Tombstone	$ 347.2
DiGiorno Rising Crust	238.1
Tony's	186.3
Totino's	157.8
Jack's	101.2

Source: *Brandweek*, June 15, 1998, p. S52, from Information Resources Inc.

★ 225 ★
Frozen Foods (SIC 2038)

Top Frozen Dinner Makers - 1998

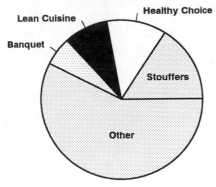

Shares of the $3.8 billion market are shown as of March 29, 1998.

	($ mil.)	Share
Stouffers	$ 596.3	15.69%
Healthy Choice	444.0	11.68
Lean Cuisine	327.7	8.62
Banquet	229.0	6.03
Other	2,203.0	57.97

Source: *Brandweek*, May 18, 1998, p. 5, from Information Resouces Inc.

★ 226 ★
Frozen Foods (SIC 2038)

Veggie Burger Market

Market shares are shown in percent.

Morningstar Farms	36.5%
Gardenburger	34.6
Other	28.9

Source: *Wall Street Journal*, May 20, 1998, p. B6.

★ 227 ★
Grain (SIC 2041)

Largest Grain Milling Companies

Shares are shown based on storage capacity.

Archer-Daniels-Midland	22.0%
ConAgra	19.0
Cargill	16.0
Cereal Processors	6.0
Others	36.0

Source: *Forbes*, November 17, 1997, p. 56, from *Beverage Digest*, Salomon Brothers Inc., *Milling and Baking News*, and Fibro.

★ 228 ★
Cereals (SIC 2043)

Ready-to-Eat Cereal Market - 1997

Market shares are shown in percent for the year ended July 20, 1997. Kellogg's has 60% of the worldwide cereal market.

Kellogg Co.	32.7%
General Mills Inc.	26.3
Post	16.6
Quaker Oats Co.	9.1
Malt-O-Meal Co.	3.7
Private label brands	10.6

Source: *Detroit News*, September 21, 1997, p. C1, from Prudential Securities.

★ 229 ★
Cereals (SIC 2043)

Top Breakfast Cereal Makers - 1997

Companies are ranked by millions of units for the 52 weeks ended October 5, 1997.

Kellogg Co.	786.7
General Mills	624.4
Kraft Foods (Post)	410.2
Quaker Oats Co.	219.8
Private label	251.1

Source: *Advertising Age*, November 1997, p. 24, from International Resources Inc.

★ 230 ★

Rice (SIC 2044)

Leading Rice Cake Makers

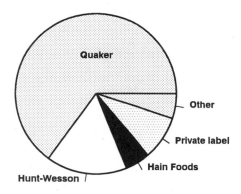

Shares are shown based on a $212.3 million market as of February 1, 1998.

	($ mil.)	Share
Quaker	$ 138.5	65.24%
Hunt-Wesson	34.3	16.16
Hain Foods	11.3	5.32
Private label	18.4	8.67
Other	9.8	4.62

Source: *Brandweek*, March 2, 1998, p. 6, from Information Resources Inc.

★ 231 ★

Rice (SIC 2044)

Top Rice Brands

Market shares are shown based on supermarket sales.

Uncle Ben's	16.8%
Rice A Roni	16.5
Minute Rice	8.9
Other	57.8

Source: *Wall Street Journal*, April 6, 1998, p. A5.

★ 232 ★

Baking Needs (SIC 2045)

Refrigerated Biscuit Dough Market - 1997

Shares of the $417.8 million market are shown for the year ended April 27, 1997.

Pillsbury	78.1%
Other	21.9

Source: *Brandweek*, June 16, 1997, p. 14, from Information Resources Inc.

★ 233 ★

Baking Needs (SIC 2045)

Refrigerated Bread Dough Market - 1997

Shares of the $196.6 million market are shown for the year ended April 27, 1997.

Pillsbury	85.4%
Other	14.6

Source: *Brandweek*, June 16, 1997, p. 14, from Information Resources Inc.

★ 234 ★

Corn Syrup (SIC 2046)

High-Fructose Corn Syrup Producers

Shares are shown in percent.

Archer-Daniels-Midland	32.0%
AE Staley	25.0
Cargill	17.0
CPC International	9.0
American Maize	8.0
Minn. Corn Processors	5.0
Others	4.0

Source: *Forbes*, November 17, 1997, p. 56, from *Beverage Digest*, Salomon Brothers Inc., *Milling and Baking News*, and Fibro.

★ 235 ★
Pet Food (SIC 2047)

Dog Food Market - 1997

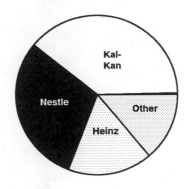

Market shares are shown in percent.

Kal-Kan	38.9%
Nestle	29.9
Heinz	17.4
Other	13.8

Source: *Advertising Age*, June 15, 1998, p. 28.

★ 236 ★
Pet Food (SIC 2047)

Pet Food Companies - 1995

Data show companies ranked by sales in millions of dollars.

	Sales ($ mil.)	Share
Ralston Purina	$ 1,471.9	15.8%
Heinz/Quaker	1,345.7	14.5
Nestle/Alpo	1,345.3	14.5
Hill's Pet Nutrition	743.3	8.0
Kal Kan	624.6	6.7
Doane	564.5	6.1
The Iams Co.	428.2	4.8
Nutro Products Inc.	228.3	2.5
Sunshine Mills	180.0	1.9
Nabisco	101.3	1.0
Other	2,270.2	24.4

Source: *Pet Product News*, November 1997, p. 12, from John Maxwell Jr. and Wheat First Securities.

★ 237 ★
Bakery Products (SIC 2050)

Bakery Product Sales - 1996

Retail sales are shown by segment.

Snack cakes and pies	32.0%
Cookies	26.0
Pastries	21.0
Vended bakery snacks	19.0
Doughnuts	2.0

Source: From the Internet, http://www.foodexplorer.com, 1997, p. 1, from Find/SVP-Prepared Foods.

★ 238 ★
Bakery Products (SIC 2050)

Largest Baked Goods Makers - 1996

Companies are ranked by sales in millions of dollars.

Nabisco Biscuit Co.	$ 3,700
Interstate Brands Corp.	3,000
The Earthgrains Co.	1,662
CPC Baking Business	1,567
Keebler Company	1,500
Flowers Industries Inc.	1,240
Sara Lee Bakery	1,000
McKee Foods Corp.	770
Pepperidge Farm Inc.	700
Metz Baking Co.	500

Source: *Bakery Production and Marketing*, July 15, 1997, p. 32.

★ 239 ★
Bakery Products (SIC 2050)

Sales in Bakery Departments

The table shows the distribution of sales at supermarket grocery stores.

White bread & rolls	14.4%
Vareity bread and rolls	14.3
Decorated cakes	10.1
Custom decorated cakes	8.2
Yeast-raised doughnuts	8.1
Sweet goods	7.8
Other	37.1

Source: *Supermarket Business*, March 1998, p. 106.

★ 240 ★

Bagels (SIC 2051)

Top Fresh Bagel Brands - 1997

Brands are ranked by sales of $331 million for the 52 weeks ended December 7, 1997.

	($ mil.)	Share
Thomas'	$ 66.1	20.0%
Lender's Bagel Shop	57.1	17.3
Sara Lee	36.4	11.0
Earth Grains	19.9	6.0
Lender's	9.5	2.9
IBC	8.4	2.5
Western Bagel	6.3	1.9
Oroweat	5.2	1.6
International	3.9	1.2
Private label	56.8	17.2
Other	61.4	18.4

Source: *Snack Food & Wholesale Bakery*, February 1998, p. 16, from Information Resources Inc.

★ 241 ★

Bakery Products (SIC 2051)

Fresh Bread Product Makers - 1997

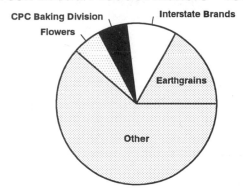

Dollar shares are shown for the 12-week period ended July 6, 1997. Figures represent Earthgrains' marketing area, not including CooperSmith territory and associated brands. Data include buns, breads, and rolls.

Earthgrains	16.50%
Interstate Brands	9.50
CPC Baking Division	6.20
Flowers	5.52
Other	62.28

Source: *Snack Food & Wholesale Bakery*, September 1997, p. 18, from Information Resources Inc.

★ 242 ★

Bakery Products (SIC 2051)

Top Shelf-Stable Snack Cake Brands - 1997

Shares are shown based on a $622 million market.

	($ mil.)	Share
Hostess (Interstate Bakeries)	$ 203.2	32.67%
Little Debbie (McKee Foods)	192.5	30.95
Tastykake (Tasty Baking Co.)	59.6	9.58
Drake's (Drake Bakeries)	50.3	8.09
Other	116.4	18.71

Source: *Advertising Age*, March 23, 1998, p. 4, from Information Resources Inc.

★ 243 ★

English Muffins (SIC 2051)

Top English Muffin Brands - 1997

Shares are shown based on sales of $392.1 million for the year ended March 1, 1998.

Thomas	62.2%
Oroweat	5.5
Wolfermans	1.3
Wonder	1.2
Sun-Maid	1.1
Pepperidge Farm	1.0
Sara Lee	0.7
Country Hearth	0.6
Earthgrains	0.6
Private label	17.3

Source: *Snack Food & Wholesale Bakery*, May 1998, p. 16, from Information Resources Inc.

★ 244 ★

Cookies (SIC 2052)

Leading Cookie Brands - 1996

Shares are shown based on $3.6 billion in supermarket sales for the 52 weeks ended December 29, 1996.

Nabisco	36.2%
Keebler	11.5
Pepperidge Farm	5.5
Archway	4.1
Private label	12.7
Other	30.0

Source: *Bakery Production and Marketing*, June 15, 1997, p. 36, from Information Resources Inc.

★ 245 ★

Cookies (SIC 2052)

Top Cookie Brands - 1997

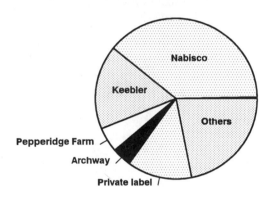

Shares of the $4.0 billion market are shown in percent.

Nabisco	39.1%
Keebler	16.6
Pepperidge Farm	5.4
Archway	4.3
Private label	13.1
Others	21.7

Source: *New York Times*, January 25, 1998, p. 4, from Goldman Sachs.

★ 246 ★

Crackers (SIC 2052)

Leading Cracker Brands - 1997

Shares of the $2.702 billion market are shown for the 52-week period ended May 18, 1997.

Nabisco Ritz	13.2%
Private label	9.0
Nabisco Premium Saltines	7.2
Nabisco Honey Maid	5.8
Sunshine Cheez-It	5.5
Nabisco Wheat Thins	5.2
Nabisco Triscuit	4.9
Pepperidge Farm Goldfish	4.8
Keebler Town House	3.3
Kraft Handi Snacks	2.9
Other	38.2

Source: *Snack Food & Wholesale Bakery*, September 1997, p. 14, from Information Resources Inc.

★ 247 ★

Bagels (SIC 2053)

Top Frozen Bagel Brands - 1997

Brands are ranked by sales of $197.3 million for the 52 weeks ended December 7, 1997.

	($ mil.)	Share
Lender's	$ 100.0	50.7%
Lender's Big 'n' Crusty	47.8	24.2
Sara Lee	17.1	8.7
Harlan Bigger Better Bagels . . .	3.2	1.6
Bagels Forever	1.5	0.8
Bagels Boys	1.0	0.5
Brooklyn Bagel Boys	0.5	0.3
Pechter	0.2	0.1
Private label	24.6	12.5
Generic	0.6	0.3
Other	0.8	0.3

Source: *Snack Food & Wholesale Bakery*, February 1998, p. 18, from Information Reources Inc.

★ 248 ★

Confectionery Products (SIC 2064)

Breath Freshener Producers - 1997

Shares are shown based on sales of breath fresheners for the second quarter of 1997. Dollar sales were $62,810,804 for that period.

Ferrero USA Inc.	29.7%
Planters/Life Savers	29.0
Warner Lambert	26.0
Callard & Bowser Ltd.	12.0
Ragold Inc.	0.9
Uniconfis Corp.	0.8
Ricola Inc.	0.6
Others	1.0

Source: *The Manufacturing Confectioner*, September 1997, p. 36.

★ 249 ★

Confectionery Products (SIC 2064)

Candy Sales by Segment

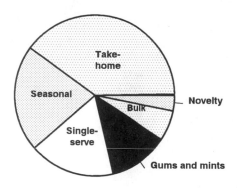

Sales are shown in percent.

Take-home	39.0%
Seasonal	21.0
Single-serve	17.0
Gums and mints	12.0
Bulk	6.0
Novelty	3.0

Source: *Grocery Headquarters*, June 1998, p. 50, from Information Resources Inc. InfoScan.

★ 250 ★

Confectionery Products (SIC 2064)

Confectionery Market by Segment - 1997

Market shares are shown for the 12 weeks ended October 5, 1997.

Chocolate	45.5%
Non-chocolate	24.7
Gum	21.3
Mints/hard roll	8.1
Other	0.4

Source: *U.S. Distribution Journal*, March/April 1998, p. 48, from MSA Distributor WATCH and American Wholesale Marketers Association.

★ 251 ★

Confectionery Products (SIC 2064)

Cough Drop/Square Makers - 1997

Shares are shown based on cough drops/squares sales for the second quarter of 1997. Dollar sales were $80,623,920 for that period.

Warner Lambert	34.0%
Quigley Corporation	10.5
Ricola Inc.	9.3
SmithKline Beecham	9.1
Ludens Inc.	7.6
A.H. Robins Co.	7.1
Procter & Gamble	4.1
J.B. Williams Co.	1.8
Blazic & Assc.	1.2
Private label	11.6
Others	3.7

Source: *The Manufacturing Confectioner*, September 1997, p. 38.

★ 252 ★

Confectionery Products (SIC 2064)

Granola/Snack Bar Market - 1997

Brand shares are shown based on $220,981,216 in sales for the second quarter of 1997.

Kelloggs Nutri-Grain	15.89%
Chewy	13.36
Kelloggs Rice Krispy Treats	10.17
Snackwell's	9.01
Store brands	5.33
Kudos	5.09

Continued on next page.

★ 252 ★ *Continued*
Confectionery Products (SIC 2064)

Granola/Snack Bar Market - 1997

*Brand shares are shown based on $220,981,216 in
sales for the second quarter of 1997.*

Golden Grahams Treats	4.73%
Nature Valley Granola Bars	4.36
Sunbelt Granola Bars	3.94
Betty Crocker Sweet Rewards	3.76
Others	24.36

Source: *The Manufacturing Confectioner*, September
1997, p. 38.

★ 253 ★
Confectionery Products (SIC 2064)

Largest Confectionery Producers - 1997

*Market shares are shown for the 24 weeks ended
October 5, 1997.*

Hershey	25.09%
M&M/Mars	18.57
Wrigley	10.83
Adams	8.01
Lifesavers	7.05
Nestle	6.12
Sunmark	5.19
Sathers	2.84
Tootsie Roll	1.85
Ferrero U.S.A.	1.60
Others	13.0

Source: *U.S. Distribution Journal*, March/April 1998, p.
48, from MSA Distributor WATCH and American
Wholesale Marketers Association.

★ 254 ★
Confectionery Products (SIC 2064)

Leading Energy Bars - 1997

PowerBar

Balance Bar

Clif Bar

*Brands are ranked by sales in millions of dollars.
Powerbar controls 52% of the market.*

PowerBar	$ 95
Balance Bar	42
Clif Bar	23

Source: *New York Times*, November 22, 1997, p. B1,
from the companies and Spence Information Services.

★ 255 ★
Confectionery Products (SIC 2064)

Leading Novelty Candy Makers - 1997

*Sales of novelty candies reached $56.3 million for
the third quarter of 1997. Company shares are shown
in percent.*

Sunmark Inc.	27.6%
Pez Candy	10.5
Sathers Co., Inc.	8.3
The Topps Company	4.7
Tootsie Roll Industries	4.4
Cap Toys Inc.	4.2
Ce De Candy Inc.	4.0
Necco	3.6
Just Born Inc.	3.5
Private label	2.9
Other	26.3

Source: *The Manufacturing Confectioner*, January 1998,
p. 19, from Information Resources Inc.

★ 256 ★
Confectionery Products (SIC 2064)

Leading Plain Mint Producers - 1997

*Sales of plain mints reached $46.0 million for the
third quarter of 1997. Company shares are shown in
percent.*

Planters/LifeSavers	36.3%
Brach and Brock	18.6
Van Melle USA Inc.	14.8
Sathers Co. Inc.	4.2
Farley Candy Co.	4.1

Continued on next page.

★ 256 ★ *Continued*
Confectionery Products (SIC 2064)

Leading Plain Mint Producers - 1997

Sales of plain mints reached $46.0 million for the third quarter of 1997. Company shares are shown in percent.

Richardson Brands Inc.	2.8%
Hershey Chocolate USA	2.2
Callard & Bowser Ltd.	2.1
Necco	1.3
Private label	7.7
Other	5.9

Source: *The Manufacturing Confectioner*, January 1998, p. 18, from Information Resources Inc.

★ 257 ★
Confectionery Products (SIC 2064)

Leading Sugar Free/Sugarless Candies - 1997

Sales of sugar free/sugarless candies reached $15.5 million for the third quarter of 1997. Brand shares are shown in percent.

LifeSavers Delites	14.0%
Sweet N Low	13.8
Estee	12.3
Sorbee	9.2
GoLightly	6.1
Fifty 50	5.7
Square Shooters	4.0
Sweet 'N Low Lil Bits	3.9
Bobs	3.7
Private label	5.6
Other	21.7

Source: *The Manufacturing Confectioner*, January 1998, p. 19, from Information Resources Inc.

★ 258 ★
Confectionery Products (SIC 2064)

Novelty Candy Market - 1997

Brand shares are shown based on $50,037,048 in sales for the second quarter of 1997.

Pez	12.2%
Sweet Tarts	9.5
Sathers	5.8
Sunmark Spree	4.5
Topps Push Pop	3.4%
Willy Wonka Nerds	3.4
Necco	3.3
Farley's	3.2
Hot Tamales	3.2
Other	51.5

Source: *The Manufacturing Confectioner*, September 1997, p. 38.

★ 259 ★
Confectionery Products (SIC 2064)

Plain Mint Market - 1997

Brand shares are shown based on $47,406,888 in sales for the second quarter of 1997.

LifeSavers	34.6%
Van Melles Mentos	13.9
Brach	10.1
Brock	9.3
Sathers	4.5
Farley's	4.3
Richardson After Dinner	3.0
Hershey's TasteTations	2.4
Private label	7.8
Others	10.1

Source: *The Manufacturing Confectioner*, September 1997, p. 36.

★ 260 ★

Confectionery Products (SIC 2064)

Top Caramel Corn Brands - 1997

Brands are shown ranked by sales in millions of dollars for the 52-week period ended April 27, 1997. Shares are shown in percent.

	Sales ($ mil.)	Share
Franklin Crunch n' Munch . . .	$ 49.1	16.5%
Cracker Jack	33.6	11.3
Houston Foods	33.0	11.1
Smart Foods	21.2	7.1
Golden Harvest	18.4	6.2
Chester's	11.7	3.9
Fiddle Faddle	9.6	3.2
Vic's	8.0	2.7
Wise	7.2	2.4
Private label	25.5	8.6
Other	79.6	27.0

Source: *Snack Food & Wholesale Bakery*, July 1997, p. 17, from Information Resources Inc.

★ 261 ★

Confectionery Products (SIC 2064)

Top Hard Sugar Candy Brands - 1997

Shares are shown based on sales of $75.8 million for the year ended January 4, 1998. Figures include packaged and rolled candy.

Jolly Rancher	13.1%
Werthers	12.5
LifeSavers	11.5
Hershey's TasteTations	7.5
Tootsie Roll Pops	7.0
Pearson Nips	6.6
Charms Blow Pop	4.6
Private label	5.6
Others	31.6

Source: *The Manufacturing Confectioner*, April 1998, p. 20.

★ 262 ★

Confectionery Products (SIC 2064)

Top Hard Sugar Candy Makers - 1997

| Leaf North America |
| Storck USA LP |
| Planters/LifeSavers |
| Tootsie Roll Inds. Inc. |
| Hershey Chocolate |
| Charms Inc. |
| Nestle USA |
| Private label |
| Other |

Shares are shown based on sales of $75.8 million for the year ended January 4, 1998. Figures include packaged and rolled candy.

Leaf North America	13.1%
Storck USA LP	12.5
Planters/LifeSavers	12.0
Tootsie Roll Inds. Inc.	9.4
Hershey Chocolate	7.5
Charms Inc.	7.3
Nestle USA	6.6
Private label	5.6
Other	26.0

Source: *The Manufacturing Confectioner*, April 1998, p. 20, from Information Resources Inc. InfoScan.

★ 263 ★

Confectionery Products (SIC 2064)

Top Holidays for Candy Sales - 1997

Data show candy sales at food, drug, and mass channels in millions of dollars. Figures are for the 52 weeks ended October 12, 1997.

	($ mil.)	Share
Easter	$ 587.2	35.75%
Christmas	501.7	30.55
Valentine's Day	392.5	23.90
Halloween	158.3	9.64
Other	2.6	0.16

Source: *Discount Merchandiser*, January 1998, p. 52, from Information Resources, Inc.

★ 264 ★

Confectionery Products (SIC 2064)

Top Licorice Brands - 1997

Shares are shown based on sales of $183.8 million for the year ended January 4, 1998. Figures are for greater than 3.5 oz.

Y & S Twizzler	58.6%
American Licorice	16.5
Good & Plenty	6.5
Starburst Fruit Twists	5.9
Switzers	3.6
Bassets	2.8
Private label	1.2
Others	4.9

Source: *The Manufacturing Confectioner*, April 1998, p. 20, from Information Resources Inc. InfoScan.

★ 265 ★

Confectionery Products (SIC 2064)

Top Licorice Makers - 1997

Shares are shown based on sales of $183.8 million for the year ended January 4, 1998. Figures are for boxes and boxes greater than 3.5 oz.

Hershey Chocolate	59.3%
American Licorice Co.	16.5
Leaf North America	10.2
Mars Inc.	5.9
Wilkinson-Spitz Ltd.	3.0

Source: *The Manufacturing Confectioner*, April 1998, p. 20, from Information Resources Inc. InfoScan.

★ 266 ★

Confectionery Products (SIC 2064)

Top Non-Chocolate Chewy Boxed/ Bagged Candy Brands - 1997

Shares are shown based on sales of $481.9 million for the year ended January 4, 1998. Figures are for boxes and bags larger than 3.5 oz.

Starburst	13.2%
Farley's	7.7
Tootsie Roll	6.3
Skittles	5.8
Brach's	5.4
LifeSavers GummiSavers	2.9
Sathers	2.6

Brock	2.5%
Jelly Belly	2.4
Private label	5.4
Others	45.8

Source: *The Manufacturing Confectioner*, April 1998, p. 20, from Information Resources Inc. InfoScan.

★ 267 ★

Confectionery Products (SIC 2064)

Top Non-Chocolate Chewy Boxed/ Bagged Candy Producers - 1997

Shares are shown based on sales of $481.9 million for the year ended January 4, 1998. Figures are for boxes and bags larger than 3.5 oz.

Mars Inc.	19.0%
E J Brach & Sons	9.8
Tootsie Roll Inds. Inc.	7.9
Farley Candy Co.	7.7
Planters/LifeSavers	4.3
Hershey Chocolate	3.3
Just Born Inc.	3.2
Trolli Inc.	3.2
Sathers Co. Inc.	2.7
Private label	5.4
Others	33.5

Source: *The Manufacturing Confectioner*, April 1998, p. 20, from Information Resources Inc. InfoScan.

★ 268 ★

Confectionery Products (SIC 2064)

Top Non-Chocolate Chewy Candy Bar Brands - 1997

Shares are shown based on sales of $163.7 million for the year ended January 4, 1998. Figures are for less than 3.5 oz.

Skittles	12.3%
Starburst	10.9
LifeSavers GummiSavers	10.3
Van Melles Mentos	9.4
Van Melles Air Heads	7.5
Starburst Fruit Twists	5.4
Y & S Twizzler	3.9
Reese's Pieces	2.8
Tootsie Roll	2.6

Continued on next page.

★ 268 ★ *Continued*
Confectionery Products (SIC 2064)

Top Non-Chocolate Chewy Candy Bar Brands - 1997

Shares are shown based on sales of $163.7 million for the year ended January 4, 1998. Figures are for less than 3.5 oz.

Private label	2.6%
Others	32.3

Source: *The Manufacturing Confectioner*, April 1998, p. 20, from Information Resources Inc. InfoScan.

★ 269 ★
Confectionery Products (SIC 2064)

Top Specialty Nut/Coconut Candy Brands - 1997

Shares are shown based on sales of $75.8 million for the year ended January 4, 1998.

Leaf Pay Day	23.3%
Brach's	17.3
Sophie Mae	6.6
Brown & Haley Almond Roca	4.4
Pearsons	3.9
Russell Stover	3.8
Planters	3.5
Lance	3.1
Sathers	2.0
Private label	6.5
Other	25.6

Source: *The Manufacturing Confectioner*, April 1998, p. 19, from Information Resources Inc. InfoScan.

★ 270 ★
Yogurt Bars (SIC 2064)

Leading Snack/Granola Bar Makers - 1997

Sales of snack bars and granola bars reached $278.7 million for the third quarter of 1997. Company shares are shown in percent.

Kellogg USA	28.70%
Quaker	16.60
Nabisco	12.39
General Mills	11.46
Mars, Inc.	4.99
McKee Baking Co.	4.93

Powerfood	3.74%
Entenmanns	3.00
Slim Fast Foods Co.	1.36
Store brands	5.01
Other	7.82

Source: *The Manufacturing Confectioner*, January 1998, p. 19, from Information Resources Inc.

★ 271 ★
Chocolate (SIC 2066)

Chocolate Bar Market - 1997

Brands are shown ranked by dollar sales for the 52 weeks ended August 17, 1997. Data refer to 3.5 ounce chocolate bars.

M&Ms	$ 113,237,648
Hershey's Bar	74,052,528
Reese's Peanut Butter Cup	65,043,980
Snickers	60,611,856
Butterfinger Bar	26,697,240
York Peppermint Patty	25,201,836
Nestle Crunch	21,999,500
Three Musketeers	21,039,116
Russell Stover Candy Bar	20,470,052
Reese's Nutrageous	16,844,888

Source: *Discount Merchandiser*, October 1997, p. 38, from Information Resources Inc.

★ 272 ★
Chocolate (SIC 2066)

Largest Bagged/Boxed Chocolate Candy Brands - 1997

Shares are shown based on sales of $723.8 million for the year ended January 4, 1998. Data refer to bags or boxes less than 3.5 oz.

M&Ms	16.4%
Hershey's	10.4
Reese's	8.8
Snickers	8.4
Butterfinger	3.6
York Peppermint Patty	3.6
Nestle Crunch	3.0

Continued on next page.

★ 272 ★ *Continued*
Chocolate (SIC 2066)

Largest Bagged/Boxed Chocolate Candy Brands - 1997

Shares are shown based on sales of $723.8 million for the year ended January 4, 1998. Data refer to bags or boxes less than 3.5 oz.

Three Musketeers	2.9%
Russell Stover	2.8
Reese's Nutrageous	2.3
Others	37.8

Source: *The Manufacturing Confectioner*, April 1998, p. 19, from Information Resources Inc. InfoScan.

★ 273 ★
Chocolate (SIC 2066)

Largest Bagged/Boxed Chocolate Candy Makers - 1997

Shares are shown based on sales of $723.8 million for the year ended January 4, 1998. Data refer to bags or boxes less than 3.5 oz.

Hershey Chocolate	39.6%
Mars Inc.	33.4
Nestle USA	14.9
Russell Stover	2.8
Leaf North America	1.7
Tootsie Roll Inds. Inc.	1.2
Others	6.4

Source: *The Manufacturing Confectioner*, April 1998, p. 19, from Information Resources Inc. InfoScan.

★ 274 ★
Chocolate (SIC 2066)

Largest Chocolate Candy Snack/Fun Size Brands - 1997

Snickers
Kit Kat
Reese's
Milky Way
Butterfinger
Three Musketeers
M&Ms
Nestle Crunch
Twix Chocolate
Baby Ruth
Others

Shares are shown based on sales of $608.7 million for the year ended January 4, 1998.

Snickers	17.2%
Kit Kat	12.0
Reese's	10.2
Milky Way	7.8
Butterfinger	6.6
Three Musketeers	6.6
M&Ms	5.9
Nestle Crunch	5.8
Twix Chocolate	3.7
Baby Ruth	3.6
Others	20.6

Source: *The Manufacturing Confectioner*, April 1998, p. 19, from Information Resources Inc. InfoScan.

★ 275 ★
Chocolate (SIC 2066)

Leading Chocolate Candy Bar Producers - 1997

Sales of 3.5 ounce chocolate candy bars reached $192.2 million for the third quarter of 1997. Company shares are shown in percent.

Hershey Chocolate USA	38.5%
Mars Inc.	33.3
Nestle USA	17.2
Russell Stover	2.5
Leaf North America	1.5
Tootsie Roll Industries Inc.	1.2
Nabisco Foods Group	0.7

Continued on next page.

★ 275 ★ *Continued*
Chocolate (SIC 2066)

Leading Chocolate Candy Bar Producers - 1997

Sales of 3.5 ounce chocolate candy bars reached $192.2 million for the third quarter of 1997. Company shares are shown in percent.

Lindt & Sprungli A.G.	0.5%
Annabelle Candy Co. Inc.	0.3
Archibald Candy Corp.	0.3
Other	4.0

Source: *The Manufacturing Confectioner*, January 1998, p. 14, from Information Resources Inc.

★ 276 ★
Chocolate (SIC 2066)

Leading Snack-Size Chocolate Candies - 1997

Shares are shown based on dollar sales for the 52-week period ended November 9, 1997.

Snickers	17.2%
Kit Kat	12.0
Reese's	10.2
Milky Way	7.8
Butterfinger	6.6
Three Musketeers	6.6
M&M's	5.9
Nestle Crunch	5.6
Twix	3.7
Baby Ruth	3.6
Other	20.8

Source: *Discount Merchandiser*, January 1998, p. 52, from Information Resources Inc.

★ 277 ★
Chocolate (SIC 2066)

Snack/Fun Size Chocolate Candy Producers - 1997

Shares are shown based on sales of snack/fun size chocolate candies for the second quarter of 1997. Dollar sales were $73,260,416 for that period.

Mars Inc.	45.2%
Hershey Chocolate USA	32.5
Nestle USA	20.9
Leaf North America	0.9
D.L. Clark Company	0.5

Source: *The Manufacturing Confectioner*, September 1997, p. 32.

★ 278 ★
Chocolate (SIC 2066)

Top Bagged/Boxed Chocolate Candy Brands - 1997

Shares are shown based on sales of $1.40 billion for the year ended January 4, 1998. Data refer to bags or boxs larger than 3.5 oz.

M&Ms	15.0%
Hershey's	10.3
Reese's	7.8
Hershey's Kisses	6.9
Snickers	5.7
Hershey's Nuggets	4.0
York Peppermint Patty	3.3
Hershey's Sweet Escapes	2.5
Brach's	1.9
Private label	1.9
Other	40.7

Source: *The Manufacturing Confectioner*, April 1998, p. 19, from Information Resources Inc. InfoScan.

★ 279 ★

Chocolate (SIC 2066)

Top Bagged/Boxed Chocolate Candy Makers - 1997

Shares are shown based on sales of $1.40 billion for the year ended January 4, 1998. Data refer to bags or boxes larger than 3.5 oz.

	($ mil.)	Share
Hershey Chocolate	$613.66	43.7%
Mars Inc.	$374.14	26.7
Nestle USA	71.10	5.1
EJ Brach & Sons	62.93	4.5
Storck USA	28.91	2.1

Source: *The Manufacturing Confectioner*, April 1998, p. 19, from Information Resources Inc. InfoScan.

★ 280 ★

Chocolate (SIC 2066)

Top Chocolate Bar Brands in Canada - 1998

Market shares are shown based on sales for the year ended February 28, 1998.

Oh Henry	5.9%
M&M's	5.6
Coffee Crisp	4.5
Kit Kat	4.5
Caramilk	4.4
Mars	4.4
Smarties	4.4
Reese Peanut Butter Cups	3.8
Aero	3.7
Glosette	3.0
Others	55.8

Source: *Marketing Magazine*, May 25, 1998, p. 18, from industry sources.

★ 281 ★

Cocoa (SIC 2066)

Cocoa Processing Companies

Shares are shown in percent.

Archer-Daniels-Midland	17.0%
Nestle	10.0
Cargill	9.0
Others	64.0

Source: *Forbes*, November 17, 1997, p. 56, from *Beverage Digest*, Salomon Brothers Inc., *Milling and Baking News*, and Fibro.

★ 282 ★

Confectionery Products (SIC 2066)

Canada's Confectionery Leaders - 1996

Sales are shown in millions of dollars.

	($ mil.)	Share
Medicated	$ 92.1	23.09%
Gums & jellies	86.0	21.56
Boiled	67.9	17.02
Mints	54.5	13.66
Caramels	52.4	13.14
Other	46.0	11.53

Source: *Candy Industry*, January 1998, p. A12, from Datamonitor food database, local trade interviews.

★ 283 ★

Confectionery Products (SIC 2066)

Canada's Confectionery Leaders - 1997

Market shares are shown in percent.

Neilson/Cadbury 29.0%
Hershey 25.0
Nestle 25.0
Effem 17.0
Others 3.0

Source: *The Manufacturing Confectioner*, May 1998, p. 16.

★ 284 ★

Confectionery Products (SIC 2066)

Mexico's Confectionery Market - 1996

Sales are shown in millions of dollars.

	($ mil.)	Share
Boiled	$ 323.6	38.00%
Caramels	188.4	22.13
Mints	168.5	19.79
Medicated	96.9	11.38
Gums & jellies	59.6	7.00
Other	14.5	1.70

Source: *Candy Industry*, January 1998, p. A12.

★ 285 ★

Confectionery Products (SIC 2066)

Ready-to-Eat Popcorn Market

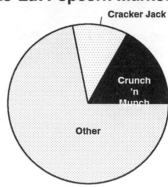

Shares of the $296.9 million market are shown in percent.

Crunch 'n Munch 16.5%
Cracker Jack 11.3
Other 72.2

Source: *Brandweek*, June 2, 1997, p. 4, from Information Resources Inc.

★ 286 ★

Confectionery Products (SIC 2066)

Top Breath Freshener Brands - 1997

Shares are shown based on sales of $259 million for the year ended January 4, 1998.

Tic Tac 29.0%
BreathSavers 27.9
Altoids 12.1
Certs 11.9
Certs Cool Mint Drops 7.3
Extra Flavor Certs 5.8
Altoids 1.4
Velamints 1.0
Smint 0.8
Ricola 0.6
Others 2.2

Source: *The Manufacturing Confectioner*, April 1998, p. 20, from Information Resources Inc. InfoScan.

★ 287 ★
Confectionery Products (SIC 2066)

Top Granola Snack Bar Brands

Brands are ranked by sales in millions of dollars for the year ended November 2, 1997.

	Sales ($ mil.)	Share
Kellogg's NutriGrain Bars . . .	$ 140.7	46.7%
Chewy	115.1	13.4
Kellogg's Rice Krispies Treats . .	98.1	11.4
Snackwell's	74.6	8.7
Kudos	43.9	5.1
Golden Grahams Treats	40.3	4.7
Nature Valley Granola Bars . . .	39.2	4.6
Sunbelt Granola Bars	33.4	3.9
Betty Crocker Sweet Rewards . .	29.2	3.4
PowerBar	28.6	3.3
Store brands	46.8	5.4

Source: *Snack Food & Wholesale Bakery*, January 1998, p. 17, from Information Resources Inc.

★ 288 ★
Confectionery Products (SIC 2066)

Top Non-Chocolate Chewy Candy Bar Makers - 1997

Shares are shown based on sales of $163.7 million for the year ended January 4, 1998. Figures are for less than 3.5 oz.

Mars Inc.	28.7%
Van Melle USA Inc.	17.0
Planters/LifeSavers	12.5
Hershey Chocolate	10.3
Tootsie Roll Inds. Inc.	4.2
Private label	2.6
Others	24.7

Source: *The Manufacturing Confectioner*, April 1998, p. 20, from Information Resources Inc. InfoScan.

★ 289 ★
Chewing Gum (SIC 2067)

Regular Chewing Gum Makers - 1997

Shares are shown based on sales of regular chewing gum for the second quarter of 1997. Dollar sales were $133,111,040 for that period.

Wm. Wrigley Jr. Co.	54.9%
Warner Lambert	22.5
Planters/LifeSavers	7.4
Amurol Confections	6.3
Leaf North America	3.1
The Topps Company Inc.	2.0
Fleer Corp.	0.5
Philadelphia Chewing Gum	0.3
Concord Confections Inc.	0.3
Private label	0.5
Others	2.2

Source: *The Manufacturing Confectioner*, September 1997, p. 36.

★ 290 ★
Chewing Gum (SIC 2067)

Regular Gum Market - 1997

Wrigley's Double Mint
Wrigley's Winterfresh
Freedent
Wrigley's Big Red
Wrigley's Juicy Fruit
Wrigley's Spearmint
Bubblicious
Bubble Yum
Cinn-A-Burst
Mint-A-Burst
Others

Brand shares are shown based on $133,111,040 in sales for the second quarter of 1997.

Wrigley's Double Mint	11.7%
Wrigley's Winterfresh	11.3
Freedent	9.2
Wrigley's Big Red	8.1
Wrigley's Juicy Fruit	7.3
Wrigley's Spearmint	7.2
Bubblicious	5.5
Bubble Yum	4.6
Cinn-A-Burst	4.0

Continued on next page.

★ 290 ★ *Continued*
Chewing Gum (SIC 2067)

Regular Gum Market - 1997

Brand shares are shown based on $133,111,040 in sales for the second quarter of 1997.

Mint-A-Burst 3.2%
Others 27.9

Source: *The Manufacturing Confectioner*, September 1997, p. 36.

★ 291 ★
Chewing Gum (SIC 2067)

Sugarless Gum Market - 1997

Brand shares are shown based on $112,065,968 in sales for the second quarter of 1997.

Wrigley's Extra 33.8%
Trident 26.3
Carefree 16.6
BreathSavers Ice Breakers 10.6
Dentyne Ice 3.9
Stick Free 3.3
Bubble Yum 2.5
Dentyne 2.1
Others 0.9

Source: *The Manufacturing Confectioner*, September 1997, p. 36.

★ 292 ★
Chewing Gum (SIC 2067)

Top Sugarless Gum Producers - 1997

Market shares are shown based on the year ended February 1, 1998.

Wrigley 34.4%
Life-Savers 33.0
Warner-Lambert 32.0
Other 0.6

Source: *Advertising Age*, March 23, 1998, p. 49, from Information Resources Inc.

★ 293 ★
Soybean Processing (SIC 2075)

Soybean Crushing Companies

| Archer-Daniels-Midland |
| Cargill |
| Bunge |
| AGP |
| Central Soya |
| Others |

Shares are shown in percent.

Archer-Daniels-Midland 31.0%
Cargill 24.0
Bunge 13.0
AGP 10.0
Central Soya 7.0
Others 15.0

Source: *Forbes*, November 17, 1997, p. 56, from *Beverage Digest*, Salomon Brothers Inc., *Milling and Baking News*, and Fibro.

★ 294 ★
Olive Oil (SIC 2079)

Top Olive Oil Producers - 1997

Shares of the $338.8 million market are shown in percent.

Bertolli USA 33.4%
Savlov 19.0
Other 47.6

Source: *Advertising Age*, May 4, 1998, p. 24.

★ 295 ★
Beverages (SIC 2080)

Largest Beverage Firms - 1997

Firms are ranked by revenues in millions of dollars.

Pepsico . . . . $ 29,292
Coca-Cola 18,868
Coca-Cola Enterprises 11,278
Anheuser-Busch 11,066
Whitman 3,250
Adolph Coors 1,822
Brown-Forman 1,584

Source: *Fortune*, April 27, 1998, pp. F-45.

★ 296 ★

Beverages (SIC 2080)

Top Beverage Categories

Sales are shown in millions of dollars for the 52-week period ended June 22, 1997.

Carbonated beverages	$ 11,597.4
Milk	9,364.2
Beer & ale	5,358.0
Juice & beverage (refrigerated)	3,424.3
Coffee	3,141.9
Bottled juices	2,585.8
Juices (frozen)	1,286.4
Bottled water	959.1
Canned juices	771.4
Aseptic juices	686.3
Isotonics	528.6
Tea, ready-to-drink	352.6

Source: *Beverage Industry*, September 1997, p. 35, from Information Resources Inc.

★ 297 ★

Beverages (SIC 2080)

Top Beverage Companies in North America - 1996

Figures represent sales in millions of dollars.

The Coca-Cola Company	$ 18,546.0
PepsiCo	10,524.0
Anheuser-Busch Companies	10,143.9
Coca-Cola Enterprises	7,921.0
The Seagram Company	6,694.0
Cadbury Schweppes	4,858.0
Philip Morris Companies	4,327.0
Southern Wine & Spirits of America	2,200.0
Panamerican Beverages Company	1,993.1
Quaker Oats Company	1,928.7

Source: *Beverage World*, July 1997, p. 60.

★ 298 ★

Beverages (SIC 2080)

Top Bottling Companies - 1996

Companies are ranked by sales in millions of dollars.

Coca-Cola Enterprises	$ 7,921.0
Pepsi-Cola Bottling Company	4,356.9
Pepsi-Cola General Bottlers	1,501.4

Coca-Cola Bottling Company (Herb Group)	$ 872.0
Honickman Affiliates	850.0
Coca-Cola Bottling Company Consolidated	773.8
Coca-Cola Bottling Company of New York	744.0
Coca-Cola Beverages Ltd.	690.0
Dr. Pepper Bottling Company of Texas	590.0
Beverage America	555.0

Source: *Beverage World*, September 1997, p. 56.

★ 299 ★

Beverages (SIC 2080)

Top Soy Beverages in Canada - 1998

Market shares are shown based on sales of 6.68 million liters for the four weeks ended March 28, 1998. Top producers include Sunrise Soya Foods, SoyaWorld Inc. and International Prosoya Corp.

Sunrise	26.2%
So Good	12.5
So Nice	12.3
Sensational Soy	9.8
Vitasoy	5.9
Soy Delight	3.5
Edensoy	1.5
Private label	13.8
Other	14.5

Source: *Marketing Magazine*, May 25, 1998, p. 19, from industry sources.

★ 300 ★
Beverages (SIC 2080)

U.S. Beverage Industry by Segment - 1996

The market is shown in percent.

Soft drinks	31.4%
Beer	25.2
Distilled spirits	15.6
Milk	8.3
Juices	6.3
Wine	6.1
Coffee	3.9
Bottled water	2.2
Tea	0.6
Powdered drinks	0.4

Source: *Beverage Industry*, March 1998, p. 41, from *Adams Liquor Handbook*.

★ 301 ★
Beer (SIC 2082)

Beer Consumption by Age - 1996

Sales are shown by age.

18-24 years old	13.9%
25-34	27.8
35-44	24.0
45-54	15.1
55-64	9.1
65 or older	10.1

Source: *New York Times*, April 18, 1998, p. B3, from Beverage Marketing.

★ 302 ★
Beer (SIC 2082)

Beer Sales by Type - 1996

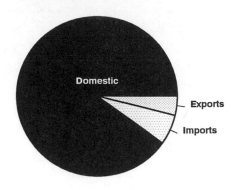

Market shares are shown in percent, based on sales of 198.7 million barrels.

Domestic	90.0%
Imports	6.0
Exports	4.0

Source: *Chicago Tribune*, October 3, 1997, p. 3, from Beer Institute and *Modern Brewery Age*.

★ 303 ★
Beer (SIC 2082)

Largest U.S. Microbrewers - 1996

Production is shown in barrels. One barrel represents 31 gallons. Microbrewers have a 2.5% share of the U.S. beer market.

Boston Beer	12,200,000
Pete's Brewing	420,000
Sierra Nevada	270,000
Redhook Ale	225,000
Pyramid Breweries	128,000
Widmer	125,000
Anchor	108,000
Full Sail	80,000
Portland	70,000
Spanish Peaks	60,000

Source: *Forbes*, July 28, 1997, p. 51, from Beer Marketer's Insights and Institute for Brewing Studies.

★ 304 ★
Beer (SIC 2082)

Leading Beer Brands - 1997

Sales are shown in millions of gallons.

Budweiser	1,119
Bud Light	710
Miller Lite	502
Coors Light	425
Busch	245
Natural Light	220
Miller Genuine Draft	171
Miller High Life	146
Busch Light	140
Milwaukee's Best	140

Source: *New York Times*, April 18, 1998, p. C1, from Impact Databank.

★ 305 ★
Beer (SIC 2082)

Leading Beers at Drugstores - 1997

Shares are shown based on sales of $660.0 million for the 52 weeks ended November 2, 1997.

Budweiser	16.1%
Bud Light	9.6
Miller Lite	9.4
Miller Genuine Draft	5.2
Coors Light	4.3
Busch	4.0
Natural Light	3.4
Miller High Life	2.9
Corona Extra	2.5
Heineken	2.3
Other	40.3

Source: *Beverage Industry*, January 1998, p. 18, from Information Resources Inc.

★ 306 ★
Beer (SIC 2082)

Leading Beers at Supermarkets - 1997

Shares are shown based on sales of $5.56 billion for the 52 weeks ended November 2, 1997.

Budweiser	13.8%
Bud Light	10.5
Miller Lite	7.5

Coors Light	7.0%
Natural Light	3.7
Miller Genuine Draft	3.4
Busch	2.9
Corona Extra	2.6
Miller High Life	2.3
Busch Light	2.1
Other	44.2

Source: *Beverage Industry*, January 1998, p. 18, from Information Resources Inc.

★ 307 ★
Beer (SIC 2082)

Leading Specialty Beer Marketers

Market shares are shown in percent.

Boston Beer	19.7%
D.G. Yuengling & Sons	7.9
Pete's Brewing	6.2
Others	66.2

Source: *Beverage World*, February 1998, p. 41, from Beverage Marketing Corp.

★ 308 ★
Beer (SIC 2082)

Microbreweries by State - 1997

Data show states ranked by number of microbreweries as of September 1997. There are 418 microbreweries operating in the United States.

California	68
Colorado	30
Washington	26
Pennsylvania	20
New York	14

Source: *Chicago Tribune*, October 8, 1997, p. C1, from Institute for Brewing Studies.

★ 309 ★
Beer (SIC 2082)

Top Beer Brands - 1997

Brands are ranked by sales in millions of barrels.

	(mil.)	Share
Budweiser	40.1	20.86%
Bud Light	23.0	11.97
Miller Lite	16.3	8.48

Continued on next page.

★ 309 ★ *Continued*
Beer (SIC 2082)

Top Beer Brands - 1997

Brands are ranked by sales in millions of barrels.

	(mil.)	Share
Coors Light	14.4	7.49%
Busch	9.3	4.84
Milwaukee's Best	6.6	3.43
Miller Genuine Graft	6.3	3.28
Miller High Life	5.4	2.81
Anheuser Busch Natural Light	4.1	2.13
Busch Light	4.0	2.08
Other	62.7	32.62

Source: *Chicago Tribune*, January 19, 1998, p. 3, from *Maxwell Consumer Report*.

★ 310 ★
Beer (SIC 2082)

Top Beer Companies

Data show millions of 31-gallon barrels sold in the United States.

Anheuser-Busch	91.1
Miller Brewing Co.	43.8
Coors	20.0
Stroh	16.7
Pabst	5.6

Source: *Detroit Free Press*, July 7, 1997, p. 8F, from Beer Marketer's Insights.

★ 311 ★
Beer (SIC 2082)

Top Beer Makers - 1997

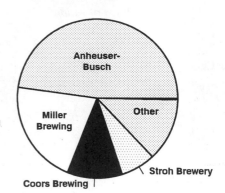

Market shares are shown in percent.

Anheuser-Busch	47.5%
Miller Brewing	21.4
Coors Brewing	10.9
Stroh Brewery	7.4
Other	12.8

Source: *Chicago Tribune*, January 19, 1998, p. 3, from *Maxwell Consumer Report*.

★ 312 ★
Beer (SIC 2082)

Top Beer Makers - Canada

The table shows the share each company claims of the market. Labatt places Molson's share at 45.9%. Molson places Labatt's share at 45.7% or 45.8% of the market.

Molson	46.65%
Labatt	46.00
Other	7.35

Source: *Marketing Magazine*, February 28, 1998, p. 1.

★ 313 ★
Wine (SIC 2084)

Best-Selling Wines

Sales are shown in thousands of dollars for the 52 weeks ended June 22, 1997. Figures are for grocery stores and drug stores.

Table wine	$ 2,450,872
Domestics	2,085,375
Varietals	1,894,117
White wine	1,055,399

Source: From the Internet, http:// winebiz.com/iri/ iri6.22.htm, October 1997, p. 1, from Information Resources Inc.

★ 314 ★
Wine (SIC 2084)

Popular Wines - 1996

Market shares are shown based on unit sales. Producer names are given in parentheses.

Carlo Rossi (E. & J. Gallo Winery)	7.6%
Franzia (The Wine Group)	7.6
Gallo Label (E. & J. Gallo Winery)	5.8
Gallo Reserve Cellars (E. & J. Gallo Winery)	4.8
Inglenook (Canandaigua Wine)	3.7
Almaden Vineyards (Canandaigua Wine)	3.5
Sutter Home (Sutter Home Winery)	3.3
Robert Mondavi (Robert Mondavi Winery)	2.7
Paul Masson (Canandaigua Wine)	1.8
Beringer (Beringer Wine Estates)	1.7
Others	57.5

Source: *New York Times*, September 4, 1997, p. C4, from *Adams Wine Handbook 1997.*

★ 315 ★
Wine (SIC 2084)

Preferred Brands of Wine

The table shows the preferred brands of wine based on a reader survey.

Cabernet Sauvignon	32.8%
Zinfandel	13.9
Pinot Noir	13.3
Merlot	9.0
Chardonnay	6.7
Syrah/Shiraz	5.9
Champagne/sparkling wine/dessert	3.1
Other	15.2

Source: *Wine Spectator*, February 28, 1998, p. 19.

★ 316 ★
Wine (SIC 2084)

Top California Wine Producers - 1996

Market shares are shown based on 750 ml bottles shipped.

Beringer	14.0%
Gallo	13.0
Sutter Home	11.0
Glen Ellen/BV	7.0
Fetzer	6.0
Kendall-Jackson	5.0
Mondavi	5.0
Others	39.0

Source: *Investor's Business Daily*, January 21, 1998, p. A4, from Gomberg, Fredrikson & Associates, and Donaldson, Lufkin & Jenrette.

★ 317 ★
Wine (SIC 2084)
Top Locations for U.S. Wineries

Central Coast, CA 250
Napa Valley, CA 240
Sonoma Valley, CA 150
New York 125
Oregon 120
Washington 95

Source: *Investor's Business Daily*, February 25, 1998, p. 1, from Cornell Unviersity School of Hotel Administration.

★ 318 ★
Liquor (SIC 2085)
Best-Selling Spirits - 1997

Sales are shown in millions of 9-liter cases.

Bacardi rum 6.800
Smironoff vodka 5.800
Absolut vodka 3.420
Jim Beam bourbon 3.400
Seagram's gin 3.210
Jack Daniel's black 3.080
7 Crown 2.840
Canadian Mist 2.780
Jose Cuervo tequila 2.680
Popov vodka 2.500
DeKuyper Cordials 2.170
Crown Royal 2.110
Gordon's vodka 1.990
E&J Brandy 1.900
Black Velvet 1.810

Source: *Chicago Tribune*, January 26, 1998, p. 3, from *Adams Handbook Advance 1998*.

★ 319 ★
Liquor (SIC 2085)
Canada's Domestic Cider Market

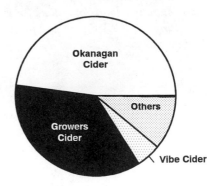

Data show shares for January to May of the years 1996 and 1997. Canadian ciders sold 512,000 9-liter cases during the first five months of 1996 and 620,000 9-liter cases during the first five months of 1997.

	1996	1997
Okanagan Cider	49.0%	48.0%
Growers Cider	35.0	36.0
Vibe Cider	0.6	5.0
Others	15.4	11.0

Source: *Marketing Magazine*, August 11, 1997, p. 3, from Association of Canadian Distillers.

★ 320 ★
Liquor (SIC 2085)
Popular Champagnes - 1997

Data show number of cases shipped to the United States.

Moet & Chandon 555,000
Veuve Clicquot 170,000
Perrier-Jouet 103,000
G.H. Mumm 100,000
Taittinger 58,800
Piper-Heidsieck 50,000

Source: *Wine Spectator*, May 31, 1998, p. 42.

★ 321 ★

Liquor (SIC 2085)

Popular Scotch Whisky Brands - 1996

Data show cases consumed. Company names are given in parentheses.

Dewar's (Guinness)	1,530,000
J&B (Grand Met)	810,000
Johnnie Walker Red (Guinness)	755,000
Clan MacGregor (William Grant & Sons)	710,000
Scoresby (Guinness)	590,000

Source: *USA TODAY*, August 1, 1997, p. B1, from Impact Databank.

★ 322 ★

Liquor (SIC 2085)

Top Imported Vodka Brands - 1996

Market shares are shown in percent.

Absolut	63.0%
Stolichnaya	20.0
Finlandia	6.0
Ketel One	4.0
Tanqueray Sterling	4.0
Other	3.0

Source: *Globe & Mail*, May 7, 1998, p. B14, from Euromonitor and Impact Database.

★ 323 ★

Liquor (SIC 2085)

Top Liquer Brands in Canada - 1998

Market shares are shown based on sales of 1.53 million 9-liter cases for the year ended March 31, 1998.

Bailey's Irish Cream	12.5%
Kahlua	10.8
Southern Comfort	5.2
Grand Marnier	4.7
Ramazzotti Sambuca	3.6
Carolans Irish Cream	3.4
Tia Maria	3.0
Amaretto Di Saronno	2.9
O'Darby Irish Cream	2.7
Luxardo Sambuca	2.6
Others	48.6

Source: *Marketing Magazine*, May 25, 1998, p. 19, from industry sources.

★ 324 ★

Liquor (SIC 2085)

Top Tequila Brands

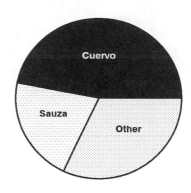

Market shares are shown in percent.

Cuervo	47.0%
Sauza	21.0
Other	32.0

Source: *Advertising Age*, April 13, 1998, p. 14, from *Market Watch*.

★ 325 ★

Liquor (SIC 2085)

Top Whisky Brands in Canada - 1997

Market shares are shown in percent. Top producers are Corby Distilleries, Seagrams, United Distillers and Alberta Distilleries.

Canadian Club	12.1%
Crown Royal	11.3
Wiser's	11.0
Corby Royal Reserve	7.1
Walker Special Old	6.9
Golden Wedding	6.4
Alberta Premium	5.9
Gibson's	5.5
Black Velvet	5.2
Seagram Five Star	5.0
Other	23.6

Source: *Marketing Magazine*, March 30, 1998, p. 9, from Association of Canadian Distillers.

★ 326 ★
Bottled Water (SIC 2086)

Bottled Water by Type

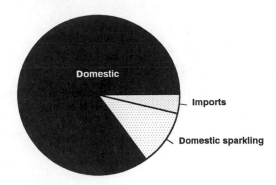

The market is shown by type.

Domestic 84.6%
Domestic sparkling 11.0
Imports 3.6

Source: *Beverage World*, October 1997, p. 56.

★ 327 ★
Bottled Water (SIC 2086)

Carbonated Water Market

Shares are shown based on sales of $511,329,000. Data include carbonated waters, club sodas, and flavored waters.

Canada Dry 12.6%
Schweppes 9.5
Vintage 6.2
Perrier 4.9
Clearly Canadian 4.7
Calistoga 2.5
Poland Spring 2.2
Polar 2.1
Mendota Springs 2.0
Private label 31.3
Other 22.0

Source: *Beverage Industry*, September 1997, p. 19, from Information Resources Inc.

★ 328 ★
Bottled Water (SIC 2086)

Leading Non-Carbonated Water Brands

Shares are shown based on sales of $1,016,212,000. Data include flavored waters.

Evian 9.1%
Poland Spring 6.7
Arrowhead 6.2
Sparkletts 3.4
Zephyrhills 3.1
Deer Park 2.9
Crystal Geyser 2.4
Hinckley & Schmitt 2.3
Ozarka 2.3
Private label 24.2
Other 37.4

Source: *Beverage Industry*, September 1997, p. 19, from Information Resources Inc.

★ 329 ★
Bottled Water (SIC 2086)

Top Bottled Water Brands - 1997

Shares are shown based on a $3.9 billion market.

Poland Spring 7.6%
Arrowhead 6.8
Evian 4.7
Sparkletts 4.7
Hinckley & Schmitt 3.1
Zephyrhills 2.8
Ozarka 2.7
Deer Park 2.5
Crystal Geyser 2.4
Crystal Springs 2.2
Other 60.5

Source: *Beverage World*, April 1998, p. 46, from Beverage Marketing Corp.

★ 330 ★

Bottled Water (SIC 2086)

Top Bottled Water Companies

Sales are shown in millions of dollars. Key brands are shown in parentheses.

Perrier Group (Arrowhead, Poland Spring, and Great Bear)	$ 966.8
Suntory International (Crystal, Belmont Spring, and Polar)	355.8
McKesson (Sparkletts)	271.9
Great Brands of Europe (Evian and Saratoga)	201.8
Crystal Geyser (Alpine Springs)	96.0

Source: *USA TODAY*, June 26, 1997, p. B1, from *Beverage Marketing*.

★ 331 ★

Bottled Water (SIC 2086)

Top Bottled Water Firms - 1997

Shares are shown based on a $3.9 billion market.

Perrier Group	28.1%
Suntory Water Group	9.2
McKesson Corporation	7.2
Danone International	5.9
Crystal Geyser	2.4
US Filter	2.3
Nora Beverages	1.8
Glacier Water Services	1.5
Pepsi-Cola	1.3
Aqua Penn	1.0
Other	39.3

Source: *Beverage World*, April 1998, p. 46, from Beverage Marketing Corp.

★ 332 ★

Soft Drinks (SIC 2086)

Diet Soft Drink Market - 1996

Shares of the $54 billion carbonated beverage market are shown in percent. Data are shown based on unit sales.

Diet Coke	8.7%
Diet Pepsi	5.7
Caffeine Free Diet Coke	1.9
Caffeine Free Diet Pepsi	1.0
Diet Dr. Pepper	0.9
Diet Mountain Dew	0.8

Diet 7 Up	0.7%
Diet Sprite	0.6
Diet Rite	0.4
Other	79.3

Source: *Advertising Age*, January 26, 1998, p. 3, from *Beverage Digest*.

★ 333 ★

Soft Drinks (SIC 2086)

Fountain Drink Market

Market shares are shown in percent.

Coke	65.0%
Pepsi	25.0
Cadbury	10.0

Source: *Wall Street Journal*, May 8, 1998, p. A3, from Sanford C. Bernstein.

★ 334 ★

Soft Drinks (SIC 2086)

Fountain Drink Market - 1996

Shares are shown in percent.

Coke	64.0%
Pepsi	21.0
Dr. Pepper/7Up	11.0
Other	4.0

Source: *USA TODAY*, November 6, 1997, p. 3B, from Beverage Marketing.

★ 335 ★

Soft Drinks (SIC 2086)

Leading Root Beers - 1997

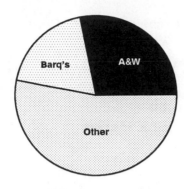

Shares are shown based on grocery sales through the first three quarters of 1997.

A&W 28.2%
Barq's 19.3
Other 52.5

Source: *Bangkok Post*, December 5, 1997, p. 19.

★ 336 ★

Soft Drinks (SIC 2086)

Leading Sports Drinks - 1997

Shares are shown for the third quarter of 1997. Company names are given in parentheses.

Gatorade (Quaker Oats) 79.0%
All Sport (PepsiCo) 9.0
PowerAde (Coca-Cola) 9.0
Other 3.0

Source: *Wall Street Journal*, January 28, 1998, p. B5A.

★ 337 ★

Soft Drinks (SIC 2086)

Low-Calorie Soft Drink Sales by City

Sales are shown in thousands of dollars for the 52 weeks ended December 28, 1997. Figures are for supermarket sales.

New York City, NY . . . . $ 182.4
Los Angeles, CA 137.6
Chicago, IL 127.2
Boston, MA 60.2
Detroit, MI 57.5
Dallas/Ft. Worth, TX 55.2
San Francisco/Oakland, CA 49.0

Source: *Beverage Industry*, March 1998, p. 37, from Information Resources Inc.

★ 338 ★

Soft Drinks (SIC 2086)

Orange Soft Drink Market - 1997

Market shares are shown in percent. Data are for supermarkets only, which account for 60% of all orange soft drink sales.

Sunkist 19.3%
Slice 12.2
Minute Maid 11.9
Private label 35.9
Other 20.7

Source: *USA TODAY*, March 31, 1998, p. B2.

★ 339 ★

Soft Drinks (SIC 2086)

Soda Market - Mexico

Market shares are shown in percent.

Coca-Cola 33.2%
Pepsi Cola 18.3
Other 48.5

Source: *National Trade Data Bank*, October 22, 1997, p. ISA970901.

★ 340 ★
Soft Drinks (SIC 2086)

Soft Drink Market - Canada

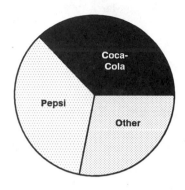

Market shares are shown in percent.

Coca-Cola	37.0%
Pepsi	35.0
Other	28.0

Source: *Forbes*, October 22, 1997, p. 212, from *Beverage Digest*.

★ 341 ★
Soft Drinks (SIC 2086)

Soft Drink Market - Mexico

Market shares are shown in percent.

Coca-Cola	64.0%
Pepsi	21.0
Other	15.0

Source: *Forbes*, October 22, 1997, p. 212, from *Beverage Digest*.

★ 342 ★
Soft Drinks (SIC 2086)

Soft Drink Producers - 1997

Shares are shown as of September 30, 1997. Cott Corp. represents more than half of the private label market.

Coca-Cola	36.8%
Pepsi	33.4
Cadbury-Schweppes	15.2
Private label	9.1
Other	5.5

Source: *Wall Street Journal*, January 6, 1998, p. B8, from *Beverage Digest*, Baseline, and company reports.

★ 343 ★
Soft Drinks (SIC 2086)

Soft Drink Sales by City

Sales are shown in thousands of dollars for the 52 weeks ended December 28, 1997. Figures are for supermarket sales.

Los Angeles, CA	$ 382.4
New York City, NY	369.0
Chicago, IL	288.5
Dallas/Ft. Worth, TX	166.8
Detroit, MI	129.5
Boston, MA	117.2
San Francisco/Oakland, CA	115.7

Source: *Beverage Industry*, March 1998, p. 37, from Information Resources Inc.

★ 344 ★
Soft Drinks (SIC 2086)

Top Diet Soft Drinks - 1997

Shares of the diet drink market are shown in percent.

Diet Coke	33.2%
Diet Pepsi	19.9
Caffeine Free Diet Coke	6.9
Caffeine Free Diet Pepsi	4.0
Diet Dr. Pepper	3.5
Diet Mountain Dew	2.9
Diet 7Up	2.3
Diet Sprite	1.9
Diet Rite	1.2
Fresca	1.1
Others	22.8

Source: *Beverage World*, March 1998, p. 39, from Beverage Markting Corporation.

★ 345 ★
Soft Drinks (SIC 2086)

Top RTD Tea Brands - 1997

Shares of the ready-to-drink tea market are shown in percent.

Lipton	34.5%
Nestea	20.4
Snapple	13.6
Arizona	9.7
Others	21.8

Source: *Beverage World*, March 1998, p. 64, from Beverage Marketing Corporation.

★ 346 ★
Soft Drinks (SIC 2086)

Top Soft Drink Brands - 1997

Market shares are shown in percent.

Coke Classic	20.6%
Pepsi-Cola	14.5
Diet Coke	8.5
Mountain Dew	6.3
Sprite	6.2
Dr. Pepper	5.9
Diet Pepsi	5.5
7Up	2.3
Caffeine Free Diet Coke	1.8
Caffeine Free Diet Pepsi	1.0
Other	27.4

Source: From the Internet, http:// biz.yahoo.com, February 12, 1998, p. 1, from *Beverage Digest*.

★ 347 ★
Soft Drinks (SIC 2086)

Top Soft Drink Makers - 1997

Shares are shown in percent.

Coca-Cola	44.1%
Pepsi-Cola	30.7
Dr. Pepper/Seven Up	14.2
Cott	2.8
National Beverage	1.9
Royal Crown	1.5
Monarch	0.8
Double-Cola	0.4
Big Red	0.2
Seagram's Mixers	0.2
Others	3.1

Source: *Beverage World*, March 1998, p. 39.

★ 348 ★
Soft Drinks (SIC 2086)

Top Soft Drinks at Convenience Stores

Market shares are shown in percent.

Mountain Dew 20-Oz	4.52%
Pepsi 2-L	4.51
Coke Classic 20-Oz	4.12
Coke Classic 2-L	3.99
Pepsi 20-oz	3.76

Coke Classic 12-PkCn	3.72%
Pepsi 12-PkCn	3.28
Others	72.10

Source: *Beverage World*, March 1998, p. 55, from Data Bank USA.

★ 349 ★
Soft Drinks (SIC 2086)

Top Soft Drinks at Supermarkets

Market shares are shown in percent.

Coke Classic 12-PkCn	8.48%
Pepsi 12-PkCn	7.42
Pepsi 2-L	5.09
Coke Classic 2-L	4.51
Pepsi 24-PjCn	4.14
Diet Coke 12-PkCn	3.48
Dr. Pepper 12-PkCn	3.10
Others	63.78

Source: *Beverage World*, March 1998, p. 55, from Data Bank USA.

★ 350 ★
Drink Mixes (SIC 2087)

Breakfast Drink Mix Market - 1997

Shares are shown based on $33 million in sales for the year ended May 25, 1997. Figures are for supermarket sales.

Tang	90.30%
Other	9.70

Source: *Brandweek*, July 14, 1997, p. 3, from Information Resources Inc.

★ 351 ★
Drink Mixes (SIC 2087)

Fruit Drink Mix Market

Shares of the $617.2 million market are shown for the year ended March 1, 1998.

Kraft	89.9%
Other	11.1

Source: *Brandweek*, April 20, 1998, p. 6, from Information Resources Inc.

★ 352 ★

Food Additives (SIC 2087)

Bulk Nutraceutical Demand - 2001

Sales are estimated in millions of dollars.

	($ mil.)	Share
Herbal extracts	$ 650	25.74%
Vitamins	650	25.74
Essential nutrients	550	21.78
Minerals	515	20.40
Other	160	6.34

Source: *Beverage World*, January 1998, p. 234, from Freedonia Group.

★ 353 ★

Food Additives (SIC 2087)

Food Additives Market by Type - 1997

- Flavors
- Nonnutritive sweeteners
- Bulking agents
- Gums and thickeners
- Emulsifiers
- Acidulants
- Colorants
- Preservatives
- Fat replacers
- Other additives

Distribution is shown based on a projected $4.73 billion market for 1997.

Flavors	24.0%
Nonnutritive sweeteners	23.0
Bulking agents	12.0
Gums and thickeners	11.0
Emulsifiers	7.0
Acidulants	6.0
Colorants	5.0
Preservatives	5.0
Fat replacers	2.0
Other additives	5.0

Source: *Chemical Week*, June 11, 1997, p. 30, from Frost & Sullivan.

★ 354 ★

Seafood (SIC 2091)

Canned Tuna Leaders - 1997

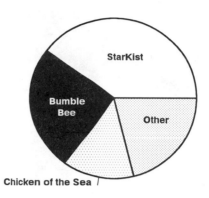

Shares are shown in percent based on sales of $1.2 billion for the year ended April 26, 1998.

	Sales ($ mil.)	Share
StarKist	$ 480.8	40.07%
Bumble Bee	300.1	25.01
Chicken of the Sea	167.3	13.94
Other	251.8	20.98

Source: *Brandweek*, June 1, 1998, p. 6.

★ 355 ★

Seafood (SIC 2091)

Seafood Sales at Supermarkets

Shares are shown based on sales. Data are estimated.

Fish	40.0%
Shrimp	31.0
Prepared entrees (cooked)	12.0
Prepared entrees (uncooked)	11.0
Lobster	3.0
Scallops	1.0
Soups	1.0
Clams & other shellfish	2.0

Source: *Supermarket Business*, November 1997, p. 77.

★ 356 ★

Frozen Fish (SIC 2092)

Frozen Fish Market - 1997

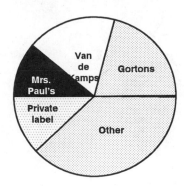

Shares of the $802.3 million market are shown in percent for the year ended May 25, 1997.

	($ mil.)	Share
Gortons	$ 169.8	21.16%
Van de Kamps	141.0	17.57
Mrs. Paul's	91.0	11.34
Private label	94.3	11.75
Other	306.2	38.17

Source: *Brandweek*, June 30, 1997, p. 9, from Information Resources Inc.

★ 357 ★

Coffee (SIC 2095)

Top RTD Coffee Brands - 1997

Shares of the ready-to-drink coffee market are shown in percent.

Frappuccino	64.1%
Nescafe	10.8
Others	25.1

Source: *Beverage World*, March 1998, p. 64, from Beverage Marketing Corporation.

★ 358 ★

Snacks (SIC 2096)

Leading Potato Chip Brands

Brand shares are shown in percent for 1993 and 1996. Company names appear in parentheses.

	1993	1996
Lay's (Frito Lay)	17.9%	28.2%
Ruffles (Frito Lay)	18.1	20.1
Pringles (Procter & Gamble)	7.7	9.9
Borden Inc. (Wise)	2.7	3.5
Eagle Thins (Eagle Snacks Inc.) . . .	6.6	1.8
Other	47.0	36.5

Source: *U.S. Distribution Journal*, August 1997, p. 36, from Datamonitor.

★ 359 ★

Snacks (SIC 2096)

Salty Snack Makers

Leading companies are shown ranked by market share. Salty snacks include corn chips, potato chips and similar products.

Frito-Lay	54.0%
Borden (Wise)	4.0
Procter & Gamble	4.0
Other	38.0

Source: *Forbes*, October 20, 1997, p. 213.

★ 360 ★

Snacks (SIC 2096)

Salty Snack Market - Mexico

Market shares are shown in percent. Barcel's figure is estimated. Sabritas is a Frito-Lay subsidiary.

Sabritas (Frito-Lay)	80.0%
Barcel	20.0

Source: *Latin Trade*, April 1998, p. 26.

★ 361 ★

Snacks (SIC 2096)

Top Pretzel Brands - 1997

Brands are shown ranked by sales in millions of dollars for the 52-week period ended May 25, 1997. Shares of the $607.9 million market are shown for that period.

	Sales ($ mil.)	Share
Rold Gold	$ 182.3	30.0%
Snyder's of Hanover	98.7	16.2
Bachman	21.9	3.6
Gardetto's	18.1	3.0
Combos	17.0	2.8
Herr's	14.8	2.4
Nabisco Pretzel Air Crisps	13.2	2.2
Snyder's of Hanover Olde Tyme	12.4	2.0
Utz	12.1	2.0
Private label	67.2	11.1

Source: *Snack Food & Wholesale Bakery*, August 1997, p. 25, from Information Resources Inc.

★ 362 ★

Snacks (SIC 2096)

Top Snack Producers in North America - 1997

Data show companywide sales of snack and bakery products in millions of dollars.

Frito-Lay Inc.	$ 9,000
Nabisco Inc.	7,031
Interstate Bakeries Corp.	3,200
Hershey Chocolate North America	3,103
M&M/Mars	2,650
Kraft Foods Inc.	2,395
Campbell Soup Co.	2,150
Keebler Corp.	2,100
Wm. Wrigley Jr. Co.	1,790
The Pillsbury Co.	1,768

Source: *Snack Food & Wholesale Bakery*, December 1997, p. 30.

★ 363 ★

Snacks (SIC 2096)

Top Tortilla Chip Brands - 1997

Shares are shown based on $1.707 billion for the year ended January 4, 1998.

	($ mil.)	Share
Doritos	$ 663.5	38.9%
Tostitos	481.7	28.2
Baked Tostitos	162.9	9.5
Santitas	55.8	3.3
Mission	32.3	1.9
Padrinos	22.1	1.3
Chi-Chi's	12.2	0.7
Herr's	9.2	0.5
Guiltless Gourmet	9.1	0.5
Other	160.3	15.2

Source: *Snack Food and Wholesale Bakery*, March 1998, p. 18, from Information Resources Inc.

★ 364 ★

Snacks (SIC 2096)

U.S. Salty Snack Market - 1997

The $11 billion market is shown in percent. Data exclude convenience stores, warehouse clubs and vending machines.

Doritos	10.0%
Lay's	7.4
Tostitos	7.1
Ruffles	6.2
Frito-Lay	4.6
Pringles	3.5
Baked Lay's	3.3
Frito-Lay Fritos	3.3
Cheetos	3.0
Rold Gold	2.5
Baked Tostitos	2.4
Private label	6.9
Other	39.8

Source: *Investor's Business Daily*, February 26, 1998, p. A4, from Information Resources Inc.

★ 365 ★

Food (SIC 2099)

Fruit Roll Up Makers - Canada

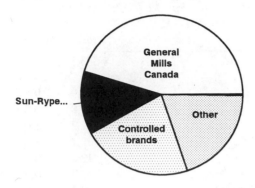

Market shares are shown in percent.

General Mills Canada 49.9%
Sun-Rype Products Ltd. 14.1
Controlled brands 24.0
Other 22.0

Source: *Marketing Magazine*, March 9, 1998, p. 13, from
A.C. Nielsen.

★ 366 ★

Food (SIC 2099)

Meat Substitute Market

Market shares are shown in percent.

Morningstar Farms 50.4%
Gardenburger 11.7
Others 37.8

Source: *Wall Street Journal*, May 20, 1998, p. B6.

★ 367 ★

Food (SIC 2099)

Portable Food Makers - Canada

Market shares are shown in percent.

General Mills Canada 19.3%
Quaker Oats Co. of Canada 16.6
Kellogg Canada 12.1
Kraft Canada 11.7

Biscuit Leclerc 4.1%
Christie 3.0
Controlled labels 22.9
Others 11.3

Source: *Marketing Magazine*, March 9, 1998, p. 13, from
A.C. Nielsen.

★ 368 ★

Food (SIC 2099)

Portable Food Market - Canada

*Spending is shown in millions of dollars for the year
ended January 3, 1998.*

	($ mil.)	Share
Granola bars	$ 100.48	37.74%
Cereal bars	59.97	22.52
Fruit snacks	58.82	22.09
Rice/corn cakes	25.73	9.66
Cereal snacks	21.24	7.98

Source: *Marketing Magazine*, March 9, 1998, p. 13, from
A.C. Nielsen MarketTrack.

★ 369 ★

Peanut Butter (SIC 2099)

Top Peanut Butter Brands - 1997

*Data show sales in millions of dollars for the 52
weeks ended November 9, 1997.*

	Sales ($ mil.)	Share
Jif	$ 229.9	31.52%
Peter Pan	86.2	11.82
Private label	152.8	20.95
Other	260.5	35.71

Source: *Advertising Age*, January 26, 1998, p. 18.

★ 370 ★

Salads (SIC 2099)

Leading Bagged Salad Producers

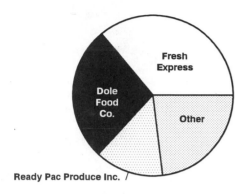

Shares are shown based on an estimated $1.0 billion market.

Fresh Express	35.6%
Dole Food Co.	27.2
Ready Pac Produce Inc.	14.2
Other	23.0

Source: *Wall Street Journal*, June 24, 1997, p. B1, from Information Resources Inc.

★ 371 ★

Snacks (SIC 2099)

Leading Fruit Snack Brands - 1997

Brands ranked by sales in millions of dollars for the 52-week period ended August 17, 1997.

	Sales ($ mil.)	Share
Betty Crocker Fruit Roll-Ups	$ 68.2	18.0%
Betty Crocker Fruit By the Foot	53.7	14.2
Betty Crocker Gushers	43.3	11.4
Betty Crocker String Thing	30.7	8.1
Farley's	30.5	8.1
Sunkist	16.4	4.3
Farley's The Roll	13.4	3.5
Farley's Dinosaur	9.9	2.6
Betty Crocker Bugs Bunny	8.2	2.2
Private label	26.0	6.9
Other	78.5	20.7

Source: *Snack Food & Wholesale Bakery*, November 1997, p. 16, from Information Resources Inc.

★ 372 ★

Syrup (SIC 2099)

Leading Syrup Brands - 1997

Shares of the $446.6 million market are shown in percent. Company names are shown in parentheses.

Log Cabin and Mrs. Butterworth's (Aurora Foods)	35.3%
Aunt Jemima (Quaker Oats Co.)	19.3
Other	45.4

Source: *Advertising Age*, October 20, 1997, p. 8, from Information Resources Inc.

★ 373 ★

Tea Bags (SIC 2099)

Tea Bag Leaders

Shares of the $599.4 million market are shown in percent.

	($ mil.)	Share
Lipton	$ 190.8	31.83%
Celestial Seasonings	71.2	11.88
Other	337.4	56.29

Source: *Brandweek*, May 18, 1998, p. 8, from Information Resources Inc.

SIC 21 - Tobacco Products

★ 374 ★
Cigarettes (SIC 2111)
Discount Cigarette Producers - 1996

Shares of the discount price segment are shown in percent.

Brown & Williamson 34.6%
R.J. Reynolds 32.0
Philip Morris 26.2
Liggett Group 4.9
Lorillard 1.8
Other 0.5

Source: *U.S. Distribution Journal*, July/August 1997, p. 21.

★ 375 ★
Cigarettes (SIC 2111)
Leading Cigarette Brands - Mexico

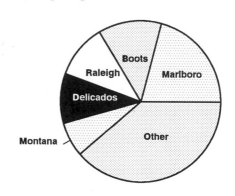

Shares are shown in percent. CLM controls 53% of the 47 billion cigarette market; Cigatam has the rest of the market.

Marlboro 21.0%
Boots 13.0
Raleigh 10.5
Delicados 10.3
Montana 6.6
Other 38.6

Source: *Financial Times*, July 28, 1997, p. 19, from industry sources.

★ 376 ★
Cigarettes (SIC 2111)
Leading Cigarette Companies - 1996

Shares are shown in percent.

Philip Morris 47.8%
R.J. Reynolds 24.6
Brown & Williamson 17.2
Lorillard 8.4
Liggett 1.9

Source: *Wall Street Journal*, September 23, 1997, p. A3, from *Market Up*.

★ 377 ★
Cigarettes (SIC 2111)

Top Cigarette Brands in Canada - 1997

Market shares are shown based on sales for the year ended August 31, 1997.

Player's Light Regular	12.5%
Du Maurier King Size	9.4
Du Maurier Regular	5.6
Player's Light King Size	4.8
Player's Regular	4.2
Du Maurier Light King Size	4.0
Export A Regular	3.5
Du Maurier Light Regular	3.0
Rothmans King Size	2.9
Export A Medium	2.7
Others	47.4

Source: *Marketing Magazine*, May 25, 1998, p. 18, from industry sources.

★ 378 ★
Cigarettes (SIC 2111)

Top Cigarette Producers

Market shares are shown for December 1997.

Philip Morris	47.80%
RJR Nabisco	25.39
Brown & Williamson	15.84
Lorillard	8.07
Other	2.90

Source: *Washington Post*, March 1, 1998, p. H1, from Sanford C. Bernstein & Co.

★ 379 ★
Cigars (SIC 2121)

Largest Cigar/Cigarillos Makers

Market shares are shown in percent.

Swisher Intl. Group	24.5%
Havatampa	23.3
Consolidated Cigar	20.5
General Cigar	17.1
John Middleton	10.0
Others	4.6

Source: *Wall Street Journal*, April 13, 1998, p. A3, from Maxwell Consumer Report *and Wheat First Butcher Singer.*

SIC 22 - Textile Mill Products

★ 380 ★
Textiles (SIC 2200)

Largest Textiles Firms

Firms are ranked by revenues in millions of dollars.

Shaw Industries	$ 3,576
Springs Industries	2,226
Burlington Industries	2,091
Mohawk Industries	1,820
Westpoint Stevens	1,820
Unifi	1,705
Interface	1,135

Source: *Fortune*, April 27, 1998, p. 56.

★ 381 ★
Hosiery (SIC 2250)

Retail Hosiery Market

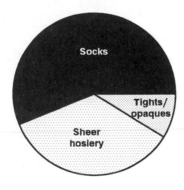

Distribution is shown based on retail sales for 1995 and 1996.

	1995	1996
Socks	54.0%	55.8%
Sheer hosiery	37.9	35.3
Tights/opaques	8.2	8.9

Source: *Nonfoods Merchandising*, September 1997, p. 11, from The National Association of Hosiery Manufacturers.

★ 382 ★
Fabrics (SIC 2261)

Leading Fireproof Fabric Makers

Shares are shown based on a 330 million pound market.

Albright & Wilson	25.0%
DuPont	25.0
Hoechst	25.0
Other	25.0

Source: *Chemical Week*, December 24, 1997, p. 23, from Albright & Wilson.

★ 383 ★
Carpets (SIC 2273)

Carpet Use in New Construction

Data show the types of carpets purchased for new construction.

Broadloom	47.0%
Carpet tile	32.0
Six-foot roll goods	21.0

Source: *Buildings*, January 1998, p. 36.

★ 384 ★
Carpets (SIC 2273)

U.S. Carpet Shipments

Shipments are estimated in millions of square yards.

	1996	1998	Share
Tufted broadloom	1,281	1,325	80.30%
Needlepunch, other	129	120	7.27
Automotive, industrial . . .	54	50	3.03
Artificial grass	37	20	1.21
Woven	22	20	1.21
Rugs, others	118	115	6.97

Source: *Textile World*, May 1998, p. 45, from U.S. Department of Commerce and Capet & Rug Institute.

SIC 23 - Apparel and Other Textile Products

★ 385 ★
Apparel (SIC 2300)

Apparel Sales by Gender - 1998

Figures are in billions of dollars for the first quarter of the year.

	($ bil.)	Share
Women	$ 20.0	54.35%
Men	11.0	29.89
Children	5.8	15.76

Source: *DNR*, June 3, 1998, p. 4, from NPD Group.

★ 386 ★
Apparel (SIC 2300)

Clothing Brands Favored by Teenagers - 1997

| Levi's |
| Calvin Klein |
| Tommy Hilfiger |
| The Gap |
| Guess |

The table shows survey responses in percent. Data include multiple responses.

Levi's	39.0%
Calvin Klein	32.0
Tommy Hilfiger	30.0
The Gap	27.0
Guess	17.0

Source: *Stores*, August 1997, p. 17, from *American Express Retail Trends Monitor*.

★ 387 ★
Apparel (SIC 2300)

Jeans Market - 1997

Shares of the $16.7 million market are shown in percent.

Levi	17.0%
Lee	10.0
Other	73.0

Source: *Brandweek*, June 16, 1997, p. 4.

★ 388 ★
Apparel (SIC 2300)

Largest Apparel Makers - 1997

Firms are ranked by revenues in millions of dollars.

Nike	$ 9,187
VF	5,222
Reebok International	3,637
Liz Claiborne	2,413
Fruit of the Loom	2,140
Nine West Group	1,865

Source: *Fortune*, April 27, 1998, pp. F-45.

★ 389 ★
Apparel (SIC 2300)

Largest Beach Apparel Makers

Firms are ranked by sales in millions of dollars.

Quiksilver	$ 151
No Fear	95
Big Dog	86
Hang Ten	81
Gotcha	74
Ocean Pacific	72

Source: *Sportstyle*, May 1998, p. 15.

★ 390 ★

Apparel (SIC 2300)

Largest Branded Apparel Makers

Sales are shown in millions of dollars.

Nike	$ 1,431
Adidas	465
Reebok	432
Russell Athletic	260
Sara Lee Casualwear	250
Fila	177
Champion	150
Discus	90

Source: *Sportstyle*, May 1998, p. 15.

★ 391 ★

Apparel (SIC 2300)

Largest Outdoor Apparel Makers

Firms are ranked by sales in millions of dollars.

Columbia	$ 250.3
Timberland	144.6
Woolrich	130.0
Patagonia	99.0
The North Face	77.5
Pacific Trail	75.0
Helly-Hansen	40.5
Gramicci	24.0
Marmot Mountain	23.0
Royal Robbins	23.0

Source: *Sportstyle*, May 1998, p. 30.

★ 392 ★

Apparel (SIC 2300)

Largest Performance Apparel Makers

Sales are shown in millions of dollars.

Speedo/Authentic Fitness	$ 200
Champion Jogbra	77
Pearl Izumi	30
Tyr	28
Insport	18
Diadora	16

Source: *Sportstyle*, May 1998, p. 13.

★ 393 ★

Apparel (SIC 2300)

Largest Ski/Snowboard Apparel Makers

Firms are ranked by sales in millions of dollars. Shares of the group are shown in percent.

	Sales ($ mil.)	% of Group
Burton	$ 40.7	17.79%
Sport Obermeyer	34.2	14.95
Snowmass Apparel	35.0	15.30
Bogner	20.0	8.74
The North Face	15.5	6.77
Roffe	13.0	5.68
Spyder	11.1	4.85
Nordica	11.0	4.81
Descente	9.5	4.15
Nils	9.5	4.15
Fila	8.2	3.58
Couloir	8.1	3.54
Fera	7.5	3.28
Marker	5.5	2.40

Source: *Sportstyle*, May 1998, p. 28.

★ 394 ★

Apparel (SIC 2300)

Sports Logo Apparel Sales - 1996

Categories are ranked by sales in millions of dollars.

T-shirts	$ 1,103
Fleece tops	665
Jackets	494
Knit shirts	352
Caps/hats	212
Shorts	92
Warmup suits	60
Fleece bottoms	52

Source: *Sporting Goods Business*, July 7, 1997, p. 16, from National Sporting Goods Association.

★ 395 ★

Apparel (SIC 2300)

Sportswear Sales by Sport - 1996

Retail sales are shown in millions of dollars.

Swimming	$ 1,800.0
Golf	1,600.0

Continued on next page.

★ 395 ★ *Continued*

Apparel (SIC 2300)

Sportswear Sales by Sport - 1996

Retail sales are shown in millions of dollars.

Camping	$ 1,300.0
Hunting	1,100.0
Fishing	902.4
Cycling	879.7
Aerobics	815.9
Downhill skiing	806.2
Running	706.8
Bowling	579.1
Martial arts	318.0
Tennis	269.6
Cross-country skiing	137.9

Source: *Women's Wear Daily*, June 12, 1997, p. 11, from National Sporting Goods Association.

★ 396 ★

Apparel (SIC 2300)

Work Apparel Market

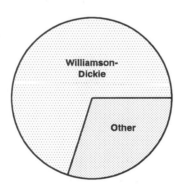

The market includes stiff khaki pants, jeans, bib overalls and chore coats for farmers, painters and mechanics.

Williamson-Dickie	70.0%
Other	30.0

Source: *Forbes*, June 15, 1998, p. 72.

★ 397 ★

Apparel (SIC 2322)

Leading Types of Men's Underwear

Shares are shown in percent.

Brief undershorts	32.1%
Boxer undershorts	27.0
Regular tee undershirts	15.1
Athletic briefs/boxer briefs	6.1
Other undershirts	15.1
Other undershorts	7.1

Source: *Body Fashions/Intimate Apparel*, February 1998, p. 11, from NPD American Shoppers Panel.

★ 398 ★

Apparel (SIC 2322)

Men's Underwear Leaders

Shares are estimated for the department store category.

Jockey	50.0%
Other	50.0

Source: *Brandweek*, June 30, 1997, p. 16.

★ 399 ★

Lingerie (SIC 2341)

Intimate Apparel Leaders

Shares are shown in percent.

Sara Lee Corporation	29.0%
VF Corp.	7.0
Warnaco Group	7.0
Maidenform Worldwide Inc.	3.5
Other	53.5

Source: *New York Times*, July 24, 1997, p. C1.

★ 400 ★
Lingerie (SIC 2341)

Intimate Apparel Sales by Segment

Data represent annual sales in millions of dollars, based on a survey of 16,000 households nationwide.

	1994	1995	1996
Bras	$ 3,117	$ 3,372	$ 3,648
Sleepwear	2,266	2,278	2,555
Panties	1,458	1,608	1,721
Robes and loungewear . . .	834	861	894
Daywear	664	648	671
Shapewear	323	339	382

Source: *Discount Merchandiser*, August 1997, p. 109, from NPD American Shopper Panel.

★ 401 ★
Window Coverings (SIC 2391)

Soft Window Coverings by Type - 1996

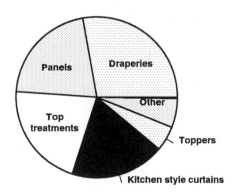

Shares are shown based on $3.2 billion in sales.

Draperies	28.0%
Panels	21.0
Top treatments	21.0
Kitchen style curtains	19.0
Toppers	5.0
Other	6.0

Source: *Bobbin*, October 1997, p. 38, from *Home Textiles Today*.

SIC 24 - Lumber and Wood Products

★ 402 ★
Fire Logs (SIC 2411)

Leading Fire Starter Brands

Shares are shown in percent.

StarterLogg	72.0%
Duraflame	9.0
Diamond	6.0
Private label	6.0
Conros	5.0
Pine Mountain	1.0
Others	1.0

Source: *Supermarket Business*, July 1997, p. 67, from Information Resources Inc. InfoScan.

★ 403 ★
Cabinets (SIC 2434)

Kitchen/Bath Cabinet Demand

Demand is shown in millions of units.

	1996	1997	1998
Repair and modeling	54.8	55.3	55.7
New construction	19.2	18.8	18.8

Source: *Wood Digest*, April 1998, p. 27, from KCMA and F.W. Dodge.

★ 404 ★
Cabinets (SIC 2434)

Largest Cabinet Makers - 1997

Companies are ranked by sales in millions of dollars.

Masco Corp.	$ 832.0
Mill's Pride	400.0
Aristokraft Inc.	250.0
American Woodmark	219.4
Schrock Cabinet Co.	200.0
Triangle Pacific Corp.	183.7
Elkay Mfg. Co., Cabinet Group	165.0

Omega Cabinets	$ 150.0
Cardell Kitchen & Bath Cabinetry	115.0
Wood-Mode Inc.	110.0

Source: *Wood & Wood Products*, April 1998, p. 48.

★ 405 ★
Hardwood (SIC 2435)

Hardwood Sales by Category

Kitchen cabinets	35.0%
Architectural woodworking	18.0
Furniture	18.0
Fixtures	13.0
Retail	13.0
Other	3.0

Source: *Forest Products Journal*, May 1998, p. 22.

★ 406 ★
Hardwood (SIC 2435)

Hardwood Sales by Region

	1995	1999
Northeast	26.0%	27.0%
West Coast	18.0	19.0
West	19.0	18.0
Southeast	13.0	14.0
Midwest	12.0	12.0
South Central	10.0	10.0
Canada, Alaska, Hawaii	2.0	2.0

Source: *Forest Products Journal*, May 1998, p. 22.

★ 407 ★
Lumber (SIC 2436)

Softwood Lumber Use

Data represent consumption in millions of board feet for 1995 and 1996.

	1995 (mil.)	1996 (mil.)	Share
New construction	19,099.2	20,212.8	40.00%
Remodeling	14,324.4	15,159.6	30.00
Other	14,324.4	15,159.6	30.00

Source: *Builder*, August 1997, pp. S-68, from American Forest and Paper Association.

★ 408 ★
Lumber (SIC 2436)

Veneer-Based Lumber Production - 1997- 1999

The table shows softwood plywood and laminated veneer lumber (LVL) production by year in millions of 3/8 inch surface measure equivalents.

	Plywood (mil.)	LVL (mil.)
1997	20,495	1,504
1998	20,000	1,856
1999	19,645	2,144

Source: *Wood Technology*, October 1997, p. 36, from *FAO Yearbook, 1998, APA Management Bulletin No. A-302, APA Economics Report E60*, and *APA Economics Report E62*.

★ 409 ★
Wood Products (SIC 2490)

Glulam Demand

Demand is shown in million board feet.

	1996	1998
Residential	134	147
Non-residential	95	104

Source: *Custom Builder*, 1998, p. 84, from Engineered Wood Association.

★ 410 ★
Wood Products (SIC 2490)

I-Joist Demand

Demand is shown in million linear feet.

	1996	1998
U.S.	444	645
Canada	54	115

Source: *Custom Builder*, 1998, p. 84, from Engineered Wood Association.

★ 411 ★
Particleboard (SIC 2493)

Medium Density Fiberboard Use by Category - 1996

Market is shown in percent.

Household furniture	26.0%
Stocking distributors	18.0
Custom laminators	13.0
Moulding	8.0
Millwork	7.0
Kitchen & bath	5.0
Partitions & fixtures	5.0
Other	18.0

Source: *Wood & Wood Products*, September 1997, p. 16, from Composite Panel Association.

★ 412 ★
Particleboard (SIC 2493)

Particleboard Use by Category - 1996

Market is shown in percent.

Household furniture	20.0%
Custom laminators	18.0
Kitchen & bath	15.0
Stocking distributors	15.0
Flooring products	10.0
Office furniture	5.0
Door core	3.0
Other	14.0

Source: *Wood & Wood Products*, September 1997, p. 16, from Composite Panel Association.

SIC 25 - Furniture and Fixtures

★ 413 ★

Furniture (SIC 2500)

Furniture Industry

Shipments are shown in millions of dollars.

	1997	1998	Share
Wood	$ 10.165	$ 10.433	47.49%
Upholstered	8.437	8.948	40.73
Metal & other	2.479	2.586	11.77

Source: *Wood Digest*, April 1998, p. S22.

★ 414 ★

Furniture (SIC 2500)

Furniture Shipments by Market

Data show furniture shipments in billions of dollars for 1997 and 1998. Figures for 1997 are estimated; figures for 1998 are projected.

	1997	1998
Residential furniture	$ 20.97	$ 21.75
Office, contract furniture	11.25	11.90

Source: *Wood & Wood Products*, January 1998, p. 15, from American Furniture Manufacturers Association and Business & Institutional Furniture Manufacturers Association.

★ 415 ★

Furniture (SIC 2500)

Furniture Spending in the Midwest

Total spending reached $8.1 billion. Distribution is shown in percent.

Sofas	23.0%
Kitchen & dining	15.0
Living room chairs	14.0
Bedrooms	13.0
Bedding	12.0
Occasional	12.0
Living room tables	6.0
Outdoor	3.0
Infants	2.0

Source: *Furniture Today*, December 29, 1997, p. 79.

★ 416 ★

Furniture (SIC 2500)

Furniture Spending in the South

Total spending reached $11.5 billion. Distribution is shown in percent.

Sofas	24.0%
Bedrooms	17.0
Bedding	14.0
Kitchen & dining	14.0
Occasional	11.0
Living room chairs	10.0

Continued on next page.

★ 416 ★ *Continued*
Furniture (SIC 2500)

Furniture Spending in the South

Total spending reached $11.5 billion. Distribution is shown in percent.

Living room tables	6.0%
Outdoor furniture	2.0
Infant furniture	2.0

Source: *Furniture Today*, December 29, 1997, p. 78.

★ 417 ★
Furniture (SIC 2500)

Largest Contract Furniture Makers

Sales are shown in millions of dollars.

Steelcase Inc.	$ 2,760
Haworth Inc.	1,510
Herman Miller Inc.	1,500
HON Industries	1,360
The Global Group	1,000
Knoll Inc.	811
Kimball Intl.	617

Source: *Wood & Wood Products*, May 1998, p. 48.

★ 418 ★
Furniture (SIC 2500)

Largest Furniture Markets

Data show sales of bedding and furniture in millions of dollars. Figures are estimated for 2001.

	1996	2001
Chicago, IL	$ 1,826.9	$ 2,455.2
Washington D.C.	1,258.7	1,895.7
New York City, NY	1,272.2	1,440.6
Atlanta, GA	931.5	1,414.8
Detroit, MI	960.2	1,246.1
Los Angeles-Long Beach, CA	1,120.0	1,204.1
Philadelphia, PA	862.8	1,007.6
Phoenix-Mesa, AZ	641.5	952.3
Nassau-Suffolk, NY	727.2	929.2
Greensboro-Winston Salem-High Point, NC	635.7	921.4

Source: *Furniture Today*, December 29, 1997, p. 32.

★ 419 ★
Furniture (SIC 2500)

Largest Furniture Markets in California

Data show sales in millions of dollars.

Los Angeles-Long Beach	$ 1,120.0
Orange County	503.0
Oakland	476.9
San Jose	436.2
San Diego	424.4
San Jose	360.0

Source: *Furniture Today*, December 29, 1997, p. 30.

★ 420 ★
Furniture (SIC 2500)

Top Furniture Makers

Companies are ranked by sales in millions of dollars. Figures include kitchen and bath cabinets, contract/office furniture, residential furniture, architectural woodwork and store fixtures.

Steelcase Inc.	$ 2,600
LifeStyle Home Furnishings	2,010
Furniture Brands International	1,620
Herman Miller Inc.	1,280
Haworth Inc.	1,150
La-Z-Boy Inc.	947
Hon Industries	813
Masco Corp.	800
Sealy Corp.	700
Klaussner Furniture Industries	640
Kimball International	639
Serta Inc.	630
Knoll Inc.	600
Sauder Woodworking	510
Ethan Allen Inc.	510

Source: From the Internet, *http://www.cabinetmag.com/fdm300.htm*, November 1997, from *Furniture Design & Manufacturing*.

★ 421 ★
Furniture (SIC 2500)

Top Furniture Makers - 1997

Companies are ranked by shipments in millions of dollars.

Furniture Brands International	$ 1,808.3
LifeStyle Furnishings International	1,693.6
La-Z-Boy	1,074.0
Klaussner	668.0
Ashley	530.0
Ladd	525.5
Ethan Allen	511.9
Sauder	475.0
Bassett	446.9
O'Sullivan	320.4

Source: *Furniture Today*, May 11, 1998, p. 25.

★ 422 ★
Furniture (SIC 2500)

Top Furniture Producers - 1996

Companies are ranked by value of furniture shipments shown in millions of dollars. The top 25 companies had a 46% share of the market.

LifeStyle Furnishings International	$ 1,733.3
Furniture Brands International	1,696.8
La-Z-Boy	985.2
Klaussner	657.0
Ladd	497.5
Sauder	475.0
Bassett	450.7
Ethan Allen	448.0
Ashley	442.0
O'Sullivan	301.1

Source: *Furniture Today*, December 29, 1997, p. 85.

★ 423 ★
Furniture (SIC 2500)

Top RTA Producers - 1997

Companies are ranked by sales in millions of dollars. RTA stands for ready-to-assemble.

Sauder	$ 475.0
Bush	325.3
O'Sullivan	320.4
Ameriwood	69.2

Source: *Furniture Today*, May 11, 1998, p. 25, from company reports.

★ 424 ★
Furniture (SIC 2511)

Wood Bedroom Furniture Imports - 1997

Data show the top sources of imports for wood bedroom furniture. Figures are in thousands of dollars.

Canada	$ 223,910
Mexico	102,693
Italy	64,729
China	28,021
Taiwan	27,926

Source: *Furniture Today*, May 11, 1998, p. 33.

★ 425 ★
Furniture (SIC 2512)

Top Upholstered Furniture Manufacturers - 1996

Companies are shown ranked by sales in millions of dollars.

Furniture Brands International	$ 850.0
La-Z-Boy Inc.	757.6
Klaussner Furniture Industries	640.0
LifeStyle Home Furnishings	500.0
KI	250.0
Flexsteel Industries, Inc.	205.0
Bassett Furniture Industries	180.0
Furniture Comfort Corp.	170.0
Washington Inc.	150.0
Rowe Furniture Corp.	142.7

Source: *Upholstery Design & Manufacturing*, May 1997, p. 22.

★ 426 ★

Furniture (SIC 2512)

Upholstered Seat Imports · 1997

Data show the top sources of imports of metal framed upholstered seats. Figures are in thousands of dollars.

Canada	$ 175,991
Taiwan	80,452
China	44,401
Italy	35,343
Mexico	22,460

Source: *Furniture Today*, May 11, 1998, p. 33.

★ 427 ★

Furniture (SIC 2514)

Metal Household Furniture Imports - 1997

China
Taiwan
Mexico
Philippines
Canada

Data show the top sources of imports of metal household furniture. Figures are in thousands of dollars.

China	$ 147,339
Taiwan	130,191
Mexico	100,182
Philippines	36,138
Canada	30,415

Source: *Furniture Today*, May 11, 1998, p. 33.

★ 428 ★

Office Furniture (SIC 2520)

Leading Federal Contractors of Office Furniture and Fixtures

Shares are shown based on $467,854,000 in purchases by the U.S. government.

Unicor	14.70%
Herman Miller Inc.	10.21
Krueger International	9.97
Haworth, Inc.	6.52
Spacesaver Corp.	5.84
Westinghouse Electric Corp. . . .	5.81

Steelcase, Inc.	4.65%
Leggett & Platt Inc.	3.42
Trendway Corp.	2.93
The Stanley Works	1.71
Others	34.24

Source: From the Internet, http:// www.govexec.com/ procure/articles/0896opgb.html, September 24, 1997, p. 2.

★ 429 ★

Office Furniture (SIC 2521)

Wood Door Market - 1997

Data are shown based on 65 million units.

Residential passage	46.00%
Closet	44.77
Residential entry	4.62
Nonresidential passage	4.31
Nonresidential entry	0.31

Source: *Wood Digest*, April 1998, p. S34.

★ 430 ★

Office Furniture (SIC 2521)

Wood Office Furniture Sales - 1997

Sales are estimated in percent.

Seating	24.3%
Desks and extensions	22.9
Storage	13.0
Panel systems	12.2
Tables	10.7
Files	3.7
Modular systems	3.1
Other	3.9

Source: *Wood Digest*, April 1998, p. S26.

★ 431 ★

Fixtures (SIC 2540)

Top Fixture Manufacturers - 1996

Data show sales in millions of dollars.

Ontario Store Fixtures	$ 216.0
Madix Store Fixtures	150.0
RHC/Spacemaster Corp.	139.0
Hamilton Fixture	76.0
Oklahoma Fixture	65.0
MET Merchandising Concepts	55.0

Continued on next page.

★ 431 ★ *Continued*

Fixtures (SIC 2540)

Top Fixture Manufacturers - 1996

Data show sales in millions of dollars.

Ready Fixtures . . . .$ 53.0
MII, Inc. Fixture Group 51.0
Goer Manufacturing Co. 42.0
Dann Dee Display Fixtures 33.0
MEG div. of Steelworks 30.0
Winslow Associates 26.0
Dillmeier Group 25.0
Russell William Ltd. 25.0
Trion Industries 25.0

Source: *VM + SD*, October 1997, p. 25.

★ 432 ★

Fixtures (SIC 2541)

Who Buys Cabinets Direct from Small Manufacturers

Sales are shown in percent, based on a survey of 175 manufacturing shops with net revenues of $5 million or less.

Builders 60.0%
Consumers 28.7
Distributors 4.5
Dealers 1.5
Dealers 1.5
Architects 1.3
Home centers 0.4

Source: *Custom Builder*, November 1997, p. 13, from *Kitchen & Bath Business*.

SIC 26 - Paper and Allied Products

★ 433 ★
Paper (SIC 2600)

Paper and Paperboard Production in North America

Production is shown in percent.

Uncoated freesheet	30.0%
Coated paper	17.0
Newsprint	17.0
Tissue	13.0
Packaging	8.0
Groundwood printing	4.0
Specialty grades	4.0
Unbleached kraft	4.0
Bristols	3.0

Source: *PIMA's Papermaker*, March 1998, p. 44.

★ 434 ★
Pulp (SIC 2611)

Pulp Production by Type - Mexico

Production is shown by type for 1995 and 1996.

	1995	1996
Chemical wood pulp	66.2%	63.4%
Chemical nonwood	29.1	30.1
Mechanical wood pulp	4.7	6.5

Source: *Pima's Papermaker*, August 1997, p. 26, from Camara Nacional de las Industrias de la Celulosa y del Papel.

★ 435 ★
Pulp (SIC 2611)

Pulp Production in Mexico - 1996

Production is shown in thousands of tons.

	Tons	Share
Bleached bagasse	153.9	30.10%
Unbleached kraft	112.9	22.08
Bleached softwood kraft	109.1	21.34
Bleached hardwood kraft	102.1	19.97
Mechanical pulp	23.2	4.54
TMP	10.1	1.98

Source: *Pima's Papermaker*, August 1997, p. 26, from CNICP.

★ 436 ★
Paper (SIC 2621)

Canada's Paper Companies - 1996

Data show pulp, paper, and converted product sales in millions of Canadian dollars. Figure for Domtar is estimated.

Abitibi-Price Inc.	$ 2,590
Stone-Consolidated	2,129
Cascades	2,101
Fletcher Challenge	1,860
Domtar	1,672
Avenor Inc.	1,656
MacMillan Bloedel Ltd.	1,626
Donohue Inc.	1,216
Repap Enterprises Inc.	1,213
Noranda Forest Inc.	1,029

Source: *PIMA's Papermaker*, June 1997, p. 63.

★ 437 ★
Paper (SIC 2621)

Largest Paper Product Makers

Firms are ranked by revenues in millions of dollars.

International Paper	$ 20,096
Georgia-Pacific	13,094
Kimberly-Clark	12,547
Weyerhaeuser	11,210
Fort James	7,259
Champion International	5,736
Boise Cascade	5,493
Mead	5,077
Stone Container	4,849
Union Camp	4,477

Source: *Fortune*, April 27, 1998, pp. F-50.

★ 438 ★
Paper (SIC 2621)

Top Kraft Paper Makers - 1997

Companies are shown ranked by capacity in thousands of tons.

	Tons (000)	Share
Stone Container	519	20.2%
Longview Fibre	500	19.4
Georgia-Pacific	340	13.2
Gaylord Container	275	10.7
International Paper	260	10.1
Union Camp	200	7.8
St. Laurent	125	4.9
Champion	100	3.9
Gilman Paper	100	3.9
Port Townsend	100	3.9
Other	54	2.0

Source: *Pulp & Paper*, November 1997, p. 11.

★ 439 ★
Paper (SIC 2621)

Top Newsprint Makers in Canada - 1997

Production is shown in thousands of tons. Total production reached 9.67 million tons.

	(000)	Share
Abitibi-Consolidated	2,650	27.40%
Donohue	1,380	14.27
Avenor	1,100	11.38
Kruger	923	9.54
Fletcher Challenge Canada	722	7.47
Other	2,895	29.94

Source: *Financial Times*, March 11, 1998, p. 22, from Canadian Pulp & Paper Association.

★ 440 ★
Paper (SIC 2621)

Top Newsprint Makers in North America - 1996

Shares are shown based on estimated annual capacity for 1996.

Abitibi-Price (Toronto, Canada)	11.4%
Avenor Inc. (Montreal, Canada)	8.7
Donohue (Quebec City, Canada)	8.5
Stone-Consolidated (Montreal, Canada)	8.3
Bowater (Greenville, SC)	8.1
Kruger (Montreal, Canada)	5.9
Fletcher Challenge Canada (Vancouver, Canada)	4.7
North Pacific Paper (Longview, WA)	4.3
Champion International (Stamford, CT)	4.3
Smurfit Newsprint (Oregon City, OR)	4.0
Other	31.8

Source: *Editor and Publisher*, October 11, 1997, p. 31, from *Pulp & Paper Week*, Canadian Pulp and Paper Association, and American Forest & Paper Association.

★ 441 ★

Paper (SIC 2621)

Top Newsprint Makers in North America - 1997

Market shares are shown in percent.

Abitibi-Consolidated	20.0%
Avenor	8.6
Donohue	8.4
Bowater	8.0
Kruger	8.0
Fletcher Challange	5.9
North Pacific Paper	4.5
Champion Intl.	4.5
Smurfit Newsprint	4.0
MacMillan Bloedel	2.9
Others	28.5

Source: *PIMA's Papermaker*, March 1998, p. 38.

★ 442 ★

Paper (SIC 2621)

Top Tissue Producers - North America

Market shares are shown in percent.

Kimberly-Clark	21.0%
Fort Howard	16.0
Procter & Gamble	14.0
James River	13.0
Georgia-Pacific	7.9
Chesapeake	4.1
Kruger	3.7
American Tissue	3.4
Perkins Papers	2.6
Jomar Mgmt.	2.0
Other	12.8

Source: *Pulp & Paper*, February 1998, p. 13.

★ 443 ★

Paper (SIC 2621)

Top Uncoated Groundwood Paper Producers - North America

Companies are ranked by annual capacity in thousands of tons. Data are estimated for 1997.

	Tons (000)	Share
Abitibi-Consolidated	1,653	30.3%
Champion International	523	9.6
Bowater	374	6.9
Alliance	369	6.8
MacMillan Bloedel	363	6.7
Fletcher Challenge	255	4.7
Tripap	248	4.5
Consolidated Papers	240	4.4
Madison Paper	225	4.1
Daishowa (North America)	195	3.6
Other	995	26.0

Source: *Pulp & Paper*, September 1997, p. 13.

★ 444 ★

Paper (SIC 2621)

U.S. Paper Companies - 1996

International Paper Co.
Kimberly-Clark Corp.
The Procter & Gamble Co.
Unisource Worldwide
James River Corp.
Georgia-Pacific Corp.
Stone Container Corp.
Champion International
The Mead Corp.
Weyerhaeuser Co.

Data show pulp, paper, and converted product sales in millions of dollars.

International Paper Co.	$ 14,003
Kimberly-Clark Corp.	13,149
The Procter & Gamble Co.	10,196
Unisource Worldwide	7,023
James River Corp.	5,690
Georgia-Pacific Corp.	5,609
Stone Container Corp.	5,142
Champion International	4,962

Continued on next page.

★ 444 ★ *Continued*

Paper (SIC 2621)

U.S. Paper Companies - 1996

Data show pulp, paper, and converted product sales in millions of dollars.

The Mead Corp.	$ 4,707
Weyerhaeuser Co.	4,648

Source: *PIMA's Papermaker*, June 1997, p. 63.

★ 445 ★

Paperboard (SIC 2631)

Largest U.S. Linerboard Producers

Firms are ranked by capacity in thousands of tons.

SSC	5,487
Georgia Pacific	2,531
International Paper	2,165
Temple Inland	2,115
Union Camp	1,845

Source: *Financial Times*, May 12, 1998, p. 28, from *Pulp & Paper Weekly*, 1998 Lockwoods Directory, Datastream, and industry analysts.

★ 446 ★

Paperboard (SIC 2631)

Top Bleached Paperboard Producers - 1997

Companies are shown ranked by production capacity in thousands of tons. Data include production of bleached packaging board and bleached bristols.

	Tons (000)	Share
International Paper Co.	2,456	34.0%
Westvaco Corp.	950	13.1
Temple-Inland Inc.	725	10.0
Potlatch Corp.	610	8.4
Georgia-Pacific Corp.	413	5.7
Champion International	295	4.1
Gulf States Paper Corp.	265	3.7
James River Corp.	225	3.1
Weyerhaeuser Corp.	220	3.0
Gilman Paper Co.	200	2.8

	Tons (000)	Share
Jefferson-Smurfit	185	2.6%
Tembec	165	2.3
Union Camp Corp.	150	2.1
St. Laurent Paperboard	132	1.8

Source: *Pulp & Paper*, October 1997, p. 13.

★ 447 ★

Paperboard (SIC 2631)

Top Linerboard Producers in North America - 1996

Market shares are shown based on capacity. Capacity is expected to reach 26.75 million short tons in 1998.

Stone Container	13.2%
Georgia-Pacific	8.9
International Paper	7.6
Inland Paperboard & Packaging	7.4
Union Camp	6.5
Weyerhaeuser	6.3
Jefferson Smurfit/CCA	6.0
Tenneco Packaging	4.6
Gaylord Container	4.5
Willamette Industries	4.4
Other	28.2

Source: *Pulp & Paper*, January 1998, p. 13.

★ 448 ★

Containerboard (SIC 2650)

Containerboard Sales - 1997

Shares are shown based on capacity.

Unbleached kraft	82.9%
Recycled	16.2
Solid bleached	0.9

Source: *Paperboard Packaging*, January 1998, p. 10, from American Forest & Paper Association.

★ 449 ★
Containerboard (SIC 2650)

Corrugated/Solid Fiber Product Shipments

Shipments are shown in billions of square feet for the first 11 months of the year.

South Central	77,136
Southeast	70,268
West	62,767
Northeast	56,866
East Central	49,186
North Central	43,100

Source: *Paperboard Packaging*, January 1998, p. 24, from Fibre Box Association.

★ 450 ★
Containerboard (SIC 2650)

Largest U.S. Corrugated Container Producers

Firms are ranked by capacity in thousands of tons.

SSC	4,872
Temple Inland	2,381
Georgia Pacific	2,175
Tenneco	1,614
Weyerhaeuser	1,424

Source: *Financial Times*, May 12, 1998, p. 28, from *Pulp & Paper Weekly*, *1998 Lockwoods Directory*, Datastream, and industry analysts.

★ 451 ★
Folding Boxes (SIC 2653)

Top End Uses for Rigid Boxes - 1997

The table shows shipments in millions of dollars. Data are estimated.

	($ mil.)	Share
Confections	$ 85.2	16.54%
Jewelry, silverware	65.6	12.74

	($ mil.)	Share
Drugs, chemicals, pharmaceuticals	$ 48.0	9.32%
Stationery, office supplies	42.4	8.23
Toys and games	29.7	5.77
Cosmetics, soap	27.5	5.34
Textiles, hosiery, apparel	26.7	5.18
Photo products, supplies	25.2	4.89
Department stores, specialty shops	21.6	4.19
Hardware, household	22.9	4.45
Food, beverages	4.2	0.82
Other	116.0	22.52

Source: *Paperboard Packaging*, January 1998, p. 37.

★ 452 ★
Folding Boxes (SIC 2657)

Largest Folding Carton Makers - 1997

Data show the number of plants.

Jefferson Smurfit	17
Rock-Tenn	16
James River	10
Simkins Industries	8
Field Container	7
Green Bay Packaging	7
Dopaco	6
Mebane Packaging Group	6
Waldorf Corp.	6

Source: *Paperboard Packaging*, January 1998, p. 34, from *Official Container Directory*.

★ 453 ★
Folding Boxes (SIC 2657)

Top End Uses for Folding Cartons - 1997

The table shows shipments in millions of dollars. Data are estimated.

	($ mil.)	Share
Dry food	$ 815.2	16.10%
Wet foods	602.8	11.91
Carriers	443.3	8.76
Paper goods	431.1	8.51
Medicinal	406.7	8.03
Retail packaging	349.7	6.91
Hardware	338.7	6.69
Perishable bakery	318.3	6.29

Continued on next page.

★ 453 ★ *Continued*
Folding Boxes (SIC 2657)

Top End Uses for Folding Cartons - 1997

The table shows shipments in millions of dollars. Data are estimated.

	($ mil.)	Share
Cosmetics	$ 293.3	5.79%
Candy	283.1	5.59
Dry bakery	273.5	5.40
Other	507.3	10.02

Source: *Paperboard Packaging*, January 1998, p. 37.

★ 454 ★
Coated Paper (SIC 2672)

Largest Coated Free-Sheet Producers in North America - 1996

Market shares are shown based on total production of 5,487,861 short tons.

S.D. Warren	21.2%
Consolidated Papers	15.5
Champion International	10.8
Mead	9.9
Potlatch	6.5
Appleton Papers	5.8
International Papers	5.8
West Linn Paper	3.3
Repap	2.3
E.B. Eddy	2.2
Other	6.0

Source: *Pulp & Paper*, March 1998, p. 13.

★ 455 ★
Coated Paper (SIC 2672)

Largest Coated Groundwood Producers in North America - 1997

Market shares are shown based on capacity.

Consolidated Papers	20.3%
Champion International	14.3
Mead	12.8
International Paper	10.6
Fletcher Challenge Canada	8.9
Bowater	8.5
Repap	6.9
Crown Vantage	5.8

Weyerhaeuser	3.8%
Other	8.0

Source: *Pulp & Paper*, May 1998, p. 13.

★ 456 ★
Food Storage (SIC 2673)

Top Food Storage Bag Brands - 1997

Shares are shown based on a $853 million market for the year ended March 1, 1998.

	($ mil.)	Share
Dow Ziploc	$ 295.5	34.64%
Hefty OneZip	125.7	14.74
Other	431.8	50.62

Source: *Advertising Age*, April 30, 1998, p. 4.

★ 457 ★
Trash Bags (SIC 2673)

Best-Selling Trash Bag Brands

Shares of the $1.0 billion market are shown for the year ended October 12, 1997.

Glad	21.0%
Hefty Cinch Sak	13.7
Hefty	7.1
Glad Handle Tie	6.4
Ruffies Sure Strength	4.6
Ruffies	3.5
Ruffies Color Scents	2.6
Glad Tie Bags	1.9
Hefty Basics	1.8
Private label	22.9
Other	14.5

Source: *Nonfoods Merchandising*, January 1998, p. 29, from Information Resources Inc.

★ 458 ★

Diapers (SIC 2676)

Leading Diaper Brands - 1997

Shares are shown based on sales of diapers and training pants for the 52 weeks ended May 25, 1996. Data include sales at drug, grocery and mass merchandise stores.

Huggies	41.4%
Pampers	24.8
Private label	16.2
Luvs	12.4
Drypers	3.1
Others	2.1

Source: *Wall Street Journal*, July 21, 1997, p. B9, from Information Resources Inc.

★ 459 ★

Diapers (SIC 2676)

Top Diaper Makers

Market shares are shown in percent.

Kimberly-Clark	35.0%
Procter & Gamble	26.0
Other	39.0

Source: *U.S./Mexico Business*, March 1998, p. 48.

★ 460 ★

Diapers (SIC 2676)

Top Diaper Makers - Mexico

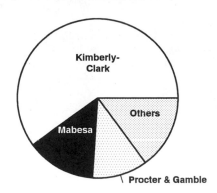

Market shares are shown for November - December.

	1996	1997
Kimberly-Clark	58.0%	60.0%
Mabesa	15.0	14.0
Procter & Gamble	17.0	11.0
Others	11.0	15.0

Source: *U.S./Mexico Business*, March 1998, p. 50, from A.C. Nielsen.

★ 461 ★

Diapers (SIC 2676)

Training Pants Manufacturers - 1997

Shares of the $400 million segment are shown for the 52 weeks ended July 27, 1997. Kimberly-Clark's top brand is Huggies; Procter & Gamble's top brands are Pampers and Luvs.

Kimberly-Clark Corp.	41.6%
Procter & Gamble Co.	37.3
Other	21.1

Source: *Advertising Age*, August 25, 1997, p. 8, from Information Resources Inc.

★ 462 ★

Feminine Hygiene Products (SIC 2676)

Leading Feminine Napkin Brands - 1997

Shares of the $1.08 billion market are shown for the 52 weeks ended July 20, 1997.

Always	39.3%
Kotex	23.8

Continued on next page.

★ 462 ★ *Continued*
Feminine Hygiene Products (SIC 2676)

Leading Feminine Napkin Brands - 1997

Shares of the $1.08 billion market are shown for the 52 weeks ended July 20, 1997.

Stayfree 12.2%
Private label 10.7
New Freedom 7.1
Carefree 5.0
Sure & Natural 1.3
Others 0.6

Source: *Advertising Age*, September 29, 1997, p. S24, from Information Resources Inc.

★ 463 ★
Feminine Hygiene Products (SIC 2676)

Leading Tampon Brands - 1997

Shares of the $647.40 million market are shown for the 52 weeks ended July 20, 1997.

Tampax 49.0%
Playtex 24.3
O.B. 10.7
Kotex 10.3
Private label 4.1

Source: *Advertising Age*, September 29, 1997, p. S24, from Information Resources Inc.

★ 464 ★
Sanitary Paper Products (SIC 2676)

Bathroom Tissue Leaders - 1997

Brands are ranked by sales in millions of dollars for the year ended November 23, 1997.

	Sales ($ mil.)	Share
Charmin	$ 1,052	30.17%
Northern	481	13.79
Scott	434	12.45
Angel Soft	373	10.70
Kleenex Cottonelle	360	10.32
Private label	387	11.10
Other	400	11.47

Source: *Wall Street Journal*, January 12, 1998, p. B1, from Information Resources Inc.

★ 465 ★
Sanitary Paper Products (SIC 2676)

Leading Bath Tissue Brands - 1997

Shares of the $3.46 billion market are shown for the 52 weeks ended July 27, 1997.

Charmin 29.3%
Northern 13.9
Scott 12.9
Private label 11.0
Angel Soft 10.9
Kleenex Cottonelle 10.4
Soft 'n Gentle 4.3
MD 2.3
Coronet 1.3
Other 3.7

Source: *Advertising Age*, September 29, 1997, p. s29, from Information Resources Inc.

★ 466 ★

Sanitary Paper Products (SIC 2676)

Leading Paper Towel Brands - 1997

Shares of the $2.25 billion market are shown for the 52 weeks ended July 27, 1997.

Bounty	37.1%
Private label	14.6
Brawny	11.4
Scott	7.6
Sparkle	7.2
Viva	6.0
Coronet	4.1
Mardi-Gras	3.8
Hi Dri	2.0
Other	6.2

Source: *Advertising Age*, September 29, 1997, p. s29, from Information Resources Inc.

★ 467 ★

Sanitary Paper Products (SIC 2676)

Retail Tissue Market - 1997

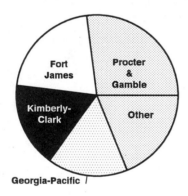

Market shares are shown in percent.

Procter & Gamble	27.0%
Fort James	21.0
Kimberly-Clark	17.0
Georgia-Pacific	16.0
Other	19.0

Source: *Pulp & Paper*, January 1998, p. 62.

★ 468 ★

Sanitary Paper Products (SIC 2676)

Top Tissue Makers - Mexico

Market shares are shown in percent.

Kimberly-Clark	55.0%
Procter & Gamble	20.0
Other	25.0

Source: *Wall Street Journal*, March 20, 1998, p. A9.

SIC 27 - Printing and Publishing

★ 469 ★
Printing (SIC 2700)

Printing and Imaging Market by Segment

Segments are ranked by sales in billions of dollars.

	($ bil.)	Share
General commercial printing . . .	$ 42.8	48.53%
Package printing	17.6	19.95
Prepress services	6.9	7.82
Forms printing	5.9	6.69
Book printing	5.2	5.90
Quick printing	4.4	4.99
Other specialty printing	5.4	6.12

Source: *Graphic Arts Monthly*, September 1997, p. 87, from Printing Industries of America.

★ 470 ★
Printing (SIC 2700)

Top Digital Prepress Companies - 1997

Companies are ranked by total annual prepress sales in millions of dollars.

Wace USA	$ 200.0
Applied Graphics Technologies	133.0
Black Dot Group	132.7
Schawk	90.8
American Color	75.0
IVA Ltd.	66.0
The Enteron Group	57.0
Kwik International Color	44.0
Color Associates	37.6
Quality House of Graphics	21.2
Graphic Technologies	20.0
Kreber Graphics	20.0

Source: *Graphic Arts Monthly*, September 1997, p. 47, from the individual companies.

★ 471 ★
Printing (SIC 2700)

Top Printing Markets - 1998

The table shows the markets that offer the largest printing potential. Figures are in billions of dollars.

Publishing	$ 10.9
Computer software	10.7
Telecommunications	8.0
Beverages	7.7
Health care	7.1
Motor vehicles	6.2
Packaged foods	5.8
Home improvements	5.4
Fashion	5.3
Financial services	4.8

Source: *American Printer*, December 1997, p. 31, from PB/BA International.

★ 472 ★
Publishing (SIC 2700)

Professional and Reference Publishing Market - Canada

Data show revenues in percent.

Law	45.0%
Medical	25.0
Business	14.0
General reference	10.0
Computer science	3.0
English & architecture	2.0
Science	2.0

Source: From the Internet, http:// www.pubcouncil.ca/ prof-ref-rev.html, October 22, 1997, p. 2.

★ 473 ★
Publishing (SIC 2700)

Top Publishing Companies - 1997

Firms are ranked by ad revenues in millions of dollars.

Time Inc.	$ 2,668.3
Conde Nast/Advance Pub..	1,086.1
Hearst Magazines	1,006.7
Hachette Filipacchi	873.8
Meredith Corp.	715.2
Gruner & Jahr	531.5
Parade Publications	516.5
Ziff-Davis	495.9
News America Corp.	469.3
Newsweek Inc.	408.5

Source: *Mediaweek*, March 2, 1998, p. 32, from Publishers Information Bureau and Competitive Media Reporting.

★ 474 ★
Newspapers (SIC 2711)

Canada's Newspaper Ownership - 1997

Hollinger	42.0%
Sun Media	13.0
Thomson	13.0
Quebecor	9.0
Independents	15.0
Other	8.0

Source: *Globe and Mail*, April 9, 1998, p. B10, from Canadian Newspaper Association.

★ 475 ★
Newspapers (SIC 2711)

Largest Newspaper Companies

Gannet	
Knight-Ridder	
Newhouse	
Dow Jones	
Times Mirror	
The New York Times	
Hearst	
McClatchy	

Data show daily circulation in millions.

Gannet	5.84
Knight-Ridder	4.05
Newhouse	2.81
Dow Jones	2.36
Times Mirror	2.31
The New York Times	2.28
Hearst	1.74
McClatchy	1.35

Source: *USA TODAY*, November 17, 1997, p. 2B, from Newspaper Association of America and McClatchy.

★ 476 ★

Newspapers (SIC 2711)

Largest Newspaper Markets

Data show the percentage of adults who read a newspaper. An estimated 59% of all adults in the 50 largest markets read a newspaper on a typical day.

Boston, MA 70.0%
Hartford-New Haven, CT 69.9
West Palm Beach, FL 68.1
Wilkes Barre-Scranton, PA 68.1
Cleveland, OH 67.1
Providence-New Bedford, R.I. 66.9
New York City, NY 66.3
Philadelphia, PA 65.7

Source: *USA TODAY*, April 15, 1998, p. 3B, from Scarborough Report.

★ 477 ★

Newspapers (SIC 2711)

Leading Tabloids by Circulation - 1997

Data represent circulation in millions.

National Enquirer 2.5
Star 2.2
Globe 1.0
National Examiner 0.5
Weekly World News 0.4

Source: *Business Week*, September 15, 1997, p. 42, from company reports and Audit Bureau of Circulations.

★ 478 ★

Newspapers (SIC 2711)

Newspaper Circulation Leaders in Canada - 1997

Market shares are shown based on circulation.

Southam 32.4%
Sun Media 13.5
Thomson 12.7
Hollinger 9.8
Quebecor 8.7
Independents 15.2
Other chains 7.8

Source: *Globe and Mail*, April 9, 1998, p. B9, from Canadian Newspaper Association.

★ 479 ★

Newspapers (SIC 2711)

Newspaper Media Firms - 1996

Firms are ranked by newspaper revenues in millions of dollars.

Gannett Co. . . . . $ 3,335.2
Knight-Ridder 2,851.9
New York Times Co. 2,335.3
Advance Publications 2,209.0
Times Mirror Co. 2,080.2
Dow Jones & Co. 1,501.8
Tribune Co. 1,336.0
Cox Enterprises 1,033.0
Hearst Corp. 865.0
E.W. Scripps 795.2

Source: *Advertising Age*, August 18, 1997, p. S8.

★ 480 ★

Newspapers (SIC 2711)

Popular Tabloids

The table shows circulation in millions.

National Enquirer	2.7
Star	2.2
Globe	1.0

Source: *Los Angeles Times*, September 4, 1997, p. 6, from Audit Bureau of Circulations.

★ 481 ★

Newspapers (SIC 2711)

Top Daily Newspapers - 1997

Data show circulation for April 1 through September 30, 1997.

Wall Street Journal	1,774,880
USA Today	1,629,665
New York Times	1,074,741
Los Angeles Times	1,050,176
Washington Post	775,894
New York Daily News	721,256
Chicago Tribune	653,554
Newsday	568,914
Houston Chronicle	549,101
Chicago Sun-Times	484,379

Source: *Chicago Tribune*, November 4, 1997, p. 5, from Audit Bureau of Circulations.

★ 482 ★

Newspapers (SIC 2711)

Top Newspapers - 1998

Data show average circulation as of March 31, 1998.

Wall Street Journal	1,820,186
USA TODAY	1,715,245
New York Times	1,110,143
Los Angeles Times	1,095,007
Washington Post	808,884

Source: *USA TODAY*, May 4, 1998, p. 11B, from Audit Bureau of Circulations.

★ 483 ★

Newspapers (SIC 2711)

Top Newspapers - Los Angeles County

Daily circulation is shown as of March 31, 1997.

Los Angeles Times	1,068,812
Investor's Business Daily	228,039
Daily News	204,493
Press-Telegram	106,485
La Opinion	103,048

Source: *Los Angeles Business Journal*, October 13, 1997, p. 24.

★ 484 ★

Newspapers (SIC 2711)

Top Sunday Newspapers - 1997

Data show circulation for April 1 through September 30, 1997.

New York Times	1,658,718
Los Angeles Times	1,361,748
Washington Post	1,102,329
Chicago Tribune	1,023,736
Philadelphia Inquirer	878,660
Detroit News & Free Press	829,178
New York Daily News	807,788
Dallas Morning News	789,004
Boston Globe	758,843
Houston Chronicle	748,036

Source: *Chicago Tribune*, November 4, 1997, p. 5, from Audit Bureau of Circulations.

★ 485 ★

Magazines (SIC 2721)

Largest Single Copy Magazine Sellers

The top single issue sellers are shown for the last six months of the year. Figures are in millions of units.

TV Guide	3.24
Family Circle	2.15
Woman's Day	2.06
Cosmopolitan	1.95
National Enquirer	1.94
Star	1.64
People	1.55
Woman's World	1.51

Continued on next page.

★ **485** ★ *Continued*

Magazines (SIC 2721)

Largest Single Copy Magazine Sellers

The top single issue sellers are shown for the last six months of the year. Figures are in millions of units.

Good Housekeeping	1.38
First for Women	1.25

Source: *Supermarket Business*, May 1998, p. 136, from Audit Bureau of Circulations.

★ **486** ★

Magazines (SIC 2721)

Magazine Media Firms - 1996

Firms are ranked by magazine revenues in millions of dollars.

Time Warner	$ 2,764.1
Reed Elsevier	1,308.4
Hearst Corp.	1,303.0
Advance Publications	1,176.0
Thomson Corp.	941.7
Ziff-Davis (Softbank)	892.0
Reader's Digest Association	831.7
International Data Group	720.0
K-III Communications Corp.	717.1
News Corp.	660.0

Source: *Advertising Age*, August 18, 1997, p. S8.

★ **487** ★

Magazines (SIC 2721)

New Magazine Topics - 1997

A total of 852 new consumer magazines were launched in 1997. The table shows the leading categories.

Sex	110
Sports	103
Media/personalities	61
Crafts/games	47
Computers	40
Special interest	36
Automotive	33

Source: *USA TODAY*, May 5, 1998, p. D1, from Oxbridge Communications.

★ **488** ★

Magazines (SIC 2721)

Top Fashion Magazines by Ad Pages

Fashion magazines are ranked by number of advertising pages. Data are for the first six months of both 1996 and 1997.

	1996	1997
Vogue	1,071	1,214
Elle	774	1,004
Harper's Bazaar	631	692

Source: *Mediaweek*, July 21, 1997, p. 6, from Publishers Information Bureau.

★ **489** ★

Magazines (SIC 2721)

Top Golf Magazines - 1997

Data show circulation.

Golf Digest	1,529,671
Golf Magazine	1,339,970
Sports Illustrated Golf Plus	440,000
Golf for Women	333,657
Golf Illustrated	284,728
Golf Tips	283,577

Source: *Advertising Age*, June 1, 1998, p. 16, from Audit Bureau of Circulations and Business Publication Audit.

★ **490** ★

Magazines (SIC 2721)

Top Internet/Computer Magazines - 1997

Magazines are ranked by ad pages.

Computer Shopper	9,348.54
Computer Reseller News	8,260.18
PC Week	7,029.03
PC Magazine	6,061.37
InformationWeek	5,226.10

Source: *Advertising Age*, June 15, 1998, p. S24.

★ 491 ★

Magazines (SIC 2721)

Top Magazines - 1997

Data show circulation for the second half of 1997.

Modern Maturity	20,390,755
Reader's Digest	15,038,708
TV Guide	13,103,187
National Geographic	9,012,074
Better Homes & Gardens	7,605,187
Family Circle	5,107,477
Good Housekeeping	4,739,592
Ladies Home Journal	4,590,155
The Cable Guide	4,544,778
Woman's Day	4,461,023
McCall's	4,216,145
Time	4,155,806
People	3,608,111
Prevention	3,310,278
Sports Illustrated	3,223,810

Source: *Advertising Age*, February 23, 1998, p. 28.

★ 492 ★

Magazines (SIC 2721)

Top Magazines by Ad Pages - 1997

Magazines are ranked by total ad pages.

PC Magazine	6,061.37
Forbes	4,662.84
Business Week	4,114.39
People	3,998.89
Fortune	3,599.77
TV Guide	3,305.05
Bride's	3,106.28
Modern Bride	3,018.98
Sports Illustrated	2,905.21
The Economist	2,900.28
PC Computing	2,818.67
Vogue	2,782.45
Time	2,781.11
Windows Magazine	2,713.44
Newsweek	2,647.21

Source: *Advertising Age*, January 26, 1998, p. 49, from Publishers Information Bureau.

★ 493 ★

Magazines (SIC 2721)

Top Magazines by Advertising Revenue - 1997

Revenues are shown in millions of dollars.

People	$ 519.5
Sports Illustrated	483.1
Time	460.5
TV Guide	445.0
Newsweek	364.0
Better Homes & Gardens	348.8
PC	294.8
Business Week	292.6
Forbes	215.4
US News & World Report	210.0
Woman's Day	209.8
Fortune	202.5
Good Housekeeping	197.6
Reader's Digest	194.9
Family Circle	190.5
Cosmopolitan	172.8
Ladies Home Journal	165.7
Vogue	137.4
Entertainment Weekly	129.5
Glamour	126.3

Source: *Los Angeles Times*, December 18, 1997, p. D4, from Publishers Information Bureau.

★ 494 ★

Magazines (SIC 2721)

Top Magazines by Non-Paid Circulation

Data show the top magazines with 1 million or more non-paid circulation for the second half of 1997.

Friendly Exchange	5,600,244
Health Monitor	4,538,216
See Magazines	2,726,574
The Costco Connection	2,563,004
Beyond the Wall	2,012,515
Rx Remedy	2,004,031
Apartment Blue Book	1,712,820

Source: *Advertising Age*, February 23, 1998, p. 28, from Audit Bureau of Circulations.

★ 495 ★
Magazines (SIC 2721)

Top Magazines in Canada - 1997

Market shares are shown based on ad revenues for the year ending December 31, 1997.

Maclean's	9.0%
Chatelaine	8.4
Canadian Living	6.0
TV Guide	5.0
Time	4.7
Reader's Digest	4.4
Flare	3.0
Report on Business Magazine	2.8
Canadian Business	2.7
Homemaker's	2.5
Others	51.5

Source: *Marketing Magazine*, May 25, 1998, p. 25, from Leading National Advertisers.

★ 496 ★
Books (SIC 2731)

Book Sales - 1997

Data show estimated sales in millions of dollars.

Professional	$ 4,156.4
Elhi	2,959.6
Higher education	2,669.7
Adult hardcover	2,410.2
Adult paperback	1,685.0
Mass market paperback	1,433.8
Book clubs	1,145.3
Religious	1,132.7
Juvenile hardcover	887.7
Subscription reference	736.5

Source: *Publishers Weekly*, March 2, 1998, p. 11, from Association of American Publishers.

★ 497 ★
Books (SIC 2731)

Book Sales by City

Los Angeles-Long Beach, CA
New York, NY
Chicago, IL
Boston, MA
Washington D.C.
Philadelphia, PA
San Francisco, CA
Seattle-Bellevue-Everett, WA
San Jose, CA
San Diego, CA

Cities are ranked by book sales in thousands of dollars.

Los Angeles-Long Beach, CA	$ 383,902
New York, NY	359,716
Chicago, IL	271,867
Boston, MA	238,116
Washington D.C.	234,589
Philadelphia, PA	161,735
San Francisco, CA	138,875
Seattle-Bellevue-Everett, WA	131,679
San Jose, CA	125,015
San Diego, CA	115,419

Source: *Christian Science Monitor*, December 9, 1997, p. 9.

★ 498 ★
Books (SIC 2731)

Children's Books Sales by Type - 1996

Sales of 536 million children's books are shown in percent.

Fiction	50.0%
Coloring/activity	25.0
Nonfiction	10.0
Educational	5.0
Religious	5.0
Book with tape/CD	2.0
Book with electronic sound pad	2.0
Reference	1.0

Source: *USA TODAY*, November 19, 1997, p. D1, from *1996 Consumer Research Study on Book Purchasing*.

★ 499 ★

Books (SIC 2731)

Largest Education Publishers - 1997

Sales are shown in millions of dollars.

Simon & Schuster	$ 1,254
McGraw-Hill	1,123
Harcourt General	685
Houghton Mifflin	656
Thomson	548
Addison Wesley Longman	513
Tribune	177
Primedia	170
Scholastic	156
Georg Von Holtzbrinck	92

Source: *New York Times*, May 26, 1998, p. C4, from Simba Information and Association of American Publishers.

★ 500 ★

Books (SIC 2731)

Leading Publishers of Hardcover Bestsellers - 1997

Shares are shown based on 1,530 hardcover bestseller positions during 1997.

Random House Inc.	22.8%
Time Warner	15.3
Penguin Putnam Inc.	13.7
Simon & Schuster	11.1
Bantam Doubleday Dell	11.0
HarperCollins	10.7
Hearst	3.0
Hyperion	2.9
Von Holtzbrinck	2.4
Grove/Atlantic Monthly	1.7
Norton	1.7
Long Street	1.6
Other	2.1

Source: *Publishers Weekly*, January 5, 1998, p. 40.

★ 501 ★

Books (SIC 2731)

Leading Publishers of Paperback Bestsellers - 1997

Shares are shown based on 1,530 paperback bestseller poitions during 1997.

Random House Inc.	23.2%
Penguin Putnam Inc.	18.8
Bantam Doubleday Dell	17.7
Simon & Schuster	14.0
Health Communications	7.0
Time Warner	6.5
Hearst	4.3
HarperCollins	2.9
Hyperion	2.7
Andrews McMeel	1.1
Other	1.8

Source: *Publishers Weekly*, January 5, 1998, p. 40.

★ 502 ★

Books (SIC 2731)

Top Book Publishers - 1996

Firms are ranked by revenue in millions of dollars. Random House and Bertelsmann are planning to merge, giving them a 26% share of the consumer book market.

Random House	$ 1,220
Simon & Schuster	911
Pearson	692
Bertelsmann	670
HarperCollins	520
Time Warner	304
Holtzbrinck	264
Hearst	158

Source: *Newsweek*, April 6, 1998, p. 39, from *Publishing Trends Newsletter*.

★ 503 ★

Books (SIC 2731)

Top Book Publishers in North America - 1996

Companies are ranked by sales in billions of dollars.

Simon & Schuster	$ 2.3
Thomson Corporation	1.5
McGraw-Hill	1.3

Continued on next page.

★ 503 ★ *Continued*

Books (SIC 2731)

Top Book Publishers in North America - 1996

Companies are ranked by sales in billions of dollars.

Random House	$ 1.3
Pearson	1.2
Time Warner	1.1
Harcourt General	1.1
Bertelsmann Group	1.0

Source: *New York Times*, March 24, 1998, p. 1, from *Subtext*.

★ 504 ★

Books (SIC 2731)

Top Elementary Textbook Makers

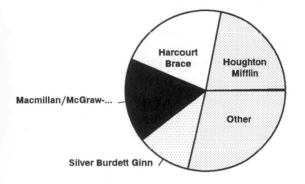

Market shares are shown in percent.

Houghton Mifflin	22.1%
Harcourt Brace	21.7
Macmillan/McGraw-Hill	16.6
Silver Burdett Ginn	10.9
Other	28.7

Source: From the Internet, http://www.bookwire.com/ subtext, December 17, 1997, p. 1.

★ 505 ★

Books (SIC 2731)

Top Math Textbook Publishers in Arkansas - 1997

Data show adoption rates for grades 1-6.

NA-W	47.0%
Macmillan/M-H	16.0
Houghton	14.0
Harcourt	13.0
Heath	3.0
Saxon	2.0

Source: From the Internet, http://www.bookwire.com/ subtext, October 1, 1997, p. 1, from Arkansas Department of Education.

★ 506 ★

Books (SIC 2731)

Top Reading Textbook Publishers in Arkansas - 1997

Data show adoption rates for grades 1-6.

Harcourt	38.0%
Heath	25.0
Macmillan/M-H	14.0
Houghton	11.0
Scott Foresman	7.0
Silver Burdett	5.0

Source: From the Internet, http://www.bookwire.com/ subtext, October 1, 1997, p. 1, from Arkansas Department of Education.

★ 507 ★

Books (SIC 2731)

Top Science Textbook Publishers in Arkansas - 1997

Data show adoption rates for grades 1-6.

Silver Burdett	46.0%
A-W	26.0
Scott Foresman	14.0
Harcourt	7.0
Scholastic	4.0
Encyclopaedia Brittanica	2.0

Source: From the Internet, http://www.bookwire.com/ subtext, October 1, 1997, p. 1, from Arkansas Department of Education.

★ 508 ★

Books (SIC 2731)

Top Social Studies Textbook Publishers in Arkansas - 1997

Data show adoption rates for grades 1-6.

Harcourt	54.0%
Macmillan/M-H	29.0
Houghton	13.0
Silver Burdett	3.0
Glencoe/M-H	1.0

Source: From the Internet, http:// www.bookwire.com/ subtext, October 1, 1997, p. 1, from Arkansas Department of Education.

★ 509 ★

Books (SIC 2731)

Top Trade Publishers

The table shows revenues in millions of dollars for 1996 and 1997. Data are estimated.

	1996	1997
Random House	$ 1,250	$ 1,250
Simon & Schuster	911	855
HarperCollins	737	740
Bantam/Doubleday/Dell	670	700
Penguin USA	306	312
Warner/Little Brown	290	295
Putnam	276	280
St. Martin's Press	160	162
Avon/Morrow	155	160
Houghton Mifflin	82	87

Source: From the Internet, http:// www.bookwire.com/ subtext/publishing.article, November 15, 1997, p. 2.

★ 510 ★

Printing (SIC 2732)

Top Book Printers

Companies are ranked by printing sales in millions of dollars.

R.R. Donnelley & Sons	$ 725.89
Quebecor Printing	560.00
Banta Corp.	238.48
Bertelsmann Industries U.S.	162.80
Golden Books Publishing	152.40
Courier Corp.	131.00
Taylor Publishing	99.00
Maple-Vail Book Mfg.	80.00

Webcrafters	$ 75.00
Landoll Inc.	71.00

Source: *Printing Impressions*, December 1997, p. 34.

★ 511 ★

Calenders (SIC 2741)

Best-Selling Types of Calenders - 1998

Annual sales of decorative calenders reach more than $5 billion. The table shows the most popular types.

Animals	25.0%
Floral	12.0
Publisher (Family Circle, etc.)	12.0
Juvenile	11.0
Art, humor	8.0
Model/celebrity, scenic	8.0
Sports	6.0
Brands (Harley Davidson, etc.)	2.0
Other	6.0

Source: *USA TODAY*, January 15, 1998, p. D1, from AT-A-GLANCE and Calender Manufacturers Association.

★ 512 ★

Publishing (SIC 2741)

Largest Yearbook Publishers

Market shares are shown in percent. "Other" refers to two other publishers.

Jostens	50.0%
Taylor Publishing	20.0
Other	30.0

Source: *Wall Street Journal*, June 25, 1998, p. A1.

★ 513 ★
Commercial Printing (SIC 2750)

Largest Printers - Sacremento, CA

Firms are ranked by number of full-time employees.

Treasure Chest	300
Terry Grimes Graphic Center of Sacremento Inc.	164
Fong and Fong Printers & Lithographers Inc.	128
Dome Printing	95
Sierra Office Supplies & Printing	92
American Lithographers	83
Fruitridge Printing and Lithography Inc.	68

Source: *Sacremento Business Journal*, February 6, 1998, p. 10.

★ 514 ★
Commercial Printing (SIC 2750)

Print Sales by Region - 1997

North Central
North Mid-Atlantic
Southeastern
Pacific
Plains
South Central
New England
South Mid-Atlantic
Mountain

Sales are estimated in millions of dollars.

North Central	$ 18.5
North Mid-Atlantic	12.4
Southeastern	11.3
Pacific	10.7
Plains	9.3
South Central	4.7
New England	4.3
South Mid-Atlantic	4.0
Mountain	2.8

Source: *American Ink Maker*, April 1998, p. 112, from National Association of Printers and Lithographers.

★ 515 ★
Commercial Printing (SIC 2750)

Top Printing Markets by City - 1996

Data show cities ranked by printing revenue in billions of dollars.

Boston, MA	$ 4.3
New York, NY	4.2
Atlanta, GA	3.9
Chicago, IL	3.9
Cincinnati, OH	3.9
Dallas, TX	3.9
Minneapolis, MN	3.9
Los Angeles, CA	3.9
Newark, NJ	3.9
Philadelphia, PA	3.7

Source: *Graphic Arts Monthly*, September 1997, p. 88.

★ 516 ★
Commercial Printing (SIC 2750)

Top Printing Markets by State - 1996

Data show states ranked by printing revenue in billions of dollars.

California	$ 11.5
New York	10.0
Illinois	9.6
Pennsylvania	7.6
New Jersey	6.3
Ohio	6.1
Texas	6.0
Wisconsin	5.2
Massachusetts	4.9
Minnesota	4.6

Source: *Graphic Arts Monthly*, September 1997, p. 88.

★ 517 ★
Commercial Printing (SIC 2750)

Top Publications Printers - 1997

Companies are ranked by printing sales in millions of dollars.

R.R. Donnelley & Sons	$ 1,121.80
Quebecor Printing	1,105.00
World Color Press	475.89
Quad/Graphics	416.80
Cadmus Communications	230.94
Brown Printing	200.00

Continued on next page.

★ 517 ★ *Continued*
Commercial Printing (SIC 2750)

Top Publications Printers - 1997

Companies are ranked by printing sales in millions of dollars.

Publishers Printing/Publishers Press	$ 151.00
Banta Corp.	119.24
Judd's Inc.	94.86
Perry Graphic Communications	93.50

Source: *Printing Impressions*, December 1997, p. 36.

★ 518 ★
Commercial Printing (SIC 2752)

Top Printers in North America - 1996

Data show total sales in millions of dollars.

R.R. Donnelley & Sons Co.	$ 6,600.0
Quebecor Printing Inc.	3,100.0
Moore Corp. Ltd.	2,500.0
Deluxe Corp.	1,896.0
World Color	1,600.0
Big Flower Press Holdings, Inc.	1,202.0
Banta Corp.	1,084.0
Quad/Graphics, Inc.	1,042.0
Standard Register	944.0
Wallace Computer Services Inc.	862.0

Source: *American Printer*, July 1997, p. 40.

★ 519 ★
Commercial Printing (SIC 2759)

Sports Cards Collectors by Region

Data show the percent of boys and girls ages 3-13 who collect sports cards in each region. Sports cards are collected by 62% of boys and 16% of girls.

West North Central	47.0%
South Atlantic	45.0
East North Central	44.0
New England	41.0
Pacific	41.0
West South Central	41.0
Middle Atlantic	38.0
East South Central	36.0
Mountain	35.0

Source: *USA TODAY*, August 4, 1997, p. C1, from NFO Research.

★ 520 ★
Commercial Printing (SIC 2759)

Top Catalog Printers

Companies are ranked by printing sales in millions of dollars.

R.R. Donnelley & Sons	$ 1,319.80
Quebecor Printing	525.00
Quad/Graphics	479.32
World Color Press	443.07
Banta Corp.	216.80
Arandell Corp.	141.22
Brown Printing	125.00
Perry Graphic Communications	59.50
Hess Management	56.00
Avanti/Case-Hoyt	56.00

Source: *Printing Impressions*, December 1997, p. 30.

★ 521 ★
Commercial Printing (SIC 2759)

Top Financial Printers

Companies are ranked by printing sales in millions of dollars.

R.R. Donnelley & Sons	$ 461.93
Bowne & Co.	303.75
Merrill Corp.	141.60
Daniels Printing	42.60
Cadmus Communications	42.34
Global Financial Press	37.00
Northstar Computer Forms	32.20
Applied Printing Technologies	21.60
Packquisition Corp.	19.80
PGI Co.	15.96

Source: *Printing Impressions*, December 1997, p. 40.

★ 522 ★
Business Forms (SIC 2761)

Business Forms Demand

Demand is shown in millions of dollars for 1997, 1998, and 1999.

	1997	1998	1999
Total forms	$ 6,384	$ 6,003	$ 5,540
Custom continuous	3,336	3,149	2,929
Unit sets	1,477	1,412	1,322
Stock continuous	1,275	1,166	1,038
Labels	886	939	970

Continued on next page.

★ 522 ★ *Continued*

Business Forms (SIC 2761)

Business Forms Demand

Demand is shown in millions of dollars for 1997, 1998, and 1999.

	1997	1998	1999
Cut sheet	$ 670	$ 692	$ 709
Form/label combos	309	343	372
Salesbooks, pegboard . . .	296	276	251
Multi-part mailer	228	212	195
Other	2,799	2,594	2,361

Source: *Purchasing*, November 6, 1997, p. 80, from International Business Forms Industry.

★ 523 ★

Greeting Cards (SIC 2771)

Greeting Card Sales by Occasion

The table shows millions of greeting cards sold for each occasion.

Christmas	2,600
Valentine's Day	900
Mother's Day	150
Easter	120
Father's Day	95
Graduation	60

Source: *New York Times*, November 20, 1997, p. C4, from Greeting Card Association.

★ 524 ★

Greeting Cards (SIC 2771)

Top Greeting Card Makers - 1996

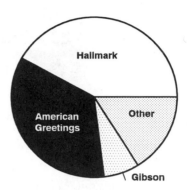

Shares are shown based on sales.

Hallmark	42.0%
American Greetings	35.0
Gibson	7.0
Other	16.0

Source: *New York Times*, November 20, 1997, p. C1, from CIBC Oppenheimer.

SIC 28 - Chemicals and Allied Products

Chemicals (SIC 2800)

Chemical Production in Canada - 1997

Production is shown in thousands of metric tons.

Ammonia	4,677
Sulfuric acid	3,995
Urea	3,291
Ethylene	3,186
Polyethylene, low-density	1,426
Sodium hydroxide	1,155
Chlorine	1,095
Ammonium nitrate	1,052
Nitric acid	1,050
Sodium chlorate	1,035

Source: *Chemical & Engineering News*, December 15, 1997, p. 26, from Statistics Canada.

Chemicals (SIC 2800)

Largest Chemicals Firms

Firms are ranked by revenue in millions of dollars.

E.I. DuPont De Nemours	$ 41,304
Dow Chemical	20,018
Occidental Petroleum	11,061
Monsanto	9,457
PPG Industries	7,379
Union Carbide	6,502

Source: *Fortune*, April 27, 1998, pp. F-45.

Chemicals (SIC 2800)

Leading Electronic Chemicals Producers

Shares are shown based on production capacity of electronic chemicals.

Ashland	50.0%
Olin	30.0
General Chemical	7.0
Mallinckrodt Baker	7.0
Other	6.0

Source: *Chemical Market Reporter*, November 17, 1997, p. 16, from Rose Associates.

Chemicals (SIC 2800)

Leading Titanium Dioxide Producers

Companies are ranked by millions of pounds produced.

	(mil.)	Share
DuPont	1,415	34.64%
Millennium	460	11.26
Kronos	355	8.69
Kemira	295	7.22
Kerr-McGee	290	7.10
Ishihara	195	4.77
Bayer	140	3.43
Thann et Mulhouse	135	3.30
Sachtleben	85	2.08
Tioxide	55	1.35
Other	660	16.16

Source: *Chemical Market Reporter*, September 15, 1997, p. 44.

★ 529 ★
Chemicals (SIC 2800)

Leading Wet Chemicals Producers - 1996

The $178.3 million market is shown in percent.

Ashland 46.0%
Olin 23.0
Mallinckrodt Baker 15.0
General Chemical 11.0
Other 5.0

Source: *Chemical Week*, July 16, 1997, p. 20, from The Information Network.

★ 530 ★
Chemicals (SIC 2800)

Paper & Pulp Chemical Market in Canada

Sales are shown in kilotons.

	1996	1997
Sodium chlorate	532	571
Sodium hydroxide	552	569
Sulphuric acid	388	407
Kaolin	390	395
Oxygen	311	319
Calcium carbonate	281	292
Sodium hydroxide	254	263

Source: *Pulp & Paper Canada*, No. 1, 1998, p. 21.

★ 531 ★
Chemicals (SIC 2800)

Paper Chemicals Market - 2000

Data show estimated end use.

Papermaking chemicals 38.0%
Specialty chemicals 24.0
Bleaching chemicals 21.0
Pulping, de-inking chemicals 17.0

Source: *Chemical Week*, February 18, 1998, p. 24, from Freedonia Group.

★ 532 ★
Chemicals (SIC 2800)

Personal Care Chemical Market - 1996

Sales are shown based on 221.6 million pounds.

Conditioning polymers 33.0%
Specialty surfactants 23.0
Thickeners 14.0
Specialty emolients 11.0
Antimicrobials 7.0
Fixative polymers 6.0
UV absorbers 4.0
Actives 2.0

Source: *Chemical Week*, November 19, 1997, p. 40, from Kline & Co.

★ 533 ★
Chemicals (SIC 2800)

Specialty Raw Material Market by Segment - 1996

Demand is shown in percent.

Conditioning polymers 32.0%
Specialty surfactants 24.0
Thickeners 14.0
Emollients 11.0
Preservatives, biostats & antidandruff
    agents 7.0
Fixative polymers 6.0
Ultraviolet absorbers 4.0
Actives 2.0

Source: *Chemical & Engineering News*, April 13, 1998, p. 24, from Kline & Co.

★ 534 ★

Chemicals (SIC 2800)

Specialty Raw Materials - 1996

Demand is shown in percent. "Other" includes antiperspirants, deodorants and makeup.

Skin care	38.0%
Hair care	29.0
Dental care	8.0
Other	25.0

Source: *Chemical & Engineering News*, April 13, 1998, p. 24, from Kline & Co.

★ 535 ★

Chemicals (SIC 2800)

Top Chemicals Companies - 1996

Sales are shown in millions of dollars.

DuPont	$ 12,300
Bayer Group	9,000
Dow Chemical	8,790
3M	6,655
BASF	6,500
Exxon Chemical	6,087
Lyondell Petrochemical	5,052
Shell Chemical	5,000
PPG Industries	4,800
Huntsman	4,500

Source: *Chemical Week*, October 22, 1997, p. 33.

★ 536 ★

Chemicals (SIC 2800)

Top Chemicals Companies - Canada

Companies are ranked by sales in millions of Canadian dollars for 1996. Shares of the group are shown in percent.

	Sales (mil.)	% of Group
Nova Chemicals	$ 3,043	18.03%
Agrium	2,485	14.72
Dow Chemical Canada	2,281	13.52
Potash Corp. Saskatchewan . . .	1,918	11.36
DuPont Canada	1,827	10.83
Methanex	1,300	7.70
Imperial Oil	875	5.18
ICI Canada	847	5.02
BASF	720	4.27
Shell Canada	606	3.59

	Sales (mil.)	% of Group
Celanese Canada	$ 561	3.32%
Petromont	414	2.45

Source: *Chemical Week*, July 23, 1997, p. 25, from *The Financial Post*.

★ 537 ★

Chemicals (SIC 2800)

Top Specialty Chemicals - 1997

Sales are shown in billions of dollars.

Industrial coatings	$ 8.3
Agricultural chemicals	7.7
Adhesives and sealants	6.4
I&I cleaners	6.1
Electronic chemicals	5.5
Specialty polymers	4.6
Food ingredients	3.3
Plastics additives	3.1
Construction chemicals	2.8
Water management	2.6
Specialty surfactants	2.0
Flavors and fragrances	1.9

Source: *Chemical Week*, January 7, 1998, p. 32, from Strategic Analysis.

★ 538 ★

Chemicals (SIC 2800)

Top U.S. Chemicals Producers

Firms are ranked by chemical sales in millions of dollars.

DuPont	$ 21.2
Dow Chemical	19.0
Exxon	12.1
General Electric	6.6
Union Carbide	6.5
Amoco	5.9
Huntsman Chemical	5.0
Celanese	4.9
BASF	4.8
Praxair	4.7

Source: *Chemical & Engineering News*, May 4, 1998, p. 22.

★ 539 ★
Chemicals (SIC 2800)

Top-Selling Categories of Fine Chemicals - 1997

Shares of the $25 billion fine chemicals market are shown in percent.

Pharmaceutical bulk actives	16.0%
Pharmaceutical intermediates	16.0
Pesticides	8.0
Other	60.0

Source: *Chemical Week*, January 21, 1998, p. 36, from Strategic Analysis.

★ 540 ★
Chemicals (SIC 2800)

U.S. Membrane Technology Demand

Demand is shown in millions of dollars.

	1995	2000
Water treatment	$ 350	$ 540
Food processing	200	300
Pharmaceuticals	150	230
Other	200	330

Source: *Chemical Engineering*, February 1998, p. 61, from Freedonia Group.

★ 541 ★
Alkalies and Chlorine (SIC 2812)

Caustic Soda Demand by End Use - North America

Demand is shown by end use.

Chemicals	48.0%
Pulp & paper	24.0
Petroleum	4.0
Other	24.0

Source: *Chemical Market Reporter*, September 1, 1997, p. 15, from Dow Chemical Company.

★ 542 ★
Alkalies and Chlorine (SIC 2812)

Chlorine Demand by End Use - North America

Demand is shown by end use. PVC stands for polyvinyl chloride.

Chemicals	45.0%
PVC	41.0
Pulp & paper	10.0
Other	4.0

Source: *Chemical Market Reporter*, September 1, 1997, p. 15, from Dow Chemical Company.

★ 543 ★
Alkalies and Chlorine (SIC 2812)

Largest Soda Ash Producers

Companies are ranked by production capacity in millions of short tons.

FMC Wyoming Corp.	3.55
General Chemical	2.40
OCI Chemical Corp.	2.30
Solvay Minerals Inc.	2.30
North American Chemical	1.45
Tg Soda Ash Inc.	1.30

Source: *Chemical Market Reporter*, July 21, 1997, p. 15, from U.S. Geological Survey.

★ 544 ★
Alkalies and Chlorine (SIC 2812)

Top Sodium Bicarbonate Makers

Capacity is shown in thousands of tons.

	Tons (000)	Market Share
Church & Dwight	430	65.45%
Rhone-Poulenc	72	10.96
FMC	70	10.65
NACC	70	10.65
Natrium	15	2.28

Source: *Chemical Market Reporter*, October 27, 1997, p. 30, from Church & Dwight.

★ 545 ★
Alkalies and Chlorine (SIC 2812)
U.S. Chloro-Alkalies Demand

The total market reached 33.5 million tons.

Chlorine 38.8%
Caustic soda 36.5
Soda ash 22.1
Caustic potash 1.3
Sodium bicarbonate 1.3

Source: *Chemical Engineering*, July 1997, p. 44, from Freedonia Group.

★ 546 ★
Industrial Gases (SIC 2813)
Electronic Gases Market - 1996

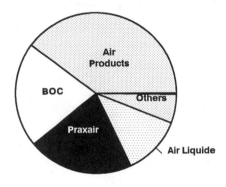

Data show shares of the $261 million market in percent.

Air Products 40.0%
BOC 21.0
Praxair 21.0
Air Liquide 12.0
Others 6.0

Source: *Chemical Week*, July 16, 1997, p. 23, from Information Network.

★ 547 ★
Industrial Gases (SIC 2813)
U.S. Industrial Gas Demand - 2001

Demand is estimated in billions of cubic feet.

	(bil.)	Share
Industrial gases	2,415	50.00%
Nitrogen	1,200	24.84
Oxygen	822	17.02
Hydrogen	210	4.35
Carbon dioxide	148	3.06
Other	35	0.72

Source: *Chemical Engineering*, February 1998, p. 64, from Freedonia Group.

★ 548 ★
Inorganic Chemicals (SIC 2819)
Bromine Market by End Use

Shares are shown in percent.

Flame retardants 47.0%
Brominated agricultural chemicals 18.0
Gasoline additives 6.0
Water treatment 6.0
Drilling fluids 5.0
Other 18.0

Source: *Chemical Market Reporter*, December 22, 1997, p. 13.

★ 549 ★
Inorganic Chemicals (SIC 2819)
Calcium Chloride Sales

Consumption is shown in percent.

Deicing 38.0%
Industrial processing 20.0
Dust control 18.0
Concrete treatment 12.0
Oil recovery 4.0
Tire ballasting 4.0
Other 4.0

Source: *Chemical Market Reporter*, April 20, 1998, p. 17, from SRI Consulting.

★ 550 ★

Inorganic Chemicals (SIC 2819)

Catalyst Demand by Sector

Data show demand in millions of dollars for 1995 and 2000.

	1995	2000
Petroleum refining	$ 903	$ 1,075
Chemical processing	822	1,135
Emissions control	517	675
Automotive	436	555
Industrial	81	120

Source: *Chemical Engineering*, July 1997, p. 57, from The Freedonia Group.

★ 551 ★

Inorganic Chemicals (SIC 2819)

Largest Dimer Acid Producers

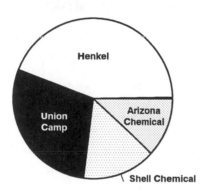

Shares are shown based on total capacity of 170 million pounds.

Henkel	44.12%
Union Camp	29.41
Shell Chemical	14.71
Arizona Chemical	11.76

Source: *Chemical Market Reporter*, March 9, 1998, p. 49.

★ 552 ★

Inorganic Chemicals (SIC 2819)

Largest Sodium Chlorate Makers

Companies are ranked by production capacity in tons per year.

Eka	286,000
CXY	140,000
Huron Tech	140,000
Kerr-McGee	138,000
Sterling Pulp	110,000
Elf Atochem	58,000
Georgia Gulf	27,000

Source: *Chemical Market Reporter*, November 10, 1997, p. 19, from SRI Consulting.

★ 553 ★

Inorganic Chemicals (SIC 2819)

Largest Sulfuric Acid Producers

Companeis are ranked by production capacity in thousands of short tons per year.

Doe Run	1,300
Kennecott	1,300
Asarco	1,005
Phelps-Dodge	880
Chino Mines	650
Cyprus Miami Mining	550
Newmont Gold	150
Savage Zinc	150

Source: *Chemical Market Reporter*, September 22, 1997, p. 33.

★ 554 ★

Inorganic Chemicals (SIC 2819)

Mexico's Inorganic Chemical Production

Production is shown in thousands of metric tons.

Sulfuric acid	3,851
Ammonia	2,600
Phosphoric acid	647
Sodium sulfate	573
Sodium hydroxide	491
Nitric acid	453
Chlorine, liquid	440
Ammonium sulfate	341

Continued on next page.

★ 554 ★ *Continued*
Inorganic Chemicals (SIC 2819)

Mexico's Inorganic Chemical Production

Production is shown in thousands of metric tons.

Hydrochloric acid	201
Ammonium nitrate	195

Source: *Chemical & Engineering News*, December 15, 1997, p. 23, from Asociation Nacional de la Industrie Quimica.

★ 555 ★
Inorganic Pigments (SIC 2819)

Iron Oxide Use in North America

Consumption is shown in percent.

Construction materials	35.0%
Paint and coatings	22.0
Plastics, rubber, paper, textiles and ceramics .	13.0
Other	30.0

Source: *Chemical Market Reporter*, November 3, 1997, p. 38, from SRI Consulting.

★ 556 ★
Plastics (SIC 2821)

Acrylic Resin Demand - 1997

Demand is shown based on a total of 2.9 million pounds.

Paints & coatings	30.0%
Construction	14.0
Plastics	11.0
Textiles	8.0
Other	37.0

Source: *Plastics News*, March 2, 1998, p. 3, from Freedonia Group Inc.

★ 557 ★
Plastics (SIC 2821)

Canada's Plastics Industry - 1996

Consumption of plastics, resins and materials is shown in tons.

Polyethylene, low-density	640,000
Polyvinyl chloride	457,000
Polypropylene	359,000
Polyethylene, low-density	345,000
Polystyrene and copolymers	148,000
ABS	76,000
Polyester, unsaturated	61,000

Source: *National Trade Data Bank*, October 22, 1997, p. ISA970801, from Canadian Plastics Industry Association.

★ 558 ★
Plastics (SIC 2821)

Engineered Plastics Market

The market is shown by end use.

Connectors & switches	53.0%
Business equipment	22.0
Information storage	15.0
Wire & cable	10.0

Source: *Design News*, May 18, 1998, p. 68, from Freeedonia Group.

★ 559 ★
Plastics (SIC 2821)

Largest Polystyrene Producers in North America

Companies are ranked by production capacity in billions of pounds.

Dow Chemical	1.6
Huntsman	1.2
BASF	1.1
Fina	1.0
Chevron	0.8
Nova Chemicals	0.8

Source: *Chemical & Engineering News*, January 19, 1998, p. 20.

★ 560 ★

Plastics (SIC 2821)

Largest Polyvinyl Chloride Makers

Firms are ranked by capacity in millions of pounds per year.

	(mil.)	Share
Shintech	2,800	18.83%
Formosa	2,265	15.23
OxyChem	2,013	13.54
Geon	1,933	13.00
Borden	1,500	10.09
Vista	1,400	9.42
Other	2,957	19.89

Source: *Chemical Market Reporter*, February 23, 1998, p. 37.

★ 561 ★

Plastics (SIC 2821)

Leading Nylon Resin Producers

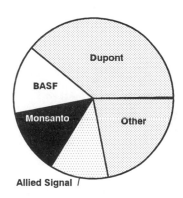

Market shares are shown in percent.

Dupont	39.2%
BASF	13.9
Monsanto	13.4
Allied Signal	11.9
Other	21.6

Source: *Chemical Market Reporter*, May 19, 1997, p. 16, from Schroder Wertheim.

★ 562 ★

Plastics (SIC 2821)

Leading S-B Latex Producers - North America

Shares are shown in percent.

Dow	33.0%
GenCorp	21.0
BASF	15.0
Reichhold	12.0
Other	19.0

Source: *Chemical Market Reporter*, December 15, 1997, p. 20, from SRI Consulting.

★ 563 ★

Plastics (SIC 2821)

Medical Plastics Market

The market is shown in percent. HDPE stands for high-density polyethylene; LDPE stands for low-density polyethylene.

Vinyl	28.0%
Polypropylene	16.0
Polystyrene	14.0
HDPE	13.0
LDPE	10.0
Other	19.0

Source: *Modern Plastics*, June 1997, p. 18, from Borealis NV.

★ 564 ★

Plastics (SIC 2821)

North American Polystyrene Use - 1996

Data show percent distribution.

Packaging & disposables	50.0%
Electrical	14.0
Institutional	11.0
Construction	9.0
Other	16.0

Source: *Chemical Market Reporter*, June 16, 1997, p. 28, from Philip Townsend Associates.

★ 565 ★
Plastics (SIC 2821)

Plastics Industry by Segment - Quebec

Data are for 1996.

Packaging	38.9%
Construction	26.0
Various products	15.7
Sports and recreation	5.1
Furniture, commercial & residential	4.0
Household, institutional & retail products	3.5
Printing & publicity	3.0
Transportation	1.9
Clothing and accessories	1.6
Electrical/electronic	0.3

Source: *Canadian Plastics*, November 1997, p. 18, from Statistics Canada.

★ 566 ★
Plastics (SIC 2821)

Polyethylene Market - North America

Companies are shown ranked by capacity in billions of pounds. Figure for Millenium Chemicals Inc./ Lyondell Petrochemical Co. represents total capacity based on the companies' proposed partnership.

Millennium Chemicals Inc./Lyondell Petrochemical Co.	6.20
Exxon Chemical Co.	4.83
Union Carbide Corp.	3.95
Dow Chemical Co.	3.79
Chevron Corp.	2.70
Phillips Petroleum Co.	2.00
Mobil Chemical Co.	1.86
Solvay Polymers Inc.	1.67
Formosa Plastics Corp. USA	0.97
Eastman Chemical Co.	0.90
Westlake Polymers	0.85
DuPont Chemical Co.	0.75

Source: *Plastics News*, October 4, 1997, p. 8.

★ 567 ★
Plastics (SIC 2821)

Polyurethane Market by End Use - 1996

Data represent demand in millions of pounds. Shares of the group are shown in percent.

	Lbs (mil.)	% of Group
Construction	1,237	29.25%
Transportation	970	22.94
Carpet cushion	524	12.39
Furniture	497	11.75
Appliances	252	5.96
Packaging	219	5.18
Bedding	181	4.28
Textiles, fibers	140	3.31
Tanks, pipes	113	2.67
Machinery	96	2.27

Source: *Chemical Week*, August 6, 1997, p. 33, from The Society of the Plastics Industry.

★ 568 ★
Plastics (SIC 2821)

Resin Consumption in Canada

Consumption is shown in millions of pounds. LDPE stands for low-density polyethylene; PVC stands for polyvinyl chloride; PP stands for polypropylene; HDPE stands for high-density polyethylene.

	1996 (mil.)	1997 (mil.)
LDPE	1,309	1,389
PVC	1,241	1,300
PP	835	882
HDPE	800	849

Source: *Modern Plastics*, January 1998, p. 78, from Kuhlike Associates.

★ 569 ★
Plastics (SIC 2821)

Top LDPE Companies - North America

Data show low-density polyethylene (LDPE) capacity in thousands of metric tons per year.

Millennium	706
Dow	515

Continued on next page.

★ 569 ★ *Continued*
Plastics (SIC 2821)

Top LDPE Companies - North America

Data show low-density polyethylene (LDPE) capacity in thousands of metric tons per year.

Chevron	418
Westlake	386
DuPont	367
Exxon	345
Eastman	295
Mobil	227
Union Carbide	227
Rexene	187
Novacor	120
AT Plastics	90
Lyondell	64

Source: *Chemical Week*, July 16, 1997, p. 10.

★ 570 ★
Plastics (SIC 2821)

Top Markets for Nylons - 1997

Data are in millions of pounds.

	(mil.)	Share
Transportation	363	29.83%
Export	158	12.98
Film	127	10.44
Electrical/electronics	100	8.22
Industrial	83	6.82
Consumer products	72	5.92
Wire & cable	56	4.60
Filaments	48	3.94
Appliances/power tools	23	1.89
Other	187	15.37

Source: *Modern Plastics*, January 1998, p. 76.

★ 571 ★
Plastics (SIC 2821)

Top Markets for Polyvinyl Chloride - 1997

Data are in millions of pounds.

Pipe & conduit extrusion	5,775
Siding	1,850
Compounders	680
Windows & doors	500

Wire & cable	450
Fittings	290
Packaging	275
Flooring (calendering)	240
Flooring (coating)	220
Paste processes	210

Source: *Modern Plastics*, January 1998, p. 70.

★ 572 ★
Plastics (SIC 2821)

TPE Demand - North America

Thermoplatic elastomer (TPE) demand is shown by end use.

Motor vehicles	31.0%
Industrial products	14.0
Construction	13.0
Consumer products	9.0
Footwear	7.0
Wire & cable	6.0
Medical products	4.0
Other	17.0

Source: *WARD'S Auto World*, August 1997, p. 66, from The Freedonia Group Inc.

★ 573 ★
Synthetic Rubber (SIC 2822)

Rubber Consumption - North America

Consumption is shown in thousands of metric tons for 1996 and 2000. Data include natural rubber and thermoplastic elastomers.

	1996	2000
Natural rubber	1,112	1,102
Styrene-butadiene	887	907
Carboxylated latex	625	641
Polybutadiene	533	553
Thermoplastic elastomers	398	494

Continued on next page.

★ 573 ★ *Continued*
Synthetic Rubber (SIC 2822)

Rubber Consumption - North America

Consumption is shown in thousands of metric tons for 1996 and 2000. Data include natural rubber and thermoplastic elastomers.

	1996	2000
Ethylene-propylene	268	279
Nitrile solid & latex	121	127
Styrene-butadiene latex	91	95
Polychloroprene	70	71
Other synthetic rubbers	431	440

Source: *Chemical & Engineering News*, September 8, 1997, p. 19, from International Institute of Synthetic Rubber Producers.

★ 574 ★
Fibers (SIC 2823)

Filament Manmade Fiber Shipments

Shipments are shown in millions of pounds.

	1996	1997	Share
Olefin	1,932	2,023	37.11%
Nylon	1,803	1,891	34.69
Polyester	1,429	1,537	28.20

Source: *America's Textile International*, February 1998, p. 53, from Fiber Economics Bureau.

★ 575 ★
Medicinals (SIC 2833)

Best-Selling Herbs - 1997

Sales are shown in millions of dollars.

Ginkgo Biloba	$ 90.2
St. John's Wort	47.8
Echinacea	22.2
Kava	2.9

Source: *Wall Street Journal*, February 26, 1998, p. B1, from Information Resources Inc.

★ 576 ★
Medicinals (SIC 2833)

Dietary Supplement Sales - 1997

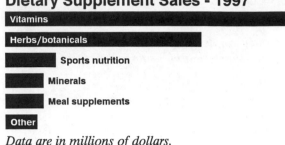

Data are in millions of dollars.

	($ mil.)	Share
Vitamins	$ 5,240	44.60%
Herbs/botanicals	3,650	31.06
Sports nutrition	990	8.43
Minerals	660	5.62
Meal supplements	650	5.53
Other	560	4.77

Source: *New York Times*, June 10, 1998, p. A18, from *Nutrition Business Jounral*.

★ 577 ★
Vitamins (SIC 2833)

Top Herbal Supplement Brands - 1996

Brands are shown ranked by sales in millions of dollars for the 52 week period ended December 29, 1996.

	Sales ($ mil.)	Share
Nature's Resource	$ 29.4	12.9%
Ginsana	26.9	11.8
Nature Made Herbal	23.4	10.3
Ginkoba	18.4	8.1
Sundown Herbal	11.9	5.2
NaturaLife Herbal	8.5	3.7
Your Life	7.3	3.2
Kwai Herbal	7.1	3.1
Garlique	6.9	3.0
Kyolic	4.8	2.1

Source: *Supermarket Business*, June 1997, p. 85, from Information Resources Inc.

★ 578 ★
Drugs (SIC 2834)

Best-Selling Drugs - 1997

The top prescription drugs are ranked by sales in millions of dollars.

Prilosec	$ 2,281.8
Prozac	1,942.0
Zocor	1,379.3
Epogen	1,200.8
Zoloft	1,195.9
Zantac	1,097.2
Paxil	949.3
Norvasc	914.8
Claritin	907.7
Vasotec	843.4

Source: *New York Times*, February 27, 1998, p. C3, from IMS America.

★ 579 ★
Drugs (SIC 2834)

Canada's Pharmaceutical Market

Breakdown shows brand name and generic product shares for 1993, 1997, and 2001.

	1993	1997	2001
Brand name	90.0%	84.0%	80.7%
Generic	10.0	16.0	19.3

Source: *Financial Times*, December 3, 1997, p. 4, from IMS Canada.

★ 580 ★
Drugs (SIC 2834)

Canada's Pharmacy Drug Sales

The table shows retail pharmacy sales for the year ended October 1997. Figures are in millions of dollars.

	($ mil.)	Share
Cardiovascular	$ 1,004	24.80%
Central Nervous System	678	16.75
Alimentary/Metabolism	627	15.49
Respiratory	388	9.58
Anti-infectives	295	7.29
Genito-urinary	219	5.41
Musculo-skeletal	174	4.30
Others	663	16.38

Source: *Financial Times*, December 22, 1997, p. 4.

★ 581 ★
Drugs (SIC 2834)

Cholesterol-Reducer Market - 1996

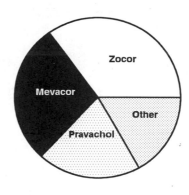

Brands are shown ranked by sales in millions of dollars.

	Sales ($ mil.)	Share
Zocor	$ 1,000.0	35.08%
Mevacor	791.9	27.78
Pravachol	564.7	19.81
Other	493.7	17.32

Source: *Advertising Age*, July 7, 1997, p. 3, from IMS America.

★ 582 ★
Drugs (SIC 2834)

Diltiazem Market - 1997

Diltiazem is a drug used to treat hypertension and angina. Data show millions of dollars.

Cardizem CD	$ 735
Dilacor XR	150
Tiazac	100
Cardizem, Cardizem SR, and generics	100

Source: *Investor's Business Daily*, December 11, 1997, p. A4, from Lazard Freres & Co. and company reports.

★ 583 ★
Drugs (SIC 2834)

External Analgesics Market - 1997

Dollar shares are shown in percent for the 52 weeks ended June 20, 1997.

Ben Gay	19.8%
FlexAll 454	8.6

Continued on next page.

★ 583 ★ *Continued*
Drugs (SIC 2834)

External Analgesics Market - 1997

Dollar shares are shown in percent for the 52 weeks ended June 20, 1997.

Aspercreme	7.8%
Icy Hot	7.1
Capzasin P	5.2
Mineral Ice	5.1
Sportscreme	3.6
Myoflex	3.1
Absorbine JR	3.1
Private label	5.5
Others	31.1

Source: *Discount Merchandiser*, October 1997, p. 59, from Information Resources Inc.

★ 584 ★
Drugs (SIC 2834)

Generic Drug Manufacturers - 1997

Data show pharmacy purchases in millions of dollars for the first quarter of 1997.

Teva USA	$ 131.349
Mylan	129.654
Apothecon (BMS)	124.939
Ivax	101.333
Schein	92.831
Geneva (Novartis)	83.493
Roxane	80.063
Barr Labs	64.370
Rugby (HMR)	62.727
Warrick (Schering)	44.225

Source: *Drug Topics*, August 1997, p. 11S, from IMS.

★ 585 ★
Drugs (SIC 2834)

Largest Drug Makers - 1997

Firms are ranked by revenues in millions of dollars.

Merck	$ 23,637
Johnson & Johnson	22,629
Bristol-Myers Squibb	16,701
American Home Products	14,196
Pfizer	12,504
Abbott Laboratories	11,883
Eli Lilly	8,518
Warner-Lambert	8,180

Schering-Plough	$ 6,778
Pharmacia & Upjohn	6,710

Source: *Fortune*, April 27, 1998, p. 56.

★ 586 ★
Drugs (SIC 2834)

Leading Cough/Cold Remedies - 1997

Shares are shown based on sales for the 52 weeks ended February 23, 1997.

Robitussin	12.4%
Nyquil	7.5
Tylenol	7.1
Alka Seltzer	6.2
Benadryl	5.9
Sudafed	5.7
Dimetapp	5.2
Formula 44	3.5
Theraflu	3.3
Private label	20.9
Other	22.3

Source: *Discount Merchandiser*, June 1997, p. 68.

★ 587 ★
Drugs (SIC 2834)

Leading Hair Growth Products - 1997

Shares of the $144.8 million market are shown for the year ended October 12, 1997.

Rogaine	58.6%
Private label	35.0
Other	6.4

Source: *Advertising Age*, December 1, 1997, p. 18, from Information Resources Inc.

★ 588 ★

Drugs (SIC 2834)

Leading Impotence Drugs - 1998

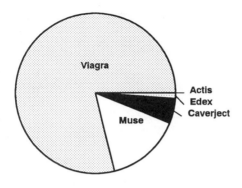

A total of 45,761 prescriptions were written for week ended April 10, 1998.

	No.	Share
Viagra	36,263	79.24%
Muse	6,716	14.68
Caverject	2,314	5.06
Edex	435	0.95
Actis	33	0.07

Source: *New York Times*, April 21, 1998, p. C4, from IMS America.

★ 589 ★

Drugs (SIC 2834)

Leading Over-the-Counter Motion Sickness Medications - 1997

Shares of the $29.9 million over-the-counter market are shown for December 7, 1997.

Dramamine	57.0%
Other	43.0

Source: *Advertising Age*, January 26, 1998, p. 4, from Information Resources Inc.

★ 590 ★

Drugs (SIC 2834)

Most Frequently Prescribed Pharmaceuticals - 1997

Products are ranked by thousands of prescriptions for the first half of 1997. Manufacturers names are shown in parentheses.

Premarin (Wyeth-Ayerst)	22,101
Trimox (Apothecon)	19,744
Sythroid (Knoll)	17,743
Lanoxin (Allen & Hansbury)	12,672
Hydrocodone with Apap (Watson)	12,006
Prozac (Dista)	11,053
Albuterol (Warrick)	10,697
Vasotec (Merck)	10,275
Zantac (Glaxo)	9,873
Prilosec (Astra Merck)	9,849

Source: *Medical Marketing & Media*, October 1997, p. 78, from *NPA Plus*.

★ 591 ★

Drugs (SIC 2834)

Pain Relief Market by Segment - 1996

Market shares are shown in percent. Acetaminophen includes Tylenol; ibuprophen includes Advil; and naproxen includes Aleve.

Acetaminophen	41.2%
Ibuprofen	25.6
Naproxen	5.6
Bayer	5.2
Other aspirin	17.8
Other	4.6

Source: *New York Times*, August 9, 1997, p. 21, from Information Resources Inc.

★ 592 ★

Drugs (SIC 2834)

Pharmacy Drug Sales

The table shows retail pharmacy sales for the year ended October 1997. Figures are in millions of dollars.

	($ mil.)	Share
Central Nervous System	$ 12,934	19.46%
Cardiovascular	12,299	18.50
Alimentary/metabolism	10,774	16.21

Continued on next page.

★ 592 ★ *Continued*

Drugs (SIC 2834)

Pharmacy Drug Sales

The table shows retail pharmacy sales for the year ended October 1997. Figures are in millions of dollars.

	($ mil.)	Share
Respiratory	$ 6,855	10.31%
Anti-infectives	6,727	10.12
Genito-urinary	4,257	6.40
Musculo-skeletal	2,484	3.74
Others	10,147	15.26

Source: *Financial Times*, December 22, 1997, p. 4.

★ 593 ★

Drugs (SIC 2834)

Popular Diabetes Drugs

Data show market shares for the month of August 1997. Figures refer to oral solid forms only.

Glucophage	24.6%
Glyburide	23.4
Glucotrol XL	15.1
Glipizide	9.4
Rezulin	7.9
Glynase prestab	4.8
Amaryl	3.1
Glyburide Micronized	2.5
Diabeta	1.9
Other	7.3

Source: *Drug Topics*, October 20, 1997, p. 24.

★ 594 ★

Drugs (SIC 2834)

Prescription Drugs Leaders

Shares are shown in percent.

Glaxo Wellcome	6.8%
Johnson & Johnson	6.2
American Home Products	6.1
Procter & Gamble	1.1
Other	79.8

Source: *New York Times*, November 4, 1997, p. C1, from Information Resources Inc., IMS America, and company reports.

★ 595 ★

Drugs (SIC 2834)

Smoking-Cessation Market - 1996

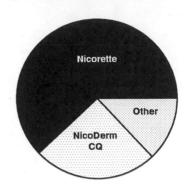

Shares are shown based on $270.5 million in sales for the year ended December 1, 1996. Data represent the over-the-counter segment only. SmithKline Beecham owns both the Nicorette and Nicoderm CQ brands.

Nicorette	62.0%
NicoDerm CQ	24.7
Other	13.3

Source: *Advertising Age*, June 30, 1997, p. S30, from Information Resources Inc.

★ 596 ★

Drugs (SIC 2834)

Stomach Remedy Market - 1997

Shares are shown for the 24 weeks ended March 9, 1997.

Pepcid AC	16.0%
Tums	11.5
Zantac 75	11.4
Mylanta	8.4
Tagamet HB 200	6.7
Pepto-Bismol	6.3
Maalox	5.9
Alka-Seltzer/Alka Mints	5.2
Rolaids	4.4
Axid AR	3.5
Mylanta AR	0.2
Private label	6.7
Other	13.8

Source: *America's Pharmacist*, October 1997, p. 81, from Information Resources Inc.

★ 597 ★

Drugs (SIC 2834)

Top Impotence Drugs

Market shares are shown as of April 17, 1998.

Viagra	94.4%
Muse	3.8
Caverject, Edex, Actis	1.7

Source: *New York Times*, April 29, 1998, p. C4, from IMS America.

★ 598 ★

Drugs (SIC 2834)

Top Pain Relievers - 1997

Brands are shown ranked by sales in millions of dollars for the 52 weeks ended June 22, 1997.

	Sales ($ mil.)	Share
Tylenol	$ 577.8	23.2%
Advil	342.3	13.7
Aleve	146.0	5.9
Excedrin	132.0	5.3
Tylenol PM	111.4	4.5
Bayer	104.4	4.2
Motrin IB	83.2	3.3
Anacin	45.4	1.8
Excedrin PM	44.8	1.8
Private label	575.7	23.1

Source: *Discount Merchandiser*, October 1997, p. 60, from Information Resources Inc.

★ 599 ★

Drugs (SIC 2834)

Top Selling Analgesics - 1997

Shares are shown based on sales of 368 million units.

Tylenol	20.0%
Advil	11.4
Aleve	4.9
Bayer	4.9
Excedrin	4.8
Tylenol PM	3.6

Motrin IB	3.5%
Excedrin PM	1.5
Ecotrin	1.3
Other	44.1

Source: *Supermarket Business*, April 1998, p. 52, from Information Resources Inc.

★ 600 ★

Drugs (SIC 2834)

Top Selling Cough/Cold Remedies - 1997

Shares are shown based on sales of 412.5 million units.

Robitussen	10.8%
Nyquil	7.2
Tylenol	6.4
Sudafed	5.4
Alka Seltzer	5.2
Benadryl	4.7
Dimetapp	4.0
Formula 44	3.4
Theraflu	3.2
Private label	30.1
Other	19.6

Source: *Supermarket Business*, April 1998, p. 52, from Information Resources Inc.

★ 601 ★

Drugs (SIC 2834)

Top Selling Stomach Remedies - 1997

Shares are shown based on sales of 368 million units.

Tums	15.1%
Pepcid AC	9.2
Mylanta	7.9
Zantac75	6.9
Pepto Bismol	6.7
Imodium	6.1
Maalox	5.0
Alka Seltzer	4.5
Tagamet	3.9
Other	34.7

Source: *Supermarket Business*, April 1998, p. 52, from Information Resources Inc.

★ 602 ★
Drugs (SIC 2834)

Top U.S. Drug Firms - 1997

Firms are ranked by sales in millions of dollars.

Bristol-Myers Squibb	$ 5,696.9
Johnson & Johnson	5,659.2
Merck & Co.	5,647.1
Glaxo Wellcome	5,536.5
American Home Products	5,329.7
Pfizer	4,949.8
Lilly	4,390.9
SmithKline Beecham	4,015.6
Novartis	3,987.8
Schering-Plough	3,810.6

Source: *Chemical Market Reporter*, March 9, 1998, p. 35, from IMS America.

★ 603 ★
Biotechnology (SIC 2836)

Leading Specialty Biocide Applications - 1997

Shares of the $1.1 billion market are shown in percent.

Water treatment	28.0%
Wood preservation	19.0
Paints & coatings	12.0
Cosmetics & toiletries	11.0
Disinfectants & sanitizers	11.0
Plastics	5.0
Food & animal feed	3.0
Pulp & paper	3.0
Metalworking	2.0
Petroleum	2.0
Hospital & medical	2.0
Other	2.0

Source: *Chemical Engineering*, January 1998, p. 56, from Kline & Co., Inc.

★ 604 ★
Biotechnology (SIC 2836)

U.S. Biotechnology Sales

Sales are shown in millions of dollars.

	1998 ($ mil.)	2003 ($ mil.)	Share
Human therapeutics . .	$ 9,120	$ 16,100	74.88%
Human diagnostics . .	2,100	3,100	14.42
Agriculture	420	1,000	4.65
Specialties	390	900	4.19
Nonmedical diagnostics	270	400	1.86

Source: *Chemical Week*, January 7, 1998, p. 35, from Consulting Resources.

★ 605 ★
Detergents (SIC 2841)

Leading Laundry Detergent Makers - 1997

Shares of the $4.3 billion market are shown in percent.

Procter & Gamble	58.0%
Unilever	20.0
Dial	6.0
Church & Dwight	5.0
Colgate Palmolive	4.0
USA Detergents	3.0
Huish	1.0
Other	3.0

Source: *Chemical Week*, January 28, 1998, p. 28, from Information Resources Inc.

★ 606 ★
Detergents (SIC 2841)

Popular Dishwasher Detergents

Data show selected sales in millions of dollars.

Cascade	$ 253
Sunlight	85
Electrasol	78
Palmolive	44

Source: *Brandweek*, June 15, 1998, p. S52, from Information Resources Inc.

★ 607 ★

Detergents (SIC 2841)

Top Liquid Detergent Brands - 1997

Market shares are shown for the 52 weeks ended October 26, 1997.

Tide	31.3%
All	11.9
Wisk	10.7
Era	7.3
Purex	6.8
Cheer	6.2
Xtra	4.8
Surf	3.4
Arm & Hammer	3.2
Private label	2.6
Other	11.8

Source: *Household and Personal Products Industry*, January 1998, p. 84, from Information Resources Inc.

★ 608 ★

Detergents (SIC 2841)

Top Powder Detergent Brands - 1997

Market shares are shown for the 52 weeks ended October 26, 1997.

Tide	42.7%
Cheer	9.7
Gain	8.5
Surf	7.3
Arm & Hammer	5.8
Wisk	4.0
Purex	3.8
Private label	2.8
All	2.3
Fab	2.3
Other	10.8

Source: *Household and Personal Products Industry*, January 1998, p. 84, from Information Resources Inc.

★ 609 ★

Soaps (SIC 2841)

Leading Personal Soap Makers - 1997

Shares of the $2 billion market are shown in percent.

Unilever	31.0%
Procter & Gamble	24.0
Dial	15.0
Colgate Palmolive	14.0
Kao	4.0
Johnson & Johnson	2.0
Other	10.0

Source: *Chemical Week*, January 28, 1998, p. 28, from Information Resources Inc.

★ 610 ★

Soaps (SIC 2841)

Men's Bath and Shower Market - 1996

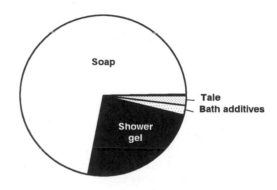

Shares are shown by type of product.

Soap	71.1%
Shower gel	24.2
Bath additives	2.3
Tale	2.3

Source: *Soap/Cosmetics/Chemical Specialties*, June 1997, p. 68, from Datamonitor Cosmetics & Toiletries Database.

★ 611 ★

Soaps (SIC 2841)

Shower Gel Market - 1997

Shares are shown for the 52 weeks ended August 24, 1997.

Oil of Olay	24.1%
Dove	13.2

Continued on next page.

143

★ 611 ★ *Continued*
Soaps (SIC 2841)

Shower Gel Market - 1997

Shares are shown for the 52 weeks ended August 24, 1997.

Caress	9.1%
Jergens	8.2
Lever 2000	7.2
Softsoap	5.2
Dial 1	4.2
Suave	4.0
Vaseline	3.2
White Rain	2.7
Other	18.9

Source: *Nonfoods Merchandising*, November 1997, p. 25, from Information Resources Inc.

★ 612 ★
Soaps (SIC 2841)

Soap Market by Segment - 1997

The $1.9 billion market is shown by category.

Deodorant bars	33.9%
Skin care bars	28.4
Body washes	16.6
Liquid soaps	14.5
Plain/pure bars	5.9

Source: *Chemical Market Reporter*, January 26, 1998, p. 13, from Information Resources Inc.

★ 613 ★
Soaps (SIC 2841)

Soap Sales - 1997

The market is shown in percent. Figures as of October 1997.

Bars	68.2%
Body washes	16.3
Other	15.5

Source: *Chemical Market Reporter*, January 26, 1998, p. 13, from Information Resources Inc.

★ 614 ★
Soaps (SIC 2841)

Top Bar Soaps - 1997

Brands are ranked by sales in millions of dollars for the 52 weeks ended September 30, 1997.

	Sales ($ mil.)	Market Share
Dove	$ 258	18.83%
Dial	191	13.94
Lever 2000	124	9.05
Irish Spring	123	8.98
Zest	112	8.18
Ivory	91	6.64
Caress	83	6.06
Other	388	28.32

Source: *Wall Street Journal*, January 20, 1998, p. B8.

★ 615 ★
Soaps (SIC 2841)

Top Soap Brands in Canada - 1998

Market shares are shown based on sales of $240.1 million for the year ended March 31, 1998.

Dove	21.6%
Ivory	11.3
Oil of Olay	9.2
Jergens	8.4
Lever 2000	8.0
Zest	6.3
Irish Spring	6.1
Dial	4.0
Palmolive	1.1
Coast	1.0
Others	23.0

Source: *Marketing Magazine*, May 25, 1998, p. 18, from industry sources.

★ 616 ★

Air Fresheners (SIC 2842)

Air Freshener Market - 1997

Shares are shown for the year ended April 27, 1997.

S.C. Johnson 56.0%
Other 44.0

Source: *Brandweek*, June 16, 1997, p. 9, from
Information Resources Inc.

★ 617 ★

Air Fresheners (SIC 2842)

Top Air Freshener Brands - 1997

Market shares are shown in percent.

Glade 59.4%
Other 40.6

Source: *Advertising Age*, June 29, 1998, p. S33.

★ 618 ★

Cleaning Preparations (SIC 2842)

Popular Cleaner Sales

Data show selected sales in millions of dollars.

Pine Sol . . . . $ 111
Lysol 88
Soft Scrub 65
Comet 56
Mr. Clean 47
Clorox Clean-Up 29
Spic and Span 28
Murphy's 22
Ajax 21
Xtra 11

Source: *Brandweek*, June 15, 1998, p. S52, from
Information Resources Inc.

★ 619 ★

Cleaning Preparations (SIC 2842)

Stain Remover Market - 1997

*Shares are shown for the 52 weeks ended September
28, 1997.*

Shout 38.5%
Spray & Wash 32.9
Wisk Away 11.3
Other 17.3

Source: *Advertising Age*, November 3, 1997, p. 17, from
Information Resources Inc.

★ 620 ★

Cleaning Preparations (SIC 2842)

Top Bathroom Cleansers - 1998

*Shares are shown of the $336.2 million market for
the year ended January 25, 1998.*

	Sales ($ mil.)	Share
Dow	$ 70.2	20.9%
Tilex	64.2	19.1
Lysol	43.6	13.0
Scrub Free	28.8	8.6
LimeAway	21.3	6.4
Comet	20.2	6.0
A-14	16.1	4.8
Shower Power	3.4	1.0
ToughAct	0.3	0.1
Simple Green	0.2	0.1
Private label	6.0	1.8

Source: *Household and Personal Products Industry*, April
1998, p. 81, from Information Resources Inc.

★ 621 ★

Cleaning Preparations (SIC 2842)

Window & Counter Cleaner Market - 1997

Brand shares are shown for the 52 weeks ended September 28, 1997. Company names are in parentheses.

Windex (S.C. Johnson) 31.2%
Formula 409 (Clorox) 18.8
Lysol (Reckitt & Col.) 7.5
Fantastik (Dow) 7.2
Private label 7.0
Glass Plus (Dow) 4.9
Cinch (Procter & Gamble) 3.7
Other 19.7

Source: *Advertising Age*, November 3, 1997, p. 17, from Information Resources Inc.

★ 622 ★

Detergents (SIC 2842)

Detergent Product Sales

Laundry powder
Laundry liquid
Dishwashing liquid
Fabric softener, liquid
Bleach
Fabric softener, sheet

Sales are shown in millions of dollars for the year ended October 26, 1997.

Laundry powder . . . . $ 2,230
Laundry liquid 2,070
Dishwashing liquid 1,340
Fabric softener, liquid 775
Bleach 647
Fabric softener, sheet 438

Source: *Chemical Market Reporter*, January 26, 1998, p. 8, from Information Resources Inc.

★ 623 ★

Cosmetics (SIC 2844)

Cosmetics Leaders - 1997

Data show department store sales in millions of dollars.

	Sales ($ mil.)	Share
Estee Lauder	$ 1,086	17.8%
Clinique	1,031	16.9
Lancome	750	12.3
Calvin Klein	366	6.0
Chanel	244	4.0
Aramis	232	3.8
Elizabeth Arden	201	3.3
Prescriptives	159	2.6
Ralph Lauren	159	2.6
Giorgio Beverly Hills	122	2.0

Source: *New York Times*, June 30, 1998, p. C1, from NPD BeautyTrends.

★ 624 ★

Cosmetics (SIC 2844)

Top Cosmetics Brands - 1997

Shares of the $2.65 billion market are shown in percent.

	Sales ($ mil.)	Share
Revlon	$ 565.8	21.2%
Cover Girl	534.8	20.0
Maybelline	410.6	15.4
L'Oreal	316.1	11.8
Almay	164.0	6.1
Max Factor	135.7	5.1
Sally Hansen	87.2	3.3
Wet 'n Wild	73.6	2.8
Bonne Belle	44.3	1.7
Natural Glow	32.8	1.2

Source: *Supermarket Business*, April 1998, p. 59, from Information Resources Inc.

★ 625 ★
Deodorants (SIC 2844)

Top Deodorant Brands - 1997

Shares of the $1.48 billion market are shown in percent.

	($ mil.)	Share
Secret	$ 217.5	14.70%
Right Guard	151.8	10.26
Mennen	125.4	8.47
Degree	109.9	7.43
Sure	102.0	6.89
Arrid	98.8	6.68
Ban	93.0	6.28
Mennen for Women	76.2	5.15
Old Spice	74.1	5.01
Soft & Dri	68.4	4.62
Other	362.9	24.52

Source: *Household and Personal Products Industry*, March 1998, p. 72, from Information Resources Inc.

★ 626 ★
Foot Care (SIC 2844)

Athlete's Foot Remedies - 1997

Shares are shown based on sales for the 52 weeks ended August 17, 1997.

Lotrimin	20.2%
Tinactin	15.4
Dr. Scholl	13.0
Desenex	12.2
Micatin	7.4
Johnson Odor Eaters	3.9
Freeman Bare Foot	3.1
Fungi Cure	2.6
Private label	9.2
Other	13.0

Source: *Discount Merchandiser*, October 1997, p. 66, from Information Resources Inc.

★ 627 ★
Foot Care (SIC 2844)

Best-Selling Athlete's Foot Medications

Market shares are shown based on unit sales for the year ended December 28, 1997.

Dr. Scholl	14.6%
Lotrimin AF	14.1
Tinactin	13.3
Desenex	10.9
Freeman Bare Foot	6.2
Micatin	5.9
Johnson Foot Care	3.9
Fungi Care	1.5
Private label	10.8
Other	18.8

Source: *Supermarket Business*, March 1998, p. 89, from Information Resources Inc.

★ 628 ★
Foot Care (SIC 2844)

Foot Care Leaders - 1997

Shares are shown based on sales for the 52 weeks ended August 17, 1997.

Dr. Scholl Foot Care Devices	42.6%
Dr. Scholl Air Pillo	8.1
Dr. Scholl Foam Ease	6.6
Private label foot care devices	5.6
Dr. Scholl Flexo Foot	4.3
Dr. Scholl Dynastep	2.9
Professional foot care devices	2.9
Dr. Scholl Work Day	2.5
Dr. Scholl Zino	2.1
Other	22.4

Source: *Discount Merchandiser*, October 1997, p. 66, from Information Resources Inc.

★ 629 ★
Foot Care (SIC 2844)

Top Selling Foot Care Brands

Shares are shown based on sales of 80.8 million units.

Dr. Scholl	36.6%
Dr. Scholl Air Pillow	14.4
Dr. Scholl Foam Ease	8.2

Continued on next page.

★ 629 ★ *Continued*
Foot Care (SIC 2844)

Top Selling Foot Care Brands

Shares are shown based on sales of 80.8 million units.

Professional Footcare	3.2%
Dr. Scholl Zino	2.4
Johnson Odor Eaters	2.4
Private label	11.9
Other	20.9

Source: *Supermarket Business*, April 1998, p. 54, from Information Resources Inc.

★ 630 ★
Fragrances (SIC 2844)

Favorite Fragrances Among African American Women

Figures are based on a survey.

White Diamonds	9.0%
Red	6.0
Giorgio	2.6
Red Door	2.2
White Linen	2.1
Eternity	2.0
Aron	1.9
CK One	1.9
Escape	1.9
Liz Claiborne	1.9

Source: *Household and Personal Product Industry*, July 1997, p. 69, from Yankelovich Partners.

★ 631 ★
Fragrances (SIC 2844)

Top Men's Fragrances - 1997

Unit shares of the prestige market.

Tommy	11.5%
Polo Sport	5.7
Eternity for Men	5.3
Obsession for Men	5.0
Pleasures for Men	4.4
Other	68.1

Source: *Women's Wear Daily*, February 1998, p. 24, from NPD BeautyTrends.

★ 632 ★
Fragrances (SIC 2844)

Top Prestige Fragrances - 1996

Market shares are shown in percent.

CK One	4.3%
Beautiful	3.8
Pleasures	3.5
Tommy	2.8
Eternity (men)	2.1
Eternity (women)	2.0
Obsession	1.9
Tresor	1.9
CK Be	1.7
Polo Sport (men)	1.6
Other	74.4

Source: *Spray Technology & Marketing*, February 1998, p. 32.

★ 633 ★
Fragrances (SIC 2844)

Top Selling Women's Fragrances - 1997

Unit shares of the prestige market.

Pleasures	5.9%
Beautiful	5.4
Tommy Girl	4.3
Tresor	3.0
Eternity	2.9
Other	78.5

Source: *Women's Wear Daily*, February 1998, p. 24, from NPD BeautyTrends.

★ 634 ★
Fragrances (SIC 2844)

Top Women's Fragrances - 1997

Sales are shown in millions of dollars.

	Sales ($ mil.)	Share
Pleasures (Estee Lauder)	$ 106	5.8%
Beautiful (Estee Lauder)	101	5.5
Tommy Girl (Tommy Hilfiger)	80	4.3
Tresor (Lancome)	54	2.9
Eternity (Calvin Klein)	53	2.9
Chanel No. 5 (Chanel)	48	2.6
White Diamonds (Elizabeth Arden)	44	2.4
White Linen (Estee Lauder)	42	2.3
Obsession (Calvin Klein)	40	2.2
Aromatics Elixir (Clinique)	37	2.0

Source: *Los Angeles Times*, May 9, 1998, p. D1, from NPD Beauty Trends.

★ 635 ★
Hair Care (SIC 2844)

Hair Coloring Leaders

Unit shares are shown in percent.

Clinique	37.3%
Lancome	21.4
Estee Lauder	17.6
Prescriptives	5.6
Chanel	2.9
Other	15.2

Source: *Women's Wear Daily*, February 1998, p. 24, from NPD BeautyTrends.

★ 636 ★
Hair Care (SIC 2844)

Hair Dye Producers

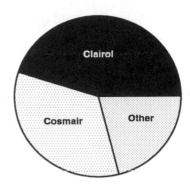

Market shares are shown in percent.

Clairol	45.1%
Cosmair	33.9
Other	21.0

Source: *Advertising Age*, February 9, 1998, p. 3, from Information Resources Inc.

★ 637 ★
Hair Care (SIC 2844)

Largest Black Hair Care Product Makers

Carson Inc.	
Soft Sheen Products Inc.	
Johnson Products	
Luster Products	
	Alberto Culver's TCB Division
	A.P. Products Ltd.

Sales are estimated in millions of dollars.

Carson Inc.	$ 110
Soft Sheen Products Inc.	95
Johnson Products	55
Luster Products	50
Alberto Culver's TCB Division	50
A.P. Products Ltd.	30

Source: *Detroit Free Press*, May 29, 1998, p. E1.

★ 638 ★
Hair Care (SIC 2844)

Popular Hair Coloring Brands

Brand shares are shown in percent for 1995 and 1996. Company names are in parentheses.

	1995	1996
Preference (Cosmair)	16.8%	16.7%
Nice 'N Easy (Clairol)	14.6	14.7
Casting (Cosmair)	7.8	7.7
Loving Care (Clairol)	7.8	7.6
Ultress (Clairol)	6.2	6.4
Just for Men (Combe)	5.2	5.5
Excellence (Cosmair)	4.4	4.7
Miss Clairol (Clairol)	4.5	4.6
Colorsilk (Revlon)	3.4	3.6
Lasting Color (Clairol)	2.8	2.7
Glints (Clairol)	2.6	2.6
Other	23.9	23.2

Source: *Soap/Cosmetics/Chemical Specialties*, June 1997, p. 60, from Datamonitor Cosmetics & Toiletries Database.

★ 639 ★
Hair Care (SIC 2844)

Top Conditioner Brands - 1997

Market shares are shown for the year ended September 28, 1997.

Pantene	14.8%
Suave	7.4
VO5	7.2
Clairol	6.7
Infusium 23	5.3
Salon Selectives	4.7
Finesse	4.7
L'Oreal	4.2
Aussie	4.0
Vidal Sassoon	3.1
Other	37.9

Source: *Household and Personal Product Industry*, December 1997, p. 62, from Information Resources Inc.

★ 640 ★
Hair Care (SIC 2844)

Top Hair Coloring Brands

Brands are ranked by sales in millions of dollars for the year ended June 6, 1997.

	Sales ($ mil.)	Share
L'Oreal Performing Preference Haircolor	$ 151	15.08%
Clairol Nice N Easy Haircolor	121	12.09
L'Oreal Excellence Haircolor	108	10.79
Just For Men	63	6.29
Clairol Natural Instincts	62	6.19
Clairol Hydrience	51	5.09
Clairol Loving Care	50	5.00
Clairol Ultress	47	4.70
L'Oreal Castings	40	4.00
Revlon Colorsilk	36	3.60
Other	272	27.17

Source: *Drug & Cosmetic Industry*, October 1997, p. 40, from Information Resources Inc.

★ 641 ★
Hair Care (SIC 2844)

Top Hair Spray Brands - 1997

Market shares are shown for the year ended September 28, 1997.

Rave	13.4%
Pantene	8.9
Salon Selective	7.4
Aquanet	7.1
Clairol	7.1
Aussie	6.7
Suave	6.3
White Rain	6.0
Finesse	3.5
Consort	2.8
Other	30.8

Source: *Household and Personal Product Industry,* December 1997, p. 62, from Information Resources Inc.

★ 642 ★
Hair Care (SIC 2844)

Top Selling Hair Coloring Brands - 1997

Shares are shown based on sales of 182.1 million units.

L'Oreal Preference	12.9%
Clairol Nice 'N Easy	12.4
L'Oreal Excellence	9.0
Revlon Colorsilk	6.4
Just For Men	5.7
Clairol Loving Care	5.5
Other	48.1

Source: *Supermarket Business,* April 1998, p. 52, from Information Resources Inc.

★ 643 ★
Hair Care (SIC 2844)

Top Selling Shampoos - 1997

Shares are shown based on sales of 606.7 million units.

Suave	15.4%
Pantene	12.0
Head & Shoulders	5.4
Clairol	5.3
Pert Plus	5.3

Johnson's	4.4%
Salon Selective	4.4
L'Oreal	3.6
Other	44.2

Source: *Supermarket Business,* April 1998, p. 54, from Information Resources Inc.

★ 644 ★
Hair Care (SIC 2844)

Top Shampoo Brands - 1997

Market shares are shown for the year ended September 28, 1997.

Pantene	15.6%
Head & Shoulders	8.1
Pert Plus	7.3
Suave	7.0
Clairol	5.8
Finesse	3.9
Neutrogena	3.9
L'Oreal	3.7
Salon Selectives	3.5
Other	41.2

Source: *Household and Personal Product Industry,* December 1997, p. 61, from Information Resources Inc.

★ 645 ★
Hair Care (SIC 2844)

Top-Selling Conditioner Brands - 1997

Shres are shown based on sales of 345 million units.

Suave	15.2%
Pantene	12.2
VO5	9.5
Clairol	5.7
Salon Selective	5.4
Finesse	3.8
Infusi23	2.9
Aussie	2.8
Vidal Sassoon	2.8
Other	39.7

Source: *Supermarket Business,* April 1998, p. 56, from Information Resources Inc.

★ 646 ★
Oral Care (SIC 2844)

Canada's Toothpaste Market

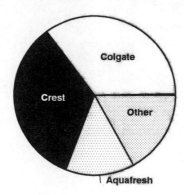

Shares are shown in percent.

Colgate	35.4%
Crest	33.7
Aquafresh	14.3
Other	16.6

Source: *Marketing Magazine*, November 10, 1997, p. 12.

★ 647 ★
Oral Care (SIC 2844)

Dentifrice Market - 1997

Brands are shown ranked by sales in millions of dollars for the 52 weeks ended July 27, 1997.

	Sales ($ mil.)	Share
Crest	$ 379.1	25.6%
Colgate	293.7	19.8
Aquafresh	168.5	11.4
Mentadent	163.9	11.1
Arm & Hammer	112.1	7.6
Sensodyn	49.0	3.3
Rembrandt	47.7	3.2
Listerine	40.8	2.8
Closeup	32.0	2.2
Ultra Brite	26.4	1.8
Pepsodent	23.7	1.6

Source: *Nonfoods Merchandising*, October 1997, p. 7, from Information Resources Inc.

★ 648 ★
Oral Care (SIC 2844)

Leading Dentifrices - 1997

Shares are shown based on units sold for the 52 weeks ended February 23, 1997.

Crest	28.8%
Colgate	20.7
Aqua Fresh	11.7
Mentadent	7.4
Arm & Hammer	6.6
UltraBrite	3.2
Closeup	2.9
Listerine	2.9
Sensodyne	1.8
Rembrandt	0.9
Other	13.1

Source: *Discount Merchandiser*, June 1997, p. 66.

★ 649 ★
Oral Care (SIC 2844)

Oral Antiseptics Market

Shares are shown in percent.

Listerine	40.7%
Scope	17.4
Plax	7.3
Act	2.4
Mentadent	2.4
Cepacol	1.6
Peroxyl	1.2
Act for Kids	1.0
Viadent	1.0
Listermint	0.6
Private label	20.4
Other	4.0

Source: *Nonfoods Merchandising*, October 1997, p. 6, from Information Resources Inc.

★ 650 ★
Oral Care (SIC 2844)

Top Mouthwash Brands - 1997

Shares are shown based on a $623.7 million market.

Listerine	40.6%
Scope	17.3
Plax	7.1
Act	2.5
Mentadent	2.1

Continued on next page.

★ 650 ★ *Continued*
Oral Care (SIC 2844)

Top Mouthwash Brands - 1997

Shares are shown based on a $623.7 million market.

Cepacol	1.6%
Peroxyl	1.2
Act for Kids	1.0
Viadent	0.9
Private label	20.4
Other	5.3

Source: *Supermarket Business*, April 1998, p. 56, from Information Resources Inc.

★ 651 ★
Oral Care (SIC 2844)

Top Toothpaste Brands - 1997

Brands are ranked by sales in millions of dollars.

Crest	$ 370.7
Colgate	312.9
Aquafresh	175.5
Mentadent	168.2
Arm & Hammer	110.7
Rembrandt	51.5
Sensodyne	49.7
Listerine	40.5
Closeup	31.9
UltraBrite	25.5

Source: *Household and Personal Products Industry*, February 1998, p. 68.

★ 652 ★
Oral Care (SIC 2844)

Top Toothpaste Producers

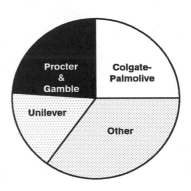

Shares of the $1.5 billion market are shown for the 52 weeks ended January 25, 1998.

Colgate-Palmolive	24.9%
Procter & Gamble	24.4
Unilever	15.9
Other	34.8

Source: *Advertising Age*, March 9, 1998, p. 51, from Information Resources Inc.

★ 653 ★
Oral Care (SIC 2844)

Top-Selling Dentifrice Brands - 1997

Sales are shown by outlet.

Crest	25.8%
Colgate	23.2
AquaFresh	12.3
Mentadent	8.1
Arm & Hammer	6.6
Closeup	3.0
UltraBrite	3.0
Listerine	2.7
Sensodyne	1.8
Other	13.5

Source: *Supermarket Business*, April 1998, p. 56, from Information Resources Inc.

★ 654 ★
Personal Care Products (SIC 2844)

Cosmetics and Toiletries Market by Sector - 1996

Sales are shown in percent.

Fragrance	19.0%
Hair care	17.0
Personal hygiene	14.0
Skin care	14.0
Makeup	11.0
Oral hygiene	11.0
Male toiletries	8.0
Shaving products	6.0

Source: *Drug & Cosmetic Industry*, June 1997, p. 29.

★ 655 ★
Personal Care Products (SIC 2844)

Personal Care Market by Segment - 1997

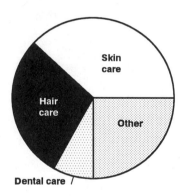

The market is shown in percent.

Skin care	38.0%
Hair care	29.0
Dental care	8.0
Other	25.0

Source: *Chemical Week*, November 19, 1997, p. 42, from Kline & Co.

★ 656 ★
Shaving Preparations (SIC 2844)

Best-Selling Shaving Creams

Market shares are shown based on unit sales for the year ended December 28, 1997.

Edge	22.9%
Colgate	16.6
Skintimate	15.2
Gillette Foamy	12.4
Gillette Satin Care	6.0
Gillette Series	5.7
Barbasol Pure Silk	1.1
Aveeno	0.5
Other	19.6

Source: *Supermarket Business*, March 1998, p. 87, from Information Resources Inc.

★ 657 ★
Shaving Preparations (SIC 2844)

Leading Shaving Cream Brands - 1997

Shares are shown based on sales for the 52-week period ended October 12, 1997.

Gillette Sensor Excel	31.6%
Edge	26.5
Skintimate	20.2
Colgate	10.5
Gillette Foamy	10.4
Gillette Satin Care	7.4
Gillette Series	7.3
Barbasol	7.3
Noxzema	3.1
Barbasol Pure Silk	1.5
Soft Shave	1.1

Source: *Discount Merchandiser*, January 1998, p. 70, from Information Resources, Inc.

★ 658 ★

Skin Care (SIC 2844)

Acne Remedies - 1997

Leading brands are shown ranked by millions of units sold for the 52 weeks ended June 27, 1997.

	Units (mil.)	Share
Clearasil	17.1	28.3%
Oxy	11.6	19.1
Neutrogena	9.8	16.2
Stridex	5.2	8.5
Noxzema	4.4	7.3
Clean & Clear	4.0	6.6
Aveeno	1.2	2.0
Exact	0.7	1.1
Stiefel	0.7	1.1
Private label	2.0	3.3

Source: *Supermarket Business*, October 1997, p. 73, from Information Resources Inc.

★ 659 ★

Skin Care (SIC 2844)

Acne/Oily Skin Treatment Market - 1996

Shares of the $263.7 million market are shown in percent.

Clearasil	25.0%
Oxy	19.0
Clean & Clear	15.0
Neutrogena	15.0
Sea Breeze	9.0
Stridex	7.0
Noxzema	7.0
Other	3.0

Source: *America's Pharmacist*, September 1997, p. 47.

★ 660 ★

Skin Care (SIC 2844)

Best-Selling Skin Care Products - 1996

- **Face cream**
- **Suntan/sunscreen products**
- **Hand & body lotions**
- **Face lotions & astringents**
- **Liquid face cleansers**
- **Lip protectors**
- **Hand creams**

Data show retail sales in thousands of dollars.

Face cream	$ 1,115,550
Suntan/sunscreen products	759,559
Hand & body lotions	711,702
Face lotions & astringents	192,667
Liquid face cleansers	153,372
Lip protectors	58,482
Hand creams	46,701

Source: *Supermarket Business*, September 1997, p. 102.

★ 661 ★

Skin Care (SIC 2844)

Leading Acne Medications - 1997

Brands are shown ranked by sales in millions of dollars for the 52 weeks ended April 27, 1997. Data include food, drug, and mass merchandiser sales.

	Sales ($ mil.)	Share
Clearasil	$ 72.297	29.4%
Oxy	52.447	21.4
Neutrogena	40.563	16.5
Stridex	18.337	7.5
Clean & Clear	15.572	6.3
Noxzema	13.821	5.6

Source: *Nonfoods Merchandising*, September 1997, p. 10, from Information Resources Inc.

★ 662 ★

Skin Care (SIC 2844)

Leading Facial Cleansers by Unit Sales - 1997

Shares are shown based on unit sales for the 52-week period ended October 26, 1997.

Noxzema	18.4%
Clean & Clear	10.7
Oil of Olay	7.9
Ponds	7.5
St. Ives	7.4
Seabreeze	6.7
Neutrogena	5.7
Freeman	5.1
Biore	2.7
Cetaphil	2.1
Other	25.8

Source: *Discount Merchandiser*, January 1998, p. 78, from Information Resources, Inc.

★ 663 ★

Skin Care (SIC 2844)

Leading Facial Moisturizers - 1997

Shares are shown based on dollar sales for the 52 weeks ended November 9, 1997.

Olay	25.3%
L'Oreal Plentitude	16.0
Ponds	14.2
Neutrogena	9.9
Alphahydroxy	5.1
Almay	4.2
Visage	4.2
Private label	1.9
Sudden Change	1.6
St. Ives	1.6
Other	16.0

Source: *Supermarket Business*, January 1998, p. 60, from Information Resources Inc.

★ 664 ★

Skin Care (SIC 2844)

Leading Hand and Body Lotions - 1997

Shares are shown based on sales for the 52-week period ended November 9, 1997.

Vaseline Intensive Care	16.2%
Jergens	8.5
Lubriderm	7.2
Suave	6.2
Curel	5.2
Nivea	5.0
Private label	5.0
Eucerin	4.5
St. Ives	3.9
Keri	2.8
Other	35.5

Source: *Discount Merchandiser*, January 1998, p. 78, from Information Resources, Inc.

★ 665 ★

Skin Care (SIC 2844)

Leading Hand/Body Lotions - 1997

Shares are shown based on sales for the 52 weeks ended March 2, 1997.

Vaseline Intensive Care	16.9%
Jergens	10.5
Lubriderm	7.6
Suave	6.0
Nivea	5.4
Curel	5.1
Eucerin	4.4
St. Ives Swiss Formula	3.9
Keri	2.4
Private label	5.4
Others	32.4

Source: *Discount Merchandiser*, June 1997, p. 71.

★ 666 ★
Skin Care (SIC 2844)

Prestige Skin Care Market

Data show dollar shares.

Clinique Dramatically Different 4-oz. lotion	4.5%
Esteee Lauder Fruition Xtra Multi complex 1.7 oz.	2.2
Clinique Clarifying 12-oz. lotion 2	1.7
Estee Lauder Advanced Night Repair 1.7 oz.	1.5
Estee Lauder 1.7-oz. Refirming Creme	1.5
Other	88.6

Source: *Household and Personal Products Industry*, May 1998, p. 82, from NPD BeautyTrends.

★ 667 ★
Skin Care (SIC 2844)

Skin Treatment Leaders

Unit shares are shown in percent.

Clarins	41.2%
Clinique	27.2
Lancome	19.0
Estee Lauder	15.3
Elizabeth Arden	4.8

Source: *Women's Wear Daily*, February 1998, p. 24, from NPD BeautyTrends.

★ 668 ★
Skin Care (SIC 2844)

Top Face Care Brands - 1998

Shares are shown for the four weeks ended February 14, 1998.

Pond's	14.6%
Biore	14.1
Oil of Olay	12.6
Other	58.7

Source: *Advertising Age*, March 9, 1998, p. 3, from A.C. Nielsen Corp.

★ 669 ★
Skin Care (SIC 2844)

Top Facial Cleansers - 1997

Shares are shown based on sales for the 52 weeks ended February 23, 1997.

Noxzema	17.2%
Ponds	9.4
Neutrogena	8.8
Oil of Olay	7.9
Clean & Clear	7.8
Seabreeze	6.7
St. Ives	5.6
Cetaphil	4.5
L'Oreal Plentitude	3.5
Freeman	3.2
Other	25.4

Source: *Discount Merchandiser*, June 1997, p. 66.

★ 670 ★
Skin Care (SIC 2844)

Top Selling Facial Moisturizers

Shares are shown based on sales of 67.4 million units.

Olay	28.2%
Ponds	13.7
L'Oreal Plentitude	12.0
Neutrogena	7.9
Alpha Hydroxy	4.0
Visage	3.9
Almay	3.6
Sudden Change	1.6
Purpose	1.3
Private label	3.7
Other	20.1

Source: *Supermarket Business*, April 1998, p. 56, from Information Resources Inc.

★ 671 ★
Skin Care (SIC 2844)

Top Selling Hand & Body Lotions

Shares are shown based on 247.8 million unit market.

Vaseline Intensive Care	18.3%
Suave	11.8
Jergens	9.8
Lubriderm	5.3

Continued on next page.

★ 671 ★ *Continued*
Skin Care (SIC 2844)

Top Selling Hand & Body Lotions

Shares are shown based on 247.8 million unit market.

St. Ives Swiss Farm 4.9%
Curel 3.9
Keri 2.2
Private label 7.4
Other 36.4

Source: *Supermarket Business*, April 1998, p. 54, from Information Resources Inc.

★ 672 ★
Sun Care (SIC 2844)

Leading Sun Care Brands - 1997

Shares are shown based on sales for the 52 weeks ended March 2, 1997.

Coppertone 14.4%
Banana Boat 13.8
Hawaiian Tropic 6.8
Bain De Soleil 6.1
Coppertone Sport 4.4
No Ad 4.4
Coppertone Water Babies 3.9
Neutrogena Glow 3.5
Neutrogena 3.1
Private label 6.7
Other 32.9

Source: *Discount Merchandiser*, June 1997, p. 71.

★ 673 ★
Sun Care (SIC 2844)

Top Selling Sun Care Brands - 1997

Shares are shown based on sales of 69.8 million units.

Banana Boat 15.2%
Coppertone 12.8
No Ad 5.7
Hawaiian Tropic 5.5
Coppertone Kids 4.1

Neutrogena 4.0%
Coppertone Sport 3.6
Private label 11.9
Other 37.2

Source: *Supermarket Business*, April 1998, p. 54, from Information Resources Inc.

★ 674 ★
Sun Care (SIC 2844)

Top Sun Care Product Makers

Market shares are shown in percent.

Schering-Plough 31.8%
Playtex Family Products Group 17.4
Other 50.8

Source: *Advertising Age*, February 23, 1998, p. 48, from Information Resources Inc.

★ 675 ★
Paints and Coatings (SIC 2851)

Automotive Coatings Market

The market is shown in millions of gallons.

OEM 38.3
Topcoat systems 22.6
Primer systems 12.5
Body panels 6.2
Underbody systems 3.2
Trim 1.9

Source: *Modern Paint and Coatings*, May 1998, p. 23, from The ChemQuest Group.

★ 676 ★
Paints and Coatings (SIC 2851)

Research Spending on Paints and Coatings - 1998

The table shows research budget allocations by type of coating.

Waterborne	40.0%
Solventborne	27.3
Two-component	14.2
Powder	11.9
UV/EB	4.2
E-coat	1.3
Plastisols	1.1

Source: *Industrial Paint & Powder*, February 1998, p. 15.

★ 677 ★
Paints and Coatings (SIC 2851)

Top Colors for Full/Intermediate Cars

Data show the percentage of vehicles manufactured in North America by color.

Medium/dark green	17.5%
White	17.0
Light brown	14.4
Black	8.0
Medium red	7.4
Medium grey	6.6
Dark red	5.2
Other	17.8

Source: *Modern Paint & Coatings*, February 1998, p. 49, from DuPont Automotive.

★ 678 ★
Paints and Coatings (SIC 2851)

Top Colors for Luxury Cars

Data show the percentage of vehicles manufactured in North America by color.

Light brown	19.8%
Medium/dark green	13.0
White metallic	12.6
Black	11.0

White	10.1%
Silver	6.7
Light green	5.7
Other	21.1

Source: *Modern Paint & Coatings*, February 1998, p. 49, from DuPont Automotive.

★ 679 ★
Paints and Coatings (SIC 2851)

Top Colors for Sports/Compact Cars

Data show the percentage of vehicles manufactured in North America by color.

Medium/dark green	20.3%
White	13.9
Black	12.9
Light brown	12.8
Bright red	9.1
Medium red	7.5
Silver	5.7
Other	20.7

Source: *Modern Paint & Coatings*, February 1998, p. 50, from DuPont Automotive.

★ 680 ★

Paints and Coatings (SIC 2851)

Top Colors for Trucks

Data show the percentage of vehicles manufactured in North America by color.

White	23.2%
Medium/dark green	18.5
Black	11.2
Bright red	7.6
Medium red	7.5
Light brown	6.1
Dark red	5.2

Source: *Modern Paint & Coatings*, February 1998, p. 50, from DuPont Automotive.

★ 681 ★

Paints and Coatings (SIC 2851)

Top U.S. Paint Companies - 1996

Companies are ranked by sales in millions of dollars.

Sherwin Williams	$ 2,200
PPG Industries	1,600
ICI Americas	1,175
DuPont	950
Akzo Nobel Coatings	600
BASF	600
Valspar	600
RPM	575
Benjamin Moore	545
Lilly Industries	425

Source: *Modern Paint & Coatings*, February 1998, p. 50, from Impact Marketing Consultants.

★ 682 ★

Organic Chemicals (SIC 2865)

Largest Phenol Producers - 1997

Firms are ranked by capacity in thousands of metric tons.

	(000)	Share
AlliedSignal	450	21.01%
Aristech Chemical	315	14.71
Mount Vernon Phenol	313	14.61
Shell Chemical	310	14.47
Georgia Gulf	300	14.01
Dow Chemical	295	13.77
JLM Industries	50	2.33

	(000)	Share
Texaco Refining	43	2.01%
Kalama Chemical	34	1.59
Dakota Gasification	20	0.93
Merichem	12	0.56

Source: *Chemical & Engineering News*, April 6, 1998, p. 21, from Chemical Market Associates Inc.

★ 683 ★

Organic Chemicals (SIC 2865)

Leading Organic Pigments Producers

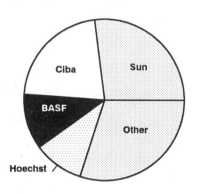

Shares are shown in percent.

Sun	27.0%
Ciba	22.0
BASF	11.0
Hoechst	10.0
Other	30.0

Source: *Chemical Market Reporter*, May 26, 1997, p. 5.

★ 684 ★

Organic Chemicals (SIC 2865)

Organic Chemical Market - 2001

The $1.56 billion market is shown by segment. "Other" includes food and beverage, cosmetics, household and personal care and petroleum refining sectors.

Printing inks 55.0%
Paints and coatings 20.0
Plastics 19.0
Textiles 2.0
Paper & paperboard 1.0
Other 3.0

Source: *Chemical Week*, March 25, 1998, p. 52, from Freedonia Group.

★ 685 ★

Organic Chemicals (SIC 2865)

Organic Chemical Production in Mexico - 1997

Production is shown in thousands of metric tons.

Ethylene 1,349
Urea 819
Terephthalic acid 578
Propylene 430
Dimethyl terephthalate 372
Ethylene glycol 340
Xylene 339

Source: *Chemical & Engineering News*, December 15, 1997, p. 23, from Asociation Nacional de la Industrie Quimica.

★ 686 ★

Organic Chemicals (SIC 2869)

Ethylene Producers by Capacity - 1997

Companies are ranked by annual capacity in billions of pounds estimated for year-end 1997.

Millennium/Lyondell 7.8
Dow Chemical 6.0
Exxon Chemical 5.9
Shell Chemical 4.7
Union Carbide 4.2
Phillips 3.9
Occidental Chemical 3.6

Chevron 3.3
Amoco Chemical 3.1

Source: *Chemical & Engineering News*, November 15, 1997, p. 20.

★ 687 ★

Organic Chemicals (SIC 2869)

Largest Chloroacetic Acid

Shares are shown based on a total capacity of 95 million pounds per year.

Dow 52.63%
Hercules 26.32
Niacet 21.05

Source: *Chemical Market Reporter*, December 22, 1997, p. 28.

★ 688 ★

Organic Chemicals (SIC 2869)

Largest Maleic Anhydride Producers

Firms are ranked by capacity in millions of pounds per year.

	(mil.)	Share
Huntsman	230	39.66%
Ashland	130	22.41
Bayer	120	20.69
Amoco	100	17.24

Source: *Chemical Market Reporter*, March 30, 1998, p. 33.

★ 689 ★

Organic Chemicals (SIC 2869)

Largest Perchloroethylene Makers

Shares are shown based on a total production capacity of 335 million pounds.

Vulcan 39.44%
PPG 35.21
Dow 25.35

Source: *Chemical Market Reporter*, December 15, 1997, p. 37.

★ 690 ★

Organic Chemicals (SIC 2869)

Largest Vinyl Acetate Makers

Production is shown in millions of pounds.

Celanese	1,213
Millennium	800
Union Carbide	720
DuPont	575
Celanese Mexicana	232
Celanese Canada	187

Source: *Chemical Market Reporter*, March 23, 1998, p. 37.

★ 691 ★

Organic Chemicals (SIC 2869)

Leading Monosodium Glutamate Producers

Shares are shown in percent.

Ajinomoto	55.0%
Miwon	13.0
Takeda	13.0
ADM	10.0
Others	9.0

Source: *Chemical Market Reporter*, August 15, 1997, p. 12.

★ 692 ★

Organic Chemicals (SIC 2869)

Polyolefin Foam Market in North America - 1997

The market is shown by application.

Protective packaging	47.0%
Automobiles	18.0
Sporting & recreational goods	10.0
Medical	3.0
Others	22.0

Source: *Rubber World*, March 1998, p. 17.

★ 693 ★

Organic Chemicals (SIC 2869)

Top Formaldehyde Producers

Production is shown in thousands of metric tons.

Borden Packaging	1,166
Georgia-Pacific	1,114
Celanese	785
Neste Resins	413
DuPont	409
Borden Chemicals	395
Perstorp	163
Spurlock	125
ISP	90
Monsanto	82

Source: *Chemical Week*, May 6, 1998, p. 30, from SRI International.

★ 694 ★

Organic Chemicals (SIC 2869)

Top Formaldehyde Producers in Canada

Production is shown in thousands of metric tons.

Neste	203
Borden	186
Celanese	160
ARC	77
Unires	55
Woodchem	25

Source: *Chemical Week*, May 6, 1998, p. 30, from SRI International.

★ 695 ★

Organic Chemicals (SIC 2869)

Top Formaldehyde Producers in Mexico

Production is shown in thousands of metric tons.

	(000)	Share
Adhesivos	75	60.48%
Resistol	37	29.84
Others	12	9.68

Source: *Chemical Week*, May 6, 1998, p. 30, from SRI International.

★ 696 ★

Phosphates (SIC 2874)

Leading Ammonium Phosphate Producers

Shares are shown based on a 10 million ton capacity.

IMC Agrico	33.0%
Cargill	13.0
CF Industries	12.0
Potash Corp.	9.0
Farmland/Hydro	7.0
Mississippi Chemical	4.0
Simplot	4.0
U.S. Agri-Chem	4.0
Other	14.0

Source: *Chemical Market Reporter*, August 4, 1997, p. 15, from IMC Global.

★ 697 ★

Insecticides (SIC 2879)

Ant/Roach Insecticide Market - 1997

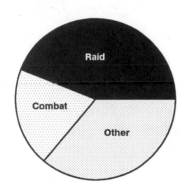

Market shares are shown in percent.

Raid	44.0%
Combat	20.0
Other	36.0

Source: *Advertising Age*, April 13, 1998, p. 8.

★ 698 ★

Adhesives (SIC 2891)

Adhesives and Sealants Market

The $9.2 billion market is shown in percent. Data are for North America.

Industry assembly	24.0%
Packaging	23.0
Construction	16.0
Wood bonding	12.0
Transportation	11.0
Consumer	6.0
Other	8.0

Source: *Chemical Week*, March 18, 1998, p. 22, from Einhorn & Associates.

★ 699 ★

Adhesives (SIC 2891)

Adhesives Demand

Demand is shown in millions of pounds.

	1996	2001	Share
Construction	4,975	5,619	39.99%
Packaging	4,843	5,551	39.51
Nondurable goods	1,324	1,515	10.78
Durable goods and other	1,165	1,365	9.72

Source: *Purchasing*, May 7, 1998, p. 87, from Freedonia Group.

★ 700 ★

Ink (SIC 2893)

Largest Ink Producers - 1997

Sales are estimated for the first nine months of the year. Sun's sales exceed the listed figure.

Sun Chemical	$ 1,000
Flint Ink	700
INX International	305
The Alper Ink Group	150
The Ink Company	135
SICPS	75
Superior Printing Ink	75
Quad/Graphics	70
Thrall (Nazdar)	70
Siegwerk USA	65

Source: *Graphic Arts Monthly*, March 1998, p. 72.

★ 701 ★

Ink (SIC 2893)

Printing Ink Consumption by Type

The estimated market is shown in percent.

	1995	2000
Lithographic	51.72%	51.07%
Flexographic	21.00	22.24
Gravure	17.31	16.27
Screen process	7.39	8.26
Letterpress	2.58	2.16

Source: *American Ink Maker*, September 1997, p. 36.

★ 702 ★

Carbon Black (SIC 2895)

Top Carbon Black Makers

Companies are ranked by capacity in millions of pounds per year of furnace black.

Cabot	940
Columbian Chemicals	690
Continental Carbon	560
Degussa	480
Engineered Carbons	560
Sid Richardson	755

Source: *Chemical Market Reporter*, September 29, 1997, p. 37.

★ 703 ★

Fire Retardants (SIC 2899)

Who Produces Polyurethane Foam

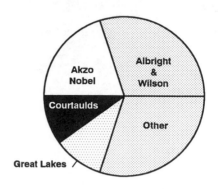

Shares are shown based on a 176 million pound market.

Albright & Wilson	30.0%
Akzo Nobel	20.0
Courtaulds	10.0
Great Lakes	10.0
Other	30.0

Source: *Chemical Week*, December 24, 1997, p. 23, from Albright & Wilson.

★ 704 ★

Salt (SIC 2899)

Leading Markets for Salt Consumption

Shares are shown in percent.

Chemical use	42.0%
De-icing	34.0
Distributors	9.0
Industrial	7.0
Agricultural	3.0
Food	3.0
Other	2.0

Source: *Chemical Market Reporter*, December 1, 1997, p. 40, from U.S. Geological Survey.

★ 705 ★

Treated Materials (SIC 2899)

Radiation Cured Material Market

The market is valued at $450 million. Data are for 1997.

Coatings 50.0%
Inks 34.0
Adhesives 16.0

Source: *Chemical Week*, April 15, 1998, p. 29, from Kusumgar, Nerlfi & Growney.

SIC 29 - Petroleum and Coal Products

★ 706 ★
Fuels (SIC 2911)

Leading Gasoline Companies - 1996

Shares are shown based on gross sales of 123 billion gallons.

Mobil	9.67%
Exxon	9.58
Shell	9.36
Citgo	9.17
Texaco	8.10
Amoco	7.85
Chevron	6.92
Marathon	5.83
Sun	4.65
Phillips	4.08
Others	24.79

Source: *Chicago Tribune*, November 22, 1997, p. 4, from *National Petroleum News Market Facts*.

★ 707 ★
Petroleum Refining (SIC 2911)

Largest Petroleum Refiners

Firms are ranked by revenues in millions of dollars.

Exxon	$ 122,379
Mobil	59,978
Texaco	45,187
Chevron	36,376
Amoco	32,836
USX	21,057
Atlantic Richfield	19,272
Phillips Petroleum	15,424

Source: *Fortune*, April 27, 1998, p. 56.

★ 708 ★
Petroleum Refining (SIC 2911)

Largest U.S. Refineries

Companies are ranked by crude refining capacity in barrels per calender day,

Shell Oil Co.	1,054,300
Exxon Co. USA	1,052,000
Chevron USA Products Inc.	1,049,000
Amoco Oil Co.	1,009,700
Mobil Oil Corp.	953,000
Tosco Corp.	876,895
Sun Refining & Marketing Co.	692,000
Citgo Petroleum Corp.	607,350
Star Enterprise	600,000
Koch Refining Co.	562,000

Source: *Oil & Gas Journal*, December 22, 1997, p. 38.

★ 709 ★
Petroleum Refining (SIC 2911)

U.S. Refined Products

Sales are shown in thousands of barrels.

	(000)	Share
Gasoline	210,152	30.59%
Distillate	134,764	19.62
Natural gas liquids & LRG	101,584	14.79

Continued on next page.

★ **709** ★ *Continued*

Petroleum Refining (SIC 2911)

U.S. Refined Products

Sales are shown in thousands of barrels.

	(000)	Share
Unfinished oils	88,689	12.91%
Residual	41,790	6.08
Kerosine jet fuel	39,767	5.79
Kerosine	6,342	0.92
Special naphthas	2,113	0.31
Naphtha jet fuel	1,672	0.24
Other refined products	60,129	8.75

Source: *Oil & Gas Journal*, January 26, 1998, p. 75.

★ **710** ★

Lubricants (SIC 2992)

Top Motor Oils - 1997

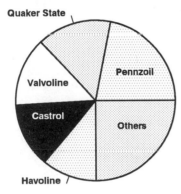

Market shares are shown in percent.

Pennzoil	21.5%
Quaker State	14.5
Valvoline	14.4
Castrol	13.2
Havoline	11.3
Others	25.1

Source: *Wall Street Journal*, April 16, 1998, p. A3, from companies and NPD Group.

SIC 30 - Rubber and Misc. Plastics Products

★ 711 ★
Tires (SIC 3011)

Farm Tire Market in North America

The size of the market is estimated in thousands of units.

	1996	1997
Fronts/implement	1,785	1,874
Drive (bias)	812	841
Drive (radial)	138	151

Source: *Tire Business*, February 2, 1998, p. 11, from Bridgestone/Firestone Inc. and Goodyear.

★ 712 ★
Tires (SIC 3011)

Leading Tire Brands on New Cars

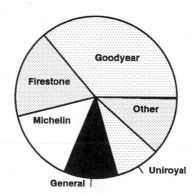

Data show the top brands on new passenger vehicles in the United States and Canada.

Goodyear	36.5%
Firestone	17.9
Michelin	15.4
General	10.7
Uniroyal	8.6
Other	11.9

Source: *New York Times*, March 28, 1998, p. B1, from *Modern Tire Dealer*.

★ 713 ★
Tires (SIC 3011)

Light Truck Tire Producers

Market shares are shown for 1996. Data are for North America. Goodyear also commands a 22% share of the highway truck tire market.

Goodyear	14.0%
BF Goodrich	9.0
Firestone	8.0
Michelin	8.0
Cooper	6.0
General	6.0
Bridgestone	5.0
Kelly-Springfield	5.0
Dunlop	3.0
Mastercraft	3.0
Uniroyal	3.0
Other	30.0

Source: *Tire Business*, September 1, 1997, p. 22.

★ 714 ★
Tires (SIC 3011)

Passenger Tire Producers

Market shares are shown for 1996. Data are for North America.

Goodyear	17.0%
Firestone	10.0
Michelin	10.0
BF Goodrich	5.0
Cooper	5.0
General	5.0
Bridgestone	4.0
Kelly-Springfield	4.0
Uniroyal	4.0
Other	36.0

Source: *Tire Business*, September 1, 1997, p. 22.

★ 715 ★
Tires (SIC 3011)

Replacement Tire Market - 1996

Shares are shown in percent.

Goodyear 16.0%
Firestone 9.0
Michelin 8.0
Bridgestone 3.5
Other 63.5

Source: *Wall Street Journal*, July 3, 1997, p. B4, from *Modern Tire Dealer*.

★ 716 ★
Tires (SIC 3011)

Tire Manufacturers - North America

Shares are shown based on 281.7 million units shipped in 1996. Data include both original equipment and replacement tires.

Goodyear 32.00%
Michelin/Uniroyal Goodrich 23.50
Bridgestone/Firestone 15.00
Continental General Tire 11.00
Cooper Tire & Rubber Co. 6.75
Other 11.75

Source: *Tire Business*, September 1, 1997, p. 9, from Fundamental Research Inc.

★ 717 ★
Tires (SIC 3011)

Top Tire Makers - 1996

Market shares are shown for 1996. Data are for North America.

Goodyear 29.2%
Michelin/Uniroyal Goodrich 21.1
Bridgestone/Firestone 19.6
Cooper 6.5
Continental General Tire 6.3
Others 17.3

Source: *Tire Business*, December 8, 1997, p. 21.

★ 718 ★
Tires (SIC 3011)

U.S. Replacement Tire Shipments

Shipments are shown in millions of units.

	1997	1998
Passenger	179.0	182.2
Light truck	29.2	30.4
Medium & wide base truck . .	12.6	13.4

Source: *Rubber & Plastics News*, January 26, 1998, p. 13, from Fundamental Research Inc.

★ 719 ★
Athletic Footwear (SIC 3021)

Athletic Footwear Market - 1997

Shares are shown in percent.

Nike 47.0%
Reebok 15.0
Adidas 6.0
Fila 6.0
Converse 3.0
Other 23.0

Source: *Boston Globe*, February 6, 1998, p. C1, from Sporting Goods Intelligence.

★ 720 ★
Athletic Footwear (SIC 3021)

Leading Athletic Shoe Companies

Shares are shown in percent.

Nike	43.3%
Reebok	15.8
Fila	7.4
Adidas	5.2
New Balance	2.7
Keds	2.7
Converse	2.6
Airwalk	2.1
LA Gear	1.9
ASICS	1.8
Other	14.5

Source: *Chicago Tribune*, December 9, 1997, p. 10, from Sporting Goods Intelligence.

★ 721 ★
Athletic Footwear (SIC 3021)

Sports Shoe Sales by Type - 1996

The market is shown in percent. Total sales reached $14.1 billion. Women purchased 45% of all shoes, followed by men with 42%. "Other" includes soccer, football, and cheerleading.

Basketball	21.0%
Cross-training	19.0
Running	12.0
Leisure	11.0
Walking	8.0
Hiking	7.0
Tennis	6.0
Aerobic	4.0
Sport sandals	2.0
Baseball	2.0
Other	8.0

Source: *USA TODAY*, August 18, 1997, p. C1, from The NPD Group Inc.

★ 722 ★
Athletic Footwear (SIC 3021)

Top Sports Shoe Makers - 1997

Firms are ranked by sales in millions of dollars.

Nike	$ 3,770
Reebok	1,280
Adidas	500
Fila	484
Converse	280
New Balance	260
Airwalk	255
Keds	180

Source: *Time*, March 30, 1998, p. 51, from *Sporting Goods Business*.

★ 723 ★
Athletic Footwear (SIC 3021)

Training Shoe Sales by Gender - 1996

Sales are shown in millions of pairs.

	($ mil.)	Share
Women's	135.3	39.76%
Men's	120.1	35.29
Children's	84.9	24.95

Source: *The Guardian*, February 7, 1998, p. 24.

★ 724 ★
Athletic Footwear (SIC 3021)

Women's Athletic Shoe Market

Shares are shown in percent.

Nike	33.0%
Reebok	18.0
Fila	5.0
Easy Spirit	4.0
Keds	3.0
Adidas	3.0

Continued on next page.

★ 724 ★ *Continued*
Athletic Footwear (SIC 3021)

Women's Athletic Shoe Market

Shares are shown in percent.

LA Gear	2.0%
New Balance	2.0
Avia	2.0
Rockport	2.0
Other	26.0

Source: *Sporting Goods Business*, September 1997, p. 28, from ASD and Target Smart Inc.

★ 725 ★
Footwear (SIC 3021)

Shoe Care Market by Category - 1997

More casual shoes are owned by adults 18 years or older than any other type of shoe. The average number of sports shoes owned is 2.8 pairs; the average number of casual shoes is 4 pairs; the average number of dress shoes is 3.9 pairs. Shares are shown based on $120 million in sales for the 52 weeks ended May 4, 1997.

Polishes	41.0%
Laces	29.0
Non-polish chemicals	22.0
Accessories	8.0

Source: *Nonfoods Merchandising*, October 1997, p. 8, from Kiwi Brands and Information Resources Inc.

★ 726 ★
Footwear (SIC 3021)

Top Segments in the Protective Footwear Market

The market is shown in millions of dollars.

	($ mil.)	Share
Occupational	$ 1,300	38.29%
Recreational	1,100	32.40
Agricultural	730	21.50
Sporting	265	7.81

Source: *Investor's Business Daily*, August 12, 1997, p. A3, from LaCrosse.

★ 727 ★
Belts and Hoses (SIC 3052)

Leading Belt and Hose Markets - Northeast Central

Sales are shown in millions of dollars.

Plumbing, heating & air conditioning	$ 20.8
Paper mills	12.9
Industrial organic chemicals	11.4
Petroleum refining	10.3
Automotive stampings	10.2

Source: *Industrial Distribution*, December 1997, p. 55.

★ 728 ★
Plastic Products (SIC 3080)

Plastic Use in Sporting Goods

Data represent millions of pounds.

Camping, fishing, and hunting	65.52
Water sports	60.80
Golf	14.00

Continued on next page.

★ 728 ★ *Continued*
Plastic Products (SIC 3080)
Plastic Use in Sporting Goods

Data represent millions of pounds.

Exercise equipment	11.29
Archery	5.39
Playground equipment	4.65
Bicycling	3.96
Basketball	2.28
Hockey	2.17
Bowling	1.01
Baseball	0.59
Football	0.03

Source: *Design News*, August 25, 1997, p. 57.

★ 729 ★
Plastic Film (SIC 3081)
Stretch Film Producers - 1997

Market shares are shown in percent.

AEP Industries Inc.	20.3%
Atlantis Plastics Inc.	16.0
Tenneco Packaging	15.7
Huntsman Packaging Corp.	15.0
ITW Auto-Sleeve	7.3
Intertape Polymer Group Inc.	6.0
Paragon Films Inc.	6.0
Other	13.7

Source: *Plastics News*, February 2, 1998, p. 3, from AEP.

★ 730 ★
Plastics (SIC 3082)
Plastics Tube, Rod & Shape Shipments by State

States are ranked by shipments in millions of dollars.

Illinois	$ 378
New York	333
Ohio	284
New Jersey	252
California	239
Pennsylvania	234
Indiana	175
Massachusetts	148
Virginia	137
Michigan	119

Source: *Plants Sites & Parks*, May-June 1997, p. 95, from Probe Economics Inc.

★ 731 ★
Plastics (SIC 3083)
Laminated Plastics Sheet & Shape Shipments by State

States are ranked by shipments in millions of dollars.

California	$ 236
North Carolina	219
South Carolina	180
Wisconsin	134
Tennessee	132

Source: *Plants Sites & Parks*, May-June 1997, p. 98, from Probe Economics Inc.

★ 732 ★
Plastic Pipes (SIC 3084)
Plastic Pipe Shipments by State

States are ranked by shipments in millions of dollars.

California	$ 342
North Carolina	258
Indiana	180
Florida	166
Georgia	166
Oklahoma	142

Continued on next page.

★ 732 ★ *Continued*
Plastic Pipes (SIC 3084)

Plastic Pipe Shipments by State

States are ranked by shipments in millions of dollars.

Kentucky	$ 128
Iowa	100
Kansas	84
Nebraska	80

Source: *Plants Sites & Parks*, May-June 1997, p. 94, from Probe Economics Inc.

★ 733 ★
Plastic Pipes (SIC 3084)

PVC Pipe Market - 1997

Demand is shown based on a 5.7 billion pound market. Figures are for North America.

Water	37.0%
Sewer	23.0
Drain, waste, vent	17.0
Conduit	14.0
Irrigation	5.0
Other	4.0

Source: *Plastics News*, May 18, 1998, p. 3, from Geon Co.

★ 734 ★
Plastic Bottles (SIC 3085)

Plastic Bottle Shipments by State

States are shown ranked by plastic bottle shipments in millions of dollars.

Ohio	$ 683
California	612
Illinois	589
New Jersey	454
Texas	398
Pennsylvania	272
Connecticut	221
Kentucky	216
Missouri	192
Georgia	170

Source: *Plants Sites & Parks*, May-June 1997, p. 107, from Probe Economics Inc.

★ 735 ★
Baby Care (SIC 3089)

Leading Baby-Cup Producers

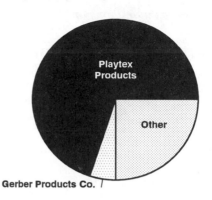

Gerber Products Co.

Shares are shown in percent. Baby-cups are also known as "sippy cups", a cross between a baby bottle and an adult cup. The market has annual sales of $300 million.

Playtex Products	70.0%
Gerber Products Co.	5.0
Other	25.0

Source: *Wall Street Journal*, August 19, 1997, p. B1.

★ 736 ★
Condoms (SIC 3089)

Leading Condom Brands Sold in Drugstores

Shares are shown based on units sold in drugstores.

Trojans	55.0%
Lifestyles	13.0
Sheik	7.0
Ramses	5.0
Other	20.0

Source: *America's Pharmacist*, July 1997, p. 51, from A.C. Nielsen.

★ 737 ★
Plastic Products (SIC 3089)

Plastic Mold Production by State

Shipments are shown in millions of dollars.

	($ mil.)	Share
Michigan	$ 687.8	21.99%
Ohio	387.6	12.39
Illinois	357.1	11.42

Continued on next page.

★ 737 ★ *Continued*
Plastic Products (SIC 3089)

Plastic Mold Production by State

Shipments are shown in millions of dollars.

	($ mil.)	Share
Pennsylvania	$ 234.7	7.50%
California	192.4	6.15
Wisconsin	184.1	5.89
Indiana	155.8	4.98
New Jersey	106.2	3.40
Minnesota	103.5	3.31
New York	88.0	2.81
Other	630.6	20.16

Source: *Plastics News*, March 21, 1998, p. 21, from Probe Economics.

SIC 31 - Leather and Leather Products

★ 738 ★

Footwear (SIC 3140)

Largest Casual Footwear Makers - 1997

Firms are ranked by sales in millions of dollars.

Rockport	$ 405
Easy Spirit	360
Dexter	300
Skechers	240
Airwalk	210
Hush Puppies	175
Keds	175
Vans	121
Lugz	90
Birkenstock	75
Tommy Hilfiger	75

Source: *Sportstyle*, May 1998, p. 24.

★ 739 ★

Footwear (SIC 3140)

Largest Rugged Footwear Makers - 1997

Firms are ranked by sales in millions of dollars.

Timberland	$ 434
Nike ACG	210
Wolverine	200
Rocky	91
Lacrosse	88
Hi-Tec USA	57
Reebok	42
Adidas	37
Vasque	34
Merrell	30

Source: *Sportstyle*, May 1998, p. 24.

SIC 32 - Stone, Clay, and Glass Products

★ 740 ★
Building Materials (SIC 3200)
Largest Building Material Makers

Firms are ranked by revenues in millions of dollars.

Owens-Illinois . . . . $ 4,680
Owens Corning 4,373
Corning 4,129
USG 2,874
Armstrong World Ind. 2,199

Source: *Fortune*, April 27, 1998, pp. F-45.

★ 741 ★
Ceramics (SIC 3200)
Advanced Ceramic Components by Type

Data show millions of dollars for 1996 and 2001.

	1996	2001
Electronic ceramics	$ 4,164	$ 6,290
Chemical processing/ environmental-related	1,261	1,658
Ceramic coatings	525	750
Structural ceramics	365	542

Source: *The American Ceramic Society Bulletin*, October 1997, p. 38, from Business Communications Co. Inc.

★ 742 ★
Glass (SIC 3211)
Flat Glass Demand - 2000

Demand is shown by segment. Data are projections based on total demand of 6.175 billion square feet.

Construction 52.1%
Motor vehicles 26.2
Specialty 18.1
Other 2.9

Source: *Ceramic Industry*, August 1997, p. 36, from The Freedonia Group Inc.

★ 743 ★
Glass Containers (SIC 3221)
Glass Beverage Container Demand - 1996

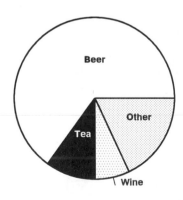

Distribution is shown based on total demand of 29 billion units.

Beer 65.0%
Tea 10.0
Wine 7.0
Other 18.0

Source: *Glass Industry*, September 1997, p. 16.

★ 744 ★
Glass (SIC 3229)

Largest Window Extruders - 1997

Sales are shown in millions of dollars.

Royal Group Technologies Ltd.	$ 230
Mikron Industries Inc.	130
Veka Inc.	92
Chelsea Building Products	63
CertainTeed Corp.	61

Source: *Plastics News*, June 15, 1998, p. 14.

★ 745 ★
Glassware (SIC 3231)

Top Selling Crystal Stemware Patterns - 1998

Share of sales are shown for fourth quarter ending January 31, 1998.

Lismore	10.08%
Araglin	3.92
Park Lane	3.32
Lady Anne	3.25
Stephanie	3.72
Arctic Lights	3.02
Hanover Gold	2.90
Flame D'Amore	2.15
Debut Gold	1.85
Monroe	1.61

Source: *HFN*, May 18, 1998, p. 35, from Maycomber Associates.

★ 746 ★
Cement (SIC 3241)

Leading Cement Companies - 1996

Market shares are shown in percent.

Holnam	12.5%
Lafarge	7.8
Southdown	6.0
Ash Grove Cement	5.7
Others	68.0

Source: *Washington Post*, August 29, 1997, p. K2, from National Association of Home Builders.

★ 747 ★
Cement (SIC 3241)

Top Cement Producers - 1997

Companies are ranked by capacity in millions of metric tons.

	(mil.)	Share
Holnam	11.7	12.7%
Lafarge	7.4	8.1
Southdown	6.6	7.2
Blue Circle	5.7	6.2
Ash Grove	5.5	6.0
Essroc	4.8	5.3
Lone Star Industries	3.6	4.0
California Portland	3.5	3.8

Source: *Wall Street Journal*, March 19, 1998, p. A3, from Portland Cement Association.

★ 748 ★
Ceramics (SIC 3250)

Ceramic Components Market - 1996

Shares are shown by type of component.

Electronic	65.9%
Chemical & environmental	20.0
Coatings	8.3
Structural	5.8

Source: *Ceramic Industry*, September 1997, p. 85.

★ 749 ★

Ceramic Tiles (SIC 3253)

Top Nations for Ceramic Imports - 1996

Data show tile imports to the United States in millions of square feet.

Italy	298
Mexico	222
Spain	175
Brazil	60
Venezuela	28
Japan	14
Other	83

Source: *Custom Builder*, January 1998, p. 59, from U.S. Department of Commerce.

★ 750 ★

Ceramics (SIC 3253)

Tile Sales by Category - 1996

Sales of $771 million are shown distributed in percent.

Glazed	74.4%
Unglazed	25.6

Source: *Ceramic Industry*, August 1997, p. 17, from U.S. Department of Commerce.

★ 751 ★

Refractories (SIC 3255)

Clay Refractory Sales - 1996

The value is shown in millions of dollars.

Bricks and shapes	$ 559,275
Unshaped clay refractories	329,747
Other refractory raw materials	23,950
Clay refractories	31,954

Source: *Ceramic Industry*, November 1997, p. 46.

★ 752 ★

Cookware (SIC 3263)

Cookware Sales by Type

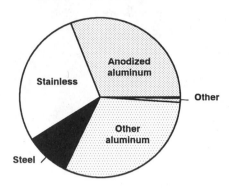

Data show sales at department stores.

Anodized aluminum	31.0%
Stainless	28.0
Steel	9.4
Other aluminum	30.5
Other	1.1

Source: *Discount Merchandiser*, May 1998, p. 104, from NPD Group.

★ 753 ★

Abrasives (SIC 3291)

Abrasives Use by Northeast Central

Sales are shown in millions of dollars.

Motor vehicles parts & accessories	$ 65.8
Motor vehicles & car bodies	47.9
Internal combustion engines	40.9
Construction machinery	27.1
Gray & ductile iron foundries	25.2

Source: *Industrial Distribution*, February 1998, p. 81.

SIC 33 - Primary Metal Industries

★ 754 ★

Metals (SIC 3300)

Largest Metals Firms

Firms are ranked by revenues in millions of dollars.

Alcoa	$ 13,482
Reynolds Metals	6,900
Inland Steel Industries	5,047
Bethlehem Steel	4,631
LTV	4,446

Source: *Fortune*, April 27, 1998, p. 56.

★ 755 ★

Steel (SIC 3312)

Steel Shipments by Market - 1997

Total shipments reached 79.11 million tons for the first nine months of the year. Distribution is shown in percent.

Service centers/distributors	20.5%
Automotive	13.5
Construction	13.4
Converting, processing	8.7
Containers, packaging	3.9
Oil, gas, petrochemical	3.0
Electrical equipment	2.3
Exports	2.3
Machinery	1.6
Appliances, utensils, cutlery	1.5
Other	28.2

Source: *New Steel*, January 1998, p. 50, from American Iron & Steel Institute.

★ 756 ★

Steel (SIC 3312)

Top Integrated Steel Producers - 1997

Production is shown in thousands of tons. AK Steel Corp. was a top producer but data were unavailable.

U.S. Steel Group	12,350
Bethlehem Steel Corp.	9,599
LTV Corp.	8,094
National Steel Corp.	6,527
Inland Steel Co.	5,814
Stelco Inc.	5,108
Dofasco Inc.	4,621
Weirton Steel Corp.	2,874
Rouge Industries, Inc.	2,837
Geneva Steel Co.	2,433
Algoma Steel Inc.	2,346
Acme Metals Inc.	750
Wheeling-Pittsburgh Steel Corp.	663

Source: *American Metal Market*, February 12, 1998, p. 1.

★ 757 ★

Steel (SIC 3312)

U.S. Steel Imports - 1997

Imports are shown in tons.

	Tons	Share
European Union	7,482,286	24.02%
Latin America	7,113,523	22.83
Asia	5,262,844	16.89
Canada	4,775,166	15.33
Oceania	576,750	1.85
Africa	388,339	1.25
Other European countries	5,557,678	17.84

Source: *New Steel*, April 1998, p. 12, from American Iron and Steel Institute.

★ 758 ★
Steel (SIC 3315)

Stainless Steel Market - 1997

Consumption is shown in net tons.

Sheet	1,734,651
Plate	282,509
Bar	251,499
Rod	113,052
Wire	47,329

Source: *Purchasing*, May 7, 1998, p. 44B, from Specialty Steel Industry of North America.

★ 759 ★
Steel (SIC 3316)

Leading Imported Steel Products - 1997

Imports are shown in tons.

Blooms, billets, slabs & ingots	6,358,322
Hot-rolled sheet	5,101,194
Cold-rolled sheet	3,690,586
Wire rod	2,236,642
Hot-dip-galvanized sheet and strip . . .	1,827,229
Coiled plate	1,550,666
Cut-to-length plate	1,387,943

Source: *New Steel*, April 1998, p. 14, from American Iron and Steel Institute.

★ 760 ★
Silver (SIC 3339)

Silver Market by End Use - 1997

Demand is shown by market.

Jewelry & flatware	33.0%
Photography	32.0
Electronics & industrial	30.0
Other	5.0

Source: From the Internet, http:// www.hotcopper.com.au/hottips1/_disc/0000005f.htm, December 2, 1997, p. 1, from CPM Group.

★ 761 ★
Aluminum (SIC 3341)

Who Uses Aluminum Mill Products - 1996

Production is shown by market.

Transportation	32.0%
Packaging	26.0
Construction	16.0
Consumer goods	8.0
Electrical	8.0
Machinery	7.0
Other	3.0

Source: *Purchasing*, November 6, 1997, p. 32B5, from Aluminum Association.

★ 762 ★
Silver (SIC 3341)

Silver Use in Photography - 1996

Data represent millions of ounces consumed.

	(mil.)	Share
Commercial photography	114.5	50.89%
Medical X-rays	52.9	23.51
Graphic arts	39.0	17.33
Dental & industrial X-rays	18.6	8.27

Source: *American Metal Market*, June 16, 1997, p. 11A, from CPM Group.

SIC 34 - Fabricated Metal Products

★ 763 ★

Metal Products (SIC 3420)

Largest Metal Product Producers

Firms are ranked by revenues in millions of dollars.

Gillette	$ 10,062
Crown Cork & Seal	8,495
Fortune Brands	7,001
Tyco International	6,598
ITW	5,220
Masco	3,760
Newell	3,234
Stanley Works	2,670
U.S. Industries	2,401
Ball	2,389

Source: *Fortune*, April 27, 1998, p. 56.

★ 764 ★

Cutlery (SIC 3421)

Leading Cutlery Makers

Market shares are shown in percent.

Zwilling J.A. Henckels	65.0%
Others	35.0

Source: *Bangkok Post*, May 5, 1998, p. 8.

★ 765 ★

Razor Blades (SIC 3421)

Best-Selling Razors

Market shares are shown based on unit sales for the year ended December 28, 1997.

Gillette Sensor Excel	29.6%
Schick Silk Effects	12.9
Schick Tracer FX	10.9
Gillette Sensor	10.1
Gillette Sensor for Women	8.2
Personal Touch	5.8
Schick Tracer	5.0

Gillette Atra Plus	4.6%
Gillette Trac II Plus	4.5
Other	8.4

Source: *Supermarket Business*, March 1998, p. 87, from Information Resources Inc.

★ 766 ★

Razor Blades (SIC 3421)

Disposable Razor Market - 1997

Shares of the $420 million market are shown in percent.

Gillette Custom Plus	14.9%
Bic Disposable	13.3
Gillette Good News	11.9
Schick Slim Twin	11.5
Gillette Good News Plus	8.9
Gillette Daisy Plus	7.4
Gillette Good News Pivot	4.1
Bic Twin Select Sensor	3.5
Gillette Microtrack	2.8
Private label	6.8
Other	14.9

Source: *Supermarket Business*, April 1998, p. 59, from Information Resources Inc.

★ 767 ★

Razor Blades (SIC 3421)

Leading Brands of Razor Blades - 1997

Shares are shown based on sales for the 52-week period ended October 12, 1997.

Gillette Sensor Excel	31.6%
Schick Silk Effects	12.2
Gillete Sensor	10.6
Schick Tracer FX	9.7
Gillette Sensor for Women	8.3

Continued on next page.

★ 767 ★ *Continued*
Razor Blades (SIC 3421)

Leading Brands of Razor Blades - 1997

Shares are shown based on sales for the 52-week period ended October 12, 1997.

Gillette Atra Plus	5.9%
Gillette Trac II	5.9
Personal Touch	4.5
Schick Tracer	3.9
Gillette Sensor Excel for Women	3.3
Other	4.1

Source: *Discount Merchandiser*, January 1998, p. 70, from Information Resources Inc.

★ 768 ★
Razor Blades (SIC 3421)

Top Razor Blade Makers - 1998

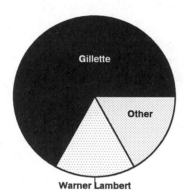

Market shares are shown for the first two months of the year.

Gillette	67.0%
Warner Lambert	16.0
Other	17.0

Source: *Wall Street Journal*, April 14, 1998, p. B1.

★ 769 ★
Razor Blades (SIC 3421)

Top Refill Razor Blade Brands - 1997

Shares are shown based on a $638 million market.

Gillette Sensor	23.9%
Gillette Sensor Excel	22.4
Gillette Atra Plus	7.1
Gillette Sensor for Women	6.4

Gillette Sensor Excel for Women	5.0%
Shick Tracer FX	5.0
Gillette Trac II Plus	4.8
Schick Silk Effects	4.3
Gillette Trac II	3.7
Private label	4.2
Other	13.2

Source: *Supermarket Business*, April 1998, p. 59, from Information Resources Inc.

★ 770 ★
Scissors (SIC 3421)

Leading Scissor Brands - 1997

Shares are shown based on sales for the 13 weeks ended March 29, 1997.

Fiskars	45.3%
DuraSharp	7.2
Cut-Rite	6.4
Singer	4.1
Kane	3.7
Crayola	2.5
Other	30.8

Source: *Supermarket Business*, July 1997, p. 47, from A.C. Nielsen.

★ 771 ★
Tool Boxes (SIC 3469)

Tool Box Sales

Dollar shares are shown in percent.

Portable	58.0%
Workbench	18.0
Combo	7.0
Cabinet	5.0
Tool set	5.0

Source: *Do-It-Yourself Retailing*, June 1998, p. 77, from Vista Sales and Marketing.

★ 772 ★
Guns (SIC 3484)

Largest Pistol Producers

Data show unit production.

Smith & Wesson	241,906
Sturm, Ruger & Co.	197,489
Beretta USA Corp.	158,858

Continued on next page.

★ 772 ★ *Continued*
Guns (SIC 3484)

Largest Pistol Producers

Data show unit production.

Colt Mfg. Co.	118,462
Lorcin Engineering	83,463
Arms Technology Inc.	51,351
Phoenix Arms	48,381
Davis Industries	45,171
Daniel Wayne	35,711
Arcadia Machine & Tool	23,413

Source: From the Internet, http:// www.afn.org, January 1997, p. 1.

★ 773 ★
Guns (SIC 3484)

Largest Revolver Producers

Data show unit production.

Smith & Wesson	258,223
Sturm, Ruger & Co.	148,439
Colt Mfg. Co. Inc.	40,085
North American Arms	34,365
H&R 1871, Inc.	10,641
Mil Inc.	893

Source: From the Internet, http:// www.afn.org, January 1997, p. 1.

★ 774 ★
Valves (SIC 3491)

Top Markets for Industrial Valves - 1998

The market is shown in percent.

Chemicals	17.44%
Water and sewage	17.20
Petroleum production	12.71
Petroleum refining	10.81
Power generation	10.71
Pulp & paper	7.01
Oil & gas transmission	5.61
Commercial construction	5.01
Gas distribution	2.4

Source: *In Tech*, February 1998, p. 18, from Valve Manufacturers Association of America.

★ 775 ★
Conveyors (SIC 3496)

Conveyor Sales - Northeast Central

Sales are shown in millions of dollars.

Farm machinery & equipment	$ 53.2
Meat packing plants	32.5
U.S. Postal Service	24.2
Concrete work	16.8
Iron ores	14.8

Source: *Industrial Distribution*, March 1998, p. 81, from Industrial Market Information Inc.

★ 776 ★
Powdered Metal (SIC 3499)

Top Markets for Powdered Metal - 1996

Sales are shown in percent.

Automotive	69.0%
Recreation, tools, and hobby	11.4
Household appliances	6.1
Industrial motors/controls, hydraulics	3.7
Hardware	2.3
Business machines	1.2
Others	6.3

Source: *WARD'S Auto World*, September 1997, p. 78, from Powder Metallurgy Parts Association.

SIC 35 - Industry Machinery and Equipment

★ 777 ★
Industrial Equipment (SIC 3500)

Commercial/Industrial Equipment Market - 1996

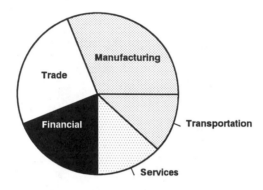

The market reached sales of $7.1 billion.

Manufacturing	31.0%
Trade	25.0
Financial	19.0
Services	13.0
Transportation	12.0

Source: *Electronic Business*, November 1997, p. 25, from Freedonia Group.

★ 778 ★
Industrial Equipment (SIC 3500)

Largest Farm/Industrial Equipment Makers

Firms are ranked by revenue in millions of dollars.

Caterpillar	$ 18,925
Deere	12,791
Dresser Industries	7,458
Ingersoll-Rand	7,103
Case	6,024
American Standard	6,008
Cummins Engine	5,625

Black & Decker	$ 4,941
Dover	4,548
Parker Hannifin	4,091

Source: *Fortune*, April 27, 1998, pp. F-53.

★ 779 ★
Lawn and Garden Equipment (SIC 3524)

Outdoor Power Equipment Shipments

Types of equipment are shown ranked by thousands of units shipped. Figures are projected for 1997 and 1998.

	1996	1997	1998
Walk-behind power mowers	5,355	5,416	5,549
Lawn tractors, front engine	1,123	1,155	1,217
Garden tillers	316	304	315
Garden tractors, riding	194	174	185
Riding mowers, rear engine	130	101	90

Source: *Discount Store News*, September 1, 1997, p. 27, from Outdoor Power Equipment Institute.

★ 780 ★
Lawn and Garden Equipment (SIC 3524)

Popular Types of Trimmers

Data show units sold in percent.

Hedge trimmers	41.0%
String trimmers	38.0
Edgers	21.0

Source: *Do-It-Yourself Retailing*, July 1997, p. 90, from Vista Information Services.

★ 781 ★

Lawn and Garden Equipment (SIC 3524)

Push Mower Market

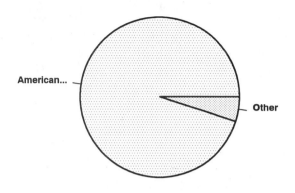

Shares are shown in percent.

American Lawn Mower Co. 95.0%
Other 5.0

Source: *Wall Street Journal*, August 7, 1997, p. B1.

★ 782 ★

Lawn and Garden Equipment (SIC 3524)

Small Tractor Sales

Data show retail sales.

	1996	1997
<40 HP	48,138	52,983
40 to 99 HP	41,213	45,744
100 to 139	21,217	23,956
4wd	4,427	5,908

Source: *Diesel Progress*, April 1998, p. 16, from Equipment Manufacturers Institute.

★ 783 ★

Construction Equipment (SIC 3531)

Construction Machinery Sales in North America

Data show unit sales.

	1997	1998	Share
Material handling/ lifting machinery . .	186,185	192,655	36.09%
Earthmoving machinery	144,340	149,275	27.97
Farm machinery and other	187,000	191,825	35.94

Source: *Diesel Progress*, December 1997, p. 15, from Yengst Associates Inc.

★ 784 ★

Construction Equipment (SIC 3531)

Skid-Steer Loader Market

Market shares are estimated in percent.

Melroe 40.0%
Case 16.0
Holland 16.0
Mustang 14.0
Other 14.0

Source: *Diesel Progress*, January 1998, p. 8.

★ 785 ★

Construction Equipment (SIC 3536)

Leading Boom Lift Producers

Market shares are shown in percent.

JLG Industries 41.0%
Genie 17.0
Grove Manlift 15.0
Snorkel Economy 11.0
Others 16.0

Source: *Wall Street Journal*, August 21, 1997, p. B4, from Midland Walwyn Capital Inc. and IDD Tradeline International.

★ 786 ★

Construction Equipment (SIC 3536)

Leading Scissor Lift Producers

Market shares are shown in percent.

JLG Industries 24.0%
Skyjack 19.0
Upright 15.0
Grove Manlift 9.0
Snorkel Economy 8.0
Mayville Engineering 8.0
Others 17.0

Source: *Wall Street Journal*, August 21, 1997, p. B4, from Midland Walwyn Capital Inc. and IDD Tradeline International.

★ 787 ★

Cranes and Hoists (SIC 3536)

Crane Market - North America

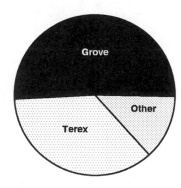

Grove

Other

Terex

Shares of the market are shown in percent.

Grove 50.0%
Terex 35.0
Other 13.0

Source: *Wall Street Journal*, September 30, 1997, p. B4, from Baseline and company reports.

★ 788 ★

Machine Tools (SIC 3540)

Top Markets for Cutting Tools & Abrasives - 1997

Data show projected consumption in millions of dollars.

Motor vehicle parts & accessories . . . . $ 398.2
Construction machinery 294.2
Industrial machinery . . . . $ 282.2
Motor vehicles & car bodies 231.2
Aircraft engines & engine parts 218.8
Farm machinery & equipment 197.7
Internal combustion engines 157.7
Special dies, tools, jigs & fixtures 148.5
Metal cutting machine tools 134.1
Aircraft 132.4

Source: *Industrial Distribution*, December 1997, p. 54, from Industrial Market Information.

★ 789 ★

Drills (SIC 3546)

Corded Drill Sales

Sales are shown in percent.

Regular corded drills 75.0%
Hammer drills 17.0
Other drills 8.0

Source: *Do-It-Yourself Retailing*, June 1998, p. 77, from Vista Sales and Marketing.

★ 790 ★

Food Machinery (SIC 3559)

Beverage Machinery Demand in Mexico

There are a number of manufacturers in the beverage industry, including 220 soda bottlers and 3,000 bottled water producers. Demand for beverage processing equipment is shown in percent.

Coca-Cola 18.9%
Cerveceria Modelo 14.9
Pepsi Cola 9.8
Cerveceria Cuauhtemoc-Moctezuma 9.1
Bonafont 5.5
Mundet 4.9
Electropura 2.9
Santa Maria 2.5
Other bottled water firms 6.1
Other soda bottlers 25.2

Source: *National Trade Data Bank*, October 22, 1997, p. ISA970901.

★ 791 ★

Plastics Machinery (SIC 3559)

Plastics Machinery Sales

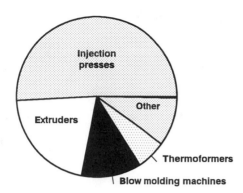

Sales are estimated to grow from $1.55 billion in 1996 to $3.15 billion in 2006. Data are shown for 1996.

Injection presses	51.0%
Extruders	21.0
Blow molding machines	12.0
Thermoformers	6.0
Other	10.0

Source: *Plastics News*, January 26, 1998, p. 3, from Freedonia Group Inc.

★ 792 ★

Plastics Machinery (SIC 3559)

Rotomolders Market - North America

Distribution is shown based on $1.2 billion in sales for 1997.

Proprietary	62.40%
Custom	30.10
Captive	4.35
Other	3.15

Source: *Plastics News*, October 18, 1997, p. 11.

★ 793 ★

Power Transmission (SIC 3568)

Power Transmision Sales - Northeast Central

Sales are shown in millions of dollars.

Paper mills	$ 328.1
Plastics products	237.1
Blast furnaces & steel mills	222.7
Motor vehicle parts & accessories	172.7
Industrial organic chemicals	144.3

Source: *Industrial Distribution*, April 1998, p. 75, from Industrial Market Information Inc.

★ 794 ★

Business Machines (SIC 3570)

Leading Federal Contractors of Office Machines

Shares are shown based on $120,495,000 in purchases by the U.S. government.

Federal Data Corp.	13.16%
Xerox Corp.	13.15
Pulsar Data Systems, Inc.	9.09
Pitney Bowes Inc.	8.45
Minolta Corp.	4.94
Eastman Kodak Co.	3.70
Loral Corp.	3.22
Canon USA Inc.	2.96
Sin Do System Co. Ltd.	2.24
Daimler-Benz AG	1.45
Others	37.64

Source: From the Internet, http:// www.govexec.com/ procure/articles/0896opgb.html, September 24, 1997, p. 3.

★ 795 ★

Computers (SIC 3571)

Business PC Leaders - 1997

Market shares are shown in percent.

Compaq	15.7%
Dell	12.8
IBM	9.5
Hewlett-Packard	8.0
Toshiba	5.6
Others	48.4

Source: *Business Week*, May 25, 1998, p. 56, from Dataquest Inc.

★ 796 ★

Computers (SIC 3571)

Commercial Desktop PC Market - Canada

Market shares are shown for the fourth quarter of 1996.

IBM	20.3%
Compaq	17.7
Dell	9.4
Apple	7.7
Hewlett-Packard	4.9
Digital	3.6
Seanix	3.4
Sidus	3.4
AST	2.9
NEC	1.6
Packard Bell	0.3
Others	25.0

Source: From the Internet, http:// www.bizlink.com, April 1997, p. 1.

★ 797 ★

Computers (SIC 3571)

Computer Damages - 1997

A total of 1.5 million desktops and laptops PCs were stolen, damaged or destroyed in 1997, with losses of more than $2.5 billion.

Accidents	35.0%
Theft	26.0
Power surge	18.0
Lightning	6.0
Shipping/transit	2.0

Water/flood	2.0%
Fire	1.0
Other	10.0

Source: *USA TODAY*, June 1, 1998, p. B1, from Safeware.

★ 798 ★

Computers (SIC 3571)

Consumer Desktop PC Market - Canada

Market shares are shown for the fourth quarter of 1996.

IBM	9.9%
Compaq	3.4
Apple	6.5
Dell	0.8
AST	7.4
Seanix	2.4
Hewlett-Packard	0.3
Packard Bell	4.6
NEC	3.2
Sidus	0.9
Other	60.7

Source: From the Internet, http:// www.bizlink.com, April 1997, p. 1.

★ 799 ★

Computers (SIC 3571)

Corporate PC Sales

Data show share of PC sales to Fortune 1000 companies as of May 1998.

IBM	23.0%
Compaq	20.0
Dell	16.0
H-P	15.0
Clones	9.0
Other	17.0

Source: *Wall Street Journal*, June 18, 1998, p. B8, from Computer Intelligence.

★ 800 ★
Computers (SIC 3571)

Desktop PC Market by Shipments

Shares are shown based on unit shipments for the second quarters of both 1996 and 1997.

	2Q 1996	2Q 1997
Compaq	10.1%	12.0%
IBM	8.0	8.1
Hewlett-Packard	4.7	6.4
Dell	4.1	5.7
Packard Bell/NEC	NA	5.5
Other	73.1	62.3

Source: *VAR Business*, October 1, 1997, p. 16, from Dataquest Inc.

★ 801 ★
Computers (SIC 3571)

Education PC Leaders - 1997

Market shares are shown in percent.

Apple	27.2%
Compaq	13.2
Dell	10.7
Gateway	7.8
IBM	6.9
Others	34.2

Source: *Business Week*, May 25, 1998, p. 56, from Dataquest Inc.

★ 802 ★
Computers (SIC 3571)

Handheld Computer Market - 1996

Shares are shown in percent.

Palm Computing (3COM)	62.0%
Hewlett-Packard	16.0
Apple	7.0
Casio	3.0
Compaq	1.0
Other	11.0

Source: *Computer Reseller News*, October 13, 1997, p. 153, from Dataquest Inc.

★ 803 ★
Computers (SIC 3571)

Home PC Leaders - 1997

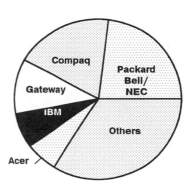

Market shares are shown in percent.

Packard Bell/NEC	23.3%
Compaq	18.8
Gateway	11.1
IBM	7.0
Acer	5.9
Others	33.9

Source: *Business Week*, May 25, 1998, p. 56, from Dataquest Inc.

★ 804 ★
Computers (SIC 3571)

Largest Markets for Computers - 1997

Consumption is shown for the first six months of the year.

Business	55.0%
Home	33.0
Government	7.0
Education	5.0

Source: *Investor's Business Daily*, March 25, 1998, p. A8, from International Data Corp.

★ 805 ★
Computers (SIC 3571)

Leading Desktop Computers

Company shares are shown based on sales for the third quarter of 1997. Figures refer to the small and midsize market.

Compaq	12.0%
Acer	11.0

Continued on next page.

★ 805 ★ *Continued*
Computers (SIC 3571)

Leading Desktop Computers

Company shares are shown based on sales for the third quarter of 1997. Figures refer to the small and midsize market.

Dell	5.0%
Apple	4.0
Hewlett-Packard	4.0
IBM	4.0
Gateway	3.0
In-house	38.0
Other	19.0

Source: *Computer Reseller News*, November 10, 1997, p. 69.

★ 806 ★
Computers (SIC 3571)

Leading Educational PC Vendors - 1997

Shares are shown for the first quarter of 1997.

Apple	29.6%
Dell	9.6
Compaq	9.1
IBM	7.3
Gateway 2000	6.6
Other	37.8

Source: *Newsweek*, August 18, 1997, p. 27, from PC Data and Dataquest Inc.

★ 807 ★
Computers (SIC 3571)

Leading Handheld Computer Makers

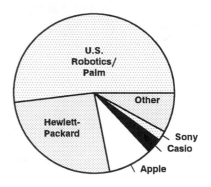

Shares of the 700,000 unit market are shown in percent.

U.S. Robotics/Palm	52.0%
Hewlett-Packard	26.0
Apple	9.0
Casio	3.0
Sony	2.0
Other	8.0

Source: *St. Louis Post-Dispatch*, September 24, 1997, p. 5C, from Dataquest Inc.

★ 808 ★
Computers (SIC 3571)

Leading Notebook Computers

Company shares are shown based on sales for the third quarter of 1997. Figures refer to the small and midsize market.

Toshiba	29.0%
IBM	9.0
Acer	8.0
Compaq	8.0
Apple	4.0
AST	4.0
Dell	4.0
Fujitsu	4.0
In-house	6.0
Other	24.0

Source: *Computer Reseller News*, November 10, 1997, p. 69.

★ 809 ★
Computers (SIC 3571)

Leading PC Companies

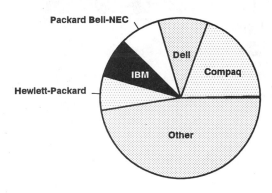

Shares are shown in percent.

Compaq	19.1%
Dell	10.3
Packard Bell-NEC	8.2
IBM	8.0
Hewlett-Packard	7.1
Other	47.3

Source: *USA TODAY*, November 25, 1997, p. B1, from Dataquest Inc.

★ 810 ★
Computers (SIC 3571)

Leading Vendors of Unix Servers - 1996

Data show units shipped.

	Units	Share
Hewlett-Packard	105,758	21.0%
Sun Microsystems	100,974	20.0
IBM	87,375	17.3
Compaq	46,576	9.2
Digital	34,509	6.8

Source: *InternetWeek*, September 8, 1997, p. 8, from Gartner Group.

★ 811 ★
Computers (SIC 3571)

Macintosh Computer Manufacturers

Data show shares for the last quarter of 1996 and the first two quarters of 1997.

	4Q 1996	1Q 1997	2Q 1997
Apple Computer	75.37%	71.15%	80.98%
Power Computing	10.31	12.20	9.73
Motorola	8.23	9.34	5.10
Umax	6.09	7.31	4.18

Source: *Wall Street Journal*, September 3, 1997, p. A3, from Dataquest Inc.

★ 812 ★
Computers (SIC 3571)

Network Computer Makers - 1997

Market shares are shown based on shipments.

Wyse	28.5%
IBM	19.5
Network Computing Devices	13.8
Tektronix	12.8
Hewlett-Packard	10.4
Other	15.3

Source: *Investor's Business Daily*, April 8, 1998, p. A8, from International Data Corp.

★ 813 ★
Computers (SIC 3571)

PC Laptop Market

Shares are shown for the third quarters of 1996 and 1997.

	3Q 1996	3Q 1997
Toshiba	26.1%	21.2%
Compaq	9.3	15.7
IBM	11.5	12.4
Dell	4.1	6.1
Acer	8.2	5.0
Packard Bell NEC	5.0	4.4
Fujitsu	1.9	3.4

Continued on next page.

★ 813 ★ *Continued*
Computers (SIC 3571)

PC Laptop Market

Shares are shown for the third quarters of 1996 and 1997.

	3Q 1996	3Q 1997
Hitachi	2.6%	3.3%
Micron	3.7	3.2
Gateway	2.0	2.8
Other	25.6	22.5

Source: *Los Angeles Times*, November 17, 1997, p. D6, from International Data Corp.

★ 814 ★
Computers (SIC 3571)

PC Leaders - 1998

Shares are shown for the first quarter of the year.

	Units (000)	Share
Compaq	1,378	17.3%
Dell	941	11.8
Gateway	654	8.2
Packard Bell-NEC	630	7.9
IBM	626	7.9

Source: *Wall Street Journal*, April 27, 1998, p. B6, from International Data Corp.

★ 815 ★
Computers (SIC 3571)

RISC-Based Systems Manufacturers - 1996

Companies are ranked by thousands of units shipped. RISC stands for reduced instruction set computer.

Sun Microsystems	315
Hewlett-Packard	155
Silicon Graphics	69
IBM	67
Digital	55
Other	179

Source: *Computer Reseller News*, October 13, 1997, p. 3.

★ 816 ★
Computers (SIC 3571)

Top Computer Firms - 1997

Firms are ranked by revenues from information technology equipment, software, services and components. Compaq and Digital are expected to merge.

IBM	$ 78.5
Compaq/Digital	37.5
Hewlett-Packard	37.0
NEC	35.0
Fujitsu	30.0
Hitachi	23.5

Source: *USA TODAY*, January 27, 1998, p. B1, from International Data Corp. and company reports.

★ 817 ★
Computers (SIC 3571)

Top Computer Shippers - 1997

Market shares are shown based on unit shipments.

Compaq	16.0%
Dell	9.4
Packard Bell-NEC	8.8
IBM	8.7
Gateway 2000	6.9
Others	50.2

Source: *Chicago Tribune*, January 27, 1998, p. 5, from Bloomberg News, Commodity Systems Inc., *Market Guide*, and Securities Data Co.

★ 818 ★
Computers (SIC 3571)

Top Markets for Network Computers - Canada

Data show shipments in thousands of units for 1996, 1998, and 2000.

	1996	1998	2000
Consumer	100.0	7,500.0	70,500.0
Commercial	383.1	3,444.7	6,768.4
Educational	2.0	292.3	940.0

Source: *Computing Canada*, February 2, 1998, p. 26, from Zona Research Inc.

★ 819 ★
Computers (SIC 3571)

Top Notebook Makers - 1997

Market shares are shown in percent.

Toshiba	19.6%
IBM	11.8
Compaq	10.4
Fujitsu	6.6
Acer	6.4
NEC	6.0
Dell	4.3
Other	34.9

Source: *Investor's Business Daily*, April 23, 1998, p. A8, from Dataquest Inc.

★ 820 ★
Computers (SIC 3571)

Top School Computer Makers

Market shares are shown in percent.

Apple	53.0%
IBM	16.0
Compaq	4.0
Dell	2.0
Gateway 2000	2.0
Other	23.0

Source: *Electronic School*, January 1998, p. A8.

★ 821 ★
Workstations (SIC 3571)

Leading Manufacturers of Workstation Based Systems - 1997

Shares are shown in percent.

Sun	37.1%
Hewlett-Packard	19.2
IBM	14.0
Compaq	8.0
Digital	7.8
Other	13.9

Source: *PC Week*, December 22, 1997, p. 3, from Computer Intelligence.

★ 822 ★
Workstations (SIC 3571)

Leading Workstations - 1997

Company shares are shown based on sales for the third quarter of 1997. Figures refer to the small and midsize market.

Compaq	11.0%
Acer	9.0
Hewlett-Packard	9.0
Sun	9.0
IBM	6.0
Dell	3.0
Digital	3.0
Apple	2.0
In-house	36.0
Other	12.0

Source: *Computer Reseller News*, November 10, 1997, p. 69.

★ 823 ★
Workstations (SIC 3571)

NT Workstation Producers - 1997

Shares are shown based on 61,384 units shipped during the first quarter of 1997.

Hewlett-Packard	37.0%
Compaq Computer	29.0
Digital Equipment	14.0
Intergraph	13.0
Other	7.0

Source: *Informationweek*, July 28, 1997, p. 26, from Dataquest Inc.

★ 824 ★

Computer Data Storage (SIC 3572)

AC Drive Market

The North American market is shown by type of system. The entire market, including hardware, software and services is expected to reach $1.16 billion in 1998.

Product 77.5%
Package 14.0
System 8.5

Source: *Design News*, February 2, 1998, p. 44, from Automation Research Corp.

★ 825 ★

Computer Data Storage (SIC 3572)

Disk Drive Leaders - 1997

Market shares are shown in percent.

IBM 23.9%
Seagate 23.1
Quantum 15.5
Western Digital 13.3
Fujitsu 7.1
Maxtor 4.5
Samsung 2.3

Source: *Investor's Business Daily*, June 18, 1998, p. 8A, from DiskTrend Inc.

★ 826 ★

Computer Data Storage (SIC 3572)

Flash Memory Card Producers - 1996

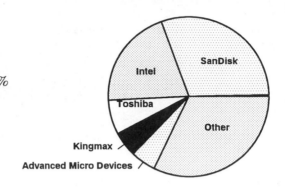

Shares are shown based on shipments.

SanDisk 30.0%
Intel 20.0
Toshiba 7.0
Kingmax 5.4
Advanced Micro Devices 5.2
Other 32.4

Source: *Investor's Business Daily*, November 17, 1997, p. A10, from Disk/Trend Inc.

★ 827 ★

Computer Data Storage (SIC 3572)

Hard Disk Drive Producers - 1996

Shares are shown based on a total of 106 million units shipped in 1996.

Seagate 28.0%
Quantum 23.0
Western Digital 18.0
IBM 10.0
Maxter 5.0
Other 16.0

Source: *Computerworld*, June 16, 1997, p. 63, from TrendFocus, Inc.

★ 828 ★
Computer Data Storage (SIC 3572)

Largest CD-ROM Drive Producers

Market shares are shown for the fourth quarter of the year.

Toshiba	15.0%
Mitsui	12.0
Goldstar	10.0
Panasonic/Matsushita	9.0
Hitachi	8.0
NEC	7.0
Samsung	7.0
Sony	7.0
Others	25.0

Source: *E-Media Professional*, June 1998, p. 12.

★ 829 ★
Computer Data Storage (SIC 3572)

Mainframe Data Storage Market - 1997

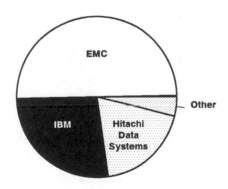

Shares are estimated.

EMC	50.0%
IBM	27.0
Hitachi Data Systems	19.0
Other	4.0

Source: *Computerworld*, November 24, 1997, p. 3, from Meta Group Inc.

★ 830 ★
Computer Data Storage (SIC 3572)

Removable Storage Drive Market

Data show the low-end removable storage drive market. Figures are in thousands of units.

	1996	1998	Share
Iomega/Zip	3,633	13,031	87.49%
LS-120/SuperDisk	91	1,414	9.49
Sony HiFD	NA	273	1.83
Others	433	177	1.19

Source: *Electronic News*, June 8, 1998, p. 50, from International Data Corp.

★ 831 ★
Computer Data Storage (SIC 3572)

Top Computer Disk Drive Makers - 1997

Market shares are shown based on shipments.

Seagate Technology	23.5%
Quantum	20.3
Western Digital	18.8
IBM	11.3
Fujitsu	8.6
Maxtor	6.5
Other	11.0

Source: *Investor's Business Daily*, March 4, 1998, p. A8, from International Data Corp.

★ 832 ★
Computer Data Storage (SIC 3572)

Top Unix Storage System Companies - 1997

Companies are shown ranked by revenue in millions of dollars.

	Revenue ($ mil.)	Share
Sun Microsystems	$ 1,672	18.6%
IBM	1,357	15.1
Hewlett-Packard	1,198	13.3
EMC	1,172	13.0

Continued on next page.

★ 832 ★ *Continued*
Computer Data Storage (SIC 3572)

Top Unix Storage System Companies - 1997

Companies are shown ranked by revenue in millions of dollars.

	Revenue ($ mil.)	Share
Digital Equipment	$ 688	7.6%
Compaq	261	2.9
NCR	259	2.9
Other	2,790	26.6

Source: *InfoWorld*, October 20, 1997, p. 6, from International Data Corp.

★ 833 ★
Computer Peripherals (SIC 3575)

Best Selling 17-Inch Monitors for VARs

Distribution is shown in percent, based on sales by Value Added Resellers.

ViewSonic	24.0%
CTX	17.0
MAG Innovision	16.0
NEC	11.0
Samsung	11.0
Sony	10.0
Panasonic	6.0
Mitsubishi	5.0

Source: *VAR Business*, September 1, 1997, p. 36.

★ 834 ★
Computer Peripherals (SIC 3577)

Ink-Jet Cartridge Replacement Market - 1998

The replacement market for ink-jet cartridges is expected to reach $6.5 billion in revenues. This market has become highly competitive as companies that specialize in replacement parts fight printer companies for market share. Data show estimated shares as a percentage of all units sold.

Manufacturers' brands	78.0%
Other	22.0

Source: *New York Times*, April 20, 1998, p. C5, from CAP Ventures.

★ 835 ★
Computer Peripherals (SIC 3577)

Largest Computer Peripheral Makers

Firms are ranked by revenues in millions of dollars.

Seagate Technology	$ 8,940
Quantum	5,319
Western Digital	4,178
EMC	2,938
Lexmark International	2,494

Source: *Fortune*, April 27, 1998, pp. F-47.

★ 836 ★
Computer Peripherals (SIC 3577)

Largest Monitor Makers

Companies are ranked by revenues in millions of dollars.

ViewSonic	$ 708.0
NECT	662.0
Sony	448.0
CTX	306.0
Mag InnoVision	262.0

Source: *Computer Reseller News*, April 20, 1998, p. 120, from Stanford Resources Inc.

★ 837 ★
Computer Peripherals (SIC 3577)

LCD Equipment Market by Segment

The market is estimated in millions of dollars. LCD stands for liquid crystal displays.

	1997 ($ mil.)	2003 ($ mil.)
Portable computers	$ 7,400	$ 10,400
Desktop monitors	397	7,500
Handheld computers	119	715
Camcorders	379	421
Digital still cameras	131	313
GPS (aftermarket)	145	290
Financial terminals	136	255

Source: *Computer Reseller News*, January 26, 1998, p. 91, from Stanford Resources.

★ 838 ★
Computer Peripherals (SIC 3577)
LOM Leaders - 1997

Data show the leading makers of LAN on motherboard (LOM) products. Total shipments reached 10.2 million units.

AMD	27.0%
Texas Instruments	25.0
Intel	24.0
3Com	21.0
Other	3.0

Source: *Investor's Business Daily*, April 16, 1998, p. A9, from International Data Corp.

★ 839 ★
Computer Peripherals (SIC 3577)
Multifunction Peripheral Producers - 1996

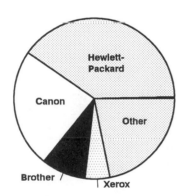

Market shares are shown based on 1.4 million units.

Hewlett-Packard	40.0%
Canon	24.0
Brother	9.0
Xerox	5.0
Other	22.0

Source: *Investor's Business Daily*, January 22, 1998, p. A8, from CAP Ventures Inc. and MFP Report.

★ 840 ★
Computer Peripherals (SIC 3577)
Suspension Assembly Producers

Market shares are shown in percent.

Hutchinson Technology	70%
Other	30

Source: *Forbes*, January 26, 1998, p. 85.

★ 841 ★
Computer Peripherals (SIC 3577)
Toner Cartridge Market - 1998

The market for replacement cartridges has become heated because of the growing number of computer printers. Companies that specialize in replacement parts are fighting printer manufacturers for market share. Data show estimated shares as a percentage of all units sold.

Manufacturers' brands	73.0%
Others	27.0

Source: *New York Times*, April 20, 1998, p. C5, from CAP Ventures.

★ 842 ★
Computer Printers (SIC 3577)
Largest Computer Printer Makers - 1997

Companies are ranked by revenues in millions of dollars.

Hewlett-Packard	$ 4,300
Epson	720
Canon USA	590
Lexmark	460
Xerox	397
Okidata	266
Apple	227
IBM	207
Tektronix	133
Genicom	112

Source: *Computer Reseller News*, April 20, 1998, p. 118.

★ 843 ★
Computer Printers (SIC 3577)

Leading Manufacturers of Page Printers - 1996

Market shares are shown in percent. Companies shipped 2.8 million units in 1996.

Hewlett-Packard	62.8%
Lexmark	7.8
Okidata	6.8
NEC	6.4
Brother	4.7
Other	11.5

Source: *Purchasing*, August 14, 1997, p. 94, from Dataquest Inc.

★ 844 ★
Computer Printers (SIC 3577)

Top Computer Printers

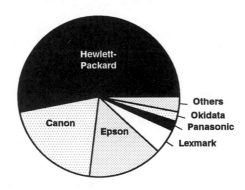

Market shares are shown as of December 1997.

Hewlett-Packard	53.0%
Canon	20.0
Epson	15.0
Lexmark	5.0
Panasonic	2.0
Okidata	2.0
Others	3.0

Source: *Investor's Business Daily*, February 25, 1998, p. A8, from Computer Intelligence InfoCorp.

★ 845 ★
Automated Teller Machines (SIC 3578)

Largest Independent ATM Companies

Companies are ranked by number of automated teller machines (ATMs) operated or serviced.

Access Cash International Inc.	3,500
McLane Co.	3,500
Card Capture Services Inc.	3,400
Hanco Systems Inc.	2,000
Nationwide Money Services	1,200

Source: *Wall Street Journal*, December 4, 1997, p. B1, from *Bank Network News* and company reports.

★ 846 ★
Postage Meters (SIC 3579)

Leading Manufacturers of Postage Meters

Shares are shown in percent.

Pitney Bowes	85.0%
Other	15.0

Source: *Purchasing*, August 14, 1997, p. 88.

★ 847 ★
Heating and Cooling (SIC 3585)

Gas Furnace Leaders - 1996

Shares are shown based on shipments of 2,871,256 units.

Carrier	21.0%
Goodman	14.0
Rheem	14.0
International Comfort Products	11.0
Lennox	10.0
Trane	10.0
York	9.0
Nordyne	4.0
Others	7.0

Source: *Appliance*, September 1997, p. 82.

Heating and Cooling (SIC 3585)

Heating Replacement Market in Indiana

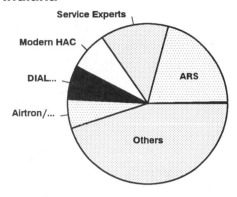

The market is shown based on heating replacement permits for single-family homes.

ARS	20.5%
Service Experts	13.8
Modern HAC	7.5
DIAL ONE Hoosier	6.8
Airtron/GroupMAC	5.8
Others	45.6

Source: *Air Conditioning, Heating & Refrigeration News*, June 22, 1998, p. 3.

★ 849 ★
Heating and Cooling (SIC 3585)

Home Cooling Market

There are 66.6 million single-family homes. Data show the types of air conditioning.

Central air conditioning	47.0%
Window units	25.0
None	28.0

Source: *Air Conditioning, Heating & Refrigeration News*, April 13, 1998, p. 16.

★ 850 ★
Heating and Cooling (SIC 3585)

Room Air Conditioner Makers - 1996

Shares are shown based on shipments of 4,525,000 units.

Fedders	27.0%
Electrolux (Frigidaire)	22.0
Whirlpool	20.0%
Matsushita	7.0
Amana	5.0
Carrier	5.0
Friedrich	5.0
Sharp	3.0

Source: *Appliance*, September 1997, p. 82.

★ 851 ★
Heating and Cooling (SIC 3585)

Top Dehumidifier Makers - 1996

Shares are shown based on shipments of 976,900 units.

Electrolux (Frigidaire)	32.0%
Whirlpool	29.0
MCD	17.0
Fedders	7.0
W.C. Wood	6.0
Samsung	4.0
Ebco	3.0
Others	2.0

Source: *Appliance*, September 1997, p. 82.

★ 852 ★
Heating and Cooling (SIC 3585)

Unitary HVAC Leaders

Market shares are estimated in percent.

Carrier Corp.	22.0%
Goodman Mfg.	17.0
Rheem Mfg.	13.0
The Trane Company	12.0
York International	12.0
Lennox Industries	11.0
Nordyne	4.0

Source: *Air Conditioning, Heating & Refrigeration News*, April 13, 1998, p. 14, from Air Conditioning and Refrigeration Institute.

★ 853 ★

Refrigerators and Freezers (SIC 3585)

Largest Refrigerated Display Case Makers

Shares are shown based on shipments of 318,500 units.

Hussman Corporation	43.0%
Kysor/Warren	20.0
Tyler Refrigeration	15.0
Hill/Phoenix	13.0
Others	9.0

Source: *Appliance*, September 1997, p. 83.

★ 854 ★

Defoamers (SIC 3590)

Defoamers Demand by Industry

Pulp & paper
Water treatment
Petroleum
Paints & coatings
Other

Data show demand in millions of dollars for 1996 and 2001.

	1996	2001	Share
Pulp & paper	$ 159	$ 210	32.56%
Water treatment	88	115	17.83
Petroleum	85	110	17.05
Paints & coatings	49	60	9.30
Other	113	150	23.26

Source: *Chemical Engineering*, October 1997, p. 75.

★ 855 ★

Pumps (SIC 3594)

Pump Sales by End Market - 2000

Sales are estimated in millions of dollars.

	($ mil.)	Share
Process manufacturers	$ 2,700	40.91%
Public utilities	2,000	30.30
Resource extraction industries	875	13.26
Construction sector	300	4.55
Other	725	10.98

Source: *Purchasing*, April 9, 1998, p. 54, from Freedonia Group.

★ 856 ★

Robots (SIC 3599)

Robot Use by Industrial Application - 1996

Distribution is shown based on 78,000 robots.

Spot welding	30.0%
Material handling	27.0
Coating	18.0
Arc welding	13.0
Material removal	4.0
Assembly	3.0
Dispensing	3.0
Inspection	1.0

Source: *Assembly*, October 1997, p. 34, from Robotic Industries Association.

★ 857 ★

Robots (SIC 3599)

Robotic Accessories Market - 1997

Market is shown in percent. Demand for automation accessories reached an estimated $500 million.

Slides	47.8%
Pick and place	26.5
Grippers	15.9
Rotary actuators	5.8
Exchange units	4.0

Source: *Assembly*, October 1997, p. 38, from Advanced Technology Advisors.

SIC 36 - Electronic and Other Electric Equipment

★ 858 ★

Electronics (SIC 3600)

Consumer Electronics Market - 1998

The market is shown in percent.

Computers 51.0%
Printers 12.0
Software 12.0
Cordless phones 5.0
PC peripherals 3.8
Answering devices 3.6
Modems 3.6
Monitors 3.3
Other 5.7

Source: *Investor's Business Daily*, March 10, 1998, p. 4,
from Consumer Electronics Manufacturers Association.

★ 859 ★

Electronics (SIC 3600)

Electronics Market - 1997

*Categories are shown ranked by factory sales in
millions of dollars for the first six months of 1997.*

Electronic components . . . . $ 70,500
Computers, peripherals 42,249
Telecommunications 29,689
Industrial electronics 16,772
Defense communications 14,142
Electromedical equipment 5,291
Consumer electronics 4,918
Other products 35,372

Source: *Assembly*, September 1997, p. 13, from U.S.
Department of Commerce.

★ 860 ★

Electronics (SIC 3600)

Top Contract Manufacturers

*Companies are ranked by revenues in millions of
dollars.*

SCI Systems Inc. . . . . $ 4,544.7
Solectron Corp. 2,817.1
Celestica Inc. 2,600.0
Jabil Circuit Inc. 863.3
AVEX Electronics Inc. 717.0
Manufacturers Services Ltd. 475.0
DOVatron (DII) 458.9
Flextronics International 448.3
Bull Electronics 400.0
Micron Custom Manufacturing 373.6

Source: *Purchasing*, May 22, 1997, p. 42, from
Technology Forecasters Inc.

★ 861 ★

Electrical Equipment (SIC 3624)

Leading Graphite Electrode Producers

Shares are shown in percent. Data are estimated.

SGL Carbon AG and Ucar International
Inc. 60.0%
Carbide/Graphite Inc. 20.0
Other 20.0

Source: *Investor's Business Daily*, November 24, 1997, p.
A3.

★ 862 ★
Household Appliances (SIC 3630)
Leading Appliance Companies

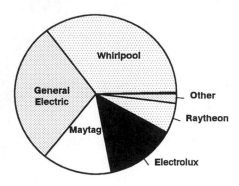

The market earned $271 million in net income for 1996. Company shares are shown in percent.

Whirlpool	35.0%
General Electric	29.3
Maytag	14.4
Electrolux	13.5
Raytheon	6.2
Other	1.6

Source: New York Times, June 13, 1997, p. C2, from Merrill Lynch.

★ 863 ★
Household Appliances (SIC 3630)
Top Major Appliances - 1997-98

Data show manufacturers' total shipments in units forecasted for 1997 and 1998.

	1997	1998
Microwave ovens	9,455,000	9,595,000
Refrigerators	9,167,000	9,135,000
Washers	7,039,000	7,131,000
Dryers	5,497,000	5,574,000
Dishwashers	4,852,000	4,887,000
Disposers	4,660,000	4,717,000
Electric ranges	4,293,000	4,360,000
Room air conditioners	4,210,000	4,237,000
Gas ranges	2,819,000	2,846,000
Freezers	1,688,000	1,697,000
Dehumidifiers	878,000	965,000
Compactors	109,000	109,000

Source: HFN, December 22, 1997, p. 54, from Association of Home Appliance Manufacturers.

★ 864 ★
Cooking Equipment (SIC 3631)
Range Shipments by Type - 1998

Shipments are shown in thousands of units.

Electric ranges	
Free standing	3,252
Built-in	647
Surface cooktops	461
Gas ranges	
Free standing	2,474
Surface cooktops	297
Built-in	74

Source: Appliance Manufacturer, January 1998, p. 74.

★ 865 ★
Cooking Equipment (SIC 3631)
Top Electric Range Makers - 1996

Shares are shown based on shipments of 4,281,000 units.

GE	45.0%
Whirlpool	20.0
Maytag (Magic Chef, Hardwick, Jenn Air)	15.0
Electrolux (Frigidaire)	10.0
Raytheon (Caloric)	6.0
Others	4.0

Source: Appliance, September 1997, p. 83.

★ 866 ★
Cooking Equipment (SIC 3631)
Top Gas Range Makers - 1996

Shares are shown based on shipments of 2,830,000 units.

GE (Roper)	30.0%
Maytag (Magic Chef, Hardwick, Jenn Air)	22.0
Electrolux (Frigidaire)	19.0
Raytheon (Caloric)	13.0
Whirlpool	7.0
Brown	3.0
Peerless Premier	3.0
Others	3.0

Source: Appliance, September 1997, p. 83.

★ 867 ★
Cooking Equipment (SIC 3631)

Top Microwave Oven Makers - 1996

Shares are shown based on shipments of 9,060,000 units.

Sharp	26.0%
Samsung	20.0
LG Electronics	17.0
Matsushita	15.0
MCD	9.0
Sanyo	6.0
Others	7.0

Source: *Appliance*, September 1997, p. 83.

★ 868 ★
Cooking Equipment (SIC 3631)

Top Outdoor Grill Makers - 1996

Shares are shown based on shipments of 5,285,000 units.

Sunbeam Outdoor Products	45.0%
Bradley	30.0
Thermos/Structo	14.0
Weber-Stephen	5.0
Others	5.0

Source: *Appliance*, September 1997, p. 83.

★ 869 ★
Cooking Equipment (SIC 3631)

Top Range Hood Makers - 1996

Shares are shown based on shipments of 9,060,000 units.

Broan	73.0%
Nutone	15.0
Watertown Metal Products	11.0
Others	1.0

Source: *Appliance*, September 1997, p. 83.

★ 870 ★
Refrigerators and Freezers (SIC 3632)

Top Built-In Refrigerator Makers - 1996

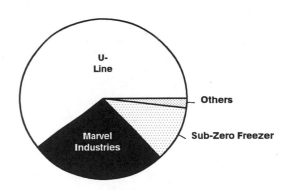

Shares are shown based on shipments of 126,000 units. Data refer to all compact, built-in and undercounter models.

U-Line	59.0%
Marvel Industries	26.0
Sub-Zero Freezer	11.0
Others	2.0

Source: *Appliance*, September 1997, p. 83.

★ 871 ★
Refrigerators and Freezers (SIC 3632)

Top Compact Refrigerator Makers - 1996

Shares are shown based on shipments of 1,070,000 units.

Sanyo	55.0%
GE/Mabe	19.0
Haier	15.0
Wanbao	7.0
Others	4.0

Source: *Appliance*, September 1997, p. 83.

★ 872 ★

Refrigerators and Freezers (SIC 3632)

Top Freezer Makers - 1996

Shares are shown based on shipments of 1,678,000 units.

Electrolux (Frigidaire)	72.0%
W.C. Wood	25.0
Sanyo	1.0
Others	2.0

Source: *Appliance*, September 1997, p. 83.

★ 873 ★

Refrigerators and Freezers (SIC 3632)

Top Refrigerator Makers - 1996

Shares are shown based on shipments of 9,045,000 units.

GE	36.0%
Whirlpool	27.0
Electrolux (Frigidaire)	16.0
Maytag (Admiral)	10.0
Raytheon (Amana)	10.0
Others	1.0

Source: *Appliance*, September 1997, p. 83.

★ 874 ★

Laundry Equipment (SIC 3633)

Top Electric Dryer Makers - 1996

Shares are shown based on shipments of 4,284,000 units.

Whirlpool	54.0%
GE	19.0
Maytag	15.0
Electrolux (Frigidaire)	7.0
Raytheon (Speed Queen)	5.0

Source: *Appliance*, September 1997, p. 83.

★ 875 ★

Laundry Equipment (SIC 3633)

Top Washer Makers

Shares are shown based on shipments of 7,129,000 units.

Whirlpool	52.0%
Maytag	19.0
GE	17.0
Electrolux (Frigidaire)	7.0
Raytheon (Speed Queen)	5.0

Source: *Appliance*, September 1997, p. 83.

★ 876 ★

Household Appliances (SIC 3634)

Coffee Maker Market - 1996

Shares are shown based on shipments of 15,000,000 units.

Mr. Coffee	32.0%
Hamilton Beach/Proctor Silex	24.0
West Bend	9.0
Black & Decker	8.0
Braun	8.0
Krups	6.0
Bunn	3.0
Others	10.0

Source: *Appliance*, September 1997, p. 84.

★ 877 ★

Household Appliances (SIC 3634)

Houseware Shipments - 1997

Shipments are shown in thousands of units.

Smoke detectors	16,000
Coffee makers, drip	15,000
Clocks, alarm	13,940
Irons, steam and spray	13,650
Carbon monoxide detectors	9,000
Clocks, kitchen wall	8,160
Can openers	7,000
Blenders, stand-type	6,250
Clocks, desk/table	6,120
Clocks, decorative wall	5,780

Source: *Appliance*, January 1998, p. 48.

★ 878 ★

Household Appliances (SIC 3634)

Largest Food Chopper Producers

Shares are shown based on shipments of 1,560,000 units.

Black & Decker	.32.0%
Hamilton Beach/Proctor Silex	.19.0
Cuisinart	.17.0
Toastmaster	.17.0
HPA/Betty Crocker	8.0
Oster/Sunbeam	5.0
Others	2.0

Source: *Appliance*, September 1997, p. 84.

★ 879 ★

Household Appliances (SIC 3634)

Largest Hair Dryer Producers

Shares are shown based on shipments of 21,150,000 units.

Conair	.42.0%
Helen of Troy	.22.0
Windmere	.11.0
Revlon	9.0
Other	.16.0

Source: *Appliance*, September 1997, p. 83.

★ 880 ★

Household Appliances (SIC 3634)

Largest Trash Compactor Producers

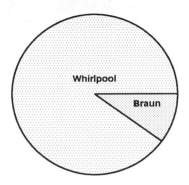

Shares are shown based on shipments of 100,000 units.

Whirlpool	.90.0%
Braun	.10.0

Source: *Appliance*, September 1997, p. 83.

★ 881 ★

Household Appliances (SIC 3634)

Leading Stand Mixer Producers - 1996

Shares are shown based on shipments of 1,230,000 units.

Oster/Sunbeam	.37.0%
KitchenAid	.33.0
Waring	9.0
Hamilton Beach/Proctor Silex	7.0
HPA/Betty Crocker	5.0
Others	9.0

Source: *Appliance*, September 1997, p. 84.

★ 882 ★
Household Appliances (SIC 3634)

Leading Toaster Makers - 1996

Shares are shown based on shipments of 10,760,000 units.

Hamilton Beach/Proctor Silex 37.0%
Toastmaster 30.0
Rival 17.0
HPA/Betty Crocker 5.0
Black & Decker 4.0
Others 7.0

Source: *Appliance*, September 1997, p. 84.

★ 883 ★
Household Appliances (SIC 3634)

Leading Waffle Iron Makers - 1996

Shares are shown based on unit shipments.

Toastmaster 39.0%
Hamilton Beach/Proctor Silex 19.0
Oster/Sunbeam 13.0
Dazey 12.0
Black & Decker 7.0
Others 10.0

Source: *Appliance*, September 1997, p. 84.

★ 884 ★
Household Appliances (SIC 3634)

Top Beard/Mustache Trimmer Makers

Shares are shown based on shipments of 2,560,000 units.

Wahl 41.0%
N.A.P. (Norelco) 28.0
Windmere 6.0
Conair 5.0
Remington 5.0
Oster 4.0
Other 11.0

Source: *Appliance*, September 1997, p. 83.

★ 885 ★
Household Appliances (SIC 3634)

Top Blender Makers - 1996

Shares are shown based on shipments of 6,180,000 units.

Hamilton Beach/Proctor Silex 47.0%
Oster/Sunbeam 29.0
Braun 10.0
HPA/Betty Crocker 5.0
Waring 5.0
Others 4.0

Source: *Appliance*, September 1997, p. 84.

★ 886 ★
Household Appliances (SIC 3634)

Top Breadmaker Producers - 1996

Shares are shown based on shipments of 2,900,000 units.

Welbilt 24.0%
West Bend 18.0
Real 12.0
Oster/Sunbeam 11.0
Toastmaster 9.0
Others 26.0

Source: *Appliance*, September 1997, p. 84.

★ 887 ★

Household Appliances (SIC 3634)

Top Curling Iron Producers

Shares are shown based on shipments of 14,000,000 units.

Conair	35.0%
Helen of Troy	18.0
Windmere	14.0
Revlon	11.0
Other	22.0

Source: *Appliance*, September 1997, p. 83.

★ 888 ★

Household Appliances (SIC 3634)

Top Hand Mixer Makers

- Hamilton Beach/Proctor Silex
- Black & Decker
- Oster/Sunbeam
- HPA/Betty Crocker
- West End
- KitchenAid
- Rival
- Others

Shares are shown based on shipments of 5,280,000 units.

Hamilton Beach/Proctor Silex	24.0%
Black & Decker	15.0
Oster/Sunbeam	13.0
HPA/Betty Crocker	11.0
West End	10.0
KitchenAid	6.0
Rival	6.0
Others	15.0

Source: *Appliance*, September 1997, p. 84.

★ 889 ★

Household Appliances (SIC 3634)

Top Iron Makers - 1996

Shares are shown based on shipments of 15,600,000 units.

Black & Decker	38.0%
Hamilton Beach/Proctor Silex	29.0
Oster/Sunbeam	17.0
Rowenta	7.0
N.A.P. (Norelco)	5.0
Others	4.0

Source: *Appliance*, September 1997, p. 84.

★ 890 ★

Household Appliances (SIC 3634)

Top Lighted Make-Up Mirror Makers

Shares are shown based on shipments of 661,000 units.

Remington/Clairol	28.0%
Conair	21.0
Windmere	17.0
Hartman	12.0
Other	22.0

Source: *Appliance*, September 1997, p. 83.

★ 891 ★

Household Appliances (SIC 3634)

Top Men's Shaver Producers

Shares are shown based on shipments of 6,840,000 units.

N.A.P.	51.0%
Remington	22.0
Braun	16.0
Matsushita	7.0
Other	4.0

Source: *Appliance*, September 1997, p. 83.

★ 892 ★

Vacuum Cleaners (SIC 3635)

Top Hand-Held Vacuum Cleaner Makers

Shares are shown based on shipments of 5,470,000 units.

Royal	39.0%
Black & Decker	32.0
Hoover	10.0
Eureka	6.0
Other	13.0

Source: *Appliance*, September 1997, p. 82.

★ 893 ★

Vacuum Cleaners (SIC 3635)

Top Vacuum Cleaner Makers

Shares are shown based on shipments of 15,980,000 units.

Hoover	34.0%
Eureka	28.0
Royal	10.0
Matsushita	9.0
Kirby	4.0
Bissell	3.0
Electrolux	3.0
Others	9.0

Source: *Appliance*, September 1997, p. 82.

★ 894 ★

Vacuum Cleaners (SIC 3635)

Top Wet/Dry Vacuum Makers

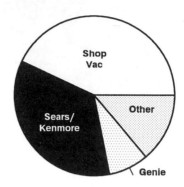

Shares are shown based on shipments of 3,825,000 units.

Shop Vac	43.0%
Sears/Kenmore	35.0
Genie	8.0
Other	14.0

Source: *Appliance*, September 1997, p. 82.

★ 895 ★

Dishwashers (SIC 3639)

Top Dishwasher Producers - 1996

Shares are shown based on shipments of 4,841,000 units.

GE	40.0%
Whirlpool	39.0
Maytag	13.0
Electrolux (Frigidaire)	8.0

Source: *Appliance*, September 1997, p. 83.

★ 896 ★

Household Appliances (SIC 3639)

Space and Water Heater Shipments - 1997

Data show millions of units shipped through August 1997. Shipments of gas boilers reached $99,762; figures for units shipped were not available.

Gas water heaters 3.0
Electric water heaters 2.7
Gas furnaces 1.7

Source: *Contractor*, November 1997, p. 5, from Gas Appliance Manufacturers Association.

★ 897 ★

Household Appliances (SIC 3639)

Top Can Opener Producers

Shares are shown based on shipments of 6,9100,000 units.

Rival 26.0%
Hamilton Beach/Proctor Silex 24.0
Black & Decker 13.0
Oster/Sunbeam 13.0
HPA/Betty Crocker 8.0
Other 16.0

Source: *Appliance*, September 1997, p. 84.

★ 898 ★

Household Appliances (SIC 3639)

Top Disposal Makers - 1996

Shares are shown based on shipments of 4,582,000 units.

In-Sink-Erator 67.0%
Anaheim Manufacturing 28.0
Watertown Metal Products 4.0
Maytag 1.0

Source: *Appliance*, September 1997, p. 83.

★ 899 ★

Household Appliances (SIC 3639)

Top Water Heater Makers - 1996

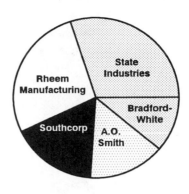

Shares are shown based on shipments of 8,905,000 units.

State Industries 30.0%
Rheem Manufacturing 27.0
Southcorp 17.0
A.O. Smith 15.0
Bradford-White 11.0

Source: *Appliance*, September 1997, p. 83.

★ 900 ★

Lighting (SIC 3645)

Outdoor Lighting Shipments

Shipments of attached and nonattached lighting units are shown for 1994 through 1997. Data represent thousands of units shipped and are estimated for 1996 and 1997. Nonattached lighting includes garden patio and pool lights that are not permanently installed.

	Attached (000)	Non. (000)
1994	4,840	2,328
1995	3,918	2,614
1996	4,043	2,592
1997	3,772	2,875

Source: *Discount Store News*, August 4, 1997, p. 21, from Economic Industry Reports.

★ 901 ★

Consumer Electronics (SIC 3651)

Consumer Electronics Sales at Discount Stores - 1997

Distribution is shown based on sales of $6,110,853,000 at discount stores in 1997.

Home office equipment	26.09%
Audio equipment	21.01
Televisions	17.86
Videocassette recorders	8.25
Blank videotapes	7.63
Video game software	5.75
Blank audiotapes	5.67
Video game modules cartridges	4.54
Miscellaneous	3.20

Source: *Discount Merchandiser*, June 1997, p. 43.

★ 902 ★

Consumer Electronics (SIC 3651)

Home Theater Sales - 1998

Factory sales are shown in millions of dollars for the first quarter of the year.

TVs, 25-inch & larger	$ 981
Projection TVs	323
Hi-fi VCRs	299
VHS videotapes	132
Audio/video receivers, amplifiers	101
Speakers	99
Audio tapes	66
DVD players	48
Compact tape formats	36

Source: *Investor's Business Daily*, June 2, 1998, p. A8, from Consumer Electronics Manufacturers Association.

★ 903 ★

Consumer Electronics (SIC 3651)

Largest TV Electronics Firms

Data show selected firms ranked by revenues in millions of dollars.

Motorola	$ 29,794
Eastman Kodak	14,538
TRW	10,831
Texas Instruments	9,750
Musicland	1,768
LSI Logic	1,290
CDW Computer Centers	1,276

Source: *TV Digest*, January 26, 1998, p. 18.

★ 904 ★

Consumer Electronics (SIC 3651)

Leading Audio Brands at Food Stores

Shares are shown based on volume.

Fuji	33.9%
Maxwell	19.5
TDK	13.4
Memorex	9.1
Sony	8.3
JVC	6.1
Others	9.7

Source: *Supermarket Business*, October 1997, p. 4, from Information Resources Inc.

★ 905 ★

Consumer Electronics (SIC 3651)

Projection Display Makers

Market shares are shown in percent.

Focus Systems	22.0%
Epson	18.0
Proxima	12.0
Sharp	12.0
Lightwave Inc.	10.0
Other	26.0

Source: From the Internet, http:// www.cgiamcity.com/ portland/stories/010598/story6.html, January 5, 1998, p. 1.

★ 906 ★

Consumer Electronics (SIC 3651)

Top Camcorder Makers - 1996

Shares are shown based on shipments of 3,634,038 units.

Sony	. 27.0%
Thomson	. 22.0
Matsushita (Panasonic, Quasar)	. 17.0
JVC	. 15.0
Sharp	. 7.0
Canon	. 3.0
Hitachi	. 3.0
N.A.P.	. 3.0
Others	. 3.0

Source: *Appliance*, September 1997, p. 82.

★ 907 ★

Consumer Electronics (SIC 3651)

Top CD Player Makers - 1996

Shares are shown based on shipments of 2,915,000 units.

Sony	. 27.0%
Pioneer	. 13.0
Matsushita (Panasonic, Technics)	. 11.0
Kenwood	. 7.0
JVC	. 6.0
RCA	. 4.0
Denon	. 3.0
Onkyo	. 3.0
Other	. 26.0

Source: *Appliance*, September 1997, p. 82.

★ 908 ★

Consumer Electronics (SIC 3651)

Top DVD Disc Companies - 1997

Total shipments reached 1.53 million units. Market shares are shown as of March 8, 1998. DVD stands for digital video disc.

Warner Home Video	. 50.68%
Columbia	. 16.72
Disney	. 7.73
Universal Home Video	. 7.14
Live Home Entertainment	. 6.52
Image	. 2.59
Republic	. 1.54
Simitar	. 1.46
Other	. 5.62

Source: *Los Angeles Times*, March 18, 1998, p. D7, from VideoScan.

★ 909 ★

Consumer Electronics (SIC 3651)

Top TV Makers - 1996

Shares are shown based on shipments of 22,383,300 units.

Thomson (RCA/GE)	. 23.0%
N.A.P.	. 15.0
Zenith	. 13.0
Sony	. 9.0
Sanyo	. 6.0
Sharp	. 6.0
Matsushita (Panasonic, Quasar)	. 4.0
Toshiba	. 4.0
Mitsubishi	. 3.0
Other	. 17.0

Source: *Appliance*, September 1997, p. 82.

★ 910 ★

Consumer Electronics (SIC 3651)

Top VCR Makers - 1996

Shares are shown based on shipments of 14,803,733 units. N.A.P. includes Magnavox, Sylvania, Philco and Philips.

Thomson (RCA/GE)	. 21.0%
N.A.P.	. 11.0
Matsushita (Panasonic, Quasar)	. 9.0
Sony	. 7.0
JVC	. 6.0

Continued on next page.

★ 910 ★ *Continued*

Consumer Electronics (SIC 3651)

Top VCR Makers - 1996

Shares are shown based on shipments of 14,803,733 units. N.A.P. includes Magnavox, Sylvania, Philco and Philips.

Sharp	5.0%
Zenith	5.0
LG Electronics	4.0
Sanyo/Fisher	4.0
Toshiba	4.0
Others	24.0

Source: *Appliance*, September 1997, p. 82.

★ 911 ★

Consumer Electronics (SIC 3651)

Top Video Disc Player Makers - 1996

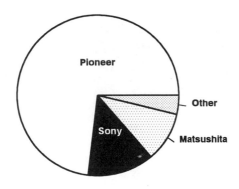

Shares are shown based on shipments of 154,354 units.

Pioneer	73.0%
Sony	13.0
Matsushita	10.0
Other	4.0

Source: *Appliance*, September 1997, p. 82.

★ 912 ★

Prerecorded Music (SIC 3651)

Best-Selling Albums - 1997

Artists are ranked by the millions of copies sold. Album titles are shown in parentheses. Sales are shown as of December 24, 1997.

The Spice Girls (Spice)	5.3
Jewel (Pieces of You)	4.3

Garth Brooks (Sevens)	3.4
Puff Daddy (No Way Out)	3.4
Hanson (Middle of Nowhere)	3.2
The Notorious B.I.G. (Life After Death)	3.2
The Wallflowers (Bringing Down the Horse)	3.1
Celion Dion (Falling Into You)	3.0
Space Jam (soundtrack)	2.9
LeAnn Rimes (You Light Up My Life)	2.9

Source: *Entertainment Weekly*, January 30, 1998, p. 33, from Soundscan.

★ 913 ★

Prerecorded Music (SIC 3651)

Top Country Music Distributors - 1997

Market shares are shown in percent.

WEA	28.7%
Universal	17.7
BMA	16.6
EMI	14.0
PolyGram	7.5
Independents	6.2

Source: *Financial Times*, March 28, 1998, p. 3, from *Billboard*.

★ 914 ★

Prerecorded Music (SIC 3652)

Music Market by Genre - 1996

Sales are shown in percent.

Rock	33.0%
Country	15.0
Rhythm and blues	12.0
Pop	9.0
Rap	9.0
Others	22.0

Source: *Financial Times*, September 27, 1997, p. 23, from Recording Industry Association of America.

★ 915 ★
Prerecorded Music (SIC 3652)

Music Sales by Format - 1997

Sales are shown in millions of dollars.

	($ mil.)	Share
CDs	$ 9,915.1	81.03%
Cassettes	1,522.7	12.44
Music videos	323.9	2.65
CD singles	272.7	2.23
Cassette singles	133.5	1.09
Vinyl singles	35.6	0.29
LPs/EPs	33.3	0.27

Source: *Billboard*, February 28, 1998, p. 81, from RIAA Market Research Committee.

★ 916 ★
Prerecorded Music (SIC 3652)

Music Sales by Segment - 1997

Data show sales in millions of units.

CDs	753.1
Cassettes	172.6
CD singles	66.7
Cassette singles	42.2
Music videos	18.6
Vinyl singles	7.5
LPs/EPs	2.7

Source: *TV Digest*, February 22, 1998, p. 15, from Recording Industry Association of America.

★ 917 ★
Prerecorded Music (SIC 3652)

Popular Formats for Prerecorded Music

Data show music sales by format for 1994, 1995, and 1996.

	1994	1995	1996
Full-length CDs	58.4%	65.0%	68.4%
Full-length cassettes	32.1	25.1	19.3
Singles (all types)	7.4	7.5	9.3
Music videos	0.8	0.9	1.0
Vinyl LPs	0.8	0.5	0.6
Other	0.5	2.0	1.4

Source: *Discount Merchandiser*, August 1997, p. 114.

★ 918 ★
Prerecorded Music (SIC 3652)

Top Album Distributors - 1998

Market shares are shown for the first three months of the year.

Sony	19.5%
WEA	17.8
Indies	16.3
EMD	12.6
PGD	11.9
BMG	11.5
Universal	10.5

Source: *Billboard*, April 18, 1998, p. 43, from Soundscan.

★ 919 ★
Prerecorded Music (SIC 3652)

Top Country Music Distributors - 1998

Market shares are shown for the first three months of the year.

WEA	23.5%
BMG	17.5
Universal	15.2
EMD	14.8
PGD	12.7
Sony	10.8
Indies	5.5

Source: *Billboard*, April 18, 1998, p. 43, from Soundscan.

★ 920 ★

Prerecorded Music (SIC 3652)

Top R&B Music Distributors - 1998

Market shares are shown for the first three months of the year.

BMG	21.2%
EMD	17.6
PGD	15.1
Sony	13.9
Universal	11.4
WEA	11.3
Indies	9.5

Source: *Billboard*, April 18, 1998, p. 43, from Soundscan.

★ 921 ★

Prerecorded Music (SIC 3652)

Top Record Companies - 1997

Shares are shown based on albums sold from January 1 through November 9, 1997. Catalog sales are not included.

WEA	17.68%
BMG	14.21
UNI	13.64
EMD	13.48
Sony	12.04
PolyGram	11.71
Other	17.24

Source: *Los Angeles Times*, November 13, 1997, p. D6, from SoundScan.

★ 922 ★

Prerecorded Music (SIC 3652)

Top Singles Distributors - 1998

Market shares are shown for the first three months of the year.

BMG	23.5%
Sony	21.9
WEA	17.7
PGD	15.4
EMD	9.3
Universal	7.1
Indies	5.0

Source: *Billboard*, April 18, 1998, p. 43, from Soundscan.

★ 923 ★

Prerecorded Music (SIC 3652)

Vinyl LP Market

Data show the number of vinyl LPs (long-playing albums) sold by year. Figure for 1997 represents unit sales through June 29, 1997.

1994	625,000
1995	794,000
1996	1,100,000
1997	2,200,000

Source: *Time*, July 14, 1997, p. 20, from SoundScan, Inc.

★ 924 ★

Prerecorded Music (SIC 3652)

Who Buys Music

Sales are shown by age group for 1995 and 1996.

	1995	1996
10-14 years	8.0%	7.9%
15-19 years	17.1	17.2
20-24 years	15.3	15.0
25-29 years	12.3	12.5
30-34 years	12.1	11.4
35-39 years	10.8	11.1
40-44 years	7.5	9.1
45+ years	16.1	15.1

Source: *Discount Merchandiser*, August 1997, p. 114.

★ 925 ★

Fax Machines (SIC 3661)

Leading Fax Machine Makers - 1996

Market shares are shown in percent.

Sharp	24.8%
Brother	24.6
Panasonic	13.8
Hewlett-Packard	11.9
Canon	7.5
Others	14.4

Source: *Purchasing*, April 23, 1998, p. 100, from Dataquest Inc.

★ 926 ★
Modems (SIC 3661)

Leading Macintosh Modem Makers

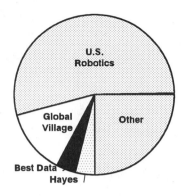

The market for Mac desktop modems is shown by company.

U.S. Robotics 54.0%
Global Village 13.0
Best Data 4.0
Hayes 4.0
Other 25.0

Source: From the Internet, http:// www.usr.com/ real.chart-d.html, September 13, 1997, p. 1, from VisionQuest 2000.

★ 927 ★
Modems (SIC 3661)

Leading Modem Manufacturers - 1997

Shares are shown based on retail sales.

3Com-U.S. Robotics 52.0%
Hayes 10.0
3Com-MCC 8.0
Diamond 6.0
Motorola 6.0
Global Village 4.0
Zoom 3.0
Boca 2.0
Best Data 1.0
NewCom 1.0
Other 7.0

Source: *Chicago Tribune*, October 3, 1997, p. C3, from VisionQuest 2000.

★ 928 ★
Modems (SIC 3661)

Modem Sales by Speed

Shares are shown based on sales.

28.8 and 33.6 kilobits 64.5%
56 kilobits 29.5
14.4 kilobits 6.0

Source: *New York Times*, November 24, 1997, p. C4, from Dataquest Inc.

★ 929 ★
Telecommunications Equipment (SIC 3661)

Carrier Switch Manufacturers

Shares are shown in percent.

Newbridge Networks 36.0%
Cisco 20.3
Nortel 11.7
Alcatel 7.5
Acend Communications 5.3
Other 19.2

Source: *InternetWeek*, September 29, 1997, p. 115, from Vertical Systems Group.

★ 930 ★
Telecommunications Equipment (SIC 3661)

Frame Relay Access Device Companies - 1996

Shares of the $346 million market are shown in percent.

Micom 19.3%
Motorola 15.5
Cisco 13.8
Hypercom 12.1
ACT Networks 11.3
Others 28.0

Source: *Computerworld*, November 17, 1997, p. 63, from International Data Corp.

★ 931 ★

Telecommunications Equipment (SIC 3661)

Internet Networking Equipment Producers - 1996

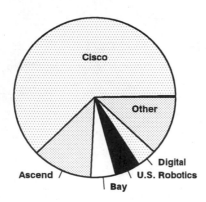

The market was valued at $2.0 billion.

Cisco	62.0%
Ascend	12.0
Bay	5.0
U.S. Robotics	5.0
Digital	4.0
Other	12.0

Source: *Network Computing*, January 15, 1998, p. 28, from Dataquest Inc.

★ 932 ★

Cable Boxes (SIC 3663)

Cable Box Sales - 1998

Sales are shown in millions of units.

Advanced analog	4.67
Pay-per-view ready analog	4.37
Digital	4.30
Non pay-per-view analog	0.11

Source: *USA TODAY*, December 16, 1997, p. 6B, from Paul Kagan Associates.

★ 933 ★

Telecommunications Equipment (SIC 3663)

Largest Cellular Phone Makers

Shares are shown based on shipments of 7,200,000 units.

Motorola/Pulsar	43.0%
Nokia-Mobira	11.0
AT&T	7.0

Audiovox	5.0%
NEC	5.0
GE/Ericsson	4.0
Radio Shack	4.0
Others	20.0

Source: *Appliance*, September 1997, p. 82.

★ 934 ★

Telecommunications Equipment (SIC 3663)

Largest Cordless Phone Makers - 1996

Shares are shown based on shipments of 20,903,000 units.

AT&T	26.0%
GE	16.0
Sony	11.0
Uniden	11.0
BellSouth	8.0
Panasonic	7.0
Radio Shack	4.0
Southwestern Bell	4.0
Cobra	3.0
Others	10.0

Source: *Appliance*, September 1997, p. 82.

★ 935 ★

Telecommunications Equipment (SIC 3663)

PC Card Pager Market

The market is shown by installed base.

Alphanumeric PC cards	0.02
Narrowband-PCS PC cards	0.00

Source: *Sales & Field Force Automation*, January 1998, p. 62, from Yankee Group.

★ 936 ★

Telecommunications Equipment (SIC 3663)

Top Headset Makers - North America

Market shares are shown in percent.

Plantronics	65.0%
Other	35.0

Source: *Investor's Business Daily*, January 21, 1998, p. A4.

★ 937 ★
Wireless Communications (SIC 3663)

Largest Wireless Equipment Makers

Market shares are shown for digital, cellular and PCS equipment.

Lucent	38.0%
Ericsson	23.0
Nortel	21.0
Motorola	13.0
Nokia	5.0
Hughes	1.0

Source: *RCR*, March 23, 1998, p. 1, from Yankee Group.

★ 938 ★
Wireless Communications (SIC 3663)

Portable Digital Phone Makers

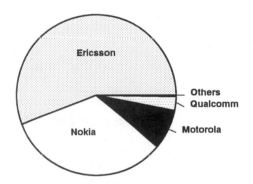

Shares are shown based on shipments.

Ericsson	55.7%
Nokia	33.0
Motorola	8.0
Qualcomm	2.9
Others	0.4

Source: *Investor's Business Daily*, March 10, 1997, p. A6, from Dataquest Inc.

★ 939 ★
Data Communications (SIC 3669)

Ethernet Workgroup Switch Makers

Shares refer to switched 10Mbps and 100 Mbps ports for the first quarter of 1997. Figures are shown based on 2.348 million ports.

3Com	28.0%
Cisco	22.0
Bay Networks	9.0
Others	41.0

Source: From the Internet, http:// www.3com.com/ solutions/documents/guides/600268.htm, 1997, p. 1, from Dell'Oro LANscape.

★ 940 ★
Data Communications (SIC 3669)

Fast Ethernet Hub Manufacturers - 1997

Shares are shown based on revenue for the first half of 1997.

3Com	41.0%
Bay	16.0
Intel	11.0
Cisco	8.0
Accton	5.0
SMS	3.0
Other	16.0

Source: *VAR Business*, October 1, 1997, p. 86, from In-Stat.

★ 941 ★
Data Communications (SIC 3669)

Fast Ethernet NIC Manufacturers - 1997

Shares are shown based on revenue for the first half of 1997. NIC stands for network interface cards.

3Com	45.0%
Intel	30.0
Xircom	4.0
Compaq	3.0
SMS	3.0
Other	15.0

Source: *VAR Business*, October 1, 1997, p. 86, from In-Stat.

★ 942 ★

Data Communications (SIC 3669)

Fast Ethernet Switch Manufacturers - 1997

Shares are shown based on revenue for the first half of 1997.

Cisco	45.0%
3Com	25.0
Bay	10.0
Cabletron	8.0
D-Link	3.0
Intel	1.0
Others	29.0

Source: *VAR Business*, October 1, 1997, p. 86, from In-Stat.

★ 943 ★

Data Communications (SIC 3669)

Internet Network Equipment Market - 1996

Data show equipment sales of $2.1 billion by type.

Routers	58.8%
Access equipment	24.6
LAN switches	10.9
WAN switches	3.6
LAN hubs	2.1

Source: *Investor's Business Daily*, October 30, 1997, p. A10.

★ 944 ★

Data Communications (SIC 3669)

Leading High-Speed ATM Access Vendors

Yurie Systems

NetEdge Systems

ADC Kentrox

3Com

Digital Link

Other

Shares are shown in percent.

Yurie Systems	31.0%
NetEdge Systems	27.0
ADC Kentrox	23.0
3Com	12.0
Digital Link	3.0
Other	4.0

Source: *InternetWeek*, January 12, 1998, p. 23, from Dataquest Inc.

★ 945 ★

Data Communications (SIC 3669)

Leading Push Technology Vendors - 1997

Company shares are shown in percent. Push technology allowed users to set up channels and have news and information delivered directly to their computers. The technology is now being used to solve more conventional business problems.

Desktop Data	51.2%
PointCast	18.7
BackWeb Technologies	8.1
Marimba	6.9
Individual Inc.	5.6
Wayfarer Communications	4.4
Other	5.1

Source: *Infoworld*, January 26, 1998, p. 81, from International Data Corp.

★ 946 ★

Data Communications (SIC 3669)

Leading Vendors of High-End Routers

Shares are shown based on the $764.9 million market for high-end routers. Figures refer to sales to Internet service providers.

Cisco	95.0%
Bay	4.6
Other	0.4

Source: *InternetWeek*, December 8, 1997, p. 14, from Dataquest Inc.

★ 947 ★

Data Communications (SIC 3669)

Leading Vendors of LAN Connectors - 1997

Shares are shown in percent for the fourth quarter of 1997. LAN stands for local area network.

3Com	45.0%
Intel	37.0
Compaq	11.0
Hewlett-Packard	4.0
Other	3.0

Source: *Wall Street Journal*, February 24, 1998, p. B4, from Dell'Oro Group.

★ 948 ★

Data Communications (SIC 3669)

NIC Market Leaders - 1997

Market shares are shown in percent. NIC stands for network interface card.

3Com	44.0%
Intel	14.0
D-Link	10.0
IBM	6.0
SMC	4.0
Other	22.0

Source: *VAR Business*, March 30, 1998, p. 40, from In-Stat.

★ 949 ★

Data Communications (SIC 3669)

PBX Services to Hotels - 1997

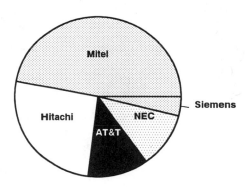

Shares are shown for the leading providers of private branch exchange (PBX) services to hotels.

Mitel	47.3%
Hitachi	25.7
AT&T	12.2
NEC	10.8
Siemens	4.1

Source: *Hotel & Motel Management*, June 16, 1997, p. 41.

★ 950 ★

Data Communications (SIC 3669)

Remote Access Concentrators Market - 1996

Shares are shown in percent.

Ascend	59.7%
U.S. Robotics	28.0
Cisco	8.8
Shiva	1.6
3Com	0.4
Others	1.5

Source: *Computer Reseller News*, November 24, 1997, p. 101, from Dataquest Inc.

★ 951 ★
Data Communications (SIC 3669)

Switch Port Market - 1998

Data show estimated unit shipments, in thousands.

	Units	Share
Ethernet	44,500	97.02%
ATM LAN	871	1.90
Token ring	467	1.02
FDDI	28	0.06

Source: *Business Communications Review*, June 1998, p. 34, from Dell'Oro Group.

★ 952 ★
Data Communications (SIC 3669)

Switched Ethernet Leaders - 1997

Market shares are shown in percent.

Cisco	37.3%
3Com	15.7
Cabletron	13.8
Bay	10.4
Xylan	3.0
Fore	2.4
Others	17.4

Source: *InternetWeek*, March 30, 1998, p. 25, from Dell'Oro Group.

★ 953 ★
Data Communications (SIC 3669)

Top Router Vendors - 1997

Market shares are shown in percent.

Cisco	64.0%
Bay Networks	10.0
3Com	4.0
IBM	2.0
Motorola	2.0
Other	18.0

Source: *Internet Computing*, May 1998, p. 28, from Dell'Oro Group.

★ 954 ★
Data Communications (SIC 3669)

Who Sells Networking Equipment - 1996

Shares are shown for vendors of networking equipment used by Internet service providers and backbone operators.

Cisco	61.8%
Ascend	12.5
Bay	5.4
U.S. Robotics	5.4
Digital	3.7
3Com	2.9
Cascade	2.4
Livingston	1.5
Others	4.4

Source: *InternetWeek*, December 8, 1997, p. 51, from Dataquest Inc.

★ 955 ★
Security Equipment (SIC 3669)

Top Carbon Monoxide Detector Makers - 1996

Shares are shown based on shipments of 6,300,000 units.

BRK/First Alert	61.0%
American Sensors (Dicon)	16.0
Jameson (Coleman)	5.0
Others	18.0

Source: *Appliance*, September 1997, p. 84.

★ 956 ★
Security Equipment (SIC 3669)

Top Smoke Detector Makers

Shares are shown based on shipments of 16,000,000 units.

BRK/FirstAlert	50.0%
Jameson (Coleman)	35.0
American Sensors (Dicon)	4.0
Fymetrics	3.0
Others	8.0

Source: *Appliance*, September 1997, p. 84.

★ 957 ★

Semiconductors (SIC 3674)

Flash Memory Market

The market is shown in percent.

Clients thin/Internet/STB	27.0%
Networking	19.0
Office automation	12.0
Hand held	9.0
Industrial/HDD	9.0
Telecom	7.0
Audio	6.0
Games	4.0
DSC	3.0
Other	4.0

Source: *Electronic News*, June 1, 1998, p. 34.

★ 958 ★

Semiconductors (SIC 3674)

Graphics Chip Market - 1997

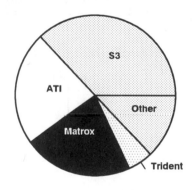

Market shares are shown for the third quarter of 1997.

S3	37.0%
ATI	23.0
Matrox	22.0
Trident	5.0
Other	13.0

Source: *Investor's Business Daily*, January 26, 1998, p. A4, from Jon Peddie Associates.

★ 959 ★

Semiconductors (SIC 3674)

Largest Digital Signal Processors

Market shares are shown in percent.

Texas Instruments	45.0%
Lucent Technologies Inc.	28.0
Analog Devices Inc.	12.0
Motorola Inc.	12.0
Other	3.0

Source: *Wall Street Journal*, June 10, 1998, p. B6.

★ 960 ★

Semiconductors (SIC 3674)

Largest Processor Producers - 1997

Shares are shown based on total revenues of $20.05 billion.

Intel	93.3%
Advanced Micro Devices	3.9
National Semiconductor	1.5
IBM Microelectronics	0.8
Others	0.5

Source: *InfoWorld*, June 15, 1998, p. 8, from Dataquest Inc.

★ 961 ★

Semiconductors (SIC 3674)

Memory Chip Market - 1997

The market is shown in percent.

DRAMs	69.0%
SPRAMs	14.0
Flash EEPROM	8.0
ROM	3.0
Logic	2.0
Other	4.0

Source: *Investor's Business Daily*, April 23, 1998, p. A8, from BancAmerica Robertson Stephens.

★ 962 ★

Semiconductors (SIC 3674)

Microprocessor Market - 1997

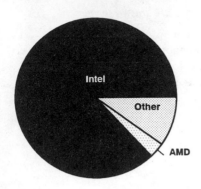

Shares are shown based on sales of $21.4 billion.

Intel 87.0%
AMD 3.2
Other 9.8

Source: *Investor's Business Daily*, June 1, 1998, p. A8, from Dataquest Inc.

★ 963 ★

Semiconductors (SIC 3674)

Microprocessor Sales - 1998

Distribution is shown based on shipments of 100 million microprocessors.

Pentium II 64.0%
Pentium 35.0
Pentium Pro 1.0

Source: *Informationweek*, July 21, 1997, p. 20, from Southcoast Capital Corp.

★ 964 ★

Semiconductors (SIC 3674)

Monthly Wafer Starts in the Southwest

Data show percent of U.S. capacity.

Texas 10.0%
Arizona 8.0
Utah 5.0
New Mexico 3.0
Colorado 1.0

Source: From the Internet, http:// www.semi/org, February 1998, p. 1, from SEMI.

★ 965 ★

Semiconductors (SIC 3674)

Multiprocessor Server Market

Sales are shown by platform.

Windows NT 50.0%
Unix 24.0
NetWare 16.0
Other 10.0

Source: *InfoWorld*, March 9, 1998, p. 88.

★ 966 ★

Capacitors (SIC 3675)

Capacitor Sales by Type

Data show capacitor sales in millions of dollars.

	1995 ($ mil.)	2000 ($ mil.)	Share
Ceramic	$ 860	$ 1,130	40.00%
Tantalum	460	600	21.24
Aluminum	400	520	18.41
Variable	45	50	1.77
Other	525	525	18.58

Source: *Purchasing*, June 19, 1997, p. 40, from The Freedonia Group Inc.

★ 967 ★

Connectors (SIC 3678)

Canada's Market for Connectors - 1996

Demand is shown in percent.

Computers and peripherals 26.2%
Telecom/datacom 15.3
Automotive 14.2
Industrial 12.3
Military 7.4
Others 24.6

Source: *National Trade Data Bank*, October 31, 1997, p. ISA970901.

★ 968 ★

Connectors (SIC 3678)

Top Access Concentrator Producers - 1997

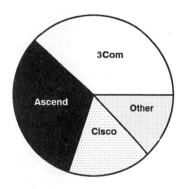

Shares are shown based on a $1.76 billion market.

3Com	37.7%
Ascend	32.3
Cisco	16.8
Other	13.2

Source: *Investor's Business Daily*, February 24, 1998, p. A9, from Dataquest Inc.

★ 969 ★

Batteries (SIC 3691)

Top Battery Brands - 1997

Market shares are shown in percent for the first quarter of the year.

Duracell	41.6%
Everready	36.5
Rayovac	10.2
Other	11.7

Source: *Brandweek*, June 30, 1997, p. 6, from Prudential Securities.

SIC 37 - Transportation Equipment

★ 970 ★
Autos (SIC 3711)

Auto Fleet Registrations - 1996

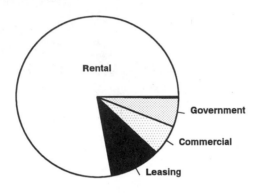

The business vehicle fleet is shown by segment. California has the highest growth in total units in operation. The states with the fastest growing concentration of fleet vehicles was Arizona and Colorado.

Rental	78.0%
Leasing	10.0
Commercial	6.0
Government	6.0

Source: From the Internet, http:// www.fleet-central.com, November 1997, p. 1, from *Automotive Fleet Fact Book*.

★ 971 ★
Autos (SIC 3711)

Auto/Light Truck Market - 1998

Market shares are shown in percent.

General Motors	29.4%
Ford Motor	24.9
Chrysler	17.2
Other	28.2

Source: *USA TODAY*, March 18, 1998, p. B1, from Autodata.

★ 972 ★
Autos (SIC 3711)

Business Car Fleets

The business vehicle fleet is shown by segment

	(000)	Share
Rental	1,590	32.0%
Business	1,295	26.0
Government	1,209	25.0
Utility	376	8.0
Police	274	6.0
Taxi	130	3.0

Source: From the Internet, http:// www.fleet-central.com, November 1997, p. 1, from *Automotive Fleet Fact Book*.

★ 973 ★
Autos (SIC 3711)

Canada's Auto Sales - 1998

Sales are shown for the first three months of the year.

GM	45,430
Ford	21,779
Chrysler	19,866
Honda	17,180
Toyota	17,036
Volkswagen	6,721
Mazda	4,748
Hyundai	4,601
Nissan	4,085
Volvo	1,860

Source: *Globe and Mail*, April 7, 1998, p. B6.

★ 974 ★
Autos (SIC 3711)

Electric Car Sales in New York

The table shows the number of vehicles each manufacturer is required to sell during the 1998 model year.

Ford	1,920
General Motors	1,920
Toyota	1,440
Honda	1,120
Other	1,600

Source: *Wall Street Journal*, December 16, 1997, p. B1, from *New York Department of Conservation Report*.

★ 975 ★
Autos (SIC 3711)

Leading Canadian Car Companies - 1996

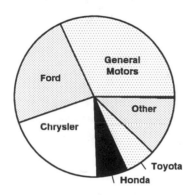

Market shares are shown in percent.

General Motors	32.3%
Ford	23.1
Chrysler	20.4
Honda	6.3
Toyota	6.3
Other	11.6

Source: *Canadian Business*, July 1997, p. 24.

★ 976 ★
Autos (SIC 3711)

Leading Vehicles in Canada - 1996

Data show the number of vehicles on the road.

Chevrolet Cavalier	41,715
Pontiac Sunfire	36,218
Ford Escort	34,377
Toyota Corolla	28,870
Ford Taurus	25,164
Pontiac Grand Am	23,962
Dodge Intrepid	22,993
Honda Accord	20,512
Honda Civic Sedan	19,207
Toyota Camry	18,940

Source: *National Trade Data Bank*, November 3, 1997, p. ISA970901.

★ 977 ★
Autos (SIC 3711)

Luxury Vehicle Market - 1998

Unit sales are shown for the first three months of the year.

Lincoln	47,299
Cadillac	43,168
Mercedes-Benz	40,365
BMW	30,939
Lexus	28,463

Source: *Wall Street Journal*, April 8, 1998, p. B6, from companies.

★ 978 ★
Autos (SIC 3711)

Minivan Market - North America

Shares are shown based on minivan sales for 1996 and 1997. Data for 1997 are projected.

	1996	1997
Chrysler	44.8%	42.4%
Ford	28.5	27.0
General Motors	19.1	20.7
Other	7.7	9.9

Source: *Marketing Magazine*, October 13, 1997, p. 28, from DesRosiers Automotive Consultants Inc.

★ 979 ★

Autos (SIC 3711)

New Car Leaders - 1997

Shares are shown for the year ended May 7, 1998.

GM	31.4%
Ford	24.4
Chrysler	16.4
Mercedes	1.2
Japanese	22.3
Other European	3.3
Koreans	1.0

Source: *Investor's Business Daily*, May 5, 1998, p. 1, from WARD's Automotive Reports.

★ 980 ★

Autos (SIC 3711)

New Car Registrations in Detroit, MI

The table shows new car registrations in the Detroit area by country of origin for January through July 1997. Japanese cars accounted for an estimated 37% share of the U.S. market during that period.

United States	81.0%
Japan	15.0
Other foreign	3.0

Source: *USA TODAY*, November 17, 1997, p. 3B, from The Polk Co.

★ 981 ★

Autos (SIC 3711)

Passenger Cars in Corporate Fleets - 1996

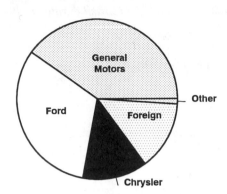

Data show passenger car fleet registrations in percent. "Foreign" includes Honda/Acura, Hyundai, Lexus, Mazda, Mitsubishi, Nissan, Subaru, Toyota, and Volvo.

General Motors	40.0%
Ford	32.0
Chrysler	13.0
Foreign	14.0
Other	1.0

Source: *Purchasing*, November 6, 1997, p. 96, from American Automobile Manufacturing Association.

★ 982 ★

Autos (SIC 3711)

Top Automobiles in Canada - 1997

Market shares are shown based on sales of 741,549 units for the year ended December 31, 1997.

GM Cavalier	6.7%
Honda Civic	6.6
GM Sunfire	6.1
Ford Escort	4.6
Toyota Corolla	4.6
Chrysler Neon	4.5
Toyota Camry	3.3
Chrysler Intrepid	3.1
Ford Taurus	3.1
Pontiac Grand Am	3.1
Others	54.3

Source: *Marketing Magazine*, May 25, 1998, p. 22, from *Canadian Auto World*.

★ 983 ★
Autos (SIC 3711)

Top Car Makers - 1997

Market shares are shown in percent.

General Motors	31.1%
Ford	25.2
Chrysler	15.2
Toyota/Lexus	8.1
Honda/Acura	6.2
Nissan/Infiniti	4.8
VW/Audi	1.1
Hyundai	0.7
Other	7.6

Source: *Los Angeles Times*, April 10, 1998, p. D4, from *Automotive News*.

★ 984 ★
Autos (SIC 3711)

Top Car Makers in Mexico - 1996

Sales are shown by company. Figures include local production and imports.

Volkswagen	51,180
General Motors	47,934
Nissan	40,475
Ford	33,624
Chrsyler	22,626

Source: *Washington Post*, March 20, 1998, p. F1, from American Automobile Manufacturers Association.

★ 985 ★
Autos (SIC 3711)

Top Car Producers in California - 1998

Figures are for the first three months of the year.

General Motors	25.0%
Ford	20.6
Chrysler/Daimler-Benz	14.2
Toyota	13.7
Honda	11.1
Other	15.4

Source: *Los Angeles Times*, May 8, 1998, p. D1, from Autodata, *Automotive News*, and J.D. Power & Associates.

★ 986 ★
Autos (SIC 3711)

Top Car/Light Truck Makers

Market shares are shown by year.

	1996	1997
GM	31.33%	31.09%
Ford	25.39	25.18
Chrysler	16.19	15.20
Toyota	7.66	8.11
Honda	5.57	6.20
Nissan	4.95	4.80
Others	8.90	9.41

Source: *Detroit Free Press*, January 9, 1998, p. E1, from Autodata Corp.

★ 987 ★
Autos (SIC 3711)

Top Full-Size Cars - 1997

Data show unit sales for January 1 through September 1, 1997.

Buick LeSabre	102,423
Dodge Intrepid	101,367
Nissan Maxima	85,859
Ford Crown Victoria	77,125
Mercury Marquis	71,686
Pontiac Bonneville	52,921
Ford Thunderbird	52,671
Buick Century	52,514
Toyota Avalon	49,810
Olds Delta	45,782

Source: *Automotive Industries*, October 1997, p. 127, from Autofacts Group.

★ 988 ★
Autos (SIC 3711)

Top Light Vehicle Makers - 1998

Figures are for the first four months of the year.

General Motors	31.4%
Ford	24.4
Chrysler	16.4
Toyota	7.8
Honda	6.3
Nissan	3.6
Other	10.1

Source: *New York Times*, May 23, 1998, p. B1, from WARD's Auto Info Bank and Bloomberg Financial Markets.

★ 989 ★
Autos (SIC 3711)

Top Luxury Auto Makers - 1997

Data show units sold through the first 10 months of 1997.

Cadillac	152,714
Lincoln	133,162
BMW	103,324
Mercedes	94,956
Acura	94,427
Lexus	79,891
Infiniti	54,891
Audi	26,876
Land Rover	19,660
Jaguar	15,486

Source: *Automotive News*, November 24, 1997, p. 3.

★ 990 ★
Autos (SIC 3711)

Top Luxury Cars - 1997

Data show unit sales for January 1 through September 1, 1997.

Cadillac DeVille/Concours	66,428
Lincoln Town Car	58,160
Volvo 850/S70/V70	49,972
Buick Electra/Park Ave.	44,576
Lexus ES250/ES300	42,213
BMW 3-series	36,998

Chrysler LHS	27,642
Mercedes E-class	27,232
Cadillac Seville	23,513
BMW 5-series	21,168

Source: *Automotive Industries*, October 1997, p. 121, from Autofacts Group.

★ 991 ★
Autos (SIC 3711)

Top Mid-Size Cars - 1997

Data show unit sales for January 1 through September 1, 1997.

Toyota Camry	275,794
Honda Accord	236,372
Ford Taurus	231,696
Chevrolet Lumina	165,640
Pontiac Grand Am	141,713
Ford Contour	111,168
Nissan Altima	103,380
Pontiac Gran Prix	99,792
Chevrolet Malibu	91,886
Mercury Sable	78,328

Source: *Automotive Industries*, October 1997, p. 103, from Autofacts Group.

★ 992 ★
Autos (SIC 3711)

Top Minivans in Canada - 1997

Market shares are shown based on sales of 231,765 units for the year ended December 31, 1997.

Chrysler Caravan/Voyager	39.0%
Ford Windstar	22.5
GM Venture/Trans/Silohuette	14.2
GMC Astra/Safari	12.6
Ford Aerostar	4.0
Toyota Sienna	1.7
Ford Villager	1.5
Nissan Quest	1.4
Chrysler Town and Country	1.0
Mazda MPV	0.9
Others	1.2

Source: *Marketing Magazine*, May 25, 1998, p. 22, from *Canadian Auto World*.

★ 993 ★
Autos (SIC 3711)

Top Passenger Cars - 1997

Data show unit sales.

Toyota Camry	397,156
Honda Accord	384,609
Ford Taurus	357,162
Honda Civic	315,546
Chevrolet Cavalier	302,161
Ford Escort	283,898
Saturn	250,810
Chevrolet Lumina	228,451
Toyota Corolla	218,461
Pontiac Grand Am	204,078

Source: *Chicago Tribune*, January 8, 1998, p. 3, from Ward's AutoInfoBank.

★ 994 ★
Autos (SIC 3711)

Top Small Cars - 1997

Data show unit sales for January 1 through September 1, 1997.

Chevrolet Cavalier	222,627
Honda Civic	221,914
Ford Escort	200,053
Saturn	175,457
Toyota Corolla	159,867
Nissan Sentra	94,909
Dodge Neon	80,211
Pontiac Sunfire	73,516
Volkswagen Jetta	62,487
Plymouth Neon	57,005

Source: *Automotive Industries*, October 1997, p. 115, from Autofacts Group.

★ 995 ★
Autos (SIC 3711)

Top Sport Utility Vehicle Models in Canada - 1997

Market shares are shown based on sales of 152,379 units for the year ended December 31, 1997.

Ford Explorer	15.1%
GMC Blazer/Jimmy	13.2
Chrysler Jeep Grand Cherokee	11.3
Honda CRV	9.7
Toyota RAV4	7.5%
Nissan Pathfinder	6.0
GM Tahoe/Yukon	5.6
Ford Bronco/Expedition	5.2
Toyota 4Runner	4.9
Jeep Cherokee	4.5
Others	17.0

Source: *Marketing Magazine*, May 25, 1998, p. 22, from *Canadian Auto World*.

★ 996 ★
Autos (SIC 3711)

Top Sports Cars - 1997

Data show unit sales for January 1 through September 1, 1997.

Ford Mustang	79,952
Chrysler Sebring	64,729
Chevrolet Camaro	41,601
Mitsubishi Eclipse	34,869
Dodge Avenger	23,371
Pontiac Firebird	21,361
Nissan 200SX	19,655
Mazda Miata	14,525
Ford Probe	13,266
Honda Prelude	12,611

Source: *Automotive Industries*, October 1997, p. 133, from Autofacts Group.

★ 997 ★
Autos (SIC 3711)

Top Vehicle Makers - Washington

Data show top auto companies ranked by share of new truck sales for February 1998.

Ford	29.40%
Chevrolet	18.17
Dodge	14.79
Toyota	10.26
Jeep	7.01
Other	20.37

Source: *Seattle Times*, April 3, 1998, p. I1, from *The MaxIS Report*.

★ 998 ★
Autos (SIC 3711)

Top-Selling Light Trucks - 1997

Models are ranked by number of vehicles sold or leased for January through July 1997.

Ford F-series	448,348
Chevrolet CK	305,963
Ford Explorer	220,350
Dodge Ram	199,983
Dodge Caravan	181,192
Ford Ranger	174,145
Jeep Grand Cherokee	140,225
Ford Windstar	131,785
Chevrolet S10	123,438
Ford Expedition	122,882

Source: *Detroit Free Press*, August 8, 1997, p. 8E, from company reports.

★ 999 ★
Autos (SIC 3711)

Types of Alternative-Fuel Vehicles in Use

The table shows number of alternative-fuel vehicles in use by type of fuel. Data are for 1995, 1996, and 1997. LPG stands for liquefied petroleum gas; CNG for compressed natural gas; LNG for liquefied natural gas; M85 for 85% methanol, 15% gasoline; M100 for 100% methanol; E85 for 85% ethanol, 15% gasoline; and E95 for 95% ethanol, 5% gasoline.

	1995	1996	1997
LPG	259,000	266,000	273,000
CNG	50,218	62,805	81,747
M85	18,319	19,636	19,787
E85	1,527	3,575	5,859
Electric	2,860	3,306	3,925
LNG	603	715	955
E95	136	341	341
M100	386	155	130

Source: *National Petroleum News*, November 1997, p. 34, from U.S. Energy Information Administration.

★ 1000 ★
Trucks (SIC 3711)

Top Pickup Trucks - 1997

The table shows unit sales for January 1 through September 1, 1997.

Ford F-series	482,577
Chevrolet C/K	342,555
Dodge Ram	201,373
Ford Ranger	200,615
Chevrolet S-10	140,505
GMC Sierra	109,258
Toyota Tacoma	96,452
Nissan pickup	87,604
Dodge Dakota	86,688
GMC Sonoma	30,223

Source: *Automotive Industries*, October 1997, p. 95, from Autofacts Group.

★ 1001 ★
Trucks (SIC 3711)

Top Sport Utility Vehicles - 1997

Data show unit sales for January 1 through September 1, 1997.

Ford Explorer	249,750
Jeep Grand Cherokee	164,930
Chevy Blazer	141,987
Ford Expedition	136,727
Toyota 4Runner	87,967
Jeep Cherokee	83,113
Chevy Tahoe	74,718
Chevy Suburban	61,719
Jeep Wrangler	58,750
GMC Jimmy	54,533

Source: *Automotive Industries*, October 1997, p. 89, from Autofacts Group.

★ 1002 ★
Trucks (SIC 3711)

Top Vans - 1997

Data show unit sales for January 1 through September 1, 1997.

Dodge Caravan	205,303
Ford Windstar	137,857
Plymouth Voyager	113,064
Ford Econoline	103,171
Chevy Van	55,649

Continued on next page.

★ 1002 ★ *Continued*

Trucks (SIC 3711)

Top Vans - 1997

Data show unit sales for January 1 through September 1, 1997.

Chevy Astro	52,983
Chrysler Town & Country	51,118
Chevy Venture	46,005
Dodge Ram Van	42,493
Mercury Villager	40,984

Source: *Automotive Industries*, October 1997, p. 109, from Autofacts Group.

★ 1003 ★

Buses (SIC 3713)

Largest Bus Makers

Market shares are shown for 35- and 40- footers.

TMC	18.3%
Flxible	17.0
Orion	16.7
Gillig	15.4
Nova BUS	10.3
New Flyer	10.3
Ikarus	4.8
Neoplan	4.5
MCI	2.3
AVS	0.1
Thomas	0.1
Other	0.2

Source: *Metro Magazine Fact Book*, 1998, p. 15, from APTA.

★ 1004 ★

Buses (SIC 3713)

Top Bus Producers in Mexico

Shares are shown based on 6,455 buses produced in the first four months of the year.

Dina	26.86%
Mercedes Benz	21.30
Kenworth	21.29
Ford	8.15
General Motors	8.15
Navistar	7.00
Chrysler	2.79
OISA	2.03
Volvo	1.00

Scania	0.61%
OshMex	0.60
International	0.22

Source: *National Trade Data Bank*, September 24, 1997, p. ISA970901, from *Auto Motores Informa*.

★ 1005 ★

Trucks (SIC 3713)

Canada's Truck Sales - 1998

Sales are for the first three months.

Chrysler	43,923
GM	41,743
Ford	36,378
Toyota	6,511
Honda	3,337
Nissan	2,800
Mazda	1,362
Subaru	822
Suzuki	748
Mercedes	579

Source: *Globe and Mail*, April 7, 1998, p. B6.

★ 1006 ★

Trucks (SIC 3713)

Class 8 Heavy Truck Producers - North America

Companies are ranked by number of Class 8 trucks produced in 1997, 1999, and 2001. Data are estimated. Ford has sold its operations to Freightliner.

	1997	1999	2001
Freightliner	62,194	75,869	78,021
Paccar	45,120	38,596	41,303
Navistar	41,298	33,141	30,691
Mack	28,204	23,376	22,830
Volvo	20,216	17,976	18,900
Ford	11,970	0	0
Other	5,310	4,929	5,587

Source: *Financial Times*, December 4, 1997, p. 6, from DRI and McGraw-Hill.

★ 1007 ★
Trucks (SIC 3713)

Class 8 Truck Leaders

Market shares are shown in percent.

	Units	Share
Freightliner	50,282	28.2%
Navistar	34,404	19.3
Mack	22,375	12.5
Peterbilt	20,277	11.4
Kenworth	17,988	10.1
Volvo	17,292	9.7
Ford (Sterling)	12,645	7.3
Western Star	2,306	1.3
Other	982	0.2

Source: *Traffic World*, March 9, 1998, p. 17.

★ 1008 ★
Trucks (SIC 3713)

Heavy Truck Market - 1997

Shares are shown in percent for the first half of 1997.

Freightliner	36.1%
Paccar	21.7
Navistar	19.0
Mack	12.3
Volvo/GM	9.6
Western Star	1.3

Source: *Wall Street Journal*, October 3, 1997, p. B4, from Baseline, company reports, and *Automotive News Magazine*.

★ 1009 ★
Trucks (SIC 3713)

Medium Truck Producers - North America

Companies are ranked by number of Class 4-7 trucks produced in 1997, 1999, and 2001. Data are estimated.

	1997	1999	2001
Navistar	61,999	57,235	59,498
Ford	52,157	46,077	51,211
GMC	42,390	35,793	35,725
Freightliner	20,412	18,581	21,772
Volvo	439	610	630

Source: *Financial Times*, December 4, 1997, p. 6, from DRI and McGraw-Hill.

★ 1010 ★
Trucks (SIC 3713)

Top Class 3,4,5 Truck Sellers - 1997

Market shares are shown in percent. Data show vehicles with a gross vehicle weight of 10,001 - 19,500 pounds.

Dodge	33.4%
Ford	30.3
Isuzu	10.1
Chevrolet	6.9
General Motors	5.6
Navistar	4.5
Others	9.2

Source: *Beverage World*, March 1998, p. 108, from American Automobile Manufacturers Association.

★ 1011 ★
Trucks (SIC 3713)

Top Class 6 Truck Sellers - 1997

Market shares are shown in percent. Data show vehicles with a gross vehicle weight of 19,501 - 26,000 pounds.

Freightliner	31.2%
General Motors	17.4
Ford	14.4
Chevrolet	10.3
Navistar	8.2
Isuzu	5.0
Others	13.5

Source: *Beverage World*, March 1998, p. 108, from American Automobile Manufacturers Association.

★ 1012 ★
Trucks (SIC 3713)

Top Class 7 Truck Sellers - 1997

Market shares are shown in percent. Data show vehicles with a gross vehicle weight of 26,001 - 33,000 pounds.

Navistar	48.5%
Ford	22.9
General Motors	11.4
Freightliner	8.6
Others	8.6

Source: *Beverage World*, March 1998, p. 108.

★ 1013 ★
Trucks (SIC 3713)

Used Truck Market in Washington - 1998

Data show market shares in Western Washington for January 1998.

Ford Explorer	5.70%
Chevrolet Blazer S10	4.52
Dodge Caravan	4.15
Ford Ranger	3.74
Plymouth Voyager	3.69
Toyota 4x4	3.56
Nissan 1/2 Ton	3.35
Ford Aerostar	3.05
Jeep Grand Cherokee	2.89
F-150 4WD	2.81
Other	62.54

Source: *Seattle Times*, March 20, 1998, p. I1, from *The MaxIS Report*.

★ 1014 ★
Auto Parts (SIC 3714)

Car Lock/Key Market - North America

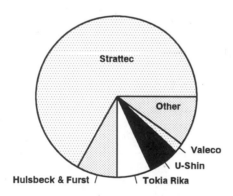

Shares of sales to the Big Three automakers are shown in percent.

Strattec	67.0%
Hulsbeck & Furst	8.0
Tokia Rika	7.0
U-Shin	6.0
Valeco	2.0
Other	10.0

Source: *Investor's Business Daily*, October 30, 1997, p. A4, from Strattec Security.

★ 1015 ★
Auto Parts (SIC 3714)

Heavy Truck Transmission Market

Shares are shown in percent.

Eaton Corp.	70.0%
Rockwell Automotive	14.0
Dana Corp.	7.0
Mack Trucks Inc.	5.0
Allison Transmission	3.0

Source: *Automotive News*, August 25, 1997, p. 16, from Rockwell Automotive.

★ 1016 ★
Auto Parts (SIC 3714)

Manufacturers of Axles for Heavy Trucks - North America

Shares are estimated.

Rockwell	41.0%
Eaton	39.0
Dana	12.0
Other	8.0

Source: *WARD'S Auto World*, August 1997, p. 63, from Power Systems Research.

★ 1017 ★
Auto Parts (SIC 3714)

Manufacturers of Clutches for Heavy Trucks - North America

Shares are estimated.

Dana	80.0%
Rockwell	12.0
Eaton	8.0

Source: *WARD'S Auto World*, August 1997, p. 63, from Power Systems Research.

★ 1018 ★
Auto Parts (SIC 3714)

Manufacturers of Manual Transmissions for Heavy Trucks - North America

Shares are estimated.

Eaton	72.0%
Rockwell	16.0
Dana	6.0
Other	6.0

Source: *WARD'S Auto World*, August 1997, p. 63, from Power Systems Research.

★ 1019 ★
Auto Parts (SIC 3714)

North American Automotive Seating Market

Market shares are shown in percent.

Johnson Controls Inc.	31.0%
Lear Corp.	28.0
Magna Interior Systems	10.0
Ford APO	6.0
Delphi Interior & Lighting	5.0
TS Tech	4.0
All others	16.0

Source: *WARD'S Auto World*, August 1997, p. 62, from CSM Corp.

★ 1020 ★
Auto Parts (SIC 3714)

Powertrain Mount Market - North America

Data show shares based on 51 million mount units. "Other" refers primarily to Japanese manufacturers.

Delphi Automotive Systems	29.0%
Cooper Tire & Rubber Co. (Engineered Products Division)	13.0
Paulstra CRC Corp.	9.0
Standard Products Co.	7.0
BTR AVS USA	6.0
Freudenber-NOK G.P.	6.0
Goodyear	5.0
Yale-South Haven Inc./Trelleborg Industri A.B.	5.0

Bridgestone APM Co.	4.0%
Other	16.0

Source: *Rubber & Plastics News*, October 20, 1997, p. 46.

★ 1021 ★
Auto Parts (SIC 3714)

Top OEM Parts Makers - North America

Companies are ranked by original equipment manufacturer sales in millions of dollars. Visteon Automotive Systems ranked second but did not release figures.

Delphi Automotive Systems	$ 19,950
Dana Corp.	4,974
Johnson Controls Inc.	4,950
Lear Corp.	4,672
Delco Electronics Corp.	4,350
Magna International Inc.	3,740
TRW Inc.	3,516
Robert Bosch Corp.	3,300
Chrysler Component Operations	3,000
Eaton Corp.	2,913

Source: *Automotive News*, March 30, 1998, p. 19.

★ 1022 ★
Auto Parts (SIC 3714)

U.S. Engine Market

The market is estimated for 1997-2002.

Gas	97.9%
Diesel	2.1

Source: *Automotive Industries*, March 1998, p. 17, from Autofacts.

★ 1023 ★
Aircraft (SIC 3721)

Top Regional Aircraft - 1998

Data show percent of total seating capacity.

Saab 340	16.2%
Embraer EMB-120 Brasilia	11.6
Bombardier Dash 8-100/200	10.7
Raytheon Beech 1900	9.1
Aerospatiale/Alenia ATR 42	7.7

Continued on next page.

★ 1023 ★ *Continued*
Aircraft (SIC 3721)

Top Regional Aircraft - 1998

Data show percent of total seating capacity.

Bombardier Regional Jet 7.4%
Aerospatiale/Alenia ATR 72 . . . . . . 6.6
Jetstream J31/J32 . . . . 5.9
BAe 146/Avro RJ 3.7
Jetstream J41 . . . . 3.0
Other 18.1

Source: *Aviation Week & Space Technology*, May 18, 1998, p. 57, from AvStat Associates Inc. for the Regional Airline Assn.

★ 1024 ★
Railroad Equipment (SIC 3743)

Leading Railway Car Producers

Market shares are shown for 1995-June 1996. Data are for light rail vehicles, commuter railcars, locomotives and heavy railcars.

ABB Daimler-Benz 21.3%
Breda 19.2
Kawasaki 15.4
M-K (Amerail) 14.3
Bombardier 14.1
Siemens-Duewag 8.7
Nippon-Sharyo 4.2
Other 2.8

Source: From the Internet, http:// www.transit-center.com, 1997, p. 1.

★ 1025 ★
Railroad Equipment (SIC 3743)

North American Freight Car Fleet

Data show the types of freight cars in the 1,516,258 car fleet.

Covered hoppers 28.3%
Tank cars 15.7
Boxcars 15.0
Gondolas 14.9
Hoppers 11.8
Flat cars 11.1
Refrigerators 2.4
Others 0.8

Source: *Railway Age*, September 1997, p. 50, from *Age of Freight Cars*.

★ 1026 ★
Railroad Equipment (SIC 3743)

Rail Equipment Purchases - 1997

Data show the number of cars purchased by each company.

Chicago (METRA) 102
Toronto (TTC) 72
Monterrey (Metrorrey) 70
Newark (NJ Transit) 64
Portland (Tri-Met) 25
Toronto (GO Transit) 25
Boston (MBTA) 17

Source: *Railway Age*, January 1998, p. 60.

★ 1027 ★
Railroad Equipment (SIC 3743)

Railcar Deliveries by Type of Car

Data are estimated for 1997, 1998, and 1999.

	1997	1998	1999
Covered hoppers	18,200	16,400	15,300
Tank cars	8,500	9,000	9,000
Gondolas	6,500	6,500	6,700
Flat cars	4,000	5,500	6,500
Open hoppers	3,300	4,800	5,300
Boxcars	1,000	1,000	1,000
Other	200	<100	<100

Source: *Railway Age*, July 1997, p. 18, from Economic Planning Associates.

★ 1028 ★
Bicycles (SIC 3751)

Bicycle Manufacturers - 1997

Dollar shares are shown for January through June 1997.

Huffy 33.5%
Dynacraft 15.9
Roadmaster 15.8
Murray 15.5
Kent 2.2
Rand International 2.2
Other 14.9

Source: *Playthings*, September 1997, p. 14, from The NPD Group - TRSTS Report.

★ 1029 ★
Motorcycles (SIC 3751)

Motorcycle Market - 1996

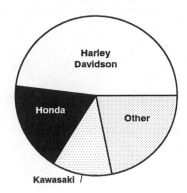

Company shares are shown in percent.

Harley Davidson 48.0%
Honda 18.0
Kawasaki 12.0
Other 22.0

Source: *Investor's Business Daily*, October 21, 1997, p. B14.

★ 1030 ★
Motorcycles (SIC 3751)

Street Bike Market

Shares of the $2.1 billion market are shown in percent. "Other" includes BMW, Ducati, Triumph, Buell and Moto Guzzi. Harley has a 52% share of the cruiser market and a 58% share of the touring bike market.

Harley-Davidson 39.0%
Suzuki/Kawasaki/Yamaha 35.0
Honda 22.0
Other 4.0

Source: *Inc.*, November 1997, p. 47.

★ 1031 ★
Aerospace (SIC 3761)

Leading Markets for U.S. Aerospace Exports - 1995- 1966

Sales are shown in percent.

Asia 41.34%
Europe 39.65
Middle East 7.22
Canada 7.09
Latin America 4.10
Central Europe 0.61

Source: *World Trade*, October 1997, p. 118, from Aerospace Industries Association.

★ 1032 ★
Aerospace (SIC 3761)

Top Aerospace Firms - Canada

Firms are ranked by value of contracts in billions of dollars.

Boeing Corp. . . . . $ 7,000.0
Lockheed Martin 758.0
Space Systems/Loral Inc. 288.2
AlliedSignal 253.0
Honeywell 202.7
United Technologies Corp. 111.8
Dynacs Engineering 74.9
Harris Corp. 46.8
Teledyne 40.0
Astro Aerospace 15.1

Source: *Aviation Week & Space Technology*, December 8, 1997, p. 84.

★ 1033 ★
Aerospace (SIC 3761)

Top Defense Contractors - 1997

Firms are ranked by contract awards in billions of dollars.

Lockheed Martin . . . . $ 11.6
Boeing 9.6
Northrop Grumman 3.5
General Dynamics 3.0
Raytheon 2.9

Source: *Washington Post*, March 24, 1998, p. C2, from U.S. Defense Department.

★ 1034 ★
Trailers (SIC 3799)

Race Car Transporter Market

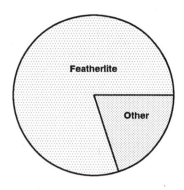

The market is shown in percent.

Featherlite 80.0%
Other 20.0

Source: *Investor's Business Daily*, May 16, 1998, p. A4.

SIC 38 - Instruments and Related Products

★ 1035 ★
Medical Instruments (SIC 3841)

Insulin Pump Market

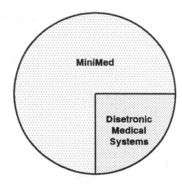

Shares are shown based on a $100 million market.

MiniMed	75.0%
Disetronic Medical Systems	25.0

Source: *Investor's Business Daily*, May 7, 1998, p. A4, from company reports.

★ 1036 ★
Bandages (SIC 3842)

Top First Aid Bandage Brands

Shares of the 167.4 million unit market are shown in percent.

Band-Aid	23.2%
Johnson & Johnson	12.1
Curad	7.0
3M Comfort Strips	4.4
Curity	4.0
J&J King	3.4
3M Comfort Strips	3.2
Band Aid Sport Strips	2.1
Private label	15.9
Other	47.9

Source: *Supermarket Business*, April 1998, p. 58, from Information Resources Inc.

★ 1037 ★
First Aid Kits (SIC 3842)

Leading First Aid Product Makers

Market shares are shown in percent.

J&J Band-Aid	49.0%
3M Nexcare	17.0
Beiersdorf Curad	15.7
Private label	14.3
Other	4.0

Source: *America's Pharmacist*, May 1998, p. 47, from Information Resources Inc.

★ 1038 ★
First Aid Kits (SIC 3842)

Top First-Aid Brands

Market shares are shown for the year ended October 12, 1997. Data refer to tape, bandages, gauze and cotton.

Band Aid	23.0%
Johnson & Johnson	13.2
Curad	5.8
Johnson & Johnson King Sterile	4.6
3M Active Strips	4.2
Curity	4.1
Steripads	3.3
3M Comfort Strip	2.9
Band Aid Sport Strip	2.8
3M	2.2
Private label	12.7
Other	21.2

Source: *Nonfoods Merchandising*, January 1998, p. 13, from Information Resources Inc.

★ 1039 ★

First Aid Kits (SIC 3842)

Top First-Aid Ointments

Market shares are shown for the year ended October 12, 1997.

Neosporin Plus	14.0%
Neosporin	10.4
Betadine	3.8
Solarcaine	3.6
Becton Dickinson	2.8
Polysporin	2.4
Bactine	2.1
Mycitracin	2.0
Fruit of the Earth	1.9
Balmex	1.8
Private label	34.6
Other	20.6

Source: *Nonfoods Merchandising*, January 1998, p. 13, from Information Resources Inc.

★ 1040 ★

First Aid Kits (SIC 3842)

Top-Selling First Aid Ointments

Shares are shown based on sales of 198.1 million units.

Neosporin Plus	5.4%
Neosporin	4.3
Becton Dickinson	2.6
Solarcaine	1.2
Bactine	1.0
Private label	62.8
Other	22.7

Source: *Supermarket Business*, April 1998, p. 58, from Information Resources Inc.

★ 1041 ★

Wheelchairs (SIC 3842)

Top Wheelchair Producers - 1997

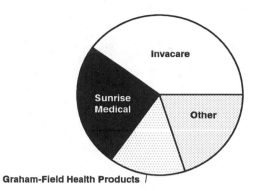

Graham-Field Health Products

Shares of the $525 million market are estimated in percent. The entire home medical equipment market is valued at $2.5 billion.

Invacare	40.0%
Sunrise Medical	25.0
Graham-Field Health Products	15.0
Other	20.0

Source: *New York Times*, January 28, 1998, p. C1, from company reports and analysts estimates.

★ 1042 ★

Electromedical Equipment (SIC 3845)

Leading M.R.I. Manufacturers - 1996

Distribution of sales is shown by company. M.R.I. stands for magnetic resonance imaging.

General Electric	38.0%
Siemens	24.0
Hitachi	12.0
Picker	11.0
Phillips	9.0
Fonar	1.0
Other	5.0

Source: *New York Times*, July 12, 1997, p. 21.

★ 1043 ★

Optical Goods (SIC 3851)

Contact Lens Care Market

The table shows annual spending on lens care products in millions of dollars. Approximately 26 million Americans use contact lenses.

	($ mil.)	Share
Soft lens care	$ 750	55.56%
Disinfecting solutions	375	27.78
Enzymatic cleaners	125	9.26
Daily cleaners	100	7.41

Source: *Supermarket Business*, September 1997, p. 41.

★ 1044 ★

Optical Goods (SIC 3851)

Leading Contact Lens Brands

Shares of the $865 million market are shown in percent.

Bausch & Lomb/Polymer	37.0%
Alcon	27.0
Ciba Vision	15.0
Allergan/Barnes-Hind	14.0
Private label	6.0
Other	1.0

Source: *America's Pharmacist*, March 1997, p. 47, from A.C. Nielsen.

★ 1045 ★

Optical Goods (SIC 3851)

Leading Eye/Lens Care Solutions - 1997

Shares are shown based on sales for the 52 weeks ended March 2, 1997.

Bausch & Lomb Renu	13.1%
Alcon Opti Free	10.2
Private label	7.9
Ciba Vision Aosept	6.8
Bausch & Lomb Sensitive Eye	4.1
Visine	3.9
Boston Clean	3.0
Bausch & Lomb	2.7
Alcon Opti Free Express	2.5
Hypotears	2.3
Other	43.5

Source: *Discount Merchandiser*, June 1997, p. 69.

★ 1046 ★

Optical Goods (SIC 3851)

U.S. Eyewear Sales

Data show retail sales in billions of dollars.

	1996	2001
Prescription lenses	$ 7.2	$ 9.7
Prescription frames	4.6	5.9
Non-prescription eyewear	3.0	4.1
Contact lenses	1.9	2.1

Source: *USA TODAY*, December 22, 1997, p. B1, from Packaged Facts and FIND/SVP.

★ 1047 ★

Cameras (SIC 3861)

Leading Disposable Camera Producers - 1997

Shares are shown based on mass merchandiser, food and drug store sales for the four-week period ended November 9, 1997.

Kodak	66.0%
Fuji	16.0
Other	18.0

Source: *New York Times*, December 11, 1997, p. C10, from Information Resources Inc.

★ 1048 ★

Movie Projectors (SIC 3861)

Movie Projector Market

Market shares are shown in percent.

Ballantyne of Omaha Inc.	65.0%
Other	35.0

Source: *Wall Street Journal*, February 20, 1998, p. B1.

★ 1049 ★

Photocopiers (SIC 3861)

Leading Federal Contractors of Duplicating Machines

Shares are shown based on $133,696,000 in purchases by the U.S. government.

De La Rue Giori Sa	31.70%
Xerox Corp.	11.00
Minolta Corp.	4.17

Continued on next page.

★ 1049 ★ *Continued*
Photocopiers (SIC 3861)

Leading Federal Contractors of Duplicating Machines

Shares are shown based on $133,696,000 in purchases by the U.S. government.

Canon USA Inc.	4.07%
Pitney Bowes Inc.	3.91
Man Roland Inc.	3.85
Eastman Kodak Co.	3.66
George Fischer Foundry Systems	2.43
Renco Group Inc.	2.38
Sin Do System Co. Ltd.	2.02
Others	30.81

Source: From the Internet, http:// www.govexec.com/ procure/articles/0896opgb.html, September 24, 1997, p. 2.

★ 1050 ★
Photocopiers (SIC 3861)

Plain Paper Copier Market

Shares are shown in percent.

Canon	29.4%
Xerox	23.3
Sharp	13.1
Mita	6.2
Minolta	4.6
Konica	4.1
Ricoh	4.0
Lanier	3.9
Toshiba	2.9
Other	8.4

Source: From the Internet, http:// www.usa.canon.com/ copiers/mktsharecopier.html, June 10, 1997, p. 1, from Dataquest Inc.

★ 1051 ★
Photographic Film (SIC 3861)

Best-Selling Film - 1997

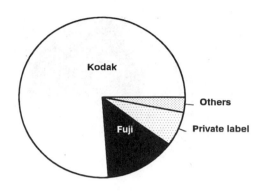

Market shares are shown for 35mm film sales.

	1996	1997
Kodak	79.2%	75.6%
Fuji	11.1	14.1
Private label	6.8	7.1
Others	3.0	3.0

Source: *Wall Street Journal*, January 16, 1998, p. A4, from retail scanner data.

★ 1052 ★
Photographic Film (SIC 3861)

Leading Types of Photographic Film - 1997

Shares are shown in percent. APS stands for advanced photo system.

35mm color print	71.3%
110 cartridge	6.9
35mm black & white	4.9
Disc cartridge	1.2
Instant print	3.3
APS	2.5
35mm slide	3.8
Medium format	4.6

Source: *Supermarket Business*, February 1998, p. 52, from *Photo Marketing Association 1997 Consumer Photographic Survey*.

★ 1053 ★

Photographic Film (SIC 3861)

Photographic Film Market - 1997

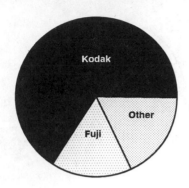

Shares are shown in percent.

Kodak	66.0%
Fuji	15.9
Other	18.1

Source: *Los Angeles Times*, September 21, 1997, p. D12, from Prudential Securities.

★ 1054 ★

Photographic Film (SIC 3861)

Top Film Brands - 1997

Brands are shown ranked by sales in millions of dollars for the 52-week period ended June 22, 1997. Data include food, drug, and mass merchandiser sales.

	Sales ($ mil.)	Share
Kodak Gold	$ 312.076	18.9%
Kodak Gold Plus	290.469	17.6
Polaroid	234.048	14.2
Fuji	129.577	7.8
Polaroid 600 Plus	118.860	7.2
Kodak Film	112.670	6.8
Kodak Royal Gold	92.295	5.6
Private label	89.705	5.4
Kodak Kodacolor	87.998	5.3
Polaroid Spectra	44.475	2.7

Source: *Discount Merchandiser*, September 1997, p. 66, from Information Resources Inc.

★ 1055 ★

Sunglasses (SIC 3861)

What We Spend on Sunglasses - 1997

Total sales of sunglasses reached $2.6 billion in 1997. The table shows the share of sales by price range.

Up to $30	37.0%
$31-$50	16.0
$51-$75	8.0
$76-$100	21.0
$101 and up	18.0

Source: *USA TODAY*, April 17, 1998, p. B1, from Sunglass Association of America.

SIC 39 - Miscellaneous Manufacturing Industries

★ 1056 ★

Flatware (SIC 3914)

Best-Selling Flatware Patterns

Data show share of sales for the fourth quarter ending January 31, 1998.

Juillard	5.63%
Easton	4.53
Dover	4.19
Golden Juillard	4.01
Michaelangelo	3.29
Chateau	2.84
Camber	2.36
Golden Aquarius	2.21
Golden Kenwood	2.12
Capello	2.02

Source: *HFN*, April 13, 1998, p. 41, from *Macomber Report*.

★ 1057 ★

Flatware (SIC 3914)

Flatware Market - 1996

The $752.85 million market is shown in percent.

Upstairs stainless steel	54.5%
Sterling silver	20.0
Housewares stainless steel	17.5
Silverplate	8.0

Source: *HFN*, July 21, 1997, p. 28.

★ 1058 ★

Musical Instruments (SIC 3931)

Best-Selling Musical Accessories - 1997

Sales are shown in millions of dollars.

Cases/bags	$ 96.0
Lighting	52.0
Stands	43.0
Reeds	28.3
Instrument pickups	17.4
Harmonicas	14.0
Tuners/metronomes	12.0

Source: *Music Trades*, April 1998, p. 115.

★ 1059 ★

Musical Instruments (SIC 3931)

Grand Piano Sales - 1997

Sales are shown by size.

Under 5'0"	6,620
5' to 5'5"	10,841
5'6" to 5'10"	5,770
5'11" to 6'4"	2,915
6'4" to 7'10"	1,985
7'11" and over	225

Source: *Music Trades*, April 1998, p. 109.

★ 1060 ★

Musical Instruments (SIC 3931)

Largest Music Industry Suppliers - 1997

The leading suppliers are ranked by estimated sales in millions of dollars. Data are for North America.

Yamaha Corporation of America	$ 781.0
Harman Int. (Professional Div.)	475.0
Telex Communications (EVI Audio)	362.9
Peavey Electronics	325.0
Steinway Musical Instruments	277.8
Shure Brothers	210.0
Fender Musical Instruments	193.0
Roland Corp. USA	150.0
Baldwin Piano & Organ	143.1
Kaman Music	130.0
Gibson Guitar Corp.	120.1
Kawai America Corporation	105.0

Source: *Music Trades*, April 1998, p. 126.

★ 1061 ★

Musical Instruments (SIC 3931)

Music Product Sales by State - 1996

Data show dollar sales.

California	$ 926,625,926
New York	498,526,323
Florida	445,724,656
Texas	445,270,168
Illinois	308,472,498
Pennsylvania	246,076,597
Ohio	225,785,418
New Jersey	223,527,818
Michigan	215,748,531
Maryland	210,124,981

Source: *Music Trades*, August 1997, p. 130.

★ 1062 ★

Musical Instruments (SIC 3931)

Musical Instrument Sales - 1997

Retail sales are shown in millions of dollars. Total industry sales grew from $5.7 billion in 1996 to $6.1 billion in 1997.

	($ mil.)	Share
Sound reinforcement	$ 757.6	12.42%
Acoustic pianos	713.8	11.70
Fretted instruments	$ 710.8	11.65%
School music products	628.3	10.30
Print music	433.5	7.11
Single unit amplifiers	362.0	5.93
Electronic music products	322.8	5.29
Microphones	312.3	5.12
Percussion products	311.7	5.11
Other	1,547.2	25.36

Source: *Music Trades*, April 1998, p. 84.

★ 1063 ★

Musical Instruments (SIC 3931)

Top-Selling Horns - 1997

Data show unit sales.

Clarinets	141,538
Trumpets	137,767
Flutes	127,576
Trombones	56,811
Alto sax	56,700
Tenor sax	10,985
French horn	9,514
Coronets	9,155
Tubas	4,466
Sousaphones	2,315

Source: *Music Trades*, April 1998, p. 110.

★ 1064 ★

Toys and Games (SIC 3942)

Beanie Baby Sales - 1997

Unit sales are shown by relationship to recipient to purchaser.

Daughter	25.0%
Self	24.0
Not related	14.0
Grandchild	13.0
Son	13.0
Multiple family members	4.0
Other family members	7.0

Source: *Playthings*, April 1998, p. 18, from NPD Group-Toy Market Index.

★ 1065 ★
Toys and Games (SIC 3942)

Doll Market - 1997

Shipments are shown in millions of dollars.

	($ mil.)	Share
Fashion dolls/clothes/ accessories	$ 1,167	55.23%
Large dolls	328	15.52
Mini dolls	163	7.71
Large doll accessories	77	3.64
Mini doll accessories	65	3.08
Doll houses/furniture	59	2.79
Soft dolls	43	2.04
Remaining dolls/accessories	211	9.99

Source: *Playthings*, April 1998, p. 36, from Toy Manufacturers of America.

★ 1066 ★
Toys and Games (SIC 3942)

Leading Manufacturers of Plush Toys - 1997

Shares are shown in percent for November 1997.

Mattel	58.1%
Hasbro Toy Group	6.0
Dan-Dee Imports	5.7
Microsoft	5.7
Earthwood	2.5
Play by Play Toy	2.2
Thinkaway Toys	2.0
Other	17.8

Source: *Playthings*, February 1998, p. 22.

★ 1067 ★
Toys and Games (SIC 3942)

Top Action Figure Makers - 1997

Market shares are shown for the first nine months of 1997.

Hasbro	59.0%
Bandai America	12.5
Toy Biz	5.6
Mattel	4.6
Thinkaways Toys	4.6
Playmates Toys	3.6
Other	10.1

Source: *Playthings*, December 1997, p. 14.

★ 1068 ★
Toys and Games (SIC 3944)

Best Selling Licensed Properties - 1997

Percentages indicate dollar share of toy industry based on sales for August 1997. Data do not include video games.

Barbie	6.4%
Star Wars	2.9
Sesame Street	1.7
Lego (basic, themed, freestyle)	1.5
Winnie the Pooh	1.5
Hot Wheels	1.4
Batman	1.1
Jurassic Park	1.0
Tamagotchi	1.0
NASCAR	1.0
Other	80.5

Source: *Playthings*, November 1997, p. 51.

★ 1069 ★

Toys and Games (SIC 3944)

Electronic Sports Game Makers - 1997

Electronic Arts	
Sony	
Acclaim	
Sega	
Midway	
Nintendo	
Other	

The video sports game market is shown for the 12 months ended September 30, 1997. Leading console systems are Nintendo 64, Sony Playstation, and Sega Genesis.

Electronic Arts	45.0%
Sony	15.0
Acclaim	9.0
Sega	9.0
Midway	4.0
Nintendo	3.0
Other	15.0

Source: *New York Times*, November 17, 1997, p. C5, from Electronic Arts and The NPD Group.

★ 1070 ★

Toys and Games (SIC 3944)

Mini Vehicle Manufacturers - 1997

Dollar shares are shown for January to June 1997.

Mattel	28.3%
Galoob Toys	28.1
Racing Champions	14.7
Tyco (Mattel)	11.0
Ertl	2.4
Hasbro Toy Group	2.3
Playing Mantis	2.1
Other	11.1

Source: *Playthings*, October 1997, p. 18, from The NPD Group - TRSTS Report.

★ 1071 ★

Toys and Games (SIC 3944)

Sports Activities Manufacturers - 1997

Dollar shares are shown for June 1997.

Hasbro Toy Group	16.6%
General Sportcraft	11.4
Mattel	9.0
Franklin Sports	7.3
Little Tikes	6.5
Toymax	4.0
Other	45.2

Source: *Playthings*, September 1997, p. 14, from The NPD Group - TRSTS Report.

★ 1072 ★

Toys and Games (SIC 3944)

Top Counties for Spending on Toys and Games - 1997

Counties are ranked by spending in millions of dollars.

Los Angeles County, CA	$ 890.1
Cook County, IL	566.5
Harris County, TX	333.7
Orange County, CA	273.8
San Diego County, CA	269.1
Maricopa County, AZ	257.6
Dallas County, TX	221.5
Kings County, NY	216.9
Wayne County, MI	216.3
Queens County, NY	208.1

Source: *Wall Street Journal*, December 26, 1997, p. B8, from National Decision Systems and Claritas Inc.

★ 1073 ★
Toys and Games (SIC 3944)

Top PC Game Joystick Producers - 1997

Market shares are shown in percent.

Microsoft	25.0%
Logitech	14.0
Mouse Systems	13.0
InterAct Accessories	12.0
Advanced Gravis	11.0

Source: *Investor's Business Daily*, May 21, 1998, p. A8, from PC Data Inc.

★ 1074 ★
Toys and Games (SIC 3944)

Top PC Gamepad Producers - 1997

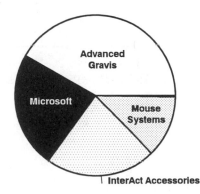

Market shares are shown in percent.

Advanced Gravis	36.0%
Microsoft	20.0
InterAct Accessories	19.0
Mouse Systems	11.0

Source: *Investor's Business Daily*, May 21, 1998, p. A8, from PC Data Inc.

★ 1075 ★
Toys and Games (SIC 3944)

Top Video Game Brands - 1998

Shares are shown for the first quarter of the year.

Sony Playstation	66.3%
Nintendo 64	29.6
Sega Saturn	4.1

Source: *New York Times*, May 25, 1998, p. C4, from *NPD TRSTS Video Games Report*.

★ 1076 ★
Toys and Games (SIC 3944)

Top Video Hardware Brands - 1998

Shares are shown for the first quarter of the year.

Sony Playstation	67.9%
Nintendo 64	30.7
Sega Saturn	1.5

Source: *New York Times*, May 25, 1998, p. C4, from *NPD TRSTS Video Games Report*.

★ 1077 ★
Toys and Games (SIC 3944)

Toys and Games Market by Segment

Shares are shown in percent. Total sales reached $13.9 billion.

Dolls	14.8%
Activity toys	13.9
Games/puzzles	9.7
Cars/boats	9.1
Stuffed animals	7.8
Action figures	6.0
Toys that are ridden	5.7
Other	23.2

Source: *New York Times*, December 20, 1997, p. B1, from Toy Manufacturers Association of America.

★ 1078 ★
Toys and Games (SIC 3944)

Video Game Hardware Market - 1997

The market is shown by company.

Sony	53.0%
Nintendo	39.0
Sega	8.0

Source: *The Guardian*, March 14, 1998, p. 3.

★ 1079 ★
Toys and Games (SIC 3944)

Virtual Pets Market - 1997

Shares are shown based on unit sales for the months of May, June and July 1997.

	May	June	July
Tamagotchi	86.0%	52.0%	34.0%
Nano Pets	7.0	23.0	42.0
Giga Pets	7.0	25.0	24.0

Source: *Playthings*, November 1997, p. 18, from The NPD Group.

★ 1080 ★

Toys and Games (SIC 3944)

Water/Pool/Sand Toy Makers - 1997

Shares are shown for June 1997.

Intex	37.6%
Aqua Leisure	9.3
General Foam Plastic	7.6
Tony Trading	6.6
Empire	6.5
Florida Pool Products	5.3
Kidpower	4.8
Other	22.3

Source: *Playthings*, September 1997, p. 14, from The NPD Group - TRSTS Report.

★ 1081 ★

Sporting Goods (SIC 3949)

Camping Equipment Market in Canada

Sales are shown by region.

Ontario	38.0%
Quebec	23.0
Prairies	19.5
British Columbia	13.5
Atlantic Provinces	6.0

Source: *National Trade Data Bank*, October 22, 1997, p. ISA970901.

★ 1082 ★

Sporting Goods (SIC 3949)

Golf Ball Producers - 1996

Shares are shown based on 70 million dozens of balls produced.

Spalding	34.3%
Fortune Brands	32.1
Wilson	12.0
Dunlop	9.9
Bridgestone	5.3
Hansberger	2.6
Hogan	1.4
Sunset	1.1
AvTech	0.6
Karstan	0.4
Geo	0.3

Source: *Rubber & Plastics News*, October 20, 1997, p. 18, from Southerland Golf Inc.

★ 1083 ★

Sporting Goods (SIC 3949)

Largest Golf Equipment Makers - 1996

Companies are ranked by sales in millions of dollars.

Titleist/Foot-Joy/Cobra	$ 677
Callaway	466
Spalding/Etonic	361
Taylor Made	251
Wilson	140
Maxfli/Dunlop	121

Source: *Brandweek*, January 26, 1998, p. 31, from *Golf Pro*.

★ 1084 ★

Sporting Goods (SIC 3949)

Largest Inline Skate Makers - 1997

Firms are ranked by sales in millions of dollars. Shares of the group are shown in percent.

	Sales ($ mil.)	% of Group
Rollerblade	$ 168	34.78%
Roller Derby	46	9.52
First Team	44	9.11
Bauer	43	8.90

Continued on next page.

★ 1084 ★ *Continued*
Sporting Goods (SIC 3949)

Largest Inline Skate Makers - 1997

Firms are ranked by sales in millions of dollars.
Shares of the group are shown in percent.

	Sales ($ mil.)	% of Group
K2	$ 39	8.07%
Variflex	30	6.21
Seneca Sports	23	4.76
Mission	20	4.14
Oxygen	17	3.52
Roces	16	3.31
National	13	2.69
CCM	12	2.48
Brookfield	12	2.48

Source: *Sportstyle*, May 1998, p. 25.

★ 1085 ★
Sporting Goods (SIC 3949)

Largest Outdoor Equipment Makers - 1997

Firms are ranked by sales in millions of dollars.

Brunswick Outdoor Recreation Group . .	$ 700.0
Coleman	515.0
American Recreation	143.0
Jansport	114.5
Eastpak	66.0
Johnson Worldwide	60.0
The Outdoor Recreation Group	41.0
Eagle Creek	33.8
The North Face	26.6
Henderson Products	25.0

Source: *Sportstyle*, May 1998, p. 32.

★ 1086 ★
Sporting Goods (SIC 3949)

Largest Ski Equipment Makers - 1997

Firms are ranked by sales in millions of dollars.

Salomon	$ 95.0
Rossignol	55.5
K2	35.0
Dynastar	32.3
Tecnica	30.5
Marker	29.0

Nordica	$ 25.9
Head USA	21.6
Volkl	15.0
Atomic	14.0

Source: *Sportstyle*, May 1998, p. 28.

★ 1087 ★
Sporting Goods (SIC 3949)

Largest Snowboard Equipment Makers - 1997

Firms are ranked by sales in millions of dollars.
Shares of the group are shown in percent.

	Sales ($ mil.)	% of Group
Burton	$ 62.0	30.53%
K2	27.0	13.29
Airwalk	22.0	10.83
Ride	19.4	9.55
Sims	13.6	6.70
Morrow	11.1	5.47
Mervin	10.4	5.12
Salomon	10.0	4.92
Vans	8.6	4.23
Lamar	6.4	3.15
Nitro	5.6	2.76
Rossignol	5.0	2.46
Wintersticks	2.0	0.98

Source: *Sportstyle*, May 1998, p. 28.

★ 1088 ★
Sporting Goods (SIC 3949)

Leading Producers of Soccer Balls - Canada

Shares are shown in percent.

Umbro	13.0%
Mitre	10.0
Cooper	9.0
Spalding	9.0
Other	59.0

Source: *National Trade Data Bank*, June 2, 1997, p. IMI970630.

★ 1089 ★

Sporting Goods (SIC 3949)

Sporting Goods Sales at Discount Stores - 1997

Distribution is shown based on sales of $5,640,691,000 at discount stores in 1997.

Fishing & camping supplies 32.48%
Firearms & supplies 11.98
Team sports goods 11.58
Marine supplies, water sports 8.94
Bicycles 8.35
Sports apparel & footwear 7.58
Racquet & golf goods 6.07
Exercise equipment 4.90
Miscellaneous 8.12

Source: *Discount Merchandiser*, June 1997, p. 43.

★ 1090 ★

Sporting Goods (SIC 3949)

Sporting Goods Sales by Category - 1996

Categories are shown ranked by sales in billions of dollars. Total sports equipment sales reached $15.7 billion.

	Sales ($ bil.)	Share
Exercise machines	$ 2.6	16.56%
Golf	2.2	14.01
Firearms/hunting	1.7	10.83
Fishing	1.6	10.19
Camping	1.5	9.55
In-line skating	0.6	3.82
Other	5.5	35.03

Source: *Los Angeles Times*, November 13, 1997, p. D5, from Sporting Goods Manufacturers Association.

★ 1091 ★

Sporting Goods (SIC 3949)

Top Sports Equipment Categories - 1996- 97

Data show manufacturers' sales in millions of dollars. Figures are estimated for 1996 and 1997.

	1996	1997	Share
Golf	$ 2,295	$ 2,410	15.19%
Exercise	2,070	2,215	13.96

	1996	1997	Share
Camping	$ 1,500	$ 1,530	9.64%
In-line skates	625	685	4.32
Bowling/billiards	430	443	2.79
Water sports	515	540	3.40
Baseball/softball	350	365	2.30
Tennis	245	258	1.63
Archery	260	255	1.61
Soccer	20	215	1.36
Other	6,691	6,950	43.80

Source: *Discount Merchandiser*, February 1998, p. 44, from *Sporting Goods Manufacturers Association Market Recreation Report*.

★ 1092 ★

Pens (SIC 3951)

Popular Kinds of Pens

Data show annual sales of $1.7 billion in percent.

Ballpoint pens 43.0%
Markers/highlighters 16.0
Roller pens 14.0
Mechanical pens 11.0
Coloring markers (water based) 6.0
Porous point (thinline markers) 4.0
Fountain pens 3.0

Source: *Potentials in Marketing*, May 1997, p. 59, from Writing Instrument Manufacturers Association.

★ 1093 ★

Fasteners (SIC 3965)

U.S. Fastener Sales

Sales are shown in billions of dollars.

	1996	2001
Standard	$ 6.43	$ 7.30
Aerospace	1.05	1.58

Source: *Assembly*, March 1998, p. 18, from Freedonia Group.

★ 1094 ★
Toothbrushes (SIC 3991)

Toothbrush Market - 1997

Brands are shown ranked by sales in millions of dollars for the 52 weeks ended July 27, 1997.

	Sales ($ mil.)	Share
Oral B	$ 139.7	24.7%
Colgate	109.6	19.4
Reach	94.4	16.7
Crest	54.0	9.6
Mentadent	47.4	8.4
Aquafresh	30.2	5.3
Butler	14.6	2.6
Tek	5.7	1.0
Dentax	5.6	1.0
Private label	38.6	6.8

Source: *Nonfoods Merchandising*, October 1997, p. 7, from Information Resources Inc.

★ 1095 ★
Candles (SIC 3999)

Types of Candles Sold in Supermarkets

Shares are shown in percent.

Birthday	25.0%
Votives	20.0
Numerals	16.0
Tapers	12.0
Wax container	11.0
Citronella	5.0
Tea light	4.0
Pillar	2.0
Other	5.0

Source: *Nonfoods Merchandising*, November 1997, p. 21, from GuildHouse and American Greetings Corp.

★ 1096 ★
Cotton Swabs (SIC 3999)

Cotton Swab Market - Canada

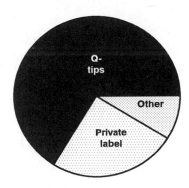

Shares are shown based on a $7.3 million market for the year ended January 3, 1998.

Q-tips	66.0%
Private label	25.0
Other	9.0

Source: *Marketing Magazine*, April 20, 1998, p. 3.

★ 1097 ★
Pet Products (SIC 3999)

Top Flea Remedy Producers - 1997

Market shares are estimated in percent.

Advantage	45.0%
Program	25.0
Other	30.0

Source: *Advertising Age*, May 11, 1998, p. 18, from IMS America.

SIC 40 - Railroad Transportation

★ 1098 ★
Transportation (SIC 4000)

Largest Transportation Firms in Washington D.C.

Companies are ranked by revenues in millions of dollars.

US Airways Group Inc.	$ 8,513.8
Banner Aerospace Inc.	389.1
World Airways Inc.	309.4
WorldCorp Inc.	216.1
Atlantic Coast Airlines Inc.	205.4

Source: *Washington Post*, April 27, 1998, p. 37.

★ 1099 ★
Railroads (SIC 4011)

Largest Community Carload Shippers - 1998

Railroad	
Union Pacific	
CSX	
BNSF	
Norfolk Southern	
Conrail	
Canadian National	
Canadian Pacific	
Illinois Central	
Kansas City Southern	

Figures show number of carloads for the first three months of the year.

Union Pacific	1,212,461
CSX	1,088,787
BNSF	1,067,231
Norfolk Southern	794,377
Conrail	608,732
Canadian National	444,734
Canadian Pacific	385,305
Illinois Central	196,121
Kansas City Southern	168,530

Source: *Journal of Commerce*, April 13, 1998, p. 1, from Association of American Railroads.

★ 1100 ★
Railroads (SIC 4011)

Largest Eastern Railroads - 1996

Firms are ranked by operating revenues in millions of dollars.

CSX	$ 4,909.0
NS	4,101.0
CR	3,597.2
IC	617.2
GTW	363.1

Source: *Distribution*, July 1997, p. 46, from Association of American Railroads.

★ 1101 ★
Railroads (SIC 4011)

Largest Railroads - 1997

Firms are ranked by revenue in millions of dollars.

Union Pacific	$ 11,014
CSX	10,621
Burlington No. Santa Fe	8,412
Norfolk Southern	5,165
Kansas City So. Ind.	1,058

Source: *Fortune*, April 27, 1998, p. 56.

★ 1102 ★
Railroads (SIC 4011)

Largest Western Railroads - 1996

Firms are ranked by operating revenues in millions of dollars.

BNSF	$ 8,186.9
UP	6,728.4
SP	3,030.1
SOO	668.9
KCS	491.6

Source: *Distribution*, July 1997, p. 46, from Association of American Railroads.

★ 1103 ★
Railroads (SIC 4011)

Rail Companies by Chemicals Shipped - 1996

Shares are shown based on 140.1 million tons of chemicals shipped.

UP	32.0%
CSX	15.2
BNSF	14.9
SP	11.6
NS	8.6
IC	6.1
Conrail	5.3
KCS	4.2
SOO	1.8
GTW	0.4

Source: *Chemical Week*, September 24, 1997, p. 34, from American Association of Railroads.

SIC 41 - Local and Interurban Passenger Transit

★ 1104 ★
Buses (SIC 4111)

Largest Motorcoach Fleets

Companies are ranked by total number of coaches. The top 50 fleets have about 42 percent of the total U.S.- Canadian motorcoach fleet.

Greyhound Lines Inc.	1,894
Ryder-ATE	1,280
ATC/Vancom Inc.	1,241
Laidlaw Transit Services	955
Academy Bus Tours Inc.	585
Liberty Lines Transit	419
Greyhound Canada Transportation Corp.	387
Diversified Transportation Ltd.	350
Surburban Transit Corp.	333
Holland America Line-Westours Inc.	299

Source: *Metro Magazine Fact Book*, 1998, p. 12.

★ 1105 ★
Buses (SIC 4111)

Largest Transit Bus Fleets - 1997

Firms are ranked by fleet size. Data are for Canada and the United States. The top 10 fleets have 24% of the U.S. And Canadian market.

MTA New York City Transit	3,745
New Jersey Transit Corp.	2,970
Los Angeles County MTA	2,020
Chicago Transit Authority	1,930
Montreal Urban Community Transit Corp.	1,544
Toronto Transit Commission	1,473
Southeastern Pennsylvania Transportation Authority	1,336
Washington Metropolitan Area Transit Authority	1,285
King County Metro	1,234
Metropolitan Transit Authority of Harris County	1,179

Source: *Metro Magazine*, September/October 1997, p. 78.

★ 1106 ★
Mass Transit (SIC 4111)

Passenger Transportation in North America - 2000

Data show the estimated number of passenger miles to be traveled in 2000. Passenger miles are the number of miles traveled by a vehicle times the number of passenger in it. Figures incude all buses and trains.

Mexican private bus	65,400
Mexican transit	29,792
U.S. transit bus	20,900
Bus tours, charters U.S., Canada	19,260
U.S. heavy rail	12,480
U.S. commuter rail	10,560
Canadian transit	8,892
U.S. linehaul bus, U.S.	6,155
U.S. light rail	833
U.S. demand response	764

Source: *Metro Magazine Fact Book*, 1998, p. 9.

SIC 42 - Trucking and Warehousing

★ 1107 ★
Trucking (SIC 4210)

For-Hire Trucking Industry - 1997

Data show operating revenues by type of carrier.

LTL	$ 4,125.6
TL	1,732.6
Specialized carriers	1,124.1
Tank	319.9
Motor vehicle haulers	275.0
Refrigerated	226.3
Bulk	84.5
Other	299.6

Source: *Fleet Owner*, May 1998, p. 21, from *F&OS Motor Carrier Quarterly Report*.

★ 1108 ★
Trucking (SIC 4210)

Intercity Trucking Market

Shares show the $230 billion market by type of fleet. Data are estimated.

Private carrriage	52.6%
Truckload	28.7
Parcel	10.0
Less-than-truckload	8.7

Source: *Logistics Management*, November 1997, p. 14, from Cass Information Systems.

★ 1109 ★
Trucking (SIC 4210)

Largest Common Carriers

Sales are shown in millions of dollars.

Yellow Freight	$ 1,571
Roadway Express	1,427
J.B. Hunt Transport	1,282
ABF Freight System	1,102
Consolidated Freight	1,098
Overnite Transport	961
Con-Way Express	816

Source: *Tire Business*, May 11, 1998, p. 11, from Truck Fleet Management and 1996 PACE Study.

★ 1110 ★
Trucking (SIC 4210)

Largest LTL Carriers - 1997

Carriers are ranked by LTL (less-than-truckload) revenue in billions of dollars.

Roadway Express	$ 2.67
Yellow Freight	2.54
Consolidated Freightways	2.30
US Freightways Corp.	1.56
Con-Way Transportation Services	1.47

Source: *Traffic World*, February 9, 1998, p. 15.

★ 1111 ★
Trucking (SIC 4210)

Top Automobile Carriers - 1996

Companies are ranked by revenue in thousands of dollars.

Commercial Carriers	$ 481,693
Allied Systems	257,623
Active Transportation	190,179
Cassens	175,648
Leaseway Motorcar	152,291

Continued on next page.

★ 1111 ★ *Continued*
Trucking (SIC 4210)

Top Automobile Carriers - 1996

Companies are ranked by revenue in thousands of dollars.

Morgan Drive Away	$ 132,208
Hadley Auto	84,423
E & L Transport	78,915
Jack Cooper	74,472
Pacific Motor Trucking	50,019

Source: *Distribution*, July 1997, p. 36.

★ 1112 ★
Trucking (SIC 4210)

Top Less-Than-Truckload Carriers - Midwest

Companies are ranked by 1996 revenues in thousands of dollars.

American Freightways	$ 729,042
U.S.F. Holland	595,400
U.S.F. Dugan	148,500
Crouse Cartage	107,502
Hyman Freightways	98,671

Source: *Distribution*, July 1997, p. 26.

★ 1113 ★
Trucking (SIC 4210)

Top Less-Than-Truckload Carriers - Northeast & Middle Atlantic

Companies are ranked by 1996 revenues in thousands of dollars.

Estes Express	$ 317,898
U.S.F. Red Star	196,400
New Penn	181,871
N E M F	117,651
Pitt Ohio Express	114,100
Wilson Trucking	82,799
Ward Trucking	67,273

Source: *Distribution*, July 1997, p. 26.

★ 1114 ★
Trucking (SIC 4210)

Top Less-Than-Truckload Carriers - Southeast & South Central

Companies are ranked by 1996 revenues in thousands of dollars.

Averitt Express	$ 322,069
Southeastern Freight	304,226
A A A Cooper	294,634
Saia Motor Freight	264,318
Southwestern	88,154
Milan Express	66,365
Boyd Brothers	65,523

Source: *Distribution*, July 1997, p. 26.

★ 1115 ★
Trucking (SIC 4210)

Top Less-Than-Truckload Carriers - Western & Rocky Mountain

Companies are ranked by 1996 revenues in thousands of dollars.

U.S.F. Reddaway	$ 178,000
U.S.F. Bestway	113,100
Motor Cargo	90,827
G.I. Trucking	78,420
Lynden Transport	64,320

Source: *Distribution*, July 1997, p. 28.

★ 1116 ★
Trucking (SIC 4210)

Top Motor Carriers by Revenue - 1996

Companies are ranked by revenue in millions of dollars.

United Parcel Service	$ 16,024,369
Roadway Express	2,338,974
Yellow Freight System	2,323,710
Schneider International	2,100,000
Consolidated Freightways	2,052,121
RPS Inc.	1,340,000
J.B. Hunt Transport	1,282,670
Con-Way Express Carriers	1,170,960
ABF Freight System	1,102,661
Ryder Integrated Logistics	1,073,416

Source: *World Trade*, December 1997, p. 66, from *Transportation Topics* and American Trucking Associations.

★ 1117 ★
Trucking (SIC 4210)

Trucking Market by Segment

The table shows the sources of carrier revenue.

LTL	26.1%
Truckload	22.4
Household goods	5.5
Refrigerated	4.3
Tank	3.8
Bulk	1.0
Other	36.9

Source: *Logistics*, February 1998, p. 18, from American Trucking Associations and American Trucking Trends.

★ 1118 ★
Trucking (SIC 4213)

Tank Trucking Companies - 1996

Companies are ranked by revenue in millions of dollars.

Trimac Transportation	$ 383
Chemical Leaman Tank Lines	280
MTL Inc.	236
Matlack Systems	225
DSI Transports	164
Superior Carriers	151
Dewey Group	114
Groendyke Transport	105
Bulkmatic Transport	104
Savage Industries	82
Transport Service	76
Koch Services	74

Source: *Chemical Week*, September 24, 1997, p. 41.

★ 1119 ★
Trucking (SIC 4213)

Top Trucking Groups - 1996

Data show revenues in thousands of dollars.

CNF Transportation	$ 3,662,183
Yellow Corp.	3,072,550
Caliber System	2,718,142
Consolidated Freightways Corp.	2,146,172
Ryder System	1,688,089
Arkansas Best Corp.	1,659,184
UniGroup Inc.	1,626,134
J.B. Hunt Transport Services	1,486,748

Continued on next page.

★ 1119 ★ *Continued*
Trucking (SIC 4213)

Top Trucking Groups - 1996

Data show revenues in thousands of dollars.

USFreightways Corp. . . . . $ 1,330,972
Landstar System 1,283,801

Source: *Transport Topics*, August 11, 1997, p. 1.

★ 1120 ★
Trucking (SIC 4213)

Top Trucking Groups - Canada

Data show revenues in thousands of Canadian dollars for 1996.

Trimac Transportation Services . . . . $ 382,691
Vitran Corp. 303,577
TNT North America 253,172
Newfoundland Capital Corp. 230,958
Westminster Holdings 209,000
Mullen Transportation 183,300
Cabano Kingsway 118,957

Source: *Transport Topics*, August 11, 1997, p. 24.

★ 1121 ★
Trucking (SIC 4213)

Top Trucking Groups in Less-Than-Truckload

Data show revenues in thousands of dollars for 1996.

Roadway Express . . . . $ 2,338,974
Yellow Freight System 2,323,710
Consolidated Freightways 2,052,121
Con-Way Express Carriers 1,170,960
ABF Freight Systems 1,102,661
Viking Freight 965,800
Overnite Transportation Co. 960,998
American Freightways 729,042

USF Holland . . . . $ 595,378
Watkins Motor Lines 531,135

Source: *Transport Topics*, August 11, 1997, p. 25.

★ 1122 ★
Trucking (SIC 4214)

Top Trucking Groups in Household Goods

Data show revenues in thousands of dollars for 1996.

United Van Lines . . . . $ 682,612
North American Van Lines 634,080
Allied Van Lines 449,603
Mayflower Transit 329,619
Atlas Van Lines 284,698
Bekins Van Lines Co. 191,584
Graebel Van Lines 151,773
Burnham 106,719

Source: *Transport Topics*, August 11, 1997, p. 27.

★ 1123 ★
Courier Services (SIC 4215)

Expedited Package Delivery Market - 1996

Shares are shown based on 4.7 billion expedited cargo shipments.

UPS 63.1%
Federal Express 13.4
U.S. Postal Service 6.1
RPS 4.0
All others 13.5

Source: *Transport Topics*, August 11, 1997, p. 8, from Colography Group, Inc.

★ 1124 ★
Courier Services (SIC 4215)

Largest Shipping Companies by Delivery Volume - 1997

Companies are ranked by average daily delivery volume in millions of parcels and documents as of August 8, 1997.

UPS	12.0
U.S. Postal Service	6.0
FedEx	2.8
Airborne	1.3
RPS	1.0
DHL Worldwide Express	0.5

Source: *Marketing News*, November 24, 1997, p. 2, from company reports.

★ 1125 ★
Courier Services (SIC 4215)

Leading Package Delivery Firms

Firms are ranked by revenue in millions of dollars.

United Parcel Service	$ 22,458
Federal Express	11,520
Pittston	3,394
Airborne Freight	2,914
AEI	1,546

Source: *Fortune*, April 27, 1998, pp. F-53.

SIC 43 - U.S. Postal Service

★ 1126 ★
Postal Service (SIC 4311)

Best-Selling Stamps - 1997

Bugs Bunny	
Classic American aircraft	
World of dinosaurs	
Endangered species	
Classic American dolls	

Data show the millions collected, based on a survey of 60,000 households.

Bugs Bunny	45.3
Classic American aircraft	35.6
World of dinosaurs	35.3
Endangered species	28.8
Classic American dolls	24.4

Source: *Christian Science Monitor*, January 2, 1998, p. 2, from U.S. Census Bureau.

★ 1127 ★
Postal Service (SIC 4311)

Best-Selling Stamps of All Time

Data show the millions collected, based on a survey of 60,000 households.

Elvis (1993)	124.0
Wildflowers (1992)	76.2
Rock n'Roll (1993)	75.8
Moon landing (1994)	47.9
Civil War (1995)	46.6

Source: *Christian Science Monitor*, January 2, 1998, p. 2, from U.S. Census Bureau.

★ 1128 ★
Postal Service (SIC 4311)

Self-Adhesive Stamps

Data show billions of self-adhesive stamps issued by the U.S. Postal Service for 1994 through 1997. In 1998, 90% of all stamps issued are expected to be self-adhesive.

	Units (bil.)	Share
1994	2.8	8.0%
1995	8.8	20.0
1996	30.0	60.0
1997	38.5	80.0

Source: *New York Times*, August 18, 1997, p. A12, from United States Postal Service.

★ 1129 ★
Postal Service (SIC 4311)

Types of Mail Received by Americans

The table shows the types of mail received by the average American household each week. Figures represent number of pieces.

Advertisements	17
Bills & statements	4
Personal mail	3

Source: *Time*, July 14, 1997, p. 20, from Arthur D. Little, Inc.

SIC 44 - Water Transportation

★ 1130 ★

Barges (SIC 4424)

Largest Commercial Barge Lines - 1998

Data show number of tank barges.

Kirby Corp. 513
American Commercial 449
Hollywood 255
Ingram 129

Source: *Chemical Week*, April 29, 1998, p. 15, from Sparks.

★ 1131 ★

Ports (SIC 4432)

Freight Transportation on the Great Lakes

Data show millions of tons transported annually.

Duluth 45.0
Chicago, IL 25.3
Detroit, MI 16.7
Cleveland, OH 15.4
Toledo, OH 14.1
Milwaukee, MN 3.2

Source: *Detroit News*, March 10, 1998, p. B1, from U.S. Army Corps of Engineers.

★ 1132 ★

Cruise Lines (SIC 4481)

Top Cruise Lines - 1997

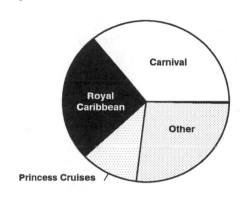

Market shares are shown in percent.

Carnival 36.0%
Royal Caribbean 26.0
Princess Cruises (P&O) 11.0
Other 27.0

Source: *Time*, May 11, 1998, p. 44.

★ 1133 ★

Ports (SIC 4491)

Largest Container Ports - North America

Ports are ranked by twenty-foot equivalent units (TEUs) for 1996. Veracruz was Mexico's leading port with 265,171 TEUs.

Long Beach, CA 3,067,334
Los Angeles, CA 2,682,802
New York/New Jersey 2,269,500
San Juan, Puerto Rico 1,640,624
Oakland, CA 1,498,202
Seattle, WA 1,473,561
Hampton Roads, VA 1,141,357
Charleston, SC 1,078,590

Continued on next page.

★ **1133 ★** *Continued*
Ports (SIC 4491)

Largest Container Ports - North America

Ports are ranked by twenty-foot equivalent units (TEUs) for 1996. Veracruz was Mexico's leading port with 265,171 TEUs.

Tacoma, WA 1,073,471
Montreal, Canada 852,530

Source: *Distribution*, July 1997, p. 74, from American Association of Port Authorities.

★ **1134 ★**
Ports (SIC 4491)

Top Eastern Ports

Ports are ranked by container traffic in thousands of twenty-foot equivalent units.

New York/New Jersey 2,269.5
Hampton Roads, VA 1,141.4
Charleston, SC 1,078.6
Port Everglades, FL 701.3
Miami, FL 656.8

Source: *Purchasing*, June 19, 1997, p. 59, from American Association of Port Authorities.

★ **1135 ★**
Ports (SIC 4491)

Top Ports - 1997

Long Beach
Los Angeles
New York
Charleston, S.C.
Seattle
Virginia Ports
Oakland, CA
Miami, FL
Houston, TX
Savannah, GA

Ports are ranked by traffic in twenty foot equivalent units.

Long Beach 2,631,495
Los Angeles 2,071,380

New York 1,677,279
Charleston, S.C. 926,823
Seattle 925,029
Virginia Ports 798,292
Oakland, CA 742,343
Miami, FL 595,780
Houston, TX 563,338
Savannah, GA 528,476

Source: *Traffic World*, March 9, 1998, p. 28, from PIERS.

★ **1136 ★**
Shipping (SIC 4491)

Top Container Carriers - 1997

Carriers are ranked by cargo transported in twenty foot equivalent units. Figures are for the first six months of the year.

Sea-Land Service Inc. 1,010,851
Evergreen Marine Corp. 920,125
Maersk Line 788,854
Hankin Shipping Co. 612,269
Hyundai Merchant Marine Co. 501,960
American President Lines 484,269
China Ocean Shipping Co. 388,263
Orient Overseas Container Line 382,486
Yangming Marine Line 357,243
Kawasaki Kisen Kalsha 347,243

Source: *World Trade*, April 1998, p. 68, from Port Import-Export Reporting Service.

SIC 45 - Transportation by Air

★ 1137 ★
Airlines (SIC 4512)

Busiest Airlines by Passenger Traffic - New York Area

The table shows number of passenger arrivals and departures for the 12 months ended May 31, 1997. Data include passenger traffic from John F. Kennedy International, La Guardia, and Newark International airports.

Continental Airlines	14,785,474
American Airlines	12,081,816
Delta Air Lines	9,096,598
United Airlines	5,998,145
Trans World Airlines	5,176,623
US Airways	4,889,213
Northwest Airlines	2,442,089
Delta Shuttle	1,937,399
Continental Express	1,730,047
British Airways	1,537,795
US Airways Shuttle	1,450,684
America West Airlines	1,126,544

Source: *Crain's New York Business*, September 8, 1997, p. 30, from Port Authority of New York and New Jersey.

★ 1138 ★
Airlines (SIC 4512)

Largest Airline Alliances

The six largest airlines have begun to form alliances. Data show combined market shares.

United-Delta	36.4%
American-US Airways	24.5
Northwest-Continental	19.8
Other	19.3

Source: *USA TODAY*, April 24, 1998, p. B1, from *Aviation Daily*.

★ 1139 ★
Airlines (SIC 4512)

Largest Regional Air Carriers - 1997

Data show carriers ranked by millions of passengers for January to June 1997.

Simmons Airlines	2.9
Comair	2.5
Continental Express	2.2
Mesa Airlines	2.1
Atlantic Southeast Airlines	1.8
Horizon Air	1.6
Piedmont Airlines	1.4
Flagship Airlines	1.4
SkyWest Airlines	1.4
Trans States Airlines	1.1
Maseba Airlines	1.1

Source: *Aviation Week & Space Technology*, November 17, 1997, p. 91, from AvStat Associates Inc.

★ 1140 ★
Airlines (SIC 4512)

Leading Passenger Airlines - Port Columbus, Ohio

Shares are shown based on 6,229,179 passenger arrivals and departures for 1996.

AmericaWest	22.0%
USAir	15.5
Delta	14.7
United	8.1
Southwest	7.8
Commuter flights	7.5
Northwest	7.3
TWA	5.7
American	4.4
Continental	4.4
ValuJet	2.2

Source: *Business First-Columbus*, January 24, 1997, p. 1, from Columbus Airport Authority.

★ 1141 ★
Airlines (SIC 4512)

Top Air Carriers - 1996

Firms are ranked by billions of revenue passenger miles. The revenue passenger mile, the standard industry measure of traffic, represents one paying passenger flown one mile.

United	116.6
American	104.5
Delta	93.9
Northwest	68.6
Continental	42.8
USAir	38.9

Source: *New York TImes*, January 27, 1998, p. C1, from Air Transport Association.

★ 1142 ★
Airlines (SIC 4512)

Top Airlines - 1997

Market shares are shown in percent.

United	19.98%
American	17.61
Delta	16.41
Northwest	11.86
Continental	7.89
US Airways	6.85
Other	19.40

Source: *Atlanta Journal-Constitution*, February 1, 1998, p. Q1.

★ 1143 ★
Airlines (SIC 4512)

Top Airlines by Revenue - 1997

Market shares are shown based on revenue passenger miles.

Delta	18.9%
United	18.2

American	18.0%
Northwest	9.9
USAir	9.1
Continental	8.1
Southwest	6.9
Others	10.9

Source: *Interavia*, April 1998, p. 32.

★ 1144 ★
Airlines (SIC 4512)

Top Airlines from Florida/Midwest

Market shares are shown based on capacity.

Northwest	27.9%
United	13.9
American	13.8
Delta	13.6
ATA	10.8
Continental	5.3
AirTran	2.9
Delta Express	2.6
Southwest	2.6
Others	6.6

Source: *Air Transport World*, December 1997, p. 48, from BACK Information Services.

★ 1145 ★
Airlines (SIC 4512)

Top Airlines from Northeast/Florida

Market shares are shown based on capacity.

US Airways	32.4%
American	16.1
Continental	13.2
Delta Express	10.1
Delta	8.3
Carnival	5.0
Southwest	3.1
TWA	3.1
Others	8.7

Source: *Air Transport World*, December 1997, p. 48, from BACK Information Services.

★ 1146 ★
Airlines (SIC 4512)

Top Airlines in Canada - 1997

Market shares are shown for the year ending December 31, 1997.

Air Canada 58.0%
Canadian Airlines International 41.0
Others 1.0

Source: *Marketing Magazine*, May 25, 1998, p. 22, from industry sources.

★ 1147 ★
Airlines (SIC 4512)

Top Airlines in Charlotte, NC - 1997

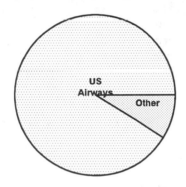

Market shares are shown in percent.

US Airways 91.0%
Other 9.0

Source: *New York Times*, March 18, 1998, p. C4, from Lehman Brothers.

★ 1148 ★
Airlines (SIC 4512)

Top Airlines in Detroit, MI - 1997

Market shares are shown in percent.

Northwest 79.0%
Other 21.0

Source: *New York Times*, March 18, 1998, p. C4, from Lehman Brothers.

★ 1149 ★
Airlines (SIC 4512)

Top Airlines in Houston, TX - 1997

Market shares are shown in percent.

Continental 80.0%
Other 20.0

Source: *New York Times*, March 18, 1998, p. C4.

★ 1150 ★
Airlines (SIC 4512)

Top Airlines in Minneapolis, MN - 1997

Market shares are shown in percent.

Northwest 82.0%
Other 18.0

Source: *New York Times*, March 18, 1998, p. C4.

★ 1151 ★
Airlines (SIC 4512)

Top Airlines in Pittsburgh, PA - 1997

Market shares are shown in percent.

US Airways 89.0%
Other 11.0

Source: *New York Times*, March 18, 1998, p. C4.

★ 1152 ★
Airlines (SIC 4512)

Top Airlines in Salt Lake City, UT - 1997

Market shares are shown in percent.

Delta 76.0%
Other 24.0

Source: *New York Times*, March 18, 1998, p. C4, from Lehman Brothers.

★ 1153 ★

Airlines (SIC 4512)

Top Airlines in St. Louis, MO - 1997

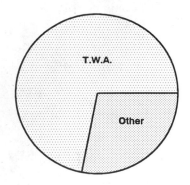

Market shares are shown in percent.

T.W.A.	72.0%
Other	28.0

Source: *New York Times*, March 18, 1998, p. C4.

★ 1154 ★

Airlines (SIC 4512)

Top Regional Airlines - 1997

Companies are ranked by number of passenger boardings, in millions.

American Eagle	12.1
Mesa Air Group	6.6
US Airways Express	6.1
Comair	5.3
Continental Express	4.9
Atlantic Southeast	3.8
Horizon Air	3.4
Mesaba Airlines	3.2

Source: *USA TODAY*, April 21, 1998, p. 6B, from Regional Airline Association.

★ 1155 ★

Airports (SIC 4512)

Top Airlines in Los Angeles County Airports - 1996

Market shares are shown in percent.

United Airlines	22.5%
Southwest Airlines	14.6
Delta Airlines	10.6
American Airlines	8.7

Northwest Airlines	3.6%
America West Airlines	3.3
Alaska Airlines	3.2
Other	33.5

Source: *Los Angeles Business Journal*, October 6, 1997, p. 22.

★ 1156 ★

Air Cargo (SIC 4513)

Air Cargo Leaders by Shipments - 1997

Market shares ae shown based on 371 million shipments. Figures are for July-September 1997.

Federal Express	46.5%
United Parcel Service	21.9
Airborne Express	20.7
U.S. Postal Service	4.6
DHL Worldwide	2.1
Emery Worldwide	0.5
BAX Global	0.3
Others	3.4

Source: *Air Cargo World*, March 1998, p. 49, from Colography Group.

★ 1157 ★

Air Cargo (SIC 4513)

Air Cargo Leaders by Weight - 1997

Market shares are shown based on 4.3 billions pounds. Figures are for July-September 1997.

Federal Express	23.6%
United Parcel Service	15.8
Airborne Express	8.8
Emery Worldwide	8.4
BAX Global	4.7
DHL Worldwide	1.5
U.S. Postal Service	0.5
Others	36.6

Source: *Air Cargo World*, March 1998, p. 49, from Colography Group.

★ 1158 ★

Air Cargo (SIC 4513)

Largest Cargo Carriers - 1997

| United Airlines |
| Northwest Airlines |
| American Airlines |
| Delta Airlines |
| Continental Airlines |

Airlines are ranked in thousands of revenue ton miles.

United Airlines	$ 2,861,730
Northwest Airlines	2,282,825
American Airlines	2,033,486
Delta Airlines	1,675,612
Continental Airlines	607,588

Source: *Air Cargo World*, April 1998, p. 78, from Air Transport Association.

★ 1159 ★

Air Cargo (SIC 4513)

Leading Federal Contractors of Air Courier Services

Shares are shown based on $145,583,000 in purchases by the U.S. government.

Federal Express Corp.	41.43%
American International Airways	17.35
Worldcorp Inc.	10.93
Sentel Corp.	5.53
Alaska Air Group Inc.	4.50
Others	20.26

Source: From the Internet, http:// www.govexec.com/ procure/articles/0896opgb.html, September 24, 1997, p. 3.

★ 1160 ★

Airports (SIC 4581)

Largest Eastern Airports - 1997

The largest airports in North America are ranked by tons of cargo transported. Figures are for the first 11 months of the year.

Miami	1,612,364
New York (JFK)	1,521,633
Newark	955,799
Atlanta	781,233
Philadelphia	450,244
Boston	401,760
Washington Dulles	321,759
Orlando	195,828
Baltimore	179,552
Charlotte	178,482

Source: *Air Cargo World*, April 1998, p. 42, from Airports Council International.

★ 1161 ★

Airports (SIC 4581)

Top Airlines at Baltimore-Washington International

Market shares are shown based on passenger traffic.

US Airways	38.9%
Southwest	19.8
United	7.7
Delta	7.5
Continental	6.3
Other	19.8

Source: *Washington Post*, May 18, 1998, p. 13, from airports.

★ 1162 ★

Airports (SIC 4581)

Top Airlines at Dulles International - 1997

Market shares are shown based on passenger traffic.

United	44.1%
Atlantic Coast	11.9
Delta	9.1
American	6.9
US Airways	5.9
Other	22.1

Source: *Washington Post*, May 18, 1998, p. 13, from airports.

★ 1163 ★

Airports (SIC 4581)

Top Airplanes at Dulles International - 1996

Market shares are shown based on enplanements. Figures refer to Washington Dulles International Airport.

United Airlines	44.44%
Atlantic Coast Airlines	14.51
USAir	9.12
American Airlines	8.62
Valujet	7.92
Delta Airlines	7.07
Other	8.32

Source: From the Internet, http://www.metwashairports.com, February 1998, p. 1.

★ 1164 ★

Airports (SIC 4581)

Top Airports by Passenger Traffic - 1996

Airports are ranked by passengers arriving and departing.

Chicago O'Hare	69,153,528
Atlanta	63,303,171
Dallas/Ft. Worth	58,034,503
Los Angeles	57,974,559
San Francisco	39,251,942
Miami	33,504,579
Denver	32,296,174
New York Kennedy	31,155,411
Detroit	30,610,993
Las Vegas	30,459,965
Phoenix	30,411,852
Newark	29,107,459

Source: *Distribution*, July 1997, p. 62, from Airports Council International and Air Transport Association.

★ 1165 ★

Airports (SIC 4581)

Top Airports for Regional Departures - 1996

Data show daily nonstop regional departures.

Dallas/Fort Worth	346
Los Angeles	313
Cincinnati	259
Boston Logan	247
Chicago O'Hare	237

Source: *USA TODAY*, October 27, 1997, p. B1, from AvStat Associates for the Regional Airline Association.

★ 1166 ★

Airports (SIC 4581)

Top Cargo Airports - 1996

Airports are ranked by metric tons of cargo enplaned and deplaned.

Memphis, TN	1,933,846
Los Angeles, CA	1,719,449
Miami, FL	1,709,906
New York JFK	1,636,497
Louisville, KY	1,368,520
Anchorage, AK	1,269,283
Chicago O'Hare	1,259,858
Newark, NJ	958,267
Atlanta, GA	800,181
Dallas/Ft. Worth, TX	774,947

Source: *Logistics Management*, October 1997, p. 18, from Air Transport Association.

★ 1167 ★

Airports (SIC 4581)

Who Controls LAX Airport

The table shows the market shares of Los Angeles International Airport, in percent.

United	30.0%
Delta	15.0
American	12.0
Other	43.0

Source: *Wall Street Journal*, January 16, 1998, p. 1.

★ 1168 ★
Airports (SIC 4581)

Who Controls Midway Airport - 1997

Data show percent of passengers.

Southwest Airlines	53.34%
America Trans Air	16.09
Northwest	8.43
Continental	3.83
Vanguard	3.44
Other	14.87

Source: *Chicago Tribune*, April 8, 1998, p. 1, from Chicago Department of Aviation.

★ 1169 ★
Airports (SIC 4581)

Who Controls Ronald Reagan Washington National Airport - 1996

Market shares are shown based on enplanements.

USAir	28.2%
Delta Airlines	17.4
American Airlines	13.5
Northwest Airlines	8.0
Continental Airlines	7.7
United Airlines	6.9
Shuttle Inc.	4.7
Trans World Airlines	3.6
Piedmont Aviation	3.4
Other	6.6

Source: From the Internet, http://www.metwashairports.com, February 1998, p. 1.

SIC 46 - Pipelines, Except Natural Gas

★ 1170 ★
Pipelines (SIC 4610)

Liquids Pipeline Companies by Total Deliveries - 1996

Companies are ranked by deliveries out of system in thousands of barrels. Data include crude oil and product deliveries.

Colonial Pipeline Co.	700,257
Texaco Pipeline Inc.	664,135
Marathon Pipe Line Co.	635,303
Shell Pipe Line Corp.	544,912
Lakehead Pipe Line Co. LP	531,448
Alyeska Pipeline Service Co.	525,507
Exxon Pipeline Co.	477,196
Amoco Pipeline Co.	445,895
Chevron Pipe Line Co.	443,524
ARCO Pipeline Co.	387,179
Santa Fe Pacific Pipelines Inc.	365,377
Sonat Pipeline Co.	346,515

Source: *Pipeline & Gas Journal*, November 1997, p. 63.

★ 1171 ★
Pipelines (SIC 4619)

Leading Pipeline Managers

Firms are ranked by revenues in millions of dollars.

Enron	$ 20,273
NGC	13,378
El Paso Natural Gas	5,638
Williams	4,410
Sonat	4,175

Source: *Fortune*, April 27, 1998, p. 56.

★ 1172 ★
Pipelines (SIC 4619)

Liquids Pipeline Companies by Product Deliveries - 1996

Companies are ranked by product deliveries in thousands of barrels.

Colonial Pipeline Co.	700,257
Santa Fe Pacific Pipelines Inc.	365,377
Buckeye Pipe Line Co. of Michigan LP	327,788
Marathon Pipe Line Co.	274,795
Williams Pipe Line Co.	236,267
Mid-America Pipeline Co.	227,867
Plantation Pipe Line Co.	212,453
Explorer Pipeline Co.	180,586
TE Products Pipeline Co. LP (TEPPCO)	179,424
Texaco Pipeline Inc.	173,246

Source: *Pipeline & Gas Journal*, November 1997, p. 46.

SIC 47 - Transportation Services

★ 1173 ★
Tourism (SIC 4720)

States Most Often Visited by Canadians - 1996

States are ranked by thousands of nights Canadians spent visiting.

Florida	35,138
New York	8,977
California	7,470
Arizona	5,611
Washington	5,171
Hawaii	4,545
Nevada	3,567
Michigan	3,356
South Carolina	2,696
Texas	2,559

Source: *Quill & Quire*, September 1997, p. 17, from Statistics Canada.

★ 1174 ★
Tourism (SIC 4720)

Top Countries for U.S. Visitors - 1996

The table shows the countries that send the most visitors to the United States. Figures are in millions of visitors.

Canada	15.3
Mexico	8.5
Japan	5.0
United Kingdom	3.1
Germany	2.0
France	1.0
Brazil	0.9
South Korea	0.8
Italy	0.6
Australia	0.5

Source: *Christian Science Monitor*, January 21, 1998, p. 2, from United States Department of Commerce.

★ 1175 ★
Tourism (SIC 4720)

Top Tourism Promoters - 1997

Spending is shown in millions of dollars. Total travel spending reached $478 million.

	($ mil.)	Share
Illinois	$ 35.3	7.38%
Hawaii	27.7	5.79
Texas	25.1	5.25
Florida	23.0	4.81
Pennsylvania	19.4	4.06
Virginia	18.3	3.83
Other	329.2	68.87

Source: *USA TODAY*, April 16, 1998, p. D1, from Travel Industry Association of America.

★ 1176 ★

Tourism (SIC 4720)

Travel Spending by State

California	
Florida	
New York	
Texas	
Illinois	
Nevada	
Hawaii	

The top states are ranked by overall spending by domestic and international travelers. Figures are in millions of dollars.

California	$ 58.3
Florida	42.9
New York	29.5
Texas	25.5
Illinois	17.3
Nevada	16.8
Hawaii	13.0

Source: *Christian Science Monitor*, November 17, 1997, p. 2, from Tourism Works for America Council.

★ 1177 ★

Travel (SIC 4720)

Business Travel Spending

Data show the breakdown of the business travel dollar.

Airfare	41.0%
Lodging	22.0
Meals	12.0
Car rental	8.0
Entertainment	5.0
Personal car costs	4.0
Ground transportation	3.0
Other	5.0

Source: *The American Saleman*, November 1997, p. 20, from Runzheimer International.

★ 1178 ★

Travel (SIC 4720)

U.S. Travel Spending - 1996

Data show the billions of dollars in spending by domestic travellers.

Foodservice	$ 91.6
Public transportation	89.5
Lodging	67.0
Auto transportation	63.1
Recreation	39.9
Retail	31.4

Source: *Washington Post*, March 25, 1998, p. C13, from Tourism Works for America Council.

★ 1179 ★

Travel Agencies (SIC 4724)

Top Travel Agencies - 1996

The table shows travel agencies ranked by gross sales in billions of dollars.

American Express	$ 9.1
Carlson Wagonlift	3.2
BTI Americas	2.5
Rosenbluth International	2.5
Maritz Travel Company	1.8

Source: *New York Times*, October 16, 1997, p. C1, from *Travel Weekly*.

★ 1180 ★

Travel Agencies (SIC 4724)

Top Travel Firms - 1997

Firms are ranked by revenues in millions of dollars.

American Express Travel Services	$ 7.9
Carlson Wagonlift Travel	3.2
BTI Americas	2.1
Rosenbluth International	2.1
Maritz Travel	1.4

Source: *St. Louis Business Journal*, February 2, 1998, p. 27A, from *Business Travel News*.

★ 1181 ★

Cruise Lines (SIC 4725)

Popular Cruise Line Destinations

Data show the most popular destinations, as ranked by travel agents.

Alaska	19.4%
Caribbean	12.8
Mediterranean	10.7
Europe	9.7
Costa Rica	5.3
South America	5.3

Source: *Christian Science Monitor*, March 30, 1998, p. 2, from American Society of Travel Agents.

SIC 48 - Communications

★ 1182 ★

Telecommunications Services (SIC 4812)

Largest Cellular Phone Markets - 1996

Los Angeles	
New York	
Chicago	
Washington, D.C./Baltimore	
Miami/West Palm Beach, FL	
	San Francisco/San Jose, CA
Detroit	
Boston	
Philadelphia	
Atlanta	

The table shows metropolitan statistical areas ranked by thousands of cellular subscribers for the end of 1996. Data are estimated.

Los Angeles	2,000
New York	1,500
Chicago	1,400
Washington, D.C./Baltimore	1,200
Miami/West Palm Beach, FL	1,100
San Francisco/San Jose, CA	936
Detroit	894
Boston	853
Philadelphia	810
Atlanta	769

Source: *Chicago Tribune*, October 6, 1997, p. C1, from RCR Publications Inc. and The Strategis Group.

★ 1183 ★

Telecommunications Services (SIC 4812)

Top Sectors in the Telecommunications Industry

Data show billions of dollars for 1997 and 2002.

	1997	2002
Local	$ 100	$ 134
Long-distance	80	107
Electronic commerce	30	80
Network management outsourcing	35	50
Wireless	28	46
Internet, intranet	3	30
Enhanced data	3	13
Frame relay	2	9
Asynchronous transfer mode	1	3
Switched multi-megabit data	1	1

Source: *Investor's Business Daily*, February 2, 1997, p. A8, from BancAmerica Robertson Stephens and International Data Corp.

★ 1184 ★

Wireless Communications (SIC 4812)

Digital Subscribers - 1997

Data are shown in thousands of subscribers. TDMA stands for Time Division Multiple Access. GSM stands for Global System for Multiple Access. CDMA stands for Code Division Multiple Access.

	1Q 1997	2Q 1997	3Q 1997
TDMA	1,634	1,804	1,986
GSM	436	631	934
CDMA	189	473	813

Source: *RCR*, January 26, 1998, p. 22, from Yankee Group.

★ 1185 ★
Wireless Communications (SIC 4812)

Largest PCS Providers in Canada - 1998

Market shares are shown based on 678,312 subscribers as of March 31, 1998. Bell Mobility covers only Ontario and Quebec. BCTel covers only British Columbia. Manitoba Telcom Services covers only Manitoba.

Cantel AT&T	47.8%
Clearnet Communications	20.9
Microcell Telecom	14.3
Bell Mobility	12.4
BCTel	3.7
Manitoba Telecom Services	0.9

Source: *Marketing Magazine*, May 25, 1998, p. 20, from industry sources.

★ 1186 ★
Wireless Communications (SIC 4812)

Leading PCS Companies by Subscribers - 1997

Shares are shown based on subscribers for the second quarter of 1997. PCS stands for personal communications services.

Sprint Spectrum	20.8%
PrimeCo	19.6
Sprint PCS	15.7
Pacific Bell	12.3
BellSouth	10.6
Western Wireless	7.4
Omnipoint	4.2
Powertel	4.2
Aerial	2.8
AT&T	1.5
GTE Wireless	0.9

Source: *Investor's Business Daily*, December 16, 1997, p. A12, from Strategis Group.

★ 1187 ★
Telephone Services (SIC 4813)

BRI/PRI Line Installation - 1997

Installation is shown by provider. BRI stands for Basic Rate ISDN. PRI stands for Primary Rate ISDN.

Bell Atlantic	45.9%
SBC	18.6
Ameritech	11.7
BellSouth	10.9
US West	7.1
GTE	5.8

Source: *Business Communications Review*, June 1998, p. 44, from International Data Corp.

★ 1188 ★
Telephone Services (SIC 4813)

Largest Independent Local Carriers

Firms are ranked by number of lines.

Teleport Communications Group Inc. . .	325,874
USN Communications Inc.	226,084
McLeodUSA	223,200
Intermedia Communications Inc.	220,587
ICG Communications Inc.	168,156

Source: *Wall Street Journal*, May 12, 1998, p. B1, from Bear Stearns & Co.

★ 1189 ★
Telephone Services (SIC 4813)

Largest Phone Companies - 1997

Firms are ranked by total business in billions of dollars.

AT&T	$ 51.4
Bell Atlantic	30.4
WorldCom/MCI	27.0
SBC Communications	24.8
BellSouth	20.6

Source: *Financial Times*, May 12, 1998.

★ 1190 ★

Telephone Services (SIC 4813)

Leading Telephone Firms - Canada

Companies are ranked by revenues in thousands of Canadian dollars.

BCE Inc.	$ 28,635,000
Bell Canada	8,700,000
Anglo-Canadian Telephone	2,815,100
BC Telecom	2,534,800
BC Tel	2,123,200
Telus Corp.	1,930,043
Call-Net Enterprises	721,700
Saskatchewan Telecommunications	698,928
Manitoba Telecom Services	601,903
Maritime Tel. & Tel. Co.	596,222

Source: *Globe and Mail's Report on Business Magazine,* July 1997, p. 162.

★ 1191 ★

Telephone Services (SIC 4813)

Local Telephone Market - New York City & Suburbs

Shares are shown based on customers in New York City, Long Island, Putnam, Rockland, and Westchester. Data are for 1996.

Bell Atlantic	87.0%
TCG	3.2
WorldCom	2.8
MCIMetro	2.3
AT&T	0.6
Frontier Telecommunications of New York	0.5
Cable & Wireless	0.3
Time Warner Communications	0.2
Other	3.1

Source: *Telecommunications*, p. 24.

★ 1192 ★

Telephone Services (SIC 4813)

Long-Distance Carriers - 1997

Shares are shown based on net income for the second quarter of 1997.

AT&T	47.9%
MCI	20.0
Sprint	9.7
Worldcom	5.5
Excel	1.9
Frontier	1.9
Others	13.1

Source: *New York Times*, August 4, 1997, p. C1.

★ 1193 ★

Telephone Services (SIC 4813)

Long-Distance Leaders in Canada - 1997

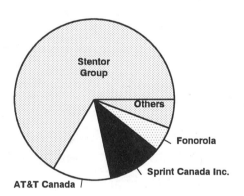

Market shares are shown for the year ended December 31, 1997.

Stentor Group	66.7%
AT&T Canada	11.5
Sprint Canada Inc.	11.0
Fonorola	4.8
Others	6.0

Source: *Marketing Magazine*, May 25, 1998, p. 21, from NBI/Michael Sone Associates.

★ 1194 ★

Telephone Services (SIC 4813)

Long-Distance Market in Mexico - 1997

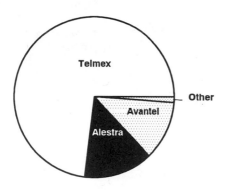

The market is shown by company. Data are based on number of phone lines. Telmex's share has dropped considerably since competition was introduced January 1997.

Telmex	73.0%
Alestra	14.0
Avantel	12.0
Other	1.0

Source: *Los Angeles Times*, March 2, 1998, p. D7, from Federal Telecommunications Commission of Mexico.

★ 1195 ★

Telephone Services (SIC 4813)

Long-Distance Service Leaders - 1997

Market shares are shown in percent.

AT&T	50.0%
MCI/WorldCom	25.0
Sprint	10.0
LCI/Qwest	1.0
Other	14.0

Source: *USA TODAY*, March 10, 1998, p. 3B.

★ 1196 ★

Telephone Services (SIC 4813)

Long-Distance Telephone Market - 2000

Shares are shown in percent. Data are estimated. At the time the source was published, WorldCom was in the process of acquiring MCI.

AT&T	44.0%
MCI	21.0
Sprint	12.0
Local phone companies	8.0
WorldCom	8.0
Other	7.0

Source: *Investor's Business Daily*, February 2, 1998, p. A8, from BancAmerica Robertson Stephens and International Data Corp.

★ 1197 ★

Telephone Services (SIC 4813)

Mexico's Telecommunications Market

Market shares are shown in percent. Others include Iusatel, Marcatel, Miditel, and Protel.

Telmex	74.2%
Alestra	14.3
Avantel	10.7
Others	0.7

Source: *Financial Times*, August 19, 1997, p. 4, from Federal Telecommunications Commission.

★ 1198 ★

Telephone Services (SIC 4813)

New Jersey's Phone Market

Shares of the business market are shown based on number of phone lines.

Bell Atlantic	99.3%
Other	0.7

Source: *Philadelphia Inquirer*, March 31, 1998, p. C1, from Atlantic-ACM.

★ 1199 ★

Telephone Services (SIC 4813)

Pennsylvania's Phone Market

Shares of the market are shown based on number of phone lines.

Bell Alantic	98.1%
Other	1.9

Source: *Philadelphia Inquirer*, March 31, 1998, p. C1, from Atlantic-ACM.

★ 1200 ★

Telephone Services (SIC 4813)

Telephone Access Line Market - 1997

Market shares are shown based on 178 million lines.

Bell Atlantic	23.0%
SBC	19.0
US West	14.0
BellSouth	13.0
Ameritech	12.0
GTE	12.0
Other	7.0

Source: *Investor's Business Daily*, May 12, 1998, p. A8, from company reports.

★ 1201 ★

Data Communications (SIC 4822)

Internet Backbone Service Providers

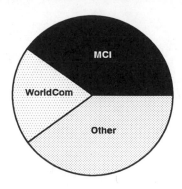

Data refer to companies who carry Internet traffic in bulk for retail Internet service providers. Shares are shown in percent. "Other" includes Sprint, BBN, GTE, and PSINet.

MCI	40.0%
WorldCom	20.0
Other	40.0

Source: *Los Angeles Times*, November 11, 1997, p. D1.

★ 1202 ★

Data Communications (SIC 4822)

Internet Network Equipment Vendors - 1996

Shares are shown based on sales of $2.1 billion.

Cisco	61.8%
Ascend	12.5
Bay	5.4
U.S. Robotics	5.4
Digital	3.7
3Com	2.9
Cascade	2.4
Others	5.9

Source: *Investor's Business Daily*, October 30, 1997, p. A10, from Dataquest Inc.

★ 1203 ★

Data Communications (SIC 4822)

Leading ATM Service Companies - 1997

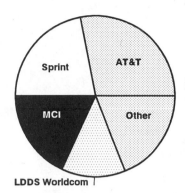

Shares are shown based on revenue.

AT&T	28.4%
Sprint	21.7
MCI	18.0
LDDS Worldcom	12.5
Other	19.4

Source: *PC Week*, October 20, 1997, p. 136.

★ 1204 ★

Radio Broadcasting (SIC 4832)

Largest Radio Companies in Canada

Data show number of stations.

CHUM Ltd.	24
Telemedia	22
Rogers Communications Inc.	20
Power Corp.	17
Nornet Broadcasting Ltd.	15

Source: *Globe & Mail*, May 1, 1998, p. B4, from Bureau of Broadcast Measurement and Canadian Association of Broadcasters.

★ 1205 ★

Radio Broadcasting (SIC 4832)

Largest Radio Markets in Canada

Data show number of stations.

Toronto	23
Vancouver	15
Edmonton	12
Calgary	9
Montreal, French	9
Winnipeg	9
Ottawa-Hill, English	8
London, Ontario	7
Hamilton	6
Quebec	6

Source: *Globe & Mail*, May 1, 1998, p. B4, from Bureau of Broadcast Measurement and Canadian Association of Broadcasters.

★ 1206 ★

Radio Broadcasting (SIC 4832)

Latin Radio Stations - Los Angeles, CA

Stations are ranked by broadcast rating.

KLVE	6.6%
KKBT	4.5
KSCA	4.4
KPWR	4.3
KRTH	3.9

Source: *Forbes*, September 22, 1997, p. 157, from The Arbitron Co.

★ 1207 ★

Radio Broadcasting (SIC 4832)

Latin Radio Stations - Miami, FL

Stations are ranked by broadcast rating.

WPOW	5.3%
WHQT	5.2
WEDR	4.9
WLYF	4.8
WAMR	4.6

Source: *Forbes*, September 22, 1997, p. 157, from The Arbitron Co.

★ 1208 ★
Radio Broadcasting (SIC 4832)

Popular Radio Formats

Data show the weekly audience in millions of listeners.

Country	43.3
New/talk, business, sports	38.9
Adult contemporary	38.8
Top 40	22.8
Oldies	22.3

Source: *USA TODAY*, April 21, 1998, p. D1, from Interep Research and Simmons.

★ 1209 ★
Radio Broadcasting (SIC 4832)

Radio Media Firms - 1996

Firms are ranked by radio revenue in millions of dollars.

CBS Corp.	$ 933.5
Evergreen Media Corp.	438.6
Walt Disney Co.	420.0
Clear Channel Communications	340.4
American Radio Systems Corp.	322.4
Jacor Communications	315.4
Capstar Broadcasting Partners	249.3
SFX Broadcasting	234.5
Chancellor Broadcasting	231.2
Cox Enterprises	191.0

Source: *Advertising Age*, August 18, 1997, p. S5.

★ 1210 ★
Radio Broadcasting (SIC 4832)

Radio Stations by State

There are 11,400 AM and FM radio stations in the United States.

	No.	Share
Texas	735	6.45%
California	678	5.95
New York	467	4.10
Florida	460	4.04
Pennsylvania	450	3.95
Illinois	380	3.33
North Carolina	376	3.30
Ohio	375	3.29
Georgia	373	3.27
Michigan	364	3.19%
Other	6,742	59.14

Source: *Business North Carolina*, December 1997, p. 92, from *Broadcasting & Cable Yearbook*.

★ 1211 ★
Radio Broadcasting (SIC 4832)

Seattle's Radio Market

Shares are shown in percent.

Entercom - Seattle	40.0%
American Radio Systems	20.0
New Century Media	11.7
Fisher Broadcasting	13.3
Sandusky Radio	11.5
Other	3.5

Source: *Mediaweek*, August 4, 1997, p. 22, from *Duncan's Radio Market Guide*.

★ 1212 ★
Radio Broadcasting (SIC 4832)

Top Radio Groups - 1996

Groups are shown ranked by estimated revenues in millions of dollars.

Hicks, Muse, Tate & Furst Holdings	$ 1,381,300
CBS Corp.	1,010,250
Jacor Communications Inc.	445,800
Clear Channel Communications	408,850
American Radio Systems License Corp.	383,850
ABC Radio Inc.	306,250
Cox Radio Inc.	216,525
Emmis Broadcasting Corp.	140,250
Heftel Broadcasting Corp.	137,650
Susquehanna Corp.	126,700

Source: *Chicago Tribune*, September 1, 1997, p. 3-1, from BIA Research.

★ 1213 ★
Radio Broadcasting (SIC 4832)

Top Radio Groups in Canada - 1997

Market shares are shown based on 516.5 million hours tuned in for Fall 1997.

Standard	8.3%
Telemedia	8.3
CHUM	7.2
WIC	7.2
Rogers	6.3
Radiomutuel	5.0
Shaw	4.7
Metromedia Plus	4.1
Rawico	2.7
Newcap	1.7
Others	44.5

Source: *Marketing Magazine*, May 25, 1998, p. 25, from industry sources and BBM Bureau of Measurement survey.

★ 1214 ★
Radio Broadcasting (SIC 4832)

Top Radio Stations - Los Angeles County

Stations are ranked by 1996-97 audience share. By revenue, Los Angeles was the top radio market in 1996.

KLVE-FM	6.4%
KKBT-FM	4.7
KPWR-FM	4.5
KFI-AM	4.1
KSCA-FM	4.1
KRTH-FM	3.7
KOST-FM	3.7

Source: *Los Angeles Business Journal*, October 13, 1997, p. 21.

★ 1215 ★
Radio Broadcasting (SIC 4832)

Top Radio Stations - New York City, NY

Data show average quarterly share.

WQIT	6.1%
WLTW	6.0
WCBS	4.7
WKTU	4.7
WSKQ	4.3

Source: *Crain's New York Business*, September 22, 1997, p. 20.

★ 1216 ★
Radio Broadcasting (SIC 4832)

Top Radio Stations in Detroit, MI - 1997

Stations are ranked by revenues in millions of dollars.

WJR	$ 20.0
WNIC	20.0
WJLB	18.0
WWJ	16.0
WOMC	15.0

Source: *Crain's Detroit Business*, May 18, 1998, p. 18.

★ 1217 ★
Radio Broadcasting (SIC 4832)

Top Radio Stations in New York - 1998

Market shares are shown for January 1 - April 1, 1998.

WLTW-FM	6.6%
WSKQ-FM	6.1
WQHT-FM	5.5
WHTZ-FM	4.7
WCBS-FM	4.6
WXRK-FM	4.3
WRKS-FM	4.2

Source: *New York Times*, May 18, 1998, p. C7, from Arbitron.

★ 1218 ★
Radio Broadcasting (SIC 4832)

Top Stations - Asheville, NC

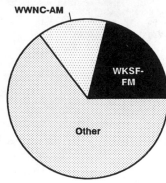

WWNC-AM

WKSF-FM

Other

Market shares are shown based on a 15 minute period.

WKSF-FM 21.3%
WWNC-AM 14.3
Other 64.4

Source: *Business North Carolina*, December 1997, p. 92, from Arbitron Co.

★ 1219 ★
Radio Broadcasting (SIC 4832)

Top Stations - Greensboro/High Point/ Winston- Salem, NC

Market shares are shown based on a 15 minute period.

WTQR-FM 10.7%
WJMH-FM 8.2
WKZL-FM 6.2
Other 74.9

Source: *Business North Carolina*, December 1997, p. 92, from Arbitron Co.

★ 1220 ★
Television Broadcasting (SIC 4833)

Ad Spending by Network

Spending is shown in thousands of dollars.

NBC . . . . $ 5,230,304
ABC 4,109,132
CBS 3,099,798
Fox 2,368,304
WB 270,888
UPN 168,172

Source: *Adweek*, May 18, 1998, p. 13, from Competitive Media Reporting.

★ 1221 ★
Television Broadcasting (SIC 4833)

Largest TV Broadcasters in Canada - 1997

Market shares are shown based on 466.7 million hours tuned in for Spring 1997.

CTV 25.1%
TVA 15.1
CBC 12.1
BBS Ontario 11.1
SRC: Societe Radio-Canada 10.0
Global TV (Ontario only) 6.3
TQS: Television Quatre Saisons 4.5
BCTV 4.2
Others 11.6

Source: *Marketing Magazine*, May 25, 1998, p. 25, from Television Bureau of Canada and BBM Bureau of Measurement survey.

★ 1222 ★
Television Broadcasting (SIC 4833)

Leading Hispanic Broadcasters

Firms are ranked by revenues in millions of dollars.

Grupo Telvisa . . . . $ 1,500
Univision 245
TV Azteca 238
Telemundo 203
Heftel Broadcasting 71
Grupo Radio Centro 48

Source: *Forbes*, September 22, 1997, p. 156, from Standard & Poor's and company reports.

★ 1223 ★
Television Broadcasting (SIC 4833)

Popular English Language Stations in Canada

The audience share is shown in percent for September 1 - November 9, 1997.

Baton	12.1%
CanWest/Global	9.9
CBC	8.6
CHUM	5.7
CTV	5.1

Source: *Financial Post*, November 22, 1997, p. 10, from CBC Research.

★ 1224 ★
Television Broadcasting (SIC 4833)

Spanish Television Market

Market shares are shown in percent.

Univision Communications	83.0%
Telemundo Group	17.0

Source: *New York Times*, June 15, 1998, p. C7.

★ 1225 ★
Television Broadcasting (SIC 4833)

Top Television Groups - 1997

Groups are ranked by FCC share. The groups have been ranked by their coverage of Nielsen's 98 million U.S. TV homes as calculated for regulatory purposes.

Fox Television Stations Inc.	34.9%
Paxson Communications Corp.	30.9
CBS Stations Inc.	30.8
NBC Inc.	26.9
Tribune Broadcasting	26.5

ABC Inc.	23.9%
Chris-Craft Industries Inc./BHC Communications Inc./United Television	18.7
Gannett Broadcasting	16.5
USA Broadcasting Inc.	15.5
A.H. Belo Corp.	14.2

Source: *Broadcasting & Cable*, April 6, 1998, p. 46.

★ 1226 ★
Television Broadcasting (SIC 4833)

Top TV Stations in Canada

Market shares are shown in percent.

CFCF	26.9%
Global	10.0
CBC	8.4
NBC	7.3
Other U.S.	14.1
Specialty channels	15.0
Other	18.3

Source: *Marketing Magazine*, March 9, 1998, p. 13.

★ 1227 ★
Television Broadcasting (SIC 4833)

TV Media Firms - 1996

Firms are ranked by TV revenues in millions of dollars.

NBC TV (General Electric Co.)	$ 4,940.0
Walt Disney Co.	4,005.0
CBS Corp.	3,390.0
News Corp.	2,500.0
Tribune Co.	681.0
Gannett Co.	641.5
BHC Communications (Chris-Craft)	446.3
Cox Enterprises	391.0
Viacom	390.3
Univision Holdings	370.3

Source: *Advertising Age*, August 18, 1997, p. S5.

★ 1228 ★

Cable Broadcasting (SIC 4841)

Cable Market in Canada

Shares are shown based on number of cable subscribers.

Rogers	29.0%
Shaw	18.5
Videotron	18.5
Cogeco	9.0
Moffat	4.1
Fundy	2.4
Other	18.5

Source: *Globe and Mail*, December 3, 1997, p. B6, from Canadian Cable Television Association.

★ 1229 ★

Cable Broadcasting (SIC 4841)

Cable TV Industry Leaders

Market shares are shown based on subscribers.

TCI	29.0%
Time Warner	18.0
MediaOne	8.0
Comcast	7.0
Cablevision	5.0
Cox	5.0
Other	25.0

Source: *Investor's Business Daily*, January 19, 1998, p. A8, from Federal Communications Commission and Paul Kagan Associates Inc.

★ 1230 ★

Cable Broadcasting (SIC 4841)

Cable TV Media Firms - 1996

Firms are ranked by cable TV revenues in millions of dollars.

Time Warner	$ 9,000.0
Tele-Communications Inc.	5,954.0

Viacom	$ 2,013.7
Comcast Corp.	1,878.1
U.S. West Media Group	1,726.0
Walt Disney Co.	1,690.0
Cox Enterprises	1,460.3
Cablevision Systems Corp.	1,315.1
USA Network	591.5
Discovery Communications	557.0

Source: *Advertising Age*, August 18, 1997, p. S5.

★ 1231 ★

Cable Broadcasting (SIC 4841)

Largest Cable Companies - 1997

Companies are ranked by number of subscribers as of September 1997.

Tele-Communications Inc.	14,306,000
Time Warner Cable	12,400,000
US West Media Group	5,100,000
Comcast Cable Communications Inc.	4,300,000
Cox Communications	3,296,830
Cablevision Systems Corp.	2,886,000
Adelphia Communications Corp.	1,907,715
Jones Intercable Inc.	1,471,328
Century Communications Corp.	1,273,000
Marcus Cable	1,216,752

Source: *TV Digest*, December 8, 1997, p. 4.

★ 1232 ★

Cable Broadcasting (SIC 4841)

Largest Cable Households

Data show the areas with the most cable households.

Hartford-New Haven, CT	77.0%
Biloxi-Gulfport, MI	76.6
Anniston, AL	76.2
Tuscaloosa, AL	75.4
Victoria, TX	74.8
West Palm Beach-Fort Pierce, FL	74.1

Source: *USA TODAY*, May 6, 1998, p. B1, from Polk.

★ 1233 ★

Cable Broadcasting (SIC 4841)

Largest Multiple System Operators - 1997

Companies are ranked by number of basic service subscribers.

Tele-Communications Inc.	14,799,746
Time Warner Cable	7,457,000
MediaOne	5,095,948
Time Warner Entertainment- Advance/Newhouse	4,500,000
Comcast	3,868,072
Cox Communications	3,275,267
Cablevision Systems	2,807,575
Adelphia Communications	1,885,425
Jones Intercable	1,519,287
Century Communications	1,471,397

Source: *Cablevision*, October 20, 1997, p. 59.

★ 1234 ★

Cable Broadcasting (SIC 4841)

Multichannel Market

The market is shown in percent. MMDS stands for multichannel multipoint distribution service. DBS stands for direct broadcasting services.

	1997	2002
Cable	65.0%	67.0%
Non-subscribers	26.0	15.0
DBS	7.0	14.0
MMDS	2.0	4.0

Source: *Cablevision*, February 9, 1998, p. 21, from Strategis Group.

★ 1235 ★

Cable Broadcasting (SIC 4841)

Prime Time Cable Stations - 1997

The table shows prime time ratings for 1997. One rating point represents about 700,000 households.

TNT	2.2
USA	2.0
Nickelodeon	1.9
TBS Superstation	1.8
ESPN	1.5
Lifetime	1.5
A&E	1.3

Cartoon	1.3
Discovery	1.2
Family	1.1

Source: *Atlanta Journal-Constitution*, January 8, 1998, p. F2, from Turner Broadcasting System Research and Nielsen Media Research.

★ 1236 ★

Cable Broadcasting (SIC 4841)

Top Cable Systems by City

Cities are ranked by number of basic cable subscribers.

New York, NY	1,004,801
Long Island, NY	642,738
Orlando, FL	543,049
San Diego, CA	475,950
Phoenix, AZ	450,303
Bronx/Brooklyn, NY	438,465
Puget Sound, WA	424,500
Chicago suburbs, IL	371,739
Denver, CO	369,844
Tampa/St. Petersburg, FL	336,844

Source: *Cablevision*, October 20, 1997, p. 61.

★ 1237 ★

Satellite Broadcasting (SIC 4841)

Leading DBS Providers

Figures are shown based on 6 million subscribers. DBS stands for direct broadcast satellite.

DirecTV	42.8%
PrimeStar	31.5
EchoStar	9.1
USSB	2.2
Others	14.4

Source: *Investor's Business Daily*, July 23, 1997, p. A1.

★ 1238 ★
Satellite Broadcasting (SIC 4841)
Satellite Television Leaders

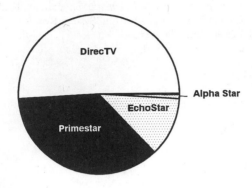

The small dish satellite market is shown by company. Approximately 60% of DirecTV subscribers also subscribe to U.S. Satellite Broadcasting.

DirecTV 51.0%
Primestar 36.0
EchoStar 12.0
Alpha Star 1.0

Source: *New York Times*, September 23, 1997, p. A6, from *Sky Report* and Media Business Corp.

★ 1239 ★
Satellite Broadcasting (SIC 4841)
Satellite TV Broadcasters - 1998

Market shares are shown as of March 1998.

DirecTV/USSB 40.0%
PrimeStar 23.0
EchoStar 14.0
C-band (large dish systems) 23.0

Source: *Investor's Business Daily*, May 11, 1998, p. A8, from Merrill Lynch and Pierce, Fenner & Smith Inc.

★ 1240 ★
Television Broadcasting (SIC 4841)
Canada's Specialty TV Channels

The market is shown by type.

	1997	2000
Canadian conventional	56.0%	52.0%
Canadian specialty	23.0	30.0
U.S. specialty	6.0	5.0
U.S. conventional	15.0	3.0

Source: *Globe and Mail*, March 21, 1998, p. B5, from Nielsen People Meter and Initiative Media.

★ 1241 ★
Television Broadcasting (SIC 4841)
Largest English-Language Specialty Channels in Canada

Figures show subscribers as of August 31, 1997.

Weather 8,167,204
Newsworld 7,316,000
YTV 7,150,000
TSN 6,401,276
CMT 6,290,810
Vision 6,115,792
MuchMusic 6,048,240

Source: *Globe and Mail*, March 21, 1998, p. B5, from Canadian Radio-Television and Telecommunications Commission.

SIC 49 - Electric, Gas, and Sanitary Services

Electricity Sales by End User - 1995

The table shows sales in percent. "Other" includes electricity used for street lighting, by governmental bodies and by rail systems.

Residential 34.6%
Industrial 33.6
Commercial 28.6
Other 3.2

Source: *Nation's Business*, September 1997, p. 22, from U.S. Energy Information Administration.

Largest Publicly Owned Utilities

Data show billions of kilowatt-hours supplied.

New York Power Authority 40.49
Los Angeles Department of Water and
  Power 22.07
Salt River Project 21.95
South Carolina Public Service Authority . . 16.02
Puerto Rico Electric Power Authority . . . 15.62

Source: *New York Times*, July 11, 1997, p. C3, from American Public Power Association.

Leading Electric Utilities - Canada

Companies are ranked by revenues in thousands of Canadian dollars.

Ontario Hydro . . . . $ 8,938,000
Hydro-Quebec 7,760,000
B.C. Hydro & Power 2,269,000
CanUtilities Holdings 1,838,900
Canadian Utilities 1,837,500

TransAlta Corp. . . . . $ 1,811,100
TransAlta Utilities 1,230,300
New Brunswick Power Corp. 1,110,260
Manitoba Hydro-Electric Board 1,038,900
Saskatchewan Power Corp. 999,000

Source: *Globe and Mail's Report on Business Magazine*, July 1997, p. 162.

Leading Northern Utilities

Market shares are shown based on capacity greater than 15 megawatts.

Consolidated Edison Co. 17.96%
Northeast Utilities 13.49
New York Power Authority 12.11
Niagara Mohawk Power Corp. 11.46
Long Island Lighting Co. 7.87
New England Electric Systems Inc. 7.52
Boston Edison Co. 5.41
New York State Electric & Gas Corp. . . . 4.07
United Illuminating Co. 2.25
Other 17.86

Source: *Public Utilities Fortnightly*, February 1, 1998, p. 8, from POWERdat Database.

Leading Western Utilities

Market shares are shown based on capacity greater than 500 megawatts.

Bonneville Power Administration 15.5%
Pacific Gas & Electric Co. 9.7
Southern California Edison Co. 8.0
PacifiCorp. 5.9
Western Area Power Administration 5.7
Los Angeles Dept. of Water & Power . . . 4.3

Continued on next page.

★ 1246 ★ *Continued*
Utilities (SIC 4911)

Leading Western Utilities

Market shares are shown based on capacity greater than 500 megawatts.

AES Corp.	3.2%
Arizona Public Service Co.	3.1
Salt River Project	3.0
Other	41.6

Source: *Public Utilities Fortnightly*, February 1, 1998, p. 12, from POWERdat Database.

★ 1247 ★
Utilities (SIC 4911)

Top Electricity Marketers - 1996

Market shares are shown in percent.

Enron Power Marketing Inc.	25.6%
Duke/Louis Dreyfus LLC	12.0
LG&E Power Marketing Inc.	7.8
Electric Clearinghouse Inc.	6.3
Citizens Lehman Power Sales	5.0
Vitol Gas & Electric	4.5
Koch Power Services Inc.	4.3
Aquila Power Corp.	2.9
DuPont Power Marketing	2.3
CNG Power Services Corp.	2.1
Others	27.1

Source: *Public Utilities Fortnightly*, July 1, 1997, p. 11, from Edison Electric Institute and Regulatory Research Services.

★ 1248 ★
Utilities (SIC 4911)

Top Utilities

Pacific Gas & Electric
Southern Company
Edison International
Commonwealth Edison
Consolidated Edison
Entergy
Public Service Electric & Gas

Companies are ranked by revenue in billions of dollars.

Pacific Gas & Electric	$ 9.6
Southern Company	9.2
Edison International	8.4
Commonwealth Edison	6.9
Consolidated Edison	6.5
Entergy	6.3
Public Service Electric & Gas	6.2

Source: *Public Utilities Fortnightly*, November 15, 1997, p. 30, from Newton-Evans Research Co.

★ 1249 ★
Pipelines (SIC 4922)

Top Energy Service Providers - Canada

Companies are ranked by assets in billions of dollars.

Duke	$ 23.00
Enron	23.00
TransCanada	14.50
Williams	13.90
El Paso	9.00

Source: *Wall Street Journal*, January 27, 1998, p. B10.

★ 1250 ★
Utilities (SIC 4922)

Gas Utilities by Gas Sales - 1996

Companies are ranked by millions of cubic feet.

Northern Illinois Gas Co.	328,961
Southern California Gas Co.	315,313
Consolidated Natural Gas Company Distribution	294,171

Continued on next page.

★ 1250 ★ *Continued*
Utilities (SIC 4922)

Gas Utilities by Gas Sales - 1996

Companies are ranked by millions of cubic feet.

Public Service Electric & Gas Co. 292,801
Consumers Power Co. 265,136
Pacific Gas & Electric Co. 264,439
Atlanta Gas Light Co. 210,264
Michigan Consolidated Gas Co. 206,951
Columbia Gas of Ohio Inc. 198,644
Atmos Energy Corp. 177,317

Source: *Pipeline & Gas Journal*, November 1997, p. 46.

★ 1251 ★
Utilities (SIC 4922)

Gas Utilities by Operating Revenue - 1996

Companies are ranked by operating revenue in thousands of dollars.

Southern California Gas Co. . . . . . $ 2,421,981
Consolidated Natural Gas Company
Distribution 1,905,512
Pacific Gas & Electric Co. 1,898,348
Public Service Electric & Gas Co. . . . 1,880,994
Northern Illinois Gas Co. 1,610,227
Brooklyn Union Gas Co. 1,432,002
Columbia Gas of Ohio Inc. 1,323,876
Consumers Power Co. 1,275,303
Atlanta Gas Light Co. 1,217,600
Michigan Consolidated Gas Co. 1,080,813

Source: *Pipeline & Gas Journal*, November 1997, p. 48.

★ 1252 ★
Utilities (SIC 4924)

Gas Distribution Utilities by Customers

Firms are ranked by number of customers.

Southern California Gas Co. 4,789,942
Pacific Gas & Electric Co. 3,677,000
Northern Illinois Gas Co. 1,863,003
Consolidated Natural Gas Company
Distribution 1,841,147
Public Service Electric & Gas Co. . . . 1,522,401

Consumers Power Co. 1,502,372
Entex (Division of NorAm Energy
Corp.) 1,394,716
Atlanta Gas Light Co. 1,394,500
Lone Star Gas Co. 1,300,000
Columbia Gas of Ohio Inc. 1,286,350
Michigan Consolidated Gas Co. 1,169,690
Brooklyn Union Gas Co. 1,125,843

Source: *Pipeline & Gas Journal*, November 1997, p. 50.

★ 1253 ★
Water Services (SIC 4941)

Canada's Water Use

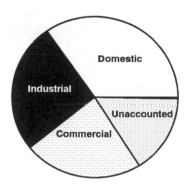

Data show how portable and raw water is used.

Domestic 35.0%
Industrial 26.0
Commercial 23.0
Unaccounted 16.0

Source: *National Trade Data Bank*, September 16, 1997, p. ISA970801.

★ 1254 ★
Water Services (SIC 4941)

Water Treatment Market - 1997

The market is valued at $2.8 billion.

Cooling water 31.0%
Process 25.0
Boiler water 22.0
Waste & supply 22.0

Source: *Chemical Week*, May 13, 1998, p. 47, from Kline & Co.

★ 1255 ★
Water Services (SIC 4941)

Where Los Angeles Gets Water

Yearly water usage is 650,000 acre feet.

LA aquaduct 65.0%
Metropolitan Water District 20.0
Local ground water 15.0

Source: *New York Times*, April 23, 1998, p. C1, from Metropolitan Water District of Southern California and Los Angeles Department of Water and Power.

★ 1256 ★
Waste Management (SIC 4953)

Largest Trash Disposal Firms

| Waste Management |
| Browning-Ferris Ind. |
| USA Waste |

Firms are ranked by revenues in millions of dollars.

Waste Management . . . . $ 9,273
Browning-Ferris Ind. 5,783
USA Waste 2,614

Source: *Fortune*, April 27, 1998, p. 56.

SIC 50 - Wholesale Trade - Durable Goods

Wholesale Trade - Auto Parts (SIC 5013)

Largest Auto Part Wholesalers - 1997

Data represent number of stores.

Genuine Parts	752
General Parts	728
APS	300
O'Reilly	240
Fisher Auto	238
Hahn Automotive	194
MAWDI (Mid-Atlantic)	109
Mid-State	108
Strafco	102
Crow-Burlingame	101

Source: *Automotive Marketing*, July 1997, p. 46.

Wholesale Trade - Auto Parts (SIC 5013)

Top Auto Parts Buying Groups - Canada

Market shares are shown in percent.

Engine Rebuilders Inc.	23.4%
Modern Sales	16.9
Kerr Machine Shop Group	16.1
Bestbuy Distributors Limited	14.4
Across Canada	10.1
Uni-select Inc.	7.7
Independent Distributors	4.0
Replacement Parts Depot	3.2
Buchanan Automotive	2.6
Eastern Automotive	0.9
Other	0.7

Source: *National Trade Data Bank*, November 3, 1997, p. ISA970901.

Wholesale Trade - Office Supplies (SIC 5044)

Largest Office Superstores - 1997

| Office Depot |
| Staples |
| OfficeMax |

Firms are ranked by total sales in billions of dollars.

Office Depot	$ 6.72
Staples	5.18
OfficeMax	3.77

Source: *Discount Store News*, March 23, 1998, p. 6, from company reports.

Wholesale Trade - Office Supplies (SIC 5044)

Leading Office Supply Stores - 1996

Data represent sales in millions of dollars.

Office Depot	$ 6,069
Staples	3,968
OfficeMax	3,179
Arvey Paper & Supplies	85

Source: *Discount Store News*, July 7, 1997, p. 80.

★ 1261 ★

Wholesale Trade - Computers (SIC 5045)

PC Distribution by Channel - 1996

Shares of the $46.32 billion market are shown in percent.

Outbound dealers	24.0%
Retailers	22.0
Direct vendors	20.0
Traditional dealers	16.0
Value added resellers	12.0
Direct dealers	3.0
Other	3.0

Source: *Computerworld*, September 22, 1997, p. 33, from Merrin Information Services, Inc.

★ 1262 ★

Wholesale Trade - Hospital Equipment (SIC 5047)

Largest GPOs

Group-purchasing organizations (GPOs) are ranked by number of acute-care hospitals they supply.

Premier Inc.	1,682
Amerinet	1,493
Novation	1,400
Medecon Services	770
Health Services Corp.	679
Joint Purchasing Corp.	382

Source: *Business Week*, March 16, 1998, p. 76, from SMG Marketing Group and American Hospital Association.

★ 1263 ★

Wholesale Trade - Metals (SIC 5051)

Largest Metal Service Centers - 1997

Sales are shown in billions of dollars. Data are for North America.

Ryerson Tull Inc.	$ 2.8
Thyssen Inc.	2.5
North American Metals Distribution Group	1.3
MacSteel Service Centers USA	1.2
Russel Metals Inc.	1.2
Reliance Steel & Aluminum Co.	1.1
Samuel, Son & Co.	1.1
EMJ	1.0

Source: *Purchasing*, May 7, 1998, p. 44B.

★ 1264 ★

Wholesale Trade - Electronics (SIC 5060)

Largest Electronics Wholesalers in North America - 1997

Firms are ranked by calender sales in millions of dollars.

Arrow Electronics Inc.	$ 5,000.0
Avnet Inc.	4,390.0
Future Electronics	2,200.0
VEBA Electronics	1,895.0
Pioneer-Standard Electronics Inc.	1,600.0
Marshall Industries	1,305.0
Bell Industries Inc.	895.0
Premier Farnell	726.0
Kent Electronics Corp.	634.0
Bell Microproducts Inc.	534.0

Source: *Purchasing*, April 23, 1998, p. 62.

★ 1265 ★

Wholesale Trade - Electronics (SIC 5060)

Largest VA Electronics Distributors

The largest providers of value-added companies are ranked by sales in millions of dollars.

Arrow Electronics Inc.	$ 2,750.0
Avnet Inc.	1,536.5
VEBA Electronics	795.9
Pioneer-Standard Electronics Inc.	544.0
Marshall Industries	456.8

Source: *Purchasing*, April 23, 1998, p. 50.

SIC 51 - Wholesale Trade - Nondurable Goods

★ 1266 ★
Wholesale Trade - Drugs (SIC 5122)

Top Drug and Medical Supply Distributors

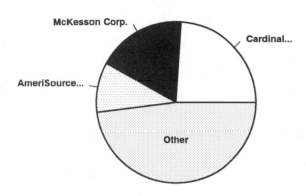

Data are shown in billions of dollars.

	($ bil.)	Share
Cardinal Bergen Health Inc.	$ 20.0	24.39%
McKesson Corp.	14.5	17.68
AmeriSource Health Corp.	8.0	9.76
Other	39.5	48.17

Source: *New York Times*, August 26, 1997, p. C2, from Montgomery Securities.

★ 1267 ★
Wholesale Trade - Drugs (SIC 5122)

Wholesale Drug Market

Data show market shares before the merger of Cardinal Health and Bergen Brunswig.

McKesson Corp.	25.0%
Bergen Brunswig	18.0
Cardinal Health	17.0
AmeriSource Health Corp.	14.0
Other	26.0

Source: *Wall Street Journal*, August 26, 1997, p. B4, from A.G. Edwards.

★ 1268 ★
Wholesale Trade - Food (SIC 5140)

Top Food Distributors - Canada

Companies are ranked by revenues in thousands of Canadian dollars.

George Weston	$ 12,807,000
Loblaw Cos.	9,869,200
Oshawa Group	6,383,500
Provigo Inc.	5,704,300
Canada Safeway	4,795,900
Westfair Foods	3,364,498
Metro-Richelieu Inc.	3,266,000
Empire Co.	2,946,863

Source: *Globe and Mail's Report on Business Magazine*, July 1997, p. 168.

★ 1269 ★
Wholesale Trade - Groceries (SIC 5140)

Largest Grocery Distributors - Canada

Companies are ranked by revenues in thousands of dollars.

Loblaw Cos. Ltd.	$ 9,356,100
Provigo Inc.	6,207,200
The Oshawa Group	5,727,800
Canada Safeway Ltd.	4,456,700
Jim Pattison Group	3,106,000
Metro-Richelieu	2,722,700
Great Atlantic and Pacific Co.	2,709,200
Empire Co. Ltd.	2,361,600

Source: From the Internet, http://www.thomaslargesinger.com, 1997, p. 5, from *Financial Post*.

★ 1270 ★

Wholesale Trade - Groceries (SIC 5140)

Top Food Retailers/Wholesalers

Companies are ranked by annual sales in millions of dollars.

Kroger Co.	$ 26.5
Wal-Mart Superstores	25.0
Safeway	22.0
American Stores Co.	19.4
Supervalu	17.1
Fleming Cos.	15.4
Fred Meyer Inc.	14.9
Albertson's	14.8
Ahold USA	14.0
Winn-Dixie Stores	13.2

Source: *SN*, November 17, 1997, p. 1.

★ 1271 ★

Wholesale Trade - Beverages (SIC 5141)

How Bottled Water is Distributed

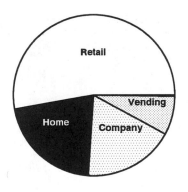

Distribution is shown by channel.

Retail	53.2%
Home	20.6
Company	18.4
Vending	7.8

Source: *Beverage World*, October 1997, p. 56, from Beverage Marketing Corp.

★ 1272 ★

Wholesale Trade - Chemicals (SIC 5160)

Top Chemical Distributors - North America

Companies are ranked by sales in millions of dollars.

Van Waters & Rogers	$ 1,680
Ashland Chemical	1,380
Chemcentral	822
Soco Chemical	560
Ells & Everard	500
Holland Chem. International	426
JLM Marketing	250
Harcros Chemicals	220
Great Western Chemical	200
Helm	188
Canada Colors & Chemicals	145
Holtrachem	139

Source: *Chemical Week*, October 8, 1997, p. 54.

SIC 52 - Building Materials and Garden Supplies

★ 1273 ★
Retailing - Home Improvement (SIC 5211)

Home Improvement Market Leaders - 1997

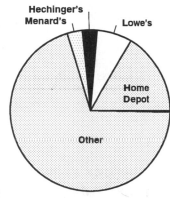

Market shares are shown in percent.

Home Depot	16.9%
Lowe's	7.1
Hechinger's	2.9
Menard's	2.5
Other	70.6

Source: *New York Times*, May 13, 1998, p. C4, from *National Home Center News*.

★ 1274 ★
Retailing - Home Improvement (SIC 5211)

Home Improvement Sales

Homeowners are expected to spend an average of $2,929 on home improvement projects in 1998. Data show where customers prefer to shop, based on a survey.

Home improvement superstores	61.0%
Home furnishings/decorating stores	31.0
Department stores	22.0
Hardware stores	17.0
Lumber yards	17.0
Gardening store/nursery	14.0

Specialty stores	12.0%
Discount mass merchandisers	6.0

Source: *Discount Merchandiser*, April 1998, p. 115, from American Express Retail Trends Monitor.

★ 1275 ★
Retailing - Home Improvement (SIC 5211)

Top Home Improvement Chains - 1997

Firms are ranked by sales in billions of dollars.

Home Depot	$ 22.69
Lowe's	10.14
Hechinger/Builder's Square	4.18
Menard Inc.	3.50
Payless Cashways	2.29
84 Lumber Inc.	1.60
HomeBasc Inc.	1.48
Carolina Holdings	1.30
Sears Hardware	1.27
Lanoga Corp.	0.99

Source: *New York Times*, May 13, 1998, p. C4, from *National Home Center News*.

★ 1276 ★
Retailing - Home Improvement (SIC 5211)

Where Home Remodeling/Repair Professionals Buy Supplies

Data are based on a survey of 763 residential remodeling and repair professionals.

Lumber/building material dealer	28.0%
Wholesaler/distributor	24.0
Specialty store	17.0
Warehouse home center	15.0
Home center	8.0
Hardware store	4.0
Manufacturer	1.0

Continued on next page.

★ 1276 ★ *Continued*
Retailing - Home Improvement (SIC 5211)

Where Home Remodeling/Repair Professionals Buy Supplies

Data are based on a survey of 763 residential remodeling and repair professionals.

Catalog/mail order	1.0%
Other	1.0

Source: *Home Improvement Market*, November 1997, p. 20, from Home Improvement Research Institute.

★ 1277 ★
Retailing - Paint and Wallpaper (SIC 5231)

Paint, Glass, and Wallpaper Sales by Outlet - 1996

Distribution is shown based on total mass merchandiser sales of $12.269 billion.

Paint, glass, wallpaper stores	44.0%
Home centers	26.4
Discount stores	14.7
Hardware stores	13.9
Miscellaneous general merchandise stores	0.8
Variety stores	0.2

Source: *Discount Merchandiser*, July 1997, p. 51.

★ 1278 ★
Retailing - Hardware (SIC 5251)

Hardware and Tools Sales by Outlet - 1996

Distribution is shown based on total mass merchandiser sales of $29.988 billion.

Hardware stores	32.5%
Home centers	26.4
Discount stores	19.8
Wholesale clubs	6.6
Department stores	3.8
Non-store retailers	3.8
Auto and home supply stores	1.7
Drug and proprietary stores	1.6
Supermarkets and grocery stores	1.3
Miscellaneous general merchandise stores	1.3
Variety stores	0.6
Household appliance stores	0.6

Source: *Discount Merchandiser*, July 1997, p. 50.

★ 1279 ★
Retailing - Hardware (SIC 5251)

Top Hardware Chains in Canada - 1997

Market shares are shown based on sales of $18 billion for the year ending December 31, 1997.

Canadian Tire	27.8%
Home Hardware Stores	10.6
Home Depot Canada	8.1
Beaver Lumber	4.2
Revelstoke Home Centres	3.1
Reno Depot	2.8
Alpa Lumber	1.9
Cashway Building Centres	1.6
Lansing Buildall	1.0
Kent Building Supplies	1.0
Others	37.9

Source: *Marketing Magazine*, May 25, 1998, p. 24, from *Hardware Merchandising*.

★ 1280 ★
Retailing - Lawn & Garden (SIC 5261)

Lawn and Garden Sales by Outlet - 1996

Distribution is shown based on total mass merchandiser sales of $19.179 billion.

Garden supply stores	27.2%
Discount stores	21.8
Home centers	14.2
Florists	11.5
Hardware stores	8.4
Non-store retailers	4.8
Supermarkets and grocery stores	4.3
Auto and home supply stores	2.6
Drug and proprietary stores	2.4
Department stores	1.2
Miscellaneous general merchandise stores	0.9
Variety stores	0.7

Source: *Discount Merchandiser*, July 1997, p. 50.

★ 1281 ★

Retailing - Nursery Products (SIC 5261)

Lawn & Garden Sales by Segment

Sales are estimated in millions of dollars.

	1997	1998	Share
Green goods	$ 19.1	$ 21.6	26.28%
Chemicals	11.2	11.7	14.23
Power equipment	9.2	9.8	11.92
Fertilizers	8.3	8.5	10.34
Watering equipment	7.8	8.2	9.98
Lawn furniture	6.4	6.8	8.27
Accessories	4.9	5.6	6.81
Tools	4.0	4.2	5.11
Trim-a-tree	4.0	4.2	5.11
Snow removal	1.6	1.6	1.95

Source: *Nursery Retailer*, February/March 1998, p. 62.

★ 1282 ★

Retailing - Nursery Products (SIC 5261)

Lawn & Garden Sales by State - 1997

Total sales are expected to reach $41.1 billion in 1997. Distribution is shown by state.

California	10.3%
New York	8.0
Texas	6.1
Pennsylvania	5.3
Illinois	5.2
Ohio	4.9
Michigan	4.2
Florida	4.0
New Jersey	3.3
Massachusetts	2.3
Other	46.2

Source: *Nursery Retailer*, February/March 1998, p. 64.

SIC 53 - General Merchandise Stores

★ 1283 ★
Retailing (SIC 5300)

Canada's Top Retail Sectors - 1997

Automotive
Food
General merchandise
Clothing
Drugs
Furniture
Other

Sales are shown in millions of dollars.

	($ mil.)	Share
Automotive	$ 88,321	37.95%
Food	56,331	24.20
General merchandise	25,914	11.13
Clothing	13,115	5.64
Drugs	12,615	5.42
Furniture	11,759	5.05
Other	24,683	10.61

Source: *Globe & Mail*, February 21, 1998, p. B1, from Statistics Canada.

★ 1284 ★
Retailing (SIC 5300)

Largest Retail Markets

Market volume is shown in thousands of dollars.

Chicago	$ 72,346,774
Los Angeles-Long Beach	66,704,137
New York	52,341,532
Philadelphia	47,088,399
Washington, D.C.	45,936,307

Source: *Sales & Marketing Management*, September 1997, p. 17.

★ 1285 ★
Retailing (SIC 5300)

Largest Retailers - North America

Sales are shown in billions of U.S. dollars.

Wal-Mart	$ 104,859
Sears	38,236
Kmart	31,437
Dayton Hudson	25,371
Costco	19,214

Source: *Discount Store News*, July 7, 1997, p. 3.

★ 1286 ★
Retailing (SIC 5300)

Largest Retailers in Washington D.C.

Companies are ranked by revenues in millions of dollars.

Giant Food Inc.	$ 4,230.6
Dart Group Corp.	663.8
Trak Auto Corp.	346.0
Crown Books Corp.	287.7
Cort Business Services Corp.	287.2

Source: *Washington Post*, April 27, 1998, p. 47.

★ 1287 ★
Retailing (SIC 5300)

Largest Specialty Retailers - 1997

Firms are ranked by revenues in millions of dollars.

Home Depot	$ 24,156
Costco	21,874
Toys 'R Us	11,038
Republic Industries	10,306
Lowe's	10,137
Limited	9,189
Best Buy	7,771
Circuit City Group	7,664

Continued on next page.

★ 1287 ★ *Continued*
Retailing (SIC 5300)

Largest Specialty Retailers - 1997

Firms are ranked by revenues in millions of dollars.

TJX	$ 7,389
Office Depot	6,718

Source: *Fortune*, April 27, 1998, p. 56.

★ 1288 ★
Retailing (SIC 5300)

Mass Retail Sales - 1997

Mass retailing outlets are ranked by sales in billions of dollars.

Discount stores	$ 171.9
Specialty discounters	61.6
Off-price apparel	17.2
Consumer electronics	16.9
Automotive	8.8
Toys	7.7
Stationery superstores	7.1
Sporting goods	3.9
Wholesale clubs	41.9
Combination drugstores	21.6
Combination supermarkets	14.4
Deep-discount drugstores	7.2
Catalog showrooms	6.4

Source: *Discount Merchandiser*, June 1997, p. 30.

★ 1289 ★
Retailing (SIC 5300)

Types of Chain Stores

The $736,850,160,000 chain store market is shown in percent.

Supermarkets	26.0%
Discount stores	17.1
Hard lines stores	10.2
Department stores	7.8
Sears, Penney, Ward	7.2
Warehouse wholesale clubs	5.7
Drug stores	5.5
Home centers	5.5
Supercenters	4.7
Apparel stores	3.1
Nonstore retailers	2.3
Convenience stores	2.2

Military exchanges	0.9%
Shoe stores	0.9
Catalog showrooms	0.5
Variety stores	0.4

Source: *Chain Store Age*, August 1997, p. 3A, from company reports.

★ 1290 ★
Department Stores (SIC 5311)

Department Store Sales by Type - 1997

Discount	62.4%
Conventional	22.0
National chain	15.6

Source: *USA TODAY*, June 2, 1998, p. B1, from International Mass Retail Association.

★ 1291 ★
Department Stores (SIC 5311)

Leading Department Stores - Canada

Data show shares for 1996.

Wal-Mart	24.0%
Zellers	23.0
Sears Canada	18.0
Bay	15.0
Eaton's	12.0
Kmart	8.0

Source: *Toronto Star*, February 7, 1998, p. C1.

★ 1292 ★

Department Stores (SIC 5311)

Top Department Stores in Canada - 1997

Market shares are shown for the year ending December 31, 1997.

Wal-Mart Canada	27.6%
Zellers	22.6
Sears Canada	18.5
The Bay	15.0
T. Eaton Co.	9.4
Kmart Canada	6.9

Source: *Marketing Magazine*, May 25, 1998, p. 24, from Statistics Canada and Kubas Consultants.

★ 1293 ★

Convenience Stores (SIC 5331)

Best-Selling Convenience Store Products - 1996

Shares of sales are shown in percent.

Tobacco	26.4%
Fast food	13.9
Beer	12.6
Soft drinks	10.1
Milk & milk products	4.7
Candy & gum	4.1
Salty snacks	3.8
Publications	3.2
Groceries	3.0
Bread & cakes, packaged	3.0
Other	15.2

Source: *National Petroleum News*, June 1997, p. 15.

★ 1294 ★

Convenience Stores (SIC 5331)

Convenience Store Leaders - Central Pennsylvania

Data show the top retailers in Central Pennsylvania which sell groceries, health & beauty care, drugs, general merchandise and tobacco products. Data are for 1996.

Shurefine	18.53%
Giant/Carlisle	17.56
Weis Markets	16.75
Kmart	4.58

CVS	3.43%
Festival Foods	3.28
Wal-Mart	2.89
Turkey Hill	2.61
Other	30.37

Source: From the Internet, http://foodmark.sju.edu, 1997, p. 1.

★ 1295 ★

Convenience Stores (SIC 5331)

Convenience Store Leaders - Delaware

Data show the top retailers in Delaware which sell groceries, health & beauty care, drugs, general merchandise and tobacco products. Data are for 1996.

Acme Markets	19.58%
ShopRite	10.57
Pathmark	8.43
Thriftway/Shop 'n Bag	7.83
Wawa	6.14
SuperFresh/A&P	6.08
Genuardi's	4.84
Rite Aid	3.99
Other	32.54

Source: From the Internet, http://foodmark.sju.edu, 1997, p. 1.

★ 1296 ★

Convenience Stores (SIC 5331)

Convenience Store Leaders - Northern Pennsylvania

Data show the top retailers in Northern Pennsylvania which sell groceries, health & beauty care, drugs, general merchandise and tobacco products. Data are for 1996.

Weis Markets	22.92%
Insalaco's	11.27
Shurefine	6.74
Bi-Lo/Riverside	5.54
Wegman's	5.23

Continued on next page.

★ 1296 ★ *Continued*
Convenience Stores (SIC 5331)

Convenience Store Leaders - Northern Pennsylvania

Data show the top retailers in Northern Pennsylvania which sell groceries, health & beauty care, drugs, general merchandise and tobacco products. Data are for 1996.

Wal-Mart (SuperCenter)	4.50%
CVS	4.37
Kmart	3.68
Other	35.75

Source: From the Internet, http:// foodmark.sju.edu, 1997, p. 1.

★ 1297 ★
Convenience Stores (SIC 5331)

Leading Convenience Store Companies - 1996

Companies are shown ranked by sales in thousands of dollars.

The Southland Corp. (7-Eleven) . . .	$ 6,868,912
Circle K (Tosco)	3,900,000
Ultramar Diamond Shamrock	2,472,000
Super America Group (Ashland) . . .	1,928,000
Casey's General Store	1,100,000
Kroger	948,000
E-Z Serve	861,642
Dairy Mart	585,746
Crown Central Petroleum	485,000
Uni-Marts	333,812

Source: *Chain Store Age*, August 1997, p. 19A, from company reports.

★ 1298 ★
Convenience Stores (SIC 5331)

Top Convenience Stores - Washington D.C.

Companies are shown ranked by sales in millions of dollars for 1997. Data include stores that sell groceries, health and beauty products, pharmaceuticals, general merchandise, and tobacco.

	Sales ($ mil.)	Share
Giant Food	$ 2,540.0	29.7%
Safeway	1,620.0	18.9
Shoppers Food Warehouse . . .	801.7	9.4
CVS	658.2	7.7
7-Eleven	355.1	4.2
Costco	279.8	3.3
Food Lion	214.5	2.5
Kmart	190.5	2.2
Wal-Mart	186.0	2.2
Rite Aid	173.0	2.0

Source: *Washington Post*, February 3, 1998, p. D3, from *Food World*.

★ 1299 ★
Discount Merchandising (SIC 5331)

Largest Discount Chains - 1997

Companies are ranked by fiscal year sales in millions of dollars.

	($ bil.)	Share
Wal-Mart/Sam's	$ 104.5	48.0%
Kmart	31.9	15.0
Target	20.4	9.0
Costco	18.5	9.0
Meijer	8.0	4.0
Fred Meyer	3.8	2.0
BJ's Wholesale	3.1	1.0
Shopko	2.6	1.0
Caldor	2.4	1.0
Ames	2.2	1.0

Source: *Discount Merchandiser*, April 1998, p. 35, from company reports and A.G. Edwards & Sons Inc.

★ 1300 ★

Discount Merchandising (SIC 5331)

Largest Supercenters - 1998

*Firms are ranked by sales in billions of dollars.
Market shares are shown in percent.*

	Sales ($ bil.)	Share
Wal-Mart	$ 32.5	62.0%
Meijer	9.0	17.0
Kmart	4.3	8.0
Fred Meyer	4.2	8.0
Target	0.8	2.0

Source: *Discount Merchandiser*, April 1998, p. 35, from company reports and A.G. Edwards & Sons Inc.

★ 1301 ★

Discount Merchandising (SIC 5331)

Leading Discount Department Stores - Canada

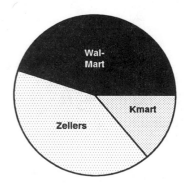

Shares of the $8.9 billion market are shown for 1997.

Wal-Mart	45.0%
Zellers	41.0
Kmart	14.0

Source: *Globe & Mail*, February 7, 1998, p. B5, from CIBC Wood Gundy.

★ 1302 ★

Discount Merchandising (SIC 5331)

Top Discount Retailers - 1996

Companies are ranked by sales in millions of dollars.

Wal-Mart Stores	$ 55,540
Kmart	26,678

Sears Merchandise Group	$ 21,657
Sam's Warehouse Club	19,700
Wal-Mart Supercenter	19,300
Costco	19,214
Target	17,623
Best Buy	7,770
Meijer	7,350
Circuit City	7,154

Source: *Discount Store News*, July 7, 1997, p. 55.

★ 1303 ★

General Merchandising (SIC 5331)

Largest General Merchandisers - 1997

Firms are ranked by revenues in millions of dollars.

Wal-Mart Stores	$ 119,299
Sears Roebuck	41,296
Kmart	32,183
J.C. Penney	30,546
Dayton Hudson	27,757
Federated Dept. Stores	15,668
May Dept. Stores	12,685
Dillard's	6,817
Nordstrom	4,852
Harcourt General	3,692

Source: *Fortune*, April 27, 1998, pp. F-50.

★ 1304 ★

General Merchandising (SIC 5331)

Largest Variety Chains - 1996

Data show sales in millions of dollars.

F.W. Woolworth Corp.	$ 1,000
McCrory's Stores	450
Variety Wholesalers	293
Bill's	238
Ocean State Jobbers	117
D & K Stores Inc.	68
Shirokiya	56
Perry Brothers	42
P.M. Place	41

Source: *Discount Store News*, July 7, 1997, p. 77.

★ 1305 ★

General Merchandising (SIC 5331)

Top Mass Merchandisers

Companies are ranked by estimated total volume in billions of dollars.

Wal-Mart	$ 74.840
Kmart	31.437
Sam's Club	19.785
Home Depot	19.536
PriceCostco	19.214
Target	17.853
Toys "R" Us	9.932
Best Buy	7.771
Circuit City	7.154
Meijer's	7.100

Source: *Discount Merchandiser*, June 1997, p. 51.

SIC 54 - Food Stores

★ 1306 ★
Grocery Stores (SIC 5411)

Alberta's Grocery Market - 1997

Data show the change in market shares during the 1997 Canada Safeway strike in Alberta. Non-grocery includes Price Club, Wal-Mart, and drugstores. Calgary Co-op includes other co-ops.

	During April-May	Post July-Aug.
Canada Safeway	13.0%	29.0%
Non-grocery	18.0	18.0
Calgary Co-op	17.5	12.5
Real Canadian Superstore	17.5	15.0
IGA	15.0	11.0
Other	7.5	6.5

Source: *Marketing Magazine*, October 27, 1997, p. 32, from NPD Group Canada Inc.

★ 1307 ★
Grocery Stores (SIC 5411)

Chicago's Top Grocery Stores - 1996

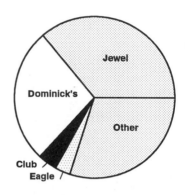

Market shares are shown in percent.

Jewel	36.0%
Dominick's	27.0
Club	4.0
Eagle	3.0
Other	30.0

Source: *Investor's Business Daily*, February 19, 1998, p. A4, from company reports.

★ 1308 ★
Grocery Stores (SIC 5411)

Largest Food Retailers

Companies are ranked by revenues in billions of dollars.

Kroger	$ 26.5
Wal-Mart Superstores	25.0
Safeway	22.4
American Stores	19.2
Ahold USA	18.5
SuperValu	16.9
Fleming	15.4
Albertson's	14.7

Continued on next page.

★ **1308** ★ *Continued*

Grocery Stores (SIC 5411)

Largest Food Retailers

Companies are ranked by revenues in billions of dollars.

Winn-Dixie Stores	$ 13.2
Fred Meyer	12.8

Source: *Washington Post*, May 21, 1998, p. D4, from Bloomberg News and *Restaurant News*.

★ **1309** ★

Grocery Stores (SIC 5411)

Largest Supermarket Chains - 1997

Companies are ranked by fiscal year sales in millions of dollars.

	($ bil.)	Share
Kroger	$ 27.9	7.0%
Safeway	24.6	6.0
American Stores	19.5	5.0
Fred Meyer	16.0	4.0
Albertson's	15.9	4.0
Winn-Dixie	14.2	4.0
Ahold USA	11.9	3.0
Publix	11.3	3.0
Food Lion	10.9	2.0
A&P	10.6	2.0

Source: *Discount Merchandiser*, April 1998, p. 35, from company reports and A.G. Edwards & Sons Inc.

★ **1310** ★

Grocery Stores (SIC 5411)

Supermarket Sales by Segment - 2000

Data show estimated sales. GM stands for general merchandise. HBC stands for health & beauty care.

Dry grocery	24.7%
Produce	12.7
Meat	12.3
Deli	7.8
Dairy	6.1

Frozen	5.5%
Bakery	4.0
Seafood	1.6
GM/HBC/Other	25.3

Source: *SN*, October 27, 1997, p. 22, from PMA/Cornell University Freshtrack.

★ **1311** ★

Grocery Stores (SIC 5411)

Top Grocery Chains - 1996

Data show sales in billions of dollars. Figure for Safeway is estimated for 1997 to show acquisition of Vons.

Kroger	$ 25.17
Safeway	22.78
American Stores	18.68
Albertson's	13.78
Winn-Dixie Stores	12.96

Source: *Wall Street Journal*, August 6, 1997, p. B4, from company reports, *Donaldson, Lufkin & Jenrette Food & Drug Handbook*, and Baseline.

★ **1312** ★

Grocery Stores (SIC 5411)

Top Grocery Stores in Canada - 1997

Market shares are shown based on $44.5 billion in sales for the year ending December 31, 1997.

Loblaw Companies	19.5%
Agora Food Merchants	10.2
Provigo	9.3
Canada Safeway	8.4
Membership Club Stores	7.8
Metro-Richelieu	6.7
Corporate A&P	5.7
Co-op	4.2
Overwaitea Food Group	4.2
Other	24.0

Source: *Marketing Magazine*, May 25, 1998, p. 23, from *Canadian Grocer*.

★ 1313 ★

Grocery Stores (SIC 5411)

Top Supermarkets in Washington D.C. - 1997

Market shares are shown in percent.

Giant Food	44.9%
Safeway	27.1
Shoppers Food Warehouse	13.5
Magruders	2.7
Food Lion	2.6
Whole Foods/Fresh Fields	2.5
Super Fresh/AP	2.3
Weis Markets	2.1
IGA	1.3
Sutton Place Gourmet	0.7
Other	0.3

Source: *Washington Post*, May 20, 1998, p. A8, from *Food World*.

★ 1314 ★

Fruit Markets (SIC 5431)

North Carolina's Fruit Markets

There are an estimated 320 markets, stalls and farms that sell fresh fruit from May to October.

Wake	13
Johnston	10
Moore	9
Rockingham	9
Union	9
Guilford	8
Robeson	8
Wayne	8

Source: *Business North Carolina*, May 1998, p. 84, from United States Department of Agriculture.

★ 1315 ★

Bagel Shops (SIC 5461)

Top Bagel Chains - 1996

Chains are ranked by outlets at the end of 1996.

Bruegger's	450
Einstein/Noah's	315
Manhattan Bagel	296
Chesapeake Bagel	156
Big Apple Bagel	118

Source: *Restaurant Business*, May 15, 1997, p. 132, from Rodman & Renshaw Inc. and Restaurant Business.

SIC 55 - Automotive Dealers and Service Stations

★ 1316 ★
Auto Dealerships (SIC 5511)

Top Car Dealerships - Los Angeles County

Firms are ranked by new car sales in 1996.

Longo Toyota	15,339
Galpin Ford	11,678
Norm Reeves Honda	6,218
Toyota of Cerritos	4,427
Don Knott Ford	3,790
Goudy Honda	3,104

Source: *Los Angeles Business Journal*, September 22, 1997, p. 43.

★ 1317 ★
Retailing - Auto Parts (SIC 5531)

Auto Parts Retail Market - Canada

Shares of the do-it-yourself automotive market are shown in percent.

Canadian Tire	40.0%
Wholesale parts distributors	20.0
Department stores	7.0
New car dealers	7.0
Service stations	7.0
Other	19.0

Source: *Marketing Magazine*, July 28, 1997, p. 3, from Automotive Industry Association of Canada.

★ 1318 ★
Retailing - Auto Parts (SIC 5531)

Largest Auto Part Retailers - 1997

Data represent number of stores.

AutoZone	1,516
Advance	688
Parts America (Western Auto)	619
Pep Boys/Parts USA	604

CSK (Northern)	580
Chief Auto	548
Discount Auto	383
Trak Auto	286
Hi-Lo	191
Super Shops	164

Source: *Automotive Marketing*, July 1997, p. 42.

★ 1319 ★
Retailing - Auto Parts (SIC 5531)

Top Auto Parts Chains - 1996

Companies are ranked by sales in millions of dollars.

Genuine Parts	$ 3,030
Sears Tire Group	2,300
AutoZone	2,240
The Pep Boys	1,820
Western Auto/Parts America	1,600
Penske Auto Center Inc.	820
CSK Auto Inc.	793

Source: *Chain Store Age*, May 1998, p. 50, from Automotive Aftermarket Suppliers and Chain Store Guide Information Services.

★ 1320 ★
Retailing - Tires (SIC 5531)

Largest Commercial Dealerships - 1996

Tire Centers Inc.

Fletcher's Cobre Tire

Kal Tire

Treadco Inc.

Les Schwab Tire Centers Inc.

Purcell Tire & Rubber Co.

Companies are ranked by sales in millions of dollars. Figures are for North America.

Tire Centers Inc.	$ 240.0
Fletcher's Cobre Tire	235.0
Kal Tire	159.0
Treadco Inc.	144.2
Les Schwab Tire Centers Inc.	121.0
Purcell Tire & Rubber Co.	106.0

Source: *Tire Business*, December 8, 1997, p. 21.

★ 1321 ★
Retailing - Tires (SIC 5531)

Largest Independent Dealerships - 1996

Companies are ranked by sales in millions of dollars. Figures are for North America.

Discount Tire Co. Inc.	$ 739.0
Les Schwab Tire Centers Inc.	562.8
Penske Auto Centers Inc.	350.0
Tire Kingdom Inc.	209.8
Winston Tire-Auto Service & Repair	148.0

Source: *Tire Business*, December 8, 1997, p. 21.

★ 1322 ★
Retailing - Tires (SIC 5531)

Top Tire Dealerships - North America

Companies are ranked by 1996 retail sales in millions of U.S. dollars.

Discount Tire Co. Inc.	$ 739.0
Les Schwab Tire Centers Inc.	562.8
Penske Auto Centers Inc.	350.0
Tire Kingdom Inc.	209.8
Winston Tire-Auto Service & Repair	148.0

Merchant's Inc.	$ 142.0
Tire Centers Inc.	112.0
Morgan Tire & Auto Inc./Don Olson Tire	98.1
Team Tires Plus Ltd.	70.8
Fountain Tire	70.6

Source: *Tire Business*, October 1, 1997, p. 17.

★ 1323 ★
Gas Stations (SIC 5541)

Gas Stations by State - 1998

Data show number of outlets. There are a total of 182,596 outlets in the United States.

Texas	15,074
California	11,258
Florida	9,024
North Carolina	7,816
Louisiana	7,424
Georgia	7,356

Source: *National Petroleum News*, May 1998, p. 8.

★ 1324 ★
Gas Stations (SIC 5541)

Gas Stations by Type - 1996

Data show types of gas stations.

Convenience stores	72.0%
Gas only/gas with incidentals	12.0
Gas with repair-service garage	12.0
Truck stops	3.0
Other	1.0

Source: *Wall Street Journal*, October 14, 1997, p. B4, from Society of Independent Gasoline Marketers of America and company reports.

SIC 56 - Apparel and Accessory Stores

★ 1325 ★

Retailing - Apparel (SIC 5600)

Leading Clothing Stores - Canada

Companies are ranked by revenues in thousands of Canadian dollars.

Dylex Ltd.	$ 1,243,308
Suzy Shier	572,481
Reitmans	409,673
Mark's Work Wearhouse	225,868
Pantorama Industries	159,892
Chateau Stores of Canada	141,975

Source: *Globe and Mail's Report on Business Magazine*, July 1997, p. 166.

★ 1326 ★

Retailing - Apparel (SIC 5600)

States with the Most Clothing Stores

Data show the number of clothing stores in each state. There are a total of 142,372 clothing stores nationwide.

California	15,387
New York	11,408
Texas	9,723
Florida	9,713
Pennsylvania	6,521
Illinois	6,386
New Jersey	5,300
Ohio	5,233
Michigan	4,908
North Carolina	4,137

Source: *Business North Carolina*, February 1997, p. 68, from U.S. Bureau of the Census.

★ 1327 ★

Retailing - Apparel (SIC 5611)

Men's and Boys' Clothing Sales by Outlet - 1996

Distribution is shown based on total mass merchandiser sales of $58.861 billion.

Department stores	29.6%
Discount stores	23.7
Family apparel stores	15.7
Men's and boys' wear stores	13.3
Off-price apparel stores	5.8
Non-store retailers	4.8
Sporting goods stores	3.3
Miscellaneous general merchandise stores	1.0
Women's ready-to-wear stores	0.9
Supermarkets and grocery stores	0.7
Drug and proprietary stores	0.6
Variety stores	0.6

Source: *Discount Merchandiser*, July 1997, p. 49.

★ 1328 ★
Retailing - Apparel (SIC 5611)

Men's Underwear Sales by Outlet

Shares are shown in percent.

Discount stores	45.7%
Chain stores	18.5
Department stores	10.9
Specialty stores	6.3
Direct mail	3.7
Other	14.8

Source: *Body Fashions/Intimate Apparel*, February 1998, p. 11, from NPD American Shoppers Panel.

★ 1329 ★
Retailing - Apparel (SIC 5621)

Women's and Girls' Clothing Sales by Outlet - 1996

Distribution is shown based on total mass merchandiser sales of $121.768 billion.

Department stores	30.8%
Women's ready-to-wear stores	23.8
Discount stores	16.2
Family apparel stores	10.1
Off-price apparel stores	9.8
Non-store retailers	4.8
Supermarkets and grocery stores	1.4
Sporting goods stores	1.0
Variety stores	0.7
Miscellaneous general merchandise stores	0.7
Drug and proprietary stores	0.4
Men's and boy's wear stores	0.3

Source: *Discount Merchandiser*, July 1997, p. 49.

★ 1330 ★
Retailing - Apparel (SIC 5632)

Bra Sales by Channel - 1997

Sales are shown in percent for January to April 1997. Data are based on a survey of 16,000 households nationwide.

Discount stores	28.9%
Chain stores	20.4
Specialty stores	17.0
Department stores	16.8
Other	16.9

Source: *Discount Merchandiser*, August 1997, p. 109, from NPD American Shopper Panel.

★ 1331 ★
Retailing - Apparel (SIC 5632)

Maternity Bra Sales by Outlet - 1997

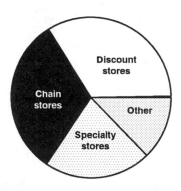

Sales are shown in percent. The $67.5 million nursing bra market is only 1.71 percent of the total bra market.

Discount stores	33.6%
Chain stores	31.9
Specialty stores	21.9
Other	12.6

Source: *Body Fashions/Intimate Apparel*, June 1998, p. 13, from NPD American Shoppers Panel.

★ 1332 ★

Retailing - Apparel (SIC 5641)

Infants' Clothing Sales by Outlet - 1996

Distribution is shown based on total mass merchandiser sales of $10.631 billion.

Discount stores	37.0%
Department stores	36.5
Childrens' and infants' wear stores	13.2
Family apparel stores	8.6
Women's ready-to-wear stores	4.7

Source: *Discount Merchandiser*, July 1997, p. 49.

★ 1333 ★

Retailing - Apparel (SIC 5651)

Largest Off-Price Apparel Chains - 1996

The table shows companies ranked by sales in millions of dollars.

T.J. Maxx	$ 3,958
Marshalls	2,731
Ross Stores	1,690
Burlington Coat Factory	1,611
Goody's Family Clothing	819
Kids "R" Us	790
Stein Marts	616
Filene's Basement	545
Dress Barn	516
The Men's Warehouse	484

Source: *Discount Store News*, July 7, 1997, p. 73.

★ 1334 ★

Retailing - Apparel (SIC 5651)

Largest Specialty Clothing Retailers - North Carolina

Data show sales in millions of dollars.

Sara Lee Direct Outlet Stores	$ 17,719.0
Cato Corp.	490.0
Overton's Inc.	64.0
Brody Brothers Dry Good Inc.	30.8
World of Clothing Inc.	24.0
Omega Sports Inc.	14.0
Tanner Companies Inc.	13.0
R&M Sporting Goods Inc.	10.5

Young Generations Inc.	$ 10.0
Durham Sporting Goods Co.	8.4

Source: *Business North Carolina*, February 1997, p. 68, from *Chain Store Guide*.

★ 1335 ★

Retailing - Shoes (SIC 5661)

Largest Sports Shoe Retailers - 1996

Foot Locker

SportsAuthority

Footaction USA

Athlete's Foot

Finish Line

Companies are ranked by net sales in millions of dollars.

Foot Locker	$ 2,300.0
SportsAuthority	635.5
Footaction USA	515.7
Athlete's Foot	350.0
Finish Line	332.0

Source: *Chain Store Age*, October 1997, p. 58.

SIC 57 - Furniture and Homefurnishings Stores

★ 1336 ★
Retailing - Furniture (SIC 5712)

Largest Rent-to-Own Furniture Stores - 1997

Market shares are shown based on 7,000 stores.

Thom Americas	18.4%
Renters Choice	10.0
Alrenco	5.4
Aaron Rents	3.1
Central Rents	2.4
Rent Way	2.4
Champion Rent-To-Own	1.9
Bestway Rental	0.8
Rainbow Rentals	0.8
Other	54.8

Source: *Investor's Business Daily*, March 27, 1998, p. A4, from company reports and Wheat First Butcher Singer.

★ 1337 ★
Retailing - Furniture (SIC 5712)

Top Furniture Retailers

Companies are ranked by sales of furniture and bedding in millions of dollars.

Heilig-Meyers	$ 994.6
Levitz	940.5
J.C. Penney	738.0
Montgomery Ward	732.0
Sears	730.7
Office Depot	679.7
Wal-Mart	660.0
Ethan Allen Home Interiors	629.9
La-Z-Boy	474.4
Havertys	438.6

Source: *Furniture Today*, December 29, 1997, p. 50.

★ 1338 ★
Retailing - Furniture (SIC 5712)

Top Furniture Stores

Heilig-Meyers
Levitz
Sears HomeLife
Pier 1 Imports
Havertys
Rooms To Go

Companies are ranked by sales in millions of dollars. The top 100 companies had a 41% share of the market.

Heilig-Meyers	$ 1,021.5
Levitz	960.7
Sears HomeLife	658.0
Pier 1 Imports	550.7
Havertys	456.9
Rooms To Go	450.0

Source: *Furniture Today*, December 29, 1997, p. 42.

★ 1339 ★
Retailing - Furniture (SIC 5712)

Top Furniture Stores - Midwest

Companies are ranked by 1996 sales in millions of dollars.

Art Van	$ 410.0
Slumberland	132.0
Nebraska Furniture Mart	122.0
Harlem Furniture	72.6

Source: *Furniture Today*, December 29, 1997, p. 49.

★ 1340 ★
Retailing - Furniture (SIC 5712)

Top Furniture Stores - Northeast

Companies are ranked by 1996 sales in millions of dollars.

Jordan's Furniture	$ 114.4
Raymour & Flanigan	107.6
ABC Carpet & Home	95.0
Sleepy's	71.0

Source: *Furniture Today*, December 29, 1997, p. 49.

★ 1341 ★
Retailing - Furniture (SIC 5712)

Top Furniture Stores - South

Companies are ranked by 1996 sales in millions of dollars.

Rooms To Go	$ 450.0
W.S. Badcock	295.8
Finger Furniture	128.0
Furnitureland South	113.0

Source: *Furniture Today*, December 29, 1997, p. 49.

★ 1342 ★
Retailing - Furniture (SIC 5712)

Top Multimarket and Specialty Furniture Retailers - 1996

Firms are ranked by 1996 sales in millions of dollars.

Heilig-Meyers	$ 1,002
Levitz	961
Sears Homelife	657
Pier 1 Imports	551
Haverty	457
Rooms to Go	450
Value City	450
Ikea	412

Source: *New York Times*, September 12, 1997, p. C1, from Bloomberg Financial Markets, company reports, and *Furniture Today Market Research*.

★ 1343 ★
Retailing - Floor Coverings (SIC 5713)

Largest Carpet and Rug Retailers - 1997

Home Depot
Shaw Industries
Sears
Lowe's
Wal-Mart

Stores are ranked by sales in millions of dollars.

Home Depot	$ 1,600
Shaw Industries	650
Sears	402
Lowe's	390
Wal-Mart	315

Source: *Wall Street Journal*, March 31, 1998, p. B1, from *Floor Focus*.

★ 1344 ★
Retailing - Floor Coverings (SIC 5713)

Rug Sales by Outlet

Retail sales reached $1.65 billion.

Home centers	20.0%
Mass merchants	20.0
National chains	20.0
Department stores	13.0
Specialty stores	10.0
Catalogs	6.0
Furniture stores	6.0
Other	5.0

Source: *HFN*, March 16, 1998, p. 40.

★ 1345 ★
Retailing - Upholstery (SIC 5714)

Upholstery Sales by Outlet

Total retail sales reached $8.44 billion.

Furniture stores	65.0%
National chains	14.0
Department stores	11.0
Sofa specialty stores	6.0
Designers	1.5
Other	2.5

Source: *HFN*, March 16, 1998, p. 24.

★ 1346 ★

Retailing - Window Coverings (SIC 5714)

Soft Window Covering Sales by Channel - 1996

Shares are shown based on $3.2 billion in sales.

Department stores	27.0%
Discount	24.0
National Chains	15.0
Specialty chains	8.0
Custom decorating shops	7.0
Catalogs	6.0
Home improvement stores	6.0
Individual specialty stores	4.0
Warehouse clubs	1.0
Other	2.0

Source: *Bobbin*, October 1997, p. 38, from *Home Textiles Today*.

★ 1347 ★

Retailing - Homefurnishings (SIC 5719)

Bedding Sales by Outlet

Total retail sales reached $6.5 billion.

Furniture stores	42.0%
Sleep shops	24.0
Department stores	11.0
National chains	8.0
Warehouse clubs	6.0
Other	9.0

Source: *HFN*, March 16, 1998, p. 24.

★ 1348 ★

Retailing - Homefurnishings (SIC 5719)

Cookware Sales by Channel - 1997

Market shares are shown in percent.

Wal-Mart	17.9%
Grocery stores	11.1
Department stores	8.7
Kmart	8.7

Target	7.7%
Mail order	6.2
Kitchen specialty stores	4.0
Factory outlets	2.7
Door to door	2.4
Warehouse clubs	1.9
Other	6.0

Source: *HFN*, January 5, 1998, p. 41.

★ 1349 ★

Retailing - Homefurnishings (SIC 5719)

Mattress Sales by Outlet - 1996

Total sales reached 18.3 million mattresses and 14.4 million box springs.

Furniture stores	49.0%
Sleep shops	24.0
Department stores and national chains	20.0
Warehouse clubs	5.0
Other (includes phone sales)	2.0

Source: *Philadelphia Inquirer*, March 1, 1998, p. D1, from International Sleep Products Association, *Furniture Today*, and *1997 Philadelphia Scarborough Report*.

★ 1350 ★

Retailing - Appliances (SIC 5722)

Coffeemaker Sales by Outlet

Distribution is shown in percent.

Wal-Mart	28.5%
Kmart	12.7
Department stores	10.6
Target	7.1
Mail-order	5.9
Catalog showroom	4.0
Warehouse clubs	3.0
Other discounters	4.2
Other	24.0

Source: *HFN*, December 1, 1997, p. 28.

★ 1351 ★
Retailing - Appliances (SIC 5722)

Iron Sales by Outlet

Retail sales reached $295 million.

Mass merchants	53.0%
Discounters	20.0
Department stores	13.0
Catalogs	9.0
Other	5.0

Source: *HFN*, March 16, 1998, p. 62.

★ 1352 ★
Retailing - Appliances (SIC 5722)

Kitchen Tool Sales by Outlet - 1997

Retail sales reached $650 million.

Mass merchants	36.0%
Supermarkets	22.0
Specialty stores	15.0
Department stores	9.0
Other	18.0

Source: *HFN*, March 16, 1998, p. 58.

★ 1353 ★
Retailing - Appliances (SIC 5722)

Small Electric Appliances Sales by Outlet - 1996

Distribution is shown based on total mass merchandiser sales of $10.562 billion.

Discount stores	37.5%
Wholesale clubs	15.9
Drug and proprietary stores	13.3
Department stores	11.5
Miscellaneous general merchandise stores	4.6
Supermarkets and grocery stores	3.9
Catalog showrooms	3.6

Hardware stores	3.2%
Auto and home supply stores	2.8
Household appliance stores	2.7
Variety stores	1.0

Source: *Discount Merchandiser*, July 1997, p. 50.

★ 1354 ★
Retailing - Homefurnishings (SIC 5722)

Cleaning Tool Sales by Outlet

Retail sales reached $702.3 million.

Mass merchants	36.0%
Supermarkets	28.0
Hardware/home centers	27.0
Other	9.0

Source: *HFN*, June 1, 1998, p. 42.

★ 1355 ★
Retailing - Electronics (SIC 5731)

DVD Player Sales

Retail sales reached $120 million.

Consumer electronics	80.0%
National chains	12.0
Mass merchants	5.0
Department stores	2.0
Warehouse clubs	1.0

Source: *HFN*, March 16, 1998, p. 77.

★ 1356 ★
Retailing - Electronics (SIC 5731)

Where People Buy Wireless Phones

Sales are shown by outlet.

Specialty wireless store	21.0%
Wireless company store	21.0
Wireless services provider	17.0
Small electronics store	10.0
Large electronics store	8.0
From an offer through work	6.0
Other	15.0

Source: *Discount Store News*, March 9, 1998, p. 8, from Consumer Electronics Manufactrers Association.

★ 1357 ★

Retailing - Computers (SIC 5734)

PC Sales by Retail Category - 1996

Sales of $26.8 billion are shown distributed by retail category.

Computer superstores	38.4%
Consumer electronics stores	22.3
Office products superstores	15.3
Discount department stores	5.0
Warehouse clubs	4.5
Other	14.5

Source: *Los Angeles Times*, November 17, 1997, p. D4.

★ 1358 ★

Retailing - Computers (SIC 5734)

Top Computer Chains - 1996

Data show sales in millions of dollars.

CompUSA	$ 3,830
Computer City	2,064
Software Etc.	150

Source: *Discount Store News*, July 7, 1997, p. 75.

★ 1359 ★

Retailing - Software (SIC 5734)

Where Entertainment Software is Sold - 1996

Sales of interactive entertainment software are shown by type of retailer.

Mass merchandiser	25.0%
Toy store chains	25.0
Software stores	21.0
Electronics stores	10.0
Computer stores	8.0
Entertainment media stores	6.0
Catalog store/mail order	4.0
Office supply stores	1.0

Source: *USA TODAY*, February 24, 1998, p. B1, from Access Media International.

★ 1360 ★

Retailing - Music (SIC 5735)

Music Sales by Channel

The market earned $12.5 billion in 1996 and is expected to reach $22 billion in 2002.

	1996	2002
Retail stores	82.7%	80.0%
Online	0.1	7.5
Other direct marketing	17.2	12.5

Source: *New Media*, August 4, 1997, p. 13, from http://www.jup.com.

★ 1361 ★

Retailing - Music (SIC 5735)

Online Music Market - 1996

Shares are shown in percent. Online music sales are estimated to grow from $18.2 million in 1996 to $47 million in 1997.

CDnow	33.0%
Tower Records	14.0
Music Boulevard	12.0
Others	41.0

Source: *Financial Times*, August 7, 1997, p. 6, from Jupiter Communications and industry estimates.

★ 1362 ★

Retailing - Music (SIC 5735)

Recorded Music Sales by Outlet - 1996

Sales are shown in percent.

Record stores	49.9%
Tape/record clubs	14.3
Mail order	2.9
Other stores	31.5

Source: *USA TODAY*, August 12, 1997, p. B1, from Veronis, Suhler & Associates.

★ 1363 ★

Retailing - Music (SIC 5736)

Leading Music Store Chains

Chains are ranked by number of outlets.

Music Go Round	43
Guitar Center	36

Continued on next page.

★ 1363 ★ *Continued*

Retailing - Music (SIC 5736)

Leading Music Store Chains

Chains are ranked by number of outlets.

Fletcher Music Centers 31
Brook Mays/H&H Music Co. 23
Music + Arts Center 23
Paul A. Schmitt Music Co. 19
Sam Ash Music Co. 19
Daddy's Junky Music 18
Baldwin Piano & Organ Co. 13
Schroeder's Keyboard City 13
Jordan Kitts Music 12
J.W. Pepper & Son 11
Mcfadyen Music 11
Sherman, Clay & Co. 10

Source: *Music Merchandising Review*, December 1997, p. 26.

★ 1364 ★

Retailing - Musical Instruments (SIC 5736)

Largest Music Product Firms - 1996

Companies are ranked by estimated revenues in millions of dollars. Products include instruments, equipment, and sheet music.

Guitar Center . . . . $ 213.3
Sam Ash Music Corp. 165.7
Brook Mays/H&H Music 58.5
Musicians Friend 53.0
Schmitt Music Company 43.6
Washington Music Center 42.6
Fletcher Music Center 42.5
Sherman Clay & Company 40.7
Thoroughbred Music 38.6
Hermes Music 38.6

Source: *Music Trades*, August 1997, p. 86.

★ 1365 ★

Retailing - Musical Instruments (SIC 5736)

Music Products Retailers by State - 1996

States are ranked by number of music products retailers.

California 862
Florida 391

Texas 346
Illinois 307
New York 277
Pennsylvania 257
Michigan 214
Ohio 193
New Jersey 193
Georgia 178
Washington 160

Source: *Music Trades*, September 1997, p. 130.

SIC 58 - Eating and Drinking Places

★ 1366 ★
Foodservice (SIC 5812)

Largest Food Service Companies

Firms are ranked by revenues in millions of dollars.

McDonald's	$ 11,409
Prosource	3,901
Darden Restaurants	3,172
Advantica	2,609
Viad	2,417
Wendy's International	2,037

Source: *Fortune*, April 27, 1998, pp. F-50.

★ 1367 ★
Foodservice (SIC 5812)

Leading F&B Spenders - Airports/ Airlines

Companies are ranked by food and beverage (F&B) sales in millions of dollars for 1996.

LSG Lufthansa Service/Sky Chefs	$ 1,530.0
Host Marriott Services Corp.	1,015.0
Dobbs International Services	750.0
Ogden Aviation Services	192.0
CA One	184.5
United Airlines	17.3

Source: *Restaurants and Institutions*, August 15, 1997, p. 80, from individual companies.

★ 1368 ★
Foodservice (SIC 5812)

Leading F&B Spenders - Military

Food and beverage (F&B) purchasing is shown by service branch in millions of dollars for 1996.

U.S. Army Center of Excellence, Subsistence	$ 366.4
Naval Supply Systems Command	271.1
Army & Air Force Exchange Service	110.0
U.S. Air Force APF Food Operations	$ 84.7
U.S. Air Force Clubs	82.7
U.S. Marine Corps Food Service Section	69.0
U.S. Navy MWR Division	65.0
U.S. Army Community & Family Support Centers	53.6
U.S. Marine Corps MWR Support Activity	24.0
U.S. Navy Exchange Service Command	17.1

Source: *Restaurants and Institutions*, August 15, 1997, p. 78, from individual service branches.

★ 1369 ★
Foodservice (SIC 5812)

Leading F&B Spenders - Prisons

Food and beverage (F&B) purchasing is shown by prison system in millions of dollars for 1996.

California Dept. of Corrections	$ 136.0
Federal Bureau of Prisons	86.6
Texas Dept. of Criminal Justice	60.0
Florida Dept. of Corrections	52.0
New York State Dept. of Corrections	40.0
Pennsylvania Dept. of Corrections	38.0
Illinois Dept. of Corrections	36.8
Ohio Dept. of Corrections	36.0
Michigan Dept. of Corrections	34.4
Virginia Dept. of Corrections	29.9

Source: *Restaurants and Institutions*, August 15, 1997, p. 74, from individual systems.

★ 1370 ★
Foodservice (SIC 5812)

Leading F&B Spenders - School Districts

Food and beverage (F&B) purchasing is shown by school district in millions of dollars for the 1996-1997 academic year.

New York City Board of Education	$ 91.0
Los Angeles Unified School District	83.0
Chicago Public Schools	63.0
Dade County Schools (Miami, FL)	37.0
Philadelphia School District	23.8
Broward County Schools (Fort Lauderdale, FL)	19.1
Hawaii Statewide School System (Honolulu, HI)	19.0
Hillsborough County Schools (Tampa, FL)	17.1
Dallas Independent School District	14.9

Source: *Restaurants and Institutions*, August 15, 1997, p. 64, from individual districts.

★ 1371 ★
Foodservice (SIC 5812)

Leading F&B Spenders - Universities

Food and beverage (F&B) purchasing is shown by university in millions of dollars for the 1996-1997 academic year.

Pennsylvania State University	$ 20.8
Michigan State University	15.1
Brigham Young University	12.5
Harvard University	9.1
University of Notre Dame	9.1
Purdue University	8.8
University of Maryland	7.9
University of Illinois	7.5

Source: *Restaurants and Institutions*, August 15, 1997, p. 70, from individual universities.

★ 1372 ★
Restaurants (SIC 5812)

Fast Food Sales by City

Sales are shown in billions of dollars.

Chicago, Il	$ 2.6
Los Angeles/Long Beach CA	2.3
Atlanta, GA	1.7
Washington D.C.	$ 1.7
Detroit, MI	1.6
Houston, TX	1.4
New York, NY	1.4
Phoenix/Mesa, AZ	1.2
Dallas, TX	1.1
Philadelphia, PA	1.0

Source: *Restaurant Business*, October 1, 1997, p. 92.

★ 1373 ★
Restaurants (SIC 5812)

Fast-Food Restaurant Sales - Canada

Sales are shown by segment in 1997.

Burger	13.6%
Pizza	11.8
Coffee/doughnut/specialty	4.6
Chicken	4.2
Varied menu	1.2
Other sandwich	3.8
Other fast food	3.7

Source: *Globe & Mail*, February 23, 1998, p. B9, from Canadian Restaurant and Foodservice Association.

★ 1374 ★
Restaurants (SIC 5812)

Italian Restaurants by Sales - 1996

Data show sales in millions of dollars.

The Olive Garden	$ 1,300.0
Sbarro	437.6
Pizzeria Uno	246.0
Romano's Macaroni Grill	226.9
Fazoli's	219.7
Mazzio's	150.8
Bertucci's	128.0
Papa Gino's	128.0
The Spaghetti Warehouse	87.3
Old Spaghetti Factory	81.0

Source: *Restaurants and Institutions*, July 15, 1997, p. 117.

★ 1375 ★
Restaurants (SIC 5812)
Largest Burger Restaurants - Canada

Data show the number of outlets.

McDonald's 1,050
A&W 498
Harvey's 350
Burger King 261
Wendy's 245

Source: *Globe & Mail*, February 23, 1998, p. B9.

★ 1376 ★
Restaurants (SIC 5812)
Largest Ice Cream Sellers

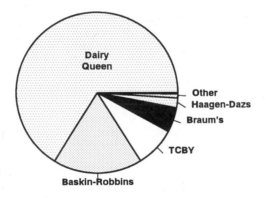

Companies are ranked by sales in millions of dollars. Dairy Queen also sells hamburgers and other food items. Sales at stores primarily selling ice cream and frozen yogurt reached $3.9 billion.

	($ mil.)	Share
Dairy Queen	$ 2,600	66.67%
Baskin-Robbins	700	17.95
TCBY	300	7.69
Braum's	200	5.13
Haagen-Dazs	80	2.05
Other	20	0.51

Source: *Los Angeles Times*, March 19, 1998, p. 3, from Technomic.

★ 1377 ★
Restaurants (SIC 5812)
Leading Burger Chains - 1996

Shares are shown based on U.S. retail sales.

McDonald's 41.9%
Burger King 19.2
Wendy's 11.0
Hardee's 7.6
Jack-In-the-Box 3.2
Others 17.1

Source: *Financial Times*, July 16, 1997, p. 13, from company reports and Technomic Inc.

★ 1378 ★
Restaurants (SIC 5812)
Leading Chicken Chains

Data show shares of aggregate sales of chicken chains in the Nation's Restaurant News list of top 100 restaurants.

KFC 57.09%
Boston Market 17.08
Popeyes Famous Fried Chicken 9.75
Chick-fil-A 8.34
Churchs Chicken 7.74

Source: *Nation's Restaurant News*, June 23, 1997, p. 144.

★ 1379 ★
Restaurants (SIC 5812)
Leading Dinner-House Chains

Data show shares of aggregate sales of dinner-house chains in the Nation's Restaurant News list of top 100 restaurants.

Red Lobster 15.66%
Applebee's Neighborhood Grill & Bar . . . 13.18
Olive Garden 11.08
Chili's Grill & Bar 10.75
Outback Steakhouse 8.80
T.G.I. Friday's 8.09
Ruby Tuesday 4.72
Lone Star Steakhouse & Saloon 3.98
Bennigan's 3.96
Romano's Macaroni Grill 2.98

Source: *Nation's Restaurant News*, June 23, 1997, p. 170.

★ 1380 ★

Restaurants (SIC 5812)

Leading Family Chains

Data show shares of aggregate sales of family chains in the Nation's Restaurant News list of top 100 restaurants.

Denny's	21.22%
Shoney's	13.99
Big Boy Restaurant & Bakery	10.84
International House of Pancakes	9.14
Cracker Barrel Old Country Store	8.42
Perkins Family Restaurants	7.78
Friendly's Ice Cream	6.84
Bob Evans Restaurants	6.59
Waffle House	6.02
Coco's	3.19
Steak 'n Shake	3.15
Village Inn	2.82

Source: *Nation's Restaurant News*, June 23, 1997, p. 150.

★ 1381 ★

Restaurants (SIC 5812)

Leading Pizza Chains

Data show shares of aggregate sales of pizza chains in the Nation's Restaurant News list of top 100 restaurants.

Pizza Hut	46.42%
Domino's Pizza	21.67
Little Caesars Pizza	13.43
Papa John's Pizza	5.83
Sbarro, The Italian Eatery	3.77
Round Table Pizza	3.63
Chuck E. Cheese's	2.76
Godfather's Pizza	2.50

Source: *Nation's Restaurant News*, June 23, 1997, p. 134.

★ 1382 ★

Restaurants (SIC 5812)

Pizza Chains by Sales - 1996

Companies are ranked by sales in millions of dollars.

Pizza Hut	$ 7,481.0
Domino's Pizza	2,800.0
Little Caesars	2,000.0

Papa John's	$ 619.2
Round Table Pizza	370.6
Chuck E. Cheese	265.0
Godfather's Pizza	250.0
Piccadilly Circus Pizza	220.0
Pizza Inn	204.0
California Pizza Kitchen	176.0

Source: *Restaurants and Institutions*, July 15, 1997, p. 113.

★ 1383 ★

Restaurants (SIC 5812)

Popular Ethnic Foods

Data show ethnic food categories ranked by share of eating occasions. "Other" includes Scandinavian, Caribbean, Middle Eastern, Thai, Vietnamese, Japanese (sushi), Indian, and Korean foods.

Italian	25.0%
Mexican	18.7
Cantonese	11.8
Chinese, other than Cantonese	8.2
Tex-Mex	7.5
Soul food	5.7
German	3.9
Cajun/Creole	3.7
Greek	2.7
Japanese	2.3
French	2.0
Other	8.5

Source: *Los Angeles Times*, October 2, 1997, p. D5, from National Restaurant Association.

★ 1384 ★

Restaurants (SIC 5812)

Steak/Barbeque Chains by Sales - 1996

Data show sales in millions of dollars.

Outback	$ 1,077.0
Sizzler	750.0
Golden Coral	710.9
Ponderosa	633.0
Ryan's	597.6
Lone Star	471.0
Western Sizzlin'	330.0
Tony Roma's	321.4

Continued on next page.

★ 1384 ★ *Continued*
Restaurants (SIC 5812)

Steak/Barbeque Chains by Sales - 1996

Data show sales in millions of dollars.

Quincy's	$ 259.2
Stuart Anderson's	255.0

Source: *Restaurants and Institutions*, July 15, 1997, p. 115.

★ 1385 ★
Restaurants (SIC 5812)

Top Asian Restaurants - 1996

Data show sales in millions of dollars.

Panda Express	$ 145.7
Benihana	118.5
Manchu Wok	80.9
Yoshinoya Beef Bowl	56.7
Sizzling Wok	40.0
Leean Chin	28.8

Source: *Restaurants and Institutions*, July 15, 1997, p. 117.

★ 1386 ★
Restaurants (SIC 5812)

Top Cafeterias by Sales - 1996

Data show sales in millions of dollars.

Old Country Buffet	$ 526.0
Luby's	450.1
Piccadilly	277.7
Morrison's Fresh Cooking	270.0
Furr's Family Dining	189.5
HomeTown Buffet	170.7
K&W Cafeterias	95.0
Fresh Choice	76.7
MCL Cafeterias	56.3
Country Harvest Buffet	53.0

Source: *Restaurants and Institutions*, July 15, 1997, p. 117.

★ 1387 ★
Restaurants (SIC 5812)

Top Chicken Restaurants - 1996

Data show sales in millions of dollars.

KFC	$ 8,200.0
Popeyes	755.0
Churches	667.8
Chick-fil-A	570.0
Kenny Rogers Roasters	265.0
El Pollo Loco	225.0
Bojangles'	214.3
Grandy's	144.0
Lee's Famous Recipe	138.6
Mrs. Winner's	96.3

Source: *Restaurants and Institutions*, July 15, 1997, p. 115.

★ 1388 ★
Restaurants (SIC 5812)

Top Contract Chains

Data show shares of aggregate sales of contract chains in the Nation's Restaurant News list of top 100 restaurants.

Marriott Management Services	29.80%
Aramark Global Food/Leisure Services	25.79
Compass Group USA	10.22
Sodexho U.S.A.	6.64
Dobbs International Services	6.39
LSG Lufthansa Service/Sky Chef	4.00
The Wood Co.	3.41
Ogden Entertainment Services	3.34
Host International (proprietary)	2.94
Daka Restaurants	2.79
Restaura Inc.	2.64
Service Master Food Management Services	2.04

Source: *Nation's Restaurant News*, June 23, 1997, p. 174.

★ 1389 ★
Restaurants (SIC 5812)

Top Dinner Houses - 1996

Data show sales in millions of dollars.

Applebee's	$ 1,540.0
T.G.I. Friday's	1,145.2
Chili's	1,104.0
Ruby Tuesday	546.0

Continued on next page.

★ 1389 ★ *Continued*
Restaurants (SIC 5812)

Top Dinner Houses - 1996

Data show sales in millions of dollars.

Bennigan's	$ 448.0
Hooters	325.0
Red Robin	293.6
The Ground Round	285.9
Houlihan's	241.6
Planet Hollywood	222.5

Source: *Restaurants and Institutions*, July 15, 1997, p. 115.

★ 1390 ★
Restaurants (SIC 5812)

Top Fast Food Chains - 1996

McDonald's

Burger King

Pizza Hut

Taco Bell

Wendy's

Companies are ranked by sales in billions of dollars.

McDonald's	$ 16.4
Burger King	7.5
Pizza Hut	4.9
Taco Bell	4.4
Wendy's	4.3

Source: *Newsweek*, November 17, 1997, p. 58, from Technomic Inc. and company reports.

★ 1391 ★
Restaurants (SIC 5812)

Top Grill-Buffet Chains

Data show shares of aggregate sales of grill-buffet chains in the Nation's Restaurant News list of top 100 restaurants.

Golden Corral	22.81%
Ponderosa Steakhouse	21.83
Ryan's Family Steak House	19.38
Sizzler	17.33
Western Sizzlin'	10.33
Quincy's Family Steakhouse	8.31

Source: *Nation's Restaurant News*, June 23, 1997, p. 164.

★ 1392 ★
Restaurants (SIC 5812)

Top Independent Restaurants - 1997

Restaurants are ranked by food & beverage sales in millions of dollars.

Tavern on the Green	$ 34.15
The Rainbow Room	34.00
Smith & Wollensky	23.50
Bob Chinn's Crabhouse	20.62
Sparks Steakhouse	20.40
Joe's Stone Crab	18.00
The 21 Club	15.72
Fulton's Crab House	15.40
Scoma's Restaurant	14.05
The Manor	14.00

Source: *Restaurants & Institutions*, April 1, 1998, p. 72.

★ 1393 ★
Restaurants (SIC 5812)

Top Restaurant Parent Companies - 1996

Companies are ranked by sales in millions of dollars. Data are for parent companies owning more than one restaurant "concept" on Retaurants and Institutions' 400 list.

PepsiCo Foodservice	$ 20,630.0
Grand Metropolitan PLC	9,097.0
Flagstar Cos. Inc.	3,345.1
Darden Restaurants	3,200.0
Allied Domecq PLC	2,648.1
International Dairy Queen	2,582.0
Carlson Hospitality Worldwide	2,558.2
ITT Corp.	1,990.0
Marriott Corp.	1,832.0
Shoney's Inc.	1,717.7

Source: *Restaurants and Institutions*, July 15, 1997, p. 67.

★ 1394 ★
Restaurants (SIC 5812)

Types of Hamburger Restaurants

The burger market is shown by type of restaurant.

Quick service	91.0%
Midscale	7.0
Upscale	2.0

Source: *Washington Post*, February 5, 1998, p. E5, from National Restaurant Association.

★ 1395 ★
Retailing - Food (SIC 5812)

Canada's Food Store Sales - 1997

Total food store sales reached $52.45 billion.

Ontario	31.5%
Quebec	26.0
British Columbia	14.8
Alberta	11.1
Other	16.6

Source: From the Internet, http://www.thomaslargesinger.com, 1997, p. 5, from *Canadian Grocer*.

★ 1396 ★
Retailing - Snacks (SIC 5812)

Snack Sales by Outlet

Sales are shown by outlet.

Supermarkets	45.6%
Warehouse clubs	12.5
Convenience stores	12.0
Mass merchandisers	11.2

Grocery stores	6.9%
Drug stores	4.9
Vending	2.5
Other	4.4

Source: *Discount Merchandiser*, March 1998, p. 72, from Snack Food Association.

★ 1397 ★
Retailing - Beverages (SIC 5813)

Retail Soft Drink Sales

Sales are shown by outlet.

Supermarkets	31.0%
Fountain	27.3
Convenience stores	11.6
Vending machines	11.3
Mass merchants	7.7
Restaurants	3.0
Other	8.1

Source: *Investor's Business Daily*, May 18, 1998, p. A4, from Beverage Marketing Corp.

★ 1398 ★
Retailing - Beverages (SIC 5813)

RTD Tea Sales by Channel

Sales are shown for the year ended March 1, 1998.

Food	$ 370.9
Drug	32.9
Mass	31.2

Source: *Beverage World Periscope*, April 30, 1998, p. 17, from Information Resources Inc.

★ 1399 ★
Retailing - Beverages (SIC 5813)

Where Soft Drinks Are Sold

Supermarkets	43.0%
Fountains	24.0
Convenience/gas stores	16.0
Vending	11.0
Mass merchandisers	3.0
Drug stores	2.0

Source: *Wall Street Journal*, May 8, 1998, p. A3, from Sanford C. Bernstein.

SIC 59 - Miscellaneous Retail

★ 1400 ★

Drug Stores (SIC 5912)

Largest Drug Store Chains - 1997

Companies are ranked by number of stores.

CVS	3,985
Rite Aid	3,925
Eckerd	2,832
Walgreen	2,328
Medicine Shoppe	1,066

Source: *New York Times*, February 10, 1998, p. C2, from National Association of Chain Drug Stores.

★ 1401 ★

Drug Stores (SIC 5912)

Top Drug Store Chains - 1997

The table shows revenue in billions of dollars. Data are for the 12 months ended October 30, 1997. Figure for CVS does not include Arbor Drugs.

Walgreen	$ 13.40
Rite-Aid	11.77
CVS	11.11
Eckerd	8.80
American Drug	5.23

Source: *Wall Street Journal*, February 10, 1998, p. A3, from National Association of Chain Drug Stores.

★ 1402 ★

Drug Stores (SIC 5912)

Top Drug Stores - Detroit, MI

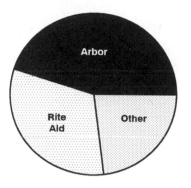

Market shares are shown in percent.

Arbor	45.2%
Rite Aid	31.5
Other	23.3

Source: *Oakland Press*, January 18, 1998, p. D1.

★ 1403 ★

Drug Stores (SIC 5912)

Top Drug Stores in Canada - 1997

Market shares are shown based on sales of $12.6 billion for the year ended December 31, 1997.

Shoppers Drug Mart	31.7%
Medis Health	16.6
Jean Coutu	13.5
Pharmasave Drugs	4.2
Pharma Plus Drugmarts	3.5
Lawton Drug Stores	1.6
Overwaitea Food Group	1.2

Continued on next page.

★ 1403 ★ *Continued*
Drug Stores (SIC 5912)

Top Drug Stores in Canada - 1997

Market shares are shown based on sales of $12.6 billion for the year ended December 31, 1997.

Warehouse Drugstore	1.1%
Rexall Drug Stores	0.8
United Pharmacists Enterprises	0.7
Others	25.1

Source: *Marketing Magazine*, May 25, 1998, p. 23, from *Pharmacy Post* and A.C. Nielsen.

★ 1404 ★
Drug Stores (SIC 5912)

Types of Pharmacies in Canada

Data show number of outlets.

Drugstore (retail)	9,893
Hospital	2,350
Industrial	339
Nursing home	230
Government	64
Home	39

Source: From the Internet, http://www.mmslists.com/c43pharmacusts_canada.html, June 17, 1997, p. 2.

★ 1405 ★
Retailing - Bandages (SIC 5912)

Where Bandages Are Sold

Sales are shown by outlet.

	($ mil.)	Share
Drug	$ 184.1	44.80%
Food	128.9	31.37
Mass	97.9	23.83

Source: *Supermarket Business*, April 1998, p. 58, from Information Resources Inc.

★ 1406 ★
Retailing - Cosmetics (SIC 5912)

Where Cosmetics Are Purchased

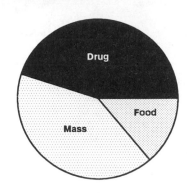

Sales are shown by retail class.

	($ mil.)	Share
Drug	$ 1,187.5	44.74%
Mass	1,087.8	40.99
Food	378.7	14.27

Source: *Supermarket Business*, April 1998, p. 59, from Information Resources Inc.

★ 1407 ★
Retailing - Cough/Cold Medicine (SIC 5912)

Cough/Cold Remedies Sales by Retail Channel - 1997

Data show sales in millions of dollars for the 52 weeks ended February 23, 1997.

	($ mil.)	Share
Drug	$ 741.1	41.72%
Food	670.1	37.72
Mass	365.2	20.56

Source: *Discount Merchandiser*, June 1997, p. 68.

★ 1408 ★
Retailing - Drugs (SIC 5912)

Analgesic Sales by Outlet

Sales are shown by outlet.

Drugstores	36.6%
Food stores	36.4
Mass merchandisers	27.0

Source: *America's Pharmacist*, January 1998, p. 63, from Information Resources Inc.

★ 1409 ★

Retailing - Drugs (SIC 5912)

Where Prescriptions Are Dispensed

Data are for the first half of 1997.

Chain stores	51.0%
Independent	29.0
Food stores	11.0
Long-term care	5.0
Mail order	4.0

Source: *Medical Marketing & Media*, October 1997, p. 76, from IMS America.

★ 1410 ★

Retailing - Fire Logs (SIC 5912)

Fire Log Sales by Outlet

Unit sales are shown by outlet for the 52 weeks ending January 4, 1998.

Food stores	66.53%
Mass merchandisers	24.36
Drug stores	9.11

Source: *Discount Merchandiser*, March 1998, p. 62, from Information Resources Inc.

★ 1411 ★

Retailing - Foot Care Products (SIC 5912)

Where Foot Care Products Are Sold

Sales are shown by outlet.

	($ mil.)	Share
Drug	$ 125.7	44.83%
Mass	95.4	34.02
Food	59.3	21.15

Source: *Supermarket Business*, April 1998, p. 54, from Information Resources Inc.

★ 1412 ★

Retailing - Hair Care Products (SIC 5912)

Where Conditioners Are Sold

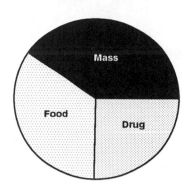

Sales are shown by outlet.

	($ mil.)	Share
Mass	$ 344.3	40.14%
Food	295.5	34.45
Drug	217.9	25.41

Source: *Supermarket Business*, April 1998, p. 56, from Information Resources Inc.

★ 1413 ★

Retailing - Hair Care Products (SIC 5912)

Where Hair Coloring Products Are Purchased

Sales are shown by percent.

Drugstores	44.1%
Mass merchandisers	36.4
Supermarkets	19.6

Source: *Women's Wear Daily*, February 1998, p. 28, from NPD BeautyTrends.

★ 1414 ★

Retailing - Oral Care (SIC 5912)

Dentifrice Market by Retail Channel - 1997

Data show dentifrice sales in millions of dollars for the 52 weeks ended February 23, 1997.

	($ mil.)	Share
Food.	$ 702.2	48.29%
Mass.	466.8	32.10
Drug.	285.0	19.60

Source: *Discount Merchandiser*, June 1997, p. 66.

★ 1415 ★

Retailing - Oral Care (SIC 5912)

Where Mouthwash is Sold

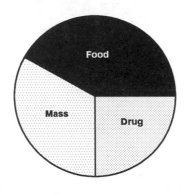

Sales are shown by outlet.

	($ mil.)	Share
Food.	$ 261.0	41.85%
Mass.	207.7	33.30
Drug.	155.0	24.85

Source: *Supermarket Business*, April 1998, p. 56, from Information Resources Inc.

★ 1416 ★

Retailing - Personal Care Products (SIC 5912)

Refillable Razor Sales by Outlet

Sales are shown by retail class.

	($ mil.)	Share
Food.	$ 246.4	38.63%
Mass.	237.3	37.20
Drug.	154.2	24.17

Source: *Supermarket Business*, April 1998, p. 59, from Information Resources Inc.

★ 1417 ★

Retailing - Personal Care Products (SIC 5912)

Where Facial Moisturizer is Sold

Sales are shown by outlet.

	($ mil.)	Share
Drug.	$ 221.4	45.16%
Mass.	176.8	36.06
Food.	92.1	18.78

Source: *Supermarket Business*, April 1998, p. 56, from Information Resources Inc.

★ 1418 ★

Retailing - Personal Care Products (SIC 5912)

Where Hand/Body Lotions Are Sold

Sales are shown by outlet.

	($ mil.)	Share
Mass.	$ 327.1	38.96%
Drug.	285.0	33.94
Food.	227.5	27.10

Source: *Supermarket Business*, April 1998, p. 54, from Information Resources Inc.

★ 1419 ★

Retailing - Shampoo (SIC 5912)

Shampoo Market by Retail Channel - 1997

Data show shampoo sales in millions of dollars for the 52 weeks ended February 23, 1997.

	($ mil.)	Share
Food	$ 578.7	39.94%
Mass	565.7	39.05
Drug	304.4	21.01

Source: *Discount Merchandiser*, June 1997, p. 64.

★ 1420 ★

Retailing - Sun Care Products (SIC 5912)

Where We Buy Suntan Lotion

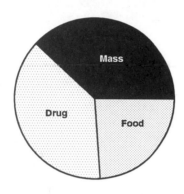

Sales are shown by outlet.

	($ mil.)	Share
Mass	$ 160.1	38.32%
Drug	158.3	37.89
Food	99.4	23.79

Source: *Supermarket Business*, April 1998, p. 54, from Information Resources Inc.

★ 1421 ★

Retailing - Sporting Goods (SIC 5941)

Canada's Sporting Goods Industry

Data show sales in the $5.1 billion apparel and equipment industry.

Sporting good chains/athletic specialty	45.0%
Discount/dept. stores	20.0
Canadian Tire	8.0
Other	27.0

Source: *Marketing Magazine*, June 1, 1998, p. 2.

★ 1422 ★

Retailing - Sporting Goods (SIC 5941)

Fitness Specialty Retailers - 1997

Companies are ranked by number of stores projected for year-end 1997.

BusyBody Fitness Warehouse	66
Omni Fitness	16
Exercise Equipment Centers	15
Push Pedal Pull	13
The Gym Source	12

Source: *Sporting Goods Business*, May 12, 1997, p. 30.

★ 1423 ★

Retailing - Sporting Goods (SIC 5941)

In-Line Specialty Retailers - 1996

Companies are ranked by sales in millions of dollars.

Blades	$ 7.0
Skate 2000	3.9
Modern Skate & Surf	3.5
Retro Sports	2.9
Nuvo	2.2

Source: *Sporting Goods Business*, May 12, 1997, p. 36.

★ 1424 ★

Retailing - Sporting Goods (SIC 5941)

Largest Sporting Goods Stores - 1997

Sales are shown in millions of dollars.

Foot Locker	$ 2,200
Sports Authority	1,500
L.L. Bean	1,086
J.C. Penney	1,000

Continued on next page.

★ 1424 ★ *Continued*
Retailing - Sporting Goods (SIC 5941)

Largest Sporting Goods Stores - 1997

Sales are shown in millions of dollars.

Champs Sports	$ 700
Gart Sports	669
Footaction	608
Dick's Sporting Goods	550
Athlete's Foot	540
REI	536
Jumbo Sports	529
Just For Feet	479
Lady Foot Locker	479
Finish Line	439
Forzani Group	439

Source: *Sportstyle*, May 1998, p. 12.

★ 1425 ★
Retailing - Sporting Goods (SIC 5941)

Leading Sporting Goods Retailers - 1996

Data represent sales in millions of dollars.

The Sports Authority	$ 1,271
JumboSports	624
SportMart	515
Dick's Clothing & Sporting Goods	425
Big 5 Sporting Goods	400
Academy Sports	367
Oshman's	366
Modell's Sporting Goods	292
Dunham's Athleisure	200
Gart Sports	180

Source: *Discount Store News*, July 7, 1997, p. 82.

★ 1426 ★
Retailing - Sporting Goods (SIC 5941)

Licensed Specialty Retailers - 1996

Going To The Game	
The Pro Image	
Bradley Specialty Retail	
Prime Sports/Fan Fair	
Fanzz	

Companies are ranked by sales in millions of dollars.

Going To The Game	$ 47
The Pro Image	40
Bradley Specialty Retail	30
Prime Sports/Fan Fair	28
Fanzz	14

Source: *Sporting Goods Business*, May 12, 1997, p. 32.

★ 1427 ★
Retailing - Sporting Goods (SIC 5941)

Soccer Specialty Retailers - 1997

Companies are ranked by number of stores projected for year-end 1997.

Soccer Master	32
TSI	14
Soccer Post	10
Soccer World	7
Soccer Village	3

Source: *Sporting Goods Business*, May 12, 1997, p. 28.

★ 1428 ★
Retailing - Sporting Goods (SIC 5941)

Sporting Goods Retailers - 1997

Companies are ranked by projected sales in millions of dollars.

Foot Locker	$ 2,570
L.L. Bean	1,071
The Sports Authority	1,550
Champs Sports	712
JumboSports	675
Footaction	660

Continued on next page.

★ 1428 ★ *Continued*
Retailing - Sporting Goods (SIC 5941)

Sporting Goods Retailers - 1997

Companies are ranked by projected sales in millions of dollars.

Dick's	$ 560
Sportmart	533
REI	506
Just For Feet	497

Source: *Sporting Goods Business*, May 12, 1997, p. 29.

★ 1429 ★
Retailing - Sporting Goods (SIC 5941)

Top Soccer Specialty Chains - 1997

Soccer Post
TSI
Soccer Master
Soccer World
Soccer Village

Retailers are shown ranked by projected sales in millions of dollars.

Soccer Post (New Jersey)	$ 12.5
TSI (North Carolina)	8.7
Soccer Master (Missouri)	6.5
Soccer World (California)	4.0
Soccer Village (Ohio)	2.0

Source: *Sporting Goods Business*, June 23, 1997, p. 16.

★ 1430 ★
Retailing - Books (SIC 5942)

Book Sales by Outlet - 1996

Data show sales in percent.

Big chain bookstores	25.0%
Book clubs	18.0
Independent/small chains	18.0
Discount stores	9.0
Warehouse/price clubs	6.0
Food/drug stores	5.0
Mail order sellers	5.0
Used bookstores	4.0
Other	10.0

Source: *USA TODAY*, July 10, 1997, p. D1, from *1996 Consumer Research Study on Book Purchases*.

★ 1431 ★
Retailing - Books (SIC 5942)

Book Sales by Outlet - 1997

Distribution is shown in percent. Barnes & Noble and Borders account for nearly 25% of sales.

Chain bookstores	25.0%
Book clubs	20.0
Independent bookstores	17.0
Mail order/Internet	6.0
Wholesale price clubs	6.0
Mass merchandisers	6.0
Food/drug stores	4.0
Others	16.0

Source: *USA TODAY*, June 11, 1998, p. D1.

★ 1432 ★
Retailing - Books (SIC 5942)

Largest On-line Book Retailers

On-line book retailing is a $290 million-a-year industry. Market shares are shown in percent. Amazon.com's share actually exceeds the figure shown.

Amazon.com	50.0%
Barnes & Noble	6.0
Other	44.0

Source: *USA TODAY*, March 25, 1998, p. B1, from Cowles/Simba Information.

★ 1433 ★
Retailing - Greeting Cards (SIC 5943)

Greeting Card Sales by Outlet - 1997

Sales are shown by percent.

Card/gift stores	33.0%
Mass merchandisers	21.0
Drug stores	18.0
Supermarkets	16.0
Variety	2.0
Department stores	1.0
Other	9.0

Source: *Discount Merchandiser*, March 1998, p. 3, from American Greetings.

★ 1434 ★

Retailing - Party Goods (SIC 5943)

Party Good Sales by Outlet

Sales are shown by percent.

Mass	38.0%
Supermarkets	22.0
Party supply	21.0
Card/gift stores	8.0
Department stores	4.0
Drug stores	3.0
Other	4.0

Source: *Supermarket Business*, May 1998, p. 126, from American Greetings Research.

★ 1435 ★

Retailing - Stationery (SIC 5943)

Stationery and Greeting Card Sales by Outlet - 1996

Distribution is shown based on total mass merchandiser sales of $20.858 billion.

Stationery stores	28.8%
Discount stores	26.3
Wholesale club	14.1
Drug and proprietary stores	13.7
Supermarkets and grocery stores	5.8
Non-store retailers	2.8
Department stores	2.7
Variety stores	2.4
Bookstores	2.3
Miscellaneous general merchandise stores . .	1.1

Source: *Discount Merchandiser*, July 1997, p. 52.

★ 1436 ★

Retailing - Jewelry (SIC 5944)

Best-Selling Colored Gemstones

Data show the top sellers, based on a survey. Retailers claim that colored gemstone jewelry account for an average of 17.5% of overall sales.

Sapphires	35.4%
Rubies	16.5
Emeralds	13.5
Amethysts	10.5
Blue topaz	7.5
Tanzanite	3.8

Source: From the Internet, http://www.gemstone.org/ pastmarket.html, 1996, p. 1, from *National Jeweler*.

★ 1437 ★

Retailing - Jewelry (SIC 5944)

Jewelry and Watches Sales by Outlet - 1996

Distribution is shown based on total mass merchandiser sales of $27.523 billion.

Jewelry stores	59.9%
Department stores	12.9
Discount stores	11.2
Catalog showrooms	6.6
Non-store retailers	3.9
Miscellaneous general merchandise stores . .	3.6
Gift, novelty and souvenir shops	1.5
Variety stores	0.4

Source: *Discount Merchandiser*, July 1997, p. 51.

★ 1438 ★

Retailing - Jewelry (SIC 5944)

Leading Jewelry/Hard Line Retailers - 1996

Data show sales in millions of dollars.

Service Merchandise	$ 3,955
Lechmere	850
Best Products	538
K's Merchandise	184
L. Luna & Son	120
Brendle's	92
Witmark	72
Brand Names Sales Inc.	50

Source: *Discount Store News*, July 7, 1997, p. 76.

★ 1439 ★
Retailing - Hobby Products (SIC 5945)

Leading Arts/Crafts Stores - 1996

Data show sales in millions of dollars.

Michaels Stores	$ 1,378
Farm-Centers of America	929
Frank's Nursery & Crafts	531
Hobby Lobby	440
Ben Franklin Retail Stores	357
House of Fabrics	255
MJ Designs	231
Old America Stores	136
Rag Shops	84
Northwest Fabrics & Crafts	82

Source: *Discount Store News*, July 7, 1997, p. 79.

★ 1440 ★
Retailing - Toys (SIC 5945)

Top Toy Stores - 1997

- Toys R Us
- Wal-Mart
- Kmart
- Target
- Kay-Bee
- Other

Shares are shown for the fiscal year ended February 1, 1997.

Toys R Us	20.9%
Wal-Mart	15.8
Kmart	7.5
Target	6.2
Kay-Bee	5.0
Other	44.6

Source: *Wall Street Journal*, November 5, 1997, p. B4, from Baseline, Tactical Retail Solutions Inc., and company reports.

★ 1441 ★
Retailing - Toys (SIC 5945)

U.S. Toy Retailers

Market shares are estimated in percent.

	1997	1998
Toys R Us	20.3%	20.0%
Wal-Mart	15.6	16.1
Other	64.1	63.9

Source: *Financial Times*, May 29, 1998, p. 17, from Tactical Retail Monitor.

★ 1442 ★
Retailing - Toys (SIC 5945)

Where We Buy Children's Action Games - 1996

Data show distribution of 22,789,000 units sold at retail. Dollar sales reached $213,488,000.

Discount	51.0%
National toy chains	31.0
Food drug	3.0
Variety	3.0
Catalog showrooms	2.0
Department stores	2.0
All other toy stores	2.0
Other outlets	6.0

Source: *Playthings*, July 1997, p. 26, from NPD Group Inc. Toy Market Index.

★ 1443 ★
Mail Order (SIC 5961)

Business to Business Catalog Sales

Sales are shown in billions of dollars.

	1997	2002
Catalog retailers	$ 18.7	$ 25.1
Printing & publishing	1.7	2.4
Auto dealers/service stations	1.2	1.9
Government enterprises	1.1	1.7
Chemicals/allied products	0.7	1.0
Industrial machinery & equipment	0.6	0.9
Security/commodity brokers	0.6	0.9

Source: *Business Marketing*, January 1998, p. 19, from Direct Marketing Association.

★ 1444 ★

Mail Order (SIC 5961)

Largest U.S. Catalog Businesses

Companies are ranked by worldwide sales through mail order. Figures are in millions of dollars.

Dell Computer Corporation	$ 5,815.0
Gateway 2000	5,050.0
J.C. Penney	3,424.0
Hewlett-Packard Direct Marketing Division	1,920.0
Fingerhut	1,545.4
Micro Warehouse	1,543.0
Micron Electronics	1,235.0
McMaster Carr	1,200.0
W.W. Grainger	1,200.0
Federated Dept. Stores/Macy's	1,155.0
Viking Office Products	1,055.8
Lands' End	1,031.5
L.L. Bean	948.6
Spiegel	891.7
Medco Containment Services	851.2
Computer Discount Warehouse	835.1
Scholastic Books	824.6

Source: *Direct Marketing*, September 1997, p. 39.

★ 1445 ★

Mail Order (SIC 5961)

Largest U.S. Mail Order Businesses

United Services Automobile Association	
Dell Computer Corporation	
Tele-Communications Inc.	
Gateway 2000	
Time Warner Cable Group	
AARP	
J.C. Penney	
GEICO	
Hewlett-Packard Direct Marketing Division	
AT&T Communications	

Companies are ranked by worldwide sales through mail order. Figures are in millions of dollars.

United Services Automobile Association	$ 5,950.0
Dell Computer Corporation	5,815.0
Tele-Communications Inc.	5,341.4
Gateway 2000	5,050.0
Time Warner Cable Group	4,253.7

AARP	$ 3,472.0
J.C. Penney	3,424.0
GEICO	3,045.2
Hewlett-Packard Direct Marketing Division	1,920.0
AT&T Communications	1,900.0

Source: *Direct Marketing*, September 1997, p. 39.

★ 1446 ★

Mail Order (SIC 5961)

Top Mail Order Companies - 1996

Data represent sales in millions of dollars.

Dell Computer Corp.	$ 7,554.0
Gateway 2000	5,035.0
J.C. Penney	3,772.0
Digital Equipment	3,300.0
Micro Warehouse	1,916.0
Spiegel	1,681.0
Fingerhut	1,638.0
Viking Office Products	1,182.3
Lands' End	1,112.0
Computer Discount Warehouse	927.9

Source: *Catalog Age*, August 1997, p. 60.

★ 1447 ★

Vending Machines (SIC 5962)

Leading Vending Machine Suppliers

Relative shares are shown in percent. Figures are based on the top 200 firms.

M&M/Mars	27.76%
Hershey Chocolate	18.50
Frito-Lay	11.07
Nabisco Foods Group	8.46
Nestle Enterprises	6.20
President Baking	2.89
Other	25.12

Source: *The Manufacturing Confectioner*, May 1998, p. 46.

★ 1448 ★
Retailing - Candy (SIC 5993)

Canada's Confectionery Sales by Channel - 1997

Sales are shown in percent.

Grocery	18.0%
Drug	15.0
Prov. mass merchandisers and wholesale clubs	12.0
Gas	4.0
Other grocery and variety	34.0
Other channels	16.0

Source: *The Manufacturing Confectioner*, May 1998, p. 16.

★ 1449 ★
Retailing - Tobacco (SIC 5993)

Cigar Sales by Outlet

Drug stores	
C-store	
Supermarket	
Mass	
Other	

Drug stores	26.0%
C-store	16.0
Supermarket	8.0
Mass	5.0
Other	45.0

Source: *Supermarket Business*, June 1998, p. 112, from Cigar Association of America.

★ 1450 ★
Retailing - Tobacco (SIC 5993)

Tobacco Sales by Outlet

Sales are shown by type of outlet. "Other" includes kiosks, duty-free shops, and vending machines.

Convenience stores	45.0%
Supermarkets	18.0
Tobacco stores	10.0
Discount stores	6.0
Drug stores	5.0
Other	16.0

Source: *Wall Street Journal*, September 30, 1997, p. B1, from Cannondale Associates.

★ 1451 ★
Retailing - Magazines (SIC 5994)

Magazine Sales by Outlet

Sales are shown by outlet.

Supermarkets	41.0%
Mass merchandisers	12.0
Drug stores	10.0
Convenience stores	9.0
Book stores	4.0
Newsstands	4.0
Terminals	3.0
Other	17.0

Source: *Supermarket Business*, May 1998, p. 138, from CDPA and Magazine Publishers of America.

★ 1452 ★
Pet Products (SIC 5999)

Pet Supplies Sales at Discount Stores - 1997

Distribution is shown based on sales of $1,301,878,000 at discount stores in 1997.

Litter	20.35%
Food treats	18.71
Flea, tick products	16.48
Accessories	13.36
Toys	11.97
Grooming products	8.85
Miscellaneous	10.28

Source: *Discount Merchandiser*, June 1997, p. 43.

★ 1453 ★
Pet Stores (SIC 5999)

Leading Pet Supply Stores - 1996

Data represent sales in millions of dollars.

Petsmart	$ 1,501
Petco	500
Pet Supplies Plus	163
Petland Inc.	112
Pet Care	102
Pet Food Warehouse	64
SuperPetz	55

Source: *Discount Store News*, July 7, 1997, p. 80.

★ 1454 ★

Retailing - Baby Products (SIC 5999)

Top Baby Store Chains - 1996

The table shows companies ranked by sales in millions of dollars.

Baby Superstore	$ 445
Lil' Things	100
Babes "R" Us	16

Source: *Discount Store News*, July 7, 1997, p. 75.

★ 1455 ★

Retailing - Candles (SIC 5999)

Candle Sales by Outlet

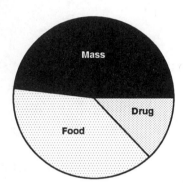

Sales are shown by outlet.

Mass	47.55%
Food	39.25
Drug	13.20

Source: *Discount Merchandiser*, May 1998, p. 108, from Information Resources Inc.

★ 1456 ★

Retailing - Pet Products (SIC 5999)

Cat Maintenance Sales by Outlet

Sales are shown by outlet.

Supermarkets	63.0%
Discount	57.0
Pet stores	21.0
Pet superstores	16.0
Garden/Feed	8.0
Warehouse	7.0

Source: *Discount Merchandiser*, June 1998, p. 86.

★ 1457 ★

Retailing - Pet Products (SIC 5999)

Cat Toy Sales by Outlet

Sales are shown by outlet.

Discount	28.0%
Supermarkets	21.0
Pet stores	9.0
Pet superstores	9.0
Garden/feed	1.0
Warehouse	1.0

Source: *Discount Merchandiser*, June 1998, p. 86, from American Pet Products Manufacturers Association.

★ 1458 ★

Retailing - Pet Products (SIC 5999)

Dog Accessories Sales by Outlet

Sales are shown by outlet.

Discount	51.0%
Pet superstores	21.0
Pet stores	18.0
Supermarkets	11.0
Garden/feed	9.0
Warehouse	4.0

Source: *Discount Merchandiser*, June 1998, p. 86, from American Pet Products Manufacturers Association.

★ 1459 ★

Retailing - Pet Products (SIC 5999)

Dog Maintenance Sales by Outlet

Sales are shown by outlet.

Discount stores	53.0%
Supermarkets	29.0
Pet superstores	25.0
Pet stores	22.0
Garden/Feed	10.0
Warehouse	3.0

Source: *Discount Merchandiser*, June 1998, p. 86, from American Pet Products Manufacturers Association.

★ 1460 ★

Retailing - Pet Products (SIC 5999)

Fish Accessories Sales by Outlet

Sales are shown by outlet.

Pet stores 40.0%
Discount 29.0
Pet superstores 20.0
Garden/feed 3.0
Supermarket 1.0

Source: *Discount Merchandiser*, June 1998, p. 86, from American Pet Products Manufacturers Association.

★ 1461 ★

Retailing - Religious Supplies (SIC 5999)

Best-Selling Products at Christian Retailers

Sales are shown in percent.

Books 25.0%
Music 19.0
Gifts 13.0
Bibles 12.0
Cards 5.0
Curriculum 5.0
Church supplies 4.0
Videos 3.0
Other 14.0

Source: *Washington Post*, November 7, 1997, p. D2, from Christian Retailing.

SIC 60 - Depository Institutions

★ 1462 ★
Banking (SIC 6020)

California's Largest Financial Institutions

Firms are ranked by assets in billions of dollars.

BankAmerica	$ 260.2
Wells Fargo	97.4
American Savings Bank	67.3
Home Savings of America	46.5
California Federal Bank	31.3

Source: *The Economist*, April 18, 1998, p. 68, from SNL Securities.

★ 1463 ★
Banking (SIC 6020)

California's Thrift Industry

Market shares are shown in percent.

BankAmerica	21.0%
Washington Mutual/H.F. Ahmanson	17.0
Other	62.0

Source: *The Economist*, March 21, 1998, p. 5.

★ 1464 ★
Banking (SIC 6020)

California's Top Banks

Market shares are shown in percent.

BankAmerica	20.6%
Washington Mutual	17.0
Wells Fargo	13.8
Golden State Bancorp	6.4
Union Bank	5.2
Other	37.0

Source: *Los Angeles Times*, March 18, 1998, p. D1, from California Bankers Association, California Department of Financial Institutions, SNL Securities, and FDIC.

★ 1465 ★
Banking (SIC 6020)

California's Top Banks by Deposits

Market shares are shown in percent.

BankAmerica Corp.	20.0%
Wells Fargo & Co.	14.4
Ahmanson	9.0
Washington Mutual	9.0
Other	47.6

Source: *Wall Street Journal*, October 6, 1997, p. A15, from SNL Securities.

★ 1466 ★
Banking (SIC 6020)

Canada's Top Banks by Assets

Market shares are shown for the fiscal year ended October 31, 1997.

Royal Bank of Canada	20.0%
Canadian Imperial Bank of Commerce	19.4
Bank of Montreal	17.0
Bank of Nova Scotia	15.9
Toronto-Dominion Bank	11.2
National Bank of Canada	5.4
Other	11.1

Source: *Wall Street Journal*, April 16, 1998, p. A17, from Canadian Bankers Association.

★ 1467 ★
Banking (SIC 6020)

Canada's Top Banks by Deposits

Market shares are shown in percent.

Royal Bank of Canada	21.0%
Bank of Montreal	18.0
Canadian Imperial Bank of Commerce	17.0
Bank of Nova Scotia	17.0
Toronto-Dominion Bank	13.5
National Bank of Canada	5.3
Other	8.8

Source: *Wall Street Journal*, April 16, 1998, p. A17, from Canadian Bankers Association.

★ 1468 ★
Banking (SIC 6020)

Canada's Top Banks by Loans

Market shares are shown for the fiscal year ended October 31, 1997.

Royal Bank of Canada	20.6%
Canadian Imperial Bank of Commerce	19.2
Bank of Nova Scotia	16.4
Bank of Montreal	15.2
Toronto-Dominion Bank	13.6
National Bank of Canada	6.2
Other	8.8

Source: *Wall Street Journal*, April 16, 1998, p. A17, from Canadian Bankers Association.

★ 1469 ★
Banking (SIC 6020)

Commercial Banks by Market Capitalization - 1997

Citicorp
NationsBank
BankAmerica
Chase Manhattan
First Union

Data show market capitalization in billions of dollars as of June 25, 1997.

Citicorp	$ 56.2
NationsBank	48.6
BankAmerica	46.2
Chase Manhattan	42.5
First Union	26.4

Source: *Fortune*, July 21, 1997, p. 25, from *Bloomberg Business News*.

★ 1470 ★
Banking (SIC 6020)

Largest Banking Firms

Data show assets in billions of dollars. Figures include all pending mergers. These companies account for 34% of U.S. banking assets.

BankAmerica	$ 568.7
Chase Manhattan	365.5
Citicorp	310.9
J.P. Morgan	262.2
Banc One	239.5
First Union	204.9
Washington Mutual	150.0
Bankers Trust	140.1
Wells Fargo	97.5
Norwest	90.4

Source: *Washington Post*, April 14, 1998, p. C1, from Sheshunoff.

★ 1471 ★

Banking (SIC 6020)

Largest U.S. Banks - 1997

Companies are ranked by assets in billions of dollars.

Citigroup	$ 697
NationsBank/BankAmerica	525
Chase Manhattan	366
JP Morgan	262
Banc One/First Chicago	230
First Union	206
Washington Mutual	151
Bankers Trust New York	140
Wells Fargo	97
Norwest	89

Source: *The Sunday Times*, April 19, 1998, p. 3, from Keefe Bruyette & Woods.

★ 1472 ★

Banking (SIC 6020)

Largest Virginia Banks - 1997

Banks are shown ranked by deposits in millions of dollars as of August 25, 1997.

	Deposits ($ mil.)	Share
First Union Corp	$ 12,492	17.3%
Wachovia Corporation	9,759	13.5
Nationsbank Corp	9,737	13.5
Crestar Financial Corp	9,195	12.8
First Virginia Banks	6,260	8.7
F&M National Corporation . .	1,570	2.2

	Deposits ($ mil.)	Share
BB&T Corp	$ 1,481	2.1%
Capital One Bank	1,076	1.5
Mainstreet Bankgroup	938	1.3
Life Bancorp	706	1.0

Source: *Financial Times*, September 9, 1997, p. 3, from SNL Securities LC.

★ 1473 ★

Banking (SIC 6020)

Leading Banks in Florida - 1997

Shares are shown based on deposits. Figures represent pending acquisitions as of December 31, 1997.

NationsBank	31.2%
First Union	17.1
SunTrust Bank	10.4
SouthTrust	5.3
Washington Mutual	4.0
AmSouth	2.8
Huntington Bancshares	2.3
Citicorp	1.3
BankAtlantic	1.1
Colonial BancGroup	1.0
Other	23.5

Source: *Wall Street Journal*, January 2, 1998, p. 14, from SNL Securities.

★ 1474 ★

Banking (SIC 6020)

Leading Banks in Leveraged Loans - 1997

Shares are shown based on volume of leveraged loans for the first three quarters of 1997.

Chase Manhattan	31.2%
Bankers Trust	20.1
NationsBank	16.7
Citicorp	15.9
BankAmerica	12.2
Toronto Dominion	9.5

Continued on next page.

★ 1474 ★ *Continued*

Banking (SIC 6020)

Leading Banks in Leveraged Loans - 1997

Shares are shown based on volume of leveraged loans for the first three quarters of 1997.

J.P. Morgan	8.8%
Bank of New York	8.6
Bank of Nova Scotia	7.9
Goldman Sachs	7.9

Source: *American Banker*, October 13, 1997, p. 7, from Securities Data Co.

★ 1475 ★

Banking (SIC 6020)

Leading Mexican Banks by Loans Past- Due - 1997

Shares are shown for June 1997.

Banamex	25.6%
Bancomer	22.3
Bancrecer	11.0
Serfin	10.9
Internacional	6.9
Confia	5.5
Promex	5.4
Atlantico	4.4
Mexicano	2.4
Banorte	2.3
BBV	1.9
Citibank	0.4
Inbursa	0.4
Other	0.6

Source: *Financial Times*, December 16, 1997, p. 4, from Salomon Brothers.

★ 1476 ★

Banking (SIC 6020)

Popular Banking Services - 1995

Data show the percent of people using each service.

Savings account	70.0%
24-hour teller card	51.0
Interest checking	47.0
Home mortgage	33.0
Auto loan	25.0
IRA	25.0

Source: *Bank Marketing*, March 1998, p. 15, from Scarborough Research and USData.com Inc.

★ 1477 ★

Banking (SIC 6020)

Top Banking Companies

Companies are ranked by assets in billions of dollars.

Chase Manhattan	$ 366.5
Citicorp	300.3
NationsBank	285.6
J.P. Morgan & Co.	269.6
BankAmerica	257.7
First Union	155.1
Bankers Trust	140.0
Banc One Corp.	122.4
First Chicago NBD	113.3
Wells Fargo	97.6

Source: *Christian Science Monitor*, November 21, 1997, p. 2, from SNL Securities.

★ 1478 ★

Banking (SIC 6020)

Top Banks - Seattle/Tacoma, WA

Market shares are shown based on deposits.

Seafirst Bank	28.0%
Washington Mutual	18.0
U.S. Bancorp.	14.0
Other	40.0

Source: *American Banker*, April 8, 1998, p. 5, from Pacific Crest Securities.

★ 1479 ★
Banking (SIC 6020)

Top Banks - Washington

Market shares are shown based on deposits.

Seafirst Bank	22.8%
Washington Mutual	15.4
U.S. Bancorp	13.8
Other	48.0

Source: *American Banker*, April 8, 1998, p. 5, from Pacific Crest Securities.

★ 1480 ★
Banking (SIC 6020)

Top Banks by Assets - 1997

Data represent assets in billions of dollars as of June 30, 1997.

Chase Manhattan	$ 352.0
Citicorp	304.3
Nationsbank	284.4
BankAmerica	258.4
J.P. Morgan	250.5

Source: *New York Times*, August 30, 1997, p. 1, from SNL Securities.

★ 1481 ★
Banking (SIC 6020)

Top Banks by Assets - 1997

Banks are ranked by assets in millions of dollars.

Citigroup	$ 697.5
BankAmerica/NationsBank	567.9
Chase Manhattan	365.5
J.P. Morgan	262.2
Banc One/First Chicago	239.5
First Union/CoreStates	205.7
Bankers Trust New York	140.1
Wells Fargo	97.5
Norwest	88.5
Fleet Financial	85.5

Source: *Wall Street Journal*, April 14, 1998, p. A14, from companies and SNL Securities.

★ 1482 ★
Banking (SIC 6020)

Top Banks in Canada - 1997

Royal Bank of Canada
Bank of Montreal
CIBC
Bank of Nova Scotia
Toronto Dominion Bank
National Bank of Canada
Laurentian Bank of Canada
Canadian Western Bank
Others

Market shares are shown based on deposits for the year ending October 31, 1997.

Royal Bank of Canada	21.1%
Bank of Montreal	17.5
CIBC	16.9
Bank of Nova Scotia	16.9
Toronto Dominion Bank	13.5
National Bank of Canada	5.3
Laurentian Bank of Canada	1.3
Canadian Western Bank	0.2
Others	7.3

Source: *Marketing Magazine*, May 25, 1998, p. 20, from Canadian Bankers Association.

★ 1483 ★
Banking (SIC 6020)

Top Banks in Florida - 1997

Market shares are shown in percent.

Barnett Banks	19.77%
First Union Corp.	17.10
NationsBank Corp.	12.19
Suntrust Banks	10.36
Washington Mutual	3.99
Amsouth Bancorp	2.84
Southtrust Corporation	2.76
HF Ahmanson	1.91
Citicorp	1.31
Bankatlantic Bancorp	1.05
Others	26.72

Source: *Financial Times*, September 1, 1997, p. 17.

★ 1484 ★

Banking (SIC 6020)

Top Banks in Syndicated Loans - 1996

Shares are shown in percent.

Chase Manhattan Corp.	20.0%
J.P. Morgan & Co.	12.0
BankAmerica Corp.	11.0
Citicorp	10.0
NationsBank Corp.	8.0
Other	39.0

Source: *US Banker*, July 1997, p. 50, from Loan Pricing Corp. and Gold Sheets.

★ 1485 ★

Banking (SIC 6020)

Top North American Banks

NationsBank	
Citicorp	
BankAmerica	
Chase Manhattan	
First Union	
Banc One	
Norwest	
Wells Fargo	
U.S. Bancorp.	
Bank of Montreal/Royal Bank	

Banks are ranked by market capitalization in billions of dollars as of January 16, 1998.

NationsBank	$ 57.7
Citicorp	54.8
BankAmerica	47.3
Chase Manhattan	44.5
First Union	43.7
Banc One	31.6
Norwest	28.0
Wells Fargo	27.9
U.S. Bancorp.	27.0
Bank of Montreal/Royal Bank	26.6

Source: *Financial Post*, January 24, 1998, p. 3.

★ 1486 ★

Banking (SIC 6020)

Top U.S. Banks - 1997

Banks are ranked by assets in millions of dollars as of December 31, 1997.

Chase Manhattan	$ 365.5
Citicorp	310.9
NationsBank	264.4
J.P. Morgan	262.2
BankAmerica	260.2
First Union	157.3
Washington Mutual/H.F. Ahmanson	149.5
Bankers Trust	140.1
Banc One	115.9
First Chicago NBD	114.1

Source: *The Economist*, March 21, 1998, p. 5, from Keefe, Bruyette & Woods.

★ 1487 ★

Banking (SIC 6020)

Top U.S. Banks by Deposits

Banks are ranked by deposits in billions of dollars. Figures are as of December 1997. BankAmerica and NationsBank have a pending merger as do Banc One and First Chicago NBD.

Citicorp	$ 199.1
Chase Manhattan	193.7
BankAmerica	172.0
Nationsbank	171.1
First Union	137.1
Banc One	85.2
Wells Fargo	72.2
First Chicago NBD	68.5

Source: *New York Times*, April 14, 1998, p. A1, from SNL Securities.

★ 1488 ★
Banking (SIC 6020)

Virginia's Banking Market

Shares are shown in percent.

First Union	15.4%
NationsBank	12.0
Wachovia	12.0
Crestar	11.3
First Virginia	7.7
Other	41.6

Source: *Washington Post*, October 20, 1997, p. B12, from *Bloomberg News*, company reports, and Danielson Associates.

★ 1489 ★
Banking (SIC 6020)

Who Holds Our Money - 1996

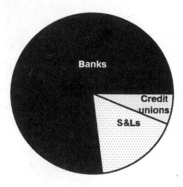

The table shows the distribution of total assets in the United States.

Banks	77.04%
S&Ls	17.30
Credit unions	5.65

Source: *Chicago Tribune*, February 26, 1998, p. 1, from Credit Union National Association and FDIC.

★ 1490 ★
Savings Institutions (SIC 6035)

Largest Savings Institutions - 1997

Firms are ranked by revenues in millions of dollars.

Washington Mutual	$ 7,524
H.F. Ahmanson	3,733
Golden West Fin. Corp.	2,914
California Federal Bank	2,466
Dime Bancorp	1,528

Source: *Fortune*, April 27, 1998, p. 56.

★ 1491 ★
Savings Institutions (SIC 6035)

Largest Savings Institutions in Milwaukee - 1997

Data show millions of dollars in assets as of December 31, 1997.

First Fleet Financial	$ 5,909.5
Mutual Savings Bank	1,825.9
St. Francis Bank F.S.B.	1,598.0
North Shore Bank	1,194.4
Advantage Bank F.S.B.	1,026.0
Guaranty Bank S.S.B.	803.7
Wauwatosa Savings Bank	667.0
West Allis Savings Bank	414.6
Great Midwest Bank	365.6
The Equitable Bank S.S.B.	343.3

Source: *The Business Journal*, February 20, 1998, p. 31.

★ 1492 ★
Savings Institutions (SIC 6035)

Top Savings and Loan Banks

The table shows banks ranked by total assets in billions of dollars.

Washington Mutual	$ 97.1
H. F. Ahmanson	55.5
Golden West Financial	39.6
California Federal	31.6
Dime Bancorp	21.8
Charter One Financial	19.8

Continued on next page.

★ 1492 ★ *Continued*
Savings Institutions (SIC 6035)

Top Savings and Loan Banks

The table shows banks ranked by total assets in billions of dollars.

Golden State Bancorp	$ 19.7
Sovereign Bancorp	17.6
GreenPoint Financial	13.1
Bank United	12.5

Source: *New York Times*, February 6, 1998, p. C4, from NationsBanc Montgomery.

★ 1493 ★
Credit Unions (SIC 6060)

Largest Credit Unions - Georgia

Bans are ranked by assets in millions of dollars as of June 30, 1997.

Delta Employees	$ 1,110.0
Atlanta Postal	868.6
Georgia Telco	614.7
Associated and Federal Employees	452.6
Robins Federal	439.1
Lockheed Georgia Employees Federal	317.5
Atlantic Coast Federal	281.4
AGE Federal	213.5
Georgia Federal	174.8
CDC Federal	117.6

Source: *Atlanta Journal-Constitution*, March 1, 1998, p. D4, from Georgia Credit Union Affiliates.

★ 1494 ★
International Banking (SIC 6081)

Top Foreign Banks in Canada

Firms are ranked by revenue in thousands of Canadian dollars.

Hongkong Bank of Canada	$ 1,536,000
Citibank Canada	405,035
Union Bank of Switzerland	293,020
Societe Generale	218,167
Banque National de Paris	163,242
Bank of Tokyo-Mitsubishi	162,496
Bank of America Canada	157,886

Credit Suisse First Boston Canada	$ 153,638
Credit Lyonnais Canada	137,328
Banca Commerciale Italiana	126,920
Swiss Bank Corp.	113,496

Source: *Globe and Mail's Report on Business Magazine*, July 1997, p. 156.

★ 1495 ★
International Banking (SIC 6081)

Top Foreign Banks in the United States

Banks are ranked by assets in billions of dollars as of June 30, 1997.

Bank of Tokyo-Mitsubishi	$ 83.6
ABN Amro	60.7
Societe Generale	52.1
Credit Lyonnais	43.5
HSBC Holdings	39.1

Source: *American Banker*, February 19, 1998, p. 1.

★ 1496 ★
International Banking (SIC 6081)

Who Has the Most Foreign Bank Offices

Countries are ranked by number of foreign banks in the United States. Japan had $357.5 billion in assets in the United States as of June 1997.

Japan	58
Italy	19
Korea	19
Germany	15
United Kingdom	15
France	14

Source: *The Banker*, March 1998, p. 58, from U.S. Federal Reserve Bank.

SIC 61 - Nondepository Institutions

Credit Cards (SIC 6141)

Credit Card Leaders - 1997

Shares are shown based on outstanding debts.

Citicorp	15.0%
Bank One	13.0
MBNA America	10.0
Discover	8.0
Chase Manhattan	8.0
NationsBank	5.0
Household	4.0
Capital One	3.0
Fleet Financial	3.0
American Express	2.0
Others	72.0

Source: *Financial Times*, May 28, 1998, p. 17, from RAM Research Group.

★ 1498 ★
Credit Cards (SIC 6141)

Largest Credit Card Issuers - 1997

Citicorp.	
Banc One-First Chicago NBD	
MBNA	
Novus	
Chase Manhattan	
American Express	
Bank America-NationsBank	
Household Finance	
Fleet Financial	
Capital One Financial	

Firms are ranked by outstanding loans in billions of dollars. Figures reflect all pending mergers.

Citicorp.	$ 64.86
Banc One-First Chicago NBD	56.56
MBNA	44.51

Novus	$ 34.68
Chase Manhattan	32.83
American Express	31.42
Bank America-NationsBank	21.49
Household Finance	17.54
Fleet Financial	13.97
Capital One Financial	13.62

Source: *New York Times*, April 14, 1998, p. C10, from *Nilson Report*.

★ 1499 ★
Credit Cards (SIC 6141)

Largest Credit Card Processors

Data show credit card volume in billions of dollars.

First Data	$ 232.5
NPD	74.0
Paymentech	45.7
BA Merchant Services	28.8
Nova	24.5
National Data	22.7
Fifth Third Bank	21.2

Source: *Wall Street Journal*, June 19, 1998, p. A4, from *Nilson Report*.

★ 1500 ★
Credit Cards (SIC 6141)

Top Credit Card Issuers - 1997

Data are in billions of dollars. The top 10 firms have 64% of the market. This figure should jump to 72% after pending mergers are completed. Bank One includes First USA and Chase Manhattan includes Bank of New York.

Citibank	$ 48.2
MBNA America	44.5
Bank One	38.6
Discover	36.0
Chase Manhattan	32.5

Continued on next page.

★ 1500 ★ *Continued*
Credit Cards (SIC 6141)

Top Credit Card Issuers - 1997

Data are in billions of dollars. The top 10 firms have 64% of the market. This figure should jump to 72% after pending mergers are completed. Bank One includes First USA and Chase Manhattan includes Bank of New York.

First Chicago NBD	$ 18.0
Household	17.3
AT&T Universal	15.3
Capital One	13.6
Advanta	11.2

Source: *Washington Post*, April 25, 1998, p. D1, from CardWeb.

★ 1501 ★
Credit Cards (SIC 6141)

Top Credit Cards - 1997

Market shares are shown in percent. Figures include credit and debit cards.

Visa	49.62%
MasterCard	25.24
American Express	18.45
Other	6.69

Source: *Wall Street Journal*, March 24, 1998, p. A3.

★ 1502 ★
Loan Arrangers (SIC 6150)

Factoring Leaders - 1997

Firms are ranked by volume in millions of dollars.

BNY Financial	$ 15,125
CIT Group/Coml. Svs.	13,700
NationsBank	8,200
Heller Financial	7,400
Republic Bsns. Credit	5,600
Congress-Talcott Corp.	4,000
SunTrust Bank	3,273

Source: *DNR*, February 27, 1998, p. 4.

★ 1503 ★
Loan Arrangers (SIC 6150)

Largest Agricultural Banks - 1996

Banks are ranked by total farm loans in thousands of dollars.

Wells Fargo Bank N.A.	$ 1,710,985
Bank of America National Trust & S.A.	1,373,000
Sanwa Bank California	715,594
U.S. Bank of Washington N.A.	406,191
Seattle-First NB	343,000
Norwest Bank South Dakota N.A.	327,855
Boatmens First NB of Kansas	327,470
U.S. Bank of Idaho	319,479
First Security Bank N.A.	310,182
Key Bank of Washington	286,792

Source: *Agri Finance*, July 1997, p. 10, from Federal Reserve System.

★ 1504 ★
Loan Arrangers (SIC 6162)

Canada's Business/Government Loans - 1997

Market shares are shown in percent.

Royal Bank	20.3%
Bank of Nova Scotia	18.7
CIBC	15.1
Bank of Montreal	14.7
Toronto-Dominion Bank	11.8
Other	19.4

Source: *Financial Times*, April 22, 1998, p. 14, from Price Waterhouse.

★ 1505 ★
Loan Arrangers (SIC 6162)

Leading Mexican Banks by Loans - 1997

Shares are shown for June 1997.

Bancomer	20.1%
Banamex	18.8
Serfin	14.1
Bancrecer	10.2
Internacional	6.4
Mexicano	5.8
BBV	5.2

Continued on next page.

★ 1505 ★ *Continued*
Loan Arrangers (SIC 6162)

Leading Mexican Banks by Loans - 1997

Shares are shown for June 1997.

Atlantico	4.2%
Confia	4.2
Promex	3.1
Banorte	2.7
Inbursa	1.4
Citibank	1.2
Quadrum	0.1
Other	2.5

Source: *Financial Times*, December 16, 1997, p. 4, from Salomon Brothers.

★ 1506 ★
Mortgage Loans (SIC 6162)

Canada's Residential Mortgagers - 1997

Market shares are shown in percent.

Royal Bank	23.3%
Bank of Nova Scotia	18.2
CIBC	17.5
Bank of Montreal	15.5
Toronto-Dominion Bank	13.3
Other	12.2

Source: *Financial Times*, April 22, 1998, p. 14, from Price Waterhouse.

★ 1507 ★
Mortgage Loans (SIC 6162)

Largest Bank Home Equity Lenders

Companies are ranked by loans outstanding at the end of the third quarter of 1997. Figures are in billions of dollars.

BankAmerica	$ 11.25
First Union	11.10
Banc One	8.86
Nationsbank	7.15
Wells Fargo	6.59

Source: *New York Times*, March 5, 1998, p. C1, from *Home Equity News*.

★ 1508 ★
Mortgage Loans (SIC 6162)

Largest Non-Bank Home Equity Lenders

Companies are ranked by loans outstanding at the end of the third quarter of 1997. Figures are in billions of dollars.

ContiFinancial	$ 5.68
Money Store	5.50
IMC Mortgage	4.57
First Plus Financial	3.05
Advanta Mortgage	2.63

Source: *New York Times*, March 5, 1998, p. C1, from *Home Equity News*.

★ 1509 ★
Mortgage Loans (SIC 6162)

Top Residential Mortgage Lenders - 1997

Companies are shown ranked by servicing volume in millions of dollars as of June 30, 1997.

	Vol. ($ mil.)	Share
Norwest Mortgage	$ 191,131	4.96%
Countrywide Home Loans, Inc.	165,472	4.30
Chase Manhattan Mortgage	163,202	4.24
Fleet Mortgage	121,000	3.14
NationsBanc Mortgage	119,510	3.10
GE Capital Mortgage Services	101,632	2.64
HomeSide Lending, Inc.	91,630	2.38
BankAmerica Mortgage	84,450	2.19
First Nationwide	64,737	1.68
Mellon Mortgage Co.	64,578	1.68

Source: *US Banker*, October 1997, p. 71, from Database Products Group.

Mortgage Loans (SIC 6162)

Top Subprime Loan Originators - 1997

Shares are shown based on $60.0 billion for the first six months of 1997.

The Money Store	5.6%
Associates First Capital	5.5
ContiMortgage Corporation	4.1
AMRESCO Residential Credit	3.1
FIRSTPLUS	3.1
IMC Mortgage Company	2.9
Advanta Mortgage	2.6
Green Tree Financial	2.5
Beneficial Corporation	2.4
EquiCredit	2.2
Long Beach Mortgage	2.2
United Companies	2.2
Other	61.6

Source: *Mortgage Banking*, October 1997, p. 52, from *Inside B&C Lending*

SIC 62 - Security and Commodity Brokers

★ 1511 ★
Investment Banking (SIC 6211)

Biggest Wall Street Firms by Fees Brokers - 1996

Firms are ranked by number of fees brokers at the end of 1996.

Merrill Lynch	14,424
Morgan Stanley, Dean Witter, Discover	11,728
Smith Barney, Salomon Brothers	11,518
Paine Webber	6,226
A.G. Edwards	6,019

Source: *New York Times*, September 25, 1997, p. C9, from Securities Data Co. and Securities Industry Association.

★ 1512 ★
Investment Banking (SIC 6211)

Investment Banks by Market Capitalization - 1997

Data show market capitalization in billions of dollars as of June 25, 1997.

Salomon Brothers	$ 6.2
Lehman Brothers	4.3
Bear Stearns	4.1
Donaldson Lufkin & Jenrette	3.5
Paine Webber	3.4

Source: *Fortune*, July 21, 1997, p. 25, from *Bloomberg Business News*.

★ 1513 ★
Investment Banking (SIC 6211)

Largest Brokerage Firms - 1997

Firms are ranked by number of brokers as of January 1, 1997.

Merrill Lynch	14,424
Smith Barney	10,818
Dean Witter	9,080

Paine Webber	6,226
Prudential	6,124
A.G. Edwards	6,019
Fidelity Brokerage	5,316
Charles Schwab	4,944
Edward Jones	3,580
Morgan Stanley	2,649

Source: *Wall Street Journal*, July 16, 1997, p. C1, from Securities Industry Association.

★ 1514 ★
Investment Banking (SIC 6211)

Largest Debt Managers

Market shares are shown in percent.

Merrill Lynch	17.4%
Morgan Stanley Dean Witter	14.1
Goldman Sachs	13.1
Salomon Smith Barney	12.7
Ceredit Suisse First Boston	7.5
Other	35.2

Source: *Financial Times*, June 15, 1998, p. 14, from Securities Data.

★ 1515 ★
Investment Banking (SIC 6211)

Largest Investment Banks - 1997

Firms are ranked by dollar value of deals in billions of dolalrs. Figures are for North America, agent-only loans priced 150 basis points over Libor, except in the case of Credit Suisse First Boston, which reported only loans that are 125 basis points or higher.

Merrill Lynch	$ 36.28
Lehman Brothers	11.50
Goldman, Sachs	11.36
Donaldson, Lufkin & Jenrette	10.00
Credit Suisse First Boston	7.40
Morgan Stanley, Dean Witter, Discover	3.48
Salomon Smith Barney	2.26

Source: *Bloomberg*, March 1998, p. 36.

★ 1516 ★
Investment Banking (SIC 6211)

Largest Managers of Information Technology IPOs

Data show the leading managers of initial public offerings in the field of information technology. Market shares are shown in percent.

Morgan Stanley Dean Witter	20.7%
Goldman Sachs	13.9
BT Alex. Brown	7.9
Donaldson, Lufkin & Jenrette	6.1
Salomon Smith Barney	5.9
Bancamerica Robertson Stephens	5.2
Nationsbanc Montgomery Securities	4.6
Hambrecht & Quist	4.4
Lehman Brothers	3.6
Other	27.7

Source: *Red Herring*, March 1998, p. 42.

★ 1517 ★
Investment Banking (SIC 6211)

Largest Online Traders

Market shares are shown in percent.

Schwab.com	30.0%
Etrade.com	14.0
Waterhouse.com	8.0
Datek.com	8.0
Fidelity.com	7.0%
Dljdirect.com	5.0
Quickwaynet.com	5.0
Ameritrade.com	5.0
Discoverbrokage.com	4.0
Others	14.0

Source: *Time*, May 11, 1998, p. 48, from Piper Jaffray.

★ 1518 ★
Investment Banking (SIC 6211)

Largest Securities Firms by Announced Deals - 1997

Data show value of announced deals in billions of dollars.

Merrill Lynch	$ 160.9
Goldman, Sachs	158.9
Morgan Stanley Dean Witter	123.9
Salomon Smith Barney	84.4
Credit Suisse First Boston	66.5
Donaldson, Lufkin & Jenrette	59.2
Bear, Stearns	56.5
Lehman	56.4
J.P. Morgan	55.2
Lazard	47.2

Source: *USA TODAY*, September 25, 1997, p. 3B, from Securities Data, Associated Press, and Securities Industry Association.

★ 1519 ★
Investment Banking (SIC 6211)

Largest Securities Firms by Debt/ Stock Issues - 1997

Data show proceeds from debt/stock issues in billions of dollars.

Merrill Lynch	$ 138.8
Salomon Smith Barney	118.2
Goldman, Sachs	96.4
Morgan Stanley Dean Witter	93.1
Lehman Brothers	88.1
J.P. Morgan	77.1

Continued on next page.

★ 1519 ★ *Continued*

Investment Banking (SIC 6211)

Largest Securities Firms by Debt/ Stock Issues - 1997

Data show proceeds from debt/stock issues in billions of dollars.

Credit Suisse First Boston	$ 46.4
Bear, Stearns	43.1
Donaldson, Lufkin & Jenrette	30.6
Chase Manhattan	21.8

Source: *USA TODAY*, September 25, 1997, p. 3B, from Securities Data, Associated Press, and Securities Industry Association.

★ 1520 ★

Investment Banking (SIC 6211)

Largest Securities Firms by IPO Issues - 1997

Goldman, Sachs

Morgan Stanley Dean Witter

Merrill Lynch

J.P. Morgan

Credit Suisse First Boston

Bear, Stearns

Lehman

Donaldson, Lufkin & Jenrette

Salomon Smith Barney

Montgomery Securities

Data show proceeds from IPO issues in billions of dollars. IPO stands for initial public offerings.

Goldman, Sachs	$ 4.1
Morgan Stanley Dean Witter	3.4
Merrill Lynch	2.7
J.P. Morgan	1.4
Credit Suisse First Boston	1.4
Bear, Stearns	1.1
Lehman	1.0
Donaldson, Lufkin & Jenrette	0.9
Salomon Smith Barney	0.9
Montgomery Securities	0.8

Source: *USA TODAY*, September 25, 1997, p. 3B, from Securities Data, Associated Press, and Securities Industry Association.

★ 1521 ★

Investment Banking (SIC 6211)

Largest Securities Firms by Stock Issues - 1997

Data show proceeds from stock issues in billions of dollars.

Morgan Stanley Dean Witter	$ 11.0
Goldman, Sachs	10.2
Merrill Lynch	9.1
Salomon Smith Barney	6.3
Donaldson, Lufkin & Jenrette	4.7
Bankers Trust	4.3
Lehman Brothers	3.9
Credit Suisse First Boston	3.4
J.P. Morgan	2.3
Montgomery Securities	2.3

Source: *USA TODAY*, September 25, 1997, p. 3B, from Securities Data, Associated Press, and Securities Industry Association.

★ 1522 ★

Investment Banking (SIC 6211)

Largest Securities Firms by Underwriting Fees - 1997

Data show underwriting fees in millions of dollars.

Merrill Lynch	$ 833.9
Goldman, Sachs	759.2
Morgan Stanley Dean Witter	545.3
Salomon Smith Barney	498.4
Donaldson, Lufkin & Jenrette	346.0
Lehman Brothers	340.1
Credit Suisse First Boston	255.9
Bankers Trust	228.8
J.P. Morgan	211.8
Bear, Stearns	151.4

Source: *USA TODAY*, September 25, 1997, p. 3B, from Securities Data, Associated Press, and Securities Industry Association.

★ 1523 ★
Investment Banking (SIC 6211)

Largest Wall Street Firms by Capital - 1996

| Merrill Lynch |
| Morgan Stanley, Dean Witter, Discover |
| Salomon Smith Barney |
| Lehman Brothers |
| Goldman, Sachs |
| Bear, Stearns |
| Paine Webber |
| Donaldson, Lufkin & Jenrette |

Firms are ranked by capital in billions of dollars for year-end 1996.

Merrill Lynch	$ 33.0
Morgan Stanley, Dean Witter, Discover . . .	23.7
Salomon Smith Barney	22.4
Lehman Brothers	19.8
Goldman, Sachs	17.7
Bear, Stearns	9.5
Paine Webber	4.9
Donaldson, Lufkin & Jenrette	3.4

Source: *New York Times*, September 25, 1997, p. A1, from Securities Industry Association.

★ 1524 ★
Investment Banking (SIC 6211)

Leading Managers of High-Yield Bonds - 1998

Market shares are shown for the first quarter of the year.

Morgan Stanley Dean Witter	14.6%
Donaldson Lufkin & Jenrette	13.3
Salomon Smith Barney	11.6
Merrill Lynch	8.9
Goldman Sachs	6.9
Chase Manhattan	6.6
Bear Stearns	6.0
Bankers Trust	6.0
Lehman Brothers	5.9

Source: *American Banker*, April 6, 1998, p. 12, from Securities Data Co.

★ 1525 ★
Investment Banking (SIC 6211)

Leading Online Stock Brokers - 1997

Shares are shown based on daily online transactions for January to March 1997. There were an average of 95,500 online transactions each day during that period.

Charles Schwab	35.0%
E*Trade	13.0
Fidelity	13.0
Quick & Reilly	10.0
DLJ	6.0
Discover	4.0
AmeriTrade	3.0
Others	16.0

Source: *Informationweek*, October 20, 1997, p. 122, from Piper Jaffray Research.

★ 1526 ★
Investment Banking (SIC 6211)

On-Line Financial Transactions - 2000

The table shows the estimated types of revenues generated by on-line transactions.

Credit cards	51.0%
Electronic checks	17.0
Electronic cash	16.0
Smart cards	13.0
Other	3.0

Source: *American Banker*, January 16, 1998, p. 14, from Jupiter Communications.

★ 1527 ★
Investment Banking (SIC 6211)

Online Investment Accounts - 1997

Data show types of online investment accounts distributed in percent.

Discount brokers	79.0%
Mutual-fund providers	16.0
Full-service brokers	5.0

Source: *Christian Science Monitor*, November 17, 1997, p. B4, from Forrester Research.

★ 1528 ★

Investment Banking (SIC 6211)

Top Common Equity Financers - Canada

RBC Dominion

Nesbitt Burns

CIBC Wood Gundy

ScotiaMcLeod

Midland Walwyn

First Marathon

TD Securities

Other

Market shares are shown in percent.

RBC Dominion	14.1%
Nesbitt Burns	13.8
CIBC Wood Gundy	12.8
ScotiaMcLeod	8.4
Midland Walwyn	7.1
First Marathon	5.7
TD Securities	5.1
Other	32.4

Source: *Globe & Mail*, January 5, 1998, p. B4.

★ 1529 ★

Investment Banking (SIC 6211)

Top Corporate Debt Financers - Canada

Market shares are shown in percent.

RBC Dominion	19.0%
Nesbitt Burns	18.0
CIBC Wood Gundy	17.0
Other	46.0

Source: *Globe & Mail*, January 5, 1998, p. B4.

★ 1530 ★

Investment Banking (SIC 6211)

Top Electricity Traders - 1997

Companies are ranked by sales in megawatt hours. Figures are for the second quarter of 1997.

Enron Power Marketing	$ 37.7
Electric Clearinghouse	17.4
Vitol Gas & Electric	12.9
Duke/Louis Dreyfus	11.2
Aquila Power	11.8

Source: *Public Utilities Fortnightly*, November 15, 1997, p. 49, from Power Marketing Association.

★ 1531 ★

Investment Banking (SIC 6211)

Top Financers in Canada

Market shares are shown in percent. Figures include all common equity, investment trusts, preferred share and debt issues.

RBC Dominion	16.0%
Nesbitt Burns	14.8
CIBC Wood Gundy	14.5
ScotiaMcLeod	11.5
Midland Walwyn	6.7
Other	36.5

Source: *Globe & Mail*, January 5, 1998, p. B4.

★ 1532 ★

Investment Banking (SIC 6211)

Top Traders in Canada

Data show the top traders of blocks of 10,000 or more shares, worth more than $1 million.

RBC Dominion	15.6%
Nesbitt Burns	12.0
CIBC Wood Gundy	11.6
ScotiaMcLeod	8.3
First Marathon	7.9
Griffiths McBurney	5.5
TD Securities	5.4
Midland Walwyn	5.1
Other	19.1

Source: *Globe and Mail*, April 8, 1998, p. B14, from TSE, ME, and VSE.

★ 1533 ★
Investment Banking (SIC 6211)

Top Wall Street Firms by Equity Capital

Data show firms ranked by equity capital in billions of dollars.

Morgan Stanley/Dean Witter	$ 12.8
Salomon Smith Barney Holdings Inc.	8.9
Merrill Lynch	7.3
Goldman Sachs	5.8
Lehman Brothers	4.1
Bear Stearns	3.6
Paine Webber Group	1.8
Donaldson, Lufkin & Jenrette	1.8

Source: *Wall Street Journal*, September 25, 1997, p. A6, from Securities Industry Association and Baseline.

★ 1534 ★
Investment Banking (SIC 6211)

Who Provides 401(k) Plans - 1997

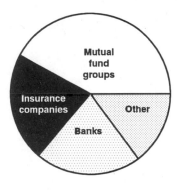

Data show estimated market share by provider.

Mutual fund groups	42.0%
Insurance companies	22.0
Banks	21.0
Other	15.0

Source: *National Underwriter*, April 27, 1998, p. 1, from Spectrem Group.

★ 1535 ★
Mutual Funds (SIC 6211)

Largest Mutual Fund Groups

Groups are ranked by market shares as of January 1997.

Fidelity Distributors	12.26%
Vanguard Group	9.49
American Fund Distributors	7.26
Franklin Distributors	5.30
Putnam Financial Services	4.98
Merrill Lynch Asset Management	2.99
T. Rowe Price Investment Services	2.57
AMEX Asset Mgmt.	2.22
AIM Distributors Inc.	1.95
Other	50.98

Source: From the Internet, http://www.mfcafe.com/market/msp_top50.html, March 1998, p. 2.

★ 1536 ★
Mutual Funds (SIC 6211)

Largest Mutual Funds - 1997

Funds are ranked by assets in billions of dollars as of May 31, 1997.

CREF Stock Account	$ 89
Fidelity Magellan	56
Vanguard Index 500	39
Investment Co. of America	35
Washington Mutual Investors	30

Source: *Fortune*, July 21, 1997, p. 31.

★ 1537 ★
Mutual Funds (SIC 6211)

Top Mutual Fund Groups in Canada - 1998

Market shares are shown based on total assets for the year ended March 31, 1998.

Investors Group	11.0%
Trimark Investment Management	9.0
Royal Mutual Funds	8.8
Mackenzie Financial	7.5
Templeton Management	5.9
Fidelity Investments Canada	4.6
AGF Management	4.5
TD Asset Management	4.5
CIBC Securities	4.0

Continued on next page.

★ 1537 ★ *Continued*
Mutual Funds (SIC 6211)

Top Mutual Fund Groups in Canada - 1998

Market shares are shown based on total assets for the year ended March 31, 1998.

CT Investment Management	3.7%
Others	36.5

Source: *Marketing Magazine*, May 25, 1998, p. 20, from Investment Funds Institute of Canada.

★ 1538 ★
Mutual Funds (SIC 6211)

Top Mutual Fund Managers - 1997

Firms are ranked by billions of dollars in U.S. assets under management as of August 31, 1997.

Fidelity Investments	$ 521.9
Vanguard Group	310.6
Capital Research & Management	227.1
Merrill Lynch Asset Management	187.9
Franklin/Templeton & Mutual Series	165.2
Putnam Funds	161.0
Federated Investors	101.3
AIM/Invesco	93.9
Dreyfus Corp./Mellon Bank	88.5
Morgan Stanley, Dean Witter	87.0

Source: *The Economist*, October 25, 1997, p. 9, from Investment Company Institute.

★ 1539 ★
Mutual Funds (SIC 6211)

Who Manages Mutual Funds - Canada

Shares are shown in percent.

Brokers/dealers	47.1%
Banks	25.0
Agencies	10.8
Trust companies	5.0
Direct to public	4.7
Life insurance	3.7
Unions/associations	2.7
Credit unions	0.5

Source: *Globe & Mail*, January 31, 1998, p. B8, from Investment Funds Institute of Canada.

★ 1540 ★
Underwriting (SIC 6211)

Canada's Top Underwriters by Bonus Credit - 1997

Underwriters are ranked by value of total financings in millions of dollars. Data include all corporate bonus credit.

CIBC Wood Gundy Securities	$ 7,989
RBC Dominion Securities	6,760
Nesbitt Burns	5,751
ScotiaMcLeod	5,344
TD Securities	4,863

Source: *Financial Post*, January 24, 1998, p. 21.

★ 1541 ★
Underwriting (SIC 6211)

Canada's Top Underwriters by Corporate Equity - 1997

Underwriters are ranked by value of total financings in millions of dollars.

RBC Dominion Securities	$ 8,143
CIBC Wood Gundy Securities	8,127
Nesbitt Burns	5,774
ScotiaMcLeod	4,260
Midland Walwyn Capital	2,638

Source: *Financial Post*, January 24, 1998, p. 28.

★ 1542 ★
Underwriting (SIC 6211)

Canada's Top Underwriters by Full Credit - 1997

Underwriters are ranked by value of total financings in millions of dollars.

RBC Dominion Securities	$ 16,226
CIBC Woody Gundy Securities	13,133
Nesbitt Burns	11,275
ScotiaMcLeod	7,796
Goldman, Sachs & Co.	5,612

Source: *Financial Post*, January 24, 1998, p. 28.

★ 1543 ★
Underwriting (SIC 6211)

Largest Acquisition-Related Private Placements

Market shares are shown in percent.

CIBC Wood Gundy Securities	21.3%
Credit Suisse First Boston	12.8
Merrill Lynch	10.7
Chase Manhattan	9.8
NationsBank	7.2
Other	38.2

Source: *Investment Dealers Digest*, March 2, 1998, p. 22.

★ 1544 ★
Underwriting (SIC 6211)

Largest Convertible Debt Underwriters - 1997

Goldman Sachs & Co.	
Salomon Smith Barney	
Merrill Lynch & Co.	
Credit Suisse First Boston	
Donaldson, Lufkin & Jenrette	
Other	

Market shares are shown in percent.

Goldman Sachs & Co.	27.5%
Salomon Smith Barney	16.4
Merrill Lynch & Co.	12.9
Credit Suisse First Boston	11.3
Donaldson, Lufkin & Jenrette	8.8
Other	23.1

Source: *Investment Dealers Digest*, January 26, 1998, p. 23.

★ 1545 ★
Underwriting (SIC 6211)

Largest Debt & Equity Underwriters

Firms are ranked by value of underwriting in millions of dollars. Figures are in millions of dollars for January - October 1997.

Donaldson Lufkin	$ 2,378
Merrill Lynch	2,373
Goldman Sachs	2,065

Smith Barney	$ 1,726
Lehman Brothers	1,082
Bear, Stearns	1,046
JP Morgan	519
CIBC Wood Gundy	447
UBS	294
Salomon Brothers	225

Source: *Broadcasting & Cable*, December 1, 1997, p. 56, from Securities Data.

★ 1546 ★
Underwriting (SIC 6211)

Largest IPO Underwriters - 1997

Market shares are shown in percent.

Goldman, Sachs & Co.	14.1%
Morgan Stanley Dean Witter	11.0
Merrill Lynch & Co.	10.4
Donaldson, Lufkin & Jenrette	5.4
Salomon Smith Barney	5.2
Other	53.9

Source: *Investment Dealers Digest*, January 26, 1998, p. 22.

★ 1547 ★
Underwriting (SIC 6211)

Largest Media/Telecom Underwriters - 1997

Market shares are shown in percent. Data are equity-related and full credit is given to book managers.

Merrill Lynch	23.4%
Salomon Smith Barney	18.2
Morgan Stanley Dean Witter	18.1
Goldman, Sachs	12.5
Bankers Trust	6.6
Other	21.2

Source: *Investment Dealers Digest*, March 9, 1998, p. 28.

★ 1548 ★

Underwriting (SIC 6211)

Largest Yankee Private Placements

Market shares are shown in percent.

Merrill Lynch	13.4%
Credit Suisse First Boston	8.8
Morgan Stanley Dean Witter	6.0
JP Morgan & Co. Inc.	5.8
Goldman, Sachs	5.7
Other	60.3

Source: *Investment Dealers Digest*, March 2, 1998, p. 22.

★ 1549 ★

Underwriting (SIC 6211)

Leading 144A Private Placement Underwriting - 1997

Market shares are shown in percent. Data exclude CDs and deposit notes.

Merrill Lynch	8.8%
Goldman, Sachs	8.4
Morgan Stanley Dean Witter	8.4
Salomon Smith Barney	7.3
Credit Suisse First Boston	7.0
Lehman Brothers	6.8
Bear, Stearns	6.8
Other	46.5

Source: *Investment Dealers Digest*, February 2, 1998, p. 12.

★ 1550 ★

Underwriting (SIC 6211)

Leading IPO Managers - 1998

Managers of initial public offerings are ranked by share of first quarter earnings.

Merrill Lynch	21.0%
Friedman, Billings, Ramsey	10.9
Morgan Stanley, Dean Witter	8.3
Goldman Sachs	8.0
CS First Boston	6.9
Donaldson, Lufkin & Jenrette	6.4
Bankers Trust	4.0
Other	34.5

Source: *American Banker*, April 8, 1998, p. 21, from Securities Data Co.

★ 1551 ★

Underwriting (SIC 6211)

Top Bank Underwriters - 1997

Market shares are shown in percent.

Merrill Lynch & Co.	17.5%
JP Morgan & Co.	15.6
Salomon Smith Barney	14.8
Morgan Stanley Dean Witter	12.3
Goldman, Sachs & Co.	11.6
Other	28.2

Source: *US Banker*, February 1998, p. 68, from Securities Data Co.

★ 1552 ★

Underwriting (SIC 6211)

Top Corporate Underwriters - 1997

Data show firms ranked by total corporate proceeds raised in billions of dollars.

Merrill Lynch	$ 208.1
Salomon Smith Barney	167.0
Morgan Stanley Dean Witter	139.5
Goldman, Sachs	137.3
Lehman Brothers	121.0
J.P. Morgan	104.0
Credit Suisse First Boston	104.0
Bear, Stearns	57.5
Donaldson, Lufkin & Jenrette	46.0
Chase Manhattan	33.1

Source: *Washington Post*, January 1, 1998, p. C4, from Securities Data.

★ 1553 ★
Underwriting (SIC 6211)

Top Junk Bond Issuers - 1997

Market shares are shown in percent.

Donaldson, Lufkin & Jenrette 21.2%
Salomon Smith Barney 16.9
Merrill Lynch & Co. 15.7
Morgan Stanley Dean Witter 14.5
Lehman Brothers 7.5
Other 24.2

Source: *Investment Dealers Digest*, January 26, 1998, p. 22.

★ 1554 ★
Underwriting (SIC 6211)

Top Tech Underwriters - 1997

Managers are ranked by proceeds in millions of dollars.

Goldman, Sachs . . . . $ 1,064.9
Morgan Stanley Dean Witter 760.4
Salomon Smith Barney 692.3
Lehman Brothers 590.2
BankAmerica 566.1
SBC Warburg Dillon Read 445.4
Hambrecht & Quist 408.3

Source: *Investment Dealers Digest*, February 9, 1998, p. 23, from Securities Data Co.

★ 1555 ★
Underwriting (SIC 6211)

Top Underwriters - 1998

Underwriters are ranked by number of new issues in billions of dollars.

Merrill Lynch . . . . $ 83.9
Smith Barney 68.6
Morgan Stanley Dean Witter 62.6
Goldman, Sachs 61.3
Lehman Brothers 40.5

Source: *New York Times*, April 14, 1998, p. C11, from Securities Data Co.

★ 1556 ★
Venture Capital (SIC 6211)

Venture Capital - 1997

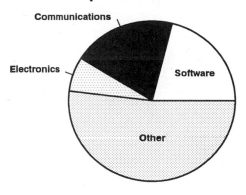

Investments are shown by sector.

	($ bil.)	Share
Software	$ 2.6	21.31%
Communications	2.4	19.67
Electronics	0.8	6.56
Other	6.4	52.46

Source: *New York Times*, April 6, 1998, p. C3, from *Coopers & Lybrand Money Tree Report*.

★ 1557 ★
Venture Capital (SIC 6211)

Venture Capital Investment by Region

Data show share of investments.

Silicon Valley 29.0%
New England 12.0
Southeast 10.0
New York metro 8.0
Upper Midwest 8.0
Texas 7.0
Other 26.0

Source: *USA TODAY*, April 21, 1998, p. B1, from Price Waterhouse National Venture Capital Survey.

★ 1558 ★
Venture Capital (SIC 6211)

Venture Capital Investment in Georgia - 1997

Data are shown by sector.

Software and information	25.3%
Health care	24.5
Communications	23.8
Consumer	7.8
Others	18.6

Source: *Atlanta Journal-Constitution*, March 22, 1998, p. H1, from Price Waterhouse.

★ 1559 ★
Venture Capital (SIC 6211)

Venture Capital Investments by State - 1997

Investments are shown in billions of dollars.

California	$ 4.560
Massachusetts	1.220
Texas	0.809
Florida	0.433
New York	0.433
Illinois	0.396
Colorado	0.364
New Jersey	0.362
Washington	0.360
Pennsylvania	0.339

Source: *Investor's Business Daily*, March 18, 1998, p. A8, from Coopers & Lybrand.

★ 1560 ★
Securities Exchanges (SIC 6231)

Options Market - 1997

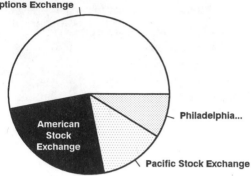

The market is shown in percent.

Chicago Board Options Exchange	53.0%
American Stock Exchange	25.0
Pacific Stock Exchange	13.0
Philadelphia Stock Exchange	9.0

Source: *New York Times*, March 10, 1998, p. C1, from The Options Clearing Corporation.

★ 1561 ★
Securities Exchanges (SIC 6231)

Stock Options Market

Market shares are estimated in percent.

Chicago Board of Options Exchange	43.0%
AMEX	30.7
Pacific Stock Exchange	17.0
PHLX	9.1
NYSE	1.7

Source: *Philadelphia Inquirer*, January 11, 1998, p. E1, from Philadelphia Stock Exchange.

★ 1562 ★

Securities Exchanges (SIC 6231)

U.S. Stock Exchange Market

The market is shown based on dollar volume.

	($ bil.)	Share
NYSE	$ 4,064	50.00%
Nasdaq	3,302	40.63
AMEX	91	1.12
Other	671	8.26

Source: *Financial Times*, March 13, 1998, p. 21, from
Nasdaq, NYSE, and AMEX.

★ 1563 ★

Financial Services (SIC 6289)

Largest Financial Information Providers

Data show the number of terminals installed.

Reuters	386,000
Dow Jones Markets	94,000
Bloomberg	91,500
Bridge	75,000

Source: *Wall Street Journal*, March 20, 1998, p. B4, from
companies.

SIC 63 - Insurance Carriers

★ 1564 ★
Insurance (SIC 6300)

Annuity Sales by Insurance Companies - 1997

Insurance companies are ranked by annuity sales in billions of dollars.

Hartford Life Ins. Co.	$ 9.73
TIAA-CREF	7.09
Nationwide Life Ins. Co.	4.94
American General Life Ins. Co.	4.85
Equitable Life Assurance Society of the U.S.	4.00
American Skandia Life Assurance Corp.	3.73

Source: *National Underwriter*, February 9, 1998, p. 1.

★ 1565 ★
Insurance (SIC 6300)

How We Buy Insurance

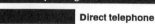

Independent agents/brokers

Tied or captive agents

Direct telephone

Direct electronic

Bundled

Other

Distribution is shown in percent for 1997 and 2003.

	1997	2003
Independent agents/brokers	51.0%	43.0%
Tied or captive agents	32.0	26.0
Direct telephone	5.9	12.0
Direct electronic	0.1	6.0
Bundled	1.0	3.0
Other	10.0	10.0

Source: *Best's Review*, October 1997, p. 104.

★ 1566 ★
Insurance (SIC 6300)

Insurance Market

Distribution is shown by policy.

	1997	2001
Personal P/C	60.0%	47.0%
Individual life	35.0	23.0
Group P/C	1.0	15.0
Group life	1.0	10.0
Long term care	0.0	2.5
Individual health	2.0	1.5
Group health	1.0	1.0

Source: *Best's Review*, May 1998, p. 30, from Datamonitor Survey Trends, 1997.

★ 1567 ★
Insurance (SIC 6300)

Largest Insurance Companies - 1996

Companies are shown ranked by net premiums written in thousands of dollars.

State Farm Mutual Auto	$ 25,060,214
Allstate Insurance	17,737,328
State Farm Fire & Casualty	8,081,212
Farmers Insurance Exchange	5,244,409
Continental Casualty	5,217,847
Nationwide Mutual Insurance	5,066,513
Liberty Mutual Insurance	4,160,306
St. Paul Fire & Marine	3,453,164
United Services Auto Association	3,184,376
American Family Mutual Insurance	2,782,426

Source: *National Underwriter*, July 21, 1997, p. 9.

★ 1568 ★

Insurance (SIC 6300)

Largest Reinsurers - 1997

Firms are ranked by net premiums in millions of dollars for the first six months of the year.

General Re	$ 1,522.2
American Re	1,467.5
Employers Re	863.4
Berkshire Hathaway	720.6
Transatlantic/Putnam	517.7
Everest Re	482.4
St. Paul Re	428.5

Source: *Business Insurance*, September 8, 1997, p. 23.

★ 1569 ★

Life Insurance (SIC 6311)

Largest Life Insurance Firms

Companies are ranked by assets in billions of dollars.

Prudential of America	$ 178.62
Metropolitan Life	162.48
Teachers Insurance and Annuity	86.36
New York Life	62.73
Northwestern Mutual Life	62.68
Connecticut General Life	62.28
Principal Mutual Life	56.84
Equitable Life Assurance	54.74

Source: *New York Times*, February 13, 1998, p. C3.

★ 1570 ★

Life Insurance (SIC 6311)

Largest Life Insurance Firms - Canada

Firms are ranked by assets in millions of Canadian dollars.

Manulife Financial	$ 47,243
Sun Life Assurance	45,567
Great-West Life Assurance	28,000
Mutual Group	27,821
London Insurance Group	24,811
Canada Life Assurance	22,361

Desjardins-Laurentine Life	.$ 7,643
Industrial Alliance Life	7,466
Metropolitan Life Insurance	6,663
Crown Life Insurance	5,800

Source: *Globe and Mail*, October 9, 1997, p. B6.

★ 1571 ★

Life Insurance (SIC 6311)

Top Canadian Life Insurance Firms - 1996

Data show year-end assets in billions of U.S. dollars.

Manufacturers Life Insurance	$ 34.0
Sun Life Assurance	32.8
Great-West Lifeco	20.2
Mutual Group	20.0
London Insurance Group	17.9

Source: *Wall Street Journal*, August 20, 1997, p. A4.

★ 1572 ★

Life Insurance (SIC 6311)

Top Life Insurance Firms in Canada - 1996

Market shares are shown based on total assets of $307.9 million for the year ended October 31, 1996.

Sun Life Assurance	.23.5%
Manufacturers Life Insurance	21.4
Great West Life Assurance	13.1
Canada Life Assurance	10.3
Mutual Life Assurance	10.1
London Life Insurance	8.0
Crown Life Insurance	2.1
Maritime Life Assurance	1.5
Imperial Life Assurance	1.4
Empire Life Insurance	0.8
Others	7.8

Source: *Marketing Magazine*, May 25, 1998, p. 20, from Canadian Bankers Association.

★ 1573 ★

Health Insurance (SIC 6321)

Health Care Payments in Michigan

Data show how Michiganders pay for health care.

Traditional insurance 44.0%
HMOs 22.0
Medicaid/Medicare 21.0
Uninsured 13.0

Source: *Detroit Free Press*, May 22, 1998, p. 11A, from Michigan Health & Hospital Association.

★ 1574 ★

Health Insurance (SIC 6321)

Largest Health Care Companies - 1997

Firms are ranked by revenue in millions of dollars.

Columbia/HCA Healthcare . . . . . $ 18,819
United Healthcare 11,794
Pacificare Health Sys. 8,983
Tenet Healthcare 8,691
Humana 7,880
Foundation Health Sys. 7,235
Medpartners 6,331

Source: *Fortune*, April 27, 1998, pp. F-53.

★ 1575 ★

Dental Insurance (SIC 6324)

Dental Insurance Market - 1996

The market is estimated in percent.

Dental indemnity 65.51%
Dental HMO 19.21
Dental PPO 13.64
Dental referral networks 1.64

Source: From the Internet, http:// nahu.org/hiu/3-97-19.htm, March 1997, p. 1, from *Health Insurance Underwriter*.

★ 1576 ★

Health Plans (SIC 6324)

Health Plans in Georgia - 1997

Coverage is shown in percent.

Preferred provider 25.9%
Medicare/Medicaid 24.8
HMO 10.6
Point of service 10.2
Private, traditional fee-for-service 8.4
No insurance 20.0

Source: *Atlanta Journal-Constitution*, March 15, 1998, p. D5, from Harkey & Associates Inc.

★ 1577 ★

Health Plans (SIC 6324)

HMO Penetration by Region

Market penetration is shown in percent.

Pacific 36.3%
Northeast 28.2
Mid Atlantic 25.6
Mountain 24.5
East North Central 21.7
West North Central 18.3
South Atlantic 16.7
East South Central 15.6

Source: *OR Manager*, March 1998, p. 37.

★ 1578 ★

Health Plans (SIC 6324)

Inpatient Admission Leaders in Atlanta, GA

Market shares are shown in percent.

Promina 27.0%
Emory University System of Healthcare . . . 12.0
Columbia/HCA's Georgia Division 9.0
Other 52.0

Source: *Hospitals & Health Networks*, March 20, 1998, p. 39.

★ 1579 ★

Health Plans (SIC 6324)

Inpatient Admission Leaders in Baltimore, MD

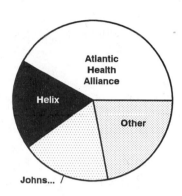

Market shares are shown in percent.

Atlantic Health Alliance	42.4%
Helix	17.9
Johns Hopkins Health System	17.8
Other	21.9

Source: *Hospitals & Health Networks*, March 20, 1998, p. 42.

★ 1580 ★

Health Plans (SIC 6324)

Inpatient Admission Leaders in Chicago, IL

Market shares are shown in percent.

Northwestern Healthcare Network	13.1%
Accord Health Network	12.9
Advocate	10.0
Rush System for Health	8.6
Other	55.4

Source: *Hospitals & Health Networks*, March 20, 1998, p. 42.

★ 1581 ★

Health Plans (SIC 6324)

Inpatient Admission Leaders in Denver, CO

Market shares are shown in percent.

Columbia Continental	33.3%
Centura Health	20.6
Exempla Healthcare	19.7
Other	26.4

Source: *Hospitals & Health Networks*, March 20, 1998, p. 42.

★ 1582 ★

Health Plans (SIC 6324)

Inpatient Admission Leaders in Detroit, MI

Market shares are shown in percent.

Detroit Medical Center	20.0%
Henry Ford Health System	19.0
Oakwood Healthcare System	8.0
Other	53.0

Source: *Hospitals & Health Networks*, March 20, 1998, p. 42.

★ 1583 ★

Health Plans (SIC 6324)

Inpatient Admission Leaders in Minneapolis, MN

Market shares are shown in percent.

Allina Health System	27.8%
Fairview Health System	25.4
HealthEast	7.2
HealthSystem Minnesota	6.0
Other	33.6

Source: *Hospitals & Health Networks*, March 20, 1998, p. 39.

★ 1584 ★
Health Plans (SIC 6324)

Inpatient Admission Leaders in Norfolk/ Virginia Beach/ Newport News, VA

Market shares are shown in percent.

Sentara	27.0%
Bon Secours Health Systems	14.0
Riverside Health Systems	11.0
Tidewater Health Care	6.0
Other	42.0

Source: *Hospitals & Health Networks*, March 20, 1998, p. 42.

★ 1585 ★
Health Plans (SIC 6324)

Inpatient Admission Leaders in San Diego, CA

Market shares are shown in percent.

Catholic Healthcare West	23.9%
ScrippsHealth	20.6
Sharp Healthcare	19.9
UCSD Healthcare Network	17.1
Kaiser Permanente	7.1
Mercy Healthcare Sacremento	6.6
Other	4.8

Source: *Hospitals & Health Networks*, March 20, 1998, p. 39.

★ 1586 ★
Health Plans (SIC 6324)

Largest For-Profit Health Care Systems - 1996

Data show the number of staffed acute-care beds.

Columbia/HCA Healthcare Corp.	57,000
Quorum Health Group	22,235
Tenet Healthcare Corp.	16,666
Principal Hospital Co.	4,331
Community Health Systems	3,275

Source: *Washington Post*, February 13, 1998, p. G2, from *Modern Healthcare*.

★ 1587 ★
Health Plans (SIC 6324)

Largest HMOs

Data show millions of enrollees.

Blue Cross & Blue Shield	11.0
Kaiser Foundation Health Plans	7.8
Aetna-U.S. Healthcare	4.0
PacifiCare/FHP	4.0
United HealthCare	3.7
Health Systems International	3.4
Prudential Health Care Plans	2.4
Cigna Health Plans	2.3
Humana	1.8
Oxford Health Plans	1.5

Source: *USA TODAY*, December 30, 1997, p. 2B, from Interstudy.

★ 1588 ★
Health Plans (SIC 6324)

Largest HMOs in Illinois

HMOs (health maintenance organizations) are ranked by number of members.

United Healthcare of Illinois	486,569
HMO Illinois	471,788
Humana Health Plan	293,396
Rush Prudential HMO	173,705
Health Alliance Medical Plans (Carle)	114,858
American Health Care Providers	55,887
FHP	53,027
Group Health Plans	50,412
Rockford Health Plans (CliniCare)	48,672
Blue Advantage	47,890

Source: *Chicago Tribune*, October 29, 1997, p. C2, from Illinois State Medical Society.

★ 1589 ★

Health Plans (SIC 6324)

Largest Managed Care Firms

Companies are ranked by number of full-risk, managed care covered lives.

United HealthCare/Humana	10.4
Kaiser Permanente	9.0
Cigna	6.3
Aetna	5.2
Foundation Health	4.4

Source: *Wall Street Journal*, May 29, 1998, p. A3, from companies and Baseline.

★ 1590 ★

Health Plans (SIC 6324)

Leading HMOs - Michigan

Market shares are shown in percent for 1996.

Blue Cross HMOs	25.5%
HAP	22.2
Physicians Health Plan	8.7
Care Choices	7.5
The Wellness Plan	6.9
Priority Health	5.8
HealthPlus	4.7
M-Care	4.6
OmniCare	4.6
SelectCare	3.9
Other HMOs	5.5

Source: *Health Care Weekly Review*, July 30, 1997, p. 1, from *Michigan Managed Care Review*.

★ 1591 ★

Health Plans (SIC 6324)

Managed Care Companies by Medicare Enrollments - 1996

Data show Medicare enrollments as of July 1, 1996.

Pacificare of California	591,993
Kaiser Foundation (California)	472,972
Humana of Florida	218,693
Health Net (California)	115,688
Oxford (New York)	88,100

Source: *New York Times*, August 2, 1997, p. 19, from The Henry J. Kaiser Family Foundation and Interstudy.

★ 1592 ★

Health Plans (SIC 6324)

Top Health Plans - Hawaii

Market shares are shown based on enrollment.

HMSA	43.3%
Kaiser	13.6
Quest	13.1
Champus	3.8
Active military coverage	3.0
Medicare	1.8
Other	10.3
Uninsured	9.0
Unknown	2.1

Source: From the Internet, http://mano.icsd.hawaii.gov/health, 1996, p. 1.

★ 1593 ★

Health Plans (SIC 6324)

Top Health Plans - Philadelphia

Market shares are shown in percent.

	Dec. 1996	Dec. 1997
Keystone Mercy	31.0%	48.0%
Health Partners	24.0	23.0
HMA	18.0	15.0
Oxford	12.0	14.0
Others	15.0	--

Source: *Philadelphia Inquirer*, February 28, 1998, p. D7, from Pennsylvania Department of Insurance and Public Welfare and Hospital Association of Pennsylvania.

★ 1594 ★

Auto Insurance (SIC 6331)

Auto Insurance Market by Type of Agent

Shares are shown in percent.

Exclusive agents	60.0%
Independent agents	28.0
Direct response	12.0

Source: *Forbes*, February 23, 1998, p. 108, from Conning & Co.

★ 1595 ★
Auto Insurance (SIC 6331)

Commercial Auto Insurers - 1996

Shares are shown based on $18.283 billion in direct premiums written.

CNA Insurance Group	5.2%
Travelers P.C. Group	4.8
Zurich Insurance Group U.S.	4.6
State Farm Group	3.6
St. Paul Cos.	3.5
Liberty Mutual Group	2.8
Nationwide Group	2.7
Old Republic Gen. Group	2.6
Progressive Group	2.5
Hartford Insurance Group	2.4
Other	65.3

Source: *Best's Review*, October 1997, p. 38.

★ 1596 ★
Auto Insurance (SIC 6331)

Largest Insurers by Total Auto Lines - 1996

Shares are shown based on $127.440 billion in direct premiums written.

State Farm Group	18.8%
Allstate Insurance Group	10.8
Farmers Insurance Group	5.2
Nationwide Group	3.7
Progressive Group	2.8
USAA Group	2.7
Berkshire Hathaway	2.4
Travelers P.C. Group	2.1
Liberty Mutual Group	1.8
CNA Insurance Group	1.6
Other	48.1

Source: *Best's Review*, October 1997, p. 36.

★ 1597 ★
Auto Insurance (SIC 6331)

Private Passenger Auto Insurers - 1996

Shares are shown based on $109.157 billion in direct premiums written.

State Farm Group	21.4%
Allstate Insurance Group	12.4

Farmers Insurance Group	5.9%
Nationwide Group	3.9
USAA Group	3.1
Progressive Group	2.8
Berkshire Hathaway	2.7
American Family Insurance Group	1.7
Liberty Mutual Group	1.7
Travelers P.C. Group	1.7
Other	42.7

Source: *Best's Review*, October 1997, p. 35.

★ 1598 ★
Disaster Insurance (SIC 6331)

Disaster Insurance Providers - South Carolina

Market shares are shown in percent.

Insurance Services Office Inc.	59.50%
South Carolina Reinsurance Facility	42.50
Other	8.00

Source: From the Internet, http://www.state.s.us, January 1998, p. 2.

★ 1599 ★
Liability Insurance (SIC 6331)

General Liability Insurance Writers - 1996

Shares are shown based on $24,194,670,000 in direct premiums written.

Amer. Intern. Group	18.4%
CNA Ins. Group	6.1
Chubb Grp. of Ins. Cos.	5.7
Travelers PC Group	4.9
Zurich Ins. Group-U.S.	4.4
Reliance Ins. Group	3.7
St. Paul Cos.	3.2
Nationwide Group	2.8
Fireman's Fund Cos.	2.5
Talegen/TRG Ins. Grps.	2.4
Amer. Financial Group	2.0
Cigna Group	1.9
Other	42.0

Source: *Best's Review*, November 1997, p. 64.

★ 1600 ★

Liability Insurance (SIC 6331)

Largest D&O Liability Insurance Leaders

The market for directors and officers (D&O) liability insurance is shown by company. Shares are shown based on volume of premiums.

AIG	30.0%
United Educators	15.0
Chubb	9.0
Exec. Risk/Aetna	9.0
Aegis	4.0
Coregis	4.0
Other	29.0

Source: *Association Management*, December 1997, p. 21, from Watson Wyatt Woldwide.

★ 1601 ★

Malpractice Insurance (SIC 6331)

Top Medical Malpractice Insurers - 1996

Market shares are shown in percent.

St. Paul	9.1%
CNA	6.9
Medical Liability Mutual of New York	6.0
Health Care Indemnity	4.4
Medical Protective	4.2
The Doctor's Co.	3.2
American Continental	3.0
AIG	2.9
Physicians Reciprocal	2.6
Norcal Mutual	2.5
Other	44.8

Source: *American Medical News*, February 16, 1998, p. 33, from Corning & Co. and A.M. Best & Co.

★ 1602 ★

Property Insurance (SIC 6331)

Largest Property & Casualty Insurers

Companies are ranked by direct-written premiums in billions of dollars.

State Farm	$ 34.2
Allstate	18.0
CNA	9.9
American International Group	9.8
Farmers	9.8

Source: *Wall Street Journal*, October 14, 1997, p. A19, from Insurance Information Institute.

★ 1603 ★

Property Insurance (SIC 6331)

Largest Property Insurance Underwriters - 1997

Shares are shown based on industry capacity.

Hartford Fire	23.5%
Hartford Steam Boiler	23.5
Zurich Insurance Co.	23.5
Lloyd's Syndicate 362	7.0
American Re-Insurance	5.0
Firemans Fund	5.0
Other	12.5

Source: *Business Insurance*, December 22, 1997, p. 1, from Industrial Risk Insurers.

★ 1604 ★

Property Insurance (SIC 6331)

Leading Property/Casualty Writers - 1996

Shares are shown based on $270.924 billion in direct premiums written.

State Farm Group	12.6%
Allstate Insurance Group	6.6
American Intern. Group	3.6
CNA Insurance Group	3.6
Farmers Insurance Group	3.6
Nationwide Group	3.2
Travelers P.C. Group	3.2

Continued on next page.

★ 1604 ★ *Continued*
Property Insurance (SIC 6331)

Leading Property/Casualty Writers - 1996

Shares are shown based on $270.924 billion in direct premiums written.

Hartford Insurance Group	2.0%
Liberty Mutual Group	2.0
Zurich Insurance Group-U.S.	2.0
Others	57.6

Source: *Best's Review*, August 1997, p. 33, from A.M. Best & Co.

★ 1605 ★
Property Insurance (SIC 6331)

Top P/C Insurers in Canada - 1997

Shares of the property/casualty market are shown in percent.

Royal & Sun Alliance	6.35%
Co-operators Group	6.22
ING Canada	5.82
AXA Canada Inc.	4.59
State Farm Insurance Co.	4.16
Zurich Canada	3.79
Guardian Group of Cos.	3.22
Liberty Mutual Group	3.15
Dominion of Canada	2.87
Lombard Canada Group	2.50
Other	57.33

Source: *Canadian Insurance*, April 1998, p. 19.

★ 1606 ★
Workers Compensation Insurance (SIC 6331)

Workers' Compensation Insurance Writers - 1996

Shares are shown based on $27,098,363,000 in direct premiums written.

Liberty Mutual Group	7.2%
Amer. Intern. Group	6.6
CNA Ins. Group	5.6
Travelers PC Group	4.5
Hartford Ins. Group	4.3
Kemper Ins. Cos.	4.2
Nationwide Group	3.6
Zurich Ins. Group-U.S.	3.2

Fireman's Fund Cos.	2.4%
Business Ins. Group	2.3
Reliance Ins. Group	1.9
Cigna Group	1.6
Other	52.6

Source: *Best's Review*, November 1997, p. 91.

★ 1607 ★
Workers Compensation Insurance (SIC 6331)

Workers' Compensation Insurance Writers - North Dakota

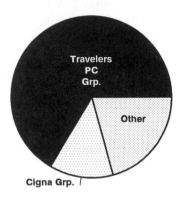

Shares are shown based on $1,230,000 in direct premiums written for 1996.

Travelers PC Grp.	66.7%
Cigna Grp.	12.7
Other	20.6

Source: *Best's Review*, November 1997, p. 92.

★ 1608 ★
Fidelity Insurance (SIC 6351)

Fidelity Insurance Leaders - 1996

Firms are ranked by direct-written premiums in thousands of dollars.

CUNA Mutual Group	$ 154,548
Chubb Group of the Ins. Cos.	137,302
Amer. Intern. Group	119,525
Travelers PC Group	99,879
Zurich Ins. Group-U.S.	61,865
CNA Ins. Group	44,301

Continued on next page.

★ 1608 ★ *Continued*
Fidelity Insurance (SIC 6351)

Fidelity Insurance Leaders - 1996

Firms are ranked by direct-written premiums in thousands of dollars.

St. Paul Cos. . . . .$ 44,301
Reliance Ins. Group 31,232
Capsure Group 28,159
Hartford Ins. Group 24,239

Source: *Best's Review*, September 1997, p. 72.

★ 1609 ★
Fidelity Insurance (SIC 6351)

Leading Fidelity Insurance Writers - Hawaii

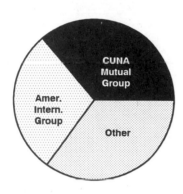

Shares are shown based on $5,218,000 in direct premiums written for 1996.

CUNA Mutual Group 36.0%
Amer. Intern. Group 29.0
Other 35.0

Source: *Best's Review*, September 1997, p. 75.

★ 1610 ★
Fidelity Insurance (SIC 6351)

Leading Fidelity Insurance Writers - New York State

Shares are shown based on $129,528,000 in direct premiums written for 1996.

Amer. Intern. Group 23.6%
Chubb Group of Ins. Cos. 22.5
Other 53.9

Source: *Best's Review*, September 1997, p. 75.

★ 1611 ★
Fidelity Insurance (SIC 6351)

Leading Fidelity Insurance Writers - Vermont

Shares are shown based on $10,474,000 in direct premiums written for 1996.

ICI Mutual Ins. Co. 85.1%
CUNA Mutual Group 3.8
Other 11.1

Source: *Best's Review*, September 1997, p. 75.

★ 1612 ★
Surety Insurance (SIC 6351)

Surety Insurance Writers - 1996

Firms are ranked by direct premiums written in thousands of dollars.

CNA Ins. Group . . . . $ 229,569
Reliance Ins. Group 178,745
Zurich Ins. Group-U.S. 162,966
USF&G Group 162,509
Travelers PC Group 152,977
St. Paul Cos. 138,516
Amer. Intern. Group 107,734
Safeco Ins. Cos. 100,739
Fireman's Fund Cos. 97,458
Chubb Group of Ins. Cos. 74,379
Hartford Ins. Group 71,753
Amwest Ins. Group 67,884
Frontier Ins. Group Inc. 63,609
Capsure Group 61,524
Liberty Mutual Group 50,690
Amer. Financial Group 48,818
Jupiter Holdings Group 39,066
International Fidelity 35,221
Kemper Ins. Cos. 32,241
Ohio Casualty Group 30,552

Source: *Best's Review*, September 1997, p. 70.

★ 1613 ★

Pensions (SIC 6371)

Top 401(k) Administrators - 1996

Data show plans and assets under management at year-end in billions of dollars.

Fidelity Investments . . . . $ 120
Vanguard Group 68
State Street Bank 58
Merrill Lynch 35
Bankers Trust 33

Source: *Wall Street Journal*, August 20, 1997, p. C1, from Cerulli Associates.

★ 1614 ★

Pensions (SIC 6371)

Top Pension Funds

The top funds and sponsors are ranked by assets in millions of dollars.

California Public Employees . . . . . $ 127,656
New York State Common 95,812
General Motors 90,600
California State Teachers 78,900
Florida State Board 71,940
New York State Teachers 68,738
Texas Teachers 64,221
New Jersey Division 59,933
General Electric 56,915
Federal Retirement Thrift 55,491

Source: *Pensions & Investments*, January 26, 1998, p. 28.

SIC 64 - Insurance Agents, Brokers, and Service

★ 1615 ★

Insurance Brokers (SIC 6411)

Top Brokers to Business - 1996

Data show revenue generated by U.S. based clients in millions of dollars.

Marsh & McLennan Cos. Inc.	$ 3,751.876
Aon Group Inc.	1,981.500
Sedgwick Group P.L.C.	639.675
Willis Corroon Group P.L.C.	599.430
Arthur J. Gallagher & Co.	411.011
Acordia Inc.	336.983
USI Insurance Services Corp.	163.300
Hilb, Rogal & Hamilton Co.	156.618
Poe & Brown Inc.	118.680
Jardine Lloyd Thompson Group P.L.C.	110.159

Source: *Business Insurance*, July 21, 1997, p. 3.

SIC 65 - Real Estate

★ 1616 ★
Commercial Real Estate (SIC 6512)

Largest Commercial Property Managers - Los Angeles County

Companies are ranked by rentable area in millions of square feet. Data include all commercial and industrial buildings already existing, under construction, or under renovation.

Cushman & Wakefield/Premisys	8.69
CB Commercial/Koll Management Services	6.84
Tooley	6.32
Insignia Commercial Group	5.15
Charles Dunn	3.29
Hines	2.68
Prentiss Properties Services	2.27
Compass Management & Leasing	2.09
Heitman Properties	1.93
PM Realty Group	1.90

Source: *Los Angeles Times*, October 29, 1997, p. D9, from Realty Information Group and CoStar.

★ 1617 ★
Commercial Real Estate (SIC 6512)

Largest Commercial Property Owners - Los Angeles County

Companies are ranked by developed office and industrial area in millions of square feet as of October 1997. Data do not include retail space.

Majestic Realty	23.0
Boeing	12.8
Watson Land	9.6
Arden Realty	6.6
Maguire Partners	6.6
Crow Investment Trust	4.9
Douglas Emmett	4.7
Shuwa Investments	4.3
J.H. Snyder	3.6
John Hancock Mutual Life Insurance	3.4

Source: *Los Angeles Times*, November 5, 1997, p. D9, from individual companies and CoStar.

★ 1618 ★
Commercial Real Estate (SIC 6512)

Largest Commercial Property Owners - Orange County, CA

Companies are ranked by developed office and industrial area in millions of square feet as of October 1997. Data do not include retail space.

Irvine Co.	12.4
Boeing	5.8
Kilroy Realty	3.6
Olen Properties	3.6
Hughes Aircraft	3.4
Catellus Development	3.2
Spieker Properties	2.8

Continued on next page.

★ 1618 ★ *Continued*
Commercial Real Estate (SIC 6512)

Largest Commercial Property Owners - Orange County, CA

Companies are ranked by developed office and industrial area in millions of square feet as of October 1997. Data do not include retail space.

Lucky Food Centers	2.5
Security Capital Industrial Trust	2.3
Steelcase	2.0
Warland Investments	2.0

Source: *Los Angeles Times*, November 5, 1997, p. D9, from individual companies and CoStar.

★ 1619 ★
Commercial Real Estate (SIC 6512)

Who Owns Commercial Real Estate

Shares are shown based on a $3.929 trillion market. REIT stands for real estate investment trust.

Corporations	43.1%
Partnerships	25.6
Not-for-profits	10.5
Government	6.0
REITs	3.6
Institutional investors	3.3
Financial institutions	2.9
Individuals	2.6
Other	2.6

Source: *Forbes*, December 29, 1997, p. 72, from AEW Capital Management.

★ 1620 ★
Shopping Centers (SIC 6512)

Top Shopping Center Managers - 1997

Firms are ranked by millions of square feet of gross leasable area managed.

Simon DeBartolo Group Inc.	138.6
General Growth Properties Inc.	90.1
Urban Shopping Centers	56.9
The Rouse Co.	44.2
Kimco Realty Corp.	43.3
Westfield Corp. Inc.	41.9
The Richards E. Jacobs Group	40.5
ERE Yarmouth Retail Retail Group	37.5

Developers Diversified Realty Corp.	33.4
First Washington Management Inc.	32.4

Source: *Shopping Center World*, March 1998, p. 5.

★ 1621 ★
Shopping Centers (SIC 6512)

Top Shopping Center Owners

Firms are ranked by millions of square feet of gross leasable area.

Simon DeBartolo Group Inc.	105.7
ERE Yarmouth	55.5
General Growth Properties Inc.	49.6
Heitman Retail Properties/Heitman Capital Management	47.5
Kimco Realty Corp.	42.1
The Rouse Co.	41.3
The Richard E. Jacobs Group Inc.	39.8
Westfield Corp. Inc.	39.1
Benderson Development Co. Inc.	32.2
The Cafaro Co.	31.3

Source: *Shopping Center World*, January 1998, p. 38.

★ 1622 ★
Shopping Centers (SIC 6512)

Top Strip Center Managers - 1997

Data show gross leasable area managed in square feet.

Kimco Realty Corp.	36,746,993
Trammell Crow Co.	28,855,746
Benderson Development Co. Inc.	28,575,000
Developers Diversified Realty Corp.	28,468,385
RD Management	20,628,630
Insignia Commercial Group Inc./ Insignia Retail Group	20,000,000
Koll Real Estate Group	19,040,939
Simon DeBartolo Group	18,900,000
New Plan Realty Trust	18,264,395
Weingarten Realty Investors	15,757,686
Faison & Associates	15,713,694

Source: *Shopping Center World*, August 1997, p. 54.

★ 1623 ★

Shopping Centers (SIC 6512)

Top Strip Centers Owners - 1997

Data show gross leasable area owned in square feet.

Kimco Realty Corp.	35,775,307
Benderson Development Co. Inc.	28,575,000
Developers Diversified Realty Corp.	25,258,212
New Plan Realty Trust	18,900,000
RD Management	18,678,630
Weingarten Realty Investors	16,888,075
Simon DeBartolo Group	16,616,018
Glimcher Realty Trust	13,597,857
Roebling Investment Co.	13,168,710
Federal Realty Investment Trust	12,236,368

Source: *Shopping Center World*, August 1997, p. 62.

★ 1624 ★

Real Estate (SIC 6531)

Largest Commercial Property Developers

Firms are ranked by millions of square feet of property managed. Figures include residential, office, retail and hotel space.

Insignia Financial Group	339.38
ERE Yarmouth	330.00
Trammell Crow Company	278.00
Lincoln Properties Company	209.50
LaSalle Partners Limited	152.90

Source: *Buildings*, August 1997, p. 44.

★ 1625 ★

Real Estate (SIC 6531)

Top Real Estate Brokerages - Los Angeles County

Companies are shown ranked by sales volume in millions of dollars for the nine months ended September 30, 1997.

Coldwell Banker Jon Douglas Co.	$ 6,852
Fred Sands Realtors	2,682
RE/MAX Beach Cities Realty	841
John Aaro & Associates	739
Dilbeck Realtors - Better Homes & Gardens	602
Shorewood Realtors Inc.	602
RE/MAX Palos Verdes Realty	508

MacGregor Realty Inc.	$ 396
Podley Doan Inc.	348
RE/MAX of Valencia	293

Source: *Los Angeles Business Journal*, October 20, 1997, p. 17.

★ 1626 ★

Real Estate (SIC 6531)

Top Real Estate Firms in Wahington D.C.

Companies are ranked by revenue in millions of dollars.

Ryland Group Inc.	$ 1,649.8
NVR Inc.	1,188.3
Rouse Co.	933.2
Fortress Group	445.3
CarrAmerica Realty Corp.	367.9

Source: *Washington Post*, April 27, 1998, p. 40.

SIC 67 - Holding and Other Investment Offices

★ 1627 ★

Bank Holding Companies (SIC 6712)

Largest Bank Holding Companies - 1997

Companies are ranked by total assets in millions of dollars as of June 30, 1997.

Chase Manhattan Corp.	$ 352,033
Citicorp	304,293
Nations Bank	284,367
BankAmerica Corp.	258,363
J.P. Morgan & Co.	250,490
First Union Corp.	205,000
Bankers Trust New York Corp.	128,948
Banc One Corp.	115,492
First Chicago NBD Corp.	112,595
Wells Fargo & Co.	100,180

Source: *New York Times*, November 19, 1997, p. C4, from Keefe, Bruyette & Woods, Inc.

★ 1628 ★

Franchises (SIC 6794)

Largest Homebased Franchises - 1997

Companies are ranked by number of homebased franchises.

Jeni-King	6,030
Coverall Cleaning Concepts	4,588
ServiceMaster	4,322
Chem-Dry	4,074
Snap-On Tools	4,014
Novus Windshield Repair	2,577
CleanNet USA Inc.	2,108
Merry Maids	1,062
Malco Tools	1,043
Servpro	917

Source: *Entrepreneur*, October 1997, p. 164.

★ 1629 ★

Franchises (SIC 6794)

Types of Franchises - Mexico

Distribution is shown for the end of 1996. "Others" includes car rental, hotels, and other services.

Retail sales of non-food products	32.0%
Restaurants and bars	19.0
Fast food outlets	17.0
Basic services (dry cleaning, auto repair, etc.)	15.0
Others	17.0

Source: *Business Mexico*, September 1997, p. 30, from Mexican Franchise Association.

★ 1630 ★

Franchising (SIC 6794)

Largest U.S. Franchises

Data show number of units.

McDonald's Corp.	22,270
Southland Corp. (7-Eleven)	16,286
Subway	13,000
Burger King Corp.	8,253
KFC Corp.	8,187
Pizza Hut Inc.	7,200
Tandy Corp. (Radio Shack)	6,779
Jani-King International	6,189
Taco Bell Corp.	5,644
International Dairy Queen Inc.	5,347

Source: *Los Angeles Times*, June 3, 1998, p. D7, from International Franchise Association.

★ 1631 ★
Real Estate Investment Trusts (SIC 6798)

Largest REITs

| Equity Office Properties Trust |
| Equity Residential Properties |
| Crescent Real Estate Equities |
| Starwood Lodging |
| Simon DeBartolo Group |

Companies are ranked by equity market capitalization in billions of dollars.

Equity Office Properties Trust	$ 7.76
Equity Residential Properties	4.44
Crescent Real Estate Equities	4.43
Starwood Lodging	3.66
Simon DeBartolo Group	3.47

Source: *Financial Times*, March 16, 1998, p. 9, from Morgan Stanley Dean Witter.

★ 1632 ★
Real Estate Investment Trusts (SIC 6798)

Top Sectors for Real Estate Investment Trusts - Los Angeles County

Data show assets in millions of dollars as of September 30, 1997.

	($ mil.)	Share
Office	$ 2,359	37.88%
Retail	1,654	26.56
Industrial/self-storage	887	14.24
Hospitality	439	7.05
Apartment	387	6.21
Other	501	8.05

Source: *Los Angeles Times*, December 17, 1997, p. D7, from Alliance Capital and CB Commercial.

SIC 70 - Hotels and Other Lodging Places

★ 1633 ★

Hotels (SIC 7011)

Largest Bay Area Hotels

Data show number of guest rooms.

San Francisco Hilton and Towers	1,896
San Francisco Marriott	1,500
The Westin St. Francis	1,189
Parc Fifty Five Hotel	1,008
Hyatt Regency San Francisco	805

Source: *San Francisco Business Times*, March 13, 1998, p. 23.

★ 1634 ★

Hotels (SIC 7011)

Largest Economy Hotel Chains

Companies are shown ranked by number of guest rooms.

Days Inns of America	163,761
Ramada Limited	131,731
Super 8 Motels	98,286
Motel 6	84,273
Howard Johnson International	55,953
Econo Lodge	45,886
Travelodge	42,544
Red Roof Inns	29,966
Knights Inn	18,080
Budgetel Inns	15,294

Source: *Hotel & Motel Management*, February 2, 1998, p. 37.

★ 1635 ★

Hotels (SIC 7011)

Largest Hotel Markets - 1997

Data show cities ranked by number of hotel rooms for January 1 through June 30, 1997.

Las Vegas	105,800
Orlando	87,200
Los Angeles-Long Beach	79,100
Atlanta	70,300
Chicago	69,400
Washington D.C.	68,500
New York	65,800
Dallas	47,600
San Diego	46,600
Anaheim-Santa Ana	44,300
San Francisco	42,900
Houston	41,100

Source: *Hotels*, November 1997, p. 4, from Smith Travel Research.

★ 1636 ★

Hotels (SIC 7011)

Largest Hotel/Casino Companies

Firms are ranked by revenue in millions of dollars.

Marriott International	$ 12,034
ITT	6,658
Hilton Hotels	5,316
Harrah's Entertainment	1,619
Mirage Resorts	1,418

Source: *Fortune*, April 27, 1998, pp. F-53.

★ 1637 ★

Hotels (SIC 7011)

Leading Cities for New Hotel Rooms

Data show cities ranked by share of new hotel rooms planned.

Dallas	4.7%
Atlanta	3.9
Phoenix	3.3
Chicago	3.2
Houston	3.0
Raleigh/Durham/Chapel Hill	2.4
Nashville	2.3
Charlotte/Gastonia	2.2
Orlando	2.2
Kansas City, MO	1.9

Source: *USA TODAY*, October 28, 1997, p. 12B, from Coopers & Lybrand Lodging Research Network, F.W. Dodge, Smith Travel Research, and Bear Stearns.

★ 1638 ★

Hotels (SIC 7011)

Top Hotel Chains in Canada - 1997

Market shares are shown for the year ended December 31, 1997.

Choice Hotels Canada	5.9%
Best Western International	4.2
Holiday Inn Worldwide	4.2
Canadian Pacific Hotels	3.6
ITT Sheraton Canada	3.5
Delta Hotels & Resorts	2.6
Travelodge	2.4
Ramada Franchise Canada	1.8
Days Inn Canada	1.6
Radisson Hotels International	1.4
Others	68.8

Source: *Marketing Magazine*, May 25, 1998, p. 22, from Hotel Association of Canada.

SIC 72 - Personal Services

★ 1639 ★
Laundromats (SIC 7215)

Laundromat Purchases - 1998

The table shows the percent of operators planning to purchase each item.

At least one top loader	49.0%
At least one dryer	41.0
At least one double-loader	11.0
At least one triple loader	7.8

Source: *American Coin-Op*, April 1998, p. 18.

★ 1640 ★
Laundromats (SIC 7215)

U.S. Laundromat Use - 1996

Data show the percent of adults who used a laundromat in the last six months.

18 to 24	12.6%
25 to 34	10.3
35 to 44	8.7
45 to 54	7.6
55 to 64	5.9
65 and older	4.8

Source: *American Demographics*, January 1998, p. 38, from Mediamark Research.

★ 1641 ★
Tax Preparation (SIC 7291)

How We Will Prepare Our Returns - 1998

Use a professional preparer	58.0%
Do it themselves	24.0
Do own with tax software	9.0
Use an Internet site	1.0
Don't know	8.0

Source: *USA TODAY*, February 25, 1998, p. B1, from Market Facts for Money Insider.

SIC 73 - Business Services

★ 1642 ★

Advertising (SIC 7310)

Ad Spending by Category - Canada

Categories are shown ranked by media spending on television, daily newspapers, magazines, radio and out-of-home advertising in millions of Canadian dollars. Data are for 1996.

Retail	$ 892.4
Automotive (cars, minivans, trucks, vans, dealer associations)	508.4
Business equipment & services	445.3
Food	400.3
Entertainment	321.1
Financial services & insurance services	273.3
Travel & transportation	213.4
Restaurants, catering services, night clubs	210.0
Local automotive dealer advertising	152.7
Cosmetics & toiletries	119.5
Drug products	108.9
Automotive (oil companies & related services)	105.7
Brewers & related products	102.7
Media (television, radio, out of home)	92.0
Home entertainment	61.8

Source: *Marketing Magazine*, October 20, 1997, p. 46, from A.C. Nielsen.

★ 1643 ★

Advertising (SIC 7310)

Advertising Expenditures by Media Channel - 1998

Projected ad spending is shown in millions of dollars. Major media channels are expected to spend a total of $111.925 billion in 1998.

Newspapers	$ 40,140
Network tv	14,876
Magazines	14,504
Radio	11,524
Spot tv (local)	11,251
Spot tv (national)	9,825
Cable tv	6,231
Outdoor	1,933
Syndication	1,641

Source: *Adweek*, September 8, 1997, p. 6, from Zenith Media Worldwide.

★ 1644 ★
Advertising (SIC 7310)

Internet Ad Spending - 1997

Spending is shown by category.

Consumer related	31.0%
Computing products	30.0
Financial services	18.0
Telecom	11.0
New media	10.0

Source: *Business Marketing*, April 1998, p. 3, from IAR Internet Advertising Revenue Report.

★ 1645 ★
Advertising (SIC 7310)

Leading Markets for Ad Spending - 1996

Distribution is shown in percent.

Television	22.0%
Newspapers	21.0
Magazines	9.0
Radio	7.0
Other	38.0

Source: *Boston Globe*, September 7, 1997, p. C1, from Salomon Brothers Inc.

★ 1646 ★
Advertising (SIC 7310)

Top Ad Categories - 1997

Categories are ranked by ad spending in millions of dollars.

Automotive	$ 1,821.6
Direct response	1,458.2
Toiletries & cosmetics	1,139.7
Computers, office equipment	1,095.9
Business & consumer services	1,070.4
Drugs & remedies	935.2
Apparel, footwear & accessories	791.2
Food & food products	739.5
Travel, hotels & resorts	610.8
Retail	470.7

Source: *Mediaweek*, March 2, 1998, p. 32, from Publishers Information Bureau and Competitive Media Reporting.

★ 1647 ★
Advertising (SIC 7310)

Top Ad Categories in Mexico - 1996

Firms are ranked by spending in millions of dollars.

Media	$ 6,552.0
Commerce & services	3,340.1
Government	1,946.0
Beverages	1,620.2
Household products	1,203.7

Source: *Advertising Age International*, May 11, 1998, p. 19.

★ 1648 ★
Advertising (SIC 7310)

Top Advertisers in Canada - 1996

Firms are ranked by spending in millions of dollars.

General Motors Corp.	$ 8.19
IBM Corp.	6.02
L'Oreal	4.00
Bank of Montreal	3.59
Philip Morris Co.	3.24

Source: *Advertising Age International*, May 11, 1998, p. 19.

★ 1649 ★
Advertising (SIC 7310)

Top Advertisers in Mexico - 1996

Firms are ranked by spending in millions of dollars.

Videovisa Videocentro	$ 81.1
Procter & Gamble Co.	55.0
Colgate-Palmolive Co.	53.5
Loteria Nacional	52.4
Organizacion Bimbo	47.1

Source: *Advertising Age International*, May 11, 1998, p. 19.

★ 1650 ★
Advertising (SIC 7310)

Top Advertising Markets - 1997

Cities are ranked by advertising billings in millions of dollars. Connecticut and New Jersey have no dominant city.

New York City	$ 37,697.2
Chicago, IL	11,214.4
Los Angeles, CA	7,394.0
Detroit, MI	6,760.9
San Francisco, CA	5,789.7
Minneapolis, MN	5,091.9
Boston, MA	4,104.4
Dallas, TX	2,606.0
New Jersey	1,907.5
Connecticut	1,792.6

Source: *Advertising Age*, April 24, 1998, p. S13.

★ 1651 ★
Advertising (SIC 7311)

Top Ad Firms in Canada - 1996

Market shares are shown based on revenues for the year ended December 31, 1996.

BBDO Canada	5.1%
Cossette Communication-Marketing	5.0
MacLaren McCann Canada	3.7
Young & Rubicam	3.3
Leo Burnett	2.6
Ogilvy & Mather	2.5
FCB Canada	2.4
Vickers & Benson	1.9
Palmer Jarvis	1.7
Publicis-BCP	1.6
Others	70.2

Source: *Marketing Magazine*, May 25, 1998, p. 20.

★ 1652 ★
Advertising (SIC 7311)

Top Ad Firms in Canada - 1997

Firms are ranked by gross income in millions of dollars.

MacLaren McCann Canada	$ 54,998
Cossette Communication Marketing	48,415
Y&R/Saint-Jacques Vallee	46,761
BBDO Canada	38,711

DDB Group Canada/Heather Reid & Assoc.	$ 31,151
Ogilvy & Mather	26,419
FCB Canada	24,109
Leo Burnett Co.	21,633
Vickers & Benson Advertising	21,306
Carlson Marketing	21,100

Source: *Advertising Age*, April 24, 1998, p. S21.

★ 1653 ★
Advertising (SIC 7311)

Top Ad Firms in Mexico - 1997

Firms are ranked by gross income in millions of dollars.

McCann-Erickson Mexico	$ 24,183
Young & Rubicam	15,513
Publicidad Ferrer y Asociados	11,843
Leo Burnett	11,572
J. Walter Thompson Mexico City	10,804
Panamer/Graficoncepto (O&M)	9,603
BBDO/Mexico	7,705
Bozell	6,977
Ammirati Puris Lintas Mexico	6,817
Grey Mexico	5,839

Source: *Advertising Age*, April 24, 1998, p. S34.

★ 1654 ★
Advertising (SIC 7311)

Top Marketing Agencies - Canada

Agencies are shown ranked by gross revenues in Canadian dollars for 1996.

BBDO Canada Inc.	$ 56,675,000
Cossette Communication-Marketing	55,829,000
MacLaren McCann Canada Inc.	41,242,000
The Young & Rubicam Group of Cos. Ltd.	36,532,000
Leo Burnett Company Ltd.	28,755,213
Ogilvy & Mather (Canada) Ltd.	27,072,661
FCB Canada Ltd.	26,553,023
Wolf Group Ltd.	25,463,280
Vickers & Benson Advertising Ltd.	20,908,000
Palmer Jarvis Inc.	19,304,872

Source: *Marketing Magazine*, May 26, 1997, p. 14.

★ 1655 ★

Advertising (SIC 7312)

Leading Outdoor Ad Spenders - 1996

Companies are ranked by outdoor ad spending in millions of dollars.

Philip Morris Cos.	$ 81.8
B.A.T. Industries	46.6
RJR Nabisco	29.4
General Motors Corp.	23.1
McDonald's Corp.	19.7
Anheuser-Busch Cos.	15.7
Loews Corp.	15.5
Seagram Co.	10.6
HFS	10.4
Grand Metropolitan	7.6
Walt Disney Co.	7.6
Bass	7.1
BankAmerica Corp.	6.5
PepsiCo	6.4
Guinness	6.3

Source: *Advertising Age*, September 29, 1997, p. s48, from Competitive Media Reporting.

★ 1656 ★

Advertising (SIC 7312)

Top Outdoor Ad Firms - 1997

Firms are ranked by billings in millions of dollars.

Leo Burnett Co.	$ 166.0
Long Haymes Carr	117.6
Grey Advertising	97.5
Saatchi & Saatchi	72.0
Y&R Advertising	66.0
BBDO Worldwide	64.5
Ogilvy & Mather Worldwide	59.0
DDB Needham Worldwide	57.6
Bates Worldwide	50.0
McCann-Erickson Worldwide	42.1

Source: *Advertising Age*, April 27, 1998, p. S41.

★ 1657 ★

Advertising (SIC 7313)

Leading Computer Firms by Newspaper Ad Spending

Firms are ranked by dollars spent on newspaper advertising for January through February 1997.

Computer City	$ 4,210,354
CompUSA Computer Superstore	3,208,425
J & R Computer World	742,389
NCA Computer Prods Store	503,577
Elek Tek Inc. Computer Store	417,880
Egghead Discount Software Store	374,572
Micron Electronics Computer Store	363,729
Comp U Tech Computers & Electronics Store	336,090
PSINet Computer Svc.	189,208
Computown Computer Store	156,362

Source: *Editor & Publisher*, June 21, 1997, p. 84.

★ 1658 ★

Advertising (SIC 7313)

Leading Magazine Ad Spenders - 1996

Companies are ranked by magazine ad spending in millions of dollars.

General Motors Corp.	$ 456.4
Philip Morris Cos.	343.1
Ford Motor Co.	280.2
Procter & Gamble Co.	280.2
Chrysler Corp.	269.5
Time Warner	156.4
Johnson & Johnson	154.6
Toyota Motor Corp.	126.1
Unilever	125.2
Nestle	118.9
IBM Corp.	84.1
Joh. A Benckiser	81.5
Walt Disney Co.	78.4
Sony Corp.	77.2
B.A.T. Industries	75.6

Source: *Advertising Age*, September 29, 1997, p. s42, from Competitive Media Reporting.

★ 1659 ★
Advertising (SIC 7313)

Leading Network Television Ad Spenders - 1996

Companies are ranked by network television ad spending in millions of dollars.

General Motors Corp.	$ 613.9
Procter & Gamble Co.	589.5
Johnson & Johnson	504.8
PepsiCo	423.4
Philip Morris Cos.	403.1
McDonald's Corp.	372.0
Ford Motor Co.	319.7
Grand Metropolitan	294.4
Chrysler Corp.	280.5
Walt Disney Co.	267.2
American Home Products Corp.	247.0
Warner-Lambert Co.	242.8
Unilever	238.9
AT&T Corp.	222.7
Nestle	214.0

Source: *Advertising Age*, September 29, 1997, p. s50, from Competitive Media Reporting.

★ 1660 ★
Advertising (SIC 7313)

Top Ad Firms for Consumer Magazines - 1997

Firms are ranked by ad billings in millions of dollars.

Leo Burnett Co.	$ 513.8
Y&R Advertising	325.6
Grey Advertising	322.4
Saatchi & Saatchi	313.7
McCann-Erickson Worldwide	313.1
BBDO Worldwide	310.0
J. Walter Thompson Co.	239.1
DDB Needham Worldwide	231.3
Ogilvy & Mather Worldwide	231.0
Foote, Cone & Belding	230.0

Source: *Advertising Age*, April 27, 1998, p. S41.

★ 1661 ★
Advertising (SIC 7313)

Top Ad Firms for Newspapers - 1997

Firms are ranked by ad billings in millions of dollars.

Bernard Hodes Group	$ 572.2
Nationwide Advertising Service	329.4
McCann-Erickson Worldwide	201.1
TMP Worldwide	199.6
J. Walter Thompson Co.	151.2
Allied Advertising	137.1
Y&R Advertising	129.6
Ogilvy & Mather Worldwide	127.7
Grey Advertising	127.3
Foote, Cone & Belding	105.0

Source: *Advertising Age*, April 27, 1998, p. S41.

★ 1662 ★
Advertising (SIC 7313)

Top Ad Firms for Sunday Magazines - 1997

Firms are ranked by ad billings in millions of dollars.

Ogilvy & Mather Worldwide	$ 26.0
TBWA Chiat/Day	19.5
CommonHealth	9.4
Draft Worldwide	9.1
BBDO Worldwide	8.3
Foote, Cone & Belding	7.7
D'Arcy Masius Benton & Bowles	6.9
Y&R Advertising	4.1
Wickersham Hunt Schwanter	4.0
Wunderman Cato Johnson	3.7

Source: *Advertising Age*, April 27, 1998, p. S41.

★ 1663 ★
Advertising (SIC 7313)

Top Cable TV Ad Firms - 1997

Firms are ranked by billings in millions of dollars.

Grey Advertising	$ 290.3
BBDO Worldwide	259.8
Y&R Advertising	255.5
Leo Burnett Co.	243.3
D'Arcy Masius Benton & Bowles	230.0
Foote, Cone & Belding	210.0

Continued on next page.

★ 1663 ★ *Continued*
Advertising (SIC 7313)

Top Cable TV Ad Firms - 1997

Firms are ranked by billings in millions of dollars.

McCann-Erickson Worldwide	$ 205.6
Ogilvy & Mather Worldwide	204.9
J. Walter Thompson Co.	202.1
DDB Needham Worldwide	183.9

Source: *Advertising Age*, April 27, 1998, p. S41.

★ 1664 ★
Advertising (SIC 7313)

Top Local Newspaper Ad Spenders - 1996

Companies are ranked by local newspaper ad spending in millions of dollars.

Federated Department Stores	$ 339.5
May Department Stores Co.	326.1
Circuit City Stores	250.3
Sears, Roebuck & Co.	193.1
Dayton Hudson Corp.	158.8
Dillard Department Stores	126.9
Time Warner	124.0
Walt Disney Co.	118.7
J.C. Penney Co.	105.2
Kmart Corp.	97.9
AT&T Corp.	95.1
Tandy Corp.	82.3
General Motors Corp.	74.1
The Wiz	68.1
Montgomery Ward & Co.	67.1

Source: *Advertising Age*, September 29, 1997, p. s46, from Competitive Media Reporting.

★ 1665 ★
Advertising (SIC 7313)

Top Network TV Ad Firms - 1997

Firms are ranked by billings in millions of dollars.

Y&R Advertising	$ 1,325.5
D'Arcy Masius Benton & Bowles	1,320.0
BBDO Worldwide	1,110.9
McCann-Erickson Worldwide	1,108.1
J. Walter Thompson	1,100.9
Leo Burnett Co.	1,099.8
Ogilvy & Mather Worldwide	962.0

Foote, Cone & Belding	$ 825.0
Saatchi & Saatchi	730.8
Grey Advertising	686.1

Source: *Advertising Age*, April 27, 1998, p. S41.

★ 1666 ★
Advertising (SIC 7313)

Top Spot Radio Ad Firms - 1997

Firms are ranked by billings in millions of dollars.

McCann-Erickson Worldwide	$ 135.0
BBDO Worldwide	130.7
Bozell Worldwide	128.0
DDB Needham Worldwide	124.6
Foote, Cone & Belding	120.0
Saatchi & Saatchi	111.6
Y&R Advertising	88.5
TBWA Chiat/Day	88.4
Bates Worldwide	84.6
Grey Advertising	83.2

Source: *Advertising Age*, April 27, 1998, p. S41.

★ 1667 ★
Advertising (SIC 7313)

Top Spot TV Ad Firms - 1997

Firms are ranked by billings in millions of dollars.

McCann-Erickson Worldwide	$ 721.2
BBDO Worldwide	667.4
Saatchi & Saatchi	656.6
J. Walter Thompson Co.	634.0
TBWA Chiat/Day	565.4
Y&R Advertising	522.1
Foote, Cone & Belding	520.0
Bozell Worldwide	513.3
Grey Advertising	511.5
DDB Needham Worldwide	384.1

Source: *Advertising Age*, April 27, 1998, p. S41.

★ 1668 ★
Advertising (SIC 7319)

Largest Dental Advertisers - 1997

Companies are ranked by share of advertising spending.

Dentsply International Incorporated	3.69%
Espe-Premier	2.54
3M	2.25
Ultradent Products Incorporated	2.13
Bisco Dental Products	2.10
Other	87.29

Source: *Medical Marketing & Media*, April 1998, p. 62, from PERQ/HCI Journal Ad Review.

★ 1669 ★
Advertising (SIC 7319)

Largest Fashion/Beauty Advertisers - 1997

Firms are ranked by media expenditures in millions of dollars.

Nike	$ 211.2
L'Oreal	160.0
Levi's	100.1
Revlon	95.9
Cover Girl	91.3
Oil of Olay	84.2
Maybelline	83.4
Estee Lauder	71.0
Neutrogena	67.6
De Beers Diamonds	60.4

Source: *Women's Wear Daily*, May 15, 1998, p. 8, from Competitive Media Reporting.

★ 1670 ★
Advertising (SIC 7319)

Largest Laboratory Advertisers - 1997

Companies are ranked by share of advertising spending.

Sigma Diagnostics	6.90%
Boehringer Mannheim Diagnostics	3.98
Abbot Diagnostics	2.90
Inova Diagnostics Incorporated	2.37
Beckman Instruments Incorporated	2.26
Other	81.59

Source: *Medical Marketing & Media*, April 1998, p. 62, from PERQ/HCI Journal Ad Review.

★ 1671 ★
Advertising (SIC 7319)

Largest Magazine Advertisers - 1997

Spending is shown in millions of dollars for the first 11 months of the year.

General Motors	$ 535
Procter & Gamble	333
Philip Morris	319
Chrysler	286
Ford Motor	248

Source: *New York Times*, March 2, 1998, p. C7, from Competitive Media Reporting.

★ 1672 ★
Advertising (SIC 7319)

Largest Network Advertisers - 1997

Spending is shown in millions of dollars for the first 11 months of the year.

General Motors	$ 729
Procter & Gamble	599
Philip Morris	432
Pepsico	378
Johnson & Johnson	370

Source: *New York Times*, March 2, 1998, p. C7, from Competitive Media Reporting.

★ 1673 ★
Advertising (SIC 7319)

Largest Newspaper Advertisers - 1997

Spending is shown in millions of dollars for the first 11 months of the year.

Ford Motor	$ 483
Federated Stores	383
General Motors	366
May Dept. Stores	305
News Corp.	304

Source: *New York Times*, March 2, 1998, p. C7, from Competitive Media Reporting.

★ 1674 ★
Advertising (SIC 7319)

Largest Nursing Advertisers - 1997

Companies are ranked by share of advertising spending.

Nurses Service Organization	4.58%
Florida	3.88
California	3.01
Johnson & Johnson Medical Division	1.89
Medical Express	1.85
Other	84.79

Source: *Medical Marketing & Media*, April 1998, p. 62, from PERQ/HCI Journal Ad Review.

★ 1675 ★
Advertising (SIC 7319)

Largest Ophthalmology Advertisers - 1997

Companies are ranked by share of advertising spending.

Allergan Pharmaceuticals	8.22%
Pharmacia & Upjohn Inc.	6.36
Allergan Inc.	5.83
Alcon Laboratories Inc.	5.74
Alcon Surgical	5.07
Other	68.78

Source: *Medical Marketing & Media*, April 1998, p. 64, from PERQ/HCI Journal Ad Review.

★ 1676 ★
Advertising (SIC 7319)

Largest Optometry Advertisers - 1997

Companies are ranked by share of advertising spending.

Sola Optical Usa	3.31%
Vision Expo	2.43
Marchon Eyewear	2.38
Transitions Optical	2.03
Luxottica Group	1.99
Other	87.86

Source: *Medical Marketing & Media*, April 1998, p. 64, from PERQ/HCI Journal Ad Review.

★ 1677 ★
Advertising (SIC 7319)

Largest Pharmacy Advertisers - 1997

Companies are ranked by share of advertising spending.

Pfizer Laboratories	2.96%
Wyeth-Ayerst	2.70
Novartis Inc.	2.45
Pfizer and Eisai Inc.	1.58
ESI Lederle Inc.	1.44

Source: *Medical Marketing & Media*, April 1998, p. 66, from PERQ/HCI Journal Ad Review.

★ 1678 ★
Advertising (SIC 7319)

Largest Radiology Advertisers - 1997

Companies are ranked by share of advertising spending.

Hitachi Medical Corporation	4.32%
Nycomed Inc.	3.83
Siemens Medical Systems Inc.	3.46
Bracco Diagnostics	3.31
GE Medical Systems	3.25

Source: *Medical Marketing & Media*, April 1998, p. 66, from PERQ/HCI Journal Ad Review.

★ 1679 ★
Advertising (SIC 7319)

Largest Telecom Firms by Ad Spending - 1997

AT&T Corp.

MCI Communications Corp.

Sprint Corp.

Bell Atlantic Corp.

SBC Communications Corp.

Marketers are ranked by spending in millions of dollars.

AT&T Corp.	$ 476
MCI Communications Corp.	455
Sprint Corp.	291
Bell Atlantic Corp.	210
SBC Communications Corp.	195

Source: *Advertising Age*, May 4, 1998, p. 20, from Competitive Media Reporting.

★ 1680 ★
Advertising (SIC 7319)

Sportswear Companies by Ad Spending - 1996

The table ranks companies by advertising expenditures in thousands of dollars. Companies shown include sportswear, bathing suits, beach wear, and exercise/athletic wear producers.

Levi Strauss Assoc. Inc.	$ 120,057.8
VF Corp.	67,157.1
Nike Inc.	22,349.7
Sara Lee Corp.	16,448.4
Gap Inc.	15,868.8
Polo/Ralph Lauren Corp.	14,987.0
Russell Corp.	12,482.6
Calvin Klein Ind. Inc.	9,998.1
Guess Inc.	8,400.2
Farley Ind.	8,235.0

Source: *Sporting Goods Dealer*, July 1997, p. 35, from Competitive Media Reporting and Publishers Information Bureau.

★ 1681 ★
Advertising (SIC 7319)

Top Ad Firms for Business Publications - 1997

Firms are ranked by ad billings in millions of dollars.

Ammirati Puris Lintas	$ 105.6
Saatchi & Saatchi	104.5
Ogilvy & Mather Worldwide	98.1
Bernard Hodes Group	78.0
McCann-Erickson Worldwide	70.4
J. Walter Thompson Co.	45.3
Goldberg Moser O'Neill	35.0
Anderson & Lembke	30.4
BBDO Worldwide	28.9
Foote, Cone & Belding	27.0

Source: *Advertising Age*, April 27, 1998, p. S41.

★ 1682 ★
Advertising (SIC 7319)

Top Ad Firms for Farm Publications - 1997

Firms are ranked by billings in millions of dollars.

Saatchi & Saatchi	$ 21.3
Bader Rutter & Associates	7.9
Creswell Munsell Fuitz & Zirbel	3.3
Rhea & Kaiser Marketing Communications	3.2
Valentine Radford Communications	3.1
McCormick Advertising Agency	2.5
NKH&W	2.5
Freebairn & Co.	1.7
Rubin Postaer & Associates	1.6
WestWayne	1.6

Source: *Advertising Age*, April 27, 1998, p. S41.

★ 1683 ★
Advertising (SIC 7319)

Top Ad Firms for Medical Journals - 1997

Firms are ranked by billings in millions of dollars.

Klemtner Advertising	$ 152.8
Foote, Cone & Belding	40.0
Cline Davis & Mann	36.5
Lyons Lavey Nickel & Swift	35.2
McCann-Erickson Worldwide	30.4

Continued on next page.

★ 1683 ★ *Continued*
Advertising (SIC 7319)

Top Ad Firms for Medical Journals - 1997

Firms are ranked by billings in millions of dollars.

CommonHealth	$ 21.8
Sudler & Hennessey	15.2
Abelson-Taylor	11.4
KPR	11.1
Lowe McAdams Healthcare	7.9

Source: *Advertising Age*, April 27, 1998, p. S41.

★ 1684 ★
Advertising (SIC 7319)

Top Advertisers - 1997

Spending is shown in millions of dollars.

General Motors Corp.	$ 2,226.9
Procter & Gamble Co.	1,703.0
Philip Morris Cos.	1,319.0
Chrysler Corp.	1,311.8
Ford Motor Co.	973.1

Source: *Advertising Age*, March 30, 1998, p. S7, from Competitive Media Reporting and Publishers Information Bureau.

★ 1685 ★
Advertising (SIC 7319)

Top Drug Advertisers - 1997

Glaxo Wellcome
Merck & Co.
Bristol-Myers Squibb Co.
Pfizer
Schering-Plough Corp.

Marketers are ranked by ad spending in millions of dollars for the first 11 months of the year.

Glaxo Wellcome	$ 147.6
Merck & Co.	114.5
Bristol-Myers Squibb Co.	99.8
Pfizer	86.3
Schering-Plough Corp.	70.2

Source: *Advertising Age*, March 16, 1998, p. S26, from Competitive Media Reporting.

★ 1686 ★
Advertising (SIC 7319)

Top Retail Advertisers - 1996

Spending is shown in millions of dollars.

Sears Roebuck & Co.	$ 555.2
Federated Department Stores Inc.	405.2
May Department Stores Co.	398.8
Circuit City Stores Inc.	372.1
J.C. Penney Co. Inc.	294.1

Source: *Shopping Center World*, June 1997, p. 8, from Competitive Media Reporting.

★ 1687 ★
Advertising (SIC 7319)

Top Web Advertisers - 1997

Companies are ranked by advertising expenditures in millions of dollars. Figures are for the first six months of 1997.

Microsoft	$ 15.9
IBM	7.2
Excite	6.4
Yahoo!	3.7
Netscape	3.6
Infoseek	3.3
Ziff-Davis	3.3
Lycos	3.0
CBS SportsLine	2.9
Nynex	2.5

Source: *Investor's Business Daily*, January 21, 1998, p. A8, from Jupiter Communications.

★ 1688 ★
Advertising (SIC 7319)

Top Web Revenue Leaders - 1997

Companies are ranked by advertising revenues in millions of dollars. Figures are for the first six months of 1997.

Yahoo!	$ 24.0
Netscape	19.2
Infoseek	15.0
CNET	12.1
Lycos	10.6
Excite Network	10.1
ZDNet	9.3
MSN	7.5

Continued on next page.

★ 1688 ★ *Continued*
Advertising (SIC 7319)

Top Web Revenue Leaders - 1997

Companies are ranked by advertising revenues in millions of dollars. Figures are for the first six months of 1997.

CMPnet . . . .$ 6.6
WebCrawler 6.0

Source: *Investor's Business Daily*, January 21, 1998, p. A8, from Jupiter Communications.

★ 1689 ★
Advertising (SIC 7319)

Top Yellow Page Ad Firms

Firms are ranked by billings in millions of dollars.

TMP Worldwide . . . . $ 709.6
Wahlstrom & Co. 154.7
Berry Network 146.2
Ketchum Directory Advertising 141.0
Ruppman National Yellow Pages 53.7
D'Arcy Masius Benton & Bowles 40.0
BJK&E Yellow Pages 38.8
Bozell Worldwide 26.5
Saatchi & Saatchi 23.1
Wunderman Cato Johnson 22.5

Source: *Advertising Age*, April 27, 1998, p. S41.

★ 1690 ★
Advertising (SIC 7319)

Toronto's Ad Spending - 1997

Spending is shown in millions of dollars.

	($ mil.)	Share
Television	$ 620	37.92%
Daily newspapers	560	34.25
Radio	140	8.56
Weekly newspapers	130	7.95
Magazines	110	6.73
Outdoor/transit	75	4.59

Source: *Globe and Mail*, June 13, 1998, p. B5, from Media Buying Services Ltd.

★ 1691 ★
Collection Agencies (SIC 7322)

Debt Collection Industry

Sales are shown among the top 6,300 agencies.

Top 10 agencies 18.0%
Top 11-50 agencies 13.0
Top 51-100 agencies 6.0
All other agencies 63.0

Source: *Investor's Business Daily*, September 23, 1997, p. A4, from Robinson-Humphrey Co., M. Kaulkin & Associates, and company reports.

★ 1692 ★
Direct Marketing (SIC 7331)

Direct Selling Market

Data show percent of sales by product.

Personal care products (cosmetics, jewelry, skin care)	38.8%
Home/family care products (cleaning products, cookware, cutlery)	34.4
Services/miscellaneous/other	10.3
Wellness products (weight loss products, vitamins)	9.2
Leisure/educational products (books, encyclopedias, toys/games)	7.3

Source: *Bangkok Post*, September 8, 1997, p. 5, from Direct Selling Association.

★ 1693 ★
Direct Marketing (SIC 7331)

Largest Direct Response Agencies - 1997

Firms are ranked by revenues in millions of dollars.

Omnicom Group	$ 4,154.2
DIMAC	192.4
Wunderman Cato Johnson Worldwide	124.7
DraftDirect Worldwide	118.3
Rapp Collins Worldwide	100.0
Bronner Slosberg Humphrey	83.2
Ogilvy One	57.8
Grey Direct	45.9
Customer Development Corp.	38.6
Targetbase Marketing	38.0

Source: *Adweek*, March 30, 1998, p. 54.

★ 1694 ★
Direct Marketing (SIC 7331)

Top Mail Service Firms - Phoenix

Firms are ranked by thousands of pieces of mail processed in the Valley.

ADVO Inc.	1,050
PSI Group	243
Al White's Mailing Inc.	175
Precision Direct Inc.	160
Val-Pak of Arizona Inc.	143
International Mail Processing	141
Business Helpers Mail Center	94

Mailings Inc. of Arizona	67
Mailer's Choice Inc.	57
HMI Associates Inc.	50

Source: *The Business Journal - Serving Phoenix and the Valley of the Sun*, December 5, 1997, p. 30.

★ 1695 ★
Janitorial Services (SIC 7349)

Largest Markets for Janitorial Services

Data show market size in millions of dollars. Shares of the group are shown in percent.

	Size ($ mil.)	% of Group
Industrial	$ 2,700	18.19%
Educational	1,900	12.80
Commercial	1,800	12.13
Health care	1,600	10.78
Contract cleaners	1,300	8.76
Restaurants/clubs	1,200	8.08
Retail	1,000	6.74
Residential	760	5.12
Governmental	608	4.10
Recreation	608	4.10
Transportation	608	4.10
Hotels/motels	456	3.07
Religious	304	2.05

Source: *Industrial Distribution*, August 1997, p. 64, from International Sanitary Supply Association.

★ 1696 ★
Rental Services (SIC 7353)

Equipment Rental Companies

Companies are ranked by equipment replacement value in millions of dollars.

Hertz Equipment Rental Corp.	$ 1,100.0
Essex Crane Rental Corp.	400.0
All Erection & Crane Rental	350.0
Prime Equipment	348.0
American Equipment Co.	316.0
Rental Service Corp.	250.5

Continued on next page.

★ 1696 ★ *Continued*
Rental Services (SIC 7353)
Equipment Rental Companies

Companies are ranked by equipment replacement value in millions of dollars.

GE Capital	$ 250.0
Carlisle Construction Co.	240.0
BET Plant Services (USA)	215.0
Bragg Crane & Rigging Co.	155.0

Source: *Construction Equipment*, September 1997, p. 58.

★ 1697 ★
Leasing (SIC 7359)
Largest Truck Leasers - 1997

Firms are ranked by revenues in millions of dollars.

Ryder System	$ 5,351
Amerco	1,425

Source: *Fortune*, April 27, 1998, p. 56.

★ 1698 ★
Temp Agencies (SIC 7361)
Largest Temp Agencies - 1997

Firms are ranked by revenues in millions of dollars.

Manpower	$ 7,259
Olsten	4,113
Kelly Services	3,853
Accustaff	2,425
Interim Services	1,608
CDI	1,497
Volt Info. Sciences	1,402

Source: *Fortune*, April 27, 1998, p. 56.

★ 1699 ★
Temp Agencies (SIC 7361)
Largest Temporary IT Staffers - 1997

Companies are ranked by revenues in millions of dollars.

AccuStaff Inc.	$ 781
Keane Inc.	624
Metamor Worldwide Inc.	577
Renaissance Worldwide Inc.	527
Analysts International Corp.	516

Cap Gemini America	$ 434
Computer Task Group	408
Ciber Inc.	407
Compuware Corp.	387
Computer Horizons Corp.	335

Source: *Informationweek*, May 18, 1998, p. 239, from Updata Capital Inc.

★ 1700 ★
Temp Agencies (SIC 7361)
Temporary Staffing Companies - 1996

Companies are ranked by U.S. sales in billions of dollars.

Manpower Inc.	$ 2.94
Adecco S.A.	2.50
Kelly Services Inc.	2.46
Olsten Staffing Services	1.83
CDI Corp.	1.52
AccuStaff Inc.	1.47
Interim Services Inc.	1.10
Aerotek	1.00
Norrell Corp.	0.99

Source: *Wall Street Journal*, November 6, 1997, p. B4, from *Staffing Industry Report*.

★ 1701 ★
Temp Agencies (SIC 7361)
Temporary Staffing Market - 1997

The $88.6 billion market is shown by segment.

PEO services	25.0%
Clerical	18.0
Technical	17.0
Industrial	15.0
Professional	7.0
Medical	5.0
Other	13.0

Source: *Investor's Business Daily*, March 26, 1998, p. A5, from company reports and Staffing Industry Analysts Inc.

★ 1702 ★

Employee Leasing (SIC 7363)

Largest Employee Leasing Firms - Phoenix

Firms are ranked by number of employees under contract.

Americare Employers Group Inc.	10,800
Consolidated Personnel Srvices Inc.	6,000
Sunwest P.E.O. Inc.	5,050
Inter West Personnel Inc.	4,200
Diversified Human Resources Inc.	3,000
Employee Solutions Inc.	2,500
Enterprising Solutions	2,000

Source: *The Business Journal - Serving Phoenix and the Valley of the Sun*, November 4, 1997, p. 24.

★ 1703 ★

Software (SIC 7372)

Best-Selling Software for Preschoolers/ Kindergarteners - 1997

Preschool and kindergarten software is the fastest growing segment of the market for educational software for home computers. Data show the topsellers ranked by sales in in millions of dollars. Total educational software sales reached $512.1 million.

Jumpstart First Grade	$ 8.90
101 Dalmations Animated Storybook	7.69
National Geographic Complete	7.51
Ready to Read With Pooh	7.44
American Girls Premiere Special Edition	7.29
Jumpstart Preschool	6.00
Jumpstart Kindergarten	5.93
Jumpstart Second Grade	5.52
Toy Story Activity Center	5.50
Sesame Street Elmo's Preschool	5.29

Source: *New York Times*, April 3, 1998, p. C1, from PC Data.

★ 1704 ★

Software (SIC 7372)

Business Chat Software

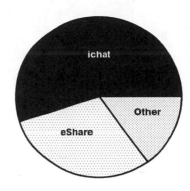

Market shares are estimated in percent.

ichat	55.0%
eShare	30.0
Other	15.0

Source: *Los Angeles Times*, June 1, 1998, p. D1.

★ 1705 ★

Software (SIC 7372)

Business Software Vendors - 1998

Shares are shown based on unit sales for the month of 1998.

Microsoft	17.1%
Symantec	13.6
IBM	9.9
Others	59.4

Source: From the Internet, http:// www.techweb.com, March 5, 1998, p. 1.

★ 1706 ★

Software (SIC 7372)

Chemical Enterprise Software Market - 1996

The market is shown based on revenues.

SAP A.G.	50.0%
Oracle	14.0
J.D. Edwards	10.0
SSA Inc.	8.0
Intentia	6.0
Other	12.0

Source: *Chemical & Engineering News*, September 15, 1997, p. 15, from Advanced Manufacturing Research.

★ 1707 ★

Software (SIC 7372)

Corporate Computing

The market is shown in percent.

	1997	2002
Windows NT	16.0%	43.0%
Proprietary	58.0	32.0
Unix	26.0	25.0

Source: *Investor's Business Daily*, April 23, 1998, p. A9, from Unisys Corp.

★ 1708 ★

Software (SIC 7372)

Corporate Software Sales

Market shares of sales to corporations are shown for November 1997.

Microsoft	59.5%
Lotus	10.3
Novell	4.0
Attachmate	3.3
IBM	2.6
Symantec	2.5

Source: *Computer Reseller News*, January 26, 1998, p. 87, from PC Data.

★ 1709 ★

Software (SIC 7372)

Educational Software Publishers - 1996

Companies are shown ranked by sales of "electronic instructional materials" to grades K-12. Figures are in millions of dollars. In addition to computer software, data also include videocassettes, videodisks, paid satellite TV programs, and Internet-based instruction.

	Sales ($ mil.)	Share
Computer Curriculum	$ 97	18.5%
Jostens Learning	91	17.3
CUC Software	40	7.6
Educational Management Group	40	7.6
McGraw-Hill	37	7.0
IBM	25	4.8
Learning Co.	22	4.2
Optical Data	20	3.8
TRO Learning	20	3.8
Scholastic	13	2.5
Broderbund	12	2.3

Source: *Wall Street Journal*, November 17, 1997, p. R22, from Cowles and Simba Information.

★ 1710 ★

Software (SIC 7372)

Educational Software Vendors - 1998

Shares are shown based on unit sales for the month of January 1998.

Cendant Software	31.9%
The Learning Company	26.5
Others	41.6

Source: From the Internet, http:// www.techweb.com, March 5, 1998, p. 1.

★ 1711 ★

Software (SIC 7372)

Enterprise Applications Market - 1996

Shares are shown based on $13.8 billion in revenue for 1996.

SAP A.G.	17.0%
Oracle Corp.	5.0
Parametric Technology Corp.	5.0
IBM Engineering Technical Solutions	4.0
J.D. Edwards World Solutions Co.	4.0
Other	65.0

Source: *PC Week*, July 21, 1997, p. 88, from Advanced Manufacturing Research.

★ 1712 ★

Software (SIC 7372)

ERP Software Companies

Shares of the enterprise resource planning (ERP) market are shown based on revenue.

SAP	33.0%
Oracle	10.0
J.D. Edwards	7.0
PeopleSoft	6.0
Baan	5.0
SSA	5.0
Other	34.0

Source: *Informationweek*, September 1, 1997, p. 15, from Advanced Manufacturing Research.

★ 1713 ★

Software (SIC 7372)

Financial Software Vendors - 1998

Shares are shown based on unit sales for the month of 1998.

Intuit	75.5%
Block Financial	19.3
Others	5.2

Source: From the Internet, http:// www.techweb.com, March 5, 1998, p. 1.

★ 1714 ★

Software (SIC 7372)

Firewall Software Market for VARs

Shares are shown based on value added resellers' (VARs) sales of firewall software.

AltaVista	29.0%
Check Point	16.0
Raptor	16.0
TIS	11.0
Cyberguard	9.0
Secure	9.0
Other	10.0

Source: *VARBusiness*, July 15, 1997, p. 14.

★ 1715 ★

Software (SIC 7372)

Groupware Market - 1996

Brand shares are shown based on 10.5 million new users.

Lotus Notes	41.0%
Novell GroupWise	20.0
Microsoft Exchange	19.0
SoftArc FirstClass	6.0
TeamWare Office	4.0
Others	10.0

Source: *Network World*, June 16, 1997, p. 1, from International Data Corp.

★ 1716 ★

Software (SIC 7372)

Internet Browser Market - 1997

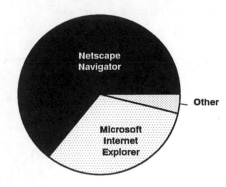

Shares are shown for the 10 months ended June 30, 1997.

Netscape Navigator	64.0%
Microsoft Internet Explorer	32.0
Other	4.0

Source: *Washington Post*, September 30, 1997, p. C1, from Zona Research.

★ 1717 ★

Software (SIC 7372)

Internet Browser Market in Canada - 1997

Market shares are shown in percent.

Netscape Navigator	72.0%
Microsoft Explorer	15.0
Other	13.0

Source: From the Internet, http://www.efni.com/~lightspd/prophead/fig1.html, September 13, 1997, p. 7.

★ 1718 ★

Software (SIC 7372)

Internet Server Software Leaders - 1997

Shares are shown based on units installed.

Netscape	35.0%
Microsoft	30.0
Apache	8.0
NCSA	8.0
Lotus	2.0
Novell	2.0
Other	15.0

Source: *Computer Reseller News*, April 20, 1998, p. 130, from Zona Research Inc.

★ 1719 ★

Software (SIC 7372)

Largest CAD/CAM CAE Software Leaders - 1997

Market shares are shown in percent.

Parametric Technology Corporation	17.9%
IBM EngineeringTechnology Solutions	16.9
SDRC	6.8
Dassault Systemes	6.7
Computervision	5.1
Autodesk Inc.	4.9
EDS Unigraphics	4.7
Other	3.5

Source: *Automotive Manufacturing & Production*, February 1998, p. 55, from Daratech Inc.

★ 1720 ★

Software (SIC 7372)

Largest Computer Security Firms

Firms are ranked by revenue in millions of dollars. Data for Trusted Information Systems is for the first nine months of 1997.

Security Dynamics Technologies	$ 135.9
Check Point Software Technologies	83.0
Axent Technologies	80.0
Secure Computing	48.7
Trusted Information Systems	28.0

Source: *InternetWeek*, March 9, 1998, p. 47.

★ 1721 ★
Software (SIC 7372)

Largest Document Managers

The table shows the market shares of the leading Web-based document management vendors.

Documentum Inc.	14.7%
PC DOCS Group	13.8
Altris Software Inc.	7.9
Information Dimensions Inc.	7.7
Interleaf Inc.	6.7
Other	49.2

Source: *PC Week*, January 26, 1998, p. 80, from International Data Corp.

★ 1722 ★
Software (SIC 7372)

Largest PC Game Publishers - 1997

Market shares are shown in percent.

Cendant Software	16.0%
Electronic Arts	11.0
GT Interactive	8.0
Microsoft	6.0
Broderbund	5.0
Hasbro Interactive	5.0
Activision	4.0
Mattel	4.0
Virgin	4.0
Other	32.0

Source: *Wall Street Journal*, March 16, 1998, p. B1, from PC Data Inc.

★ 1723 ★
Software (SIC 7372)

Largest Software Companies - Los Angeles County

Firms are ranked by number of local employees.

CUC Software	700
Candle Corp.	637
Activision Inc.	380
CCH Inc.	350
CyberMedia	220

Source: *Los Angeles Business Journal*, September 29, 1997, p. 42.

★ 1724 ★
Software (SIC 7372)

Largest System Utility Publishers - 1997

Data are in millions of dollars.

Symantec	$ 115.3
Network Associates	58.2
Microsoft	44.3
Cybermedia	33.6
Computer Associates	19.7

Source: *Computer Reseller News*, April 20, 1998, p. 175, from PC Data Inc.

★ 1725 ★
Software (SIC 7372)

Leading Anti-Virus Software - 1997

Shares of the retail market are shown in percent. Figures are as of October 1997. In the corporate market, McAfee leads with a 47% share of dollar sales. In the distributor market the company has a 41% dollar share.

Symantec	50.0%
McAfee	36.0
Dr. Solomon	5.0
Touchstone	5.0
IBM	2.0
Other	2.0

Source: From the Internet, http:// biz.yahoo.com/ prnews97/10/16, October 16, 1997, p. 1, from PC Data.

★ 1726 ★
Software (SIC 7372)

Leading Corporate Firewalls

Brands are shown ranked by results of a poll of 212 network managers asked "Which of the following firewalls does your organization use?"

Check Point's Firewall-1	20.8%
TIS' Gauntlet	15.6
Raptor Systems' Eagle	11.8
Cisco's PIX	11.8
Secure Computing's Sidewinder	9.0
Other	31.0

Source: *Network World*, January 26, 1998, p. 14, from Zona Research.

★ 1727 ★
Software (SIC 7372)

Leading Design & Illustration Programs Used by Magazine Publishers

Based on a survey of art departments at magazine publishers, the table shows the percent of respondents who reported using each program. The sum of the figures exceeds 100% because the survey allowed multiple responses.

Adobe Illustrator	88.6%
Macromedia FreeHand	23.7
Adobe Photoshop	19.3
Corel Draw	7.9
Other	7.0

Source: *Folio*, September 1, 1997, p. 53.

★ 1728 ★
Software (SIC 7372)

Leading Internet/Intranet Server Companies - 1996

Data show 2.15 million licenses by company.

Netscape	43.0%
Microsoft	39.0
Other	18.0

Source: *Investor's Business Daily*, July 15, 1997, p. A6, from Zona Research Inc.

★ 1729 ★
Software (SIC 7372)

Leading Java Software Vendors - 1997

Shares are shown based on an estimated $58.9 million market.

Microsoft	28.0%
Symantec	22.0
Sun	15.0
IBM	14.0
Visigenic	7.0
Other	14.0

Source: *Network World*, December 8, 1997, p. 39, from Zona Research.

★ 1730 ★
Software (SIC 7372)

Leading Operating Systems

The market is shown for home PCs.

	Jan. 1997	Jan. 1998
Windows 95	37.0%	59.0%
Windows 3.1	33.0	22.0
DOS	15.0	9.0
Other	15.0	10.0

Source: *Wall Street Journal*, May 14, 1998, p. B1, from Odyssey L.P. and Dataquest Inc.

★ 1731 ★
Software (SIC 7372)

Leading Producers of Software Sold to Corporations

Shares are shown based on unit sales.

Microsoft	61.8%
Novell	15.1
Lotus	5.6
Other	17.5

Source: *Computer Reseller News*, June 23, 1997, p. 117, from PC Data.

★ 1732 ★
Software (SIC 7372)

Leading Telecom Software Makers

Shares of the $10.5 billion market are shown in percent.

Bellcore	16.0%
Lucent Technologies	11.4
Cincinnati Bell	8.5
Andersen Consulting	7.1
Bell Sygma	6.6
EDS	6.6
Sun Microsystems	4.0
Hewlett-Packard	3.7
Cap Gemini	3.5
IBM	2.9
Nortel	2.9
Others	26.8

Source: *USA TODAY*, January 28, 1998, p. 6B, from Dataquest Inc.

★ 1733 ★
Software (SIC 7372)

Leading Web Servers - 1998

Shares are shown for January 1998.

Apache	45.0%
Microsoft IIS	21.0
Netscape Enterprise	5.0
NCSA	4.0
Other	25.0

Source: *Network World*, January 12, 1998, p. 31, from Netcraft.

★ 1734 ★
Software (SIC 7372)

OLAP Vendors

Online analytical processing (OLAP) shares are shown in percent.

Oracle	19.0%
Hyperion Software	18.0
Comshare	12.0
Cognos	9.0
Arbor Software	5.0
Other	37.0

Source: *Informationweek*, October 20, 1997, p. 20, from *The OLAP Report*.

★ 1735 ★
Software (SIC 7372)

Operating Systems for Workstations - 1997

Market shares are shown in percent.

Unix	52.0%
Windows NT	23.0
NetWare	6.0
Proprietary/other	19.0

Source: *Investor's Business Daily*, June 4, 1998, p. A8, from Dataquest Inc.

★ 1736 ★
Software (SIC 7372)

Operating Systems Leaders - 1997

Market shares are shown based on unit sales.

Microsoft Windows	86.0%
Apple	4.6
DOS	2.3
Other	7.1

Source: *Business Week*, January 19, 1998, p. 60.

★ 1737 ★
Software (SIC 7372)

Operating Systems Market - 1997

Market shares are shown for the third quarter of 1997. OS/2 has less than 1% of the market.

Windows95 . . . . 63.0%
MacOS 33.0
DOS 2.0
Windows 2.0
OS/2 . . . . 1.0

Source: *USA TODAY*, December 10, 1997, p. B1, from NPD SofTrends.

★ 1738 ★
Software (SIC 7372)

PC Game Producers - 1997

Market shares are shown in percent. Figures are shown based on software unit shipments.

Cendant 15.7%
Electronic Arts 11.4
Microsoft 5.8
Hasbro Interactive 5.5
Broderbund 5.1
LucasArts 4.7
Virgin 4.4
Activision 4.0
Learning Co. 4.0
Others 31.3

Source: *Investor's Business Daily*, May 21, 1998, p. A8, from PC Data Inc.

★ 1739 ★
Software (SIC 7372)

PC Operating Systems

Shares are shown in percent. Microsoft Windows includes Windows 95 and 3.x.

Microsoft Windows 83.0%
Other 17.0

Source: *USA TODAY*, October 23, 1997, p. 14A, from Information Data Corp.

★ 1740 ★
Software (SIC 7372)

Personal-Finance Software Market - Canada

Shares are shown in percent. Approximately 750,000 Canadian households use personal-finance software.

Quicken 65.0%
Microsoft Money 30.0
Other 5.0

Source: *Marketing Magazine*, July 21, 1997, p. 4.

★ 1741 ★
Software (SIC 7372)

Photo-Editing Software Market - 1997

Market shares are shown in percent.

Adobe Systems 39.0%
Microsoft 19.0
Management Graphics Inc. 16.0
The LivePix Co. 12.0
Meta-Creations Corp. 7.0
Other 7.0

Source: *Investor's Business Daily*, April 27, 1998, p. A8.

★ 1742 ★
Software (SIC 7372)

Server Software Leaders - 1997

Data show an estimated 3.3 million units of new server software will be sold in 1997.

Windows NT server 39.8%
NetWare 27.2
OS/2 . . . . 26.8
Unix 21.7
Other 4.5

Source: *PC Week*, June 1, 1998, p. 84, from International Data Corp.

★ 1743 ★
Software (SIC 7372)

Speech Recognition Market

Market shares are shown in percent.

ViaVoice 68.0%
Other 32.0

Source: *Wall Street Journal*, April 13, 1998, p. 4B.

★ 1744 ★
Software (SIC 7372)

Streaming Video Market

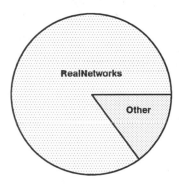

Market shares are shown in percent.

RealNetworks 85.0%
Other 15.0

Source: *Informationweek*, June 8, 1998, p. 102.

★ 1745 ★
Software (SIC 7372)

Supply-Chain Software Market - 1996

Shares of the $271 million market are shown in percent.

i2 Technologies 19.0%
Manugistics 15.0
Numetrix 8.0
E3 Associates 5.0
Logility 4.0
Other 49.0

Source: *Electronic Business*, December 1997, p. 19, from Advanced Manufacturing Research.

★ 1746 ★
Software (SIC 7372)

Top Corporate E-Mail Vendors - 1996

Vendors are shown ranked by millions of new e-mail users. Brands are given in parentheses.

IBM/Lotus (Notes, cc:Mail, and
  Officevision) 8.4
Netscape (Netscape Mail) 5.5
Microsoft (Exchange and Mail) 4.4
Qualcomm (Eudora Pro) 2.9
Novell (Groupwise) 2.2
Software.com (Post.Office and Intermail) . . 1.2

Source: *Reseller Management*, June 1997, p. 46, from International Data Corp.

★ 1747 ★
Software (SIC 7372)

Top Drawing and Painting Software Vendors - 1997

Data represent unit sales.

Corel 37,379
Visio 21,127
Macromedia 20,287
Adobe 16,883
Fractal 12,734

Source: *Computer Reseller News*, August 11, 1997, p. 129, from PC Data.

★ 1748 ★
Software (SIC 7372)

Top ERP Vendors

Market shares are shown in percent.

	1997	1998
SAP AG	36.0%	37.0%
Oracle Corp.	12.0	13.0
PeopleSoft Inc.	7.0	9.0
J.D. Edwards Inc.	7.0	7.0
Baan Co.	6.0	6.0
Other	32.0	24.0

Source: *PC Week*, February 23, 1998, p. 84, from Advanced Manufacturing Research Inc.

★ 1749 ★
Software (SIC 7372)

Top Office Suite Sellers - 1997

Shares are estimated based on unit sales.

Microsoft 70.0%
Corel 26.5
Lotus 3.7

Source: *New York Times*, June 15, 1998, p. C6, from PC Data.

★ 1750 ★
Software (SIC 7372)

Top Software Companies - North America

Data show revenue in millions of U.S. dollars for 1995. Total software sales in North America reached 6.9 billion in 1996.

Microsoft Corp. . . . . $ 7,400
Novell Inc. 1,900
Adobe Systems Inc. 762
Autodesk Inc. 534
Intuit Inc. 503
Symantec Corp. 438
Attachmate Corp. 415
Softkey International 255
Borland International Inc. 208
GT Interactive Software 204

Source: *Smart Computing*, May 1997, p. 92, from *1996 Soft.letter 100*.

★ 1751 ★
Software (SIC 7372)

Top Software Firms - 1997

Market shares are shown based on sales of $22.8 billion.

Microsoft 57.0%
Adobe 4.0
Novell 3.8
Autodesk 2.8
Network Associates 2.6
Intuit 2.5

Symantec 2.4%
GT Interactive 2.3
Netscape 2.3
Others 20.3

Source: *Investor's Business Daily*, May 14, 1998, p. A8, from Hart Teeter Research and Softletter.

★ 1752 ★
Software (SIC 7372)

Top-Selling Computer Games - 1993-1997

Data show sales in millions of units for both the Mac and PC platforms.

MYST 3.1
Doom II 1.7
Microsoft Flight Simulator 1.7
Doom Shareware 1.3
Sim City 2000 . . . . 1.0
7th Guest 0.9
Warcraft II 0.8
Dark Forces 0.8
Sim City Classic 0.8
Ultimate Doom 0.7

Source: *New York Times*, October 27, 1997, p. C5, from PC Data.

★ 1753 ★
Software (SIC 7372)

U.S. Software Security Market

The market is shown by segment in millions of dollars.

	1996	1998	2000
Disaster recovery . . .	$ 236.31	$ 357.51	$ 540.38
Consulting/services . .	192.50	297.31	480.91
Encryption	135.54	188.70	270.36
Firewalls	103.15	153.94	230.49
Digital IDs	005.50	007.59	011.57

Source: *Reseller Management*, December 1997, p. 42, from Zona Research.

★ 1754 ★

Software (SIC 7372)

Voice Recognition Market - 1997

Market shares are shown in percent.

IBM	51.0%
Lernout & Hauspie Speech Products	25.0
Dragon Systems	10.0
Other	14.0

Source: *Investor's Business Daily*, June 8, 1998, p. A9, from PC Data.

★ 1755 ★

Software (SIC 7372)

Web Browser Market

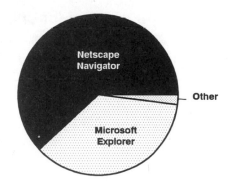

Shares are shown in percent.

Netscape Navigator	62.0%
Microsoft Explorer	36.0
Other	2.0

Source: *Investor's Business Daily*, October 21, 1997, p. A1, from Zona Research Inc.

★ 1756 ★

Software (SIC 7372)

Web Server Leaders

Shares are shown based on a survey of 1,681,868 public sites.

Apache	44.74%
Microsoft	18.86
Netscape	11.11
NCSA	4.42
O'Reilly & Associates	2.87
Other	18.0

Source: *Internetweek*, December 8, 1997, p. 1, from NetCraft Consultancy.

★ 1757 ★

Integrated Systems (SIC 7373)

CRS Market

Companies are shown ranked by the number of CRS (customer reservations system) terminals in the United States.

	Terminals	Share
Galileo	48,921	25.2%
Sabre	2,920	41.6
Worldspan	1,200	18.0
Amadeus	29,470	15.2

Source: *Air Transport World*, June 1997, p. 1, from *Travel Distribution Report* and Amadeus.

★ 1758 ★

Networks (SIC 7373)

Business Intranet Use - 1997

End use is shown in percent. Figures are based on a survey of 3,000 businesses.

Electronic mail	47.0%
Communications	12.0
General business	5.0
Information management	4.0
User support	4.0
Document management	3.0
Personnel	3.0
Research	2.0
Other	20.0

Source: *Investor's Business Daily*, April 7, 1998, p. A8, from Computer Intelligence Infocorp.

★ 1759 ★
Networks (SIC 7373)

Largest Midrange Servers - 1997

Companies are ranked by revenues in millions of dollars.

IBM	$ 2,600
Hewlett-Packard	1,800
Sun	1,300
Digital	628
Compaq	500
NCR	479
Tandem	304

Source: *Computer Reseller News*, April 20, 1998, p. 110.

★ 1760 ★
Networks (SIC 7373)

Leading Network VARs

Value added resellers (VARs) are ranked by revenue in millions of dollars.

CompuCom Systems Inc.	$ 2,000
Vanstar Corp.	1,800
Anixter Inc.	1,675
Wang Laboratories	1,050
CIC Systems Inc.	450
Pomeroy Computer Resources	336
ESSC (Enterprising Services Solutions)	290
Sarcom Inc.	235
Bell Atlantic Network Integration	200
Centron DPL Company	185

Source: *VAR Business*, August 15, 1997, p. 80.

★ 1761 ★
Networks (SIC 7373)

Leading RDMS Vendors for NT

Shares are shown in percent. RDMS stands for Relational Database Management Systems.

Microsoft	40.0%
Oracle	35.0
Sybase	10.0
IBM	5.0
Informix	5.0
Other	5.0

Source: *Digital Systems Report*, 1997, p. 28.

★ 1762 ★
Networks (SIC 7373)

Leading RDMS Vendors for Unix

Shares are shown in percent. RDMS stands for Relational Database Management Systems.

Oracle	55.0%
Informix	20.0
Sybase	9.0
IBM	3.0
Other	13.0

Source: *Digital Systems Report*, 1997, p. 28.

★ 1763 ★
Networks (SIC 7373)

PC Server Leaders - 1996

Shares are shown based on total revenues of $1.9 billion.

Compaq	29.5%
IBM	13.1
Hewlett-Packard	7.7
Gateway 2000	7.2
Digital	5.5
Dell	5.2
Other	31.8

Source: *Computer Reseller News*, September 29, 1997, p. 281, from Dataquest Inc.

★ 1764 ★

Networks (SIC 7373)

PC Server Leaders - 1997

Market shares are shown based on shipments for the fourth quarter of the year.

Compaq	37.0%
IBM	13.8
Dell	12.5
Hewlett-Packard	10.2
Gateway	3.5
Others	23.0

Source: *Wall Street Journal*, June 18, 1998, p. 4B, from International Data Corp.

★ 1765 ★

Networks (SIC 7373)

PC Server Market - 1997

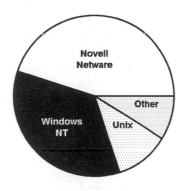

Market shares are shown based on operating system shipments.

Novell Netware	45.0%
Windows NT	35.0
Unix	11.0
Other	9.0

Source: *Investor's Business Daily*, March 3, 1998, p. A9, from Dataquest Inc.

★ 1766 ★

Networks (SIC 7373)

Top Intranet Web Servers

Market shares are shown in percent.

Windows NT	55.0%
Unix	36.0
Novell	4.0
Other	5.0

Source: *Business Week*, January 19, 1998, p. 60, from Zona Research.

★ 1767 ★

Networks (SIC 7373)

Top NT Server Producers

Market shares are shown in percent. VAR stands for value-added reseller.

Compaq	35.6%
Hewlett-Packard	8.7
Dell	8.2
Gateway 2000	5.1
IBM	4.9
DEC	2.6
Micron	2.2
BYO VARs	35.6

Source: *Computer Reseller News*, February 16, 1998, p. 117, from Computer Intelligence Inc.

★ 1768 ★

Networks (SIC 7373)

Top Server Vendors - 1997

Market shares are shown based on unit sales.

SCO OpenServer	33.1%
Hewlett-Packard HP-UX	11.0
IBM AIX	11.0
Sun Solaris	10.9
SCO UnixWare	7.1
Digital UNIX	4.6
Sun Solaris x86	3.5
Other	18.7

Source: *Performance Computing*, June 1998, p. 16, from International Data Corp.

★ 1769 ★

Networks (SIC 7373)

Wireless LAN Market

Market shares are shown in percent.

Lucent	41.0%
Aironet	17.0
Proxim	15.0
Symbol	9.0
Breesecom	4.0
Other	14.0

Source: *Computer Reseller News*, March 23, 1998, p. 87, from Business Research Group.

★ 1770 ★

Software (SIC 7373)

Database Software Leaders - 1996

Market shares are shown in percent.

Oracle	38.4%
IBM	21.8
Informix	9.7
Sybase	6.9
Computer Associates	5.0
Microsoft	4.0

Source: *Business Week*, January 19, 1998, p. 60, from Dataquest Inc.

★ 1771 ★

Information Technology (SIC 7375)

ECN Market

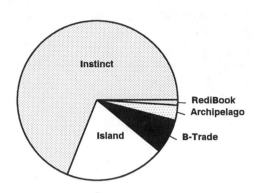

ECN stands for electronic communications networks. ECNs are private trading networks used for trading on the Nasdaq. Figures are for February 1998.

Instinct	69.0%
Island	20.0
B-Trade	7.0
Archipelago	3.0
RediBook	1.0

Source: *Forbes*, April 6, 1998, p. 115, from ECNs and NASD.

★ 1772 ★

Information Technology (SIC 7375)

Federal IT Spending

Spending is shown in billions of dollars.

Contracted out	$ 22.0
Services	15.3
Equipment	4.9
Software	1.5
Personnel costs	6.1

Source: *Electronic Business*, November 1997, p. 23.

★ 1773 ★
Information Technology (SIC 7375)

I.T. Spending in the United States

Distribution of $454.5 million in spending is shown in percent.

Midsize to small business	204.2%
Big business	194.7
Consumers	55.6

Source: *New York Times*, November 23, 1997, p. 1, from company reports and Yankee Group.

★ 1774 ★
Information Technology (SIC 7375)

Information Security Sales

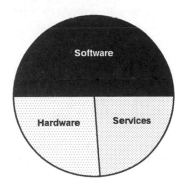

Data show sales in millions of dollars for 1996 and 2001.

	1996	2001	Share
Software	$ 745	$ 2,000	50.00%
Hardware	520	1,050	26.25
Services	340	950	23.75

Source: *Computerworld*, November 3, 1997, p. 48, from The Freedonia Group Inc.

★ 1775 ★
Information Technology (SIC 7375)

IT Spending in the Health Care Industry - 1998

Spending is shown in percent.

Corporate services	18.85%
Operations	15.97
Point of care	13.99
Product management	9.95
Dept. systems	6.27
Relationship management	6.13
Service delivery	4.44

Source: *Integration Management*, June 15, 1998, p. 4, from G2R Inc.

★ 1776 ★
Information Technology (SIC 7375)

Largest Interactive Agencies - 1997

Firms are ranked by revenues in millions of dollars.

Modem Media	$ 36,000
CKS Group	34,800
Grey New Technologies	34,170
Strategic Interactive Group	32,000
Organic Online	30,000
THINK New Ideas	26,418
1XL/BoxTop	25,000
Brand Dialogue	25,000
Thunder House Online	22,500
Poppe Tyson Interactive	22,000

Source: *Brandweek*, March 23, 1998, p. 20.

★ 1777 ★
Information Technology (SIC 7375)

Leading Electronic Data Interchange VARs

Value added resellers (VARs) are ranked by revenue in millions of dollars.

GTE Corp. (Gov't. Systems Div.)	$ 2,260
Entex Information Systems	2,148
Ernst & Young LLP	2,100
CompuCom Systems Inc.	2,000
TRW Systems Integration Group	1,700
Wang Laboratories Inc.	1,051
Keane Inc.	487
National Data Corp.	281

Continued on next page.

★ **1777 ★** *Continued*
Information Technology (SIC 7375)

Leading Electronic Data Interchange VARs

Value added resellers (VARs) are ranked by revenue in millions of dollars.

BTG Inc. . . . . $ 263
Computer Data Systems Inc. 251

Source: *VAR Business*, August 15, 1997, p. 128.

★ **1778 ★**
Information Technology (SIC 7375)

Leading Interactive Agencies - 1997

The table shows revenue in thousands of dollars. Data are estimated.

Modem Media . . . . $ 36,000
CKS Group 34,800
Grey New Technologies 34,170
Strategic Interactive Group 34,000
Organic Online 30,000
Brand Dialogue 25,000
Poppe Tyson Interactive 22,000
Eagle River 20,000
Thunder House Online 20,000
iXL 19,000

Source: *Adweek*, November 17, 1997, p. 32.

★ **1779 ★**
Information Technology (SIC 7375)

Technologies Used in Corporate Training - Canada

Data show the percentage of companies using each technology.

Computer-based training resource center . . 37.0%
CD-ROMs 32.0
Two-way video 17.0
Network distribution of courses 11.0
Internet access for training 10.0
Satellite downlink 9.0
EPSS 9.0
Desktop computer conferencing 3.0

Source: *Training & Development*, October 1997, p. 58.

★ **1780 ★**
Internet (SIC 7375)

Cities Most Wired to the Internet - 1997

Data show percent of residents who used the Internet at least once a month.

Madison, WI 48.5%
Washington D.C. 48.0
Austin, TX 43.4
Columbia, MO 43.0
Boston, MA 41.7
San Francisco, CA 41.0
San Jose, CA 41.0
Denver, CO 39.4
Reno, NV 38.5
Seattle-Tacoma, WA 38.3

Source: *Christian Science Monitor*, April 1, 1998, p. 9, from International Demographics Inc.

★ **1781 ★**
Internet (SIC 7375)

Cities with the Highest Internet User Density

Data show cities ranked by percent of population online.

San Francisco, CA 26.3%
Washington, D.C. 26.2
Austin, TX 24.4
Seattle, WA 23.0
Denver, CO 19.9
San Diego, CA 19.7
New York, NY 19.2
Atlanta, GA 18.2
Chicago, IL 17.7
Philadelphia, PA 17.1

Source: *Yahoo! Internet Life*, March 1998, p. 80, from Find/SVP.

★ **1782 ★**
Internet (SIC 7375)

Cities with the Most Internet Users

Cities are ranked by number of Internet users.

New York, NY 3,475,200
Los Angeles, CA 2,305,500
Washington, D.C. 1,860,200

Continued on next page.

★ 1782 ★ *Continued*
Internet (SIC 7375)

Cities with the Most Internet Users

Cities are ranked by number of Internet users.

San Francisco, CA	1,709,500
Chicago, IL	1,530,080
Boston, MA	1,136,690
Philadelphia, PA	1,026,000
Detroit, MI	781,440
Dallas, TX	769,500
Seattle, WA	752,100

Source: *Yahoo! Internet Life*, March 1998, p. 80, from Find/SVP.

★ 1783 ★
Internet (SIC 7375)

Domain Registrations by City

Areas are ranked by percentage of total .com, .net and .org Internet domain names registered there. Figures are as of March 31, 1998.

New York	9.50%
Washington	7.19
Los Angeles	6.86
San Francisco	3.59
Boston	3.36
San Jose, CA	2.92
San Diego	2.24
Dallas	2.19
Atlanta	2.08
Oakland, CA	2.05
Others	58.02

Source: *USA TODAY*, May 6, 1998, p. 9D, from Network Solutions Inc.

★ 1784 ★
Internet (SIC 7375)

How Canadians Pay For Online Shopping

Data show how Internet users pay for online purchases.

Credit cards	85.0%
Check or money order	14.0
Bank transfer	8.0
Electronic cards	2.0
Billed/invoiced	1.0
Other	6.0

Source: *Marketing Magazine*, May 4, 1998, p. 17, from Angus Reid Group.

★ 1785 ★
Internet (SIC 7375)

Internet Access by State

Data show the percentage of state's with Internet access. Access is defined as those 16 and older who have had Internet access in the past month and still have Internet access.

California	30.0%
District/Maryland	29.0
Illinois	29.0
Virginia	28.0
New York	26.0
Texas	24.0

Source: *Washington Post*, May 22, 1998, p. D1, from Nielsen Media Research.

★ 1786 ★
Internet (SIC 7375)

Internet Economy - 2001

The market is shown in billions of dollars.

Business to business commerce	$ 186
Infrastructure (hardware, software, development services)	58.9
Internet access (ISP fees, hosting services)	48.0
Content (advertising, subscriptions)	38.0
Consumer retail commerce	18.3
Financial services	5.0

Source: *New Media*, June 2, 1998, p. 7, from Forrester Research.

★ 1787 ★
Internet (SIC 7375)

Internet Investment by State - 1997

Data show venture capital investment in millions of dollars.

California	$ 1,218.4
Massachusetts	294.3
New York	120.4
Texas	82.5
Colorado	77.8
Pennsylvania	64.9
Washington	64.8
Virginia	43.5
Illinois	36.6
New Jersey	25.6

Source: *Investor's Business Daily*, April 27, 1998, p. A8, from Coopers & Lybrand.

★ 1788 ★
Internet (SIC 7375)

Internet Retailing - 1998

The market is estimated in percent.

Computer hardware	29.0%
Travel	23.0
Computer software	5.0
Books	4.6
Gifts, flowers	3.7
Online brokerages	3.0
Apparel	2.0
Other	29.7

Source: *Investor's Business Daily*, February 26, 1998, p. A8, from BancAmerica Robertson Stephens and Media Matrix.

★ 1789 ★
Internet (SIC 7375)

Internet Service Provider Leaders

Market shares are shown in percent.

America Online	30.0%
CompuServe	7.5
Microsoft	2.4
AT&T	2.3
Local	46.8
Other	10.9

Source: *Internet Computing*, May 1998, p. 28, from Computer Intelligence Infocorp.

★ 1790 ★
Internet (SIC 7375)

Internet Users by Age

The table shows share of users by age.

40-49	26.0%
30-39	23.0
18-24	18.0
25-29	14.0
50-64	14.0
65+	5.0

Source: *Atlanta Journal-Constitution*, February 22, 1998, p. P1.

★ 1791 ★
Internet (SIC 7375)

Internet/Intranet Market - 1996

The market is shown in percent.

Communications	58.0%
Servers	22.0
Content	10.0
Consumption	4.0
Security	4.0
Creation	2.0

Source: *Investor's Business Daily*, April 27, 1998, p. A3.

★ 1792 ★
Internet (SIC 7375)

Largest Internet Service Providers - Bay Area

Companies are ranked by number of accounts in the Bay Area, San Francisco.

America Online Inc. 350,000
Prodigy 100,000
Pacific Bell Internet Services 58,000
Compuserve Corp. 47,710
AT&T Worldnet Service 37,000
MCI 30,000
Netcom 26,000
Best Internet Communications Inc. . . . 26,000

Source: *The Business Journal - San Francisco*, February 13, 1998, p. 22.

★ 1793 ★
Internet (SIC 7375)

Largest Internet Service Providers - Mexico

Compuserve
Internet de Mexico
MPSNet
Supernet
NextGen

Providers are ranked by number of users. NextGen refers to business users.

Compuserve 16,000
Internet de Mexico 12,000
MPSNet 7,000
Supernet 3,000
NextGen 700

Source: *Business Mexico*, 1998, p. 82.

★ 1794 ★
Internet (SIC 7375)

Largest Internet Service Providers in Canada - 1997

Market shares are shown based on 2 million subscribers for the year ended August 31, 1997. "Others" includes about 400 companies.

Sympatico 20.0%
AOL Canada 5.0
PSINet Ltd. 4.0
Netcom Canada 3.0
Others 68.0

Source: *Marketing Magazine*, May 25, 1998, p. 21, from Evans Research Corporation.

★ 1795 ★
Internet (SIC 7375)

Largest Online Services

Data show firms ranked by millions of subscribers.

America Online 9.0
CompuServe 2.9
Microsoft Network 2.3
Prodigy 1.0

Source: *Los Angeles Times*, September 9, 1997, p. D1, from Nesbitt Burns.

★ 1796 ★
Internet (SIC 7375)

Leading Internet Providers

Data show millions of subscribers.

America Online 10.00
MSN 1.85
CompuServe 1.40
AT&T 1.00
Prodigy 0.90
Earthlink 0.60
Netcom 0.60
Storynet 0.33
Erol's 0.29
MindSpring 0.25

Source: *Investor's Business Daily*, April 20, 1998, p. 1, from Jupiter Communications.

★ 1797 ★
Internet (SIC 7375)

Leading Web Surfing Agencies

Agencies are ranked by spending on the World Wide Web in millions of dollars.

Department of Defense	$ 86,178
Department of Commerce	14,079
National Aeronautics and Space Administration	13,532
Environmental Protection Agency	9,622
Department of Agriculture	7,812

Source: *Investor's Business Daily*, July 21, 1997, p. A6, from U.S. General Accounting Office.

★ 1798 ★
Internet (SIC 7375)

Media Use by Web Surfers

Internet	31.0%
TV	29.0
Radio	24.0
Print	16.0

Source: *Investor's Business Daily*, April 22, 1998, p. A8, from Hambrecht & Quist.

★ 1799 ★
Internet (SIC 7375)

Most Popular Sports Web Sites

Data show number of unique visitors.

ESPN SportsZone	5,383,000
CBS SportsLine	4,996,000
CNN/SI	3,564,000
NBA	1,979,000

Source: *The Industry Standard*, May 11, 1998, p. 36, from Revelantknowledge.

★ 1800 ★
Internet (SIC 7375)

Most Visited Web Sites - 1998

The table shows the most visited Web sites of February 1998 by people 12 years and older. Data are in thousands.

yahoo.com	31,286
netscape.com	23,072

microsoft.com	17,901
excite.com	16,524
aol.com	14,130
infoseek.com	13,750
geocities.com	12,576
lycos.com	10,250
msn.com	8,276
altavista.digital.com	7,689

Source: *New Media*, May 5, 1998, p. 9, from Revelantknowledge.

★ 1801 ★
Internet (SIC 7375)

Online Shopping by Category - 1996

Categories are shown ranked by sales in millions of dollars.

	Sales ($ mil.)	Share
Computer products	$ 323	32.0%
Travel	276	24.0
Entertainment	194	19.0
Gifts	103	10.0
Apparel	89	5.0
Food and drink	78	5.0
Other	75	5.0

Source: *Success*, July/August 1997, p. 60, from Forrester Research.

★ 1802 ★
Internet (SIC 7375)

Online Users by City

Cities are shown ranked by millions of online users.

New York	3.5
Los Angeles	2.3
Washington D.C.	1.8
San Francisco	1.7
Chicago	1.5
Boston	1.1
Philadelphia	1.0
Dallas	0.8
Detroit	0.8
Seattle	0.7

Source: *Computer Reseller News*, November 10, 1997, p. 96, from Scarborough Research, Arlen Communications, and Find/SVP.

★ 1803 ★
Internet (SIC 7375)

Popular Search Engines

The table shows the percentage of home computer users who visited each Web site at least once during January 1998. Figures are based on a survey of 28,000 respondents.

Yahoo.com	39.6%
Infoseek.com	19.2
Excite.com	19.0
Lycos.com	12.9
Digital.com	9.7
Webcrawler.com	8.5
Hotbot.com	4.7
Search.com	3.5

Source: *New York Times*, March 16, 1998, p. C5, from Media Metrix Inc.

★ 1804 ★
Internet (SIC 7375)

Top Internet Service Providers - 1996

Companies are shown ranked by revenue in millions of dollars.

	Revenue ($ mil.)	Share
UUNET/MFS	$ 2,543.45	22.0%
MCI	165.00	14.0
Netcom	120.50	11.0
BBN	118.10	10.0
AT&T	116.00	10.0
PSInet	89.90	8.0
Mindspring	18.50	2.0
Other	264.45	23.0

Source: From the Internet, http:// www8.zdnet.com/ zdimag/cyberstats/1997/08/isp.html, September 29, 1997, p. 1, from Zona Research Inc.

★ 1805 ★
Internet (SIC 7375)

Top Internet Service Providers - Los Angeles

Data show the top Los Angeles County based companies ranked by number of customers.

EarthLink Network Inc.	350,000
LinkEasy Network	17,000
LinkOnline Network	10,000
PacificNet	8,000
2The Loop Internet Switch Co.	6,000
Cyberg8t Internet Services Inc.	5,000
DigitLink Network Services	1,775
Netwood Communications	1,500
4Link Network Inc.	1,300
InternetConnect	1,228

Source: *Los Angeles Business Journal*, October 27, 1997, p. 20.

★ 1806 ★
Internet (SIC 7375)

Top-Selling Online Products - 1997

Sales are shown in millions of dollars.

PC hardware and software	$ 863
Travel	654
Entertainment	298
Books and music	156
Gifts, flowers and greetings	149
Apparel and footwear	92
Food and beverages	90
Jewelry	38
Sporting goods	20
Consumer electronics	19

Source: *Los Angeles Times*, January 19, 1998, p. D4, from Forrester Research.

★ 1807 ★

Internet (SIC 7375)

U.S. Internet Use by Industry

End use is shown in percent.

Services	51.0%
Manufacturing	17.0
Wholesale trade	8.0
Retail trade	7.0
Finance, insurance and real estate	6.0
Transport and public utilities	5.0
Other	6.0

Source: *OECD Observer*, October/November 1997, p. 17.

★ 1808 ★

Internet (SIC 7375)

Where We Access the Internet

Home	
Work	
School	
Other	

Home	69.0%
Work	49.0
School	28.0
Other	16.0

Source: *Detroit Free Press*, May 15, 1998, p. 4E, from MCI LibraryLink.

★ 1809 ★

Internet (SIC 7375)

Who Provides Internet Access for Business

ISP stands for Internet Service Provider.

Local ISPs	38.0%
America Online	26.0
CompuServe	7.0
Government	3.0
AT&T	2.0
Microsoft	2.0
Netcom	2.0
Prodigy	1.0

Source: *PC Magazine*, March 10, 1998, p. 10, from Computer Intelligence/InfoBeeds.

★ 1810 ★

Mergers & Acquisitions (SIC 7375)

Leading Legal Advisors - Northeast

The table shows the leading advisers of mergers & acquisitions. Figures are in millions of dollars for the first six months of 1997.

Skadden, Arps, Slate, Meagher & Flom	$ 37,889.3
Simpson Thacher & Bartlett	33,897.3
Wachtell Lipton Rosen & Katz	30,761.0
Cravath, Swaine & Moore	24,090.0
Sullivan & Cromwell	15,777.6

Source: From the Internet, http://www.securitiesdata.com, October 1997, p. 1.

★ 1811 ★

Mergers & Acquisitions (SIC 7375)

Leading Legal Advisors on Corporate Mergers

Market shares are shown in percent. Figures are for the first six months of 1997.

Dorsey & Whitney	1.7%
Skadden, Arps, Slate, Meagher & Flom	1.3
Sullivan & Cromwell	1.0
Wachtell Lipton Rosen & Katz	0.9
Simpson Thacher & Bartlett	0.8
Shearman & Sterling	0.7
Fried, Frank, Harris, Shriver & Jacobson	0.6
Gibson Dunn & Crutcher	0.6
Richards, Layton & Finger	0.6
Other	91.8

Source: From the Internet, http://www.securitiesdata.com, October 1997, p. 1.

★ 1812 ★

Computer Services (SIC 7379)

Largest Computer Service Firms

Firms are ranked by revenues in millions of dollars.

EDS	$ 15,236
Unisys	6,636
Computer Sciences	5,616
First Data	5,235
Automatic Data Proc.	4,112

Source: *Fortune*, April 27, 1998, pp. F-47.

★ 1813 ★
Computer Services (SIC 7379)

Leading Computer Consultants

Companies are ranked by revenues in millions of dollars.

EDS Corp.	$ 14,441
Andersen Consulting	5,300
Computer Sciences Corp.	4,242
Automatic Data Processing	3,567
Ernst & Young LLP	2,100
The Sabre Group	1,600
Booz Allen & Hamilton Inc.	1,100
Litton PRC	810
American Management Systems	800
DMR Consulting Group	650

Source: *VAR Business*, August 15, 1997, p. 80.

★ 1814 ★
Computer Services (SIC 7379)

Leading Software VARs

Value added resellers (VARs) are ranked by revenues in millions of dollars.

Compuware Corp.	$ 614
Keane Inc.	487
Cincinnati Bell Information Systems	480
J.D. Edwards	478
Computervision Corp.	382
System Software Associates	341
National Computer Systems Inc.	331
Acxiom Corp.	270
Cambridge Technology Partners	237
CACI International Inc.	233

Source: *VAR Business*, August 15, 1997, p. 80.

★ 1815 ★
Computer Services (SIC 7379)

Top Computer Service Providers - 1996

Market shares are shown based on $159 billion.

IBM	9.1%
EDS	8.2
Lockheed Martin	3.7
Andersen Consulting	3.3
Computer Sciences	2.9
Other	72.8

Source: *Wall Street Journal*, February 12, 1998, p. B8, from Dataquest Inc.

★ 1816 ★
Computer Services (SIC 7379)

Value Added Resellers - North America

Companies are shown ranked by revenues in billions of dollars for 1997.

IBM Global Services	$ 15.9
EDS Corp.	14.4
Digital Equipment Corp.	6.2
General Electric Capital IT Solutions	5.5
Andersen Consulting	5.3
Computer Sciences Corp.	4.2
Automatic Data Processing	3.6
Comdisco Inc.	2.4
GTE Corp. (Government Systems Division)	2.3
Science Applications International Corp.	2.2

Source: *VAR Business*, August 15, 1997, p. 1.

★ 1817 ★
Security Services (SIC 7382)

Electronic Security Systems and Services - 1996

Firms are ranked by gross revenues in millions of dollars.

ADT Security Services Inc.	$ 993.8
SecurityLink from Ameritech	250.0
Wells Fargo Alarm Services Inc.	241.1
Honeywell Inc., Home & Building Control	223.0
Brink's Home Security Inc.	156.0
Westar Security sub. Western Resources	142.0
Republic Security Services Inc.	100.0

Continued on next page.

★ 1817 ★ *Continued*
Security Services (SIC 7382)

Electronic Security Systems and Services - 1996

Firms are ranked by gross revenues in millions of dollars.

Protection One Inc. . . . .$ 73.5
Westec Security Group 68.0
Rollins Protective Services Inc. 66.0

Source: *Security Distribution & Marketing*, May 1997, p. 84.

★ 1818 ★
Security Services (SIC 7382)

Top Security Firms - Silicon Valley

Burns International Security Services

The Wackenhut Corp.

Wells Fargo Guard Service

Pinkerton Security Services

Pedus Security Services Inc.

American Protective Services

Guardmark Inc.

Firms are ranked by number of licensed personnel.

Burns International Security Services . . . 1,457
The Wackenhut Corp. 872
Wells Fargo Guard Service 817
Pinkerton Security Services 675
Pedus Security Services Inc. 500
American Protective Services 360
Guardmark Inc. 355

Source: *The Business Journal - Serving Phoenix and the Valley of the Sun*, December 5, 1997, p. 23.

★ 1819 ★
Business Services (SIC 7389)

Corporate Training Expenditures - 1997

Total spending reached $58.6 billion. Sales are shown by expense.

Training staff salaries 70.0%
Facilities/overhead 7.0
Hardware 6.0
Seminars & conferences 6.0
Custom materials 4.0
Off-the-shelf materials 4.0
Outside services 3.0

Source: *Training*, October 1997, p. 40.

★ 1820 ★
Business Services (SIC 7389)

Leading Contract Services Used by Colleges

Data show percent of colleges that have privatized each service.

Food service 66.0%
Vending 57.7
Bookstore 39.2
Custodial, academic buildings 22.7
Laundry 22.7
Security, academic buildings 20.6

Source: *AS&U*, September 1997, p. 16.

★ 1821 ★
Business Services (SIC 7389)

Leading Contract Services Used by School Districts

Data show percent of school districts that have privatized each service.

Transportation 40.4%
Food service 21.1
Computer servicing 19.3
HVAC maintenance 19.3
Printing 15.8
Vending 14.0

Source: *AS&U*, September 1997, p. 16.

★ 1822 ★
Business Services (SIC 7389)

Top Retail Interior Design Firms - 1997

The table shows firms ranked by retail interior design fees for 1997.

Pavlik Design Team	$ 25,108,000
Callison Architecture Inc.	23,530,000
Retail Planning Associates Inc.	18,200,000
FRCH Design Worldwide	17,000,000
Gensler	10,368,000
Design Forum	9,000,000
WalkerGroup/CNI	9,000,000
Jon Greenberg & Associates Inc. . . .	7,800,000
P.E.G./Park Architects, P.C.	7,000,000
AAD	6,800,000
Bergmeyer Associates Inc.	6,500,000
JPRA Architects	6,500,000

Source: *VM + SD*, February 1998, p. 56.

★ 1823 ★
Conventions (SIC 7389)

Largest Bay Area Conventions - 1998

Data show attendance.

American Dental Association	55,000
American Academy of Family Physicians	16,000
Design Automation Conference	15,000
Experimental Biology Convention . . .	14,000
Direct Marketing Association	12,700

Source: *San Francisco Business Times*, March 13, 1998, p. 25.

★ 1824 ★
Conventions (SIC 7389)

Largest Conventions in Chicago, IL

Events are ranked by attendance.

National Restaurant Show	103,946
Print/Converflex	96,107
World Sports Expo	85,031
NPE-Plastics Expo and Conference . . .	82,634
National Hardware Show	72,300
National Manufacturing Week	65,000

Source: *Crain's Chicago Business*, March 30, 1998, p. 17.

★ 1825 ★
Conventions (SIC 7389)

Largest Trade Shows - 1997

Data show the leading industries for the top 200 trade shows.

Computers & electronics	20
Sporting goods & recreation	17
Gifts	12
Apparel	11
Food & beverage	10
Medical & healthcare	10
Automotive & trucking	8

Source: *Business Marketing*, May 1998, p. 39, from *Tradeshow Week*.

★ 1826 ★
Mergers & Acquisitions (SIC 7389)

Biggest Wall Street Firms by Mergers Handled - 1997

Firms are ranked by billions of dollars in deals handled as of September 25, 1997.

Merrill Lynch	$ 160.9
Goldman, Sachs & Co.	158.9
Morgan Stanley, Dean Witter, Discover . .	123.9
Smith Barney, Salomon Brothers	84.5
Credit Suisse First Boston	66.5

Source: *New York Times*, September 25, 1997, p. C9, from Securities Data Co. and Securities Industry Association.

★ 1827 ★
Mergers & Acquisitions (SIC 7389)

Largest Bank Deals - 1997

Sellers are shown ranked by value in billions of dollars. Acquirers are in parentheses.

U.S. Bancorp (First Bank System)	9.10
First USA (Banc One)	7.30

Continued on next page.

★ 1827 ★ *Continued*
Mergers & Acquisitions (SIC 7389)

Largest Bank Deals - 1997

Sellers are shown ranked by value in billions of dollars. Acquirers are in parentheses.

Great Western Financial (Washington
　Mutual) 7.00
Central Fidelity Banks (Wachovia) 2.30
Alex. Brown & Sons (Bankers Trust N.Y.) . . 1.90
Dauphin Deposit (Allied Irish Banks) . . . 1.40
Montgomery Securities (NationsBank) . . . 1.20
Security Capital (Marshall & Isley) 0.92
First Michigan Bank (Huntington
　Bancshares) 0.89
Collective Bancorp (Summit Bancorp) . . . 0.88

Source: *Wall Street Journal*, July 9, 1997, p. B4, from
SNL Securities.

★ 1828 ★
Mergers & Acquisitions (SIC 7389)

Largest Book Publishing Acquisitions

Acquirers are shown in parentheses. Transaction values are shown in billions of dollars. The Random House and Bertelsmann deal is a recently announced deal.

West Publishing (Thomson Corp.) . . . . $ 3.4
Macmillan (Maxwell Communications) . . . 2.5
Commerce Clearing House (Wolters
　Kluwer) 1.9
Matra-Hachette (Lagardere Group) 1.5
Harcourt Brace Jovanovich (General
　Cinema) 1.5
Random House (Bertelsmann A.G.) 1.4
News Corp. (Harper Collins) 1.3

Source: *New York Times*, March 25, 1998, p. C1.

★ 1829 ★
Mergers & Acquisitions (SIC 7389)

Largest Defense Industry Acquisitions

Acquisitions are shown ranked by deal value in billions of dollars. Buyers are in parentheses.

McDonnell Douglas Corp. (Boeing) . . . $ 14.00
Hughes Electronics defense unit
　(Raytheon) 9.00
Loral Corp. (Lockheed Martin) 9.00
Martin Marietta Corp. (Lockheed) 5.00

Rockwell International aerospace/defence
　unit (Boeing) . . . .$ 3.20
General Electric aerospace unit (Martin
　Marietta) 3.05
Westinghouse defense unit (Northrop
　Grumman) 3.00
Texas Instruments defense unit (Raytheon) . 2.95
Grumman Corp. (Northrop) 2.17

Source: *Wall Street Journal*, July 7, 1997, p. A3, from
Mergerstat and the companies.

★ 1830 ★
Mergers & Acquisitions (SIC 7389)

Largest Financial Service Deals

Deals are ranked by value of deal in billions of dollars.

Citicorp (Travelers Group) . . . . $ 82.9
Associates First Capital (Investor Group) . . 17.6
Corestates Financial (First Union Corp.) . . 17.1
Barnett Banks (NationsBank) 14.8
Allstate (Investor Group) 11.8

Source: *Wall Street Journal*, April 7, 1998, p. C1, from
Securities Data Co. and Securities Industry Association.

★ 1831 ★
Mergers & Acquisitions (SIC 7389)

Largest Merger & Acquisiton Industries

Industries are ranked by value of mergers in billions of dollars.

Financial institutions . . . . $ 24.9
Telecommunications 23.5
Business services 13.5
Machinery 11.2
Computer & ofice equipment 8.5

Source: *New York Times*, March 4, 1998, p. C1, from
Securities Data Co.

★ 1832 ★
Mergers & Acquisitions (SIC 7389)

Largest Mergers in Minnesota - 1997

Firms are ranked by value of deals in millions of dollars. Acquirers are shown in parentheses.

U.S. Bancorp Portland (U.S. Bancorp
  Minneapolis) . . . . $ 8,740
National Car Rental System Inc. (Republic
  Industries Inc.) 2,350
Cowles Media Company (McClatchy
  Newspapers Inc.) 1,400
3M/National Advertising Company
  (Outdoor Systems Inc.) 1,000
Piper Jaffray Companies Inc. (U.S.
  Bancorp) 730
Automotive Products Company (Tower
  Automotive Inc.) 725
Spine-Tech Inc. (Sulzer Medica Ltd.) . . . 618
Measurex Corporation (Honeywell Inc.) . . 600
Ceridian/Computing Devices (General
  Dynamics) 600

Source: *Corporate Report Minnesota*, March 1998, p. 86.

★ 1833 ★
Mergers & Acquisitions (SIC 7389)

Largest Telecom Mergers

Firms are ranked by value of deal in billions of dollars. Acquirers are shown in parentheses.

Ameritech (SBC Communications) . . . $ 62.0
MCI Communications (Worldcom) 37.0
Nynex (Bell Atlantic) 25.6
Lucent Technologies (Shareholders) . . . 20.0
Pacific Telesis (SBC Communications) . . . 16.7

Source: *New York Times*, May 12, 1998, p. C11, from Securities Data Co.

★ 1834 ★
Mergers & Acquisitions (SIC 7389)

Largest U.S. Mergers

Data show value of deals in billions of dollars. The Travelers Group and Citicorp deal is pending.

Travelers Group (Citicorp) . . . . $ 70.0
WorldCom (MCI Communications) 37.0
Bell Atlantic Corp. (Nynex Corp.) 25.6
RJR Nabisco (Kohlberg Kravis Roberts &
  Co.) 25.0
Walt Disney Co. (Capital Cities/ABC) . . . 19.0

Source: *Christian Science Monitor*, April 7, 1998, p. 10, from Associated Press.

★ 1835 ★
Mergers & Acquisitions (SIC 7389)

Leading M&A Advisors to the Utilities Industry - 1997

Shares are shown in percent.

Morgan Stanley 43.0%
Merrill Lynch 41.6
Salomon Smith Barney 38.0
Credit Suisse First Boston 18.3
SBC Warburg 15.0
Bear Stearns 14.0
Goldman Sachs 11.9
Petri Parkman 9.2
Blackstone 4.6
Chase Manhattan 3.1

Source: *American Banker*, January 14, 1998, p. 14, from Securities Data.

★ 1836 ★
Mergers & Acquisitions (SIC 7389)

Leading M&A Thrift Advisors - 1997

Firms are ranked by value of announced deals in millions of dollars. Figures are for the first six months of 1997.

Merrill Lynch & Co. . . . . $ 8,688.7
Lehman Brothers 7,654.2
Keefe, Bruyette & Woods Inc. 1,501.2
Sandler O'Neill & Partners 1,271.8
McDonald & Co. Securities Inc. 1,092.5

Source: *US Banker*, September 1997, p. 78, from Sheshunoff Information Services.

★ 1837 ★

Mergers & Acquisitions (SIC 7389)

Merger Activity by Industry - 1997

Data show share of total industry mergers.

Telecommunications	9.5%
Commercial banks	8.3
Investment banks	8.0
Electric, gas, and water distribution	4.8
Credit institutions	4.5
Business services	4.4
Oil & gas	4.4
Radio & TV stations	3.9
Hotels and casinos	3.8
Other	48.4

Source: *Fortune*, March 2, 1998, p. 26, from Securities Data Co.

★ 1838 ★

Mergers & Acquisitions (SIC 7389)

Top Advisers to Thrifts - 1997

Firms are ranked based on value of announced deals in millions of dollars.

Merrill Lynch & Co.	$ 11,334.30
Goldman, Sachs & Co.	8,913.60
Lehman Brothers	7,654.20
Sandler O'Neill & Partners L.P.	4,424.40
Keefe, Bruyette & Woods Inc.	3,634.40
NationsBanc Montgomery Securities Inc.	1,136.20
McDonald & Company	1,121.30
Robert W. Baird & Co. Inc.	1,064.00
Credit Suisse First Boston Corp.	1,023.30
Salomon Smith Barney Inc.	915.2

Source: *US Banker*, March 1998, p. 76, from Sheshunoff Information Services Inc.

★ 1839 ★

Mergers & Acquisitions (SIC 7389)

Top Healthcare Service Deals - 1997

Deals are ranked by value in millions of dollars. Acquirers are shown in parentheses.

Healthsource (Cigna Corp.)	$ 1,700
Horizon/CMS Healthcare Corp. (HealthSouth Corp.)	1,600
Vivra (Gambro Healthcare)	1,500
Multicare Cos. (Genesis Health Ventures)	1,400
Renal Treatment Centers (Total Renal Care Holdings)	$ 1,300
Horizon/CMS Nursing Homes (Integrated Health Services)	1,200
American Medical Response (Laidlaw)	1,100
Living Centers of America (GranCare)	1,100
Value Health (Columbia/HCA Healthcare Corp.)	1,100
RoTech Medical Corp. (Integrated Health Services)	858

Source: *Modern Physician*, February 1998, p. 9, from Irving Levin Associates.

★ 1840 ★

Mergers & Acquisitions (SIC 7389)

Top Investment Bank Mergers - 1997

Acquisitions are shown ranked by deal value in billions of dollars. Acquirers are shown in parentheses.

Morgan Stanley (Dean Witter)	$ 10.4
Salomon Brothers (Travelers Group)	9.0
Alex Brown (Bankers Trust)	1.6
Quick & Reilly (Fleet Financial)	1.6
Montgomery Securities (NationsBank)	1.2
Dillon Read (SBC Warburg)	0.6
Robertson Stephens (BankAmerica)	0.5
Wheat First Butcher (First Union)	0.5
CIBC (Oppenheimer)	0.5

Source: *Financial Times*, September 25, 1997, p. 13.

★ 1841 ★

Mergers & Acquisitions (SIC 7389)

Top Merger & Acquisition Advisors in the Chemical Industry

Firms are ranked by value of deals managed in millions of dollars.

Goldman Sachs	$ 12,770.3
SBC Warburg	11,100.0
Lazard Houses	8,147.2
J.P. Morgan	6,168.0
Credit Suisse First Boston	5,456.7
Morgan Stanley	2,641.3
Merrill Lynch	2,298.0
Dresdner Kleinwort Benson	1,731.3
Dillon, Read	1,100.0
Schroders	600.0

Continued on next page.

★ 1841 ★ *Continued*

Mergers & Acquisitions (SIC 7389)

Top Merger & Acquisition Advisors in the Chemical Industry

Firms are ranked by value of deals managed in millions of dollars.

Deutsche Morgan Grenfell	$ 150.0
Citibank	100.0
ING Barings	22.3
Coopers & Lybrand	15.8
Strand Partners	15.8

Source: *Chemical Week*, September 10, 1997, p. 24, from Securities Data Corp.

★ 1842 ★

Mergers & Acquisitions (SIC 7389)

Top Merger Advisers - 1997

Firms are ranked based on value of announced deals in millions of dollars.

Merrill Lynch & Co.	$ 45,462.6
Morgan Stanley Dean Witter Discover	37,642.4
Credit Suisse First Boston Corp.	36,356.7
JP Morgan Securities	36,036.1
Goldman, Sachs & Co.	34,494.1
NationsBanc Montgomery Securities Inc.	24,242.5
Keefe, Bruyette & Woods Inc.	11,092.7

Source: *US Banker*, March 1998, p. 73, from Sheshunoff Information Services Inc.

★ 1843 ★

Mergers & Acquisitions (SIC 7389)

Top Merger Firms - 1997

Firms are ranked by value of deals handled in billions of dollars.

Merrill Lynch	$ 267
Goldman Sachs	232
Morgan Stanley	208
Salomon Smith Barney	189
Lehman Bros.	136
Lazard Freres	126
Credit Suisse First Boston	113
JP Morgan	113
Bear Stearns	87
Donaldson Lufkin & Jenrette	70

Source: *USA TODAY*, January 2, 1998, p. 6B, from Securities Data.

★ 1844 ★

Mergers & Acquisitions (SIC 7389)

Top Mergers & Acquisitions Advisers - 1997

Firms are ranked by value of deals completed in millions of dollars.

Merrill Lynch	$ 207,219.7
Morgan Stanley	196,085.7
Goldman Sachs	185,518.5
Salomon Smith Barney	106,290.8
Credit Suisse First Boston	93,622.0
Bear Stearns	78,140.5
Lazard Houses	68,298.9
Donaldson Lufkin & Jenrette	58,465.4
J.P. Morgan	57,507.1
Lehman Brothers	51,093.9

Source: *Financial Times*, January 23, 1998, p. 2, from IFR Securities Data.

★ 1845 ★
Mergers & Acquisitions (SIC 7389)

Top Mergers in the Business Service Industry - 1997

Firms are ranked by value of deal in millions of dollars. Acquirers are shown in parentheses.

ADT Ltd. (Tyco International Ltd.) . . $ 5,269.1
PHH Corp. (HFS Inc.) 1,809.5
Pioneer Hi-Bred International (DuPont
   Co.) 1,705.6
Network General Corp. (McAfee
   Associates Inc.) 1,142.5
Prime Service Inc. (Northrop Grumman
   Corp.) 1,027.5

Source: *Mergers & Acquisitions*, March/April 1998, p. 53.

★ 1846 ★
Mergers & Acquisitions (SIC 7389)

Top Mergers in the Computer Software Industry - 1997

Firms are ranked by value of deal in millions of dollars. Acquirers are shown in parentheses.

Cooper & Chyan Technology Inc.
   (Cadence Design Systems Inc.) . . . . $ 474.8
Bellcorp (Science Applications
   International Corp.) 473.7
Epic Design Technology Inc. (Synopsys
   Inc.) 455.4
Computer Data Systems Inc. (Affiliated
   Computer Services) 383.7
SolidWorks Corp. (Dassault Systems) . . . 288.0

Source: *Mergers & Acquisitions*, March/April 1998, p. 53.

★ 1847 ★
Mergers & Acquisitions (SIC 7389)

Top Mergers in the Health Service Industry - 1997

Firms are ranked by value of deal in millions of dollars. Acquirers are shown in parentheses.

OrNda HealthCorp. (Tenet Healthcare
   Corp.) . . . . $ 3,123.4
FHP International Corp. (PacifiCare
   Health Systems Inc.) 2,000.1
Vivra Inc. (Incentive AB) 1,660.5
Healthsource Inc. (CIGNA Corp.) 1,652.7

Source: *Mergers & Acquisitions*, March/April 1998, p. 53.

★ 1848 ★
Mergers & Acquisitions (SIC 7389)

Top Mergers in the Machine Industry - 1997

Firms are ranked by value of deal in millions of dollars. Acquirers are shown in parentheses.

Thermo King Corp. (Ingersoll-Rand Co.) $ 2,560.0
Rank Xerox (Xerox Corp.) 1,632.0
Greenfield Industries Inc. (Kennametal
   Inc.) 957.0
Goulds Pumps Inc. (ITT Industries Inc.) . 922.1
United Defense (Carlyle Group) 850.0

Source: *Mergers & Acquisitions*, March/April 1998, p. 53.

★ 1849 ★
Mergers & Acquisitions (SIC 7389)

Top Mergers in the Petroleum Industry - 1997

Firms are ranked by value of deal in millions of dollars. Acquirers are shown in parentheses.

PanEnergy Corp. (Duke Power Co.) . . $ 7,666.8
NorAm Energy Corp. (Houston
   Industries Inc.) 3,648.8
Louisiana Land & Exploration
   (Burlington Resources Inc.) 2,954.3
Reading & Bates Corp. (Falcon Drilling
   Co.) 2,587.0
Monterey Resources Inc. (Texaco Inc.) . . 1,435.3
Valero Energy Corp. (PG&E Corp.) . . . 1,408.3
Chauvco Resources Ltd. (Pioneer
   Natural Resources Co.) 1,200.0

Source: *Mergers & Acquisitions*, March/April 1998, p. 53.

★ 1850 ★
Mergers & Acquisitions (SIC 7389)

Top U.S. Deals

Data show the value of deals in billions of dollars. Acquirers are shown in parentheses.

MCI (WorldCom) . . . . $ 30.0
Nynex (Bell Atlantic) 25.6
RJR Nabisco (Kohlberg Kravis Roberts) . . 25.0
Capital Cities/ABC (Walt Disney) 19.0
Pacific Telesis Group (SBC
   Communications) 16.7

Source: *USA TODAY*, October 2, 1997, p. B1.

SIC 75 - Auto Repair, Services, and Parking

★ 1851 ★

Auto Rental (SIC 7514)

Airport Car Rental Market - Atlanta, GA

Shares are shown based on airport car rental revenues by both on-airport and off-airport firms, as reported to local airport authorities. Data are for July 1, 1995, through June 30, 1996.

Hertz	29.7%
Avis	21.8
National	15.0
Alamo	14.2
Budget	11.1
Dollar	2.9
Other	5.3

Source: *Travel Weekly*, May 5, 1997, p. 33, from *Auto Rental News*.

★ 1852 ★

Auto Rental (SIC 7514)

Airport Car Rental Market - Chicago O'Hare

Shares are shown based on airport car rental revenues by both on-airport and off-airport firms, as reported to local airport authorities. Data are for July 1, 1995, through June 30, 1996.

Hertz	30.9%
Avis	25.8
National	14.9
Alamo	12.5
Budget	11.2
Dollar	4.7

Source: *Travel Weekly*, May 5, 1997, p. 33, from *Auto Rental News*.

★ 1853 ★

Auto Rental (SIC 7514)

Airport Car Rental Market - Los Angeles, CA

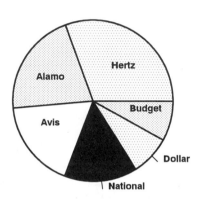

Shares are shown based on airport car rental revenues by both on-airport and off-airport firms, as reported to local airport authorities. Data are for July 1, 1995, through June 30, 1996.

Hertz	31.4%
Alamo	20.5
Avis	17.6
National	15.1
Dollar	7.9
Budget	7.6

Source: *Travel Weekly*, May 5, 1997, p. 33, from *Auto Rental News*.

★ 1854 ★

Auto Rental (SIC 7514)

Airport Car Rental Market - San Diego, CA

Shares are shown based on airport car rental revenues by both on-airport and off-airport firms, as reported to local airport authorities. Data are for July 1, 1995, through June 30, 1996.

Hertz	29.4%
Avis	20.9
Alamo	19.2
National	17.0
Budget	9.0
Dollar	4.5

Source: *Travel Weekly*, May 5, 1997, p. 33, from *Auto Rental News*.

★ 1855 ★

Auto Rental (SIC 7514)

Airport Car Rental Market - Seattle, WA

Shares are shown based on airport car rental revenues by both on-airport and off-airport firms, as reported to local airport authorities. Data are for July 1, 1995, through June 30, 1996.

Hertz	26.2%
Avis	22.4
Alamo	17.2
National	12.6
Budget	11.3
Dollar	4.9
Other	5.4

Source: *Travel Weekly*, May 5, 1997, p. 33, from *Auto Rental News*.

★ 1856 ★

Auto Rental (SIC 7514)

Top Airports for Car Rentals - 1996

Airports are ranked by revenue from car rentals in millions of dollars.

Orlando, FL	$ 344.6
Los Angeles, FL	320.6
Miami, FL	265.7
San Francisco, CA	257.3
Dallas/Ft. Worth, TX	239.6
Atlanta, GA	207.3
Phoenix, AZ	193.9
Denver, CO	176.0
Chicago (O'Hare), IL	170.7
Boston, MA	162.5

Source: *Travel Weekly*, May 26, 1997, p. 25, from *Auto Rental News*.

★ 1857 ★

Leasing (SIC 7515)

Vehicle Leasing in Canada

Market shares are shown in percent.

Vehicle manufacturers	80.2%
Auto dealers	10.1
Commercial companies	9.7

Source: *Globe and Mail*, June 8, 1998, p. B6, from Vertex Consultants Inc.

★ 1858 ★

Parking Lots (SIC 7521)

Parking Space Operators

There are 5 million privately run parking spaces. "Five firms" refers to APCOA, Allright, Standard Parking and Diamond Parking.

Central Parking	18.6%
Five firms	16.0
1,000 independents	65.4

Source: *Investor's Business Daily*, April 7, 1998, p. A4, from company reports.

★ 1859 ★
Auto Body Repair (SIC 7530)

Collision Repair Work

Data show the types of parts used in collision repair. OEM stands for original equipment manufacturer.

OEM	80.0%
Non-certified, non-OEM	12.0
Recycled OEM	5.0
CAPA-certified	3.0

Source: *Automotive Body Repair*, June 1998, p. 22, from Certified Aftermarket Parts Association.

★ 1860 ★
Auto Repair Services (SIC 7530)

Auto Repair Service Market by Outlet

The market is shown in percent.

Independent body repair shops	77.3%
New car dealerships	19.6
Franchised body repair shops	2.1
Used car dealerships	0.9
Other	0.1

Source: *BodyShop Business*, June 1997, p. 28.

★ 1861 ★
Retreading Shops (SIC 7534)

Largest Off-the-Road Tire Retreading Shops in North America - 1996

Brad Ragan Inc.	
NRI Inc.	
Purcell Tire & Rubber Co.	
Fletcher's Cobre Tire	
Shrader's Inc.	

Companies are ranked by millions of pounds of rubber consumed.

Brad Ragan Inc.	8.00
NRI Inc.	7.61
Purcell Tire & Rubber Co.	5.50
Fletcher's Cobre Tire	4.00
Shrader's Inc.	3.30

Source: *Tire Business*, December 8, 1997, p. 22.

★ 1862 ★
Retreading Shops (SIC 7534)

Largest Passenger/Light Truck Retreading Shops in North America - 1996

Companies are ranked by thousands of pounds of rubber consumed.

Les Schwab Tire Centers Inc.	4,900
Ray Carr Tires Inc.	1,310
EcoTyre Technologies Inc.	1,150
White's Tire Service of Wilson Inc.	1,060
Goodyear	946
C&J Tire Service Inc.	894
Retread Manufacturing Inc.	625

Source: *Tire Business*, December 8, 1997, p. 22.

★ 1863 ★
Retreading Shops (SIC 7534)

Largest Truck Retreading Shops in North America - 1996

Companies are ranked by millions of pounds of rubber consumed.

Goodyear	29.99
Treadco Inc.	13.68
Tire Centers Inc.	9.90
Southern Tire Mart Inc.	9.70
GCR Truck Tire Centers	6.84
Purcell Tire & Rubber Co.	6.50
Brad Ragan Inc.	5.90
Les Schwab Tire Centers Inc.	5.82
Pomp's Tire Service Inc.	5.45
Kal Tire	5.02

Source: *Tire Business*, December 8, 1997, p. 23.

★ 1864 ★
Auto Repair Services (SIC 7538)

Largest Auto Repair Chains - 1997

Chains are ranked by number of service bays.

Pep Boys	5,400
Super Shops	425
WSR	392
Grand Auto	338
Double Discount (Tire Warehouse)	225
VIP Discount	184
All-Car Distributors	151

Continued on next page.

★ 1864 ★ *Continued*

Auto Repair Services (SIC 7538)

Largest Auto Repair Chains - 1997

Chains are ranked by number of service bays.

Sun Devil Auto 131
Champion Auto (corporate only) 110
Big Wheel/Rossi 80

Source: *Automotive Marketing*, July 1997, p. 50.

★ 1865 ★

Carwashes (SIC 7542)

Top Car Wash Operators in North America

Firms are ranked by number of outlets.

Petro Canada 152
Shell Oil Company 96
Shell Oil Products Company USA 59
Tosco Marketing Company 56
Wash Depot 56
Sunoco Canada 31
Imperial Oil Company 30
British Petroleum 26
Auto Bell Car Wash 25
Octopus Car Wash 25

Source: *Auto Laundry News*, May 1998, p. 38.

★ 1866 ★

Auto Service (SIC 7549)

Aftermarket Sales - 1996

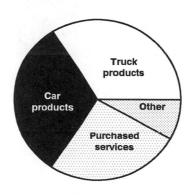

Sales are shown in billions of dollars.

	($ bil.)	Share
Truck products	$ 45.6	34.44%
Car products	41.9	31.65
Purchased services	34.6	26.13
Other	10.3	7.78

Source: *Aftermarket Business*, September 1, 1997, p. 1, from Lang Marketing Resources Inc.

SIC 78 - Motion Pictures

★ 1867 ★
Motion Pictures (SIC 7812)

Leading Film Studios by Box Office Receipts

Data show box office receipts in millions of dollars for the periods from January 1 to August 3 in both 1996 and 1997.

	1996	1997
Sony	$ 323	$ 896
Buena Vista	763	595
Universal	393	516
Fox	475	431
Warner Bros.	545	398
Paramount	369	383
New Line	118	242
Miramax	130	220
MGM	256	30

Source: *Financial Times*, August 22, 1997, p. 21, from *Variety*.

★ 1868 ★
Motion Pictures (SIC 7812)

Top Grossing Films of All Time

Data show box office grosses in millions of dollars.

Titanic	$ 471.0
Star Wars	461.0
E.T.	399.8
Jurassic Park	356.8
Forrest Gump	329.7
The Lion King	312.9
Return of the Jedi	309.2
Independence Day	306.2
The Empire Strikes Back	290.3
Home Alone	285.0

Source: *USA TODAY*, March 16, 1998, p. D1, from Exhibitor Relations Co. Inc.

★ 1869 ★
Motion Pictures (SIC 7812)

Top Grossing Movies - 1997

The table shows movies ranked by estimated gross revenue in millions of dollars. Data are for the year ended December 25, 1997.

Men in Black	$ 250
The Lost World	230
Liar Liar	180
Air Force One	170
Jerry Maguire	154
Star Wars	140
Ransom	136
101 Dalmations	136
My Best Friend's Wedding	127
Face/Off	112
Batman & Robin	107
George of the Jungle	105
Contact	101
Hercules	100

Source: *Financial Times*, December 31, 1997, p. 10, from *Hollywood Reporter*.

★ 1870 ★
Motion Pictures (SIC 7812)

Top TV-Based Video Vendors - 1998

Market shares are shown for the year ended April 5, 1998. Data refer to television-based videos.

Disney	20.6%
Fox	15.6
Paramount Home Video	10.0
Anchor Bay	7.1
Warner Home Video	6.6
PolyGram Home Video	5.5

Continued on next page.

★ 1870 ★ *Continued*
Motion Pictures (SIC 7812)

Top TV-Based Video Vendors - 1998

Market shares are shown for the year ended April 5, 1998. Data refer to television-based videos.

Hallmark Home Entertainment	4.8%
Cabin Fever	4.6
Universal Home Video	3.8
Other	21.4

Source: *Los Angeles Times*, April 15, 1998, p. D7, from VideoScan.

★ 1871 ★

Video Tapes (SIC 7812)

Children's Video Vendors - 1998

The children's video market is shown as of January 11, 1998.

Disney	20.1%
Universal Home Video	15.7
Warner Home Video	12.9
Sony/Sony Wonder	11.7
Lyon's Group	10.1
Paramount Home Video	9.5
Live Home Entertainment	4.9
Anchor Bay	4.0
Fox	3.3
Hallmark Home Entertainment	2.5
Other	5.3

Source: *Los Angeles Times*, January 20, 1998, p. D11, from VideoScan.

★ 1872 ★

Video Tapes (SIC 7812)

Exercise Video Vendors - 1997

The market is shown as of December 7, 1997.

PPI Entertainment	22.7%
Warner Home Video	22.4
BMG Video	12.7
Anchor Bay	10.3
PolyGram Home Video	7.7
Goodtimes Home Video	4.6
Sony/Sony Wonder	3.8
Healing Arts	3.0
Other	12.8

Source: *Los Angeles Times*, December 17, 1997, p. D12.

★ 1873 ★

Video Tapes (SIC 7812)

Sports Video Sales Market - 1997

Shares are shown based on sports video sales for January 1 through October 26, 1997.

Fox	26.35%
PolyGram Home Video	22.11
Warner Home Video	9.86
Orion Home Entertainment	6.03
Simitar	5.65
Goodtimes Home Video	4.06
Madacy	3.75
Prism	3.61
Paramount Home Video	2.64
PPI Entertainment	2.31
Other	13.63

Source: *Los Angeles Times*, November 5, 1997, p. D7, from VideoScan.

★ 1874 ★

Video Tapes (SIC 7812)

Theatrical Video Sales Market - 1997

Shares are shown based on theatrical video sales for January 1 through November 9, 1997.

Disney	23.30%
Warner Home Video	22.04
Fox	11.81
Universal Home Video	11.26
Columbia	10.12
Paramount Home Video	9.99
Live Home Entertainment	2.55
Anchor Bay	2.36
Other	6.57

Source: *Los Angeles Times*, November 19, 1997, p. D7, from VideoScan.

★ 1875 ★

Video Tapes (SIC 7812)

Video Market - 1997

Data show shares of video sales through the first eight months of 1997.

Disney	19.93%
Warner Home Video	19.84
Fox	9.95
Columbia	8.71
Paramount Home Video	8.54

Continued on next page.

★ 1875 ★ *Continued*
Video Tapes (SIC 7812)

Video Market - 1997

Data show shares of video sales through the first eight months of 1997.

Universal Home Video	8.29%
Anchor Bay	2.91
Sony/Sony Wonder	2.50
PolyGram Home Video	2.35
Live Home Entertainment	2.30
Other	14.68

Source: *Los Angeles Times*, September 10, 1997, p. D9, from VideoScan.

★ 1876 ★
Video Tapes (SIC 7812)

Video Sales Market by Segment

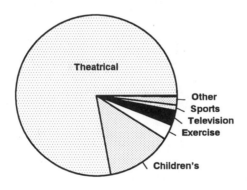

Shares are shown in percent.

Theatrical	78.0%
Children's	13.0
Exercise	3.0
Television	3.0
Sports	1.0
Other	2.0

Source: *Los Angeles Times*, November 5, 1997, p. D7, from VideoScan.

★ 1877 ★
Film Distribution (SIC 7822)

Leading Film Distributors - 1997

Shares are shown for January 6 through November 9, 1997.

Sony	23.0%
Buena Vista	14.4
Warner Bros.	11.7
Paramount	10.8
Universal	10.6
20th Century Fox	10.2
New Line	6.3
Miramax	5.8
MGM/UA	1.6
Other	5.6

Source: *Los Angeles Times*, November 11, 1997, p. D15, from Entertainment Data Inc.

★ 1878 ★
Film Distribution (SIC 7822)

Top Film Distributors - 1998

Shares are shown for January 5 - March 22, 1998.

Paramount	28.0%
Sony	13.5
Miramax	11.7
New Line	10.5
Warner Bros.	10.1
MGM/UA	5.1
Universal	4.7
20th Century Fox	3.5
Buena Vista	3.4
DreamWorks SKG	2.8
Other	6.7

Source: *Los Angeles Times*, March 24, 1998, p. D12, from A.C. Nielsen and Entertainment Data Inc.

★ 1879 ★

Movie Theaters (SIC 7832)

Largest Movie Theater Chains - Canada

Canada has an estimated 1,800-1,900 theater screens.

Cineplex Odeon Corp.	808
Famous Players Inc.	555
Independents	194

Source: *Globe & Mail*, January 17, 1998, p. B1.

★ 1880 ★

Movie Theaters (SIC 7832)

Top Movie Theater Chains

KKR/Hicks Muse

Carmike Cinemas

Cineplex Odeon/Sony

AMC Entertainment

Cinemark USA

Companies are ranked by number of screens owned.

KKR/Hicks Muse	5,347
Carmike Cinemas	2,720
Cineplex Odeon/Sony	2,600
AMC Entertainment	2,117
Cinemark USA	1,754

Source: *Wall Street Journal*, January 20, 1998, p. A3.

SIC 79 - Amusement and Recreation Services

★ 1881 ★
Concert Promotions (SIC 7922)

Largest Concert Promoters in Texas - 1997

Firms are ranked by gross revenues in millions of dollars.

PACE Concerts	$ 21.3
Universal Concerts	8.4
TNA USA	7.3
Magicworks Concerts/Magic Concert Promotion	4.0
Avalon Attractions	3.0
Beaver Prods.	2.9
462 Inc.	1.7

Source: *Amusement Business*, March 30, 1998, p. 24.

★ 1882 ★
Theatrical Entertainment (SIC 7922)

Broadway Show Seasons

The table shows gross sales in millions of dollars for the 1993-1997 seasons. Data are for shows on tour and in New York City.

1993-94	$ 1,061
1994-95	1,108
1995-96	1,246
1996-97	1,281

Source: *USA TODAY*, July 8, 1997, p. D1, from The League of American Theatres and Producers Inc.

★ 1883 ★
Theatrical Entertainment (SIC 7922)

Largest Theater Events

Radio City Christmas Spectacular
Phantom of the Opera
Phantom of the Opera
Joseph and the Amazing Technicolor Dreamcoat
Riverdance
Holyfield vs Tyson

Events are ranked by total attendance from December 2, 1996 - November 24, 1997.

Radio City Christmas Spectacular	1,045,592
Phantom of the Opera	293,101
Phantom of the Opera	182,007
Joseph and the Amazing Technicolor Dreamcoat	152,663
Riverdance	135,022
Holyfield vs Tyson	16,279

Source: *Amusement Business*, December 22, 1997, p. 69.

★ 1884 ★
Entertainers (SIC 7929)

Top Concert Promoters - 1997

Data represent all promotions by gross revenue in millions of dollars.

TNA International Ltd./TNA USA	$ 185.0
Universal Concerts	117.6
Pace Concerts	98.0
Cellar Door	95.9
Delsener/Slater Enterprises	77.5
Jam Products/Tinley Park Jam Corp.	61.0

Continued on next page.

★ 1884 ★ *Continued*
Entertainers (SIC 7929)

Top Concert Promoters - 1997

Data represent all promotions by gross revenue in millions of dollars.

Magicworks Concerts/Magic Concert Promotions	$ 42.8
Belkin Promotions	38.7
Bill Graham Presents	38.6
Metropolitan Entertainment	32.5

Source: *Amusement Business*, December 22, 1997, p. 12.

★ 1885 ★
Entertainers (SIC 7929)

Top Concert Tours - 1997

Data show touring income in millions of dollars.

Rolling Stones	$ 89.3
U2	79.9
Fleetwood Mac	36.3
Metallica	34.1
Brooks & Dunn/Reba McEntire	33.5
Garth Brooks	25.0
Tina Turner	24.8
The Artist (Prince)	24.6
Jimmy Buffett	24.4
Aerosmith	22.3

Source: *Detroit Free Press*, December 24, 1997, p. 6F, from Pollstar.

★ 1886 ★
Entertainers (SIC 7929)

Top Country Tours - 1997

Data show gross sales in millions of dollars.

Garth Brooks	$ 24.1
Brooks & Dunn/Reba McEntire	21.8
Alan Jackson	16.6
Vince Gill	8.9
George Strait	5.1
Hank William Jr./Travis Tritt	4.6
Reba McEntire	4.3
Tim McGraw	4.1
John Michael Montgomery	4.0
Clay Walker	2.4

Source: *Amusement Business*, December 22, 1997, p. 16.

★ 1887 ★
Entertainers (SIC 7929)

Top Entertainers 1996-1997

Entertainers are ranked by 1996-1997 income in millions of dollars.

Steven Spielberg	$ 313
George Lucas	241
Oprah Winfrey	201
Michael Crichton	102
The Beatles	98
Jerry Seinfeld	94
David Copperfield	85
Stephen King	84
Tom Cruise	82
Arnold Schwarzenegger	74
Harrison Ford	72
Rolling Stones	68
Tim Allen	66
John Grisham	66
Celine Dion	65
David Bowie	63
John Travolta	61
Mel Gibson	59
Siegfried & Roy	58
Sting	57

Source: *Forbes*, September 22, 1997, p. 163, from Adams Media Research, Entertainment Data Inc., *Amusement Business*, and Pollstar.

★ 1888 ★
Entertainers (SIC 7929)

Top Entertainment Promoters - 1997

Data show sole promotions by gross revenue in millions of dollars.

Universal Concerts	$ 91.3
Delsener/Slater Enterprises	38.9
Cellar Door	36.5
Electric Factory Concerts/Larry Magid Entertainment	28.0
Jam Products/Tinley Park	27.3
Contemporary Products	25.9
Bill Graham Presents	25.7
Metropolitan Entertainment	25.4
Pace Concerts	23.9
Mama Concerts & Rau	23.4

Source: *Amusement Business*, December 22, 1997, p. 12.

★ 1889 ★
Entertainers (SIC 7929)

Top Touring Acts - 1997

Data show gross sales in millions of dollars.

U2	$ 126.5
Michael Jackson	83.5
The Rolling Stones	56.5
Metallica	32.0
Fleetwood Mac	27.4
Garth Brooks	24.1
Brooks & Dunn/Reba McEntire	21.8
Tina Turner	20.3
Jimmy Buffett	18.6
Phil Collins	16.7

Source: *Amusement Business*, December 22, 1997, p. 16.

★ 1890 ★
Sports (SIC 7941)

Leading Basketball Franchises

Data show the league attendance for the Continental Basketball Association.

Sioux Falls Skyforce	145,794
Fort Wayne Fury	135,076
Grand Rapids Hoops	133,305
Idaho Stampede	127,465
La Crosse Bobcats	100,085

Source: *Los Angeles Times*, June 4, 1998, p. D1, from Continental Basketball Association.

★ 1891 ★
Sports (SIC 7941)

Leading Major League Baseball Franchises - 1996

Data show franchises ranked by millions of dollars in revenue from gate receipts, media, and stadiums for the 1996 season. Media includes all television and radio revenue. Stadium revenue includes tickets, suite rentals, concessions and parking.

New York Yankees	$ 133.3
Baltimore Orioles	105.3
Colorado Rockies	95.6
Cleveland Indians	95.4
Los Angeles Dodgers	88.6
Boston Red Sox	88.4

Texas Rangers	$ 87.7
Atlanta Braves	79.1
Chicago Cubs	76.6
Chicago White Sox	70.3
Toronto Blue Jays	70.2
St. Louis Cardinals	69.8
New York Mets	68.3
Houston Astros	62.4
Seattle Mariners	57.6
Florida Marlins	55.8
San Diego Padres	52.8
San Francisco Giants	51.8
Philadelphia Phillies	50.0
Oakland Athletics	49.4
Cincinnati Reds	45.3
Detroit Tigers	44.4
Kansas City Royals	43.1
Anaheim Angels	42.5
Milwaukee Brewers	41.6
Minnesota Twins	41.1
Montreal Expos	40.9
Pittsburgh Pirates	39.9

Source: *Financial World*, June 17, 1997, p. 47.

★ 1892 ★
Sports (SIC 7941)

Leading National Basketball Association Franchises - 1996

Data show franchises ranked by millions of dollars in revenue from gate receipts, media, and stadiums for the 1995-1996 season. Media includes all television and radio revenue. Stadium revenue includes tickets, suite rentals, concessions and parking.

New York Knicks	$ 99.9
Chicago Bulls	86.8
Portland Trail Blazers	86.1
Los Angeles Lakers	81.3
Phoenix Suns	78.8
Detroit Pistons	77.3
Boston Celtics	64.6
Cleveland Cavaliers	64.5
Houston Rockets	62.8
Orlando Magic	62.8
Utah Jazz	61.4
San Antonio Spurs	59.7
Seattle SuperSonics	55.7
Charlotte Hornets	53.7
New Jersey Nets	52.9

Continued on next page.

Sports (SIC 7941)

Leading National Basketball Association Franchises - 1996

Data show franchises ranked by millions of dollars in revenue from gate receipts, media, and stadiums for the 1995-1996 season. Media includes all television and radio revenue. Stadium revenue includes tickets, suite rentals, concessions and parking.

Sacramento Kings	$ 50.4
Toronto Raptors	49.4
Golden State Warriors	48.2
Indiana Pacers	47.8
Washington Bullets	45.9
Philadelphia 76ers	44.6
Miami Heat	44.3
Minnesota Timberwolves	44.0
Denver Nuggets	43.6
Vancouver Grizzlies	42.3
Dallas Mavericks	42.2
Atlanta Hawks	41.3
Milwaukee Bucks	36.4
Los Angeles Clippers	35.5

Source: *Financial World*, June 17, 1997, p. 48.

★ 1893 ★
Sports (SIC 7941)

Leading National Football League Franchises - 1996

Data show franchises ranked by millions of dollars in revenue from gate receipts, media, and stadiums for the 1996 season. Media includes all television and radio revenue. Stadium revenue includes tickets, suite rentals, concessions and parking.

Dallas Cowboys	$ 121.3
Miami Dolphins	95.4
San Francisco 49ers	85.9
St. Louis Rams	85.8
Kansas City Chiefs	82.0
New York Giants	80.6
Philadelphia Eagles	80.3
Chicago Bears	79.5
Oakland Raiders	79.3
Atlanta Falcons	79.2
New England Patriots	79.1
New Orleans Saints	79.0
Buffalo Bills	77.7

Baltimore Ravens	$ 75.8
San Diego Chargers	75.6
New York Jets	75.4
Carolina Panthers	75.1
Green Bay Packers	74.9
Minnesota Vikings	74.2
Denver Broncos	73.4
Pittsburgh Steelers	72.5
Cincinnati Bengals	72.1
Tampa Bay Buccaneers	72.1
Seattle Seahawks	71.2
Arizona Cardinals	71.1
Washington Redskins	70.7
Indianapolis Colts	69.7
Detroit Lions	69.4
Jacksonville Jaguars	67.3
Houston Oilers	65.7

Source: *Financial World*, June 17, 1997, p. 49.

★ 1894 ★
Sports (SIC 7941)

Leading National Hockey League Franchises - 1996

Data show franchises ranked by millions of dollars in revenue from gate receipts, media, and stadiums for the 1995-1996 season. Media includes all television and radio revenue. Stadium revenue includes tickets, suite rentals, concessions and parking.

Chicago Blackhawks	$ 73.1
New York Rangers	70.4
Detroit Red Wings	65.2
Boston Bruins	64.9
St. Louis Blues	54.8
Philadelphia Flyers	53.6
Pittsburgh Penguins	48.6
Toronto Maple Leafs	46.2
New Jersey Devils	43.6
Vancouver Canucks	42.7
San Jose Sharks	42.4
Los Angeles Kings	40.4
Montreal Canadiens	40.2
Anaheim Mighty Ducks	39.5
Calgary Flames	38.6
New York Islanders	37.1
Colorado Avalanche	36.9
Washington Capitals	36.5
Dallas Stars	33.9
Florida Panthers	32.6

Continued on next page.

★ 1894 ★ *Continued*

Sports (SIC 7941)

Leading National Hockey League Franchises - 1996

Data show franchises ranked by millions of dollars in revenue from gate receipts, media, and stadiums for the 1995-1996 season. Media includes all television and radio revenue. Stadium revenue includes tickets, suite rentals, concessions and parking.

Ottawa Senators	$31.9
Buffalo Sabres	29.3
Edmonton Oilers	27.6
Tampa Bay Lightning	25.0
Hartford Whalers	23.8
Phoenix Coyotes	20.6

Source: *Financial World*, June 17, 1997, p. 50.

★ 1895 ★

Sports (SIC 7941)

Most Popular Sports for High School Girls

Data show number of participants.

Basketball	445,869
Outdoor track and field	379,060
Volleyball	357,576
Softball	305,217
Soccer	209,287
Tennis	146,573
Cross-country	140,187
Swimming & diving	111,360
Field hockey	56,142
Golf	39,634

Source: *Detroit Free Press*, June 12, 1998, p. 2E, from National Federation of State High School Associations and Women's Sports Foundation.

★ 1896 ★

Sports (SIC 7941)

NFL Attendance - 1997

Data show average attendance as of September 16, 1997.

Buffalo Bills	79,139
Washington Redskins	78,270
Kansas City Chiefs	78,169
Denver Broncos	74,969
New York Jets	72,988
Carolina Panthers	72,633
Arizona Cardinals	71,578

Source: *South Florida Business Journal*, September 19, 1997, p. 2.

★ 1897 ★

Sports Promotion (SIC 7941)

Leading Pro Sports Golfers - 1997

Tiger Woods
Arnold Palmer
Greg Norman
Jack Nicklaus
Fred Couples
Justin Leonard
Ernie Els
Nick Faldo
Davis Love III
Corey Pavin

Golfers are ranked by millions of dollars in endorsements.

Tiger Woods	$28
Arnold Palmer	20
Greg Norman	14
Jack Nicklaus	11
Fred Couples	10
Justin Leonard	10
Ernie Els	9
Nick Faldo	8
Davis Love III	8
Corey Pavin	7

Source: *USA TODAY*, May 1, 1998, p. C1, from *Sports Business Journal*.

★ 1898 ★

Sports Promotion (SIC 7941)

Top Athlete Endorsers

Athletes are ranked by endorsement income in millions of dollars.

Michael Jordan	$ 40.0
Shaquille O'Neal	17.0
Arnold Palmer	15.0
Andre Agassi	13.0
Tiger Woods	10.0
Dale Earnhardt	8.5
Dennis Rodman	8.5
Michael Schumacher	8.0
Pete Sampras	8.0
Jack Nicklaus	8.0

Source: *Chicago Tribune*, September 10, 1997, p. 3-1, from *IEG Sponsorship Report*.

★ 1899 ★

Sports Promotion (SIC 7941)

Top Athlete-Endorsers - 1997

The table shows athletes ranked by endorsement income in millions of dollars. Data include tradition endorsement earnings, licensing royalties, exhibition and appearance fees, and income from autograph signings and speeches.

Micheal Jordan (NBA)	$ 47.0
Tiger Woods (golf)	24.0
Arnold Palmer (golf)	16.0
Dale Earnhardt (NASCAR)	15.5
Andre Agassi (tennis)	14.0
Greg Norman (golf)	13.0
Shaquille O'Neal (NBA)	12.5
Grant Hill (NBA)	12.0
Michael Schumacher (Formula One)	10.0
Michael Chang (tennis)	9.5

Source: *USA TODAY*, January 29, 1998, p. 3C, from *Forbes*.

★ 1900 ★

Racing (SIC 7948)

Auto Racing Associations by Sponsor Revenue - 1997

Data show revenue from commercial sponsorships in millions of dollars.

Formula One	$ 790
Nascar	441
Championship Auto Racing	387
Indianapolis Racing League	26

Source: *New York Times*, December 4, 1997, p. C1, from IEG Inc.

★ 1901 ★

Entertainment Facilities (SIC 7990)

Top Amphitheaters - 1997

Data show facilities ranked by gross revenue.

Pine Knob Music Theatre	$ 18,118,099
Universal Amphitheatre	13,998,188
Jones Beach Theatre	12,941,274
Shoreline Amphitheatre	10,955,844
Blockbuster-Sony Music Center	10,925,662
PNC Bank Arts Center	10,561,201
Coca-Cola Star Lake	10,554,692
World Music Theatre	10,048,432
Deer Creek Music Center	10,037,432
Riverport Amphitheatre	9,573,727

Source: *Amusement Business*, December 22, 1997, p. 42.

★ 1902 ★

Sports Participation (SIC 7990)

Participation in Outdoor Activities - 1996

Data show millions of people who participated at least once during 1996.

Freshwater fishing	45.9
Camping (tent)	38.0
Hiking/backpacking	19.9
Hunting (shotgun/rifle)	17.8
Camping (RV)	17.7
Target shooting	16.8
Saltwater fishing	14.0
Mountain biking	9.9
Fly fishing	5.7

Continued on next page.

★ 1902 ★ *Continued*
Sports Participation (SIC 7990)

Participation in Outdoor Activities - 1996

Data show millions of people who participated at least once during 1996.

Mountain/rock climbing 4.7
Trap/skeet shooting 3.7
Clay shooting (sporting) 3.1

Source: *Sporting Goods Dealer*, August 1997, p. 6, from Sporting Goods Manufacturers Association.

★ 1903 ★
Sports Participation (SIC 7990)

Popular Types of Fishing - 1996

A total of 35.2 million people fished during 1996. Data show the most popular types of fishing. People may have participated in more than one type.

Freshwater 84.0%
Saltwater 27.0
Great Lakes 6.0

Source: *USA TODAY*, August 1, 1997, p. C1, from Fishing, Hunting and Wildlife Associated Recreation.

★ 1904 ★
Health Clubs (SIC 7991)

Top Cities for Health Club Membership

| San Diego |
| San Francisco |
| Los Angeles |

The table shows cities ranked by the percentage of adults who belong to health clubs. Data are based on a survey of the 59 largest metro areas. Cities with the lowest rates of adult membership are Wilkes-Barre-Scranton, PA; Louisville, KY; and Charleston, SC.

San Diego 22.5%
San Francisco 20.0
Los Angeles 19.5

Source: *USA TODAY*, September 22, 1997, p. C1.

★ 1905 ★
Golf Courses (SIC 7992)

Top Areas for Golf Courses - 1997

The table shows the metro areas with the greatest number of private golf holes.

West Palm Beach-Boca Raton, FL 1,773
Chicago, IL 1,656
Philadelphia, PA 1,332
Riverside-San Bernardino, CA 1,242
Nassau-Suffolk, NY 1,035
Washington D.C. 1,026
Atlanta, GA 1,008
Houston, TX 1,008
Phoenix-Mesa, AZ 990
Pittsburgh, PA 945

Source: *Wall Street Journal*, April 17, 1998, p. W10, from Golf Digest Research Resource Center.

★ 1906 ★
Amusement Parks (SIC 7996)

Top Amusement Parks in North America - 1997

The table shows attendance in thousands of visitors during 1997. Data are estimated.

The Magic Kingdom 17,000
Disneyland 14,250
EPCOT at Walt Disney World 11,796
Disney-MGM Studios 10,473
Universal Studios Florida 8,900
Universal Studios Hollywood 5,400
Sea World of Florida 4,900
Busch Gardens Tampa Bay 4,200
Sea World of California 3,990
Six Flags Great Adventure 3,700

Source: *Amusement Business*, December 22, 1997, p. 82.

★ 1907 ★
Amusement Parks (SIC 7996)

Top Waterparks - 1997

Data show attendance in thousands of visitors.

Wet'n Wild (Orlando, FL) 1,300
Blizzard Beach 1,280
Typhoon Lagoon 1,260
Schlitterbahn 800

Continued on next page.

★ 1907 ★ *Continued*

Amusement Parks (SIC 7996)

Top Waterparks - 1997

Data show attendance in thousands of visitors.

Raging Waters	706
Water Country, USA	630
Six Flags Hurricane Harbor (Arlington, TX)	600
Adventure Island	533
White Water	510
Wet'n Wild (Las Vegas, NV)	450
Six Flags Hurricane Harbor (Valencia, CA)	400
Wild Rivers	400
Wyandot Lake	400
Hyland Hills Water World	350
White Water Bay	320

Source: *Amusement Business*, December 22, 1997, p. 78.

★ 1908 ★

Fairs (SIC 7999)

Largest Fairs in North America - 1997

Data show attendance in number of visitors.

State Fair of Texas	3,479,425
Houston Livestock Show & Rodeo	1,788,437
State Fair of Oklahoma	1,741,515
Canadian National Exhibition	1,705,469
Minnesota State Fair	1,683,454
Los Angeles County Fair	1,277,250
Western Washington Fair	1,265,171
Eastern States Exposition	1,226,069
Calgary Stampede	1,169,923
Tulsa State Fair	1,165,789

Source: *Amusement Business*, December 22, 1997, p. 98.

★ 1909 ★

Gambling (SIC 7999)

Casino Gaming by State - 1995

States are ranked by casino gaming revenue in billions of dollars.

Nevada	$ 7.3
New Jersey	3.7
Mississippi	1.7
Illinois	1.2
Louisiana	1.1
Missouri	0.5
Other	0.8

Source: *Financial Times*, November 21, 1997, p. 7, from Arthur Andersen.

★ 1910 ★

Gambling (SIC 7999)

Leading States for Gambling - 1995

States are ranked by consumer spending on gambling in billions of dollars. Data do not include games on oceangoing ships or Indian reservations.

Nevada	$ 7.4
New Jersey	4.8
California	2.6
Illinois	2.3
New York	2.3
Louisiana	1.9
Mississippi	1.8
Florida	1.6
Texas	1.4
Ohio	1.3

Source: *American Demographics*, May 1997, p. 38, from Christiansen and Cummings Associates, Inc.

★ 1911 ★

Gambling (SIC 7999)

Leading Types of Legalized Gambling - 1995

Data show $44 billion in consumer spending by type of gambling. Charitable games include charitable bingo.

Casinos	40.6%
Nevada/New Jersey slot machines	16.0
Riverboats	10.5
Nevada/New Jersey table games	8.7
Lotteries	34.3
Indian reservations	9.1
Parimutuels	8.4
Charitable games	3.4
Non-casino devices	3.2
Card rooms	1.7

Source: *American Demographics*, May 1997, p. 36, from Christiansen and Cummings Associates Inc.

★ 1912 ★

Gambling (SIC 7999)

Popular Games of Chance - 1996

Data show the percent of adults who participated in games of chance at least once during 1996. Charitable games include bingo.

Any game	56.0%
State-run lotteries	45.0
Casinos	20.0
Charitable games	16.0

Source: *American Demographics*, May 1997, p. 39, from Roper Starch Worldwide, Inc.

★ 1913 ★

Gambling (SIC 7999)

State Lottery Sales - 1996

New York
Texas
Massachusetts
Ohio
California
Florida
Pennsylvania
New Jersey
Illinois
Georgia

The table shows state lotteries ranked by sales in billions of dollars for fiscal year 1996.

New York	$ 3.61
Texas	3.43
Massachusetts	3.03
Ohio	2.38
California	2.30
Florida	2.06
Pennsylvania	1.67
New Jersey	1.59
Illinois	1.58
Georgia	1.54

Source: *Los Angeles Times*, November 11, 1997, p. D3.

★ 1914 ★

Golf Courses (SIC 7999)

Golf Course Types in Canada - 1996

Data show the rounds of golf played on Canadian courses.

Semi-private	49.7%
Public	31.0
Private	19.2

Source: *Globe and Mail*, April 11, 1998, p. B4, from 1996 Golf Participation in Canada Study.

★ 1915 ★

Golf Courses (SIC 7999)

Top States for Golf Courses

Data show the states with the most golf courses.

Florida 1,145
California 924
Michigan 879
New York 834
Texas 827

Source: *Christian Science Monitor*, April 9, 1998, p. 10, from National Golf Foundation and National Association of Junior Golfers.

★ 1916 ★

Ski Resorts (SIC 7999)

Ski Resort Industry

A series of sales and mergers have placed a number of popular resorts in the hands of four large companies. These companies control 23 percent of the market, based on 74 million skier days logged in the United States and Canada.

	Days (mil.)	Share
American Skiing Co.	4.9	6.62%
Vail Resorts Inc.	4.9	6.62
Intrawest Corp.	4.6	6.22
Booth Creek Ski Holdings	2.1	2.84
Other	57.5	77.70

Source: *Ski*, November 1997, p. 89.

SIC 80 - Health Services

Health Care (SIC 8000)

Largest Health Care Firms in Washington D.C.

Companies are ranked by revenues in millions of dollars.

Manor Care Inc.	$ 1,527.2
Mid Atlantic Medical Services	1,111.7
PHP Healthcare Corp.	232.3
Hanger Orthopedic Group	145.6
Sunrise Assisted Living Inc.	89.8

Source: *Washington Post*, April 27, 1998, p. 35.

Health Care (SIC 8000)

Leading Health Care Networks in Chicago - 1996

Shares are shown based on admissions.

Northwestern Healthcare Network	13.1%
Advocate Health Care	10.0
Rush System for Health	8.6
Columbia/HCA-Chicago	5.3
Loyola University Health System	4.4
University of Chicago Health System	3.1
Other	55.5

Source: *Chicago Tribune*, November 16, 1997, p. C1, from SMG Marketing Group Inc.

Health Care (SIC 8011)

Radiology Services Market

Data show expenses in percent. Market size is estimated to be between $48 billion and $72 billion.

Radiologist	20.0%
Technologist	20.0
Maintenance	15.0
Upgrades	15.0
Film	9.0
Capital charge	8.0
Contrast agents	7.0
Administrative overhead	6.0

Source: *Investor's Business Daily*, September 29, 1997, p. A4, from Tucker Anthony.

★ 1920 ★
Surgery (SIC 8011)

Where Glaucoma Surgery is Performed

Data show who performs the procedure.

Ambulatory surgery centers	48.0%
Hospital outpatient	44.7
Doctors offices	3.6
Hospital inpatient	3.4
Other	0.3

Source: *Hospitals & Health Networks*, February 20, 1998, p. 68, from *Outpatient Procedure Resource Book.*

★ 1921 ★
Surgery (SIC 8011)

Where Hernia Surgery is Performed

Data show who performs the laparoscopic repair procedure.

Hospital outpatient	75.9%
Hospital inpatient	20.2
Ambulatory surgery centers	3.2
Doctors' offices	0.3
Other	0.3

Source: *Hospitals & Health Networks*, February 20, 1998, p. 69, from *Outpatient Procedure Resource Book.*

★ 1922 ★
Surgery (SIC 8011)

Where Prostate Biopsies are Performed

Data show who performs the procedure.

Doctors' offices	69.3%
Hospital outpatient	20.2
Ambulatory surgery centers	5.4
Hospital inpatient	4.8
Other	0.2

Source: *Hospitals & Health Networks*, February 20, 1998, p. 69, from *Outpatient Procedure Resource Book.*

★ 1923 ★
Surgery (SIC 8011)

Where Skin Lesions Are Removed

Data show who performs the procedure.

Doctors' offices	82.1%
Hospital outpatient	14.1
Ambulatory surgery centers	1.6
Hospital inpatient	1.5
Other	0.7

Source: *Hospitals & Health Networks*, February 20, 1998, p. 69, from *Outpatient Procedure Resource Book.*

★ 1924 ★
Nursing Homes (SIC 8050)

Largest Nursing Facility Chains - 1997

Companies are shown ranked by total number of beds as of June 30, adjusted to reflect mergers completed as of November 24, 1997.

Beverly Enterprises	64,124
Vencor	40,869
Paragon Health Network	38,097
Genesis Health Ventures	37,700
Sun Healthcare Group	33,152
Integrated Health Services	26,217
Life Care Centers of America	25,319
ManorCare Health Services	24,335
Extendicare Health Services	20,849
The Evangelical Lutheran Good Samaritan Society	17,645

Source: *Provider*, January 1998, p. 42, from the companies.

★ 1925 ★
Nursing Homes (SIC 8050)

Largest Nursing Homes - Cleveland

Companies are ranked by number of licensed beds.

Menorah Park Center for the Aging	352
MetroHealth Center for Skilled Nursing Care	320
Harborside Healthcare - Beachwood	274
Harborside Healthcare--Westlake	256
Little Forest Medical Center	256

Source: *Crain's Cleveland Business*, February 2, 1998, p. 18.

★ 1926 ★
Senior Citizen Housing (SIC 8050)

Senior Citizen Housing by State

Data show total number of units.

	Units	Share
California	8,043	14.6%
Texas	5,333	9.6
Florida	4,807	8.7
Illinois	3,258	5.9
Pennsylvania	2,744	5.0
Michigan	2,363	4.3
Arizona	1,947	3.5
Wisconsin	1,919	3.5
North Carolina	1,737	3.1
Oregon	934	1.7

Source: *Continuum*, April 1998, p. 31, from American Senior Housing Association and Coopers & Lybrand.

★ 1927 ★
Nursing Homes (SIC 8051)

Largest Assisted Living Facilities

Firms are ranked by number of beds owned, managed or leased.

Emeritus Corporation	9,740
Alternative Living Services	9,467
Senior Lifestyle Corp.	7,307
Marriott Senior Living Services	6,573
ARV Assisted Living	6,300
Sunrise Assisted Living Inc.	5,315
Assisted Living Concepts	4,888
Greenbriar Corporation	4,379
The Fountains	4,279
Atria Communities	4,170

Source: *Contemporary Long Term Care*, April 1998, p. 64.

★ 1928 ★
Nursing Homes (SIC 8051)

Largest Nursing Facilities

Firms are ranked by number of beds owned, managed or leased.

Beverly Enterprises Inc.	63,552
Sun Healthcare Group Inc.	47,103
Integrated Health Services	42,000
Vencor Inc.	40,383
Genesis Health Ventures	39,285
Paragon Health Network	37,365
Manor Care Inc.	24,089
Extendicare Health Services Inc.	20,971
Life Care Centers of America	20,309
The Evangelical Lutheran Good Samaritan Society	17,036

Source: *Contemporary Long Term Care*, April 1998, p. 60.

★ 1929 ★
Nursing Homes (SIC 8051)

Largest Subacute Care Facilities

Firms are ranked by number of beds owned, managed or leased.

Integrated Health Services	6,000
Life Care Centers of America Inc.	5,634
Vencor Inc.	5,273
ServiceMaster Diversified Health	4,916
Extendicare Health Services Inc.	3,657
Sun Healthcare Group Inc.	3,302

Continued on next page.

★ 1929 ★ *Continued*
Nursing Homes (SIC 8051)

Largest Subacute Care Facilities

Firms are ranked by number of beds owned, managed or leased.

Mariner Health Group	1,705
Guardian Health Group	1,700
Lenox Healthcare Inc.	1,556
Paragon Health Network	1,200

Source: *Contemporary Long Term Care*, April 1998, p. 66.

★ 1930 ★
Nursing Homes (SIC 8051)

Largest Subacute Care Providers - 1997

ManorCare Health Services
Life Care Centers of America
ServiceMaster Diversified Health Services
Vencor
Integrated Health Services
Sun Healthcare Group
Summit Care Corp.
Extendicare Health Services
Mariner Health Group
Arbor Health Care Co.

Companies are shown ranked by total number of subacute beds as of June 30, 1997.

ManorCare Health Services	6,665
Life Care Centers of America	6,368
ServiceMaster Diversified Health Services	5,082
Vencor	4,825
Integrated Health Services	3,700
Sun Healthcare Group	3,323
Summit Care Corp.	2,415
Extendicare Health Services	2,407
Mariner Health Group	1,691
Arbor Health Care Co.	1,193

Source: *Provider*, January 1998, p. 46, from the companies.

★ 1931 ★
Hospitals (SIC 8060)

Largest Hospital Systems

Companies are ranked by number of hospitals owned or managed.

Columbia/HCA Healthcare	340
Quorum Health Group	259
Dept. of Veterans Affairs	151
Tenet Healthcare	123
Magellan Health Services	75

Source: *USA TODAY*, November 18, 1997, p. B1, from American Hospital Association.

★ 1932 ★
Hospitals (SIC 8060)

Largest Hospital Systems - Cleveland, OH

Hospitals are ranked by 1996 net patient revenues in millions of dollars.

Cleveland Clinic Foundation	$ 929.6
University Hospitals Health Systems	691.6
Summa Health Systems	333.5
Meridin Health System	333.0
MetroHealth System	271.8

Source: *Crain's Cleveland Business*, August 4, 1997, p. 26.

★ 1933 ★
Hospitals (SIC 8060)

Leading Types of Hospitals

Shares are shown in percent. Other specialty hospitals include long-term acute care, cancer, and surgery hospitals.

General medical-surgical	77.0%
Psychiatric	11.0
Rehab	3.5
Children's	2.6
Other specialty	2.0
Other	3.7

Source: *OR Manager*, February 1998, p. 21, from SMG Marketing Group.

★ 1934 ★

Hospitals (SIC 8060)

Top Hospitals in Chicago - 1996

Hospitals are ranked by net patient revenue in millions of dollars.

Rush-Presbyterian-St. Lukes Medical Center	$ 478.9
University of Chicago Hospitals	466.1
Northwestern Memorial Hospital	405.5
Loyola University Medical Center	374.0
Christ Hospital and Medical Center	341.3
Lutheran General Hospital	334.9
Cook County Hospital	236.7
MacNeal Hospital	235.1
University of Illinois at Chicago Medical Center	217.4
Illinois Masonic Medical Center	212.6

Source: *Crain's Chicago Business*, August 25, 1997, p. 23.

★ 1935 ★

Surgery (SIC 8060)

Cosmetic Surgery Procedures by Region - 1996

The table shows 700,000 procedures distributed in percent.

Pacific	24.0%
South Atlantic	23.0
Mid-Atlantic	17.0
East North Central	10.0
West South Central	8.0
Mountain	7.0
East South Central	5.0
West North Central	5.0
New England	2.0

Source: *USA TODAY*, August 21, 1997, p. D1, from American Society of Plastic and Reconstructive Surgeons.

★ 1936 ★

Mental Health Services (SIC 8063)

Largest Mental Health Facilities in Arizona - 1996

Facilities are ranked by number of licensed beds.

Arizona State Hospital	489
Samaritan Behavioral Health Services	275
Charter Behavioral Health System of Arizona	170
Desert Hills Center for Youth and Families	120
Westbridge Treatment Center	110
Desert Vista Behavioral Health Services	100

Source: *The Business Journal - Serving Phoenix and the Valley of the Sun*, December 19, 1997, p. 20.

★ 1937 ★

Home Care Services (SIC 8082)

Leading Home Care Services

Data show the most frequently offered services.

Cancer	1,334
AIDS	1,295
Pain	1,226
Pediatric	1,074
Cardiac	946
Psychiatric	809
At-risk pregnancy	781
Other	605

Source: *CARING Magazine*, October 1997, p. 8, from *Modern Healthcare*.

SIC 81 - Legal Services

★ 1938 ★

Legal Services (SIC 8111)

Largest Law Firms

Jones Day Reavis & Pogue

Skadden Arps Slate Meagher & Flom

Morgan Lewis & Bockius

Sidley & Austin

Latham & Watkins

White & Case

Mayer Brown & Platt

McDermott Will & Emery

Fulbright & Jaworski

Foley & Lardner

Firms are shown ranked by number of U.S. attorneys.

Jones Day Reavis & Pogue	1,074
Skadden Arps Slate Meagher & Flom	1,048
Morgan Lewis & Bockius	808
Sidley & Austin	723
Latham & Watkins	716
White & Case	700
Mayer Brown & Platt	663
McDermott Will & Emery	624
Fulbright & Jaworski	616
Foley & Lardner	605

Source: *Fortune*, October 13, 1997, p. 40, from U.S. Business Litigation.

★ 1939 ★

Legal Services (SIC 8111)

Largest Law Firms in Chicago - 1997

Firms are ranked by number of attorneys at Chicago office.

Sidley & Austin	386
Mayer, Brown & Platt	384
Winston & Strawn	316
Kirkland & Ellis	308
Jenner & Block	295
Katten, Muchin & Zavis	288
McDermott, Will & Emery	259
Lord, Bissell & Brook	250
Rudnick & Wolfe	214
Gardner, Carton & Douglas	202
Seyfath, Shaw, Fairweather & Geraldson	193
Hirshaw & Culbertson	191
Sonnenschein, Nath & Rosenthal	190
Schiff, Hardin & Waite	186

Source: *Crain's Chicago Business*, September 22, 1997, p. 21.

★ 1940 ★

Legal Services (SIC 8111)

Largest Legal Advisors in the Northeast - 1998

Firms are ranked by value of deals in millions of dollars.

Elias, Matz, Tierman & Herrick	$ 238.0
Foley, Hoag & Eli	131.8
Housley Kantarian & Bronstein	131.8
Skadden, Arps, Slate, Meagher & Flom	131.8
Critchfield, Critchfield & Johnston	102.8
Malizia, Spidi, Sloane & Fisch	102.8
Silver, Freedman & Taff	102.8

Source: *American Banker*, April 30, 1998, p. 28, from Sheshunoff Information Services.

SIC 82 - Educational Services

★ 1941 ★
Education (SIC 8200)

Foreign Students in the United States 1996- 97

Data show the home country of foreign students.

Asia	57.3%
Europe	14.8
Latin America	10.4
Middle East	6.7
North America	5.2
Africa	4.6
Oceania	0.9

Source: *Christian Science Monitor*, January 21, 1998, p. 3, from Institute for International Education.

★ 1942 ★
Education (SIC 8200)

Leading Host Countries for American Students Abroad

Countries are ranked by the number of American students hosted during the 1994-1995 school year.

United Kingdom	19,410
France	7,872
Spain	7,473
Italy	7,062
Mexico	4,715
Germany	3,504
Australia	3,346
Israel	2,621
Costa Rica	2,302
Japan	2,212

Source: *USA TODAY*, September 16, 1997, p. 13A, from Institute of International Education.

★ 1943 ★
Schools (SIC 8211)

Largest Private School Enrollments

There are a total of 4,836,442 students in private schools.

California	569,062
New York	473,119
Pennsylvania	342,298
Illinois	293,038
Ohio	246,805

Source: *AS&U*, January 1998, p. 3.

★ 1944 ★
Schools (SIC 8211)

Private Schools by State

There are a total of 26,093 private schools.

California	3,145
New York	1,985
Pennsylvania	1,846
Texas	1,353
Illinois	1,347
Florida	1,262
Michigan	1,075

Source: *AS&U*, January 1998, p. 3.

★ 1945 ★

Schools (SIC 8211)

Public School Enrollments by State

Total public school enrollment has reached 46.35 million.

California	5.86
Texas	3.90
New York	2.90
Florida	2.30
Illinois	1.99
Ohio	1.84
Pennsylvania	1.84

Source: *AS&U*, January 1998, p. 3.

★ 1946 ★

Universities (SIC 8221)

Colleges/Universities by State

There are a total of 3,706 colleges and universities in the United States.

California	349
New York	310
Pennsylvania	217
Texas	179
Illinois	169

Source: *AS&U*, January 1998, p. 3.

★ 1947 ★

Universities (SIC 8221)

Largest Colleges/Universities in Florida - 1997

Institutions are ranked by total enrollment.

Miami-Dade Community College	50,000
Florida International University	30,097
Florida Atlantic University	19,470
Palm Beach Community College	16,294
University of Miami	13,270

Broward Community College	12,500
Nova Southeastern University	10,700
Northwood University	10,176

Source: *South Florida Business Journal*, November 7, 1997, p. 32.

★ 1948 ★

Universities (SIC 8221)

Popular Colleges for Foreign Students - 1996- 1997

Data show number of foreign students enrolled for the 1996-1997 academic year.

Boston University	4,657
New York University	4,491
University of Southern California	4,183
University of Wisconsin-Madison	3,886
Columbia University	3,807
Ohio State University Main Campus	3,772
University of Texas-Austin	3,403
Harvard University	3,238
University of Michigan-Ann Arbor	3,194
University of Illinois-Champaign	3,091

Source: *Christian Science Monitor*, December 11, 1997, p. 2, from Institute of International Education.

★ 1949 ★

Libraries (SIC 8231)

Largest Libraries - 1997

Data show millions of books in circulation.

Queens Borough	15.3
Los Angeles County	14.2
Cincinnati/Hamilton County	12.6
King County (Seattle)	12.6
Columbus, Ohio	11.9
New York City	11.1

Source: *USA TODAY*, June 18, 1998, p. A1, from Public Library Association.

SIC 83 - Social Services

Child Care (SIC 8351)

Largest Child Care Management Firms - 1998

Firms are ranked by licensed capacity.

Bright Horizons	16,572
CorporateFamily Solutions	14,618
Children's Discovery Centers	14,022
KinderCare Learning Centers	5,622
Childtime Learning Centers	5,032
La Petite Academy	4,300
ARAMARK Educational Resources	4,050
Mulberry Child Care Centers	2,858
Nobel Education Dynamics	2,700
Hildebrandt Learning Centers	1,972

Source: *Child Care Information Exchange*, May 1998, p. 18.

★ 1951 ★

Child Care (SIC 8351)

Largest Child Care Organizations - North America

The table shows total licensed capacity as of January 1, 1998. Data include for-profit organizations only.

KinderCare Learning Centers	143,420
La Petite Academy	100,000
Children's World Learning Centers	74,750
Tutor Time Learning Centers	37,305
Childtime Learning Centers	27,740
Children's Discovery Centers	26,000
Nobel Education Dynamics	18,400
Kids 'R Kids International	16,500
Bright Horizons Children's Centers	15,850
CorporateFamily Solutions	14,300

Source: *Child Care Information Exchange*, January 1998, p. 15.

★ 1952 ★

Senior Citizen Housing (SIC 8361)

Largest Senior Housing Companies - 1997

Companies are shown ranked by number of units in which they have ownership interest.

Colson & Colson/Retirement Corp.	21,465
Emeritus Corporation	9,039
Nationwide Health Properties, Inc.	7,405
Host Marriott Corporation	7,200
Marriot Senior Living Services	6,800
ARV Assisted Living, Inc.	6,566
Grand Court Lifestyles, Inc.	6,297
Health and Retirement Properties Trust	5,802
ACTS, Inc.	5,520
Health Care Property Investors, Inc.	5,451
Meditrust	6,060
Senior Lifestyle Corporation	5,343

Source: *Contemporary Long Term Care*, February 1998, p. 15, from American Seniors Housing Association.

★ 1953 ★

Charities (SIC 8399)

Largest Charitable Organizations - 1997

The table shows organizations ranked by number of donors.

American Heart Association	4,100,000
American Cancer Society	1,800,000
American Red Cross	1,600,000
American Diabetes Association	1,500,000
Arthritis Foundation	534,000
Alzheimers Disease and Related Disorders Association	135,000
Juvenile Diabetes Foundation International	70,000
Lupus Foundation of America	47,000

Continued on next page.

★ 1953 ★ *Continued*

Charities (SIC 8399)

Largest Charitable Organizations - 1997

The table shows organizations ranked by number of donors.

Huntingtons Disease Society of
   America 40,000
Children and Adults with Attention
   Deficit Disorders 32,000

Source: *Association Management*, May 1997, p. 41.

★ 1954 ★

Charities (SIC 8399)

Largest Charities by Private Support - 1996

| Salvation Army |
| American Red Cross |
| American Cancer Society |
| Emory University |
| Catholic Charities USA |
| Second Harvest |
| YMCA of the USA |
| Habitat for Humanity International |
| Boys & Girls Clubs of America |
| Stanford University |

Groups are ranked by income derived from private support. Figures are in thousands of dollars.

Salvation Army . . . . $ 1,012,403
American Red Cross 479,928
American Cancer Society 426,695
Emory University 415,406
Catholic Charities USA 386,545
Second Harvest 351,376
YMCA of the USA 340,337
Habitat for Humanity International . . 334,737
Boys & Girls Clubs of America 321,757
Stanford University 312,887

Source: *The Chronicle of Philanthropy*, October 30, 1997, p. 33.

★ 1955 ★

Charities (SIC 8399)

Leading Types of Charities - 1996

Data show contributions in billions of dollars.

	($ bil.)	Share
Religion	$ 69.0	45.85%
Education	18.8	12.49
Health	13.9	9.24
Human services	12.2	8.11
Arts, cultures & humanities . . .	10.9	7.24
Gifts to foundations	8.3	5.51
Public/society benefit	7.6	5.05
Environmental/wildlife	4.0	2.66
International affairs	2.0	1.33
Other	3.8	2.52

Source: *New York Times*, December 9, 1997, p. D1, from *Giving USA 1997*.

★ 1956 ★

Charities (SIC 8399)

Top Charities by Total Income - 1996

Organizations are ranked by total income in millions of dollars.

YMCA of the USA . . . . $ 2,473.0
Catholic Charities USA 2,103.5
American Red Cross 1,813.9
Salvation Army 1,563.1
Goodwill Industries International 1,200.0
Shriners Hospitals for Children 1,047.6
Boy Scouts of America 553.5
YWCA of the USA 510.8
American Cancer Society Inc. 506.1
Planned Parenthood Federation of
   America 504.0
Girl Scouts of the USA 492.3
Boys and Girls Clubs of America 437.8

Source: *Christian Science Monitor*, December 15, 1997, p. B4, from *The NonProfit Times* and *The Chronicle of Philanthropy*.

★ 1957 ★

Charities (SIC 8399)

Top Corporate Donors - 1996

Data show contributions in dollars. Figures for information technology and pharmaceutical companies include donations of equipment, software, and drugs tabulated at retail prices; in addition, pharmaceutical companies provide financial support for many medical research programs.

Merck & Company	$ 140,500,000
IBM Corporation	100,800,000
Johnson & Johnson	88,500,000
Pfizer Inc.	85,473,901
Hewlett-Packard Co.	71,579,000
General Motors Corp.	66,700,000
Eli Lilly & Company	66,289,000
Bristol-Myers Squibb Co.	64,708,575
Microsoft Corporation	59,166,294
Intel Corporation	55,613,575

Source: *New York Times*, December 9, 1997, p. D4, from *Taft Corporate Giving Directory, 19th edition*.

★ 1958 ★

Philanthropy (SIC 8399)

Top Private Donors

The table shows donations in millions of dollars.

Ted Turner	$1,000
Kathryn Albertson	$ 660
George Soros	540
Bill Gates	210
Leonard Abramson	100
Michael & Jane Eisner	89
Mitchell Wolfson Jr.	75
Phyllis Wattis	70
Raymond Nasher	50
Dwight Opperman	50

Source: *Fortune*, February 2, 1998, p. 89.

SIC 84 - Museums, Botanical, Zoological Gardens

★ 1959 ★

Museums (SIC 8412)

Art Museum Attendance

Data show attendance for 1996-97.

Metropolitan Museum of Art (NY)	5,500,000
Museum of Modern Art (NY)	5,500,000
Boston Museum of Fine Arts	1,100,000
Philadelphia Museum of Art	1,100,000
Los Angeles County Museum of Art	602,141
National Museum of American Art (D.C.)	400,000
Seattle Art Museum	386,729

Source: *Christian Science Monitor*, January 23, 1998, p. B4.

★ 1960 ★

Museums (SIC 8412)

Top Museum Shows - 1997

Picasso: The Early Years

Renoir's Portraits

Glory of Byzantium

Cartier

Monet and the Mediterranean

Data show attendance. The Picasso show was held at the National Gallery of Art. The Renoir show was at The Art Institute of Chicago. The Monet show was held at the Kimball Museum. The other shows were held at the Metropolitan Museum of Art.

Picasso: The Early Years	530,911
Renoir's Portraits	489,423
Glory of Byzantium	460,864
Cartier	420,686
Monet and the Mediterranean	338,300

Source: *New York Times*, February 26, 1998, p. B4, from *Art Newspaper*.

SIC 86 - Membership Organizations

★ 1961 ★

Membership Organizations (SIC 8600)

Largest Membership Organizations - 1997

The table shows organizations ranked by number of members.

American Automobile Association	35,291,651
American Association of Retired Persons	32,000,000
YMCA of the USA	14,447,270
National Congress of Parents and Teachers	6,500,000
National Right to Life Committee	6,000,000
Boy Scouts of America	5,628,806
National Committee to Preserve Social Security and Medicare	5,500,000
Evangelical Lutheran Church in America	5,200,000
National Council of Senior Citizens	5,000,000
American Farm Bureau Federation	4,700,000

Source: *Association Management*, May 1997, p. 30.

★ 1962 ★

Membership Organizations (SIC 8611)

Largest Trade and Institutional Membership Organizations - 1997

The table shows organizations ranked by number of members.

National Federation of Independent Business	560,000
U.S. Chamber of Commerce	220,000
Distributive Education Clubs of America	186,000
National Association of Home Builders	185,000
Road Runners Club of America	160,000
National Pork Producers Council	100,000
American Management Association	85,000
United States Hispanic Chamber of Commerce	70,000

American Hospital Association	55,000
United States Taekwondo Union	45,000

Source: *Association Management*, May 1997, p. 32.

★ 1963 ★

Labor Organizations (SIC 8631)

Largest Labor Unions

Membership is shown in millions.

National Education Association	2.30
Teamsters	1.30
Amer. Fed. of State, County & Municipal Employees	1.20
Service Employees International Union	1.10
United Food and Commercial Workers	1.00
American Federation of Teachers	0.94
United Auto Workers	0.77

Source: *Wall Street Journal*, January 21, 1998, p. A2, from AFL-CIO, NEA, and AFT.

★ 1964 ★

Social Organizations (SIC 8641)

Popular Runners Clubs - 1997

Data show number of club members.

Road Runners Club of America	160,000
New York Road Runners Club	34,000
Atlanta Track Club	11,147

Source: *Runner's World*, September 1997, p. 72.

★ 1965 ★

Political Organizations (SIC 8651)

Lobbying Efforts by Industry

The table shows soft dollar lobbying spending in millions of dollars.

Communications	$ 14.5
Oil & gas	9.7
Insurance	9.6
Tobacco	6.7
Health care	6.6
Computer & electronics	4.5

Source: *VAR Business*, February 16, 1998, p. 57, from Common Cause.

★ 1966 ★

Religious Organizations (SIC 8661)

Largest Christian Denominations

Data show number of members.

Roman Catholic	61,200,000
Southern Baptist Convention	15,663,296
United Methodist	8,800,000
National Baptist Convention USA Inc.	8,500,000
Church of God in Christ (Pentecostal)	5,499,875
Evangelical Lutheran Church in America	5,180,910
Church of Jesus Christ of Latter Day Saints (Mormon)	5,180,910
National Baptist Convention America Inc.	4,500,000
African Methodist Episcopal	3,500,000
Presbyterian Church USA	2,631,466

Source: *Detroit News*, September 14, 1997, p. 14A.

★ 1967 ★

Religious Organizations (SIC 8661)

Largest Religions

Data show estimated millions of members.

Roman Catholic	60.3
Baptist	36.5
Methodist	13.4
Pentecostal	10.3
Lutheran	8.2
Jewish	5.3
Muslim	5.1
Mormon	5.0

Source: *USA TODAY*, June 4, 1998, p. 14A, from *Yearbook of American Churches* and *World Almanac*.

SIC 87 - Engineering and Management Services

★ 1968 ★

Engineering Services (SIC 8711)

Largest Engineering Firms - Arkansas

Data show firms ranked by number of staff members.

Garver & Garver	125
CEI Engineering Associates	104
Cromwell Architects Engineers	96
Crafton Tull & Associates	93
McClelland Consulting Engineers	91
Grubbs Garner & Hoskyn	75
Mid-South Engineering Co.	60
Anderson Engineering Consultants	56
Engineering Services	38
McGoodwin Williams & Yates	38

Source: *Arkansas Business*, October 13, 1997, p. 23, from company records and American Consulting Engineers Council of Arkansas.

★ 1969 ★

Engineering Services (SIC 8711)

Top Engineering Firms - 1996

Firms are ranked by design and planning billings in millions of dollars.

Jacobs Engineering Group	$ 354.68
Fluor Daniel Inc.	240.93
BE&K Inc.	207.46
Raytheon Engineers & Constructors	188.10
Dames & Moore	157.50
Simons International Corp.	81.00
Burns and Roe Enterprises	60.01
Day & Zimmermann International Inc.	49.95
Bechtel Group Inc.	42.18
Syska & Hennessy Inc.	38.00

Source: *Building Design & Construction*, July 1997, p. 56.

★ 1970 ★

Architectural Services (SIC 8712)

Hotel & Motel Design Firms - 1996

Firms are ranked by dollars earned from fees for lodging projects.

Wilson & Associates	$ 18,400,000
Brennan Beer Gorman Architects	11,908,000
DiLeonardo International	10,355,000
Concepts 4	9,900,000
Daroff Design and DDI Architects	5,000,000
Murphy/Jahn	5,000,000
BSW International	4,800,000
RTKL Associates	4,575,000
Bent Severin & Associates	4,514,274
Hill/Glazier Architects	4,120,000

Source: *Hotel & Motel Management*, November 3, 1997, p. 137.

★ 1971 ★

Architectural Services (SIC 8712)

Top Architectural Firms - 1996

Firms are ranked by design and planning billings in millions of dollars.

Gensler	$ 88.00
NBBJ	54.50
The Hillier Group	36.58
Ehrlich-Rominger Associates	24.25
Zimmer Gunsul Frasca Partnership	24.00
Callison Architecture Inc.	23.50
Thompson, Ventulett, Stainback & Associates	22.05
Smallwood, Reynolds, Stewart, Stewart & Assoc. Inc.	19.25
Kaplan/McLaughlin/Diaz	18.00
Corgan Associates Inc.	16.95

Source: *Building Design & Construction*, July 1997, p. 12.

★ 1972 ★

Accounting Services (SIC 8721)

Largest Accounting Firms by Partners - 1996

Firms are ranked by number of U.S. partners.

Ernst & Young 1,993
Andersen Worldwide 1,649
Deloitte & Touche 1,556
KPMG 1,509
Coopers & Lybrand 1,241
Price Waterhouse 963

Source: *New York Times*, October 18, 1997, p. B2, from *Bowman's Accounting Report*.

★ 1973 ★

Accounting Services (SIC 8721)

Largest Accounting Firms in New England - 1997

Firms are ranked by revenues in millions of dollars.

Berry, Dunn, McNeil & Parker . . . . . $ 17.1
Toflas, Fleishman. Shapriro & Co. 16.0
Blum, Shapiro & Company 13.9
Baker, Newman & Noyes 11.0
Carlin, Charron & Rosen 9.9
Feeley & Driscoll 8.5
Vitale, Caturano & Co. 7.9
Kostin, Ruffkess & Co. 7.4

Source: *Practical Accountant*, April 1998, p. 24.

★ 1974 ★

Accounting Services (SIC 8721)

Largest Accounting Firms in North Central - 1997

Firms are ranked by revenues in millions of dollars.

Crowe, Chizek and Company . . . . . . $ 97.4
Plante & Moran 86.9
Clifton Gunderson 74.8
Geo. S. Olive & Co. 58.3
Altschuler, Melvoin & Glasser 53.5
Friedman, Eisenstein, Raemer & Schwartz . . 45.5
Wipfli Ullrich Bertelson 29.0
Virchow, Krause & Company 23.6

Source: *Practical Accountant*, April 1998, p. 24.

★ 1975 ★

Accounting Services (SIC 8721)

Largest Accounting Firms in the Midwest - 1997

Firms are ranked by revenues in millions of dollars.

Baird, Kurtz & Dobson . . . . $ 90.0
Larson Allen Weishar 48.9
Maver Hoffman McCann 27.0
Elde Helmeke 19.1
Rubin, Brown Gornstein & Co. 16.7
Kennedy & Coe 15.1
Charles Bailly & Co. 12.5
Lurie Besikoff & Lapidus 12.0

Source: *Practical Accountant*, April 1998, p. 24.

★ 1976 ★

Accounting Services (SIC 8721)

Largest Accounting Firms in the Northeast - 1997

Firms are ranked by revenues in millions of dollars.

Constantin Associates . . . . $ 59.1
Richard A. Eisner & Co. 57.0
Goldstein Golub Kessler & Company 48.8
David Bertion & Co. 37.3
Reznick Fedder & Silverman 35.0
Anchin, Block & Anchin 31.5
M.R. Weiser & Co. 27.5

Source: *Practical Accountant*, April 1998, p. 30.

★ 1977 ★

Accounting Services (SIC 8721)

Top Accounting Firms by Revenue - 1996

Firms are ranked by U.S. revenues in millions of dollars.

Andersen Worldwide . . . . $ 4,511
Ernst & Young 3,570
Deloitte & Touche 2,925
KPMG 2,281
Coopers & Lybrand 2,116
Price Waterhouse 2,016

Source: *New York Times*, October 18, 1997, p. B2, from *Bowman's Accounting Report*.

★ 1978 ★
Accounting Services (SIC 8721)

Top Accounting Firms in the Southeast - 1997

Firms are ranked by fiscal year revenues in millions of dollars.

Cherry, Bekaert & Holland	$ 25.0
Dixon, Odom & Co.	21.6
Elliott, Davis & Co.	17.0
Goodman & Co.	14.4
Rachlin Cohen & Holtz	14.2
Kaufman Rossin & Co.	13.8

Source: *Practical Accountant*, April 1998, p. 33.

★ 1979 ★
Accounting Services (SIC 8721)

Top Tax Firms

Firms are ranked by tax auditing revenues in millions of dollars.

Ernst & Young	$ 1,002.4
H&R Block Tax Services Inc.	906.3
Andersen Worldwide	762.3
KPMG Peat Warwick	750.0
Deloitte & Touche	720.0
Price Waterhouse	514.8
Coopers & Lybrand	500.9
Grant Thornton	86.7
McGladrey & Pullen	86.4
Jackson Hewitt	86.2

Source: *Accounting Today*, March 16, 1998, p. 24.

★ 1980 ★
Commercial Research (SIC 8732)

Largest R&D Spenders on Computer Hardware

Data show the top spenders on research in millions of dollars.

Hewlett-Packard	$ 3,100
Motorola	2,700
Intel	2,300
Digital Equipment	1,000
Sun Microsystems	826

Source: *Computer Reseller News*, February 16, 1998, p. 118.

★ 1981 ★
Commercial Research (SIC 8732)

Largest R&D Spenders on Internet/ Communications Industries

Data show the top spenders on research in millions of dollars.

Lucent Technologies	$ 2,900.0
Cisco	698.2
Bay Networks	269.8
Cabletron Systems	161.7
Newbridge Networks	155.3
Fore Systems	55.2

Source: *Computer Reseller News*, February 9, 1998, p. 6.

★ 1982 ★
Commercial Research (SIC 8732)

Largest Research Firms - 1997

Firms are ranked by number of companies covered.

Salomon Smith Barney	1,495
Merrill Lynch	1,457
Morgan Stanley Dean Witter	1,294
Bankers Trust New York Corp.	1,190
Goldman, Sachs	1,118
Bear, Stearns	1,104
CIBC Oppenheimer	1,040
Standard & Poor's Equity Group	979
Donaldson Lufkin & Jenrette	936
Credit Suisse First Boston	920

Source: From the Internet, http://www.nelnet.com/ t25uscc.htm, May 1998, p. 2.

★ 1983 ★
Commercial Research (SIC 8732)

Largest Research Organizations

Organizations are ranked by research revenues in millions of dollars.

A.C. Nielsen Corp.	$ 1,391.6
Cognizant Corp.	1,339.1
Information Resources Inc.	456.3
NFO Worldwide Inc.	190.0
Westat Inc.	182.0
The Arbitron Co.	165.2
Maritz Marketing Research Inc.	146.0
The Kantar Group Ltd.	127.1

Continued on next page.

★ 1983 ★ *Continued*
Commercial Research (SIC 8732)

Largest Research Organizations

Organizations are ranked by research revenues in millions of dollars.

The NPD Group Inc.	$ 110.3
Market Facts Inc.	100.1

Source: *Marketing News*, June 8, 1998, p. H4.

★ 1984 ★
Commercial Research (SIC 8732)

R&D Expenditures by Source

Research funding is shown in billions of dollars for 1997 and 1998. Data are forecasted for 1998.

	1997	1998
Industry	$ 133.3	$ 142.3
Government	62.7	62.9
University, nonprofit	9.7	10.2

Source: *R&D Magazine*, January 1998, p. A, from Battelle.

★ 1985 ★
Commercial Research (SIC 8732)

Top Research Leaders - 1997

IMS Health
Information Resources Inc.
Nielsen Media Research
A.C. Nielsen Corp.
VNU Marketing Information Services
Westat
Arbitron Co.
Gallup Organization
NFO Worldwide
Maritz Marketing Research

Companies are ranked by research revenue in millions of dollars.

IMS Health	$ 378.3
Information Resources Inc.	366.7
Nielsen Media Research	358.6
A.C. Nielsen Corp.	310.0
VNU Marketing Information Services	220.0
Westat	182.0
Arbitron Co.	165.2

Gallup Organization	$ 151.4
NFO Worldwide	141.1
Maritz Marketing Research	116.8

Source: *Advertising Age*, May 25, 1998, p. S2.

★ 1986 ★
Commercial Research (SIC 8732)

Who Funds R&D - 1997

Funding is shown in percent.

Industry	66.1%
Federal government	29.2
Academia	3.0
Other nonprofit institutions	1.7

Source: *Industry Week*, January 19, 1998, p. 22, from National Science Foundation.

★ 1987 ★
Construction Management (SIC 8741)

Top Construction Managers - 1996

Managers are ranked by value of construction managed in millions of dollars.

Bovis Inc.	$ 1,944.95
Gilbane Building Co.	1,714.96
Heery International Inc.	1,246.00
Sverdrup Corp.	918.72
URS Greiner Inc.	742.50
3D/International	729.00
Barton Malow Co.	723.24
Parsons Brinckerhoff Inc.	673.97
HRH Construction Corp.	629.65
McClier	604.00

Source: *Building Design & Construction*, July 1997, p. 38.

★ 1988 ★
Marketing Services (SIC 8741)

Top Direct Response Agencies - 1996

Agencies are ranked by direct response revenues in thousands of dollars.

Rapp Collins Worldwide	$ 105,831
DIMAC Direct	88,778
Bronner Slosberg Humphrey	83,200
Wunderman Cato Johnson	81,003
Barry Blau & Partners	63,723

Continued on next page.

★ 1988 ★ *Continued*
Marketing Services (SIC 8741)

Top Direct Response Agencies - 1996

Agencies are ranked by direct response revenues in thousands of dollars.

OgilvyOne Worldwide	.$ 57,800
DraftDirect Worldwide	57,097
Carlson Marketing Group	46,440
Customer Development Corp.	37,887
Gage Marketing Group	36,738

Source: *Advertising Age*, July 21, 1997, p. 22.

★ 1989 ★
Marketing Services (SIC 8741)

Top Marketing Service Agencies - 1996

Agencies are ranked by revenues in thousands of dollars. Data include combined revenue from sales promotion and direct response.

Carlson Marketing Group	$ 160,138
Gage Marketing Group	122,460
Alcone Marketing Group	109,913
Rapp Collins Worldwide	105,831
Wunderman Cato Johnson	104,134
DIMAC Direct	88,778
Bronner Slosberg Humphrey	83,200
Barry Blau & Partners	63,723
Frankel & Co.	62,855
OgilvyOne Worldwide	57,800

Source: *Advertising Age*, July 21, 1997, p. 21.

★ 1990 ★
Marketing Services (SIC 8741)

Top Sales Promotion Agencies - 1996

Agencies are ranked by sales promotion revenue in thousands of dollars.

Carlson Marketing Group	$ 113,698
Alcone Marketing Group	109,913
Gage Marketing Group	85,722
Frankel & Co.	62,855
HMG Worldwide	46,000
TLP	38,200
Marketing Corp. of America	37,342
Cyrk	36,986

Integer Group	.$ 29,109
Ryan Partnership	27,668

Source: *Advertising Age*, July 21, 1997, p. 22.

★ 1991 ★
Management Consulting (SIC 8742)

Largest Executive Recruiters in Chicago, IL - 1997

Firms are ranked by revenue in millions of dollars.

Spencer Stuart	$ 21.1
Heidrick & Struggles Inc.	16.0
LAI	9.4
Ray & Berndtson	9.3
Korn/Ferry International	8.6

Source: *Crain's Chicago Business*, March 2, 1998, p. 19.

★ 1992 ★
Consulting Services (SIC 8748)

Top Information Technology Analysts - 1996

Firms are ranked by revenue in billions of dollars. Data for Aberdeen Group, Hurwitz Group, Jupiter Communications, and Zona Research were not available. Figure for Gartner Group includes Dataquest Inc. revenue.

Gartner Group	$ 395.0
International Data Corp.	100.0
Meta Group	36.9
Forrester Research	25.0
Giga Info. Group	13.2
The Yankee Group	7.8

Source: *Informationweek*, November 17, 1997, p. 39, from the companies.

★ 1993 ★

Human Resource Consulting (SIC 8748)

Largest Benefit Consultants

Firms are ranked by revenues in millions of dollars.

Hewitt Associates	$ 600
William M. Mercer Cos.	580
Towers Perrin	511
Watson Wyatt Worldwide	359
Coopers & Lybrand L.L.P.-The Kwasha Lipton Group	315
Aon Consulting	273
Buck Consultants Inc.	227
Deloitte & Touche/Employee Benefit Group	129
The Segal Co.	94
Sedgwick Noble Lowndes	73

Source: *Business Insurance*, December 8, 1997, p. 4.

SIC 92 - Justice, Public Order, and Safety

★ 1994 ★

Prisons (SIC 9223)

Prison Spending by State

Alabama	
Michigan	
Arizona	
California	
North Carolina	

The table shows the states that spend the highest percentage of their state budgets on prisons.

Alabama	. 16.9%
Michigan	. 15.0
Arizona	. 8.0
California	. 8.0
North Carolina	. 7.9

Source: *Utne Reader*, January-February 1998, p. 14, from *Quill*.

SIC 93 - Finance, Taxation, and Monetary Policy

★ 1995 ★

Taxation (SIC 9311)

Sources of State Money

Data show the types of tax levied.

General sales and use	33.3%
Individual income	32.1
Corporate income	7.0
Licenses	6.4
Motor fuels	6.2
Other	14.9

Source: *USA TODAY*, March 17, 1998, p. A1, from Tax Foundation.

★ 1996 ★

Taxation (SIC 9311)

Where the Tax Dollar Goes

Spending is shown in percent.

Social security	22.89%
Health & medical	19.90
National defense	15.42
Income security	14.43
Net interest	13.93
Education, training	3.48
Transportation	2.49
Veterans benefits	2.49
Other	4.98

Source: *Christian Science Monitor*, March 16, 1998, p. B2, from Tax Foundation.

SIC 94 - Administration of Human Resources

★ 1997 ★

Federal Programs (SIC 9431)

Health Spending - 1999

Spending is shown in billions of dollars.

Medicaid Part A benefits	$ 130.5
Medicaid benefits	107.7
Medicaid Part B benefits	72.7
Federal administration	4.1
Children's Health Insurance Program . . .	1.9

Source: *American Medical News*, February 16, 1998, p. 1, from U.S. Department of Health and Human Services.

SIC 95 - Environmental Quality and Housing

★ 1998 ★

Environmental Services (SIC 9510)

Environmental Services Market - Mexico

Data show millions of dollars estimated for 1995, 1996, and 1997.

	1995	1996	1997
Wastewater and potable water treatment	$ 235	$ 329	$ 565
Air pollution control	125	178	267
Solid waste management	63	90	125

Source: *Business Mexico*, September 1997, p. 39, from U.S. Department of Commerce.

★ 1999 ★

Environmental Services (SIC 9510)

Top Environmental Firms

Firms are ranked by environmental revenues in millions of dollars. Environmental revenues can be derived from such categories as design, construction, equipment and research.

Bechtel Group Inc.	$ 1,307.3
U.S. Filter Corp.	1,300.0
Foster Wheeler Corp.	1,248.0
Jacobs Engineering Group Inc.	1,038.0
ICF Kaiser International Inc.	1,017.0
CH2M Hill Cos. Ltd.	912.0
Laidlaw Environ. Services Inc.	705.7
Morrison Knudsen Corp.	703.0
Metcalf & Eddy	701.0
OHM Corp.	603.0

Source: *Engineering News-Record*, July 14, 1997, p. 65.

★ 2000 ★

Land Ownership (SIC 9512)

Where the Federal Government Owns Land

Data show land owned by the federal government as a percent of each region's total area. The government owns 24.2% of all U.S. lands.

Mountain states	46.6%
Pacific states	44.2
Appalachian states	6.6
Lake states	5.8
Delta states	5.3
Southeast	4.7
Northern plains	2.7
Northeast	2.3
Corn belt	1.7
Southern plains	1.4

Source: *Investor's Business Daily*, December 10, 1997, p. A8, from Urban Land Institute.

SOURCE INDEX

This index is divided into *primary sources* and *original sources*. Primary sources are the publications where the market shares were found. Original sources are sources cited in the primary sources. Numbers following the sources are entry numbers, arranged sequentially; the first number refers to the first appearance of the source in *Market Share Reporter*. All told, 951 organizations are listed.

Primary Sources

Accounting Today, 1979
Advertising Age, 23, 177, 184, 204, 217, 219, 229, 235, 242, 292, 294, 324, 332, 369, 372, 456, 461-463, 465-466, 479, 486, 489-492, 494, 581, 587, 589, 595, 617, 619, 621, 636, 652, 668, 674, 697, 1097, 1209, 1227, 1230, 1650, 1652-1653, 1655-1656, 1658-1667, 1679, 1681-1685, 1689, 1985, 1988-1990
Advertising Age International, 1647-1649
Adweek, 1220, 1643, 1693, 1778
Aftermarket Business, 1866
Agri Finance, 69, 1503
Air Cargo World, 61, 1156-1158, 1160
Air Conditioning, Heating & Refrigeration News, 848-849, 852
Air Transport World, 1144-1145, 1757
American Banker, 1474, 1478-1479, 1495, 1524, 1526, 1550, 1835, 1940
The American Ceramic Society Bulletin, 94-95, 97-98, 102, 741
American Coin-Op, 1639
American Demographics, 3, 1640, 1910-1912
American Ink Maker, 514, 701
American Medical News, 1601, 1997
American Metal Market, 756, 762
American Printer, 471, 518
The American Saleman, 1177
American Vegetable Grower, 44-47, 63
America's Pharmacist, 596, 659, 736, 1037, 1044, 1408
America's Textile International, 574
Amusement Business, 1881, 1883-1884, 1886, 1888-1889, 1901, 1906-1908
Appliance, 847, 850-851, 853, 865-895, 897-899, 906-907, 909-911, 933-934, 955-956
Appliance Manufacturer, 864
Arkansas Business, 1968
AS&U, 150, 1820-1821, 1943-1946
Assembly, 856-857, 859, 1093
Association Management, 1600, 1953, 1961-1962
Atlanta Journal-Constitution, 1142, 1235, 1493, 1558,

1576, 1790
Auto Laundry News, 1865
Automotive Body Repair, 1859
Automotive Industries, 987, 990-991, 994, 996, 1000-1002, 1022
Automotive Manufacturing & Production, 1719
Automotive Marketing, 1257, 1318, 1864
Automotive News, 989, 1015, 1021
Aviation Week & Space Technology, 1023, 1032, 1139
Bakery Production and Marketing, 238, 244
Bangkok Post, 335, 764, 1692
Bank Marketing, 1476
The Banker, 1496
Banks Systems + Technology, 7
Bee Culture, 67-68
Best's Review, 1565-1566, 1595-1597, 1599, 1604, 1606-1612
Beverage Industry, 203, 209-211, 296, 300, 305-306, 327-328, 337, 343
Beverage Industry Annual Manual, 207-208
Beverage World, 297-298, 307, 326, 329, 331, 344-345, 347-349, 352, 357, 1010-1012, 1271
Beverage World Periscope, 1398
Billboard, 915, 918-920, 922
Bloomberg, 1515
Bobbin, 401, 1346
Body Fashions/Intimate Apparel, 397, 1328, 1331
BodyShop Business, 1860
Boston Globe, 719, 1645
Brandweek, 169-170, 178-179, 196-197, 214-216, 220, 224-225, 230, 232-233, 285, 350-351, 354, 356, 373, 387, 398, 606, 616, 618, 969, 1083, 1776
Broadcasting & Cable, 22, 1225, 1545
Broiler Industry, 171
Builder, 108-111, 113, 115, 117-124, 126, 129, 131, 133, 135-136, 407
Building Design & Construction, 103, 143-144, 1969, 1971, 1987
Buildings, 383, 1624

Original Sources

Source Index: Original

PLACE NAMES INDEX

This index shows global regions, political entities, states and provinces, regions within countries, and cities. The numbers that follow listings are entry numbers; they are arranged sequentially so that the first mention of a place is listed first. The index shows references to more than 230 places.

Place Names Index

PRODUCTS, SERVICES, AND ISSUES INDEX

This index shows, in alphabetical order, references to products, services, and issues covered in *Market Share Reporter*, 9th Edition. More than 1,100 terms are included. Terms include subjects not readily categorized as products and services, including such subjects as *crime* and *welfare*. The numbers that follow each term refer to entry numbers and are arranged sequentially so that the first mention is listed first.

401(k) plans, 1534, 1613
Abrasives, 753
Accounting services, 1972-1979
Acetaminophen, 591
Acid, chloroacetic, 687
Acid, hydrochloric, 554
Acne remedies, 658-659, 661
Acrylonitrile-butadiene-styrene (ABS), 557
Action figures, 1067, 1077
Actuators, 857
Adhesives, 537, 698-699, 705
Advertising, 1129, 1642-1690
Advertising, magazine, 1658
Advertising, newspaper, 1657, 1664
Advertising, online, 1687
Advertising, outdoor, 1655
Advertising, television, 1659
Aerobics, 395, 721
Aerospace, 1031-1033
Agriculture, 41-42, 44-47, 63, 604
Air cargo, 1156-1159
Air conditioners, 727, 850, 863
Air fresheners, 616-617
Air pollution control, 1998
Aircraft, 788, 1023
Aircraft parts, 788
Airlines, 1137-1154
Airports, 1155, 1160-1169
Alcoholic beverages, 161, 163, 301, 303-312, 314, 316, 318, 320-325
Alkalies and chlorine, 541-545
Aluminum, 761, 966
Amethysts, 1436
Ammonia, 525, 554
Ammonium nitrate, 525, 554
Ammonium phosphate, 696
Ammonium sulfate, 554
Amusement parks, 1906-1907
Analgesics, 29, 583, 598-599, 1408
Annuities, 1564
Answering machines, 858

Antimicrobials, 532
Antiperspirants, 534, 625
Antiseptics, 649
Apparel, 1, 18, 385-400, 451, 1086-1087, 1327, 1329, 1332, 1646, 1788, 1801, 1806, 1825
Apparel, baby, 1
Apparel, intimate, 399
Apparel, men, 395, 397, 1327-1328
Apparel stores, 1289, 1326-1327, 1329, 1334
Apples, 38, 55-56, 218
Applesauce, 199
Appliance stores, 1278, 1350
Appliances, 12, 567, 755, 776, 851, 853, 862-867, 869-876, 878-882, 884-899, 1351-1353
Apricots, 199, 218
Archery, 728, 1091
Architectural services, 1970-1971
Art, 19, 1439
Asparagus, 201
Aspirin, 591
Assisted living facilities, 1927
Athlete's foot remedies, 627
Athletic footwear, 719-724
ATM access, 944
ATM switches, 1203
Audio equipment, 901, 907, 911
Audio tape, 901-902, 904
Auto body repair, 1859
Auto dealerships, 1316, 1443, 1860
Auto parts, 753, 776, 1014-1022, 1257, 1318
Auto parts stores, 1278, 1280, 1319
Auto rental, 1851-1856
Auto repair services, 1860, 1864, 1866
Automated teller machines, 845
Automation, 856-857
Autos, 967, 970-999, 1283, 1646
Autos, corporate, 970, 972, 981
Axles, 1016
Baby care, 1, 29, 458-460, 735
Baby cups, 735
Baby feeding equipment, 1

Products, Services, and Issues Index

Products, Services, and Issues Index

COMPANY INDEX

The more than 4,500 companies and institutions in this book are indexed here in alphabetical order. Numbers following the terms are entry numbers. They are arranged sequentially; the first entry number refers to the first mention of the company in *Market Share Reporter*. Although most organizations appear only once, some entities are referred to under abbreviations in the sources and these have not always been expanded.

20th Century Fox, 1877-1878
The 21 Club, 1392
2The Loop Internet Switch Co., 1805
3Com, 838, 927, 939-942, 944, 947-948, 950, 952-954, 968, 1202
3M, 535, 1668, 1832
462 Inc., 1881
4Link Network Inc., 1805
7-Eleven, 1297-1298
84 Lumber Inc., 1275
A A A Cooper, 1114
A&E, 1235
A&P, 1295, 1309
A&W Farms, 44
A&W Restaurants, 1375
A. Duda & Sons Inc., 45
Aaron Rents, 1336
ABB Daimler-Benz, 1024
ABB Lummus Global Inc., 104
Abbot Diagnostics, 1670
Abbott Laboratories, 585
ABC Carpet & Home, 1340
ABC Inc., 1220, 1225, 1834, 1850
ABC Radio Inc., 1212
Abelson-Taylor, 1683
Aberdeen Group, 1992
ABF Freight System, 1109, 1116, 1121
Abitibi-Consolidated, 439, 441, 443
Abitibi-Price Inc., 436, 440
ABN Amro, 1495
Abramson; Leonard, 1958
AC and S Inc., 158
A.C. Nielsen Corp., 1983, 1985
Academy Bus Tours Inc., 1104
Academy Sports, 1425
Access Cash International Inc., 845
Acclaim, 1069
Accord Health Network, 1580
Accton, 940
AccuStaff Inc., 1698-1700
Acend Communications, 929
Acer, 803, 805, 808, 813, 819, 822

Acme Markets, 1295
Acme Metals Inc., 756
Acordia Inc., 1615
Across Canada, 1258
ACT Networks, 930
Active Transportation, 1111
Activision, 1722-1723, 1738
ACTS, Inc., 1952
Acura, 989
Acxiom Corp., 1814
A.D. Makepeace Co., 48
Adams & Smith Inc., 154
ADC Kentrox, 944
Addison Wesley, 499, 507
Adecco S.A., 1700
Adelphia Communications Corp., 1231, 1233
Adhesivos, 695
Adidas, 390, 719-720, 722, 724, 739
Adkin Blue Ribbon Pkg. Co. Inc., 48
ADM, 691
Adobe Systems Inc., 1741, 1747, 1750-1751
Adolph Coors, 295
ADT Ltd., 1845
ADT Security Services Inc., 1817
Advance Publications, 473, 479, 486, 1318
Advanced Gravis, 1073-1074
Advanced Micro Devices, 826, 960
Advanta, 1500, 1510
Advantage Bank F.S.B., 1491
Advantica, 1366
Adventure Island, 1907
ADVO Inc., 1694
Advocate Health Care, 1580, 1918
AE Staley, 234
Aegis, 1600
AEI, 1125
AEP Industries Inc., 729
Aerotek, 1700
AES Corp., 1246
Aetna, 1589, 1600
Affiliated Computer Services, 1846
African Methodist Episcopal, 1966

Company Index

Best Buy, 1287, 1302, 1305
Best Data, 926-927
Best Internet Communications Inc., 1792
Best Products, 1438
Best Western International, 1638
Bestbuy Distributors Limited, 1258
Bestfoods, 165
Bestway Rental, 1336
BET Plant Services, 1696
Bethlehem Steel Corp., 754, 756
Betty Crocker, 878, 881-882, 885, 888, 897
Beverage America, 298
Beverly Enterprises Inc., 1924, 1928
BF Goodrich, 713-714, 717
BHC Communications, 1225, 1227
Bi-Lo, 1296
Bierlein Cos., 157
Big 5 Sporting Goods, 1425
Big Apple Bagel, 1315
Big Boy Restaurant & Bakery, 1380
Big Dog, 389
Big Flower Press Holdings, Inc., 518
Big Red, 347
Big Wheel, 1864
Bill Gates, 1958
Bill Graham Presents, 1884, 1888
Bill's, 1304
Birkenstock, 738
Bisco Dental Products, 1668
Biscuit Leclerc, 367
Bissell, 893
BJK&E Yellow Pages, 1689
BJ's Wholesale, 1299
Black & Decker, 778, 876, 878, 881-883, 888-889, 892, 897
Black & Veatch, 104
Black Dot Group, 470
Black Gold Farms, 44
Blackstone, 1835
Blades, 1423
Blaine Larsen Farms, 47
Blandin Paper, 70
Blazic & Assc., 251
Blizzard Beach, 1907
Block Financial, 1713
Bloomberg, 1563
Blue Advantage, 1588
Blue Bell, 181
Blue Circle, 747
Blue Cross HMOs, 1590
Blum, Shapiro & Company, 1973
BMA, 913
BMW, 989, 1030

BNSF, 1099, 1102-1103
BNY Financial, 1502
Boatmens First NB of Kansas, 1503
Bob Chinn's Crabhouse, 1392
Bob Evans Restaurants, 1380
Boca, 927
Boehringer Mannheim Diagnostics, 1670
Boeing, 1032-1033, 1617-1618, 1829
Bogner, 393
Boise Cascade, 437
Bojangles', 1387
Bols Wessanen U.S.A. Inc., 173
Bombardier, 1024
Bomel Construction Co. Inc., 153
Bon Secours Health Systems, 1584
Bonafont, 790
Bonneville Power Administration, 1246
Booth Creek Ski Holdings, 1916
Booz Allen & Hamilton Inc., 1813
Borden, 166, 173, 193, 217, 359, 560, 693-694
Borden Packaging, 693
Borders, 1431
Borland International Inc., 1750
Borton & Sons, Inc., 55
Bosch Corp.; Robert, 1021
Boskovich Farms Inc., 47
Boston Beer, 303, 307
Boston Bruins, 1894
Boston Celtics, 1892
Boston Edison Co., 1245
Boston Market, 1378
Boston Museum of Fine Arts, 1959
Boston Red Sox, 1891
Boston University, 1948
Bovis Inc., 143, 1987
Bowater, 440-441, 443, 455
Bowden Building Co., 119
Bowen & Bowen, 128
Bowie; David, 1887
Bowman Agricultural Enterprises, LLC, 55
Bowne & Co., 521
Boy Scouts of America, 1956, 1961
Boyd Brothers, 1114
Boys & Girls Clubs of America, 1954, 1956
Bozell Worldwide, 1653, 1666-1667, 1689
Bracco Diagnostics, 1678
Brach & Sons; EJ, 279
Brad Ragan Inc., 1861, 1863
Braden Farms, Inc., 52
Bradford-White, 899
Bradley, 868
Bradley Specialty Retail, 1426
Bragg Crane & Rigging Co., 1696

Company Index

Company Index

Earthwood, 1066
Eastern Automotive, 1258
Eastern States Exposition, 1908
Eastman Chemical Co., 566, 569
Eastman Kodak Co., 794, 903, 1049
Eastpak, 1085
Easy Spirit, 724, 738
Eaton Corp., 1015-1018, 1021, 1291
E.B. Eddy, 454
Ebco, 851
Echo Bay Mines, 79
EchoStar, 1237-1239
Eckerd, 1400-1401
Econo Lodge, 1634
EcoTyre Technologies Inc., 1862
Eddy Potash, 99
Edifice Inc., 105
Edison International, 1248
Edmonton Oilers, 1894
EDS Corp., 1732, 1812-1813, 1815-1816
EDS Unigraphics, 1719
Educational Management Group, 1709
Edward Jones, 1513
Edwards; A.G., 1511, 1513
Edwards; J.D., 1706, 1712, 1748, 1814
Effem, 283
The Egan Cos., 152
Egghead Discount Software Store, 1657
Ehrlich-Rominger Associates, 1971
Einstein's, 1315
Eisner & Co.; Richard A., 1976
Eisner; Michael & Jane, 1958
E.J. Brach & Sons, 267, 279
Eka, 552
El Paso, 1249
El Paso Natural Gas, 1171
El Pollo Loco, 1387
Elde Helmeke, 1975
Electric Clearinghouse Inc., 1247
Electric Factory Concerts, 1888
Electrolux (Frigidaire), 850-851, 862, 865-866, 872-875, 893, 895
Electronic Arts, 1069, 1722, 1738
Electropura, 790
Elek Tek Inc. Computer Store, 1657
Elf Atochem, 552
Eli Lilly & Company, 585, 1957
Elias, Matz, Tierman & Herrick, 1940
Elizabeth Arden, 623, 634, 667
Elkay Mfg. Co., Cabinet Group, 404
Ellason & Knuth Cos. Inc., 149
Elliot Co. Inc.; Davis H., 159
Elliott, Davis & Co., 1978

Ells & Everard, 1272
Els; Ernie, 1897
Elward Construction Co., 155
EMC, 829, 832, 835
EMCOR Group Inc., 144-145, 147, 152
EMD, 918-922
Emerald Homes, 123
Emeritus Corporation, 1927, 1952
Emery Worldwide, 1156
EMI, 913
EMJ, 1263
Emmis Broadcasting Corp., 1212
Emory University, 1954
Emory University System of Healthcare, 1578
Empire Co., 1080, 1268-1269
Empire Farms Inc., 44
Empire Life Insurance, 1572
Employee Benefit Group, 1993
Employee Solutions Inc., 1702
Employers Re, 1568
Encyclopaedia Brittanica, 507
Engine Rebuilders Inc., 1258
Engineered Carbons, 702
Engineering Services, 1968
Engle Homes, 112
Enron, 1171, 1249
Enron Oil & Gas Company, 87
Enron Power Marketing Inc., 1247
Ensign Resource Service Group, 93
Entenmanns, 270
Entercom, 1211
Entergy, 1248
The Enteron Group, 470
Enterprising Solutions, 1702
Entex (Division of NorAm Energy Corp.), 1252
Entex Information Systems, 1777
Environmental Protection Agency, 1797
EPCOT at Walt Disney World, 1906
Epic Design Technology Inc., 1846
Epson, 842, 844, 905
EquiCredit, 1510
The Equitable Bank S.S.B., 1491
Equitable Life Assurance, 1564, 1569
Equity Office Properties Trust, 1631
Equity Residential Properties, 1631
ERE Yarmouth, 1620-1621, 1624
Ericsson, 933, 937-938
Ernie Els, 1897
Ernst & Young LLP, 1777, 1813, 1972, 1977, 1979
Erol's, 1796
Ertl, 1070
ESI Lederle Inc., 1677
Espe-Premier, 1668

Company Index

Company Index

Company Index

Company Index

Maxfli, 1083
Maxtor, 825, 827, 831
Maxwell Communications, 1828
May Department Stores Co., 1303, 1664, 1673, 1686
Maybelline, 1669
Mayer, Brown & Platt, 1938-1939
Mayflower Transit, 1122
Maytag, 862, 865-866, 873-875, 895, 898
Mayville Engineering, 786
Mazda, 973, 981, 1005
Mazzio's, 1374
MBNA, 1497-1498, 1500
McAfee Associates, 1725, 1845
MCC, 927
McCain Foods Ltd., 166
McCann-Erickson Mexico, 1653
McCann-Erickson Worldwide, 1656, 1660-1661, 1663, 1665-1667, 1681, 1683
McCar Development, 128
McClatchy Newspapers Inc., 475, 1832
McClelland Consulting Engineers, 1968
McCormick Advertising Agency, 1682
McCrory's Stores, 1304
McDermott, Will & Emery, 1938-1939
McDonald & Co., 1836, 1838
McDonald's, 1366, 1375, 1377, 1390, 1630, 1655, 1659
McDonnell Douglas Corp., 1829
McEntire; Reba, 1886, 1889
Mcfadyen Music, 1363
McGladrey & Pullen, 1979
McGoodwin Williams & Yates, 1968
McGraw-Hill, 499, 503-504, 506, 1709
McGraw; Tim, 1886
MCI, 1003, 1192, 1195-1196, 1201, 1203, 1679, 1792, 1804, 1833-1834, 1850
MCIMetro, 1191
McKee Baking Co., 270
McKee Foods Corp., 238, 242
McKesson Corp., 330-331, 1266-1267
McKinney Drilling Co., 156
MCL Cafeterias, 1386
McLane Co., 845
McLeodUSA, 1188
McMaster Carr, 1444
Mead, 437, 444, 454-455
Measurex Corporation, 1832
Mebane Packaging Group, 452
Medco Containment Services, 1444
Medecon Services, 1262
MediaOne, 1229, 1233
Medical Express, 1674
Medical Liability Mutual of New York, 1601
Medical Protective, 1601

Medicare, 1592
Medicine Shoppe, 1400
Medis Health, 1403
Meditrust, 1952
Medpartners, 1574
Meijer's, 1299-1300, 1302, 1305
Mel Gibson, 1887
Mellon Bank, 1538
Melody Homes, 112
Membership Club Stores, 1312
Menard Inc., 1273, 1275
Menorah Park Center for the Aging, 1925
The Men's Warehouse, 1333
Mercedes, 979, 989, 1004-1005
Mercer Cos.; William M., 1993
Merchant's Inc., 1322
Merck & Co., 585, 590, 602, 1685, 1957
Mercy Healthcare Sacramento, 1585
Meredith Corp., 473
Meridin Health System, 1932
Merrill Blueberry Farms, Inc., 48
Merrill Lynch, 521, 1511, 1513-1515, 1518-1524, 1533, 1535, 1538, 1543-1553, 1555, 1613, 1826, 1835-1836, 1838, 1841-1844, 1982
Merry Maids, 1628
Mesa Airlines, 1139, 1154
Mesaba Airlines, 1154
MET Merchandising Concepts, 431
Met West Agribusiness, 51, 57
Meta-Creations Corp., 1741
Meta Group, 1992
Metallica, 1885, 1889
Metamor Worldwide Inc., 1699
Metcalf & Eddy, 1999
Methanex, 536
Metro-Richelieu Inc., 1268-1269, 1312
MetroHealth Center for Skilled Nursing Care, 1925
MetroHealth System, 1932
Metromedia Plus, 1213
Metropolitan Entertainment, 1884, 1888
Metropolitan Life, 1569-1570
Metropolitan Museum of Art (NY), 1959
Metropolitan Transit Authority of Harris County, 1105
Metz Baking Co., 238
Mexicano, 1475, 1505
MGM, 1867, 1877-1878
MHI Homes, 114
Miami-Dade Community College, 1947
Miami Dolphins, 1893
Miami Heat, 1892
Michael & Jane Eisner, 1958
Michael Chang, 1899
Michael Crichton, 1887

Company Index

Reba McEntire, 1886, 1889
Reckitt & Col., 621
Red Lobster, 1379
Red Robin, 1389
Red Roof Inns, 1634
Redhook Ale, 303
RediBook, 1771
Reebok, 388, 390, 719-720, 722, 724, 739
Reed Elsevier, 486
Regency Homes, 125
REI, 1424, 1428
Reichhold, 562
Reilly Industries, 99
Reiter Bros. Inc., 48
Reitmans, 1325
The Related Cos., 136
Reliance Insurance Group, 1599, 1606, 1608, 1612
Reliance Steel & Aluminum Co., 1263
Remington, 884, 890-891
Renaissance Worldwide Inc., 1699
Renal Treatment Centers, 1839
Renco Group Inc., 1049
Renentenbach Constructors Inc., 105
Reno Depot, 1279
Rent Way, 1336
Rental Service Corp., 1696
Renters Choice, 1336
Repap Enterprises Inc., 436, 454-455
Replacement Parts Depot, 1258
Republic, 908
Republic Bsns. Credit, 1502
Republic Industries Inc., 1287, 1832
Republic Security Services Inc., 1817
Resistol, 695
Restaura Inc., 1388
Retail Planning Associates Inc., 1822
Retread Manufacturing Inc., 1862
Retro Sports, 1423
Reuters, 1563
Revelstoke Home Centres, 1279
Revlon, 638, 879, 887, 1669
Rexall Drug Stores, 1403
Rexene, 569
Reynolds Metals, 754
Reznick Fedder & Silverman, 1976
RHC/Spacemaster Corp., 431
Rhea & Kaiser Marketing Communications, 1682
Rheem Manufacturing, 847, 899
Rhodes Homes, 116
Rhone-Poulenc, 544
Richard A. Eisner & Co., 1976
The Richard E. Jacobs Group Inc., 1620-1621
Richard Goettle Inc., 156

Richards, Layton & Finger, 1811
Richmond American, 112, 124-125, 134
Ricoh, 1050
Ricola Inc., 248, 251
Ride, 1087
Rite Aid, 1295, 1298, 1400-1402
Rival, 882, 888, 897
Riverdance, 1883
Riverside, 1296
Riverside Health Systems, 1584
RJR Nabisco, 165, 374, 376, 378, 1655, 1834, 1850
RMP Properties, 135
R.N. Rouse & Co., 105
Road Runners Club of America, 1962, 1964
Roadmaster, 1028
Roadway Express, 1109-1110, 1116, 1121
Robert Bosch Corp., 1021
Robert Mondavi Winery, 314
Robert W. Baird & Co. Inc., 1838
Robertson Stephens, 1840
Robins Co.; A.H., 251
Robins Federal, 1493
Robison-Prezioso Inc., 146
Robson Communities, 124
Roces, 1084
Rock-Tenn, 452
Rockford Health Plans (CliniCare), 1588
Rockport, 724, 738
Rockwell, 1015-1018, 1829
Rocky, 739
Rodman; Dennis, 1898
Roebling Investment Co., 1623
Roffe, 393
Rogers Communications Inc., 1204, 1213, 1228
Roland Corp. USA, 1060
Roller Derby, 1084
Rollerblade, 1084
Rolling Stones, 1885, 1887, 1889
Rollins Protective Services Inc., 1817
Romano's Macaroni Grill, 1374, 1379
Rondo Pools Inc., 160
Rooms To Go, 1338, 1341-1342
Rose Acre Farms, Inc., 65
Rosenbluth International, 1179-1180
Rosendin Electric Inc., 147
Ross Stores, 1333
Rossi, 1864
Rossignol, 1086-1087
RoTech Medical Corp., 1839
The Rottlund Co., 108
Rouge Industries, Inc., 756
Round Table Pizza, 1381-1382
The Rouse Co., 1620-1621, 1626

Sbarro, 1374, 1381
SBC Communications, 1187, 1189, 1200, 1679, 1833, 1850
SBC Warburg, 1554, 1835, 1840-1841
S.C. Johnson, 621
Scania, 1004
Schawk, 470
Scheid Vineyards and Management Co., 51
Schein, 584
Schering-Plough, 584-585, 602, 674, 1685
Schiff, Hardin & Waite, 1939
Schlitterbahn, 1907
Schmitt Music Company, 1363-1364
Schneider International, 1116
Scholastic Books, 499, 507, 1444, 1709
Schreiber Foods Inc., 173
Schrock Cabinet Co., 404
Schroders, 1841
Schroeder's Keyboard City, 1363
Schuff Steel Co., 154
Schumacher; Michael, 1898-1899
Schwab.com, 1517
Schwarzenegger; Arnold, 1887
SCI Systems Inc., 860
Science Applications International Corp., 1816, 1846
Scoma's Restaurant, 1392
ScotiaMcLeod, 1528, 1531-1532, 1540
Scott Co. of California, 145, 152
Scott Foresman, 506-507
Scripps; E.W., 479
ScrippsHealth, 1585
SCS Group L.C., 157
S.D. Warren, 454
Sea-Land Service Inc., 1136
Sea World, 1906
Seaboard Corporation, 64
Seaboard Farms, Inc., 171
Seafirst Bank, 1478-1479
Seagate Technology, 825, 827, 831, 835
The Seagram Company, 297, 325, 1655
Seagram's Mixers, 347
Sealy Corp., 420
Seanix, 796, 798
Sears, 894, 1285, 1289, 1291-1292, 1303, 1337, 1343, 1664, 1686
Sears Hardware, 1275
Sears HomeLife, 1338, 1342
Sears Merchandise Group, 1302
Sears Tire Group, 1319
Seattle Art Museum, 1959
Seattle-First National Bank, 1503
Seattle Mariners, 1891
Seattle Seahawks, 1893
Seattle SuperSonics, 1892

Sebrell/Griffin & Co., 105
Second Harvest, 1954
Secure Computing, 1714, 1720
Security Capital, 1618, 1827
Security Dynamics Technologies, 1720
SEDA Construction, 115
Sedgwick Group P.L.C., 1615
Sedgwick Noble Lowndes, 1993
Seedorff Masonry Inc., 148
Sega, 1069, 1078
The Segal Co., 1993
Seinfeld; Jerry, 1887
SelectCare, 1590
Seneca Sports, 1084
Senior Lifestyle Corp., 1927, 1952
Sentara, 1584
Sentel Corp., 1159
Seppala Homes, 113
Serfin, 1475, 1505
Serta Inc., 420
Service Employees International Union, 1963
Service Experts, 848
Service Master Food Management Services, 1388
Service Merchandise, 1438
ServiceMaster Diversified Health Services, 1628, 1929-1930
Servpro, 1628
Seyfath, Shaw, Fairweather & Geraldson, 1939
SFX Broadcasting, 1209
SGL Carbon AG, 861
Shady Knoll Gamebird Farm, 66
Shambaugh & Son Inc., 144
Shaquille O'Neal, 1898-1899
Sharp, 850, 867, 905-906, 909-910, 925, 1050
Sharp Healthcare, 1585
Sharyland Plantation, 46
Shasta Industries Inc., 160
Shaw Industries, 380, 1213, 1228, 1343
Shea Homes, 134
Shearman & Sterling, 1811
Shell Chemical, 535-536, 686, 706
Shell Oil, 708, 1865
Shell Pipe Line Corp., 1170
Shell Western E & P Inc., 87, 89
Sherman Clay & Co., 1363-1364
Sherritt International, 78
Sherwin Williams, 681
Shintech, 560
Shirokiya, 1304
Shiva, 950
Shoma Homes, 120
Shoney's Inc., 1380, 1393
Shop Vac, 894

University of Chicago Hospitals, 1934
University of Illinois, 1371
University of Illinois at Chicago Medical Center, 1934
University of Illinois-Champaign, 1948
University of Maryland, 1371
University of Miami, 1947
University of Michigan-Ann Arbor, 1948
University of Notre Dame, 1371
University of Southern California, 1948
University of Texas-Austin, 1948
University of Wisconsin-Madison, 1948
University; Pennsylvania State, 1371
University; Purdue, 1371
University; Stanford, 1954
Univision, 1222, 1227
UP, 1102-1103
UPN, 1220
UPS, 1123-1124
Urban Shopping Centers, 1620
URS Greiner Inc., 104, 1987
US Airways, 1098, 1138, 1154, 1161-1162
US Filter, 331
US Freightways Corp., 1110
US West, 1187, 1200, 1231
USA, 1235
USA Broadcasting Inc., 1225
USA Detergents, 605
USA Network, 1230
USA Waste, 1256
USAA Group, 1596-1597
USAir, 1137, 1140-1143, 1145, 1147, 1151, 1163, 1169
USF&G Group, 1612
USF Holland, 1121
USFreightways Corp., 1119
USG, 740
USI Insurance Services Corp., 1615
USN Communications Inc., 1188
USSB, 1237
USX, 707
Utah Jazz, 1892
Utilx Corp., 159
UUNET, 1804
Vail Resorts Inc., 1916
Val-Pak of Arizona Inc., 1694
Valeco, 1014
Valentine Radford Communications, 1682
Valero Energy Corp., 1849
Valspar, 681
Value City, 1342
Value Health, 1839
ValuJet, 1140, 1163
Van Melle USA Inc., 288
Van Waters & Rogers, 1272

Vancom Inc., 1104
Vancouver Canucks, 1894
Vancouver Grizzlies, 1892
Vanguard Group, 1168, 1535, 1538, 1613
Vanstar Corp., 1760
Variety Wholesalers, 1304
Variflex, 1084
Vasque, 739
Vazza Properties, 110
VEBA Electronics, 1264-1265
Veka Inc., 744
Vencor Inc., 1924, 1928-1930
Veuve Clicquot, 320
VF Corp., 16, 388, 399, 1680
Viacom Inc., 21-22, 1227, 1230
Viad, 1366
ViAVoice, 1743
Vickers & Benson Advertising Ltd., 1651-1652, 1654
Videotron, 1228
Videovisa Videocentro, 1649
ViewSonic, 833, 836
Viking Freight, 1121
Viking Office Products, 1444, 1446
Village Builders, 114
Village Homes, 112
Village Inn, 1380
Vince Gill, 1886
Vino Farms, Inc., 51
VIP Discount, 1864
Virchow, Krause & Company, 1974
Virgin, 1722, 1738
Virginia Dept. of Corrections, 1369
Visigenic, 1729
Visio, 1747
Vision Expo, 1676
Vista, 560
Vitale, Caturano & Co., 1973
Vitol Gas & Electric, 1247
Vitran Corp., 1120
Vivra Inc., 1839, 1847
VNU Marketing Information Services, 1985
Volkswagen, 973, 983-984
Volt Info. Sciences, 1698
Volvo, 973, 981, 1004, 1006-1009
Von Holtzbrinck, 500
Vons, 1311
VSI Corp., 153
The Vulcan Group, 146, 689
Wace USA, 470
Wachovia, 1472, 1488, 1827
Wachtell Lipton Rosen & Katz, 1811
The Wackenhut Corp., 1818
Waffle House, 1380

Company Index

Company Index

BRANDS INDEX

This index shows more than 1,100 brands—including names of periodicals, television programs, popular movies, and other "brand-equivalent" names. Each brand name is followed by one or more numerals; these are entry numbers; they are arranged sequentially, with the first mention of the brand shown first.

Brands Index

Ford Villager, 992
Ford Windstar, 992, 998, 1002
Formula 409, 621
Formula 44, 586, 600
Forrest Gump, 1868
Fortune, 492-493
Franco-American, 196
Franzia, 314
Frappuccino, 357
Freedent, 290
Freeman, 662, 669
Freeman Bare Foot, 626-627
French's, 215
Fresca, 344
Friendly Exchange, 494
Frito-Lay Fritos, 364
Fruit of the Earth, 1039
Fuji, 904, 1051, 1054
Fungi Care, 627
Fungi Cure, 626
Gain, 608
Gallo Label, 314
Gallo Reserve Cellars, 314
The Gap, 386
Gardetto's, 361
Garlique, 577
Gatorade, 336
General Motors Cavalier, 982
General Motors Jimmy, 995, 1001
General Motors Sierra, 1000
General Motors Sonoma, 1000
General Motors Sunfire, 982
General Motors Tahoe, 995
George of the Jungle, 1869
Gibson's, 325
Giga Pets, 1079
Gillette Atra Plus, 765, 769
Gillette Custom Plus, 766
Gillette Daisy Plus, 766
Gillette Foamy, 656-657
Gillette Good News, 766
Gillette Good News Pivot, 766
Gillette Good News Plus, 766
Gillette Microtrack, 766
Gillette Satin Care, 656-657
Gillette Sensor, 765, 769
Gillette Sensor Excel, 657, 765, 769
Gillette Sensor Excel for Women, 769
Gillette Sensor for Women, 765, 769
Gillette Series, 656-657
Gillette Trac II, 769
Gillette Trac II Plus, 765, 769
Ginkoba, 577

Ginsana, 577
Giorgio, 630
Glad, 457
Glad Handle Tie, 457
Glad Tie Bags, 457
Glade, 617
Glamour, 493
Glass Plus, 621
Glints, 638
Glipizide, 593
Globe, 477
Glosette, 280
Glucophage, 593
Glucotrol XL, 593
Glyburide, 593
Glynase, 593
Golden Grahams Treats, 252, 287
Golden Harvest, 260
Golden Wedding, 325
Golf Digest, 489
Golf for Women, 489
Golf Illustrated, 489
Golf Magazine, 489
Golf Tips, 489
GoLightly, 257
Good & Plenty, 264
Good Housekeeping, 485, 491, 493
Good Humor, 222
Goodyear, 712, 715
Gordon's vodka, 318
Gortons, 356
Grand Marnier, 323
Great Bear, 330
Green Giant, 220
Grey Poupon, 215
Groupwise, 1746
Growers Cider, 319
Guess, 386
Guiltless Gourmet, 363
Gulden's, 215
Haagen-Dazs, 180, 182-183, 185, 222
Hansen's, 208
Harlan Bigger Better Bagels, 247
Harper's Bazaar, 488
Havoline, 710
Hawaiian Punch, 208
Hawaiian Tropic, 672-673
Head & Shoulders, 643-644
Health Monitor, 494
Healthy Choice, 183, 225
Hefty, 457
Hefty Basics, 457
Hefty Cinch Sak, 457

Brands Index

Brands Index

APPENDIX I

SIC COVERAGE

This appendix lists the Standard Industrial Classification codes (SICs) included in *Market Share Reporter*. Page numbers are shown following each SIC category; the page shown indicates the first occurrence of an SIC. *NEC* stands for not elsewhere classified.

Agricultural Production - Crops

0100 Agricultural production - crops, p. 9
0110 Cash grains, p. 9
0115 Corn, p. 10
0132 Tobacco, p. 10
0161 Vegetables and melons, p. 10
0171 Berry crops, p. 11
0172 Grapes, p. 12
0173 Tree nuts, p. 12
0175 Deciduous tree fruits, p. 12
0180 Horticultural specialties, p. 14
0181 Ornamental nursery products, p. 14
0182 Food crops grown under cover, p. 14

Agricultural Production - Livestock

0213 Hogs, p. 15
0252 Chicken eggs, p. 15
0259 Poultry and eggs, nec, p. 15
0279 Animal specialties, nec, p. 15

Agricultural Services

0762 Farm management services, p. 17

Forestry

0811 Timber tracts, p. 18

Fishing, Hunting, and Trapping

0912 Finfish, p. 19
0913 Shellfish, p. 19
0971 Hunting, trapping, game propagation, p. 19

Metal Mining

1000 Metal mining, p. 21
1041 Gold ores, p. 21
1044 Silver ores, p. 21
1094 Uranium-radium-vanadium ores, p. 22

1099 Metal ores, nec, p. 22

Coal Mining

1200 coal mining, p. 23
1220 Bituminous coal and lignite mining, p. 23

Oil and Gas Extraction

1311 Crude petroleum and natural gas, p. 24
1321 Natural gas liquids, p. 25
1389 Oil and gas field services, nec, p. 25

Nonmetallic Minerals, Except Fuels

1411 Dimension stone, p. 26
1440 Sand and gravel, p. 26
1450 Clay, ceramic, & refractory minerals, p. 26
1455 Kaolin and ball clay, p. 26
1474 Potash, soda, and borate minerals, p. 27
1479 Chemical and fertilizer mining, nec, p. 27
1499 Miscellaneous nonmetallic minerals, p. 27

General Building Contractors

1500 General building contractors, p. 28
1520 Residential building construction, p. 28
1521 Single-family housing construction, p. 28
1540 Nonresidential building construction, p. 35

Heavy Construction, Except Building

1600 Heavy construction, ex. building, p. 36
1611 Highway and street construction, p. 36
1622 Bridge, tunnel, & elevated highway, p. 36

Special Trade Contractors

1700 Special trade contractors, p. 37
1711 Plumbing, heating, air-conditioning, p. 37
1721 Painting and paper hanging, p. 37
1731 Electrical work, p. 38

Appendix: SIC Nomenclature

Appendix: SIC Nomenclature

Appendix: SIC Nomenclature

APPENDIX II

ANNOTATED SOURCE LIST

The following listing provides the names, publishers, addresses, telephone and fax numbers (if available), and frequency of publications for the primary sources used in *Market Share Reporter*.

Accounting Today, 425 Park Ave., New York, NY 10018, *Telephone*: (212) 756-5155, *Fax:* (212) 756-5175, *Published:* 2x mo.

Advertising Age, Crain Communications, Inc., 220 E. 42nd St., New York, NY 10017, *Telephone:* (212) 210-0725, *Fax:* (212) 210-0111, *Published:* weekly.

Advertising Age-International, Crain Communications, Inc., 220 E. 42nd St., New York, NY 10017, *Telephone:* (212) 210-0725, *Fax:* (212) 210-0111, *Published:* weekly.

Adweek, BPI Communications, Merchandise Mart, Suite 936, Chicago, IL 60654, *Telephone:* (800) 722-6658, *Fax:* (312) 464-8540, *Published:* weekly.

Aftermarket Business, Advanstar Communications, Inc., 7500 Old Oak Blvd., Cleveland, OH 44130-3343, *Published:* monthly.

Agri Finance, Century Publishing Co., 990 Grove St., Evanston, IL 60201-4370, *Telephone:* (708) 491-6440, *Fax:* (708) 647-7055, *Published:* 9x/yr.

Air Cargo World, Journal of Commerce Inc., 1230 National Press Building, Washington D.C. 20045, *Telephone:* (202) 783-1148, *Published:* monthly.

Air Conditioning, Heating and Refrigeration News, Business News Publishing Co., P.O. Box 2600, Troy MI 48007, *Telephone:* (313) 362-3700, *Fax:* (313) 362-0317.

Air Transport World, Penton Publishing, Inc., 600 Summer St., P.O. Box 1361, Stamford, CT. 06904, *Telephone:* (203) 348-7531, *Fax:* (203) 348-4023. *Published:* monthly.

American Banker, American Banker Inc., 1 State St. , New York, NY 10023,*Telephone:* (212) 408-1480, *Fax:* (212) 943-2984. *Published:* Mon.-Fri.

The American Ceramic Society Bulletin, American Ceramic Society, 735 Ceramic Place, Westerville, OH 43081-8720, *Published:* monthly, *Price:* $50 per year for nonmembers and libraries; included in membership dues.

American Co-Op, American Trade Magazines, Inc., 500 N. Dearborn St., Chicago, IL 60610-4901, *Published:* monthly, *Price:$33* per year.

American Demographics, P.O. Box 68, Ithaca, NY 14851-0068, *Telephone:* (607) 273-6343, *Fax:* (607) 273-3196.

American Ink Maker, MacNair-Dorland Co., 445 Broadhollow Rd., Melville, NY 11747, *Telephone:* (212) 279-4456. *Published:* monthly.

American Medical News, American Medical Assn., 515 N. State St., Chicago, IL 60610, *Telephone:* (312) 464-4440, *Fax:* (312) 464-4184, *Published:* 48x/yr.

American Metal Market, Capital Cities Media Inc., 825 7th Avenue, New York, NY 10019, *Telephone:* (800) 360-7600. *Published:* daily, except Saturdays,

Sundays, and holidays, *Price:* $560 per year (U.S., Canada, and Mexico).

American Printer, Maclean Hunter Publishing Co., 29 N. Wacker Dr., Chicago, IL 60606. *Published:* monthly.

The American Salesman, National Research Bureau Inc., 424 N. 3rd St., PO Box 1, Burlington IA, 52601-0001, *Telephone:* (319) 752-5415, *Fax:* (319) 752-3421, *Published:* monthly, *Price:* $38.25.

American Vegetable Grower, Meister Publishing Co., 37733 Euclid Ave., Willoughby, OH 44094-5992, *Telephone:* (216) 942-2000, *Fax:* (216) 942-0662. *Published:* monthly.

America's Pharmacist, NARD: The National Association Representing Independent Retail Pharmacy, 205 Daingerfield Rd., Alexandria, VA 22314, *Telephone:* (703) 683-8200, *Fax:* (703) 683-3619, *Published:* monthly, *Cost:* $50.

America's Textile International, Billian Publishing, 2100 Powers Ferry NW, Ste. 300, Atlanta, GA 30339, *Telephone:* (404) 955-5656, *Fax:* (404) 952-0669. *Published:* monthly.

Amusement Business, BPI Communications Inc., Box 24970, Nashville, TN 37202, *Telephone:* (615) 321-4250, *Fax:* (615) 327-1575. *Published:* weekly.

Appliance, Dana Chase Publications Inc., 1110 Jorie Blvd., CS 9019, Ste. 203, Hinsdale, IL 60521, *Telephone:* (708) 990 - 3484, *Fax:* (708) 990 - 0078, *Published:* monthly, *Cost:* $60.

Appliance Manufacturer, Business News Publishing Co., 755 W. Big Beaver Rd., Ste. 1000, Troy, MI 48084-4900, *Telephone:* (313) 362-3700, *Fax:* (313) 244-6439. *Published:* monthly.

Arkansas Business, 201 E. Markham, P.O. Box 3686, Little Rock, AR 72203, *Telephone:* (501)372-1443 Fax: (501) 375-3623. *Published:* weekly, *Price:* $38 per year.

AS&U (American School and University), North American Publishing Co., 401 N. Broad St., Philadelphia, PA 19106, *Telephone:* (215) 238-4200, *Fax:* (215) 238-4227. *Published:* monthly.

Assembly, Hitchcock Publishing Co., 191 S. Gary Ave., Carol Stream, IL 60188, *Telephone:* (708) 665-1000, *Fax:* (708) 462 - 2225.

Association Management, American Society of Association Executives, 1575 Eye St., Washington DC 20005, *Published:* monthly, *Price:* $24 per year to members, $30 per year for nonmembers.

Atlanta Journal-Constitution, 72 Marietta St., NW Atlanta, GA 30303, *Telephone:* (404) 526 - 5151, *Published:* daily.

Auto Laundry News, E.W. Williams Publications Co., 370 Lexington Ave., New York, NY 10017-6658, *Published:* monthly, *Price:* $25 per year.

Automotive Body Repair, Capital Cities/ABC/Chilton Co., Chilton Wy., Radnor PA 19089, *Published:* monthly.

Automotive Industries, Capital Cities/ABC/Chilton Co., Chilton Way, Radnor PA 19089, *Telephone:* (215) 964-4255, *Fax:* (215) 964-4251.

Automotive Manufacturing & Production, Capital Cities/ABC/Chilton Co., Chilton Way, Radnor PA 19089, *Telephone:* (215) 964-4255, *Fax:* (215) 964 - 4251.

Automotive Marketing, Capital Cities/ABC/Chilton Co., Chilton Way, Radnor, PA 19089, *Telephone:* (215) 964-4000, *Fax:* (215) 964-4251. *Published:* monthly, *Price:* $36 per year.

Automotive News, Crain Communications Inc., 380 Woodbridge, Detroit, MI 48207 *Telephone:* (313) 446-6000, *Fax:* (313) 446-0347.

Aviation Week & Space Technology, McGraw-Hill, Inc., 1221 Avenue of the Americas, New York, NY

10020, *Telephone:* (212) 512-2294, *Fax:* (212) 869-7799. *Published:* weekly.

Bakery Production and Marketing, Cahners Publishing Co., 455 N. Cityfront Plaza Dr., Chicago, IL 60611, *Telephone:* (312) 222-2000.

Bangkok Post, Post Publishing Company Ltd., Bankok Post Building, 136 Na Ranong Road, Office Kosa Road, Klong Toei, Bangkok, Thailand 10110, *Published:* daily.

Bank Marketing, Bank Marketing Assn., 1120 Connecticut Ave., NW, Washington D.C. 20036, *Telephone:* (202) 663-5268, *Fax:* (202) 828-4540, *Published:* monthly.

The Banker, Greystoke Place, Feteer Lane, London, England EC4A IND, *Telephone:* (071) 405-6969, *Published:* monthly.

Bank Systems + Technology, Miller Freeman, 1515 Broadway, New York, NY 10036, *Telephone:* (212) 869-1300, *Fax:* (212) 302-6273.

Bee Culture, Dadant & Sons Inc., 51 S. 2nd St., Hamilton, IL 62341, *Telephone:* (217) 847-3324, *Fax:* (217) 847-3660, *Published:* monthly, *Cost:* $15.60; $24.10 foreign.

Best's Review, A.M. Best Co. Inc., Ambest Rd., Oldwick, NJ 08858, *Telephone:* (908) 439-2200, *Fax:* (908) 439-3363. *Published:* monthly.

Beverage Industry, Advanstar Communications, Inc., 7500 Oald Oak Blvd., Cleveland OH 44130, *Telephone:* (216) 243-8100, *Fax:* (216) 891-2651. *Published:* monthly, *Price:* $40 per year.

Beverage World, Keller International Publishing Corp., 150 Great Neck Rd., Great Neck, NY 11021, *Telephone:* (516) 829-9210, *Fax:* (516) 829-5414. *Published:* monthly.

Beverage World's Periscope, Keller International Publishing Corp., 150 Great Neck Rd., Great Neck, NY 11021, *Telephone:* (516) 829-9210, *Fax:* (516) 829-5414. *Published:* monthly.

Billboard, BPI Communications Inc., 1515 Broadway, 14th Fl, New York, NY 10036, *Telephone:* (212) 764-7300, *Fax:* (212) 536-5358.

Bloomberg, 499 Park Ave., New York, NY 1022, *Telephone:* (212) 980-5800, *Published:* monthly.

Bobbin, Bobbin Blenhaim Media Corp., 1110 Shop Rd., PO Box 1986, Columbia, SC 29202, *Telephone:* (803) 771-7500, *Fax:* (803) 799-1461.

Body Fashions/Intimate Apparel, Advanstar Communications Inc., 7500 Ola Oak Blvd., Cleveland, OH 44130, *Price:* $35.

Body Shop Business, Babcox Publications Inc., 11 S. Forge St., Akron, OH 44304, *Telephone:* (216) 535-7011, *Price:* $115 per year.

The Boston Globe, Globe Newspaper Co., P.O. Box 2378, Boston, MA 02107, *Telephone:* (617) 929-2000. *Published:* daily.

Brandweek, Adweek L.P., 1515 Broadway, New York, NY 10036, *Telephone:* (212) 536-5336. *Published:* weekly, except no issue in the last week of Dec.

Broadcasting & Cable, Cahners Publishing Co., 1705 DeSales Street, N.W., Washington, DC 20036, *Telephone:* (800) 554-5729 or (202) 659-2340, *Fax:* (202) 331-1732.

Broiler Industry, Watt Publishing Co., 122 S. Wesley Ave., Mount Morris, IL 61054-1497, *Telephone:* (815) 734-4171, *Fax:* (815) 734-4201. *Published:* monthly.

Builder, Hanley-Wood Inc., 655 15th St. N.W., Ste. 475, Washington, D.C. 20005, *Telephone:* (202) 737-0717, *Fax:* (202) 737-2439. *Published:* monthly.

Building Design & Construction, Cahners Publishing, 1350 E. Touhy Ave., Des Plaines, IL 60017-5080, *Telephone:* (708) 635-8800. *Published:* monthly.

Buildings, Stamats Communications Inc., 427 6th Ave., P.O. Box 1888, Cedar Rapids, IA 52406, *Telephone:* (319) 364-6167, *Fax:* (319) 364-4278, *Published:* monthly, *Price:* $50 per year.

Business Communications Review, BCR Enterprises, Inc., 950 York Rd., Hinsdale, IL 60521, *Telephone:* (800) 227-1324. *Published:* monthly.

Business First Columbus, 200 E. Rich St., Columbus, OH 43215, *Telephone:* (614) 461-4040.

Business Insurance, Crain Communications, Inc., 740 N. Rush St., Chicago IL 60611, *Published:* monthly.

The Business Journal - San Francisco, American City Business Journals, 21st St., Sacramento, CA 95814-5221, *Telephone:* (916) 447-7661, *Fax:* (916) 444-7779, *Published:* weekly, *Cost:* $36; $34 corporate.

Business Journal - Serving Phoenix and the Valley of the Sun, 3737 N. 7th St., Ste. 200, Phoenix, AZ 85014, *Telephone:* (602) 230-8400, *Fax:* (602) 230-0955, *Published:* weekly, *Cost:* $46.

The Business Journal, American City Business Journals, 2025 N. Summit Ave., Milwaukee, WI 53202, *Telephone:* (414) 278- 7788, *Fax:* (414) 278-7028.

Business Marketing, Crain Communications, 740 N. Rush St., Chicago, IL 60611, *Telephone:* (312) 649-5200, *Published:* monthly.

Business Mexico, American Chamber of Commerce, A.C., Lucerna 78, Col. Juarez, DEl. Cuauhtemoc, Mexico City, Mexico, *Telephone:* 705-0995, *Published:* monthly.

Business North Carolina, 5435 77 Center Dr., No. 50, Charlotte, NC 28217-0711 *Telephone:* (704) 523-6987 *Published:* monthly.

Business Week, McGraw-Hill Inc., 1221 Avenue of the Americas, New York, NY 10020. *Published:* weekly, *Price:* U.S.: $46.95 per year; Canada: $69 CDN per year.

Cablevision, Chilton Publications, P.O. Box 7698, Riverton, NJ 08077-7698, *Telephone:* (609) 786-0501. *Published:* twice monthly, *Price:* U.S.: $55 per year, $99 for 2 years; Elsewhere via surface mail: $85 per year, $159 for 2 years.

Canadian Business, CB Media Limited, 70 Esplanade, Second Floor, Toronto MSE IR2 Canada, *Telephone:* (416) 364-4266, *Fax:* (416) 364-2783. *Published:* monthly, *Price:* Canada: $24 per year, $60 for 3 years; Elsewhere: $40 per year, $100 for 3 years.

Canadian Insurance, Stone & Cox Ltd., 111 Peter St., Ste. 202, Toronto, ON Canada M5V 2H1, *Telephone:* (416) 599-0772, *Fax:* (416) 599-0867.

Canadian Plastics, Southam Magazine Group, 4703 Porter Ctr. Rd, Lewiston, NY 14092.

Candy Industry, Advanstar Communications, Inc., 7500 Old Oak Blvd., Cleveland, OH 44130. *Telephone:* (216) 891-2612, *Fax:* (216) 891-2651.

Catalog Age, Cowles Business Media Inc., 911 Hope St., Six River Bend Center, Box 4949, Stanford CT 06907-0949, *Telephone:* (203) 358-9900, *Published:* monthly.

Ceramic Industry, Business News Publishing Co., 5900 Harper Road, Suite 109, Solon, OH 44139, *Telephone:* (216) 498-9214, *Fax:* (216) 498-9121. *Published:* monthly, *Price:* U.S.: $53 per year; Mexico: $63; Canada: $66.71 (includes postage & GST).

Chain Store Age, Lebhar-Friedman Inc., 425 Park Ave., New York, NY 10022, *Telephone:* (212) 371-9400, *Fax:* (212) 319-4129. *Published:* monthly.

Chemical & Engineering News, American Chemical Society, Dept. L-0011, Columbus, OH 43210, *Telephone:* (800) 333-9511 or (614) 447-3776. *Published:* weekly, except last week in December, *Price:* U.S.: $100 per year, $198 for 2 years; elsewhere: $148 per year, $274 for 2 years.

Chemical Engineering, McGraw-Hill Inc., 1221 Avenue of the Americas, New York, NY 10020, *Telephone:* (212) 512-2000. *Published:* monthly.

Chemical Market Reporter , Schnell Publishing Co., Inc., 80 Broad St., New York, NY 1004-2203, *Telephone:* (212) 248-4177, *Fax:* (212) 248-4903, *Published:* weekly.

Chemical Week, Chemical Week Associates, P.O. Box 7721, Riverton, NJ 08077-7721, *Telephone:* (609) 786-0401, *Published:* weekly, except four combination issues (total of 49 issues), *Price:* U.S.: $99 per year; Canada: $129 per year. Single copies $8 in U.S. and $10 elsewhere.

Chicago Tribune, 435 N. Michigan Ave., Chicago, IL 60611, *Telephone:* (312) 222-3232. *Published:* daily.

Child Care Information Exchange, Exchange Press Inc., P.O. 2890, Redmond, WA 98073, *Telephone:* (800) 221-2864, *Published:* bimonthly, *Price:* $35 per year.

Christian Science Monitor, Christian Science Publishing Society, One Norway St., Boston, MA 02115, *Telephone:* (800) 456-2220, *Published:* daily, except weekends and holidays.

The Chronicle of Philanthropy, 1255 23rd St. NW, Ste. 775, Washington D.C. 20037, *Telephone:* (202) 466-1200, *Fax:* (202) 296-2691.

Computer Reseller News, CMP Media Inc., One Jericho Plaza, Jericho, New York 11753, *Published:* $199; Canada $224.

Computerworld, P.O. Box 2043, Marion, OH 43305-2403, *Telephone:* (800) 669-1002, *Published:* weekly.

Computing Canada, Plesman Publications Ltd., 2005 Sheppard Ave. E., 4th Fl., Willowsdale, ON, Canada M2J 5B1, *Telephone:* (416) 497-9562, *Fax:* (416) 497-9427. *Published:* biweekly.

Construction Equipment, Cahners Publishing Co., 1350 E. Touhy Ave., Des Plaines, IL 60018, *Telephone:* (708) 635-8800, *Fax:* (708) 390-2690, *Published:* monthly (with 2 annuals).

Contemporary Long Term Care, Bill Communications Inc., PO Box 3599, Akron, OH 44309-3599, *Telephone:* (216) 867-4401, *Fax:* (216) 867-0019.

Continuum, Universite de Montreal, CP 6128, Succ. A, Montreal, PQ, Canada H3C 3J7.

Contractor, Cahners Publishing Co., 44 Cook St., Denver, CO. 80206-5800, *Telephone:* (708) 390-2676, *Fax:* (708) 390-2690, *Published:* monthly.

Corporate Report Minnesota, Corporate Report Inc., 5500 Wayzata Blvd., Suite 800, Minneapolis, MN 55416, *Telephone:* (612) 591-2531. *Published:* monthly, *Price:* $29 per year, $47 for 2 years, $63 for three years. Back issues $3.95 each.

Crain's Chicago Business, Crain Communications Inc., 740 N. Rush St., Chicago, IL 60611, *Telephone:* (312) 649-5411.

Crain's Cleveland Business, Crain Communications, Inc., 1725 Merriman Rd., Ste. 300, Akron, OH 44313-5251, *Telephone:* (216) 836-9180, *Fax:* (216) 836-1005. *Published:* weekly.

Crain's Detroit Business, Crain Communications Inc., 1400 Woodbridge, Detroit, MI 48207-3187, *Telephone:* (313) 446-6000. *Published:* weekly, except semiweekly the fourth week in May.

Crain's New York Business, Crain Communications, Inc., 220 E. 42nd St., New York, NY 10017, *Telephone:* (212) 210-0100, *Fax:* (212) 210-0799. *Published:* weekly.

Custom Builder, Willows Publishing Group Inc., 38 Lafayette St., P.O. Box 998, Yarmouth, ME 04096, *Telephone:* (207) 846-0970, *Fax:* (207) 846-1561, *Published:* 6x/yr.

Dairy Foods, Gorman Publishing Co., 8750 W. Bryn Mawr Ave., Chicago, IL 60062, *Telephone:* (312) 693-3200. *Published:* monthly, except semimonthly in Aug.

Appendix: Annotated Source List

Dairy Herd Management, Miller Publishing, 12400 Whitewater Dr., Minnetonka, MN 55345, *Telephone:* (612) 931-0211.

Design News, 275 Washington St., Weston, MA 02158-1630, *Telephone:* (617) 964-3030, *Fax:* (617) 558-4402.

Detroit Free Press, Knight-Ridder, Inc., 1 Herald Plaza, Miami, FL 33132, *Telephone:* (305) 376-3800, *Published:* daily.

Detroit News, Gannett Co. Inc., 1 Gannett Dr., White Plains, NY 10604-3498, *Telephone:* (914) 694-9300, *Published:* daily.

Diesel Progress, Diesel & Gas Turbine Publications, 13555 Bishop's Ct., Brookfield, WI 53005-6286, *Telephone:* (414) 784-9177, *Fax:* (414) 784-8133, *Published:* monthly.

Digital Systems Report, Computer Economics Inc., 5841 Edison Place, Carlsbad, CA 92008, *Telephone:* (800) 326-8100, ext. 123.

Direct Marketing, Hoke Communications Inc., 224 7th St., Garden City, NY 11530, *Telephone:* (516) 746-6700, *Fax:* (516) 294-8141, *Published:* monthly, *Cost:* $56.

Discount Merchandiser, Schwartz Publications, 233 Park Ave. S., New York, NY 10003, *Telephone:* (212) 979-4860, *Fax:* (212) 979-7431, *Published:* monthly.

Discount Store News, Lebhar-Friedman Inc., 425 Park Ave, New York, NY 10022, *Telephone:* (212) 756-5100, *Fax:* (212) 756-5125, *Published:* weekly.

Distribution, Chilton Co., Chilton Way, Radnor, PA 19089, *Telephone:* (215) 964-4000. *Published:* monthly, *Price:* U.S.: $65 per year; Canada: $70 per year, Single issues $5.50, except July issue $45.

DNR (Digital News & Review), Cahners Publishing Co., 275 Washington St., Newton, MA 02158, *Telephone:* (617) 558-4243, *Fax:* (617) 558-4759, *Published:* 2x/mo.

Do-It-Yourself-Retailing, National Retail Hardware Assn., 5822 W. 74th St., Indianapolis, IN 46278-1756, *Telephone:* (317) 297-1190, *Fax:* (317) 328-4354, *Published:* monthly, *Cost:* $8; $2 single issue.

Drug & Cosmetic Industry, Advanstar Communications Inc., 7500 Old Oak Blvd, Cleveland, OH 44310, *Published:* monthly.

Drug Topics, Medical Economics Publishing Co., 5 Paragon Dr., Montvale, NJ 07645-1742, *Telephone:* (201) 358-7200, *Published:* semimonthly, only once in December.

E-Media Professional, Online Inc., 462 Danbury Road, Wilton, CT 06897-2126, *Published:* monthly, *Cost:* $55; $98 corporate.

The Economist, The Economist Bldg, 111 W. 57th St., New York, NY 10019, *Telephone:* (212) 541-5730, *Fax:* (212) 541-9378, *Published:* weekly, *Cost:* $110; $3.50 per single issue.

Editor & Publisher, 11 W. 19th St, New York, NY 10011, *Telephone:* (212) 675-4380, *Fax:* (212) 929-1259, *Published:* weekly.

Egg Industry, Watt Publishing Co., 122 S. Wesley Ave., Mount Morris, IL 61054-1497, *Telephone:* (815) 734-4171, *Fax:* (815) 734-4201, *Published:* bimonthly.

Electronic Business, CMP Publications Inc., 8773 South Ridgeline Blvd., Highlands Ranch, CO, 80126-2329, *Telephone:* (516) 562-5000, *Fax:* (516) 562-5409, *Published:* monthly.

Electronic News, Electronic News Publishing Corp., 488 Madison Ave., New York, NY 10022, *Telephone:* (212) 909-5924, *Published:* weekly, except last week of Dec.

Electronic School, Scholastic Inc., 730 Broadway, New York, NY 10003, *Telephone:* (212) 505-4900, *Fax:* (212) 260-8587.

Engineering & Mining Journal, Maclean Hunter Publishing Co., 29 Wacker Dr., Chicago, IL 60606, *Fax:* (312) 726-2574, *Published:* monthly.

Engineering News Record , McGraw-Hill Inc., Fulfillment Manager, ENR, P.O. Box 518, Highstown, NJ 08520, *Telephone:* (609) 426-7070 or (212) 512-3549, *Fax:* (212) 512-3150, *Published:* weekly, *Price:* U.S.: $89 per year; Canada: $75 per year. Single copies $5 in U.S.

Entertainment Weekly, Time-Warner Inc., 1675 Broadway, New York, NY 10019, Published: weekly.

Entrepreneur Magazine, Entrepreneur Inc., 2392 Morse Ave., Irvine, CA 92714, *Telephone:* (714) 261-2325, *Fax:* (714) 755-4211.

Financial Post, The Financial Post Company, 333 King St., East, Toronto M5A 4N2, Canada, *Telephone:* (800) 387-9011. *Published:* monthly with 5-day per week newspaper, *Price:* $182 per year; weekend mail subscription $49.95 includes magazine and annual issues.

Financial Times, FT Publications Inc., 14 East 60th Street, New York, NY 21002, *Telephone:* (212) 752-4500, *Fax:* (212) 319-0704, *Published:* daily, except for Sundays and holidays, *Cost:* $425.

Financial World, 1328 Broadway Ste. 3, New York, NY 10001-2132, *Telephone:* (212) 594-5030, *Fax:* (212) 629-0021.

Fleet Owner, Intech Publications, 707 Westchester Ave., No. 101, White Plains, NY 10604-3102, *Telephone:* (914) 949-8500, *Fax:* (212) 682-0922, *Published:* monthly, *Price:* $40.

Folio, Cowles Business Media, P.O. Box 4294, Stamford, CT 60907-0294, *Price:* U.S.: 24 issues for $96, 48 issues for $152, 72 issues for $199; Canada/Mexico: 24 issues for $116, 48 issues for $184, 72 issues for $240.

Forbes, Forbes, Inc., P.O. Box 10048, Des Moines, IA 50340-0048, *Telephone:* (800) 888-9896, *Published:* 27 issues per year, *Price:* U.S.: $54 per year; Canada: $95 per year (includes GST).

Forest Products Journal, Forest Products Society, 2801 Marshall Court, Madison, WI 53705-2295, *Published:* monthly, except combined issues in July/August and November/December, *Price:* U.S.: $115 per year; Canada/Mexico: $125; single copies $12 each plus shipping and handling.

Fortune, Time Inc., Time & Life Building, Rockefeller Center, New York, NY 10020-1393, *Published:* twice monthly, except two issues combined into a single issue at year-end, *Price:* U.S.: $57 per year; Canada: $65 per year.

Fruit Grower, Meister Publishing Co., 37733 Euclid Ave., Willoughsby, OH 44094-5992.

Furniture Today, Cahners Publishing Co., 200 S. Main St., P.O. Box 2754, High Point, NC 27261, *Telephone:* (919) 889-0113, *Published:* weekly.

Glass Industry, Ashlee Publishing Co., Inc., 310 Madison Avenue, New York, NY 10017-6098, *Telephone:* (212) 682-7681, *Fax:* (212) 697-8331, *Published:* monthly, except 2 issues in February, *Price:* U.S./Canada/Mexico: $40 per year, $50 for 2 years, $60 for 3 years.

Globe and Mail, 444 Front St. W., Toronto, ON, Canada M5V 2S9, *Telephone:* (416) 585-5000, *Fax:* (416) 585-5085, *Published:* Mon.-Sat. (morn.).

Globe and Mail's Report on Business Magazine, 444 Front St. W., Toronto, ON, Canada M5V 2S9, *Telephone:* (416) 585-5000, *Fax:* (416) 585-5085.

Graphic Arts Monthly, Cahners Publishing Company, 44 Cook St., Denver, CO 80206-5800, *Telephone*: (800) 637-6089, *Published:* monthly.

Grocery Headquarters, Delta Communications Inc., 455 N. Cityfront Plaza Drive, Chicago, IL 60611, *Telephone:* (312) 222-2000, *Fax:* (312) 222-2026, *Published:* monthly.

The Guardian, Guardian Newspapers, 119 Farrington Road, London EC1R 3ER.

Appendix: Annotated Source List

Grocery Headquarters, Delta Communications Inc., 455 N. Cityfront Plaza Drive, Chicago, IL 60611, *Telephone:* (312) 222-2000, *Fax:* (312) 222-2026, *Published:* monthly.

HFN, 7 E. 12th St., New York, NY 10003. *Published:* weekly.

Hoard's Dairyman, W.D. Hoard & Sons Co., PO Box 801, Fort Atkinson, WI 53538-0801, *Telephone*: (414) 563-5551, *Fax:* (414) 563-7298.

Home Improvement Market, Capital Cities/ABC/Chilton Co., Chilton way, Radnor PA 19089, *Telephone*: (215) 964-4270, *Published:* monthly.

Hospitals & Health Networks, Chilton Co., 737 North Michigan Avenue, Suite 700, Chicago, IL 60611, *Telephone:* (312) 440-6836, *Published:* monthly.

Hotel & Motel Management, Advanstar Communications, Inc., 7500 Old Oak Blvd., Cleveland, OH 44130, *Telephone:* (216) 826-2839.

Hotels, Cahners Publishing Co., 1350 Touhy Ave., P.O. Box 5080, Des Plaines, IL 60017-5080, *Telephone:* (708) 635-8800, *Fax:* (708) 635-6856.

Household and Personal Products Industry, Rodman Publishing, 17 S. Franklin Turnpike, Box 555, Ramsey, NJ 07446, *Telephone:* (201) 825-2552, *Fax:* (201) 825-0553, *Published:* monthly.

In-Tech, ISA Services Inc., 67 Alexander Dr., PO Box 12277, Research Triangle Park, NC 27709, *Telephone:* (919) 549-8411, *Fax:* (919) 549-8288.

Inc., Inc. Publishing Co., 38 Commercial Wharf, Boston, MA 02110, *Telephone:* (617) 248-8426, *Published:* monthly.

Industrial Distribution, Cahners Publishing Company, 275 Washington Street, Newton, MA 02158, *Telephone:* (617) 964-3030, *Published:* monthly.

Industrial Paint & Powder, Chilton Publications, 191 S. Gary Ave., Carol Stream, IL 60188, *Telephone:*

(708) 665-1000, *Fax:* (708) 462-2225, *Published:* monthly.

The Industry Standard, Internet Industry Publishing, 315 Pacific Ave., San Francisco, CA 94111-1701, *Telephone:* (415) 733-5400, *Fax*: (415) 733-5401.

Industry Week, Penton Publishing, 1100 Superior Ave., Cleveland, OH 44114-2542, *Telephone:* (216) 696-7000, *Fax:* (216) 696-7670.

Informationweek, CMP Publications, Inc., P.O. Box 1093, Skokie, IL 60076-8093, *Published:* weekly, except double issue in the last two weeks of December, *Price:* U.S./Canada: $120 per year; free to qualified persons in field of information management.

Infoworld, Infoworld Publishing Co., 155 Bovet Rd., Ste. 800, San Mateo, CA 94402, *Telephone:* (415) 572-7341, *Published:* weekly.

Integration Management, Post-Newsweek Business Information Inc., 8500 Lessburg Pike, Suite 7500, Vienna, VA 22182-2412, *Telephone*: (703) 848-2800, *Published:* monthly, except June and December.

Interavia, Swissair Centre, 31 Route de l'Aeroport, P.O. Box 437, 1215 Geneva 15, Switzerland, Switzerland, *Telephone:* (902) 788-2788, *Published:* monthly, Price: $128 per year.

Internet Computing, PO Box 55485, Boulder CO 80322-5485, *Published:* monthly.

InternetWeek, CMP Media Inc., 600 Community Drive, Manhasset, NY 11030, *Published:* weekly, *Price:* free to qualified companies.

Investment Dealers Digest, 2 World Trade Center, 18th Fl., New York, NY 10048, *Telephone:* (212)227-1200, *Fax:* (212) 321-3805.

Investor's Business Daily, P.O. Box 661750, Los Angeles, CA 90066-8950, *Published:* daily, except weekends and holidays, *Cost:* $128 per year.

Journal of Commerce, Journal of Commerce, Inc., Two World Trade Center, 27th Floor, New York, NY 10048, *Telephone:* (212) 837-7000, *Fax:* (212) 837-7035.

Latin Trade, Freedom Communications Inc., 200 South Bicauyne Blvd., Suite 1150, Miami, FL 33131, *Published:* monthly.

Logistics, 1924 W. Mall, Vancouver, BC, Canada, V6t 1Zs.

Logistics Management, 1924 W. Mall, Vancouver, BC, Canada, V6t 1Zs.

Los Angeles Business Journal, 5700 Wilshire, No. 170, Los Angeles, CA 90010, *Telephone:* (213) 549-5225, *Fax:* (213) 480-0468.

Los Angeles Times, The Times Mirror Company, Times Mirror Square, Los Angeles, CA 90053, *Telephone:* (800) LA TIMES.

The Manufacturing Confectioner, The Manufacturing Confectioner Publishing Company, 175 Rock Rd., Glen Rock, NJ 07452, *Telephone:* (201) 652-2655, *Fax:* (201) 652-3419, *Published:* 12 times per year, *Price:* $25 per year, single copies $10 each, except $25 for April and July issues.

Marketing Magazine, Maclean Hunter Canadian Publishing, P.O. Box 4541, Buffalo, NY 14240-4541, *Telephone:* (800) 567-0444, *Fax:* (416) 946-1679, *Price:* Canada: $59.50 per year, $98.50 for 2 years, $125 for 3 years; U.S.: $90 per year.

Marketing News, American Marketing Assn., 250 S. Wacker Dr., Ste. 200, Chicago, IL 60606-5819, *Telephone:* (312) 993-9517, *Fax:* (312) 993-7540, *Published:* biweekly.

Mediaweek, ADWEEK, L.P., P.O. Box 1976, Danbury, CT 06813-1976, *Telephone:* (800) 722-6658, *Published:* weekly, except first week of July, last week of August, and Last two weeks of December, *Price:* U.S.: $95 per year, $170 for 2 years; Canada: $230 per year.

Medical Marketing & Media, CPS Communications, Inc., 7200 West Camino Real, Suite 215, Boca Raton, FL 33433, *Telephone:* (407) 368-9301, *Fax:* (407) 368-7870, *Published:* monthly, *Price:* U.S.: $75 per year; Canada: $90 per year.

Mergers & Acquisitions, Securities Data Publishing, 40 West 57th Street, , New York, NY 10019.

Metro Magazine, Bobbit Publishing Co., 2512 Artesia Boulevard, Redondo Beach, CA 90278, *Published:* bimonthly, with an extra issue in October, *Price:* $25 per year.

Metro Magazine Fact Book, Bobbit Publishing Co., 2512 Artesia Boulevard, Redondo Beach, CA 90278.

Mining Engineering, Society for Mining, Metallurgy and Exploration Inc., 8307 Shafer Parkway, PO Box 625002, Littleton, CO 80127, *Telephone:* (303) 973-9550, *Fax:* (303) 973-3845.

Modern Paint & Coatings, Communication Channels Inc., 6255 Barfield Rd., Atlanta, GA 30328, *Telephone:* (404) 256-9800, *Fax:* (404) 256-3116, *Published:* monthly.

Modern Physician, Crain Communications, Inc., 740 N. Rush St., Chicago, IL 60611-2590.

Modern Plastics, McGraw-Hill, Inc., Attn. Fulfillment Manager, P.O. Box 481, Highstown, NJ 08520, *Telephone:* (800) 525-5003, *Published:* monthly, *Price:* U.S.: $41.75 per year, $62.70 for 2 years, $83.50 for 3 years; Canada:$CDN 53 per year, $CDN 80 for 2 years, $CDN 106 for 3 years.

Mortgage Banking, Mortgage Bankers Association of America, MBA Dept. 0021, Washington, DC 20073-0021, *Telephone:* (202) 861-6992, *Published:* monthly, *Price:* U.S.: $40 per year, $95 for 3 years; Canada: $42 per year.

Music Merchandising Review, 485 Seventh Ave., Suite 1400, New York, NY 10018, *Telephone:* (212) 594-0880, *Fax:* (212) 594-8556.

Music Trades, P.O. Box 432, 80 West St., Englewood, NJ 07631, *Telephone:* (201) 871-1965, *Fax:* (201) 871-0455, *Published:* monthly.

National Petroleum News, Hunter Publishing Limited Partnership, Circulation Dept., National Petroleum News, 25 Northwest Point Blvd., Suite 800, Elk Grove Village, IL 60007, *Telephone:* (708) 427-9512, *Published:* monthly, except semimonthly in June, *Price:* U.S.: $60 per year for those in petroleum marketing industry, $75 per year for others; Canada: $69 per year for those in petroleum marketing industry, $84 per year for others.

National Trade Data Bank, STAT-USA, U.S. Department of Commerce, Washington D.C., 20230, *Telephone:* (202) 482-1986, *Fax:* (202) 482-2164.

National Underwriter, The National Underwriter Co., 505 Gest St., Cincinnati, OH 45203, *Telephone:* (800) 543-0874, *Fax:* (800) 874-1916, *Published:* weekly, except last week in December, *Price:* U.S.: $77 per year, $130 for 2 years; Canada: $112 per year, $130 for 2 years.

Nation's Business, U.S. Chamber of Commerce, 1615 H St., NW, Washington D.C. 20062, *Telephone:* (202) 463-5650, *Fax*: (202) 887-3437, *Published*: :monthly.

Nation's Restaurant News, Lebhar-Friedman, Inc., Subscription Dept., P.O. Box 31179, Tampa, FL 33631-3179, *Telephone:* (800) 447-7133. *Published:* weekly on Mondays, except the first Monday in July and the last Monday in December, *Price:* $34.50 per year and $55 for 2 years for professionals in the field; $89 per year for those allied to field.

Network Computing, CMP Publications, Inc., 600 Community Dr., Manhasset, NY 11030, *Telephone:* (708) 647-6834, *Fax:* (708) 647-6838.

Network World, Network World, Inc., 161 Worcester Rd., Framingham, MA 01701-9172, *Telephone:* (508) 875-6400, *Published:* weekly.

New Media, 901 Mariner's Island Blvd., Suite 365, San Mateo, CA 94404, *Telephone:* (650) 573-5170.

New Steel, Chilton Publishing Company, One Chilton Way, Radnor, PA 19089, *Telephone:* (212) 887-8560, *Published:* monthly.

New York Times, New York Times Co., 229 W. 43rd St., New York, NY 10036, *Telephone:* (212) 556-1234. *Published:* daily.

Newsweek, The Newsweek Building, Livingston, NJ 07039-1666, *Telephone:* (800) 631-1040, *Published:* weekly, *Price:* U.S.: $41.08 per year; Canada: $61.88 per year (send to P.O. Box 4012, Postal Station A, Toronto, ON M5W 2K1).

Nonfoods Merchandising, Intl. Thomson Retail Press, 22 W. 21st. St., Box 640, New York, NY 10011, *Telephone:* (212) 741-7210, *Published:* monthly.

Nursery Retailer, Brantwood Publications, Inc., 3023 Eastland Blvd., Ste. 103, Clearwater, FL 34621-4106, *Telephone:* (813) 796-3877, *Fax:* (813) 791-4126, *Published:* 6x/yr.

Oakland Press, Great Lakes Media Inc., 48 W. Huron, Pontiac, MI 48342, *Published:* daily.

OECD Observer, Orgn. for Economic Cooperation and Development, 2001 L St. NW, Ste. 700, Washington D.C. 20036-4910, *Telephone*: (202) 785-6323, *Fax:* (202) 785-0350.

Oil & Gas Journal, PennWell Publishing CO., 3050 Post Oak Blvd, Ste. 200, Houston, TX 77056, *Telephone:* (713) 621-9720, *Fax:* (713) 963-6285.

OR Manager, 2170 S. Parker Rd., Ste. 300, Denver, CO 80231-5711, *Telephone:* (303) 755-6300.

Paperboard Packaging, Advanstar Communications Inc., 131 West First Street, Duluth, MN 55802, *Telephone:* (218) 723-9477, *Fax:* (218) 723-9437, *Published:* monthly, *Price:* U.S.: $39 per year, $58 for 2 years; Canada: $59 per year, $88 for 2 years.

PC Magazine, Ziff-Davis Publishing Co., 950 Tower Ln., Foster City, CA 94404, *Telephone:* (415) 378-5600, *Fax:* (415) 378-5675.

PC Week, Ziff-Davis Publishing Company L.P., Customer Service Dept., PC WEEK, P.O. Box 1770, Riverton, NJ 08077-7370, *Telephone:* (609) 461-210, *Published:* weekly, except combined issue at year-end, *Price:* U.S.: $160 per year; Canada/Mexico: $200 per year.

Pensions & Investments, Crain Communications Inc., 220 E. 42nd St., New York, NY 10017, *Telephone:* (212) 210-0227, *Fax:* (212) 210-0117, *Published:* monthly.

Performance Computing, Miller Freeman Inc., 600 Harrison St., San Francisco, CA 94107, *Telephone:* (415) 905-2200, *Fax:* (415) 905-2234.

Pet Product News, Fancy Publications, Inc., P.O. Box 6050, Mission Viejo, CA 92690, *Telephone:* (714) 855-8822, *Fax:* (714) 855-3045, *Published:* monthly.

Philadelphia Inquirer, Philadelphia Newspapers Inc., 400 N. Broad St., Box 8263, Philadelphia, PA 19101, *Telephone:* (215) 854-2000, *Published:* daily.

PIMA's Papermaker, Paper Industry Management Assn., 2400 E Oakton St., Arlington Heights, IL 60005, *Published:* monthly.

Pipeline & Gas Journal, Oildom Publishing Co. of Texas, Inc., 3314 Mercer St., Houston, TX 77027, *Telephone:* (713) 622-0676, *Fax:* (713) 623-4768, *Published:* monthly, *Price:* free to qualiifed subscribers; all others $15 per year.

Plants Sites & Parks, Pocral Inc., 10100 W Sample Rd., No. 201, Coral Springs, FL 33065, *Telephone:* (305) 753-2660, *Fax:* (305) 755-7048.

Plastics News, Crain Communications, 965 E. Jefferson, Detroit, MI 48207-3185, *Published:* weekly.

Playthings, Geyer-McAllister Publications, Inc., 51 Madison Ave., New York, NY 10010, *Telephone:* (212) 689-4411, *Fax:* (212) 683-7929, *Published:* monthly, except semimonthly in May.

Potentials in Marketing, Lakewood Publications Inc., 50 S. 9th St., Minneapolis, MN 55402, *Telephone:* (612) 333-0471, *Fax:* (612) 333-6526.

Practical Accountant, Faulkner & Gray, Inc., 11 Penn Plaza, 17th Floor, New York, NY 10001, *Telephone:* (800) 535-8403 or (212) 967-7060, *Published:* monthly, *Price:* U.S.: $60 per year; Elsewhere: $79 per year.

Prepared Foods, Cahners Publishing Company, 44 Cook St., Denver, CO 80217-3377, *Telephone:* (303) 388-4511, Published: monthly, except semimonthly in April, *Price:* qualified manufacturers - $41 per year; all others in U.S. - $84 per year.

Printing Impressions, North American Publishing Co., 401 N Broad St., Philadelphia, PA 19108, *Telephone:* (215) 238-5300, *Fax:* (215) 238-5457.

Professional Builder, Cahners Publishing Co., 1350 E. Touhy Ave., Des Plaines, IL 60018.

Progressive Grocer, 263 Tresser Blvd., Stamford, CT 06901, *Telephone:* (203) 325-3500, *Published:* monthly, *Price:* U.S.: $75 per year; Canada: $86 per year; single copies $9 each.

Provider, American Health Care Association, 5615 W. Cermak Rd., Cicero, IL 60650, *Published:* monthly.

Public Utilities Fortnightly, Public Utilites Reports Inc., 2111 Wilson Blvd, Ste 200, Arlington, VA 22201, *Telephone:* (703) 243-7000, *Fax:* (703) 527-5829.

Publishers Weekly, Cahners Publishing Company, ESP Computer Services, 19110 Van Ness Ave., Torrance, CA 90501-1170, *Telephone:* (800) 278-2991, *Published:* weekly, *Price:* U.S.: $129 per year; Canada: $177 per year (includes GST).

Pulp & Paper, Miller Freeman Inc., P.O. Box 1065, Skokie, IL 60076-8065, *Telephone:* (800) 682-8297, *Published:* monthly, *Price:* free to those in pulp, paper, and board manufacturing and paper converting firms; Others in U.S.: $100 per year.

Pulp & Paper Canada, Southam Business Communications Inc., P.O. Box 1144, Lewiston, NY 14092, *Published:* monthly, *Price:* Canada: $55 per year, $66 for 2 years, $78 for 3 years; U.S.: $62 per year, $91 for 2 years.

Purchasing, Cahners Publishing Company, 44 Cook St., Denver, CO 80217-3377, *Telephone:* (303) 388-4511. *Published:* semimonthly, except monthly in January, February, July, August, December, and one extra issue in March and September, *Price:* U.S.: $84.95 per year; Canada: $133.95 per year; Mexico: $124.95 per year.

Quick Frozen Foods International, E.W. Williams Publications Co., 2125 Center Ave., Ste. 305, Fort Lee, NJ 07024, *Telephone:* (201) 592-7007, *Fax:* (201) 592-7171, *Published:* quarterly.

Quill & Quire, 70 The Esplanade, 4th Fl, Toronto, ON, Canada M5E 1R2, *Telephone:* (416) 360-0044, *Fax:* (416) 360-8745, *Published:* monthly.

R&D Magazine, Cahners Publishing Company, 275 Washington St., Newton, MA 02158, *Telephone:* (708) 635-8800, *Fax:* (708) 390-2618, *Published:* monthly.

Railway Age, Simmons-Boardman Publishing, 345 Hudson St., New York, NY 10014, *Telephone:* (212) 620-7200, *Fax:* (212) 633-1165, *Published:* monthly.

RCR, RCR Publications, 777 East Speer Blvd., Denver, CO 80203.

Red Herring, Flipside Communications, 1550 Bryant Street, Ste. 950, San Francisco, CA 94103, *Telephone:* (415) 865-2277, *Fax:* (415) 865-2277, *Published:* monthly.

Reseller Management, Elsevier Science Publishing Co. Inc., 655 Avenue of the Americas, New York, NY 10010, *Telephone:* (201) 292-5100, *Fax:* (201) 292-0783.

Restaurant Business, Penton Publishing, 1100 Superior Ave., Cleveland, OH 44114, *Telephone:* (216) 696-7000, *Published:* monthly.

Restaurants & Institutions, Cahners Publishing Co., 1350 Touhy Ave., Cahners Plaza, Des Plaines, IL 60017-5080, *Telephone:* (312) 635-8800.

Rubber & Plastics News, Crain Communications, 1725 Merriman Road, Ste. 300, Akron, OH 44313, *Telephone:* (330) 836-9180, *Fax:* (33) 836-1005, *Published:* weekly.

Rubber World, 1867 W. Market St., PO Box 5485, Akron, OH 44313, *Telephone:* (216) 864-2122, *Fax:* (216) 836-1005.

Runner's World, Rodale Press Inc., 33 E Minor St, Emmaus, PA 18098, *Telephone:* (215) 967-8419, *Fax:* (215) 967-7793, *Published:* monthly.

Sacremento Business Journal, 1401 21st St., Sacramento, CA 95814-5221, *Telephone:* (916) 447-7661, *Fax:* (916) 444-7779, *Published:* weekly.

St. Louis Business Journal, American City Business Journals, 1 Metropolitan Sq., P.O. Box 647, Saint Louis, MO 63188, *Telephone:* (314) 421-6200, *Fax:* (314) 621-5031.

St. Louis Post-Dispatch, 900 N. Tucker Blvd., Saint Louis, MO 63101, *Telephone:* (314) 340-8000, *Fax:* (314) 340-3050.

Sales & Field Force Automation, CurtCo Freedom Group, 29160 Heathercliff Road, Suite 200, Mailbua, CA 90265, *Published:* monthly.

Sales & Marketing Management, Times Mirror Magazines, Inc., 2 Park Ave., New York, NY 10016, *Telephone:* (212) 592-6300, *Fax:* (212) 592-6300, Published: 15x/yr.

San Francisco Business Times, San Francisco Business Times, Inc., Embarcadero Center West, 275 Battery Street, Suite 940, San Francisco, CA 94111. *Published:* weekly, *Price:* $49 per year.

San Juan Star, P.O. Box, 364187, San Juan PR 00936-4187, *Telephone:* (809) 782-4200, *Fax:* (809) 783-5788, *Published:* daily.

Seattle Times, Knight Ridder Inc., 1 Herald Plaza, Miami, FL 33132, Telephone: (305) 376-3800, Published: daily.

Security, Cahners Publishing Co., 1350 E. Touhy Ave., Des Plaines, IL 60018, *Telephone:* (708) 635--8800, *Fax:* (708) 299-8622

Security Distribution & Marketing, Cahners Publishing Co., 1350 E. Touhy Ave., Des Plaines, IL 60018, *Telephone:* (708) 635--8800, *Fax:* (708) 299-8622.

Shopping Center World, Communications Channels, Inc., 6255 Barfield Rd., Altanta, GA 30328, *Telephone:* (404) 256-9800.

Ski, Times Mirror Magazines Inc., 2 Park Ave., New York, NY 10016, *Telephone:* (212) 779-5000, *Fax:* (212) 481-9261.

Smart Computing, Sandhills Publishing, 120 W Harvest Drive, Lincoln, NE 68521, *Published:* monthly.

SN, Fairchild Publications, 7 W. 34th St., New York, NY 10001, *Telephone:* (212) 630-4750, *Fax:* (212) 630-4760.

Snack Food & Wholesale Bakery, Stagnito Publishing Co., 1935 Shermer Rd., Ste. 100, Northbrook, IL 60062-5354, *Telephone:* (708) 205-5660, *Fax:* (708) 205-5680, *Published:* monthly, *Price:* free to qualified subscribers; $45 per year to all others.

Soap/Cosmetic/Chemical Specialties, 455 Broad Hollow Road, Melville, NY 11747-4722.

South Florida Business Journal, American City Business Journals, 7950 NW 53 St., Ste. 210, Miami, FL 33166, *Telephone:* (305) 594-2100, *Fax:* (305) 594-1892.

Sporting Goods Business, Gralla Publications, Inc., 1515 Broadway, New York, NY 10036, *Telephone:* (212) 869-1300.

Sporting Goods Dealer, Times Mirror Magazines, Inc., 2 Park Ave., New York, NY 10016, *Telephone:* (212) 779-5000, *Fax:* (212) 213-3540, *Published:* monthly.

Sportstyle, Fairchild Publications, 7 W. 34th St., New York, NY 10001, *Telephone:* (212) 630-4000, *Fax:* (212) 630-3726.

Spray Technology & Marketing, Indsutry Publications, Inc., 389 Passaic Ave., Fairfield, NJ 07004, *Telephone:* (201) 227-5151, *Fax:* (201) 227-921, *Published:* monthly.

Stores, NRF Enterprises Inc., 100 West 31st St., New York, NY 10001, *Published:* monthly, *Price:* U.S./Canada: $49 per year, $80 for 2 years, $120 for 3 years.

Success, Lang Communications, P.O. Box 3038, Harlan, IA 51537-3038, *Published:* monthly, except January and July, *Price:* U.S.: $19.97 per year, $33.97 for 2 years, $47.97 for 3 years; Canada: add $7 for postage and GST.

Successful Farming, Meredith Corp., 1716 Locust St., Des Moines, IA 50309, *Telephone:* (515) 284-3000, *Fax:* (515) 284-2700.

The Sunday Times, Times Newspapers, P.O. Box 495, Virginia Street, London E19XY.

Supermarket Business, Howfrey Communications, Inc., 1086 Teaneck Rd., Teaneck, NJ 07666, *Telephone:* (201) 833-1900, *Published:* monthly.

Supply House Times, 1350 E Touhy Ave., PO Box 5080, Des Plaines, IL 60017-5080, *Telephone*: (847) 635-8800.

Telecommunications, Horizon House Publications, Inc., 685 Canton St., Norwood, CA 02062, *Telephone:* (617) 769-9750, *Fax:* (617) 762-9071.

Textile World, Maclean Hunter Publishing Co., Circulation Dept., 29 N. Wacker Dr., Chicago, IL 60606, *Price:* U.S./Canada: $45 per year, $75 for 2 years, $105 for 3 years.

Time, Time, Inc., Time & Life Bldg., Rockefeller Center, New York, NY 10020-1393, *Telephone:* (800) 843-8463, *Published:* weekly.

Tire Business, Crain Commincations, Inc., 1725 Merriman Rd., Ste. 300, Akron, OH 44313-5251, *Telephone:* (216) 836-9180, *Fax:* (216) 836-1005.

Toronto Star, One Yong Street, Toronto, Ontario M5E 1E6, Telephone: (416) 367-2000, *Published:* daily.

Traffic World, Journal of Commerce Inc., 2 World Trade Center, 27th Fl, New York, NY 10048, *Telephone:* (212) 837-7000, *Fax:* (212) 837-7035.

Training, American Society for Training and Development Inc., 1640 King Street, P.O. Box 1443, Alexandria, VA 22313-2043, *Telephone:* (703) 683-8100, *Published:* monthly.

Training & Development, American Society for Training and Development Inc., 1640 King Street, P.O. Box 1443, Alexandria, VA 22313-2043, *Telephone:* (703) 683-8100.

Transport Topics, American Trucking Assn., 2200 Mill Road, Alexandria, VA 22314, *Telephone:* (703) 838-1770.

Travel Weekly, Reed Travel Group, 500 Plaza Dr., Secaucus, NJ 07096, *Telephone:* (201) 902-2000, *Fax:* (201) 319-1947, *Published:* 2 times/week (Mon. and Thurs.).

TV Digest, Warren Publishing Inc., 215 Ward Ct., NW, Washington D.C. 20037.

U.S. Distribution Journal, BMT Publications Inc., 7 Penn Plaza, New York, NY 10001, *Telephone:* (212) 594-4120. *Published:* monthly, plus one additional issue in Dec.

U.S./Mexico Business, 3033 Chimney Rd., Suite 300, Houston, TX 77056, *Published:* monthly, with combined issues in Jan./Feb. and July/Aug.

Upholstery Design & Manufacturing, Delta Communications Inc., 455 Cityfront Plaza Drive, Chicago, IL 60611-5503, *Telephone:* (312) 222-2000, *Fax:* (312) 222-2026.

US Banker, Kalo Communications, 60 E. 42nd St., Ste. 3810, New York, NY 10165, Telephone: (212) 599-3310.

USA TODAY, Gannett Co., Inc., 1000 Wilson Blvd., Arlington, VA 22229, *Telephone:* (703) 276-3400. *Published:* Mon.-Fri.

Utne Reader, Lens Publishing Co. Inc., The Fawkes Building, 1624 Harmon Place, Ste. 330, Minneapolis, MN 55403, *Telephone:* (612) 338-5040.

VAR Business, CMP Media Inc., 1 Jericho Plaza A, Jericho NY 11753, Telephone: (516) 733-6700, *Published:* weekly.

VM + SD (Visual Merchandising and Store Design), ST Publications Inc., 407 Gilbert Ave., Cincinnati, OH 45202, *Telephone:* (513) 421-2050, *Published:* monthly, *Price:* $39 per year.

Wall Street Journal, Dow Jones & Co. Inc., 200 Liberty St., New York, NY 10281, *Telephone:* (212) 416-2000. *Published:* Mon.-Fri.

WARD's Auto World, Ward's Communications, 28 W. Adams, Detroit, MI 48226, *Telephone:* (313) 962-4456. *Published:* monthly.

Washington Post, The Washington Post, 1150 15th St., N.W., Washington, DC 20071, *Published:* weekly, *Price:* $48 per year.

Wine Spectator, M Shanken Communications Inc., 387 Park Ave. S, 8th Fl., New York, NY 10016, *Telephone:* (212) 684-4224.

Women's Wear Daily, Fairchild Publications, 7 E. 12th St., New York, NY 10003, *Telephone:* (212) 741-4000, *Fax:* (212) 337-3225. *Published:* daily.

Wood & Wood Products, Vance Publishing Corp., 400 Knightsbridge Pkway., Lincolnshire, IL 60069, *Telephone:* (708) 634-4347, *Fax:* (708) 634-4379, Published: monthly, except semimonthly in March.

Wood Digest, Johnson Hill Press, 1233 Janesville Ave., Fort Atkinson, WI 53538, *Telephone:* (414) 563-6388, *Fax:* (414) 563-1702.

Wood Technology, Miller Freeman Inc., 600 Harrison St., San Francisco, CA 94107, *Telephone:* (415) 905-2502, *Fax:* (415) 905-2630.

World Trade, Freedom Magazines, 17702 Cowan, Ste. 100, Irvine, CA 92714-6035.

Yahoo!Internet Life, Ziff Davis Inc., One Park Ave., New York, NY 10016, *Published:* monthly.